New Frontiers of Educational Research

For further volumes:
http://www.springer.com/series/10795

Ronghuai Huang · Kinshuk
J. Michael Spector
Editors

Reshaping Learning

Frontiers of Learning Technology in a Global Context

Springer

Editors
Ronghuai Huang
Faculty of Education
Beijing Normal University
Beijing
People's Republic of China

Kinshuk
Faculty of Science and Technology
Athabasca University
Athabasca, AB
Canada

J. Michael Spector
College of Information
University of North Texas
Denton, TX
USA

ISSN 2195-3473 ISSN 2195-349X (electronic)
ISBN 978-3-642-32300-3 ISBN 978-3-642-32301-0 (eBook)
DOI 10.1007/978-3-642-32301-0
Springer Heidelberg New York Dordrecht London

Library of Congress Control Number: 2012953659

Printed on acid-free paper

Springer is part of Springer Science+Business Media (www.springer.com)

Foreword

As I sat down to gather my thoughts for the foreword to *Reshaping Learning*, I found myself reflecting on the momentous times we have lived in the past few years, and how hard it would have been to predict some of the events we have all experienced in that time, even just a half dozen years ago. That learning is changing to me is self-evident. All I need do is to look at my own experience, or that of my own family—we live in a world where the tools and resources we have in our pockets have made learning something that truly happens any time, in any place—with no particular need for a connection to schools, or courses, or programs of study.

Not only do we have ever-present access to tools that once could only be had in a lab or a studio, we use those tools constantly to enrich our communications, no matter how significant or mundane they may be. There is little need to let a claim go without a quick Internet fact-check, and we laugh as we do it, knowing that the answer to almost any obscure question is seconds away. Social media is ever-present as well, with a power to influence the course of events not only within our daily lives, but globally, in ways that few of us truly understand.

It is easy to forget that it was only about a half-dozen years ago that Facebook was opened to the public. Who among us then could have foreseen that four years later, a page entitled "We Are All Khaled Said" would be created there to commemorate the death of a young Tunisian in protest against an oppressive government. Who would have predicted then, that in the space of just a few days, hundreds of thousands of people would be motivated, at great personal risk, to travel to Tahrir Square to join in the protest, to say "no more"? Facebook was the medium they used to ensure the world was watching, and they ultimately toppled a government that had been in place for three decades—who saw that kind of influence coming from social media? By the time this book sees print, Facebook will likely have more than a billion users, spanning virtually every country and region on the planet. More than any other single platform, Facebook had redefined how we think about not only our personal stories, and has become very much a part of business, government, entertainment, science—and yes, even learning.

Six years is both no time at all, and a long time, depending on your perspective. For kids in school today, six years is equivalent to the time between when they were in middle school and when they entered college. Imagine a world where you grew up in these times? There is little doubt that your expectations of what schools could or should be would be based on your experiences, and those of the world, in those six years. There is little doubt that a young adult entering university has every expectation that their learning environment will be totally connected, totally global, and always on. For them, the past six years represent a third of their lifetimes, a long while indeed. The changes in the world, in technology, in the ways we communicate, have been formative parts of their experiences, so much so that it is impossible for most of them to consider how it must have been in a world without mobile telephones.

Six years can seem like no time at all, however, to a faculty member or school teacher who is balancing work, family, and more. Technologies that seem modern and very up-to-date, like e-mail, the Web, and office productivity tools, have been with us for far longer than six years. While they may still feel up-to-date to most of us, these tried-and-true tools are often viewed by our protégés as too slow, or too hard, or just too clunky to be of much use to them. It is all too easy to think we have it all figured out, all sewn up, when in fact, the kinds of technologies most used, most important to the people in our classrooms, are rarely part of their learning experience—and all too easy as well to expect them to become proficient on the technologies that have been part of our experience.

In this dichotomous landscape, our internecine battles over hybrid and online learning approaches can seem almost quaint in a world where the new vision of online learning is orders of magnitude more expansive, with massively open online courses with tens of thousands of students, and few if any boundaries between who is teacher and who is learner among them. At an almost breathtaking speed, previously incontrovertible constraints like the credit hour are being openly questioned at the highest levels of our institutions. Presidents and trustees of our most vaunted universities are actively considering new models of certification, ideas like micro-credits, and even concepts from social media like badging.

This is the world *Reshaping Learning* was written for, a world in which change is not only given, but everywhere, and proactively embraced. A world where the ability to manage change is seen as a distinct competitive advantage, and the learning marketplace full of alternative models. The premise of this book is that the world around us, the ways in which we live our everyday lives, the connections we make, the increasingly global community we live in—all of these are inexorably changing the ways we learn as well.

We can no longer confine learning to schools. Avocation and vocation are blending, and the ways we learn informally are influencing the ways we are to learn formally. Learning is not only in the midst of change, as the authors of the papers that follow so clearly describe, it indeed has already changed and in significant ways. The roles of teacher, professor, mentor—even students and parents—have become more important, and more challenging than ever.

Those are the kinds of changes examined here, and it is no accident that the reflections here have a distinctly global flavor. Some of the greatest challenges we face in education are unfolding in what, for a North American audience, will seem like far flung parts of the world. Nonetheless, there is widespread agreement that it will be in places like China, India, Asia, and Africa that we are going to see some of the most definitive innovations in the coming years; it is in those places that the challenges are the greatest.

Indeed, it is these sorts of challenges on which this book focuses, and it is on these sorts of challenges that we must place our focus as well. Huang, Kinshuk, and Spector have provided an outstanding analysis of what the imperatives of learning are, and what is not only possible, but key to reshaping learning. It is to us, now, that the gauntlet falls, and to us to ensure that our campuses and classrooms reflect the world as it is and as it will be.

Let's make the most of it!

Author Biography

Dr. Larry Johnson is an acknowledged expert on emerging technology and its impacts on society and education, and has written five books, seven chapters, and published more than 60 papers and research reports on the topic. He speaks regularly on the topics of creativity, innovation, and technology trends, and has delivered more than 100 keynote addresses to a long list of distinguished groups and organizations all over the world. He is the founder of the Horizon Project, which produces the acclaimed series of Horizon Reports that are used by over 1.25 million educators in 150 countries.

Preface

In this technology-mediated post-modern world, changes in the ways and means of living and working are so rapid that the world in which we live is dramatically different from what it was when we were adolescents, and our children will surely inherit a quite different world. We live and work in an environment, where technology is ubiquitously available, highly supportive, and fully penetrative. Not only have information and communications technologies (ICT) become part of our life, but ICT also has exerted considerable impact on the world in which we live. First, the boundary between physical and virtual worlds has become blurred (Huang et al. 2010). Both worlds are interdependent and interactive; increasingly, things previously clearly designated as virtual are becoming an everyday part of our physical existence. An everyday example is looking up a menu item on one's smartphone in a restaurant prior to settling on one's order—the Internet description of the item is virtual but one is about to eat the real thing. The word 'virtual' first appeared in connection with virtual computer memory, referring to random access memory (RAM) that only existed as RAM when needed or referenced, residing physically on a hard disk storage device. Virtual in that context meant something that appeared to be RAM but was not actually RAM. The term has more recently applied to classrooms—virtual classrooms are not physical classrooms but consist of groups of people who are connected via the Internet or other means and perform the same kinds of activities performed in physical classrooms. At some point, however, virtual classrooms will or have become so common and so pervasive that the distinction between physical classrooms and virtual classrooms loses its usefulness. The boundary between the physical and the virtual becomes transparent or vanishes entirely.

Our life is more and more marked with *e-things*, such as "e-business, e-commerce, e-government, e-mail, e-education, and all the other e-something" (Bengtsson n.d., p. 1). Second, information continues to be created at an exponential rate. We have entered a knowledge explosion era. New things come out endlessly, and knowledge is made available more than we can consume (Huang et al. 2010). Third, the pace of life has become quicker than ever. The availability of speedy transportation as well as Internet-based telecommunication is making it quicker still. Our world has become smaller, and our life has also been transformed to an extent that our ancestors could never imagine. To a larger extent, technology has changed, the world has changed, and life has changed.

Education has changed as well. As Johnson (2005) put it, "New technology cultivates active learning, provides new ways for students to learn, and renders a more authentic, outcome-driven, performance-based type of learning" (p. 2). Technology "has transformed both *what* young people learn today and *how* they learn" (Wagner 2008, p. 178). In the years to come, we will witness a new generation of learners, who are largely digital natives (Prensky 2001). These learners are characterized by a different mentality than that of their counterparts of older generations. They view learning differently from their teachers who are largely digital immigrants (Prensky 2001). In the eyes of many digital natives, learning is more than just going to lectures and relying on textbooks; rather, learning involves engaging in technology-mediated learning activities such as doing research on the Internet, searching, finding, and analyzing a variety of resources available in the virtual world and bringing into their own lives. Digital natives would prefer to stay connected to others virtually rather than be immersed in stacks of library books (Wagner 2008). Also, digital natives view learning as discovery and creation processes (Wagner 2008). They have developed distinctive learning styles, which "involve a preference for multi-tasking, multimedia, bite-sized content and high levels of social interaction" (Ellis and Goodyear 2010, p. 21). For these Net-Generation (Net-Gen; a.k.a., digital natives) learners, learning is technology-dependent. Their learning contexts, expectations, and practices have changed. "The increasing availability of ICT has widened the range of places in which students can learn, and they now expect greater flexibility in educational provision" (p. 21). There is no doubt that learning less and less frequently takes place as it did in the age of digital immigrants and prior generations. This change towards the virtual requires immediate attention of educational researchers and practitioners to investigate how educators can best ensure effective, efficient, and engaging learning in order to better cater to the needs of learners and knowledge workers everywhere in the new millennium.

This book is timely to educators and educational researchers across the globe for three reasons: First, the book deals in detail with the nature of learning exclusively in a technology-mediated context. Second, this volume represents the wisdom and most current research of recognized international educators and researchers in the field of educational technology, all of whom particularly address the critical and pressing educational problems that we are facing today in the digital era. Third, this volume is both informative and transformative in terms of the conceptual and practical impact of technology on current educational practices.

The book is structured into five thematic parts. Part I deals with the "*New Shape of Learning*" and sets the stage for the other parts of the book. It presents the emerging learning mode and emerging dimensions of learning in the era of transformation. It also provides the changes in schools. Part II includes chapters that present the latest research on "*New Sights of Future Students*" so that the reader can understand how students have changed today. Part III covers the developing trends of learning content and cases of learning content development. Part IV discusses various "*New Dimensions of Learning Technologies*". Part V introduces the "*Emerging Trends in Learning Technologies*"; as a result, readers will discover the trends of technologies in education and the cases of how to integrate these technologies into learning.

Part I: New Shape of Learning

The first part of the book consists of three chapters. Ronghuai Huang, Geng Chen, Junfeng Yang, and John Loewen's chapter proposes a new learning mode (connected learning) in today's information society and five laws of technology enhanced learning. It also identifies how to smoothly transform form traditional learning into connected learning.

The chapter by Erkki Sutinen introduces a scheme where technology can serve as a vehicle to combine the assets of formal and informal learning into a creative tension towards transformational learning.

The chapter by Victoria J. Marsick, Karen E. Watkins and Sarah A. Boswell draws on trends, research, and experience in organizations broadly conceived to examine schools as learning communities, with emphasis on workplace-based and field-based learning.

Part II: New Insights of Future Students

The second part of the book consists of three chapters. Chris Jones's chapter critically examines student characteristics in light of the popular discourse which describes students as part of a net generation of digital native young people. At the end of the chapter, it argues that there is no one shape for students and that digital technologies open up a range of opportunities and choices at all levels of education.

The chapter by Linda Corrin, Sue Bennett, and Lori Lockyer reports on a study which aims to further the understanding of the motivations, attitudes, and practices of young people in relation to technology.

The chapter by Margaret Martinez explores the use of adaptive learning technology, strategies and models, learning orientations, learner analytics, professional development, and the neurobiology of learning research to find innovative ways to adapt and improve learning and enhance educational, workplace, and career success for future generations.

Part III: The Future of Learning Content

The third part of the book consists of three chapters. Robby Robson's chapter examines the characteristics of the first generation of e-Learning content and discusses what might be expected from the next generation of e-Learning content and how this will affect the processes used to create it.

M. S. Vijay Kumar's chapter points out a clear need for a fresh perspective on how we think about resources and the relationships available to education to constructively leverage this new ecology blending technology and open education resources in powerful ways.

Yanyan Li, Yue Zhou, and Lanfang Zeng's chapter introduces National Pilot Curriculum (NPC) in China. It also presents the quality assessment framework to identify a curriculum as NPC, and summarizes the supporting role of the construction of NPC in promoting the quality of higher education in China.

Part IV: New Dimensions of Learning Technologies

The fourth part of the book consists of five chapters. John Traxler's chapter reviews previous research on mobile learning and then looks forward to a world where the notion of learning technology is itself becoming increasingly problematic as technology, especially mobile technology, starts to become pervasive, universal, ubiquitous, and therefore taken-for-granted, and not-worth-mentioning.

Gwo-Jen Hwang's chapter address how the e-learning has been affected by emerging technologies via reviewing several studies and applications; moreover, the strategies of applying the new approach as well as the potential research issues are discussed.

Kinshuk and Ryan Jesse's chapter discusses an implementation of an application for a mobile device to author authentic learning examples for ubiquitous learning environments, with ability to be reused.

Morris S. Y. Jong, Jimmy H. M. Lee, and Junjie Shang's chapter provides readers with a contextual view on educational use of games, particularly, computer games.

Cathie Norris, Akhlaq Hossain, and Elliot Soloway's chapter draws on the work of Project RED, a nationwide survey of classroom computer use, to identify the characteristics that distinguish between essential and supplemental use of computing devices in the classroom in 1:1 (one laptop per student) project.

Part V: Emerging Trends in Learning Technologies

The fifth and final part of this book consists of five chapters. The chapter by Yueh-Min Huang, Hsin-Chin Chen, Jan-Pan Hwang, and Yong-Ming Huang highlights the possible application of Cloud technology, SNSs, and sensing technology for e-learning, and explores the pedagogical development using these technologies.

The chapter by Longkai Wu, Chee-Kit Looi, Beaumie Kim, and Chunyan Miao proposes a holistic pedagogical model and elaborates on the design of a curriculum to establish engaging scenarios where learners could experience three holistic learning dimensions in the classroom: virtual reality immersion, agent mediation, and teacher moderation.

The chapter by Steve Chi-Yin Yuen, Gallayanee Yaoyuneyong, and Erik Johnson examines the spectrum of mobile and stationary Augmented Reality (AR) applications and delivery systems, and proposes new definitions of AR inclusive of current technologies. AR applications designed for education are discussed, as well as projects and pedagogical approaches suitable for use with AR technologies.

The chapter by Dirk Ifenthaler and Deniz Eseryel provides an overview of how complex learning may be facilitated by mobile augmented reality learning environments and discusses technological, theoretical, and assessment challenges that must be addressed by future research for mobile augmented reality learning environments to fulfill their potential.

The chapter by Regina Wasti and Rory McGreal introduces mobilizing web sites in an open university environment. It analyzes Factors considered in the implementation of mobilizing web sites including screen size, the use of advanced features, the display of large images, file formats, linking to embedded objects, and so on.

In conclusion, this compilation will benefit learners, educators, scholars, and trainers by providing them the new shape of learning and emerging developments in learning technologies. In the era of transformation from traditional learning to new learning mode, we hope readers will find ways to the new learning mode and the supporting technologies in the book.

Finally, we would like to express our gratitude to the many people; to all those who provided support, talked things over, read, wrote, offered comments, allowed us to quote their remarks, and assisted in the editing, proofreading, and design.

Ronghuai Huang
Kinshuk
J. Michael Spector

References

Johnson S (2005). Everything bad is good for you. Penguin, New York

Prensky M (2001). Digital game-based learning. McGraw Hill, New York

Ellis R, Goodyear P (2010). Students' experiences of e-learning in higher education: the ecology of sustainable innovation. Routledge, New York

Ronghuai H, Gen C, Jinbao Z, Yunwu W (2010) Research on informationization learning mode and its digital resource form[J]. Mod Distance Edu Res (6):68–73

Wagner T (2008) The global achievement gap: why even our best schools don't teach the new survival skills our children need—and what we can do about it. Basic Books, New York

Contents

Part I
New Shape of Learning

Chapter 1
The New Shape of Learning: Adapting to Social Changes in the Information Society

Ronghuai Huang, Geng Chen, Junfeng Yang and John Loewen

Abstract Changes in the way we communicate in the age of social informatization has affected the way we live, work, and consequently, the traditional ways in which we learn. This transformation requires a new way of thinking about learning. The essential difference between learning in a traditional manner, called **nibbled learning,** and information-based learning, also called connected learning, lies in the different understandings of knowledge processing. Nibbled learning is the process by which the learners pass required tests according to standard requirements and a set order of knowledge units so as to comprehensively master the learning contents within a specified period of time. Connected learning, with the characteristics of autonomy, enquiry, and collaboration, has been widely piloted and adopted in informal learning and training. In order to understand and promote connected learning, we define a learning scenario as "a comprehensive description of one or a series of learning events or learning activities", which includes four elements: learning time, learning place, learning peers and learning activities. Five typical types of learning scenario are defined; classroom lectures, individual learning, inquiry learning, learning by doing, and work-based learning. The concept of an effective learning activity is introduced followed by a description of the five conditions that make up an effective learning activity; to start with authentic

R. Huang (✉)
R&D Center for Knowledge Engineering, Beijing Normal University, Beijing 100875, China
e-mail: huangrh@bnu.edu.cn

G. Chen
Beijing Jiaotong University, Beijing 100088, China

J. Yang
Hangzhou Normal University, Hangzhou 310038, China

J. Loewen
Vancouver Island University, 900 5th Street, Nanaimo, BC, V9R 5S5, Canada

R. Huang et al. (eds.), *Reshaping Learning*, New Frontiers of Educational Research,
DOI: 10.1007/978-3-642-32301-0_1,

problems, to motivate with learning interests, to take the experience of learning activities as the explicit behaviors, critical thinking as the implicit behaviors, and tutoring and feedback as external support. A proposal is put forward that the five laws of technology enhanced learning (TEL), namely digital learning resources, virtual learning communities, learning management systems, designer psychology and learner psychology, must be met in order to carry out effective learning activities and make use of technologies to enhance learning demands. Lastly, the process of transformation of main-stream digital learning resources (such as the modes of individual task, micro courseware, hand-on processes, group coordination and similar experiences) from nibbled learning to connected learning is discussed.

Keywords Learning scenario · Learning activity · Effective learning · Technology-enhanced learning · Five laws of TEL · Social informatization · Nibbled learning · Connected learning · Digital resource form

1.1 The Need to Reshape Learning to Reflect Social Changes in Today's Information Society

The phrase "social informatization", a well-known Chinese academic construct, is relatively unknown in Western academia. One of the few references in western academia is provided by Kim and Nolan (2006) who state that "'social informatization' can be defined as the process by which the social capacity to generate, process, and transmit information increases". From a Chinese academic perspective Qi (2003), identifies that social informatization is the process by which the focus of national economic and social structures transfers from a physical space to an informational or knowledge space). In more detail, social informatization is the process by which computer information processing technology and transmission means are widely used in all sectors of society. Consequently, social interactions and methods of doing business have dramatically changed.

Social informatization is caused by the rapid development of information and communication technology. The information technology revolution, mainly represented by computers, microelectronics and communication technology is the driving source of social informatization (Shi and Lin 2009). Modern information technology with digital technology as the basic feature represents and stores the real world in the form of digital symbols and then uses computing technology to do the high-speed processing and transmission. Modern communication technology transmits digital symbols in the forms of electrical signals and optical signals at speeds faster than the human mind can register. With the spread of modern information and communication technology to all corners of the world and all aspects of people's work and life, a digital world modeled on the real world will rapidly expand. The digital world is a combination of the real world and virtual world. Therefore, to a certain extent, social informatization is the gradual coupling process of the digital world and the real world.

With the rapid development of the digital world and its gradual coupling with the real world, social informatization highlights two basic characteristics; the rapid growth of information and the accelerated pace of life. The rapid growth of information (commonly known as "information explosion") refers to the huge amounts of digital information that is accessible. The channels of access to this information are gradually increasing allowing for quicker access to information as well as access to information that was previously inaccessible. This exponential growth in information accessibility is what has led to the term "information explosion". Consequently, it takes much less time for people to access information, so at work, people "seem" to be more efficient. Conversely, a variety of irrelevant information is pushed to these same people. Social informatization makes people aware of the convenience of accessing information, but in the face of a large volume of information, individuals will also feel overwhelmed and frustrated due to the abundance of irrelevant information.

Social informatization has brought great changes to people's life styles. These changes are mainly reflected in the ways of communication, commerce and leisure. In the way of communication, traditional mail correspondence is gradually being replaced by e-mail, fixed telephone by mobile phones and face-to-face conversation by real-time online communication tools. In the way of commerce, with the growing popularity of electronic bank cards, online payments will become the main way of payment for the next generation and virtual currency will become an important part of the currency system. As more and more online stores become available, physical stores will have to combine with virtual stores in order to compete. In the aspect of leisure activities, paper reading will be partially replaced by "electronic paper reading", the increasing number of television channels will be gradually integrated with online videos. Additionally online games will become an important way of leisure for the younger generation and online dating will become an important component of socialization for young people.

Social informatization will change the way of working for many people, thereby promoting the development of newly emerging industries, particularly in the service and creative industries. The most important feature of the information age is the increased proportion of service industries and a decreased proportion of manufacturing industries. This increase of service industries, which are replacing traditional industries in every sector are supported by informatization. Creative industry is a major force in the modern service industry. Creative industry includes online videos, online games and so on. The basic philosophy of this creative industry is to provide on-demand and personalized service. The main ways of working in this new creative industry are working at home, online collaborative working and individual and small-group work.

Social informatization will change people's perspectives on their capability, knowledge and learning; because of this, the traditional way of learning will face great challenges. The new perspective of capability focuses more on the capabilities of learning, collaboration and information processing. The new perspective of knowledge is no longer limited to just knowing "what" and "why", but focuses more on knowing "where" and "how". The phrase "knowledge is power" will have a new meaning. The sources of knowledge will be expanded; the role of knowledge from books will become increasingly limited, while the role of personal experience or tacit knowledge from work and life will become more prominent. Our understanding of learning philosophy will change. As the boundary between learning and work becomes increasingly blurred, academic education prior to work will no longer be the norm and the acquisition of different diplomas on the same level at different phases of life will gradually become a reality. The new way of learning is that of informatization, with inseparable relations to information and communication technology. As one of the survival skills in the information society, the informatization way of learning has drawn more and more attention. The way of learning that simply "digests" the knowledge from books will become a way of the past. Experiential learning, with participation in activities and problem solving in groups, combined with the virtual world will gradually become the mainstream way of learning. With this transition from the old way of learning to a new learning mode, it is then important to define the characteristics of this new learning mode so that it may be used effectively to leverage the advances of the new information society.

1.2 Connected Learning: Matching Learning with Social Change

Information technology has brought many possibilities to learning in the new era. Where information technology reaches, many new learning modes emerge with a common characteristic, which is to make full use of the function of technology to accomplish learning outcomes that many not be realized in traditional learning (Li and Chen 2006/2011).

1.2.1 Transitioning from Traditional Learning to Connected Learning

A new learning method, informatization learning mode is presented as a way to fully apply and use information technology and digital resources in learning. Informatization mode refers to enriched learning experiences that are created with effective use of appropriate technologies and digital resources. If the learning process is interpreted as the process of learners' processing knowledge, the most fundamental difference between informatization learning mode and the traditional learning mode lies in the different understandings of people on how to process knowledge in one mode versus the other mode.

The traditional learning mode is mainly based on "nibbled learning" Nibbled learning is the process by which the learners pass required tests according to standard requirements and a set order of knowledge units so as to comprehensively master the learning contents within a specified period of time. In nibbled learning, the learning paths of the learners are homogeneous and linear and learning methods are single and relatively rigid which is not conducive to the fostering of innovative thinking. Long affected by the nibbled learning mode, the traditional learning mode follows three different models: teacher-centered, textbook-centered and classroom-centered. The learning contents are relatively closed and many textbooks seem to present a "maze" of knowledge, which is carefully designed according to the theoretical structures and whose framework is usually composed of outdated knowledge. Questions and answers in this model emphasize memorization. Classroom teaching seems only to help students become familiar with the maze, answering questions on the structure of the maze, providing students with knowledge on how to answer the questions about the maze, and finally giving exams to test student's knowledge about the maze. In nibbled learning, although students try hard to understand and master all the knowledge to be learned, they are used to matching the questions to the answers, "looking for" the answers in the books and "asking for" the answers from their teachers. In this sense, it seems to be a process of training students on "how to look for the answers" and how to "memorize the answers" without thoroughly thinking and analyzing the contexts of the issues; this is superficial learning.

Knowledge connected learning is proposed as being included as an integral attribute of informatization learning mode. Knowledge connected learning is the process by which the learners start from the understanding of knowledge sources and knowledge structures of the same learning objectives and gradually master within the key knowledge contents so as to master the whole learnt knowledge within the specified period of time. In connected learning, the learning paths of the learners are differentiated with both linear and non-linear paths. Flexible learning methods are more conducive to the fostering of innovative thinking and reasoning.

1.2.2 The Characteristics of Connected Learning

Knowledge connected learning is generated from the requirements of social informatization, accompanied by the changes in people's lifestyles. In traditional textbooks, the learning contents focus more on:

- the individual knowledge unit than the connection between the knowledge units;
- the knowledge in the books than the connection between the knowledge in the books and the real world; and,
- how to match the questions to the answers than the identification of the contexts of the problem and the definition of the problem.

While in the informatization learning mode, the learning content is no longer confined to the knowledge mazes in traditional textbooks, as these knowledge mazes do not work. The learning process is no longer one of matching questions and answers, but one that focuses on how to understand the problem context, how to define the problem, how to ask questions and where to find a solution to the problem and so on. Informatization learning mode has the following characteristics:

(1) One of the basic objectives of knowledge-connected learning is to develop the capability of knowledge transferability and the formation of good study habits. Knowledge transferability is an important foundation for lifelong learning, which includes the capabilities of knowledge transferability, learning with the use of technology, collaboration, information processing and so on. An important feature of the cultivation of lifelong learning capability is to foster good study habits from a young age.

(2) A problem-oriented approach is the starting point of knowledge-connected learning. Without questions, there will be no thinking and therefore no connection with knowledge, making it difficult to have deep learning.
In the traditional nibbled learning method, learners read the materials provided and listen to the teacher. The four basic steps for the learner are to preview the textbook, listen carefully to the teacher, review the materials, and to consolidate the learning by completing homework. These steps are completed in an iterative way. All the steps are based on the materials with the objective being to digest the materials provided, and the assessment of the course is to test the extent to which the student has "mastered" the materials content. Knowledge connected learning does not necessarily start from previewing materials; it may start from a problem or task. In today's society, it is difficult for the students to stay focused on the lectures provided by the teacher. Professor Naomi Baron explains that students have a very short attention span in part because of "the media that we as teachers and parents have encouraged them to spend their time with, and in part because we haven't taught them to have longer attention spans" (quoted in Carlson 2005). When giving lectures, the teacher has to change their teaching methods approximately every 15 min to "humorously" attract students' attention by changing the topic. This fact shows that nibbled learning is not suited to the student that is present in today's classroom.

(3) Open classroom is a prerequisite for connected learning.
Connected learning will expand teaching scenarios in an open classroom model. The single form of classroom teaching (the closed model) is not suitable for the requirements of today's students. With the open classroom model, individual learning with clear tasks, collaborative learning in groups with a common goal, experiential learning oriented with complicated activities and processes, and problem-based learning oriented with practical situations will become more widely used.

(4) The effective use of information technology is important for connected learning.

The personal computer, handheld devices and e-readers will become the essential equipment of students. Information technology is not only a learning support tool, but also a cognitive tool. How to use information technology in learning will become an important indicator of measuring whether students are "capable".

(5) Social interaction is an integral part of connected learning.
The interaction between teachers and students is no longer the only method of interaction. Firstly, the interaction among students from the same school as well as from different schools, have become more and more important. This interaction is facilitated by modern communication technology. Secondly, learning through interactive media will take up a larger proportion of learning. Effective human–computer interaction (HCI) will enhance learning effectiveness and efficiency. Zhang and Nunamaker (2003) observes that HCI research facilitates the design of easy-to-use interfaces that precisely present learning materials in a large variety of formats. Finally, the teacher is no longer the sole knowledge "owner". Due to the easy accessibility of information, students often know more than the teacher, so the knowledge contribution provided by the students in the teaching process is indispensable.

1.2.3 Teaching Methodology Changes Required by Connected Learning

In face of the requirements of informatization learning mode, the traditional "indoctrination" teaching mode will face huge challenges. Firstly, it is difficult for the teacher who's only experience is that of "digesting" textbook knowledge to imagine what form connected learning should be. This type of teacher will usually think that as long as they are provided with good teaching materials and resources of "high quality", students will carefully "digest" these materials. Secondly, it is difficult for teachers who are used to classroom lecturing to figure out an "interpretation" on how to organize learning activities as they usually think that as long as they provide "excellent" recorded lectures, the students will carefully "watch" them.

The teachers who do not have practical experience and who do not pursue professional development in a multi-disciplinary fashion will find their knowledge and skills insufficient to meet the demands of today's students. Finally, teachers born prior to the 1980 s are called "digital immigrants" whereas current students are called "digital natives" (Prensky 2001). The information literacy of digital immigrants is far behind that of "digital natives" which will make teaching for digital immigrants a more difficult process.

The transformation from nibbled learning to connected learning is an innovative process. The creative process will be reflected in the following aspects.

1.2.4 Preparation: From Preparing Lessons to Designing Learning Activities

The process of preparing lessons refers to all preparatory work that needs to be completed by teachers in order to deliver a teaching task. Teachers form teaching capability based on the requirements of teaching, which is an important part of the whole process of teaching and an important step for giving a good lesson. Lesson preparation has three levels of focus: a semester, a unit and a lesson. When preparing lessons, teachers have to become familiar with the syllabus and materials in order to grasp the teaching contents, to analyze the teaching tasks and to clarify the teaching objectives, to study the characteristics of the student and choose appropriate teaching methods, to design the teaching process and write lesson plans so as to prepare for class. The "three preparations" of the traditional lesson preparation in nibbled learning refer to preparing teaching materials, preparing students and preparing teaching methods. Preparing teaching materials requires the teacher to fully understand the teaching contents, preparing students requires the teacher to understand the students' mastery of associated knowledge, and preparing teaching methods requires teachers to think about how to allocate time in class and how to give effective lectures. In China, with the implementation of new curriculum reform in basic education, the contents of lesson preparation have extended from a "three preparation" method to a "five preparation" method, consisting of preparing curriculum standards, preparing teaching materials, preparing teaching methods, preparing the students and preparing the expected outcomes. Preparing curriculum standards requires teachers to think about how to implement the guidelines of the new curriculum reform and preparing the expected outcomes requires teachers to reasonably preset learning outcomes in order to flexibly respond to the changes in class. This is a big step in moving towards connected learning.

The key feature of connected learning is that it is a student-centered perspective, with one of the core indicators being to design a learning activity system based on the learning process of students. The main focus of teachers' lesson preparation is on how to design learning activities that connect possible learning outcomes with the teaching objectives, how to give consideration to both the individuality and commonality of students, how to effectively organize learning activities and how to design evaluation and so on. Giving a lecture is only one type of learning activity and therefore is only one part of the process.

1.2.5 Process: From Lecturing to Organizing Learning Activities

The focus of nibbled learning is lecturing, specifically how to give a good lecture. The issues discussed in the class in K-12 schools, such as how to lead in a new lecture, how to guide students to think, how to give a summary of the lecture and how to maintain classroom discipline and so on are all about how to give a lecture. The classroom lectures are only one part of connected learning with a very limited range of application. Individual learning, collaborative learning in groups, experiential learning and problem solving learning, are more focused on how to effectively organize activities. The effective organization of learning activities require teachers to learn more about individual students, to prepare more resources to meet the requirements of different students and to provide different kinds of evaluation methods, all of which are enormous challenges for the teachers who are used to only giving lectures. Therefore, the new learning mode requires teachers to shift their teaching focus from lecturing to organizing learning activities.

1.2.6 Evaluation: From Examinations to the Entire Learning Process

As an important part of the teaching process, evaluation is synonymous with examining the students' learning achievements, which in the traditional sense refers to academic scores which are the results of the examination. The contents of the exam are usually variants of the example exercises in the textbooks that students can remember, explain or complete such as multiple choice, fill in the blanks, definition, short answers, and comprehension questions, which only reflect "shallow learning" situations of the students. Following the traditional learning process means adding a mid-term exam and unit tests to the final exam to come up with a grade. In order to distinguish from "examination-oriented education", the hundred-point scale system of exam scores is changed to a five-point scale; this does not change the essence of the process. The evaluation of connected learning changes the understanding of learning achievements right from the beginning. Learning achievements are no longer the reflection of "superficial learning" situations, but of the reflection of "deep learning", shifting from what students have remembered, what they can explain, what they can complete of the example exercises in the textbooks, to situations where the focus is on what students have thought about, what they have experienced and whether they can ask questions and solve problems. Obviously, "deep learning" cannot be "examined" by the traditional examination method.

1.2.7 Services: From Monitoring to Providing Support for the Learning Process

The purpose of nibbled teaching mode is to train the students to navigate in a closed maze of knowledge; teaching focuses on helping students become familiar with the maze of knowledge and exams are given to evaluate student's familiarity with the maze. Another important part of this teaching process, Q&A, seems to provide advice in order to aid students' navigation. Connected learning:

- removes the learning contents from the restriction of the maze allowing a change from organizing teaching to organizing learning activities so that students' learning becomes "self-constructed";
- evaluates the process of the students ability to think, experience, and solve problems;
- changes the "Q&A" from helping students to find answers in the maze to support their learning and covers the process of guiding students to ask questions, define concepts and seek answers for problem-solving strategies.

In order to improve the teaching methods and then to foster and improve connected learning, it is necessary to identify when, where and how learning occurs.

1.3 The Learning Scenario: Identifying When, Where and How Learning Occurs

1.3.1 The Meaning of Learning from Different Perspectives

"Learning" is one of the most commonly used words in our work and daily life. Parents often tell their children to be good at "learning", as do the employers to their employees, and even the teachers to their students. However, the word "learning" does not have the exact same meaning in the above contexts, indicating that individual people may have quite different understandings of the word "learning".

What is learning? That is one of the fundamental issues in the research of learning theory. Learning theory is a branch of education and educational psychology, which describes and illustrates the learning categories, processes and learning conditions of humans and animals. Some people think that learning theory includes three types of philosophical frameworks; behaviorism, cognitivism and constructivism (Woolfolk et al. 2006). Alternatively, some people believe that cognitive learning theory includes constructivist learning theory and that humanism is the third most popular learning theory thus, the three types of learning theory should be behaviorism, cognitivism and humanism.

The representative of early behaviorism, Edward Lee Thorndike believes that learning is formed by the link of the stimulus and response in the nervous system, which is the basic theory on learning in behavioral psychology. John Watson believes that learning is the link of stimulus and response through conditioned response. Therefore, behavioral learning theory considers learning as the establishment of the link of stimulus and response (S–R), as the process of trial and error, with the emphasis on the behavioral change caused by exercise driven by reinforcement (quoted from Baum 2005). B. F. Skinner put forward the principle of operant conditioning and carried out a systematic study on the reinforcement principle, which improves the development of the theory (quoted from Slater 2004). The instructional machine and programmed instruction designed by Skinner based on the principle of operant conditioning used to be very popular; it promotes the development of audio–visual instruction, programmed instruction, and early computer assisted instruction (CAI).

Cognitive learning theory has a different view of the essence of learning. For example, Gestalt psychology (also known as traditional cognitivism) states that memory traces are left in the brain through learning and stay in the nervous system after the experience. These traces are not isolated elements, but an organized whole. Edward Chace Tolman, an expert in Sign Gestalt Theory, believes that learning should be the process of moving from a sign or a signal to a certain symbolic meaning (i.e. S–S), and the acquirement of expectation rather than the formation and link of habits. Learning achieves the objectives based on the mind map (i.e. cognitive map) or on environmental signals. Jean Piaget, the founder of constructive cognitive psychology, believes that learning is a proactive self-regulation process that has different forms at different stages of the individual development process of a learner (quoted from Cole et al. 2005). Therefore, cognitive psychology emphasizes the motivation of the individual as an organism, that learning is the personal understanding and organization of the scenario; the result of internal reflection on external stimuli with the emphasis on internal strengthening.

Constructivism is based on the internal reflection of cognitive psychology. The Piaget school and the school of social and cultural history in the former Soviet Union played a crucial role in promoting the popularity of constructivism in the United States. Piaget believes that learning is a kind of "self"-construction. Lev Vygotsky believes that learning is a "social construction", emphasizing the role of the social, cultural and historical background of the learner in the cognitive process, attaching great importance to the positions of "activity" and "social interaction" in the development of an individual's high-level cognitive ability (Santrock 2004). Therefore, knowledge is not taught by teachers but acquired by learners in certain contexts or socio-cultural contexts with the help of others (including teachers and learning peers) as well as necessary learning materials (all the pieces allowing for the construction of knowledge). Constructivist learning theory is considered one of the most important theories in fields such as computers in education and e-learning, etc.

Humanistic psychology was founded by Abraham Maslow, and is represented by Carl R. Rogers, who believe that once people have a sense of security, once they are no longer hungry, all they want to do, no matter what job or level, is to learn and grow (Maslow et al. 1998) (quoted from Farber et al. 1998). The essential difference between humanism and other academic schools is that humanism places an emphasis on the positive nature and value of an individual, rather than focusing on the individual's misbehaviors. Additionally, it emphasizes the individual's growth and development, which is referred to as self-achievement.

Humanistic learning theory is considered to be the most important theoretical support for adult learning and in-service training.

So, what is "learning" for teachers, students and parents? It is difficult to give a unified explanation in the views of behaviorism, cognitivism, constructivism, or humanism. It could be said that it is a broad concept of "learning" with a varied meaning according to different contexts. It is undeniable that "learning" in daily teaching usually refers to students listening to lectures, completing self-study and participating in group discussions. It actually refers to a learning scenario, an agreement between the teachers and students on how the students should learn. Therefore, this paper intends to categorize "learning" by learning scenarios in the hope of understanding what learning is, and how to learn effectively from another perspective.

1.3.2 The Concept of a Learning Scenario

Conole and Oliver (1998) describe learning scenarios as including the following characteristics:

- media type;
- use of media;
- the preparatory work required;
- the educational interactions which are supported;
- the delivery constraints.

Edutech Wiki defines a learning scenario as an instantiation of an instructional design model for a given subject and a given kind of situation. It basically defines what learners and other actors like the teacher should/can do with a given set of resources and tools.

In this paper, we refer to a learning scenario as a comprehensive description of one or a series of learning events or learning activities, which includes four elements; learning time, learning place, learning peers and learning activities. Commonly speaking, a learning scenario refers to the time, place, people and events of a learning activity as shown in Fig. 1.1.

Firstly, a learning activity, the first element of a learning scenario refers to the combination of both the students' and teachers' tasks needed to complete a particular learning objective (Yang 2005). For learners, a learning activity refers to the issues of what to learn (or what to "do") and how to learn (or how to "do"), which is an "activity" or "activity" series. From the perspective of a teacher or designer, a complete learning activity consists of the following components: learning objectives, activities or tasks, learning methods and operational procedures, organizational forms, ways of interaction, forms of learning outcomes, activity monitoring rules, roles and responsibilities, learning evaluation rules and evaluation criteria. Learning activities should include three basic elements:

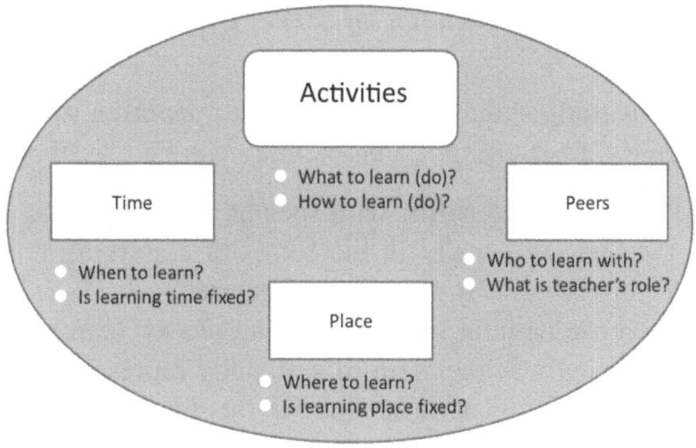

Fig. 1.1 The four elements of a learning scenario: TAPP

learning tasks, learning methods and evaluation requirements. In certain contexts, a learning activity and learning scenario are synonymous.

Secondly, learning place and learning time do not seem to be an important point of discussion in school education, but both are important in distance education and corporate training. For example, are learners learning in an established learning center (for online education) or training site (corporate training)? They may learn in the workplace or at home and for fixed or variable lengths of time. These issues are worthy of discussion. In fact, even in school education it may be, where the learning place is arranged in a regular classroom, multimedia classroom, laboratory, computer room or library, and learning time is scheduled on a weekday morning, afternoon or evening, or during the weekend, that conditions will lead to different forms of teaching organization, that the type of learning place and different time periods and duration, if it is fixed, involves not only the teaching arrangement, teaching organization and condition preparation, but also the psychological preparation of the learner. Different learning places and time periods have different "metaphors" to different learners, which will generate different psychological preparation.

Moreover, the concept of a learning peer does not seem a worthy issue for discussion in classroom teaching in schools or training institutions and organizations because in this form of collective learning, learning peers are the learner's classmates. In corporate training, learning peers are often strangers, so at the start of teaching, "ice-breakers" that aim to introduce participants to one another are very important. In distance learning, learners have difficulty in finding the same category of learning peers, and consequently, the loneliness and isolation of learning and being unable to seek the help of learning peers have become prominent issues. Similarly, even in conventional classroom teaching, it is common practice to separate students into smaller groups; this is a very important issue when organizing coordinated learning. Therefore, the important role of learning peers in learning activities is also an integral part of a learning scenario.

1.3.3 The Features of Five Typical Learning Scenarios

All learning should occur in a certain learning scenario. Although it is difficult to specify all learning scenarios, they can be classified by the following rules:

(1) Learning scenarios with specific learning places, learning events and learning peers are usually in the forms of classroom teaching or learning counseling represented by "classroom lectures";
(2) Those without specific learning places, learning events and learning peers are typically in the form of self-study represented by individual self-study; and,
(3) Those with at least one of the three elements unspecified can be further divided into three categories, which are represented by "group discussion", "learning by doing" and "learning in practical work".

This paper will discuss five typical learning scenarios: classroom lectures, self-study, inquiry learning (or group discussion), learning by doing and work-based learning (learning in practical work (shown in Table 1.1).

The phrase "classroom lectures" refers to learning in the classroom on campus or in similar learning environments. It is a collective learning behavior, usually in the form of classes. It has three typical features. First, it has a fixed teaching environment, like classrooms, meeting rooms, etc.; second, there are teachers to give face-to-face lectures, or organize classroom discussions and other forms of teaching; third, there are agreed or prepared learning contents, such as textbooks, handouts or outline, etc., which are often relatively fixed.

The scenario of "self-study" refers to the learning behaviors pre-appointed or arranged by the teacher, which are organized by the individual learner usually without teachers' instruction or mentoring. Although there may be learning peers around who may even play the role of teacher for one another, their own learning is usually carried out independently. The three basic features of self-study are specific learning contents, pre-set learning objectives, and specific evaluation requirements or evaluation methods. For example, exams for self-study learners take self-study as the main learning form, with homework and exercises as the evaluation methods and passing the exams organized by the host units as the evaluation requirements.

The scenario of "inquiry learning" refers to the learning form of participating in groups and communicating in discussion. Mayer (2004) defines inquiry learning as the process where students adopt a scientific approach and make their own discoveries; they generate knowledge by activating and restructuring knowledge schemata. De Jong (2006) adds that inquiry learning environments also ask students to take initiative in the learning process and can be offered in a naturally collaborative setting with realistic material. It can be a part of classroom teaching or a learning form at work, or be organized by learners themselves. A successful "inquiry learning" scenario usually consists of three features, which are clear inquiry topics, moderate scale of members and a powerful learning organizer.

Table 1.1 Five typical learning scenarios

Learning scenario	Learning activity	Learning place	Learning time	Learning peers
Classroom lecture (collective)	• F2f classroom lecturing • prepared teaching materials	Fixed teaching environment	Fixed time	Classmates
Individual learning (individual)	• Specific learning contents • Preset learning objectives • Specific evaluation requirements	Not fixed	Not fixed	Not fixed
Inquiry learning (group)	Specific discussion topics	Not fixed	• relatively concentrated discussion period	• Appropriate group membership • Appropriate group leader
Learning by doing (community)	• Task-oriented evaluation • Learning support	• Activity based on the environment	• Tasks matched to the objectives	Not fixed
Work-based learning (community)	• Learning contents rooted in the work • Tasks matched to the complexity of work	• "Work" place	Not fixed	• Partners • The interpersonal relationship is suitable for learning

The scenario of "learning by doing" refers to the learning form, which embeds "doing" activities in the learning activities of school education or training. "Learning by doing" places the emphasis on learning as the experience of "doing". For example, that the youth conduct "research" by imitating the research procedure of scientists is a typical "learning by doing" scenario. In the past, learning by doing may have been difficult to implement; but technological tools, such as simulations, observation using remote instruments, field work with mobile devices as data collection platforms, and connecting with mentors and research communities enables authentic learning experiences in ubiquitous learning environments (Lombardi 2007). A successful "learning by doing" activity usually consists of four elements which are learning tasks matched with learning objectives, evaluation methods matched with learning tasks, support service matched with students and the organizational form matched with the learning environment.

The scenario of "work-based learning" is a learning form that involves gaining experience through practical work. Although it emphasizes "doing" as "learning by doing", it is based on the practical working environment and working tasks rather than in "simulating" the environment. A successful "work-based learning" activity usually has three distinct features, which are learning contents rooted in the work, learning tasks matched with the working intensity, and interpersonal relationships or a learning atmosphere suitable for learning.

The five learning scenarios have their own advantages, disadvantages and impact conditions, as shown in Table 1.2.

(1) "Classroom lecture" is considered to be a common learning scenario. Most parents consider it as the most important way of learning, and it is the best way of learning when attending a class instructed by a famous teacher or a senior-class teacher. It is not difficult to organize lectures for the teaching organizers, who just have to invite a good teacher and arrange the classroom for facilitation. Neither is it for learners, because whether they are listening to the classroom lectures depends on their moods at that time and the degree of acceptability. However, listening to the classroom lectures mainly uses memory. There is often lack of communications in larger classes. The effectiveness of classroom lectures depends on the teaching skills of teachers and the existing knowledge of students as well as their interest in the contents.
(2) "Individual learning" is considered as the most flexible learning scenario, with flexible time and place, which has the added advantage of time conservation. The disadvantage is that the learners may feel lonely and may be unwilling to get help in the face of difficulty. Its impact conditions are the readability of learning materials, and the degree of linkage of learning contents to the learners' knowledge background. In addition, personal learning interest also plays a crucial role.
(3) "Inquiry learning" or "group learning" is commonly used but not often considered as a "learning" scenario. The advantages are that the participants easily generate interest and there are usually more opportunities for communications and exchanges in small-scale discussions. The disadvantages are as

Table 1.2 Basic features of the five learning scenarios

Learning scenarios	Advantages	Disadvantages	Impact conditions
Classroom lectures (collective)	• Easy to organize • "Feel" easy	• Mainly learn by memory • Fewer opportunities for communication	• Teachers' lecturing skills • Learners' interest in the contents
Individual learning (individual)	• Flexible time and place • Usually save time	• Easy to feel lonely • Difficult to get help	• The readability of materials • Personal interest in learning
Inquiry learning (group)	• Easy to generate interest • More opportunities for communication	• Spend more time • Easy to "rely on the work of others"	• Group leader's organizational capacity • Good interpersonal relationships
Learning by doing (community)	• Easy to generate interest • Good learning effects	• Difficult to get help • May not pass the "exam"	• The design of tasks • Support service for learning
Work-based learning (team)	• Learning interest generated in the work • "Apply what they have learnt"	• The conflict of "working" and "learning" • May not pass the "exam"	• Learning atmosphere of the work place • Individual learning skills

follows: it usually costs learners a lot of time, but not everyone can achieve the desired results; the "free rider" phenomenon is common as some members may complete most of the "work", while the others can easily "share" the group outcomes; and, even if each participant is required to speak, there will be situations where the learner carefully plans before their speech but may not participate afterwards. Successful inquiry learning depends on the group leader's organizational capability and interpersonal communication skills within the group.

(4) "Learning by doing" is considered as a good learning form but not easy to organize. The advantages are that participants are easy to engage, and the learning effects are good once the entire "doing" process is completed. The disadvantages are that learners are not willing to get effective help when facing difficulty and they may not pass traditional exams, which are memory-based. Successful "learning by doing" activities are highly dependent on the design of "doing" tasks and the appropriate mentoring and support provided in the learning process.

(5) "Work-based learning" is a fashionable learning method in vocational education and in-service training. Its advantage is that participants have a learning interest in the work, which usually results in "learning for practice". The disadvantage is the conflict of "working" and "learning". Working performance and learning effectiveness may not excel in parallel, or the learners may not pass the traditional exams. Successful "work-based learning" depends on the learning atmosphere of the leaner's working organization and the personal learning skills of the individual learner.

1.4 Five Laws on Technology Enhanced Learning

1.4.1 Technology Enhanced Learning (TEL) and Learning Scenarios

The traditional way of instruction includes teaching and learning, but now we can see that except for "classroom lectures", all of the other scenarios, "self-study" (such as "exams for self-study"), "inquiry learning", "learning by doing" and "work-based learning" have extended beyond this traditional way of thinking. With the popularization of the Internet learning materials are no longer the only method of distributing learning contents, nor is the blackboard the only teaching tool in the classroom. The Internet and multimedia have become an integral part of teaching and learning. Online learning has become a popular form of learning, and "blended learning" has become one of the most commonly used teaching strategies. For the public in general Technology Enhanced Learning (TEL) has become synonymous with almost all "information technology in learning" including eLearning.

The objective of TEL is to provide socio-technical innovation in learning practice for an individual or an organization in a way that is independent of learning time, place and progress, which enhances learning efficiency and input–output effectiveness. Therefore, TEL can be interpreted as providing support to any learning activity through technological means.

From traditional "blackboard and chalk" face-to-face classroom lecturing to classroom teaching supported by multimedia technology, and from online learning as the main form to the return of a more "rational" and more "realistic" blended learning, the teaching paradigm is transforming from a "teacher-centered" to a "learner-centered" paradigm, as shown in Table 1.3. The main changes are as follows:

- The instructional organization changes from how to "implement" teaching (how to give a better lecture) to "facilitating learning";
- The instructional objective changes from the delivery of knowledge to knowledge construction;
- Management changes from offering courses to creating a good learning environment;
- Quality control changes from the improvement of instructional quality (how to "teach" better) to the improvement of learning quality (how to create a better learning environment);
- Content arrangement changes from creating generic learning materials to creating personalized learning materials; and,
- Evaluation changes from "individual" evaluation to "open" evaluation.

Siemens (2004) states some significant trends in learning, including:

(1) Informal learning is a significant aspect of our learning experience. Learning now occurs in a variety of ways—through communities of practice, personal networks, and through completion of work-related tasks.
(2) Learning is a continual process, lasting for a lifetime. Learning and work related activities are no longer separate. In many situations, they are the same.
(3) Many of the processes previously handled by learning theories (especially in cognitive information processing) can now be off-loaded to, or supported by, technology. Many learning theories, especially on cognitive information processing that we used to believe in are off-loaded or supported by technology. "Know-how" and "know-what" will be replaced by "know-where", which means knowing where to find the required knowledge. Sparrow et al. (2011) have performed research on "google effects on memory". They argue that the Internet has become a primary form of external or transactive memory, where information is stored collectively outside ourselves. When faced with difficult questions, people are primed to think about computers and that when people expect to have future access to information, they have lower rates of recall of the information itself and enhanced recall instead for where to access it.

Table 1.3 The transformation of teaching paradigm

Teaching paradigm Contents for comparison	"Teacher-centered" paradigm	"Learner-centered" paradigm
Teaching organization	To "implement" teaching	"To promote deep learning"
Teaching objectives	To deliver knowledge	To construct knowledge
Management	To provide courses	To create a powerful learning environment
Quality control	To improve the quality of teaching (How to "teach" better)	To improve the quality of learning (How to create a better learning environment)
Content arrangement	To cover all learning materials	Learning materials vary with each individual
Evaluation	"individual" evaluation	"open" evaluation

In the past, in many cases, especially in the emerging fields of adult learning, vocational education, distance and open learning, learning theories such as behaviorist, cognitive or even constructivist do not give a reasonable explanation of current learning practice nor can they give guidance to instruction, instructional organization and instructional design.

Although research and development technicians and educational innovation facilitators have carried out in-depth discussion on the role of technology in education, ordinary teachers and learners have a more direct understanding of the potential role of technology. The role of technology in learning is shown most directly in the aspects of presenting learning materials, data storage, communication, management and cognitive assistance. Its specific forms are mainly that of digital learning resources, virtual learning communities, learning (teaching) management system software platforms and various related support tools. Table 1.4 describes each learning scenario and the potential role that technology plays in the scenario.

1.4.2 Conditions for Effective Learning Activities

Technology provides many potential applications for a variety of learning scenarios and generates new ways of teaching and learning. Initially, an organization or individual has high expectations on technology playing a large role in teaching and learning however, the actual effects are usually not as successful as expected.

The former president of Open University in Britain, Prof. John Daniel (2001) performed an analysis on e-learning and published his results. Firstly, in the past few years, the Internet has changed the definition of distance education. Before 1997, distance education generally referred to using broadband to implement synchronous teaching for distant learners in different places, with an emphasis on recreating the classroom environment (for example simulating face-to face-interaction). However, today the situation has changed; distance education refers to asynchronous teaching on the Internet. Secondly, the mode of asynchronous teaching on the Internet borrows from some traditional distance education concepts. In the simplest form, students study the contents of the course presented as html on the network and take online tests after each session. Third, this simple and ineffective mode of e-learning has been rejected by students. Currently, the development trend is to combine online instruction with a large number of other activities using a web based course to facilitate learning. However, this is not the only means of learning. Fourth, the experience of using a network in teaching at Open University shows that the best application of network technology in teaching is to facilitate interaction among people rather than delivering all contents of the course to the students' computer. Fifth, the value of the interactivity of the Internet and the facilitation of learning by 8,000 tutors is very valuable (Daniel 2001). Therefore, the simplest learning mode of e-learning described earlier is invalid,

Table 1.4 Learning scenarios and the potential roles of technology

Learning scenarios	Learning materials	Learning methods	Roles of the teacher	Potential roles of technology
Classroom lectures (collective)	• Materials/handouts • Presentation tools	• Listening to the teacher • Q&A/discussion	• Teaching • Q&A on site Organize discussion	• Tools for material presentation • Digital Resource Management System (data management)
Self-study (individual)	• Materials/handouts • Digital courses (online and offline)	• Read/browse	• Distance Q&A	• Digital learning resources (materials) • Virtual learning environment (for communication) • Q&A/Help Tools • Learning management system (process management)
Inquiry learning (group)	• Background materials • Study guide	• Discussion (on site and on line)	• instruct tasks/ways of discussion • Evaluation	• Digital learning resources • Virtual learning environment (for exchanges) • Learning management system (process management)
Learning by doing (community)	• Background materials • Operation guide	• Operation/experiment • Discussion	• Explicitly instruct tasks Mentoring • Evaluation	• Digital learning resources • Q&A/Help Tools • Data storage/management
Work-based learning (community)	• Background materials • Job description	• Work • Discussion • Reflection	• Explicitly instruct tasks • Mentoring • Evaluation	• Digital learning resources • Data storage/management

and the best application of network technology is to achieve interaction among people.

From the perspective of knowledge and learning in the information age, Huang et al. (2007) identify in a comparative study on e-learning between Chinese and British students that there are many differences in the methods of e-learning. Additionally the authors identify that there are differences in the methods of tutoring and in selecting learning materials. From this study, they identify the need to investigate whether e-learning really happens.

If we consider "whether learning happens" in a different perspective, it is about "effective learning". In a formal learning environment such as classroom teaching, it refers to the process by which students complete learning tasks, achieve learning objectives and self-development within a certain period of time by using appropriate learning strategies to actively process learning contents under the guidance of teachers. While in an informal learning environment, such as distance learning and e-learning, students may not be under the direct guidance of teachers, there may not be assignments, and the students may not just be using the knowledge learned in the course, but may also be applying other skills and knowledge. However, the student perception may be that a specific task does not lead towards self-development.

Are learning activities effective? Are they successful? A senior researcher at Microsoft, Randy Hinrichs (2003) points out the five indicators of any successful educational activity. They are motivation, time on task, collaboration, critical thinking and feedback.

Critical thinking is an important condition of effective learning activities, describing the learner's implicit behavior, which is difficult to observe. According to the definition of constructivist learning theory, teachers are no longer "philosophers" in the classroom, but function as a tutor and helper of learners. Therefore, "feedback" is a condition of effective learning activities. This is the external (especially tutors, instructors and service supporters) response to the external behaviors of the learners, so it is an external supporting behavior. So what are the motivation, starting point and explicit behaviors of effective learning?

The desire to learn is the driving force for intrinsic motivation, with the main emphasis on non-intellectual factors such as individual learning needs and learning passions generated in learning activities (Shi 1994). Learning interests refer to the positive understanding, willingness and emotional state of a person about learning. Learning interests can be divided into direct and indirect learning interests. Direct learning interest occurs when the student enjoys the learning process, for example via learning materials or learning activities, while indirect learning interest by the results of learning activities. The motivation of learners derives mainly from learning interests.

The starting point of learning refers to the learner's preparedness to the new learning, which is based on their existing level of knowledge and psychological development when they engage in new learning activities (Bransford et al. 2000). Obviously, the boundaries of the "level of knowledge and psychological development" become blurred for adults when learning new knowledge. Usually, based on their cognitive capability, adults can "adapt to" or "make up for" the lack of some field of knowledge through learning. Learning interests are heightened when a learner is confronted with authentic problems, when they are aware of the social significance of the learning or its relationship with or to them. Authentic problems refer to those that are closely related to the work and learning of the learners. These authentic problems may be categorized as:

(1) Helping learners solve their practical problems;
(2) Helping learners understand and deal with difficulties in their work or personal life;
(3) Helping learners to enhance their "working" capabilities; and,
(4) Helping learners develop their personal interests.

These explicit behaviors can be directly observed by for example, throwing a ball, writing, or playing the piano, while implicit behaviors cannot be easily observed without the assistance of tools or experiments (Che 2001). Learning activities should be experienced as an explicit behavior, rather than an implicit behavior. First of all, the observable learning "activities" of the learners, such as reading materials, attending lectures, watching videos, doing homework, or completing a task, etc. are the necessary conditions of "learning". Secondly, the "experience of learning activities" refers to the learners' identification of the existence of such learning activities. When participating in "non-traditional" learning activities, if the learners can identify that "they are really learning", this can increase their sense of achievement and reduce their anxiety, especially when they have completed the assigned learning activities or tasks. Therefore, it can reduce their cognitive load.

The five conditions of effective learning activities are to start with authentic problems, to motivate with learning interests or willingness, to take the experience of learning activities as the explicit behaviors, to take critical thinking as the implicit behaviors and to provide tutoring and feedback as external support, as shown in Fig. 1.2.

Fig. 1.2 The five conditions of effective learning activities

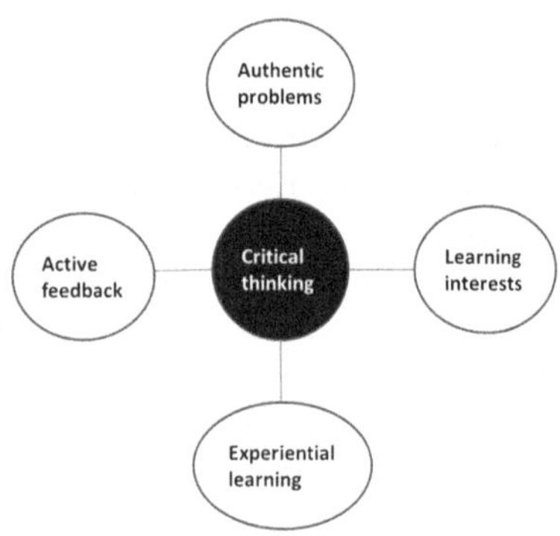

1.4.3 The Five Laws of TEL

When we consider TEL, there are three key elements; e-learning resources, virtual learning environments and learning management systems. These elements are also the fundamental components of e-learning systems. In the traditional classroom, these three elements refer to "the expansion of teaching materials", "learning places" and "classroom management".

1.4.3.1 Law 1: On Intrinsic Access to e-Learning Resources

e-Learning resources refer to multimedia materials running on multimedia computers and network environments and include digital video, digital audio, multimedia software, CD-ROM, websites, email, online learning management systems, computer simulations, online discussion, data files and databases. At present, the most typical forms of e-learning resources are multimedia materials in the form of webpages, which are usually organized according to curriculum objectives and content frameworks, and include descriptions of every part of instruction and learning activities.

In the US Ministry of Education White Papers of Educational Technology issued by the U.S. Ministry of Education, e-learning is defined as "the learning and teaching activities primarily carried out on computers and the network" (quoted from: Intelligence Development Institute of Shanghai Academy of Educational Sciences, 2001). The key to maximizing the effectiveness of e-learning is to intelligently integrate e-learning resources. The application of dynamic digital contents in instruction will increase the level of exploration and research of students. Professor He Kekang (2002) has described e-learning in this way, referring to learning and teaching activities on the Internet or in other digital formats, as achieving a brand new way of learning, making full use of learning environments with new communication mechanisms and rich resources provided by modern information technology. Such a way of learning will change the role of the teacher and the relationship between teachers and students in traditional instruction, which then fundamentally changes the structure of instruction and the nature of education.

In addition to clearly stating the need for learning and teaching activities, the above definition also implies that there should be clear educational objectives that are organized by "trained" teachers. However, it is often unconsciously interpreted that "new ways of learning can be generated by combining new communication mechanisms with e-learning resources", which implies a "common-sense" hypothesis.

Hypothesis 1 (About resources) Provided with e-learning resources of "high-quality", learners will take the initiative to browse or to "read through" all resources in order to learn more effectively than face-to-face teaching.

Due to the existence of Hypothesis 1, when we evaluate e-learning curriculum resources, curriculum resources of "high quality" usually emphasize "the integrity of the contents", "the diversity of media forms" and "the interesting presentation forms", etc.

In a great number of e-learning resources cases, the actual effects of e-learning are far behind people's expectations. From the view of learners, will they actually "seriously learn all e-learning resources"? The answer is obviously no, so Hypothesis 1 is conditional.

Law 1 (About resources) If learners take the initiative to browse or to "read through" all e-learning resources in order to learn more effectively than face-to-face teaching, the resources have to satisfy the following five basic conditions:

(a) (Required contents) The contents are of learners' interests or necessary for them to solve problems;
(b) (Moderate difficulty) The contents are of moderate difficulty and in an appropriate scale, so that cognitive "overload" will not occur;
(c) (Reasonable structure) The structure of the contents is simple and clear, which will not result in thinking "chaos" for learners;
(d) (Proper media) The media are presented in forms that are acceptable to the learners, so that they do not suffer visual strain;
(e) (Clear navigation) The navigation layout is clear with moderate depth so the learners will not get lost.

1.4.3.2 Law 2: On Virtual Learning Communities

Virtual Learning Environment (VLE) refers to a software system used to support learning and teaching in the field of education covering a variety of categories such as teaching support platforms, learning content management systems and discussion forums, etc. Virtual Learning Community (VLC) refers to a group of people who share learning as their primary purpose and share common interests or common discussion topics in a discussion forum. Wang (2005) defines VLC as a new distance education online teaching support platform based on the theory of constructivist learning, computer information processing technology, computer network resource sharing technology and multimedia information display technology. VLC is also a new type of learning structure, so it has sociological attributes as well as the basic attributes of the man–machine system. It is a combination of the requirements of modern society, scientific technology and the theory of learning and teaching. Sun (2005) describe the VLC as breaking through the limitation of time and space of traditional teaching and giving learners the possibility of developing their personalities and to collaborate, so that they can construct knowledge, experience emotion and interact with each other. The VLC has inherited and integrated relative elements of traditional communities, virtual communities and online learning and formed its own representative characteristics, which are technology, common interests and purposes, the exchange of knowledge, inquiry learning and collaborative learning. The above definitions may also be described in the following two ways:

- "VLC is based on constructive learning theory and supported by the technical platform"; and,
- "with VLC, learners can individually construct knowledge, experience emotions and interact with others".

These two descriptions imply a "common-sense" hypothesis of people.

Hypothesis 2 (Virtual Learning Environment) Provided with a "convenient" VLE, learners will communicate as if they were in a an authentic classroom environment and in fact, sometimes even better than an authentic environment.

There are many "successful" cases of virtual communities in business, entertainment and games. These cases are not only popular, but also bring promising economic benefits. It is taken for granted that the "successful" experience is as effective as in the field of education or learning. If we have not achieved the expected effects, we usually attribute this to the "inconvenience" of VLE, which needs design improvements. Therefore, almost all e-learning systems are invariably equipped with VLC, which is regarded as the core component of the system.

Then, can VLC be as "active" as an "online business community" and "game community"? The answer is no. So Hypothesis 2 is also conditional.

Law 2 (About environment) If learners want to communicate in a VLE as in the authentic classroom environment and sometimes even better than an authentic environment, the following three basic conditions are required:

(a) (Sense of belonging to the group) Win the trust of learners so that they feel it is the place where they should "come", providing a sense of "belonging to the group";
(b) (Sense of personal achievements) Provide timely feedback to the learners, so they can find the answers and acquire a sense of achievement in the VLE;
(c) (Sense of emotional identification) Allow learners to gain a sense of emotional identification and release their desire of "competition", "performance" or " conformity" in the VLE.

1.4.3.3 Law 3: On Learning Management Systems

e-Learning management platforms are used to manage e-learning resources using certain methods and technologies in the VLE. With the continuous development and evolution of e-learning, e-learning management platforms have developed from simple management systems into powerful integrated application platforms, and depending on the emphases of their functions, they are also commonly known as learning platforms or learning resource management platforms. So far, learning management systems (LMSs) have different names in accordance with different emphases:

- Content Management System (CMS): The software system consisting of a tool or a set of tools to support content management.
- Learning Content Management System (LCMS): The system consisting of creating, storing, distributing and managing the personalized learning contents in the form of learning objects.
- Learning Activity Management System (LAMS): The system used for designing, managing and delivering online collaborative learning activities, including the learning management environment, the delivery of the sequences of students' activities, the operation and monitoring of teachers to students' activities, and setting up and adapting the activity sequences.

Qian and Sun (2005) defines an LMS as the network system used to effectively manage learning resources, learners and facilitators. Dalsgaard (2006) defines an LMS as well suited for managing student enrolment, exams, assignments, course descriptions, lesson plans, messages, syllabus, basic course materials, etc. LMSs play an important role in web-based teaching, are one of the infrastructures in network education and the main tool for the implementation of network education. "All LMSs have the following functions: user registration and management, courseware directory management, learners' information data recording and reporting to the administrator, etc. An LMS can help learners to arrange schedules on learning progress and to communicate and collaborate with other learners. It can help administrators to know about, track, analyze and report on the learning status of learners" (Yang et al. 2003).

Those definitions imply a certain logical relation, which is that "as long as there is an LMS, it can effectively manage learning resources, learners and facilitators". "An LMS helps with the study plan, communication and collaborative learning". It also implies a "common sense" hypothesis of people.

Hypothesis 3 (Learning management system) If the learners store relevant information in certain structures (in the database), administrators and teachers can effectively manage the learning process.

Learning management systems are "troublesome". In many cases, such as in the scenarios of "information overload" or "you can never find what you want", it is difficult to get the statistics of the information that you want (for example, what are the student's preferences). If the information is stored in a certain format in the computer database, the function of the database system should be to effectively solve the "problem", so the learning process can be effectively managed.

However, the notion that an LMS performs as we expect has been proven to be negative in many studies. It is important for the teachers to effectively manage the learning process of learners using the LMS.

Law 3 (About the system) For the teachers to effectively manage the learning process of learners using the LMS, the following four basic conditions must be satisfied.

(a) (Process coupling) The business model and the "teaching process" are highly coupled;

(b) (Performance promotion) A service-oriented system that can solve practical problems can reduce the work intensity of teachers or lead to better performance;
(c) (Data reliability) The data is safe and reliable so as to acquire the trust of teachers;
d) (Habit formation) The "metaphors" should be clear enough for teachers to easily understand the design of the LMS and therefore quickly "form" good habits on how to manage the LMS.

1.4.3.4 Law 4: On user's Understanding of the Designer's Intention

Both e-learning resources and VLEs and LMSs are artifacts designed by people. People often consider the following hypothesis on the designer psychology.

Hypothesis 4 (Designer psychology) Usually, users can clearly understand the design intention of e-learning resources, learning support platforms and learning management systems.

So far, there are many digital curriculum resources of "high quality" and evolving learning support platforms and management information systems with "comprehensive" functions, but how many designers will admit that they do not "carefully" design? Obviously, the sub-consciousness of designers trusts that the users should understand their design intention. In fact, Hypothesis 4 is completely wrong.

Law 4 (About design) Users may not clearly understand the designer's intentions of curriculum resources, learning support platforms and management information systems. Design that does not take into account user psychology is usually considered a failure.

In order to make users understand the design intention, the following three methods can be applied:

(a) The use of "metaphor" and "common sense";
(b) Clear and concise documents;
(c) A universal standard of labels and symbols that is made public and available to teachers and students.

1.4.3.5 Law 5: On Learners Asking for Help

When the designers design e-learning resources, VLEs and LMSs, they always have a hypothesis about the learner's mindset.

Hypothesis 5 (Learner mindset) Irrelevant of distance learning or on-site learning, learners will naturally turn to the teachers for help when encountering learning difficulties in order to achieve learning objectives.

With instruction organized on campus, a specific time and location are usually arranged for tutoring and answering questions. Teachers who make their contact information public so that students may contact them when having problems are considered as "good teachers". With network education, "making the contact information of teachers, tutors and supporting staff public and appointing relevant staff on duty" is considered as the most typical form of learning support service. However, Hypothesis 5 is also completely wrong.

Law 5 (About users) Irrelevant of distance learning or on-site learning, learners may not turn to the teachers for help when encountering learning difficulties. So the "passive" type of tutoring is usually regarded as a failure.

In order to make learners turn to the teachers for help when encountering difficulties, there are three necessary conditions:

(a) Appropriate external pressure;
(b) The intimacy of teachers;
(c) Timely and effective feedback.

After clarifying the laws regarding TEL, the next step in the process then is to determine the most effective way of implementing digital resources into the connected learning paradigm.

1.5 The Transformation of Digital Resources from Nibbled Learning to Connected Learning

As Wiley (2000) digital resources are valuable in the support of learning. Digital resources are a very important component of connected learning as they fully reflect the needs of the learner, allowing for more effective learning in the current information age. The current forms of digital resources and their requirements in connected learning will now be discussed.

1.5.1 Typical Forms of Digital Resources for Nibbled Learning

Impacted by the habits of traditional teaching mode, digital resources in e-learning are stamped with the brand of nibbled teaching mode, which produces resources of "the knowledge maze" whose contents emphasize the structure of learning theories in a professional, systematic and complete way. People that conform to this idea specifically advocate for the resources organized and developed by the "experts". This preset learning mode migrates naturally from the part of nibbled teaching process to include three typical types; classroom migration resources, digitalized independent-learning resources and simple mixing resources. These correspond to the teaching forms of "classroom lectures," "self-study after class (reading materials) "and "listening to the lectures and reviewing".

1.5.1.1 Classroom Migration Resources (CMR): A Metaphor for Traditional Classroom Transfer

The main feature of this type is that teachers "move" the teaching contents from the face-to-face classroom to the Internet. Some of the lecture materials, teaching materials and electronic homework are presented in the form of web pages, some are recorded and delivered as part of the courseware using streaming media that can be watched on demand and some use the form of live video given as face-to-face lectures that may be viewed in real-time via the Internet from learning stations in other locations. All of the methods described that move classroom teaching to the Internet are referred to as the classroom migration type. With curriculum of this type, the teaching methods and structures have not been fundamentally changed, only the methods of delivering the information via an intermediary media have been changed. Chen and Yao (2006) point out that online teaching in many schools throughout China is still following the traditional teaching mode where the teachers are giving lectures as videos and the students are listening remotely using a computer monitor as the only medium. Presently, the number of students in China learning via distance education is enormous, and most of these students demonstrate weak self-study habits. Curriculum forms of this type require fewer teachers per student therefore allowing for more students. As this model is seemingly acceptable to students, its existence is reasonable. However, in this form of curriculum, the main features of online learning for the students' are passive learning, mechanical memory and the grasping of knowledge points. This does not meet the conditions of learning taking place (Huang et al. 2007). In many cases, real learning does not occur.

1.5.1.2 Digitalized Independent-Learning Resources (DIR): A Metaphor for the Digitalization of Self-Study Materials

Some online courses are presented as the type of digitalized independent-learning, which means that the teachers upload the learning materials and contents to the online curriculum platform for students' to access via self-study. In this curriculum form, teachers provide students with the learning materials, supporting exercises, review questions and assessment requirements, but they do not design corresponding learning activities for students or provide the required tutoring and support in the learning process. Curriculum of this type reflects the student-centered teaching philosophy to a certain degree, which allows for the openness and flexibility of network education, but the actual practices are not ideal. In the process of online teaching, most teachers still use network technology as the tool for displaying the learning materials. They upload these materials to the Internet for the students to read and to learn. Students often give up because of the lack of usefulness of this kind of learning. Teachers have not made full use of the advantages of the network environment; they just use the network for the sake of the network, which does not reflect the appeal of online education. Online learning emphasizes individual learning of the learners, including taking initiative. In this type of online self-study, it is difficult for the learners to identify problems and to arouse their learning interests in the face of boring learning materials, or to experience the process of social construction in the learning activities, not to mention discussion and exchanges with the teachers for timely feedback. Under these conditions, the sense of loneliness and frustration of the students will become more serious, leading to very little critical thinking and ultimately to the probability of giving up the entire process of online learning. Therefore, with curriculum of this type of online self-study, real learning is difficult to find.

1.5.1.3 Simple Mixed Resources (SMR): A Metaphor for the Mixing of Traditional and Digitalized Learning Resources

Curriculum of this type uses blended teaching, which means that teachers will move part of the teaching process and contents to the network, for example, by providing lecture notes and assignments on an LMS platform, while the other part of instruction is still carried out face to face in the classroom, or online in the "classroom migration" type. Compared with the curriculum of online self-study, the simple blended curriculum provides more learning support to online learners and it is currently the most widely used curriculum form in online teaching. The main disadvantage of the simple blended type is that teachers currently do not involve students in the constructive process of learning through the experience and interaction of systematic instructional design, in particular, the design of learning activities, so online teaching is simply blended with classroom teaching without effective integration. This means that the advantage of online learning has not been fully realized.

The above types of resources are products of the traditional teaching mode, which is a large part of nibbled learning, especially in regards to instruction delivered on campus. Firstly, these resources can provide a way of adjusting the teaching process in a class to account for the few students who do not keep up with the teaching progress or miss the class for various reasons. Secondly, they provide an effective way of accessing the resources between classes and schools for the few students with special interests and requirements, for example, facilitating students who are going to take entrance exams for postgraduate study. Thirdly, they provide an opportunity for teachers to share their teaching experience; this reduces the time of lesson preparation. However, these types of resources have little impact on promoting changes in the teaching mode, and in many cases, may even prevent it. Firstly, these resources further promote students' ability in the examination process, which reduces their interest in learning. Secondly, they provide the opportunity for some teachers to take the easy route, which further weakens their studies in the teaching materials and the teaching content. Thirdly, due to the easy accessibility of the answers, some students' understanding of the contents shows a decreased value, which will naturally lead to the decline of learning efficacy.

In the field of distance education, these resources fit to some extent into the habits of the learners that were formed in the traditional classroom. Currently, in China, the present distance learners are not qualified successful applicators of nibbled learning. With the conflicts of time in their work and learning as well as the irrelevance of what they learn compared to the requirements of actual work, the practical effects of these resources are not ideal. The field of distance education urgently calls for a new learning mode to solve the conflict of teaching and learning in the space–time separation of teachers and learners. However, as teachers and students are used to the nibbled teaching mode, this restricts the current mode of producing digital resources and the development of new learning modes.

1.5.2 Typical Forms of Digital Resources for Connected Learning

The change of learning form in China will long be affected by the influence of traditional nibbled teaching mode. This means that in the fields of e-learning and "network education", "classroom migration" and "online self-study" forms will take a long-term dominant position in learning. Any large-scale change of learning modes is a gradual process and it has quietly taken place in the informal learning environment. However, the change of teaching methods in schools is obviously falling behind it. The boundary of campus education and distance education will become increasingly blurred. In the aspect of the organization of learning activities, face-to-face learning and online learning will no longer exist in isolation, with blended learning becoming the replacement. The ideal mode of blended learning is the new learning mode, informatization learning mode.

It is widely anticipated that the new learning mode should have independence, inquiry and collaboration as its basic features. Independent learning should consist of self-planning, self-monitoring and self-evaluation. Inquiry learning should be oriented with open-ended questions and provide accurate assessments based on the definition of questions and learning outcomes. Collaborative learning should provide peer consultation, mutual inspiration and expressivity. This new concept of learning is defined by five typical forms of learning resources, specifically; mini courseware and "apps", task-oriented resources, experience-oriented resources, collaboration-oriented resources, and social learning resources. Following is a description of the components and orientations of the digital resources used to aid in organizing learning or learning materials. Of course, these five forms are not completely independent in a specific course; they are usually integrated or blended.

1.5.2.1 Mini Courseware and "Apps" (MCA)

Mini courseware and "apps" are suitable for learners who are busy working and have small slices of time available for learning as well as having little or no fixed learning location. Additionally, it is only suitable for learning less difficult courses, which only need the understanding and remembrance of some new concepts. Learning resources are mainly based on the design of mini activities. With this type, the number of learning activities may larger, but learning tasks should not be too complicated. During the process of organizing learning activities, a variety of recommended measures need to be taken. The forms of learning resources are mainly reading texts, listening to audio or watching video. These are best displayed on handheld learning terminals that support portability and are also suitable for reading. The evaluation is mainly based on objective and short-answer questions. The test results should be recorded and included as a part of the course scores.

1.5.2.2 Task Oriented Resources (TOR)

The basic characteristic of task oriented resources is to organize learning based on a series of "learning activities". From the perspective of learners, each learning activity includes four aspects; learning tasks, learning resources, evaluation methods and learning support services. Learning tasks require a clear description of the learning outcomes so that the learners can explicitly understand what they should do in the associated activity. Evaluation methods should adequately examine the completion of learning activities without focusing on the assessment of learners' memorization of the learning contents. Learning support services are extremely important, so the instructors or tutors have to understand the learning difficulties and learning environment of the learners so as to facilitate effective communication with them. There should not be too many learning activities in a course so as to reduce the cognitive burden of the learners. The basic principle of preparing learning resources is that they should be adequate and appropriate to completing the learning tasks with the result of reducing redundant resources.

1.5.2.3 Experience Oriented Resources (EOR)

Experience oriented resources are suitable for courses consisting of only a few concepts that focus on the training of operational skills. There are two types of these resources. The first resource is used to instruct and support operational skills in a real environment, and the second resource is used for virtual experiments or online drilling software. The former is used to examine the feasibility of real conditions, while the latter is used to examine the availability of virtual reality software. The forms of learning resources are mainly based on corresponding cases, clear operational instructions and specific methods of assessment and evaluation.

1.5.2.4 Collaboration Oriented Resources (COR)

Collaboration oriented resources refer to the type of learning activities that use organized groups with the primary goal of solving complex problems. The learning objectives of each individual are coherent with those of the group, and the evaluation of group members will be interdependent. The collaboration type is suitable for courses with relatively clear tasks and complex problems and ill-structured. The difficulty of this type is in how to design group-learning tasks and in grouping strategies. Sharing the group experience of completing the tasks is the foundation for the continuous development of collaborative learning in groups. The forms of learning resources are mainly based on corresponding cases, activity instructions and evaluation methods of tasks in groups.

1.5.2.5 Social Learning Resources (SLR)

Social Learning Resources are suitable for courses with open-ended questions, individual empirical knowledge and inquiry knowledge construction. The learning process usually includes problem definition, individual knowledge inquiry, group experience sharing and the expression of learning outcomes and so on. The difficulty of curriculum design includes how to evaluate the individual contribution of knowledge, how to motivate learners and how to intervene in the learning process and so on. The resources required are mainly based on the resource index, the rules and evaluation methods of experience sharing.

These five forms of resources are gradually being applied and accepted, especially in informal learning environments and related training. Over time, they will gradually become the mainstream form of learning resources.

1.6 Other Aspects on the Transmission from Nibbled Learning to Connected Learning

The construction of resources is the basis of the realization from nibbled learning to connected learning. In addition, the construction of the following aspects should be focused on in order to realize the smooth transmission from nibbled learning to connected learning.

1.6.1 Focus on the Research on Learning Psychology in the Technology Environment

First of all, it is required to study the differences of technology-based learning of different people. At present, the importance of the problem-solving capability, innovative thinking, collaborative skills, information literacy and so on has been recognized, but how to eliminate the digital gap so as to enable all learners to have effective learning with the application of technology is the important research subject for the construction of environment and resources. Secondly, it is required to further study the characteristics of learning behaviors and psychological processes of human in the technology environment, how human and technology environment achieve interaction and what factors affect the psychology of the learners (such as motivation). With the development of technology and the advancement of the study on learning psychology in technology environment, researches in the field of educational technology will no longer satisfy the simple application of the technology, so the establishment of adaptive learning and collaborative learning environment will surely become the focus of pilot researches. Technology-supported learning environment will truly reflect the characteristics of openness, sharing, interaction and collaboration and so on. In this type of learning environment, there will be more emphasis on the non-intelligent factors such as the internal emotion of learners and on the role of social interaction in learning.

1.6.2 Pay More Attention to the Design and Support of Learning Activities

To achieve the connected learning, the instructional design should not only pay attention to the design of learning resources and learning process, but also more to the design and support of learning activities. The instructional design of connected learning will focus more and more on curriculum integration, especially the integration of general disciplines and information technology. In the process of integration, how to design research-based learning activities, authentic problem-based learning activities, integrated learning activities and collaborative learning activities so as to allow the learners to integrate the knowledge of different disciplines and how to cultivate innovative talents are the key points and also the difficult points of instructional design. The learning process and activities of the learners will be designed to be more flexible. In the learning process, the mentoring role of the teachers will become more prominent, and the studies on the support for learning process will become more important. The transmission of the role of teachers from "the sage on the platform" to "the mentor by students' side" also means that the instructional plan is no longer the design of the teaching process of the teachers as in traditional instructional plans, but should be transmitted to the "learning plan", where the learning process and activities of the students will be designed as an important part.

1.6.2.1 Learning Support and Services

To promote connected learning, we have to understand the learners first, and then provide personalized support and services according to the characteristics of learners. Therefore, learner modeling, the analysis of learning characteristics and the instruction in accordance with learning characteristics should be the focus in the future research and practice.

Educational technology has paid close attention to the support for student learning in research and practice, including the aspects of student learning activities, teaching organization and teaching evaluation and so on in the context of information technology in particular in the network environment. The teachers working in the frontline of education can deeply feel the problems in teaching, and only they can solve the problems with theoretical knowledge according to actual situations. The practitioners of educational technology should provide a variety of ideas and methods to solve practical teaching problems for the teachers so as to effectively support student learning.

1.6.2.2 Training for Teachers

The supporting service for the teachers is one of the key factors in the realization of the transmission of learning methods, which relates to the issue of training for teachers. All nations in the world attach great importance to the training for teachers. In 2000, the U.S. International Educational Technology Association developed "Basic Standards on Educational Technology for All Teachers", which standardizes the basic capabilities of educational technology that should be mastered by teachers, and systematic training on educational technology for teachers is required in order to achieve the standards. In addition, the U.K., France, Singapore, South Korea and other countries also attach great importance to the trainings for teachers. According to the survey, 1/3 of the teachers in the areas with the rapid development of educational technology in China still do not quite understand or even know about the knowledge of educational technology. It also shows that most of the teachers in the frontline of teaching welcome the trainings on educational technology with strong learning motivation. Therefore, it is a guarantee of realizing the transmission of learning styles to figure out how to carry out trainings on technology-promoted learning for teachers, especially how to implement effective trainings so that teachers in the frontline will truly understand the learners and understand how to use technology to promote effective learning of the learners.

1.6.2.3 More Comprehensive Review and Study on the Application of Computer in Education

So far, countries around the world have invested a lot of manpower, materials and financial resources to research and explore the application of new technologies in the field of education. Delighted for the practice, we have to think calmly about several issues of the application of the computers in the field of education in order to obtain more comprehensive understandings.

The targets of the application: As proved in practice, computers are not equally effective in all disciplines and objects, especially related to the disciplines relevant to the humanities or the cultivation of personal emotions and those with emphasis on the cultivation of practical operation capacity. Therefore, it should be grasped that the application of computers in education should focus on which disciplines, knowledge points and learning objects and what kind of strategies should be used.

The conditions of the application: The application of computers in education should consider whether the leaders attach great importance, whether the funds can keep up, whether the teachers have basic computer skills, whether there are sufficient teaching resources to support and whether they have sufficient mental preparation and so on. There are close relationships among various conditions, so the standards and combinations of conditions vary to different regions and different schools. So the practitioners specialized in researchers on educational technology have to select different regions and different types of schools for scientific experiments by adequate investigations, field trips and comparisons, and then promote the successful experience.

The effectiveness of the application: The effectiveness of the application contains two meanings. One refers to the effects of the application of computer in education and instruction, which usually takes the evaluation results of the education and instruction as the primary reference. The other one refers to the ratio of the input and output, which is the issue of effectiveness. People have done a lot of work for the former, while they also pay more and more attention to the latter. However, there have been no practical research results on the effectiveness of the investment in the application of computers and other technologies in education so far, so it will result in the blindness of investment by people and also impede the further development of educational technology. The comprehensive study on the effectiveness of the application of computers in education will be an important part of the researches on educational technology.

References

Baum WM (2005) Understanding behaviorism: behavior, culture and evolution. Blackwell, Malden

Bransford JD, Brown A, Cocking R (2000) How people learn: brain, mind, experience, and school. National Academy Press, Washington, DC

Carlson S (2005) The net generation goes to college. Chron High Educ 52(7):A34

Che W (2001) The encyclopedia of psychological counseling (in Chinese). Science and Technology Press, Hangzhou

Chen S, Yao B (2006) The definition, development and status quo of network teaching. Adult High Educ J 4:9–12

Cole M, Cole SR, Lightfoot C (2005) The development of children. Worth Publishers, New York
Conole G, Oliver M (1998) A pedagogical framework for embedding C&IT into the curriculum. Assoc Learn Technol J 6(2):4–16
Dalsgaard C (2006) Social software: E-learning beyond learning management systems. Eur J Open Distance E-Learn. Retrieved October 12, 2011 from http://www.eurodl.org/materials/contrib/2006/Christian_Dalsgaard.htm
De Jong T (2006) Technological advances in inquiry learning. Science 312:532f
Dienil J (2001) The challenge of open university in the new century (in Chinese). Distance Educ China 1:10–14
Farber BA, Brink DC, Raskin PM (1998) The psychotherapy of Carl Rogers: cases and commentary. Guilford Press, New York
He K (2002) The essence of e-learning: Integration of information technology and curriculum. E-educ Res 1:36
Hinrichs R (2003) Learner modeling and assessment R&D for technology-enabled learning systems. Learning Federation Steering Committee, Washington, DC
Huang R, Zhang Z, Chen G, Xu Z (2007) Online learning: does learning really happens: comparison of Chinese and British online learning in intercultural context (in Chinese). Open Educ Res 13(6):12–24
Kim S, Nolan PD (2006) Measuring "social informatization": a factor analytic approach. Sociol Inq 76(2):188–209
Li M, Chen W (2006) e-Learning methods: theoretical perspective. Open Educ Res 2:18–22
Lombardi MM (2007) Authentic learning for the 21st century: an overview. Educause Learn Initiative 1(2007):1–12
Maslow AH, Stephens DC, Heil G, Bennis W (1998) Maslow on management. Wiley, New York
Mayer RE (2004) Should there be a three-strikes rule against pure discovery learning? Am Psychol 59(1):14
Prensky M (2001) Digital natives, digital immigrants Part 1. On the Horizon 9(5):1–6
Qi G (2003) Social informatization and sustainable development. J Social Theory Guide 10:53–55
Qian G, Sun S (2005) To analyzed- based learning manage system by distance learning circle theory (in Chinese). Mod Educ Technol 1:28–36
Santrock JW (2004) A topical approach to life-span development. Cognitive development approaches. McGraw-Hill, New York, pp 200–225
Shi L (1994) Learning theory (in Chinese). Peoples Education Press, Beijing
Shi Y, Lin Z (2009) Cross-national study between the level of societal informatization and the quality of life. Chin J Manag 8:1019–1028
Siemens G (2004) Connectivism: a learning theory for the digital age. Int J Instruction Tech Distance Learn. Retrieved on November 12, 2011, from http://www.itdl.org/Journal/Jan_05/article01.htm
Slater L (2004) Opening skinner's box: great psychological experiments of the twentieth century. Bloomsbury, London
Sparrow B, Liu J et al (2011) Google effects on memory: cognitive consequences of having information at our fingertips. Science 333(6043):776
Sun D (2005) On the enlightenment of engaged learning theory to construct virtual learning community (in Chinese). J Distance Educ 6:22–25
Wang L (2005) The principle and application of virtual learning community (in Chinese). High Education Press, Beijing
Wiley DA (2000) Connecting learning objects to instructional design theory: a definition, a metaphor, and a taxonomy. Learn Technol 2830(435):1–35
Woolfolk A, Winne, PH, Perry NE (2006) Educational psychology: canadian edition (3rd ed.). Scarborough, Ontario: Allyn & Bacon, Canada
Yang K (2005) Learning activity-centered instruction design (in Chinese). Publish House of Electronics Industry, Beijing, pp 82–83

Yang Z, Wu D, Liu Q (2003) Network education standards and technology (in Chinese). Tsinghua University Press, Beijing

Zhang D, Nunamaker JF (2003) Powering e-learning in the new millennium: an overview of e-learning and enabling technology. Inf Syst Frontiers 5(2):207–218

Chapter 2
Emerging Dimensions of Learning

Erkki Sutinen

Abstract Within the current global financial crisis, education has seemingly conflictive expectations as a producer of experts that can bring the globe back on track. One of the tensions lies between the formality and informality of education. While the formal approach emphasizes strict goal settings, accreditation and quality management, the proponents for informal learning call for flexibility and organic competence creation. Cases from K12 technology education with robots, contextual Information and Communication Technology education in developing countries and context-aware mobile learning games help to take the two approaches into real contexts. These examples open a scheme where technology can serve as a vehicle to combine the assets of formal and informal learning into a creative tension towards transformational learning.

2.1 Introduction

Learning and education are generally understood as the main drivers for wealth creation and poverty reduction—the problems that the developing countries need to solve in order to progress. The motivation for developing functional education is to reach the next one billion of particularly young, illiterate, unemployed people. Ordinary methods or conventional education do not suffice for the effort. At the same time, developed countries are struggling with the aging population. With a fast changing society, the elderly need to learn to cope with the surrounding

E. Sutinen (✉)
School of Computing, University of Eastern Finland, Joensuu, Finland
e-mail: erkki.sutinen@uef.fi

R. Huang et al. (eds.), *Reshaping Learning*, New Frontiers of Educational Research,
DOI: 10.1007/978-3-642-32301-0_2,

changes and new digital services that they are dependent on, and the rare young people need to get education that matches almost one-to-one with their future jobs.

Much too often, the solutions for educational challenges have been hunted for using the dimensions of formal and informal learning. Formalists have believed in multiplying what they call "the best practices". They are a synonym to introducing quality management systems to follow up their implementations devising national tests based on standards for school achievements and using technologies for streamlining learning outcomes and even processes. An informalist develops solutions that match authentic problems, and an extremist in their field could not care less about how the students can apply their skills in foreign settings. Standardization of qualifications is not an issue.

The problem is that informal and formal perspectives are not independent dimensions but represent the extremes of one dimension. In fact, the dichotomy maps the landscape of education in terms of forms. Even the contents or the spirit of learning are understood in terms of forms. From the viewpoint of integrating technology into education, the formal/informal division calls for technologies that manage a formal learning process or facilitate an informal one.

For the emerging grand challenges of learning, earlier recipes do not seem to work, including the dichotomy of formal and informal learning. The reasons are in the low number of teachers, their poor competences, lacking schooling infrastructure, too narrow or irrelevant competence spectrum of school graduates, among many others. Technology has been expected to answer to the presented problems. However, the technology used has been mainly developed with other application areas in mind, and in contexts that do not suffer from the problems described above. Therefore, it is important to identify fresh dimensions for learning that would release the imagination of educators to open the world of learning—knowledge, skills, and attitudes—to those not yet accessing it.

But how to identify the fresh dimensions? I would argue that the learning research community needs to go back to the ground and the grassroots. The explorations need to take place within the challenges, together with the learning communities. This requires risk-taking that has not really been in the focus of learning research. On the contrary, various ethical committees have made it sure that research happens in almost a vacuum, or clinical environments, and does not intervene with the learner or the learning process. Instead it observes a given, controlled learning situation, and, certainly, does not take risks. From the viewpoint of educational technology, the use of experimental methodology has meant that much of the research focuses on evaluating the use of existing technologies, or toy solutions only designed for the purpose of research. Too small a part of educational technology research aims at designing advanced technologies for real-life challenges. However, in science, it is always true that we are learning when we cross the frontiers of the current wisdom, and this involves risks.

Although money is usually one of the bottlenecks that prevent learning, it cannot solve the problem entirely. A recent article by Jansen (2011) analyzes the South African situation. Even within massive investments in education, the level of skills in mathematics and science has decreased among pupils coming from disadvantaged communities or families. Jansen requires shifting the focus from money onto educators and their professional pride. Part of this pride is openness to cross the borders by exploring new ways to tackle the challenge, and then be proud of what had been found out.

Within an action research oriented study in learning Java programming to solve a problem, the researcher got negative feedback from their teacher students. The conventional approach to learn Java per se seems to lie deep in teachers' understanding of quality teaching.

One of the key principles of the world-renown Finnish teacher education is to empower teachers. A teacher's professional pride lies in their deep understanding that they are the best teacher for their class. To a major extent, the current article is based on this foundation. The dimensions of learning have been derived from individual cases that have taken the teacher researchers to various boundaries of learning.

2.2 In the Quest for Ideal Learning

Throughout history, the quest for ideal learning has had diverse drivers. This section identifies examples of these drivers. They are characterized by varying agenda: political, economical, psychological, philosophical, and finally, technological.

An example of how *politics* can influence pedagogy is the well-known Sputnik crisis in the 1950s. During the cold war era, American pedagogy needed to back to basics from more exploratory movements. The change was based on the interpretation that the Soviet science and mathematics education had outperformed the American one: it had brought up skillful scientists that took the cold war competitor to the outer space before the U.S. The outcome of the emphasis on the basics was the orientation towards formal education.

Economical interests have a significant role on new pattern of learning, but interestingly, they might not always lead to a formal or standardized focus. The Bauhaus school (Droste 1990) that flourished in Germany in the 1920s had roots in, among others, economics. It was expected to preserve the German competitiveness with England. The school was supposed to be a barrier-breaking, interdisciplinary learning environment for novel design.

The role of *psychological* research for education is apparent. The emphasis on informal versus formal learning has a parallel in the concepts of the unconscious and the conscious. In the 1970s, the psychologist Bettelheim stated that children can elaborate their unconscious fears within conscious stories, making the traditional tales enchanting (Bettelheim 1976). The tales help the children to prepare for their future. Thus, stories can be an informal learning milieu that enriches the learning process by emotional aspects.

Especially in science and mathematics education, it is possible to identify the barrier between a formal and an informal approach. From the *philosophical* viewpoint, radical empiricism calls for an approach where learning needs to be based on immediate observation, and therefore, it cannot follow a formal process driven by theory or a given curriculum. A theory-based education squeezes down the empirical reality, informed by accepted or authorized theories (Beynon 2007). Pólya (1957) follows the empirical approach by encouraging teachers to teach mathematics in the way that it is done: by experimentation.

Technological developments have had diverse influences on pedagogy, supporting either the formal or the informal approach. An example of the formal interest is adaptive hypermedia (Brusilovsky 2001) that could basically orchestrate the learning process though a hyperspace. Papert's ideas on constructionism (Papert 1980) show how technology can open a learner in an informal setting. In his ideas of how technology can join science and art, Steve Jobs has echoed the agenda of the Bauhaus movement.

Based on the examples above, we use the attribute *formal* to refer to education that emphasizes structure, discipline, and expected outcomes, whereas *informal* learning gives a learner a foundation that she or he can play in, and learn as a side-effect.

In the following, we will see how experiences at the grassroots level can shape education in a *bottom-up* way. This approach is complementary to a more *top-down* principle of designing education based on international standards, like PISA for basic education or Shanghai lists for ranking universities. In a way, our approach takes the human rights into the centre of educational reform. It is the human situation with its all ambivalence and change in the surrounding society that maintains creative tension between formal and informal learning.

2.3 Four Seasons of Exploring Learning Approaches in Diverse Settings

The section describes four approaches that have successfully mixed formal and informal flavors of learning in real contexts. The approaches all share contexts that have been atypical platforms for learning, thus been the borderland for exploring new dimensions for learning. They cover the years 2002–2011, and the projects were located worldwide. The contexts have been arranged by seasons, indicating the stage within the overall research process and the role of the approach.

2.3.1 Spring: Preparing the ground—Kids' Club

"Kids' Club" is a technology laboratory where children between 10 and 16 years work with university students and researchers as co-designers of new technologies. The first Kids' Club following the agenda was established in 2002 at the

Fig. 2.1 Children ideating and learning in Kids' club

University of Joensuu (part of University of Eastern Finland as of 2010). Unlike a conventional afterhours technology club, the laboratory emphasizes research and an active collaboration with companies. Usually, an instance of Kids' Club has gathered twice a month throughout one school year with an overarching theme, like designing a miniature copper mine, or devising a smart door. The Kids' Clubs have had around ten children and two to three students or researchers per annum. Robots, like LEGO Mindstorms, have had a key role in shaping of the Kids' Club (Fig. 2.1) (Virnes et al. 2008).

The Kids' Club concept has been used in particularly challenging learning settings, with outstanding results. Learner groups consisted of both special education pupils with ADHD, Asperger's syndrome and autism, and an SOS children's village in Lusaka, Zambia. It has also been modified into a Seniors' Club where elderly citizens, with no prior skills in information and communication technology (ICT), have been able to design and implement digital games. The learning environments have allowed us to explore and devise novel technologies as well as pedagogical approaches to the learning process. The diverse settings have opened a novel field of study, and contributed to a set of research papers and theses.

Kids' Clubs have featured formal aspects, like curriculum and explicit learning goals. However, informal aspects of learning have dominated the concept. Children have solved authentic problems, and their work has not been formally assessed. Creativity and wide collaboration with local communities have characterized the approach. The university students, most of whom are completing a Computer Science degree, that have been involved in the Kids' Club activities have not only got course credits but, more importantly, learned valuable competences from working with particularly demanding and knowledgeable customers. Thus, the mix between formal and informal aspects has not only shaped the children's learning process, but also that of the university students.

From the viewpoint of our overall research agenda, Kids' Club prepared the ground for understanding how co-design of technology can break the conventional separation of formal and informal leaning. As a concept, it generated the dimensions describing the participation of the members of the learning community. Access, ownership and commitment cannot be classified as formal or informal aspects of learning. Besides the level of participation, Kids' Club focused our attention to the drivers of the learning process: invention, authenticity, diversity, and technology.

2.3.2 Summer: Growth by Cross-Fertilizing Formal and Informal Education—Contextualized ICT Education in Developing Countries

One of the challenges of ICT education in developing countries is that it does not match the realities of where graduates are supposed to work (Bass and Heeks 2011). Our work in Tanzania, at Tumaini University, Iringa University College, started with explorations on how ICT can be learned without the conventional approach of learning programming in the ABC style, starting from variables. Since 2002 we started the work by applying the Kids' Club approach of learning programming by building robots. Later we abstracted the approach from hands-on technologies towards context-in learning. The contextual undergraduate program in ICT started at Tumaini in 2007, and the first cohort of the three-year program consisted of 27 students. The program was built on the idea that the students, from the very first day of their studies, are working with local people that set requirements for the technology that the students, therefore, need to learn. In addition, the students get the topic for their thesis in their first year, which helps them to integrate their courses around a topic of interest (Tedre et al. 2009).

The frontier that allowed us to identify a dimension for learning at the Tumaini curriculum development process was that of courage. Most universities in developing countries have low academic self-esteem to design their own curricula that would match the surroundings. Also, private universities like Tumaini need to fund their operations by study fees. Introducing a novel program to its curriculum would present a fiscal risk by possibly resulting in a decreasing number of enrolled students.

Aiming at a university degree, the Tumaini ICT program is based on a formal approach: it follows a curriculum that has contents from the universal Computing curriculum. However, the formal aspects are balanced by informal ones.

Community outreach is a basis for problem-based theses that motivate students to explore on their own. The students also break the barriers of conventional undergraduate education by being exposed to and doing research within the user communities and novel pedagogical approaches.

Within the overall research agenda, the contextual ICT education forms the growing period which allowed us to cross-fertilize formal and informal education. The summer period of our research generated the dimensions of transformational and transactional university education. The dimension indicates the societal expectations of university education. The traditional transactional education emphasizes the values of formal education, like efficiency and standards, but does not reduce to it. Transformational education is an agent for change: education should not only serve as a wish list for future employers, but change the reality itself.

2.3.3 Autumn: Processing the Harvested Ideas—Context-Aware Mobile Learning Environments in Authentic Settings

Idea-wise, our work in context-aware mobile learning games is an application of the contextual approach in education to technology itself. Since 2006, we have created mobile games for a science festival, an open-air museum, a forest located in a biosphere region, and the Museum of Technology in Helsinki (Fig. 2.2). All of these games have shared the context-aware approach that allows the mobile game to follow the user in the environment where they are. The games are based on interactive stories that require the users to carry out tasks or solve puzzles in the surrounding environment. For example, an interactive story takes an open-air museum visitor into the 19th century where they need to locate various objects within the museum premises in order to solve the puzzle (Islas Sedano et al. 2010).

The frontier that challenged the designers of the games was in game developers' interaction with the content experts. Museums, science festivals and biosphere regions are predominantly places for informal and explorative learning. Museum curators are not usually familiar with technology. Applying technology into these settings might easily flatten the experience and narrow an otherwise free exploration into a linear path. The linearization of a path has happened for example with interactive museum guides that mostly take the visitors the fastest way from one place of interest to the next one.

Formal aspects of context-aware learning games are shown in the rules of the games that enforce the visitor to experience the context as an organized setting. Informal aspects of the games are based on the authenticity of the learning experience in an out-of-classroom surrounding.

The period with context-aware learning games allowed us to process the harvest of our earlier intervention: the observations on the importance of context in the ICT curriculum design. The approach generated the dimension of context awareness. Context awareness is an integral perspective of the design process,

Fig. 2.2 Context-aware games are designed in their user environment in close collaboration with content experts

and it applies to the availability of local resources. In addition, context awareness can be intensified in the learning experience by technical implementation.

2.3.4 Winter: Consuming the Lessons Learned for the Next Rounds—Design Milieux

Inspired by our research on using ICT for HIV and AIDS education, we have come up with a scheme of design milieux (Duveskog et al. 2012). The concept of a design milieu captures the features that promote successful design of learning environments in authentic settings. Although based on the analysis of approaches described here, the concept of a design milieu allows us to reflect upon and summarize the lessons learned from the seasons of Kids' Club, ICT education in context, and context-aware games.

Unlike most research in educational technology, the analysis of design milieux does not pay attention to how technology enhances the learning process or its outcomes. On the contrary, it concentrates on the characteristics of the environment where a given learning technology has been designed and implemented. This is an important aspect, because technology functions more and more as a tool to enhance the learning process, whereby the learning community becomes the design community rather than a user community of a set of digital learning materials. Thus, this research aspect has taken us from limits of a conventional user scenario towards a more unknown design scenario.

A design process can follow a formal pattern from specifications until an end product, and the co-designers can be assessed on their contributions to this process. However, learning as a design endeavor can be more naturally understood from the viewpoint of informal learning.

The outcome of the analysis of design milieux generated a dimension that describes a given milieu by the following characteristics:

1. Creative engagement of student designers.
2. Support from leadership.
3. Sense of ownership in process and product.
4. Freedom of expression.
5. The development of new expected and unexpected skills.
6. The variety of technical equipment and resources.
7. The appearance and quality of the intervention.
8. The achievement of goals.
9. Spin-offs.
10. The openness to outsiders and new ideas.

The exciting outcome was that a given characteristic can indicate a creative tension or conflict within the milieu. For example, the leadership can support part of the process but be overly critical of some aspects of it.

2.3.5 Synopsis of Complementary Dimensions Emerging from Explorations on the Ground

Table 2.1 summarizes the dimensions identified in the approaches presented in Sect. 2.3. It shows how different foci of the research have helped us to identify dimensions that complement each other. The different points of interest are linked to the four seasons. The preparation stage collects the aspects of what a learning process consists of: the participating learning community and the forces that drive them to learn. When informal and formal aspects of learning interact with each other in a real curriculum, the question is shifted to what outsiders expect from a (university-level) learning: should learning happen at a factory-like entity with standardized procedures or should it rather take place in an experimental unit that promotes change.

The third phase gathers the harvest as products, exemplified in our research as learning games. These games are quite logically based on the context-aware technology, because of the ground that emphasized the participation of the context

Table 2.1 Dimensions for learning generated by the four approaches

	Focus	Dimensions
Kids' club	Spring: preparing the ground	Participation: access, ownership, commitment Dynamics/drivers: invention, authenticity, diversity, technology
ICT education in context	Summer: growth by cross-fertilizing formal and informal university education	Societal expectation: transformational or transactional
Context-aware learning games	Autumn: processing the harvested ideas	Context awareness: design, resources, implementation
Design milieux	Winter: consuming the lessons learned for the next rounds	Creative tensions

and the cross-fertilization of the streams of informal and formal learning for transforming a given context. Therefore, the identified dimension focuses on various aspects of context. Finally, creative tensions identified by the study of design milieux illustrate the inherently conflictive qualities of any learning setting.

In the next section, we will analyze the dimensions more carefully, to be able to show how the educators can enrich their teaching by taking advantage of these dimensions.

2.4 Dimensions of Learning

2.4.1 Level of Participation

Our research on the Kids' Club as an open platform for technology learning has observed the importance that participation has for successful learning results. Participation can be analyzed by using the categories of access and ownership. Access means technical, attitudinal or other possibility to participate, ownership measures the level that access is relevant for self-expression. In particular, access to education or technology does not guarantee its ownership, and maximum ownership materializes as commitment, i.e., the allocation of resources to what is understood, or owned, as a relevant technology or education.

The observation is in sharp contrast to various programs that are based on the idea of delivery of technology to schools, to maximize its penetration. The delivery of technology has to be based on the demand of the learning community.

If access and ownership are dimensions independent of each other, following scenarios can be considered:

1. Minor access, minor ownership: Technology or education is rare or not available, and there is no demand for it either.
2. Minor access, major ownership: Technology or education is hard to access or difficult to use, but the few opportunities are fully used. This is usually the case for early adopters of technology. Their passion allows them to break the barriers from learning technologies and expressing themselves with it.
3. Major access, minor ownership: Technology is understood as transferred from outside and alien for the user communities. Technology might be used, because it is enforced, but it does not have a positive impact to the users' lives or they remain only users, not designers that can express themselves with it for their own purposes.
4. Major access, major ownership: Technology is available and in full use: the ideal scenario.

Even in countries where the ICT penetration at school is high, the educators might not use it, due to their low ownership (scenario 3). However, even a poor technology and low bandwidth do not prevent its functional use, if the learning community see how they can express themselves with it (scenario 2). The Kids' Club experience shows the importance for the drivers that support the ownership of the technology. They are described in the next section.

2.4.2 Drivers of the Learning Process

Another dimension identified in the Kids' Club concerns the drivers that motivate, initiate or foster a learning process. The dimension answers the questions of *what* drives, *why* learners get interested, *who* are maintaining the interest, and *how* the process is facilitated.

Invention means the outcomes of learning. Learning should always satisfy the learner's curiosity and will to find new observations, problems, solutions and insights. Therefore, invention answers the question of *what* to learn.

Authenticity tells what drives the learner to new inventions. Authentic learning is based on genuine interest and motivation that is rooted in the learner's immediate context or surrounding. Authenticity is the *why* of learning.

Diversity of the learning community is a prerequisite for innovations that solve authentic problems. A heterogeneous group of learners, the *who*, guarantee the representativeness and distribution of expertise that develops along with the learning process.

Technology is a vehicle that allows for diverse participants of the learner community to combine their skill and knowledge profiles to transform authentic problems into working inventions. It is the *how* of the learning community.

2.4.3 Societal Expectations from an Educational Institution

The five preparatory years before the launch of the contextualized ICT curriculum forced us to analyze the societal expectations of a university curriculum that both uses and teaches information and communication technology. From the early stages of development, it was required that the curriculum needs to differentiate from its many competitors that have been transferred to Tanzania without much rethinking. The university, by its rector, expressed the wish that the graduates became doers.

The design process of the contextualized ICT curriculum aimed at transformation that changes the surrounding society. The change process was to be conducted not only by competent ICT graduates, but even by students that were still taking classes, enabled by the openness of the curriculum itself. On the contrary, a conventional, transactional education serves the purposes given to the institutions from outside and beforehand.

Table 2.2 summarizes how transactional expectations from education, particularly that of a university, distinguish from transformational expectations. The aspects can be divided by three main categories. First, from the *relations'* point of view, a transactional institution follows the trends of the surrounding society, and its dependency is seen not only in its finances but also its values. It avoids risks when cooperating with its partners, and its teaching is based on textbooks rather than its own research.

Secondly, *organizational* issues distinguish institutions. A transformational university arranges teaching according to dynamic, open and flexible curricula where also its research partners can have their say. Academically, a transformational

Table 2.2 Transactional and transformational expectations from university education

		Transactional (effective within status quo)	Transformational (change)
Relations	To the trends in society	Passive to reactive follower	Active to proactive leader
	Of research to teaching	Teaching is based on repeating, presenting, performing research	Teaching is based on doing research
	To funders with respect to finances and values	Dependent	Autonomous
	To real life	Risk avoidance	Risk taking
Organization	Studies	Closed (Lehrplan)	Open (Curriculum)
	Academic	Discipline-based	Interdisciplinary
	Administrational	Hierarchy	Learning community
Students	Graduates	Qualifications	Competences
	Incoming students	Restrictive—entrance tests	Attractive—recruitment

institute favors interdisciplinary approaches where degree programs and research units cross the traditional borders of disciplines. Overall, the administration supports the institution's identity as a networked learning community.

Thirdly, the attitude towards *students* is most clearly seen in how the institution recruits new applicants and how it equips the graduates. A transactional university is superficial and formal in its selection process, whereas a transformational university is consumer-oriented and understands that it is primarily the students that choose a university, no more the other way round. Therefore, it takes risks in its student recruitment, and its flexibility in relations and organization guarantee that an excited incoming student can grow and graduate with competences that help them to outperform those with qualifications that do not measure the graduate's passion but superficial mastery of examinations.

In general, an emphasis on structures and formalities characterize a transactional educational institution. Its main task is to carry out the services to the society, according to predefined agreements. A transformational educational institution lives by its contents and spirit.

2.4.4 Aspects of Context-Awareness

The explorations with context-aware games exposed us to yet another dimension of learning, that of context-awareness. It can be measured by at least the following three aspects:

1. The design aspect describes the extent to which the design process has taken into account contextualization and participation.
2. The resources aspect indicates how well the learning environment makes use of local resources and copes with limited budgets available for small or poor user groups. In this way, it measures the sustainability of the learning intervention.
3. The technical or implementation aspect indicates the use of mobile and context-aware technologies in the intervention.

The previously identified dimensions—participatory, motivational and societal—orient towards the *people* of the learning community: their internal collaboration, their dynamics and their interrelations within the larger society. The context-aware dimension complements these dimensions, since it pays attention to how *technology* allows the learning experience to grow its roots in the surroundings where it takes place.

Like the other dimensions, the context-awareness of learning cannot be reduced to or measured by the dichotomy of formal and informal learning. Interestingly, the concept of awareness has conscious and unconscious connotations. The first connotation is used for example in issues like HIV and AIDS awareness, to refer to explicated and internalized understanding. The second one applies to the sensory use of the term: one can be aware of a sound without consciously paying attention to it.

The latent and manifest meanings of awareness are apparent also in the context-aware dimension of learning. Organic growth of learning within its surroundings, representing the aspect of resources, is often latent. However, it can be supported both formally and informally: allocating resources or making use of what is available, in improvised ways. The design aspect refers to an organized growth process of a learning intervention, and is thus manifest. Context-aware design benefits from formal and informal approaches: planned collaboration methods alongside with an open attitude and tolerance of diversity. The technical aspect shares latent and manifest viewpoints as the technologies enhance the aspects of both design and resources.

2.4.5 Creative Tensions

Our analysis of the process behind learning environments has identified a set of ten success factors for their design milieux (Sect. 2.3.4). Together, these factors define the fifth dimension of learning. It is related to the motivational or drivers dimension, because most of the identified factors measure the pull or push effects of designing successful learning environments. However, unlike the other dimension, the focus is on design, not learning.

The most interesting finding is the indication of simultaneous conflictive factors. For example, while it is important that creative designers enjoy a freedom of expression, a free context might feature conflictive characteristics of criticism and judgment. In this case, a factor that might sound counterproductive to a creative design process, might force the designer to redesign, reflect upon or re-assess their work, potentially improving the final product.

A creative tension is crucial for promoting out-of-box thinking. Our preliminary results indicate that the most exciting learning environments have been designed in milieux that have conflictive features. To some extent, this is contrary to the fairly common viewpoint that the learning environment should smoothen the learning process.

2.5 Role of Educators in Designing Technology for New Dimensions of Learning

2.5.1 The Educator's Four Agendas

Educators have a key role in reshaping education so that it meets with the challenges set for it. The dimensions analyzed in Sect. 2.4 translate to the educator's agendas that we call spring, summer, autumn, and winter.

Spring. Prepare your milieu as a living laboratory for learning. The milieu is where the learning happens, and it can also be called learning environment, context, setting, or surrounding. The term milieu emphasizes all different aspects of the place of learning, as part of the ecosystem it is embedded in. Preparing the milieu means that the educator familiarizes themselves to the milieu, to make full advantage of it. In that exercise, the educator makes use of the dimensions of participation and drivers.

The educator needs to ensure both the access (*laboratory*) and the ownership (*living*) of the technology that the learning milieu uses. Participation means that the learners feel comfortable in their environment and can express themselves so that learning becomes an activating design process for them. This requires two things: First, the teacher learns the talent profiles of the learning group, their interests, culture and background. Second, the teacher demands a technical environment that the users can learn to use for their self-expression.

The educator orchestrates the learning process by paying attention to its drivers. An ideal setting is built on a mix of formal and informal elements, like explicated principles and a creative atmosphere.

Summer. Cultivate the curriculum so that it transforms its environment. When the prerequisites of a successful learning process are guaranteed by participation and drivers, the educator starts growing the learning process so that it makes a difference in the learners' lives and their context. This requires open collaboration and negotiations with the surrounding community. The educator cannot isolate themselves within the school, but should proactively see the potential of the surroundings, which in some cases might exceed the geographical limits of the immediate neighborhood. Again, formal principles are handy to guide an informal, improvised interaction with the community.

Autumn. Harvest technologies by inviting skilled ICT professionals to co-design learning specific technological solutions within your real context. A technology-intensive learning setting is always a milieu that uses its local resources for designing new technological solutions. At this stage, a living laboratory that opened up to the rest of the community starts to produce new technologies. These solutions integrate the learning process to the surrounding, so to add authenticity, contextualization, and relevance. The educator with the rest of the learning community learns also technical skills. Like in earlier stages, part of this phase is formal with requirement analysis, specifications, and learning the technical environment, and the rest is informal exploration.

Winter. Incubate your own context as a creative design milieu, by making use of tensions. After the educator has managed to make the learning milieu a functional living laboratory that is actively involved with its wider context, also via the technologies that it has designed, the laboratory has changed into a creative design milieu. At that point, the educator starts to stimulate it by deliberately making use of the creative tensions within the milieu. This exercise can follow predefined, formal recipes, but also improvise.

To give an example of how these principles apply, let us consider a typical setting in the context of a developing country. A community multimedia center

(CMC) is a unit that is expected to serve a local community, like a village or a small town, and act as a hub for learning and using ICT. In many cases, it has reduced to a boring office with a decaying training room equipped with outdated technologies. The architecture of the building is based on traditional teaching scenario where the teacher makes the students to learn various features of software by heart. There is not only a question of what the learners benefit from the courses, but also what problems desktops solve in developing countries, in general.

To change the conventional, non-functional CMC scenario, we can follow the four principles. First, an existing CMC needs to re-position itself within the community that it serves. The CMC should not only be an access point for technology, but attract ownership and commitment among the user community. Secondly, the curricula—which does not need to restrict itself to ICT skills, but also design issues, business classes etc—needs to be rethought to transform the community as well as the CMC itself. A key issue is that the CMC needs to become proactive and take risks. Thirdly, the CMC can be a center that also designs relevant solutions to its surroundings. And last, the CMC should be a dynamic place that sparks innovation by admitting the tensions in its operations.

2.5.2 The Educator's Technical Toolbox

The educator needs the following technologies that are relevant for realizing new dimensions for learning. It is worthwhile observing that the selection contains very few mainstream educational technologies.

For participation that is more than access, the educator uses social media and tools that support dynamics and collaboration within the group, not just exchange of opinions. The collaboration can also be stimulated with hands-on technology exercise, such as designing and building robots. Technology can also intensify drivers, as tools for creativity (invention), context-aware technologies to integrate the technology to its surroundings (authenticity), or dialogue tools for understanding each other (diversity).

Whereas various database tools support the management and efficiency requirements of transactional learning, transformational learning requires information retrieval, including tools for text analysis, multiple representation, and digital stories. They also allow for analyzing and visualizing emotions.

Context awareness in design requires tools for contextualization and participation. To cope with limited resources of the context, either in poor settings or small groups, the educators can make use of various planning tools. But most importantly, for implementing tools that interact within the physical environment and integrate the learning process to it, educators need to master mobile and context-aware technologies, such as those using sensors.

2.5.3 Role of Data for Supporting New Dimensions of Learning

A general requirement for the successful use of technology relates to input and output data created in the learning process. An important aspect is data access and ownership. The latter refers to users' being proud of, protecting and taking care of their input data. This is an issue for all phases above, from creativity tools up to sensor technologies that require accurate input data. A crucial aspect of the output data is its appropriate and culturally meaningful representation; that is particularly important for learning.

It is also important to keep in mind that learning can be considered as a process that turns tacit or implicit data from the context into explicated information and knowledge that, again, can transform the very context. The learning milieu is a place or laboratory that supports this process of enhancing context awareness.

One of the key goals of learning is that it will have impact on behavior, a change in the learner or in their environment. Ideally, the learner's behavior changes from uninformed and heteronomic towards informed and autonomic. Technology should make the increasing levels of awareness transparent, from implicit and latent up to explicit and explicated; including the aspects of knowledge, attitudes and behavior.

An informal learning setting copes with uncertainty of the process, or even makes use of it. The data equivalent of uncertainty is rough data. Keeping this in mind, the information retrieval or other technologies used should not automate the refinement process of data (what happens, e.g., in Google Refine), but allow the learner to refine it by themselves, even at the cost of getting lost in the hyperspace.

The learner-controlled data refinement process should support positive filtering, *i.e.* to filter out the unnecessary extra data. Positive filtering does not mean building digital, negative filters, or barriers of prevention mechanisms blocking harmful information.

2.6 Application Areas in Developing Countries

The section shows how a few key areas, with high expectations in the developing countries, can benefit from the presented dimensions for learning. ICT is expected to penetrate throughout the society and as an overarching technology require well-trained ICT professionals. Various development projects, funded by governments from developed countries, are, after decades' of history with not only success stories, a standard tool for development.

Recently, the role of the poor, or the bottom of the pyramid (BoP), as technology users has attracted attention as a vehicle to reduce poverty. Apparently, the surprisingly high penetration of mobile technology among the poor has opened the eyes of the decision makers. The subjective power of the poor can be channeled by mobile technology in what is called crowd sourcing (Howe 2006): getting an extended community of citizens to suggest or even design the ways how their living conditions can be improved. Companies are using crowd sourcing also to get ideas for their products or future services.

Microstudies is a theoretical, not yet realized example of how the new dimensions of learning could revolutionize learning in developing countries. Unlike the traditional, certificate or degree oriented formal education, microstudying is based on learning module by module and building one's competence bottom-up.

The emphasis of the section is to show how the existing learning approaches can be significantly outperformed, by applying the dimensions seriously. The focus is on both multiplication and qualitative improvement.

2.6.1 ICT Education

As an integrating technology, ICT, in addition to biotechnology and nanotechnology, has been mentioned as one of the most potential areas that change the realities in developing countries. However, the level of ICT education in developing countries does not yet match the expectations from ICT graduates. Most ICT or Computer Science programs are still based on the international ACM/IEEE Computing Curriculum. Another problem is that ICT education is split up among institutions of varying academic levels, with only occasional interaction with each other.

For the dimension of participation, ICT education needs to emphasize ownership. The learners need to become master designers that can express themselves with whatever technology is available. This is in sharp contrast to enterprise-dependent, formal certificate programs that many ICT or Computing departments at, say, African universities arrange, on behalf of these companies. Currently, the programs focus on the accessibility of the given proprietary software.

As of the drivers, ICT education has to focus on the aspect of diversity. This is because the future graduates are expected to be able to work with diverse users, and understand their demands that might be expressed in most informal representations. Learning to make use of diversity helps also in designing ICT solutions that reflect new cultural settings, this far not exposed to ICT. These solutions might end up export products to the global community, for example, as adventure games or mobile weather forecasts based on oral stories.

ICT education, if any, needs to be transformational. In its relations to the society outside the educational institution, it needs to be proactive in initiatives, base its teaching on in-house R&D, and take whatever risks are required to cross the borders and work with companies, non-governmental organizations and individual, low-income user communities. It needs to be organized as a learning community that co-operates nationdeep from the level of primary school up to the university. ICT education, rather than being predominantly a subject of its own, needs to be a central component in interdisciplinary programs. It could be implemented through

ICT4D (Unwin 2009), game design, or e-tourism. Students need to be recruited based on their interests and pragmatic orientation, and the competences of the graduate need to match the challenges of the region and the country.

Regarding context awareness, ICT education in developing countries is the most appropriate place to focus on context-aware mobile computing. This particular area can significantly benefit areas where mobile penetration is high and people are living in informal settings. Not only for natural disasters, but positively for surrounding market opportunities, context-aware applications are functional. Tourists can also benefit from mobile applications that help them to learn and understand an alien context.

ICT education has to take place in living laboratories on-site, rather than closed ones. Therefore, the aspects of design milieux can be used to nurture ICT education.

2.6.2 Development Projects

Development projects aim at enhancing a country's capacity for wealth creation. A typical example of development projects is STIFIMO, a science, technology, and innovation program between Finland and Mozambique. The Government of Finland is funding the program by 22 million euros in 2010–14. The purpose of the program is the following:

> By the end of 2014, Ministry of Science and Technology of Mozambique with its strategic partners are running funding and support services for catalyzing and commercializing science and technology based innovations in Mozambique. Intensified and focused R&D and training activities in the areas of ICT and agriculture have turned these fields into role models on how to apply science and technology for innovations, within networks of diverse stakeholders. A few risk taking pilot initiatives have further transformed the Mozambican STI landscape.

2.6.2.1 STIFIMO Contributes to the Overall Objective

> In 2025, Mozambique is fully using science and technology for innovations that contribute towards economic growth and poverty alleviation. This means that culture of innovation has emerged and expands selected sectors of the economy and strengthens its key clusters. The national STI system is effective and efficient and well-utilized due to its quality of service. Mozambique is known for its use of and contribution to international good practices. The country has managed to turn local human and material strengths into contextualized ST-based innovations, based on demand. Proactive collaboration between the private, public and academic sectors is constantly searching for synergies and cross-overs between the sectors.

Development projects and programs are in many ways intercultural learning processes, and therefore, it makes sense to apply the dimensions of learning to them. Most of the current development projects, however, seem to follow quite simplistic patterns that leave little space for learning. This is seen in their lack of results that would benefit the developing country or region in question. A typical development project is based on a program document that formalizes, if not stagnates, the project to a set of consultancies, carried out by expatriates that almost literally follow the program document.

From the participation point of view, a development project requires commitment from the local stakeholders. From the viewpoint of a learning process, a development project is a school where all the stakeholders pay a study fee: this can be a formal prerequisite that can be acknowledged by ICT tools, in terms of used working hours, ideas, results or accomplished changes.

Development projects are driven by their authenticity. They require a bottom-up approach where problems are solved at the ground-level and functional innovations are promoted outside their sources by mobile technologies.

A transformational development project requires a learning community approach that is very far away from the conventional hierarchical administration followed in most developing countries. Stakeholders—the active student body of a development project—needs to be recruited based on their merits rather than formal statuses.

From the viewpoint of context-awareness, a development project require participatory and contextualized design, and building upon local strengths.

2.6.3 Crowd School: BoP Sourcing as a Global Learning Exercise

Kenya's becoming the world leader in mobile banking is a success story that is based on the BoP thinking (Hughes and Lonie 2007). The demand among ordinary, often poor, citizens paved the way for an industry that has in many ways reshaped the financial landscape of Kenya and other developing countries. Not only the transfer of money has become independent of one's ability to go physically to a bank, but m-banking has also revolutionized the way the products and services are marketed and paid for. This has fundamentally changed the opportunities for small-scale entrepreneurs.

Crowd sourcing means solving complex problems in parallel. In a way, a problem—whether open or closed—can be given to a global user community that start contributing to its solution(s), making use of the computing power that they have available. This means that both the individuals and their computing powers are used in parallel. As mentioned earlier, an interesting observation is the amount of the people with mobile phones in developing countries. The mobile phone users can have a substantial role in solving global problems in an orchestrated—yes, partly formal—way, participating in a global, authentic—yes, understood traditionally as an informal—learning process.

When thinking of learning from the viewpoint of a learning community, crowd sourcing can enhance learning by making a truly distributed effort where people with different talents solve problems. For example, one way to use computers for HIV and AIDS education is based on students' real life stories that they craft into a digital form. Sharing these stories on a distributed platform that possibly automatically interlaces the stories contributes to getting a bigger picture of the complexity of the HIV and AIDS phenomenon. This requires that an individual teacher works closely with the particular context, to collect the stories, but at the same time ensures that the community shares their stories within a global community.

A *crowd school* is a learning approach where a global BoP learning community combines forces to solve a given, complex problem. How could a global crowd school look like? An example that makes use of diverse schools around the globe is the Environment Online (http://www.enoprogramme.org/). It is organized around thematic assignments on environmental issues. The virtual school features concrete assignments, like tree planting and various other campaigns. A challenge is to use technology to orchestrate the tasks into massively parallel assignments within the BoP communities that use mobile technologies, and to support these assignments automatically.

Going back to our example of m-banking, we can build an analogue between money transfer and knowledge transfer. In the same way as real money is transferred in m-banking, a crowd school revolutionizes the distribution of knowledge and ideas within its network. Whereas m-banking transforms individual entrepreneurship into profits, the transfer of information and knowledge materializes into solutions and new insights in a crowd school.

Using the presented dimensions, a crowd school calls for the ownership of given problems and is driven by a hunger for invention. An outside society expects it to come up with radical openings, so it is transformational. From the context-awareness point of view, it emphasizes the use of available resources.

2.6.4 Microstudies: An Application of Microloans to Education

The concept of microstudies applies the success of microloans into education and training. Microloans have transformed the lives of masses of small-scale entrepreneurs. According to the concept, the bank is not asking for major and long-term business plan for a major loan, but the customer starts from very small amounts of a few euros. Based on the success of the entrepreneur's portfolio, they can apply for bigger loans and develop the business accordingly.

Following the microloan concept, microstudies are a sequence of modules that develop a learner's competence in a given area. The learner is expected to have a mobile phone into which they can order the required module. The building competence profile is stored digitally on a server. The learner can use the profile and history at job interviews. The learning process is not based on distant learning objectives, like those of certificates or degrees. On the contrary, the goals are simple upgrades on his or her current skills. The modules can be paid by airtime. Over the years, the learning path that consists of the sequence of modules can be transformed to a certificate or degree.

Microstudies are more individual than a crowd school, and also more formal. This can be seen in the dimensions relevant for microstudies. Reliable access is prioritized at the cost of ownership. An efficient and inspiring technical implementation can also work as the driver of a successful learning process. This is also seen in the transactional emphasis of microstudies that make the best out of available resources. This said, it is important to observe that microstudies are a cross of formal and informal education, and their requirements emphasize practical competences rather than knowledge.

2.6.5 Mapping Educational Challenges in Developing Countries onto the Dimensions of Learning

The examples presented in this section show that the dimensions can be applied in versatile ways for most diverse application areas. Table 2.3 summarizes the dimension profiles for the presented application areas. It is important to note that the creative tensions of design milieux apply to any application area, and have therefore been omitted from the analysis.

Table 2.3 shows that the identified dimensions of learning help to focus the design and teaching efforts onto the critical aspects of learning. The analysis shows that there is no one best practice or approach for improving learning. The analysis also indicates that the introduced dimensions are independent of each other, and only dependent on the requirements and demands from the intended learning context.

Once again, the idea of characterizing learning based on its formality loses meaning when brought into a context. For example, for tackling the massive challenge of inappropriate or completely lacking ICT education in developing countries, a much more fine-tuned approach is needed than organizing adaptive online courses matching the formal learning requirements.

Table 2.3 Dimensions of learning applied to a few relevant application areas in developing countries

	Participation	Drivers	Transactional versus transformational	Dimensions of context
ICT education	Ownership	Diversity	Transformational	Implementation
Development projects	Commitment	Authenticity	Transformational	Design, resources
Crowd sourcing from BoP	Ownership	Invention	Transformational	Resources
Microstudies	Access	Technology	Transactional	Resources

It is interesting to note that in a set limited to only four different scenarios, all the aspects of the presented dimensions were required. The observation means that the presented dimensions are expressive and sensitive to the differences of the environments.

2.7 Discussion

Juxtaposed with the traditional dichotomy of formal and informal learning, we have identified a set of new dimensions that an educator can make use of to intensify and diversify his or her teaching setting.

The dimensions were identified from various real life settings where new technologies were applied in living laboratories that had features from both formal and informal learning. All the interventions covered several years of research. The research agenda was, together with the learning community, to create new pedagogical approaches and related technologies and analyze their feasibility. Unlike a typical study in educational technology, we were not interested in the effect of a particular technology to learning outcomes, but diverse aspects on how the learning changes together with new technologies. One of these results is the identification of the dimensions of learning.

Retrospectively, the four different interventions and their results have been arranged with the metaphor of seasons. The four seasons focused on the roles and dynamics of a learning community (spring), how the learning community answers the expectations of its surroundings and possibly changes it (summer), how to the community co-designs new technologies that integrate learning to its physical context (autumn), and finally, how the learning community survives as a design milieu with diverse creative tensions (winter).

Rather than organized or planned beforehand, the research process was explorative and organic. It identified the dimensions of participation, drivers of learning, focus of societal expectations, context-awareness and creative tensions in the learning environment as a design milieu. These dimensions are not aligned with the dichotomy of formal and informal learning. Rather, they help to cross the boundary between formal and informal learning. This is an important finding, because the boundary easily stagnates the reforms in education. For example, ownership can be encouraged in both formal and informal settings, and authenticity is a useful driver for all learning. The derived dimensions show that the boundary is artificial, and the dimensions encourage, for example, educators to use and design versatile technologies for their particular learning settings, independently of their being formal or informal.

There are three main target groups that can benefit from the dimensions: educators, designers of educational technology and researchers.

Regarding educators, the findings emphasize the design orientation of learning and teaching. The future of education is in its functionality: the learning community learns by designing artifacts that increase their awareness of their context. The educator facilitates this process that exceeds any physical, disciplinary, maturity or other limits that traditional schooling is based on; the context is not restricted to the immediate physical surroundings. This far, various limits have usually determined the forms of education: classes, age groups, subjects, degree contents, objectives and so on. The design orientation emphasizes the roles of improvisation and inspiration. It also has an impact on the professional identity of an educator.

For a designer of technology for education, the study reminds of the need for novel technologies for learning. Basically, the learning technologies should allow the learner to elaborate their awareness of the surrounding reality. This requires advanced features for context-awareness and tools that they can use for representing the learning process, transforming raw data or tacit knowledge into more explicated forms of information. Moreover, the technologies should allow sharing this forming knowledge within the most heterogeneous and distributed learning communities, i.e., people speaking different languages, representing different world views, using the same expressions for different meanings or emotions, or the other way round. In other words, we can use the term *hermeneutic* technologies, to emphasize the importance of interpretation of observations in the learning process.

In terms of researchers, the dimensions call for more context-oriented an approach to learning. Much more than this far, the learning requires relevance, at the cost of structures. Context-orientation is a cross-disciplinary challenge where the new technical solutions go side by side with the advancing understanding of learning. Moreover, the context is a multilayered concept: an individual learner belongs to multiple contexts simultaneously that vary within the community. Technologies are required to help the learner to manage the learning process through the overlapping contexts.

Much of the article is based on contexts outside the mainstream of technology-intensive learning settings. The reason for the discrepancy lies in the research agenda of the author. For a fresh understanding of learning and the role of technology therein, researchers need to take a way outside their camp and be exposed to realities outside their comfort zones. We cannot find answers to the challenges of teaching the next billion by sitting in our well-equipped classrooms and in closed technology laboratories. The more challenging a learning context is, the more it requires a researcher to focus to find an out-of-box solution to these challenges.

The dimensions of learning were derived from a few concrete learning settings. This raises the question of the validity and generalizability of these dimensions outside these living laboratory settings. To some extent, this is a fair question, but the diversity of the settings and the length of each intervention compensates for the lack of representative sampling. Rather than a statistically oriented survey, the derivation process has been, deliberately, explorative and focused on a deep analysis of the settings in the review. To show the validity of the results, the derived dimensions of the selective study have been tested in other selected learning scenarios.

Richard Branson has challenged educators with his idea of a tented university in Africa. To think of a learning milieu as a caravan, or educators as nomads, is aligned with the dimensions identified in this study. A functional design should bend modern technology towards tools that incorporate the dimension of learning to whatever learners need to accomplish, by their minds or hands. Becoming competent in knowledge, skills, attitudes, values or behavior should not be an artificially isolated island from the rest of life, but an integral part of it. Like a tent that can be set up anywhere, the future learning milieu is as ubiquitous as a campfire in the African night. The difference is that it breaks the boundaries of what, where and how the traditions allow one to learn.

2.8 Conclusion

We have presented a set of new dimensions for learning. The dimensions are based on a few analyzed research-based learning interventions. They all took place in the borderland between formal and informal learning: in K12 after-hours technology laboratories, explorative university education in a developing country or in places where people are supposed to learn on their own, like a museum or a national park.

The set of identified dimensions emphasize different aspects of learning: the degree of the participation within the learning community, the drivers that motivate a learning process, the societal task expected from an educational institution, and the role of the surrounding context. The creative tensions as indicators of productive design milieux show that learning always takes place in a dynamic field.

Examples for the context of developing countries showed that the dimensions have potential to significantly change the traditional educational settings and cross their conventional boundaries. The role of the educators in the effort is crucial. The teachers need to rethink their roles and tasks as educators, towards the direction of becoming conductors of highly distributed learning processes.

The transformation in the educators' role requires technology. For example, technologies used in crowd-sourcing can make the world into a global think-tank that solves problems at hand. This kind of learning makes use of advanced text mining techniques for information retrieval.

But future educators do not only orchestrate global learning processes from within their immediate contexts. They turn these contexts into design milieux that produce digital and artifacts and context-aware tools for learning. A learning community for functional design reminds of the Bauhaus movement in the 1920s.

All in all, the use of the dimensions helps educators to assume varying roles, improvise, and even act globally, if needed. The flexibility is necessary for the reform of education. The reform is required by the challenges caused by reasons that look quite different from each other: fast and unexpectedly changing competence requirements of working life, the minimal or lacking educational infrastructure or missing teachers in developing countries, or the aging populations in the countries of high income.

The study shows the need of further research in the area of context-aware learning. Most of the current technologies for education are supposed to ease the administrational or pedagogical management of learning processes or provide learning and teaching resources available where and when needed. Context-aware learning technologies offer instruments that root the learning into its surroundings.

A key question is how technology can provide a cozy, homely learning environment for the masses that do not have a privilege of schooling. Social media can provide a stimulating, even addictive environment with supportive peers. However, it is a significantly harder challenge to make sure that the members of these communities get competences that match the requirements of the job markets for the lifetime of the members.

References

Bass JM, Heeks R (2011) Changing computing curricula in African universities: evaluating progress and challenges via design-reality gap analysis. Electron J Inf Syst Developing Ctries 48(5):1–39

Bettelheim B (1976) The uses of enchantment: the meaning and importance of fairy tales. Knopf, New York

Beynon M (2007) Computing technology for learning—in need of a radical new conception. J Educ Technol Soc 10(1):94–106

Brusilovsky P (2001) Adaptive hypermedia. User Model User-Adapt Interact 11(1–2):87–110

Droste M (2002) Bauhaus, 1919–1933. Bauhaus-Archiv, Museum für Gestaltung. TASCHEN GmbH, 2002

Duveskog M, Sutinen E, Cronje J (2012) Design milieux. Manuscript

Howe J (2006) The Rise of crowdsourcing. North, 14(14):1–5. http://www.clickadvisor.com/downloads/Howe_The_Rise_of_Crowdsourcing.pdf

Hughes N, Lonie S (2007) M-PESA: mobile money for the "unbanked" turning cell phones into 24-hour tellers in Kenya. Innovations (Winter/Spring) 2(1–2):63–81. http://www.mitpressjournals.org/doi/abs/10.1162/itgg.2007.2.1-2.63

Jansen JD (2011) South Africa's education system: How can it be made more productive. In: Moeletsi M (ed): Advocates for change. How to overcome Africa's challenges, Picador Africa, pp 99–114

Papert S (1980) Mindstorms: children, computers, and powerful ideas. Basic Books, New York

Pólya G (1957) How to solve it. Doubleday, Garden City

Sedano CI, Pawlowski J, Sutinen E, Naumanen M, Vinni M, Laine TH (2010) Involvement of non-technical individuals in the design of successful digital games. IEEE Multi Eng Educ Mag 5(3):10–18

Tedre M, Bangu N, Nyagava SI (2009) Contextualized IT education in Tanzania: beyond standard IT curricula. J Inf Technol Educ 8(1):101–124

Unwin T (ed) (2009) ICT4D: information and communication technology for development. Cambridge University Press, Cambridge

Virnes M, Eija K-L, Sutinen E (2008) How children's individual needs challenge the design of educational robotics. IDC 2008

Chapter 3
Schools as Learning Communities

Victoria J. Marsick, Karen E. Watkins and Sarah A. Boswell

Abstract This chapter draws on trends, research, and experience in organizations broadly conceived to examine schools as learning communities, with emphasis on workplace-based and field-based learning. While the ultimate beneficiaries of such learning are students of all ages, we take the position that students cannot learn unless teachers, leaders and other adults in schools are able to learn and share knowledge as learning communities. We use lenses we have developed over time on informal and incidental learning (Marsick and Watkins 1990; Marsick et al. 2009) and the learning organization (Watkins and Marsick 1993, 1996; Marsick and Watkins 1999) to consider workplace-based and field-based learning, facilitated by technology, in schools conceptualized as learning communities.

V. J. Marsick (✉)
Adult Learning and Leadership, Organization and Leadership,
Teachers College, New York, USA
e-mail: marsick@tc.columbia.edu

K. E. Watkins
Lifelong Education, Administration and Policy,
The University of Georgia, Athens, GA, USA
e-mail: kwatkins@uga.edu

S. A. Boswell
Consultant, Collective Learning: A Teacher Development Company,
Lawrenceville, GA, USA
e-mail: sboswell@theclteam.com

R. Huang et al. (eds.), *Reshaping Learning*, New Frontiers of Educational Research,
DOI: 10.1007/978-3-642-32301-0_3,

3.1 Case for Schools as Learning Communities

School leaders today are transforming their schools in order to help students develop twenty first century skills. According to Darling-Hammond (Umphrey 2009), a pioneer in conceptualizing schools as whole learning systems, twenty first century skills include creativity and innovation, critical thinking, problem solving, collaboration and communication. Darling-Hammond emphasizes meta-skills of learning: the need to reflect in- and on-action and the ability to learn how to learn. Darling-Hammond (1993) made the case for why such learning is important a decade ago in terms of the changing workplace in which graduates must effectively function:

> There is little room in today's society for those who cannot manage complexity, find and use resources, and continually learn new technologies, approaches, and occupations. In contrast to low-skilled work on assembly lines, which was designed from above and implemented by means of routine procedures from below, tomorrow's work sites will require employees to frame problems, design their own tasks, plan, construct, evaluate outcomes, and cooperate in finding novel solutions to problems.... Increasing social complexity also demands citizens who can understand and evaluate multidimensional problems and alternatives and who can manage ever more demanding social systems. (Darling-Hammond 1993, p. 752).

Darling-Hammond, among others, contends that schools that wish to effect twenty first century skills, need to become vibrant learning communities, engaged in whole system learning, in which teachers and leaders work and learn together, often with their students, to support learning and development.

While schools are locations for teaching and learning of younger people, schools are not always conceptualized as locations of adult learning. Drago-Severson (2009) points to research that "shows that supporting adult learning is directly and positively linked to enhancing children's achievement (Donaldson 2008; Guskey 2000; Leithwood et al. 2004; Roy and Hord 2003; Wagner 2007)" (p. 13). We join Drago-Severson (Ibid), based on our own prior work on learning cultures and systems (Watkins and Marsick 1993, 1996; Marsick and Watkins 1999) in concluding that schools need to be "true learning centers, places where adults and children are well supported in their learning and development."

Schools are also not always understood as whole systems with structures, processes, cultures and resources that interact in complicated ways to nurture or inhibit desired learning of both adults and young people. Reformers often emphasize de-contextualized "best practices," but years of experience in workplaces with organizational change demonstrate that learning and performance are greatly influenced by context and by the system in which learning takes place and work gets done.

We adopt an organizational learning view of emerging learning practices in this chapter. Technology plays a key role in developing new curricula for twenty first century skills, with many organizations offering technology-based support in curriculum development and for teaching and learning strategies keyed to desired standards. Yet teachers and schools can be unprepared to use technology, with the younger generation being more advanced in their technology sophistication than the teachers. In this chapter we examine the culture that supports the continued learning of teachers needed in this demanding context.

3.2 Organizational Learning in Schools

Much work on organizational learning emanates from outside the school system. Learning organizations serve as a means for businesses to maximize their potential. Due to economic uncertainties, building knowledge and facilitating learning became a point of survival; and the concept of learning organizations was viewed as that source of survival. Argyris (1991), echoed this thought, "[a]ny company that aspires to succeed in the tougher business environment of the 1990s must first resolve a basic dilemma: success in the marketplace increasingly depends on learning…" (p. 99). Yet Marsick and Watkins (1999) remind us that "learning is not an end in itself. It is a means to excellent products and services, … or to improve [overall outcomes]" (p. 26). Senge (1990, 2006) shared, "Learning is a process that extends [one's] capacity to create [and] be part of the generative process of life" (pp. 13–14). Learning generates new knowledge; new knowledge creates change: change that is needed to maintain a competitive edge in a rapidly changing society. Argyris (1989) stated that the quality of learning within a company yields an "intellectual capital, crucial in building an organization that is vigilant about detecting and correcting errors, dedicated to producing innovations, and ready to change to meet the demands of the environment, which itself is often changing" (p. 5).

Darling-Hammond advocated a learning approach to school change early in her work on school reform. Since then, schools with this focus have often adapted Senge's (1990, 2006) five disciplines: (1) personal mastery, (2) understanding individual and organizational mental models, (3) building a shared vision, (4) team learning, and (5) systems thinking. These practices have been adopted in some schools (Senge et al.2000). Senge (1990) defined learning organizations as "organizations where people continually expand their capacity to create the result they truly desire, where new and expansive patterns of thinking are nurtured, where collective aspiration is set free, and where people are continually learning how to learn together" (p. 3).

Garvin (1993) critiqued Senge's definition as unclear in ways that distort implementation. He instead defined learning organizations as "an organization skilled in creating, acquiring, interpreting, transferring and retaining knowledge and at purposefully modifying its behavior to reflect new knowledge and insights" (p. 80). Many others have added their voices to this discussion. Coppieters (2005) summarized one of the essential characteristics of a learning organization as "increasing the learning capacity to reach a state of continuous change or transformation" (p. 134). Bowen et al. (2006) defined a learning organization as a place that is:

> Associated with a core set of conditions and processes that support the ability of an organization to value, acquire, and use information and tacit knowledge acquired from employees and stakeholders to successfully plan, implement, and evaluate strategies to achieve performance goals. (pp. 98–99).

Bowen et al. include the structure as well as the processes when defining the learning organization. Collinson and Cooks (2007) stated, "Organizational learning is the deliberate *use* of individual, group, and system learning *to embed* new thinking and practices that continuously *renew and transform* [emphasis added] the organization in ways that support shared aims" (p. 117).

Hiatt-Michael (2001) sees the learning organization as a place where all members acquire new ideas as well as accept responsibility for the learning. Hiatt-Michael further states that the learning organization is one that focuses on "harnessing experiences of the members." Collinson and Cook (2007) also emphasize capitalizing on the knowledge of members to ground innovation within the school through the "deliberate *use* of individual, group, and, system learning *to embed* new thinking" (p. 117). The learning organization then becomes a place that could help create the shift from professional learning as an isolated venture to a collective responsibility among teachers. Bowen et al. (2007) propose "that the degree to which a school functions as a learning organization, may influence the willingness of school employees to embrace new innovations for promoting student achievement" (p. 200).

Leithwood and his colleagues (e.g., Leithwood et al. 1998; Leithwood and Seashore 1998) have done substantial research on organizational learning in schools originating in their long history of work with leadership and change. Leithwood et al. (1995) defined the learning organization in schools as

> A group of people pursuing common purposes (individual purposes as well) with a collective commitment to regularly weighing the value of those purposes, modifying them when that makes sense, and continuously developing more effective and efficient ways of accomplishing those purposes (p. 63).

Leithwood et al. (1995) and Collinson and Cook's (2007) definitions emphasize action elements that affect teaching and learning. Leithwood and colleagues have also researched links to teacher and student performance (e.g., Mulford et al. 2004; Sillins 2000).

Researchers such as Dufour (2004) and Hord and Sommers (2008) have coined the term *professional learning communities* (PLC), a growing practice in schools that incorporates many of the components of a learning organization centered on collaboration and team learning. However, in some cases PLCs have been introduced to schools as a program more so than an approach, eliminating the structures—i.e., common vision, collaborative learning culture, collaborative skills, etc.—needed to sustain its intention. Schechter (2008) stated:

> Despite the numerous conceptions of organizational learning in schools (e.g., coordinated group efforts [PLC], professional development programs, shared goals, active commitment to continuous improvement, horizontal network of information flow, open culture, teacher leadership), they are rarely translated into operational structures and processes in school reality (p. 156).

PLCs thus may not be creating the change intended and can be viewed by teachers as one more thing to do. Therefore, the concept of change by learning has not fully taken root nor is it well-conceptualized by K-12 school leaders and teachers in practice, despite academic work toward that end. Gray (2000) contended, "By understanding more about the process [of learning organizations] … a greater impetus for change can be created" (p. 238). Bowen et al. (2007) concurred, noting that "unfortunately, the concept of the learning organization is generally vague, and school personnel have few tools available to support its assessment and to inform intervention strategies" (p. 199).

Common themes across these definitions are innovation, change and a capacity for learning. Bowen et al. (2007) mentions these three themes as the key to unlock the creative and dynamic processes schools need to undergo to address the challenges faced in teaching their youth. Although schools' number one focus is creating solutions for maximizing teaching and learning for their students, they seldom look at designing a learning culture among the adults to generate innovative solutions.

Creating a place for all members to learn new ideas and accept responsibility for their learning has been a challenge in schools despite promising work on reflective practice in the classroom. The level of responsibility for learning extends to teachers meeting the necessary requirements to maintain their state certification. They tend to take courses offered from the district or nearby staff development centers that are convenient for their schedules and meet the number of hours needed; seldom is the learning geared towards the generation of new ideas and a responsibility to learn as a genuine part of growth as a professional. Typically professional learning is a very individualized task for teachers. Rarely do teachers discuss their professional learning plans among each other, let alone their learning needs.

Moreover, schools must be structured to generate complex outcomes. Human growth and development are not measured simply and occur over time at different paces for individual learners. Additionally, schools are nested systems: teachers interacting with students within and outside classrooms, groups of teachers working together within and across grades, principal and teacher shared leadership dynamics, shared governance, and relationships with parents, families, and larger communities. Therefore, building learning communities in schools cannot be effected by adopting a standardized formula without considering many factors in the school context. One promising development is the rise in sophistication and accessibility of technology as a way to enhance the capacity of the whole system to learn continuously.

3.3 Role of Technology and Informal Learning

Technology has the potential to revolutionize learning, especially given the twenty first century skills mandate, and many technology-based providers have stepped up to assist teachers meet these new demands. Technology partners often bring the world to the doors of individual schools; sites offer opportunities to learn what other teachers are doing within and beyond one's immediate geographic region. Yet teachers and schools may not be prepared to leverage the opportunities offered by technology without changing mental models and practices that extend to the way school leaders and districts are themselves structured as learning systems. In this section, we look at developments in the broader organizational world, as well as schools, that hold implications for schools as learning communities.

3.3.1 Technology's Impact on Learning Practices

Revolutions in technology enable learners to access what they want to know, when they want to know it, in the way in which they would like to learn it—deepening our reliance on informal learning approaches. Course delivery is increasingly technology-based, or blended with face-to-face formats, but even more importantly, technology enhances the ability to integrate learning into work practices and workflow. E-learning strategies escalate daily. Desktop learning, electronic performance support systems, podcasts and voice recognition systems are changing the location and capacity for delivering learning to individuals across time and space.

Bassi et al. (1998) underscored the way in which technology shifts the control and design of learning from providers to learners themselves. The evolution of Electronic Performance Support and intelligent tutoring systems (ITS) enable employees to learn what they need when the demand arises because expertise and feedback are built into these systems. According to Bassi et al. (1998), for example, the U.S. AirForce Research Center achieved "a 50 percent reduction in the amount of time to train to the same criteria" using ITS and "saw a 34 percent increase in student performance over a given amount of training time" (p. 68). ITS assesses where the learner is and presents the information based on those needs. ITS also critiques performance in real time, responding to the learner's actions and answering questions. These systems work one-on-one, adapting to unique learning needs.

Mobile devices are increasingly used to deliver professional learning. Mobile devices bring learning into the field, at the point of contact. Mobile learning research has focused on technology and design issues. Studies have also been conducted on mobile classroom training in order to foster inquiry and to engage informal learning outside the classroom as either a complement or the core of learning (Gephart et al. 2010).

Looi et al. (2010, p. 155) and Chan et al. (2006) argue the potential of mobile learning for creating "'seamless learning spaces'...marked by continuity of the learning experience across different scenarios or contexts." Mobile devices enable active learning, within context, to "explore, capture and manipulate both physical and virtual (or digital) objects," even though applications are difficult to design, implement, and research given that "students are 'on the move' across different modes of space (both physical and virtual) and time" (Looi et al.2010, p. 161).

Mobile devices support learning for self-directed individuals or for groups. Some research in schools on group-supported learning showed learning gains using this approach, but the technology can pose a problem because of screen size (Yang and Lin 2010).

Despite constraints, mobile learning is a growing component of work-based learning. Ahmad and Orton (2010), for example, studied 400 mobile phone users in IBM who found them especially helpful to access needed experts and information in the field in ways that strengthened their confidence so they could better serve clients. More work is being done on mobile learning in school settings, in part funded through the U.S. Department of Education, than is being conducted in business environments. Results of early studies are promising vis-à-vis learning outcomes and engagement (Gephart et al. 2010).

Dede (2009, pp. 67–68) describes a hybrid approach that combines real and virtual settings through "immersive simulations (that) use location-aware handheld computers (generally with global positioning system [GPS] technology) which allow users to physically move throughout a real-world location while collecting place-dependent simulated field data, interviewing virtual characters, and collaboratively investigating simulated scenarios." Early research on one of these, *Alien Contact!*, showed "high levels of student engagement, as well as educational outcomes in literacy and math equivalent to students playing a similar, engaging board game as a control condition" (Dede 2009). This is only one example of how the development of new tools escalates the possibilities for bridging and augmenting both formal and informal learning.

3.3.2 Informal Learning: Emerging Learning Practices

In many ways these trends reflect a return to the former reliance on personalized, contextualized "Go Sit By Nellie" approaches found in on-the-job training. The practices often rely on informal and incidental learning strategies, mediated by technology, that enable organizations to target learning to individual needs without the abstractness or complexities of fixed time, fixed place, trainer or Subject-Matter-Expert (SME)- reliant approaches. An extended example is IBM Learning Solutions' (2005) emerging Learning on Demand system, consisting of Work Apart Learning, Work Embedded Learning and Work Enabled Learning. Work Apart Learning is enhanced formal training linked to just-in-time learning that is increasingly self-directed. For example, modules are available online to enable self-study when new capabilities are needed. Work Embedded Learning embeds knowledge in work roles and makes it available during action. For example, sales professionals can access data bases of information, short tutorials linked to job tasks, or experts who can help with non-routine questions as they negotiate sales with customers through an enhanced electronic performance support system linked to electronic work tools. Work Enabled Learning involves coaching and self-initiated learning reviews.

Table 3.1 A learning architecture (Bersin & Associates, 2009)

Formal	Informal: on-demand	Informal: social	Informal: embedded
Instructor Led training	E-Learning	Wikis, blogs	Performance support
Virtual classroom	Search	Communities of Practice	Feedback
Games	Books, articles videos	Forums	Rotational assignments
Simulations	Podcasts	Expert directories	Quality circles
Testing and evaluation	Learning/Knowledge Portals	Social networks	After action reviews
E-Learning		Coaching and mentoring	Development planning
		Conferences and colloquia	

Mallon (2009) define informal learning as "… any learning opportunity that is accidental, ad-hoc, unplanned and which likely happens without the guidance of a discipline, such as instructional design" (p. 2). Like IBM, they also see three categories of informal learning: on-demand, social, and embedded. Table 3.1 gives their examples for each category.

3.3.3 *Informal Science Education*

Recent interest in Informal Science Education has led to considerable advancement of our understanding of the nature of informal learning, its pedagogy, and its assessment. Spurred by funding from the National Science Foundation (NSF), researchers have sought to clarify how people learn science across the lifespan. NSF defines informal learning thus: "Informal learning happens throughout people's lives in a highly personalized manner based on their particular needs, interests, and past experiences. This type of multi-faceted learning is voluntary, self-directed, and often mediated within a social context. It provides an experiential base and motivation for further activity and subsequent learning." NSF further defined a funding program that promotes "innovation in anywhere, anytime, lifelong learning, through investments in research, development, infrastructure, and capacity-building for STEM learning outside formal school settings" (nsf.gov 2012).

Bell et al. (2009) argue that informal learning has a range of learning outcomes that far exceeds those of traditional academic courses focused primarily on conceptual knowledge. "Across informal settings, learners may develop awareness, interest, motivation, social competencies, and practices. They may develop incremental knowledge, habits of mind, and identities that set them on a trajectory to learn more" [p. 27]. While many of these outcomes are also achievable in formal settings, the informal nature of the learning encourages a broader spectrum of learning. These authors look at learning outcomes that are lifelong (competencies acquired across a developmental life-span), life-wide (competencies acquired across the many settings and contexts of one's life), and life-deep (competencies and beliefs acquired from living in one's many cultures).

One model for understanding informal science education was developed focusing on visitors to a science museum, the contextual model of learning (Falk and Dierking 2000). In their model, what is learned is influenced by the personal, sociocultural, and physical context. Another intriguing framework for understanding informal learning of science that connects well to our work is the notion of the "third space.":

> Third Spaces is a theoretical construct that lends itself to nonschool learning (e.g., Gutiérrez 2008; Eisenhart and Edwards 2004). Third spaces are outside the two typical spheres of existence: home and work or home and school for children. For telecommuters, for example, a coffee shop where they spend the work day could be construed as a third space. Third spaces are places where participants' everyday and technical (or scientific) language and experiences intersect and can be the site for fascinating accounts of informal learning. (Bell et al. 2009, p. 32).

These many approaches to learning science informally again demonstrate the elasticity, ubiquitousness, and flexibility of informal learning. Whether learning occurs in a museum, from an I-pad application, through internet portals such as second life, or a field trip; the possibilities for observing, reflecting, and ultimately learning are enormous. These experiences offer so many stimuli, and the possibility of such complete immersion in the context that what is learned can barely be absorbed by the learner, let alone captured by an evaluator. It is difficult to design these environments in ways that have the potential to stimulate learning toward pre-defined outcomes.

On the one hand, over-design thwarts the learner's natural impulses. On the other, lack of design leaves learning totally random. Bell et al. (2009) recognize that the contextual, learner-centered, and social nature of informal learning make it particularly problematic to capture individual learning outcomes. "Other important features of informal environments for science learning include the high degree to which contingency typically plays a role in the unfolding of events—that is, much of what happens in these environments emerges during the course of activities and is not prescribed or predetermined" (p. 56).

Fenichel and Schweingruber (2010) propose that designers draw on distinct features of informal learning to create more effective learning experiences "These facets of learning—the development of expertise, the role of intuitive ideas and prior knowledge in gaining deep understanding, and the ability to reflect on one's own thinking—can be put to use in informal settings to build deeper, more flexible understanding" (p. 39).

Scholars of informal science education show that this type of learning is extraordinarily rich, deeply embedded in particular physical, personal, and social contexts, and exceedingly difficult to capture. Bell et al. (2009) concluded that assessments significantly under-report the learning accrued from these contexts

(p. 57). They note that outcomes include a broad range of behaviors, can be unanticipated, evident at different times, and even at different scales [e.g., group vs. individual]. Small wonder then that a phenomenon that is so wide-spread is also not well-understood. Our work is one approach to evolving a theory of informal and incidental learning.

3.3.4 Our Model of Informal and Incidental Learning

The model we developed over time (Marsick and Watkins 1990; Cseh et al. 1999; Marsick et al. 2009) grew out of scholarship and practice centered in learning from experience, self-directed learning, action research, action science and transformative learning.

We started with Dewey's (1938) cycle of problem solving through reflective thought. Reflective thought begins with a disjuncture between what is expected and what occurs, which can lead to re-thinking the nature of the problem and the directions in which one might look for solutions. Solving a problem involves one or more cycles of trial and error in which learning takes place as one seeks to achieve a desired outcome. Observation of what occurs leads to course corrections and eventually to conclusions and planning for how one will address similar situations going forward. Dewey essentially adapted the scientific method to solving problems of everyday life. We focused on the learning process of an individual and added stages of reflective learning that usually occur incidentally but that, with coaching, can deepen informal learning.

We recognize the challenges faced when individuals learn in habitual ways. Drawing on Argyris and Schön (1978) and on Mezirow (1985), we look for ways to engage learners in examining taken-for-granted understandings, assumptions, and unintended consequences. We emphasize intentionality, consciousness, proactivity, and critical reflection as facilitators of informal learning (Marsick and Watkins 1990). We drew on Lewin's (1947) understanding of learning as based on interactions among individuals and environment; and have thus increasingly placed the learning of individuals in larger social contexts, e.g., groups, communities of practice, organizations, and society.

We extended our thinking about context by drawing upon learner network theory (Poell et al. 2000). Learning varies, according to this theory, by the interests and preferences of key actors (employees, managers, HRD, etc.), mediated by "the negotiation of power among the actors" (Ibid 1999, p. 44). Poell and his colleagues propose four ideal types of networks: vertical, horizontal, external, and liberal. Informal and incidental learning takes place within three basic strategy configurations: extended training, directed reflection, or reflective innovation. Our model of informal and incidental learning depicts a cycle of learning that begins with a trigger that is framed within a particular context. Individuals interpret the experience, and seek solutions. The model emphasizes the fact that individuals generally need to learn their way through to actually implement the proposed

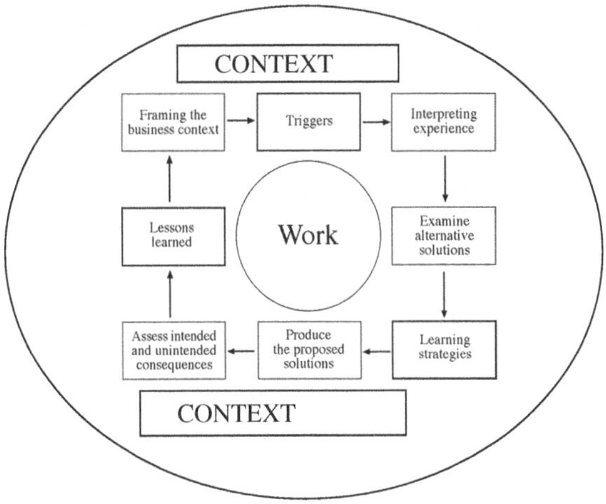

Fig. 3.1 Re-conceptualized informal and incidental learning model (1999). *Source* Cseh, Watkins, Marsick, "Informal and Incidental Learning in the Workplace". *Proceedings of the annual conference of the Academy of Human Resource Development,* 1998

solutions or strategies. Once they produce the proposed solution, it will have consequences—both those they intended, and those they did not anticipate. Assessment of those consequences enables individuals to make meaning of what happened and to derive lessons from the experience. The cycle begins again as the meaning derived from the experience permits a reframing of the initial learning trigger. Figure 3.1 below depicts our model of informal and incidental learning.

Engeström and Kerosuo (2007, pp. 336–337) underscore the need to bridge a historic divide between studies of workplace learning verus organizational learning as areas of inquiry, and the way in which "cultural–historical activity theory tends to cross and blur the divide" between the two in several ways. A unifying theory of informal learning—to which activity theory has much to contribute—must likewise bridge this divide. Our review of literature (Marsick et al. 2009) leads us to the following research-based conclusions about informal learning practices:

- Informal learning is always defined in contrast to informal learning. However, studies confirm that informal learning interacts in important ways with formal learning.
- Informal learning can be studied by examining learning activities and processes, for example, experimenting, reflection (meaning vs. action oriented), examining one's own practice, getting and using ideas from others, learning by doing, learning from mistakes, mentoring, coaching, giving and receiving feedback, or conversations with colleagues. However, there is no one "best activity" for getting results, which depend more on a range of other individual, group, community, organization, and societal factors.
- Informal learning is difficult to link directly to outcomes but some links can be identified and assessed, for example, the way that beliefs affect choices and their consequences for action taken.
- Individuals bring themselves to their learning tasks, and so, their strategies and approaches are mediated by their beliefs, values, histories, and prior socialization.

Studies support early theorizing that individual's intentionality, proactivity, and critical reflectivity affect the nature of their learning.
- Context greatly affects learning practices and choices, including triggers for learning, resources, and environmental influences. In short, the effects of context permeate the entire informal learning cycle.
- Relationships (and facilitators or barriers to engaging in relationships) are key to building informal learning communities.
- Knowledge management (both technology and person based) can become a link between individually generated informal learning—that is often highly particular to a given situation—and accessibility by a wide range of people to information and ideas for their own informal learning when the right systems, practices, structures, leadership, and culture are in place.

What we observe in these and other examples is the proliferation of informal learning approaches that are beginning to eclipse more formal learning strategies. While technology is a clear driving force, other less tangible forces support this trend toward informal and incidental learning in the workplace. One significant factor is the democratization of knowledge—the increase in accessibility through both design and technology of expert knowledge and tools.

3.3.5 Democratization of Knowledge

An exponential change in the accessibility of knowledge has been propelled by a hunger for innovation. According to von Hippel (2005), "The trend toward democratization of innovation … is being driven by two related technical trends: (1) the steadily improving *design capabilities* (innovation toolkits) that advances in computer hardware and software make possible for users; (2) the steadily improving ability of individual users to *combine and coordinate* their innovation-related efforts via new communication media such as the Internet" (p.2). These trends also impact design and delivery of work-based learning.

Design architecture, especially *option rich modular design architecture*, leads to enhanced innovation. Illustrative of this is open source coding through which communities of user designers create effective products that compete against traditional closed source coding. This represents a fundamental shift in thinking about innovation and who controls the processes of invention. The modularity of the design architecture permits innovation and collaborative knowledge creation with little specialized expertise.

These toolkit designs change the playing field because anyone can access and use the structural information that underlies much professional work. Novices have access to the same tools as experts and professionals. Not only can novices design custom homes or even legal documents—they can also work with manufacturers of these products, learn what customers want, and develop their own repertoire of potential designs and ideas.

Designers can also use tools for learners to create their own learning programs—from simple self-directed learning designs to more complex, web-enabled knowledge management tools that draw on knowledge repositories. An example, designed for reading for elementary school children, put at teachers' disposal multi-media, interactive lessons emanating from printed children's books that were almost infinitely adaptable by BOTH the teacher and the children. Children could read the story, become virtual reporters interviewing the characters who respond orally, or "google"™ various terms to learn more.

Open-ended, influence-able designs are needed that start with where learners are and can be controlled by both the learner and their guides. Electronic courses seldom draw on all available options. They resemble an electronic textbook more than a software program for learning integrated with work. By contrast, one organization envisions a desktop knowledge management system that would enable assembly line workers to access a brief 7 min learning module or a longer, more interactive learning program on the task. Workers search a "stockpile" of sample assembly designs sorted by ratings of their effectiveness. They access a tutor and continually updated information on how others rated the tutor's helpfulness. The tutor could import the novice's assembly design to his computer, make suggested changes that the novice would see as notations initialed by the tutor, and which the novice can accept or reject. The novice's proposed assembly design would be added to the in-house stockpile of possible designs. What makes tools like this so powerful is immediate, continuous updating and responsiveness to varying ability levels. These tools are fully focused on getting the task done with the requisite learning strategically targeted, modular, and "just enough." They blend formal and informal learning, capitalize on the democratization of knowledge, and support the creation of a learning community.

3.4 Whole System Impact on Learning Practices

Organizational factors influence climate for learning and may be easier to "manipulate" when stimulating informal learning than are individual-dependent variables or even learning activities themselves. Organizational factors that consistently show up as conducive to creating a rich learning environment are: (1) trust, (2) culture, (3) structure and communication, and (4) leadership/management practices. There is no single prescription as to how a *particular organization* should optimally operationalize these four factors, which typically interact with one another.

Trust is needed in order to ask candid questions, get and give feedback, communicate freely, and build learning relationships. Much informal learning is tacit and acquired while talking with, or observing, others. Informal learning is believed to promote capabilities needed to develop and exercise tacit knowledge—understanding context, problem solving, decision making, and communication. High

Performance Work literature emphasizes trust as a "pre-condition for effective learning" (Fuller et al. 2003).

Trust is often cultural. An extensive body of research on learning culture, using the Dimensions of the Learning Organization Questionnaire (DLOQ), shows that, to lead to improved results, organizational variables—leaders who model learning and effective strategic interaction with the organization's environment—matter significantly for informal learning at the system level (Watkins and Marsick 2003). Empowering people toward a collective vision and establishing systems that capture and share learning mediate these outcomes. Factors more easily shaped by professional developers—e.g., encouraging collaboration and group learning, promoting dialogue and inquiry, and creating continuous learning opportunities are helpful, but not sufficient, factors for achieving best results.

In many schools, building trust is an ongoing dilemma. Teachers often work in an environment driven by directives, with little to no input in decision making, and feedback they perceive as judgmental instead of constructive. This can generate a culture of uncertainty that fosters a privatization of practice and stifles teacher-to-teacher interaction. Some of the learning community strategies intended to provide supportive feedback such as classroom walk-throughs have instead been used as tools for punitive feedback. Learning communities must yield a level of transparency to be authentic in its process. A safe environment must be present for teachers to be willing to be transparent. "Trust…need(s) to be developed between and among staff members… in order for [them] to embark on new and seemingly risky forms of professional development" (Roy 2007, p.3). Learning communities can be the 'social exchange' where teachers can begin to genuinely practice the process of trusting over time. "A school cannot achieve relational trust simply through some workshop, retreat, or form of sensitivity training, although all of these activities can help… Trust grows through exchanges in which actions validate these expectations… In this respect, increasing trust and deepening organizational change support each other" (Bryk and Schneider 2003, p. 43).

Nevertheless these whole system strategies are essential because they impact student achievement. A recent study conducted in Lahore, Pakistan used the DLOQ to examine the learning culture in schools to see if the construct could help us differentiate between high and low performing schools (Akram et al. 2012). The headmasters and headmistresses of all the boys and girls high schools (N = 174) in one district of Lahore were selected to participate in this study. "On the basis of the schools' overall student achievement on the BISE exams, the researchers selected 30 high and 30 low performing schools. The *t* test for independent samples revealed that high performing schools demonstrated significantly higher mean scores (M = 4.96, SD = 0.66) than the low performing high schools (M = 4.57, SD = 0.82) on Strategic Leadership, $t(58) = -2.017$, $p = 0.048$, followed by Knowledge Performance (M = 4.98, SD = 0.62, as compared to M = 4.52, SD = 0.69), $t(58) = -2.69$, $p = 0.009$. No statistically significant differences were found between high and low performing schools on other dimensions of the learning culture" (p. 4). This study reinforced the critical role played by school leaders in supporting learning of teachers and of the system itself—and its ultimate relationship to increasing student achievement.

3.5 Conclusions and Implications for Work- and Field-Based Learning Practices in Schools as Learning Communities

Technology is catalyzing and mediating much learning, formal and informal, in schools that seek to transform themselves to meet new needs in this changing global environment. However, as we have argued in this chapter, we believe that whole-system work-based learning, implemented with an eye to learning of the total system in which such learning is embedded, is most conducive to the effective teaching of twenty first century skills for students.

Lick (2006) proposes three constructive elements for teacher interaction: "(a) effective communication (b) active listening (c) creating trust and credibility" (p. 92). These elements are often missing in school environments where for so long the culture has been centered around teachers working in isolation. Garmston (2005) confirms, "...teachers most often work in isolation, and professional learning programs seldom invest the time in teaching teachers to work with adults. Professional development in this area is a must"(p. 65). Carving out time from the traditional daily schedule for learning communities can be challenging yet is crucial. Ginsberg (2004) maintains that "adults need time to learn from and with each other in meaningful ways. When schools make collaborative adult learning a regular part of the school day, teachers can share and elaborate on existing knowledge. Shared learning creates a collaborative atmosphere and models life-long learning for students" (p. 89).

The seven dimenions of a learning culture provide a platform that can foster and maintain collaborative adult learning experiences. This learning culture then maximizes any learning that comes into the school or that is generated as a need of the school i.e., technology training. Using the DLOQ, schools can generate conversations around needs and begin creating interventions toward creating learning communities; tackling some of the mentioned barriers to adult learning.

Incorporating our models of informal and incidental learning and of a learning culture lead to this kind of whole system work-based learning where teachers' professional learning in technology, as well as other content and pedgogical practices, can be developed systemicly in effort to maintain a competitive edge in teaching twenty first century skills. By focusing on a broad-based conception of learning, growing leaders with the capacity to provide strategic leadership for learning, and building a culture of alignment around a collective vision, schools can become the kind of learning community that will be sufficiently agile to meet the demands of a digital world.

References

Ahmad N, Orton P (2010) Smartphones make IBM smarter, but not as expected. Train Dev 64(1):46–50

Akram M, Watkins KE, Sajid A (2012) Measuring the learning culture of high and low performing high schools in Pakistan. In: Proceedings of the Canadian international conference on education, Ontario, Canada

Argyris C (1989) Education for leading-learning. Organization Dynamics, Autumn, pp 5–15

Argyris C (1991) Teaching smart people how to learn. Harvard Bus Rev 69(3):99–109

Argyris C, Schön D (1978) Organizational learning: a theory of action perspective. Jossey-Bass, San Francisco

Bassi L, Cheney S, Lewis E (1998) Trends in workplace learning: supply and demand in interesting times. Train Dev J 5(1):58–68

Bell P, Lewenstein B, Shouse AW, Feder MA (eds) (2009) Committee on learning science in informal environments, national research council learning science in informal environments: people, places, and pursuits. National Academies Press, Washington D.C

Bowen GL, Ware WB, Rose RA (2006) The reliability and validity of the school success profile learning organization measure. Eval Program Plan 26:97–104

Bowen GL, Ware WB, Rose RA, Powers JD (2007) Assessing the functioning of schools as learning organizations. Child Schools 29(4):199–208

Bryk A, Schneider B (2003) Trust in schools: a core resource for school reform. Educ Leadersh 60(6):40–45

Chan T-W, Roschelle J, His S Kinshuk, Sharples M, et al. (2006) One-to-one technology-enhanced learning: An opportunity for global research collaboration. Res Pract Tech Enhanced Learn 1(2):3–29

Collinson V, Cook TF (2007) Organizational learning: Improving learning, teaching, and leading in school systems. Sage, Thousand Oaks

Coppieters P (2005) Turning schools into learning organizations. Eur J Teach Educ 28(2):129–139

Cseh M, Watkins KE, Marsick VJ (1999) Re-conceptualizing Marsick and Watkins' model of informal and incidental learning in the workplace. In: Kuchinke KP (ed) Proceedings of the academy of HRD. Academy of human resource development, Baton Rouge, pp 349–355)

Darling-Hammond L (1993) Reframing the school reform agenda: developing capacity for school transformation. Phi Delta Kappan 74:752–761

Dede C (2009) Immersive interfaces for engagement and learning. Science 323:66–69

Dewey J (1938) Experience and education. Collier Books, New York

Donaldson GA (2008) How leaders learn: Cultivating capacities for school improvement. Teachers College Press, New York

Drago-Severson E (2009) Leading adult learning: Supporting adult development in our schools. Corwin/Sage, Thousand Oaks, CA

Dufour R (2004) What is a professional learning community? Educ Leadersh 61(8):6–11

Eisenhart M, Edwards L (2004) Red-Eared sliders and neighborhood dogs: creating third spaces to support ethnic girls' interests in technological and scientific expertise. Child Youth Environ 14(2):156–177. http://www.colorado.edu/journals/cye/

Engeström Y, Kerosuo H, Kajamaa A (2007) Beyond discontinuity: Expansive organizational learning remembered, Management Learning 38(3):319–336. http://mlq.sagepub.com/search?author1=Anu+Kajamaa&sortspec=date&submit=Submit

Falk JH, Dierking LD (2000) Learning from museums: Visitor experiences and the making of meaning. AltaMira, Walnut Creek, CA

Fenichel M, Schweingruber HA (2010) National research council surrounded by science. National Academies Press, Washington D.C

Fullan M (1993) Changes forces: probing the depths of educational reform. Falmer, London

Fuller A, Ashton D, Felstead A, Unwin L, Walters S, Quinn M (2003) The impact of informal learning at work on business productivity. The center for labour market studies, University of Leicester

Garmston R (2005) Create a culture of inquiry and develop productive groups. J Staff Dev 26(2): 65–66
Garvin DA (1993) Building a learning organization. Harvard Bus Rev 71(4):78–91
Gephart MA, Marsick VJ, Shiotani, A (2010) Instituionalizing a performance-based learning perspective. Report prepared for Booz Allen Hamilton by the J.M. Huber Institute for Learning in Organizations, Teachers College, Columbia University, New York
Ginsberg MB (2004) Classroom walk-throughs. In: Easton LB (ed) Powerful designs for professional learning. NSDC, Oxford
Gray J (2000) How schools learn: common concerns and different responses. Res Pap Educ 15(3):235–239
Guskey TR (2000) Evaluating professional development (2nd ed.). Corwin, Thousand Oaks, CA
Gutiérrez KD (2008) Developing a sociocritical literacy in the third space. Read Res Q 43(2): 148–164
Hiatt-Michael D (2001) Schools as learning communities: a vision for organic school reform. Sch Community J 11(2):113–127
Hord SM, Sommers WA (2008) Leading professional learning communities: voices from research and practice. Corwin, Thousand Oaks
Leithwood KA, Seashore K (eds) (1998) Organizational learning in schools. Taylor & Francis, New York
Leithwood K, Jantzi D, Steinbach R (1995) An organisational learning perspective on school responses to central policy initiatives. Sch Organ 15(3):229–252
Leithwood KA, Leonard LJ, Sharratt L (1998) Conditions fostering organizational learning in schools. Educ Adm Q 34(2):243–276
Leithwood K, Seashore-Louis K, Anderson S, Wahlstrom K (2004) How leadership influences student learning. Minneapolis; Toronto, Canada: University of Minnesota, Center for Applied Research and Educational Improvement; Ontario Institute for Studies in Education
Lewin K (1947) Frontiers in group dynamics. Hum Relat 1:5–41
Lick DW (2006) A new perspective on organizational learning: creating learning teams. Eval Program Plan 29:88–96
Looi C-K, Seow P, Zhang BH, So H-J, Chen W, Wong L-H (2010) Leveraging mobile technology for sustainable seamless learning: a research agenda. Br J Educ Technol 41(2): 154–169
Mallon D (2009) Defining informal learning: A taxonomy for describing how most learning happens in today's organizations, Bersin and Associates Research Bulletin 4(46)
Marsick VJ, Watkins KE (1990) Informal and incidental learning in the workplace. Routledge, NY
Marsick VJ, Watkins KE (1999) Facilitating learning organizations: making learning count. Aldershot and Brookfield, VT
Marsick V, Watkins K, Callahan M, Volpe M (2009) Informal and incidental learning in the workplace. In: Smith MC (ed) Handbook of research on adult development and learning. Routledge Press, London, pp 570–600
Mezirow JD (1985) A critical theory of adult learning and education. In: Brookfield S (ed) Self-directed learning: from theory to practice, new directions for adult and continuing education. Jossey-Bass, San Francisco
Mulford W, Silins H, Leithwood K (2004) Educational leadership for organisational learning and improved student outcomes. Kluwer Academic Publishers. ISBN 1-4020-1987-4
Nsf. org (2012) http://www.nsf.gov/funding/pgm_summ.jsp?pims_id=504793&org=EHR&sel_org=EHR&from=fund
Poell RF, Chivers GE, Van der Krogt FJ, Wildemeersch DA (2000) Learning-network theory: organizing the dynamic relationships between learning and work. Manag Learn 31(1):25–49
Roy P, Hord S (2003) Moving NSDC's staff development standards into practice: Innovation configurations (Vol. 1). National Staff Development Council, Oxford, OH
Roy P (2007) Trust is the on-ramp to building collaboration and collegiality, the learning principal. NSDC, Oxford

Schechter C (2008) Organizational learning mechanisms: the meaning, measure, and implications for school improvement. Educ Adm Q 44(2):155–186
Senge P (1990, 2006) The fifth discipline: the art and practice of the learning organization. Doubleday, New York
Senge P et al (2000) Schools that learn: a fifth discipline fieldbook for educators, parents, and everyone who cares about education. Currency/Doubleday, New York. ISBN 0-385-492323-1
Silins (2000) Towards an optimistic future: schools as learning organizations—effects on teacher leadership and student outcomes. Paper presented at the annual AARE-NZARE conference, Sydney
IBM Learning Solutions (2005) On-demand learning: blended learning for today's evolving workforce (unpublished document). http://www-935.ibm.com
Umphrey J (2009) Toward 21st century supports: an interview with Linda Darling-Hammond. Princ Leadersh 10:18–21
Von Hippel E (2005) Democratixing innovation. MIT Press, Creative Commons
Wagner T (2007) Leading for change: Five habits of mind that count. Education Week 26(45): 29–30
Watkins K, Marsick VJ (1993) Sculpting the learning organization. Jossey-Bass, San Francisco
Watkins KE, Marsick VJ (1996) In action: creating the learning organization. American Society for Training and Development, Alexandria
Watkins K, Marsick V (eds) (2003) Making learning count! Diagnosing the learning culture in organizations, advances in developing human resources, vol 5(2). Thousand Oaks, Sage
Yang JC, Lin YL (2010) Deveopment and evaluation of an interactive mobile learning environment with shared display groupware. Educ Technol Soc 13(1):195–207

Part II
New Insights of Future Students

Chapter 4
The New Shape of the Student

Chris Jones

Abstract This chapter critically examines student characteristics in light of the popular discourse which describes students as part of a net generation of digital native young people. Digital and networked technologies have clearly changed the possibilities for students to learn and the ways in which teaching and learning can be conducted. It is also claimed that new technologies change what students are able to learn. However, the claim that there is a new generation of learners characterized by a new mentality has to be careful assessed in the light of recent empirical evidence. The idea of a generation gap between digitally native students and their digitally immigrant teachers is challenged, as are claims that pressure from this new generation forces radical institutional change on educational institutions. The chapter argues against the generational nature of the argument and separates the technological changes that are taking place from the determinist rhetoric they have been couched in. This rhetoric suggests that changes amongst students are already well understood and that their educational implications are already known and lead to generally applicable if not universal consequences. The chapter concludes by arguing that there is no one shape for students and that digital technologies open up a range of opportunities and choices at all levels of education.

C. Jones (✉)
The Institute of Educational Technology, The Open University,
Milton Keynes MK7 6AA, UK
e-mail: c.r.jones@open.ac.uk

R. Huang et al. (eds.), *Reshaping Learning*, New Frontiers of Educational Research,
DOI: 10.1007/978-3-642-32301-0_4,

4.1 Introduction

This chapter critically investigates the relationship between students and new technologies. It has become commonplace to describe students as digital natives part of a net generation. These ideas first developed in the late 1990s and early twenty-first century and have an almost viral character in the way that they circulate in academic literature gathering force from anecdotal connections with personal lives. Many adults have had the experience of being dumfounded by the apparent technological ease of sometimes extremely young people. This chapter looks for the theoretical foundations and empirical evidences that support the idea of a new generation of young people. In particular the focus of the chapter is on education and learning. If there are changes taking place in relation to new technology what are they and how do they affect students? The easy solution would be simply to repeat the widely disseminated version of students being part of a net generation composed of digital natives. The task this chapter undertakes is to critically examine these ideas and to assess whether they can be useful to educators.

The ideas that became popularized in terms of the net generation and later the idea of the digital native largely began with the work of Tapscott (1997) and the book *Growing Up Digital: The Rise of the Net Generation*. The term that has become most associated with young people and new technology, digital native, was introduced in two articles by Prensky (2001a, b). One of the earliest terms used to describe this group of young people was the generational term Millennials first developed by Howe and Strauss (2000). Alongside these 3 main terms there have been a plethora of other terms such as 'Generation Y' (Jorgensen 2003; Weiler 2005; McCrindle 2006); the 'IM Generation' referring to the Instant Message Generation (Lenhart et al. 2001); the 'Gamer Generation' (Carstens and Beck 2005); and 'Homo Zappiens' (Veen 2003) and most recently Google Generation (Rowlands et al. 2008) and the i-Generation (Rosen 2010). Although there are a wide variety of alternatives this chapter will focus on the two main terms, net generation and digital native, and treat them all as roughly interchange.

4.1.1 The Implications of the Generational Argument for Learning

In general the claims that have been made about the a new generation of young people are held in common and they argue that that because young people are growing up immersed in a world permeated with networked and digital technologies an entire generation thinks differently, learns differently, exhibits different social characteristics and has different expectations for learning. Prensky has gone further in claiming that the brains of students today are 'physically different' (Prensky 2001b). The new generation of students are portrayed as having a common set of preferences including: wanting to receive information quickly; relying on communication technologies; often multitasking and having a low tolerance for lectures; and preferring active approaches to learning (see for example Tapscott 1999; Oblinger 2003; Oblinger and Oblinger 2005).

A key assertion associated with the idea of Digital Natives is that "today's students *think and process information fundamentally differently* from their predecessors." (Prensky 2001a, p. 1 emphasis as in original). These changes to students preferences are said to be the direct consequence of technological changes which have had an impact on ways of thinking.

> Digital Natives are used to receiving information really fast. They like to parallel process and multi-task. They prefer their graphics before their text rather than the opposite. They prefer random access (like hypertext). They function best when networked. They thrive on instant gratification and frequent rewards. They prefer games to "serious" work. (Prensky 2001a, p. 2)

Prensky (2001a) also argued that there is a sharp generational divide, a 'singularity', that separates digital native students and their teachers. The net generation argument whilst similar is couched in slightly different way allowing teachers the ability to learn the new skills.

> Needless to say, a whole generation of teachers needs to learn new tools, new approaches, new skills. This will be a challenge…
>
> But as we make this inevitable transition, we may best turn to the generation raised on and immersed in new technologies. Give the students the tools and they will be the single most important source of guidance on how to make their schools relevant and effective places to learn. (Tapscott 1999, p. 11)

The net generation argument leads to a set of prescriptions for teaching and learning including a change from being 'teacher-centered' to becoming 'learner centered'. The role of the teacher is to facilitate, creating and structuring what happens in the classroom, including the tailoring of an individualized experience for the student (Tapscott 1999, p. 10). The learning preferences of these students include: bite size learning, new media and high levels of social interaction including collaboration. These prescriptions for teaching and learning were not particularly new even in 1999, and the idea that new technologies led to new kinds of learning interactions was popularized after the first wave of Internet technologies were applied to education (see for example Harasim 1990; Harasim et al. 1995; Hiltz and Turoff 1978). What was new was the central position specified for the new generation of students as the agent of change in education.

The generational nature of the argument also leads to a deficit model of professional development for teachers because they have grown up in a different world and enter the new environment as strangers. In the strong version argued by Prensky these teachers are required to try and imitate their digital native students but however, hard they try they will always retain a digital immigrant 'accent'. In Tapscott's version teachers can learn new skills under the guidance of their students. In both cases the characteristics of digital native students and their digital immigrant teachers are already established and relatively fixed. These arguments describe an unusual deficit model in which teachers are required to change and learn new skills and approaches, even though, especially in Prensky's strong version of the argument, they can never be fully successful in this endeavor and it is the students who are the source of guidance for their teachers.

The broad argument found in the discourse is that students' ways of thinking have changed, for example Dede (2005); Dede et al. (2007) claimed that technology was reshaping the mindset of students of all ages and creating a 'neo-millennial' learning style. Prensky (2001b, 2011) makes a stronger claim, that students exposed to digital technologies develop different brain structures. Prensky's (2001b) account relies on largely non-human studies of animals and a limited number of studies focused on brain changes in humans. There is a growing literature in the field of neuroscience and a review of this can be found in Bavelier et al. (2010). Overall I take the view with Ellis and Goodyear (2010) that there is currently no evidence of either a fundamental shift in learning processes or in the structure of the brain associated with growing up with digital technologies. The argument being put here is not trying to prejudge claims about the plasticity of the brain but to reject notions of the hardwiring of characteristics in students as a consequence of their early exposure to digital technologies.

It is because of these assumed changes among students that teachers were told that they had to modify their teaching practices to accommodate the learning needs of their technologically sophisticated students. The thesis argues that the pressure for change is from students but the proponents of the digital native thesis have noted that after almost a decade the change in schools and universities has been slow:

> It is inevitable … that change would finally come to our young peoples' education as well, and it has. But there is a huge paradox for educators: the place where the biggest educational changes have come is not our schools; it is everywhere else but our schools. (Prensky 2010, p. 1)

Despite the slow pace of educational change Prensky (2010) still clings to the idea that it remains an inevitable outcome of generational change. Tapscott (2009) also places education as one part of a broad wave of social and institutional change. The prescription for education that Tapscott and Williams (2010) provide situates educational reform in wider neo-liberal arguments by locating students as customers and universities as value creating centers of production.

> Change is required in two vast and interwoven domains that permeate the deep structures and operating model of the university: (1) the value created for the main customers of the university (the students); and (2) the model of production for how that value is created. First we need to toss out the old industrial model of pedagogy (how learning is accomplished) and replace it with a new model called collaborative learning. Second we need an entirely new modus operandi for how the subject matter, course materials, texts, written and spoken word, and other media (the content of higher education) are created. (Tapscott and Williams 2010, p. 10)

This relationship to market forces has led several authors to point out how commercial interests have been active in perpetuating the idea of a new generation (Buckingham and Willet 2006; Bayne and Ross 2007; Herring 2008). This suggests that the arguments presented in the digital native and net generation discourse as simply an inevitable outcome of generational change are in fact deeply political and implicated in major social choices about the place of education in contemporary society.

All the authors involved in advancing the idea of a new generation of technologically sophisticated students have argued that education is forced to change because there has been a generational shift caused by a process of technological change. In this determinist outlook technological change is seen as arising independently from society and then having an impact on other dependant domains, yet little theoretical work has been presented to support such a link. Furthermore the development of the ideas about digital natives and the net generation did not lead to the development of a research agenda and a related program of empirical work to assess the claims being put forward. This weakness in the argument was noted in Bennett et al. (2008) who conducted a review of the literature and called for empirical work to be undertaken to describe the student population and their relationships with new technologies and learning. Since Bennett et al. (2008) came to that conclusion there has been a considerable growth in empirical research in a variety of national contexts and the following section briefly reviews the outcome of these.

4.2 Empirical Research on Students and Technology

The findings from published empirical research examining the claims of the discourse surrounding a new net generation of digital natives shows that while the technological and material context is present in most of the advanced and the newly emerging industrial economies, this context does not translate in any simple way to a generational change in attitudes and natural skill levels related to the technology. Rather than supporting the idea that there is a net generation of digital natives who are naturally proficient with technology the evidence from a variety of contexts and sources shows a great variety in students' experiences with technologies.

There are several reviews of recent research available (Jones and Shao 2011; Livingstone et al. 2005; Luckin et al. 2009; Pedró 2009; Selwyn 2009; Schulmeister 2008; Staksrud et al. 2009). Jones and Shao, Pedró and Schulmeister concentrate in students in Higher Education whereas Selwyn, Livingstone, Luckin and Staksrud et al. focus on school age students. Perhaps significantly there is a marked separation between work on school age and university age students and it is rare for an author to cover both age groups unless their work spans a wide age range (Selwyn provides an exception e.g. Selwyn 2008, 2009, 2011). reviewed published literatures on young people and digital technology with a particular focus on information sciences, education and media/communication studies. Selwyn showed that young people's engagements with digital technologies were varied and often unspectacular. He also highlighted the misplaced determinism that underpins many current portrayals of young people and digital technology.

He concluded that while there is a need to keep in mind the changing lifeworlds of young people it would be helpful to steer clear of the excesses of the digital native debate.

Selwyn went on to state that there was no evidence of a serious break between young people and the rest of society. Selwyn argued that educationalists should approach the digital native literature with caution and that adults should not feel threatened by younger generations' engagements with digital technologies. He suggested that academic communities should promote more empirically grounded and socially aware portrayals of the complexity of the lives that young people develop through their engagement with digital and networked technologies. Livingstone et al. (2005) found that young people expressed confidence in their Internet use and information searching in particular but when probed more closely a nuanced picture emerged with students admitting to a range of difficulties suggesting that self-report may exaggerate both confidence and skills. In related work Staksrud et al. (2009) concluded that there were significant gaps in research and the quality and reporting of work in this area was uneven and often weak. Much of the non-academic work was quantitative and conducted by market research organizations and without more qualitative and mixed methods research they argued that the picture of children's' use of new technologies and the Internet would remain incomplete.

Pedró (2009) carried out a meta-analysis of studies from Organisation for Economic Co-operation and Development (OECD) countries. There were differences in students' technology adoption and use and that digital divides between different kinds of students still existed. Furthermore, there was not sufficient empirical evidence to support the claim that students' use of digital media had transformed the way in which they learn or their preferences and perceptions concerning teaching and learning in higher education. Neither was there enough empirical evidence to support claims about the effects of technology on cognitive development. Schulmeister (2008) concluded that many of the claims were overstated or unsupported and that users proved to be a mixture of groups rather than a single group with common characteristics. He noted that studies examining the use of computers did not always distinguish between the types, contents or functions of the media activities or include anything about the motives of the users. The age distribution of young people's preferences suggested that their actual interests were influenced by socialization and their behavior in relation to media was related to the same questions that occupied young people before the advent of contemporary media.

Jones and Shao (2011) concluded that there was no empirical evidence that there is a single new generation of young students entering Higher Education and the terms net generation and digital native did not capture the processes of change that were taking place. They argued that the complex changes that empirical work identified had an age related component, particularly with regard to newer technologies such as social networking site use (e.g. Facebook), the uploading and manipulation of multimedia (e.g. YouTube) and the use of handheld devices to access the mobile Internet. They found that demographic factors interacted with age to pattern students' responses to new technologies and that the most important of these were gender, mode of study (distance or place-based) and the international or home status of the student. They went on to conclude that the gap between students and their teachers was not fixed, nor was the gulf so large that it could not be bridged and there was little evidence that students entered university with demands for new technologies that their teachers could not meet (see also Salajan et al. 2010; Waycott et al. 2009).

Jones and Shao's review (2011) showed that students persistently reported that they preferred moderate use of Information and Communication Technologies (ICT) in their courses and argued that universities should be confident in the provision of what might seem to be basic services (see also Schulmeister 2008; Smith and Caruso 2010). Students appreciated and made use of the basic infrastructure for learning such as that provided by Learning or Course Management Systems and university library online services. Students were not found to not make extensive use of Blogs, Wikis and 3D Virtual Worlds but students who were required to use these technologies in their courses were unlikely to reject them and low use should not be taken to imply that they were inappropriate for educational use. They found no obvious or consistent demands from students for changes to pedagogy at university or evidence of a pent-up demand for greater collaboration. They also found no evidence of a consistent demand from students for the provision of highly individualised or personal university services and advice derived from generational arguments should not be used by government and government agencies to promote changes in university structure designed to accommodate a supposed net generation of digital natives. The review concluded that young students did not form a generational cohort and they did not express consistent or generationally organised demands. A key finding of this review was that political choices should be made explicit and not disguised by arguments about generational change.

Examining the detailed empirical studies showed that students were not all equally competent with technologies and their patterns of use varied considerably when they moved beyond basic and entrenched technologies to newer emerging or recently introduced technologies (Jones et al. 2010a; Kennedy et al. 2008, 2010, Van den Beemt et al. 2010a). There were variations among students even within the net generation age group and young people cluster into different user groups with different interests, preferences, and lifestyles (Bullen et al. 2011; Jones et al. 2010b; Jones and Hosein 2010; Kennedy et al. 2010; Schulmeister 2010; Van den Beemt et al. 2010b). Variation was related to other characteristics, including age, gender, socio-economic background, academic preference (major) and year of study (grade) (Brown and Czerniewicz 2008; Caruso and Kvavik 2005; Hosein et al. 2010a; Jones et al. 2010a; Kvavik 2005; Krause 2007; McNaught et al. 2009; Selwyn 2008; Smith et al. 2009; Smith and Caruso 2010; Van den Beemt et al. 2010a).

While there was considerable growth in students' access to computing technologies and online tools this was often for social and entertainment purposes rather than for learning (Oliver and Goerke 2007; Selwyn 2009) and students' use of technology for social and leisure purposes was different to their use of technologies for academic purposes (Corrin et al. 2010; Jones et al. 2010b; Jones and Ramanau 2009; Hosein et al. 2010b). Furthermore empirical studies showed that high levels of general use and skill with new technologies did not necessarily translate into preferences for increased use of technology in educational contexts. A large number of students still held conventional attitudes towards teaching (Kennedy et al. 2009; Gabriel and MacDonald 2009; Garcia and Qin 2007; Lohnes and Kinzer 2007; Margaryan et al. 2011) and research shows a consistent and long-standing finding that students would prefer moderate use of technology in the classroom (Jones 2002; Kennedy et al. 2009; Kvavik 2005; Salaway and Caruso 2007; Smith and Caruso 2010). Care needs to be taken with this finding because 'moderate use of ICT' in 2004 may have been quite different to moderate use of ICT in 2010 (Smith and Caruso 2010).

Evidence for the changing technological context comes from students use of the newer technologies, often bundled together under the term Web 2.0 (O'Reilly 2005). There was little evidence that students were significant users of either Web 2.0 or the most recent or most advanced technologies (Kennedy et al. 2007). Indeed there is some evidence that certain kinds of use of new technologies are against student wishes (Jones et al. 2010a). Age only seemed to be one of several interrelated factors, rather than the sole factor, in students' use of web 2.0 and social networking sites (Jones and Hosein 2010). Furthermore students had a pragmatic and instrumental way of using technologies, only using those technologies that were useful in terms of communication and information searching (Schulmeister 2010). Nagler and Ebner (2009) found common use of Wikipedia, YouTube and social networking sites while social bookmarking, photo sharing and microblogging were much less popular. However, while the evidence of students' natural take-up of such technologies is limited the evidence also suggests that students will make use of technologies that are requirements for their studies (Jones et al. 2010b; Smith and Caruso 2010; Kennedy et al. 2007). Taken together this evidence shows significant change in technology and in students' use but it contrasts with net generation and digital native rhetoric in which a uniform generation of students is portrayed as advanced users of new technology.

There is good evidence to suggest that there is no simple generational divide and the divisions between students and teachers have also been overdrawn (Kennedy et al. 2008, 2010; McNaught et al. 2009; Pedró 2009; Salajan et al. 2010; Waycott et al. 2009). Yet while this divide dissolves under scrutiny other digital divides show persistence (Schulmeister 2008; Hargittai 2010). Hargittai (2010); Hargittai et al. (2010) has shown the complexity and variation in people's use of the Internet and demonstrated considerable variation in students' online skills related to students' socioeconomic backgrounds. Broad demographic influences affect students' interaction with technology including gender and ethnicity as well as social class (Hargittai 2010; Jones et al. 2010a; Smith and Caruso 2010; Kennedy et al. 2010; Selwyn 2008). Access to technology is still unevenly spread and it relies on digital literacies rather than simple availability of new technology (Schulmeister 2010;

Palfrey and Gasser 2008). A persistent problem with the idea of a net generation of digital natives is that it directs attention towards divides that are not found in empirical work, and away from those divides that persist in education.

4.3 Revisions to the Original Thesis

Since the original net generation and digital native thesis was launched there have been a number of revisions, some from the original authors. Prensky (2009, 2011) recognizing that the digital native-digital immigrant distinction might have become less relevant as an increasing proportion of society has grown up exposed to digital and networked technology proposed a new term 'digital wisdom'.

> Although many have found the terms useful, as we move further into the twenty-first century when all will have grown up in the era of digital technology, the distinction between digital natives and digital immigrants will become less relevant… I suggest we think in terms of digital wisdom. (Prensky 2009, p. 1)

Unlike the strict native-immigrant distinction in which digital immigrants could never become natives, Prensky now argues that it is at least possible to acquire digital wisdom through interaction with technology. Prensky defined wisdom as '…the ability to find practical, creative, contextually appropriate, and emotionally satisfying solutions to complicated human problems.' (Prensky 2011, p. 20). However, Prensky (2011, p. 18). Still retains the still largely unsupported idea that the 'brains of those who interact with technology frequently will be restructured by that interaction'.

The move which Prensky makes has the effect of softening his previous position, which he described as a singularity separating the generations, and the idea of digital wisdom has the effect of allowing everyone to move towards digital enhancement.

> Homo sapiens digital, then, differs from today's human in two key aspects: He or she accepts digital enhancement as an integral fact of human existence, and he or she is digitally wise, both in the considered way he or she accesses the power of digital enhancements to complement innate abilities and in the way in which he or she uses enhancements to facilitate wiser decision making. Digital wisdom transcends the generational divide defined by the immigrant/native distinction. (Prensky 2011, p. 20)

Prensky still retains many of the features of his previous arguments. He retains the claim that use of digital technologies changes the brain of the user and he remains deterministic suggesting that digital enhancement is required for success. He argues that: '…in an unimaginably complex future, the digitally unenhanced person, however, wise, will not be able to access the tools of wisdom that will be available to even the least wise digitally enhanced human.' (Prensky 2011, p. 18). What Prensky has done is to move from a hard form of technological determinism, in which the divide between natives and immigrants is a necessary outcome of their exposure to technology, to a softer form of determinism in which digital enhancement is a necessary development for everyone if they are to succeed.

Palfrey and Gasser (2008) in their book *Born Digital* mounted the most sustained attempt to reclaim the term digital native as a useful academic term. Palfrey and Gasser (2008, p. 14) suggest that the term generation is an overstatement and prefer to call the new cohort a 'population'. They amplify this argument in a recent publication (Palfrey and Gasser 2011). While their intention is to reclaim the term digital native and they accept many of the criticisms of generational framing, their arguments lead to some confusion. Firstly they identify the digital native population by their access to technology, so it ceases to be a universal condition. Secondly they argue that access to new technology depends on a learned digital literacy. This argument clearly leaves a lot to be desired. From a generation who are born digital, because they grew up in a world infused with new technology, they have moved to a sub-group, a population who depend on access to technology which is itself conditioned by a digital literacy that can only be acquired through some form of informal or formal learning. The attempt to re-claim the term Digital Native has significant weaknesses and it is not clear what benefit remains in retaining the idea. The term Digital Native is at best misleading, and the authors agree that the idea of a generational change needs to be abandoned.

An alternative to the Digital Native/Digital Immigrant dichotomy was suggested by Stoerger (2009) who proposed a new metaphor, 'the Digital Melting Pot'. The aim was to redirect attention away from 'assigned' generational characteristics to the individual's diverse technological capabilities and to focus on the digital skills they might gain through experience. The Melting Pot metaphor emphasized the integration rather than the segregation of digital natives with the digital immigrants. Stoerger's (2009) aim was for to suggest that by gaining technology experience, those with low levels of competency could be transformed and educators could play a significant role in guiding individuals to acquire and enhance their technological skills. More recently, another replacement metaphor has been proposed to replace the terms natives and immigrants with 'visitors' and 'residents' (White and Le Cornu 2011). This revised metaphor replaces the 'immigrants' and 'natives' generations with an experiential divide between 'residents' and 'visitors'; resident being someone who spends a proportion of their life online, whereas a visitor is someone who uses the Web as a tool to address their specific needs. All these approaches raise questions about the causes of such a change.

4.4 Students, Technology and Causation

Writing recently Prensky (2011) has put the following case forward with regard to the causes of the new generation:

> … being a Digital Native is about growing up in a digital country or culture, as opposed to coming to it as an adult… It's not so much of 'facts' about hardware or software as having experienced so much of digital devices and interfaces that their use comes naturally and intuitively." (Prensky 2011, p. 17)

He also argues that his original use of the term was metaphorical and claims to have been shocked both by literal interpretations of the distinction and by those who criticized the term for being a broad generalization. Prensky adopts an idea about causation that links growing up with digital devices to a natural and intuitive stance towards the new technology. One aspect of this argument is its particular understanding of the relationship between technologies and change. Tapscott (2009) takes a similarly determinist position in relation to the net generation suggesting that an entire generation of young people is different to previous generations because of their experience of the bits and bytes of networked and digital technologies. Tapscott argues that because of changes in technology there have been some 'inevitable' consequences for learning. Essentially both Prensky and Tapscott argue that there has been a generational change caused by a process of technological change.

In this technological determinist account technology behaves as an independent and external structural force acting on social forms but not being conditioned by them. Selwyn (2003) writing about children's use of technology argued that the determinist discourses fundamentally fail to reflect the diversity and complexity to be found in real lives and 'the framing of children, adults and technology within these determinist discourses tends to hide the key shaping actors, the values and power relations behind the increasing use of ICT in society.' (Selwyn 2003, p. 368). Criticism of technological determinism has been longstanding (e.g. Buckingham 2006; Herring 2008) and it has been repeated in the current context (Jones 2011, 2012). One of the oddities of this way of thinking is that the technological environments experienced by digital natives were designed and developed by previous generations.

> Someone had to design, build, and upgrade the technologies that have evolved into the electronic spaces that the natives now inhabit. Interestingly, very few educational technology advocates mention that the digital immigrants were the creators of these devices and environments." (Stoerger 2009 Online)

Stoerger's contention points to two key arguments. Firstly digital technologies do not stand outside of society they are implicated in social change and secondly they embody previous social conditions in their design. This point is even more striking given the supposed divide between digital natives and the supposed immigrant nature of previous generations.

Bennett et al. (2008) are probably the most quoted critics of the original thesis and they argued that the discourse surrounding technology and generational change resembled an academic 'moral panic'. That is the digital native and net generation discourse restricts critical and rational debate and identifies the new generation a positive but threatening presence in relation to the existing academic order. The discourse provides a series of binary distinctions: new generation or old generations; technically capable and inclined or technically challenged; and finally between students and their teachers. These authors do not dismiss the potential for change related to developments in digital and networked technology, rather they argue for the collection of evidence and the adoption of a cautious attitude when advocating technologies as a vehicle for educational reform.

Educational institutions are portrayed as threatened by new Internet based technologies. Change ceases to open up a range of possibilities and becomes 'inexorable' and an 'imperative' instead:

> Universities are losing their grip on higher learning as the Internet is, inexorably, becoming the dominant infrastructure for knowledge—both as a container and as a global platform for knowledge exchange between people— and as a new generation of students requires a very different model of higher education… The transformation of the university is not just a good idea. It is an imperative, and evidence is mounting that the consequences of further delay may be dire. (Tapscott and Williams 2010, p. 18)

This rhetoric displays the characteristics of the moral panic identified by Bennett et al. (2008). In a moral panic an identified group in society is portrayed as a threat to social values and norms and the identified group are often described in sensational terms as a threat to the status quo. Digital natives and the net generation are used in education to advance otherwise contestable claims in way that suggests they are a necessity and not open to rational choice.

The determinist argument is contested by a range of alternative accounts which understand young people as active agents in the process of engagement with technology (Czerniewicz et al. 2009). Agency can also be understood to include the structural conditions that students face in educational institutions which are, like the design of digital technologies, the outcomes of decisions made within the institutions and express a form of collective agency. Research in universities reported by Jones and Healing (2010b) illustrates this process at several levels. Staff members designed and re-designed courses, embedding requirements for the appropriate use of technology, universities and the faculties and departments within them made decisions about what kinds of technology to deploy and the kinds of access students would have to these technologies. These arguments suggest expanding the notion of the agent to include persons acting not on their own behalf, as individuals, but enacting roles in collective organizations and institutions.

A further issue arises with the use of new technologies and agency within education. Students are increasingly working in settings which include active technologies that replicate some of the characteristics of human agency. Jones and Healing (2010b) point to the interactive nature of the digital networks through which education is mediated and note student reports of distraction, caused by the intervention of automated processes such as notifications from social networking sites. They conclude that there is an increasing likelihood that students will interact with humans and machines in similar ways. In addition Säljö (2010) argues that the kinds of digital devices being introduced have a different character to previous artifacts and technologies which reified and externalized information because they externalize cognitive processes.

These issues direct attention to another aspect of causation in the digital native and net generation arguments. They both assume that there is something distinctive and known about the new technologies at a general level. The term digital can be used to reference the entire collection of digital devices and their effects, and this is the way it is generally used in the digital native debate. However, it can also refer to a particular category of technological devices. Digital devices are potentially different to other kinds of artifact in the way that they can incorporate computer processing. However, the digital can also point to particular devices because while the Internet and Web depend on digital technologies, the digital extends beyond them. Many if not most digital devices are available both on and off-line in terms of a network connection. Both Prensky and Tapscott have provided accounts which suggest that it is because young people have grown up with digital technologies that they form a new generation. Prensky argued that digital natives are comfortable with digital technology because they had grown up with it and that "having experienced so much of digital devices and interfaces that their use comes naturally and intuitively" (Prensky 2011, p. 17). In his account Tapscott (2009 ,p. 2) argues that the reason for young people's natural facility with technology was that: 'they were the first to grow up surrounded by digital technology'. All these accounts assume that digital technologies have uniform and general character. Someone growing up with digital toys in one period is believed to develop skills and aptitudes that can be applied to the technologies of another period and appropriate to another level of social development. Since the digital native and net generation arguments were first developed new technologies and services have become mainstream, including wireless broadband, smartphones, social network sites (e.g., Facebook) and participatory social media (e.g., YouTube). Much of the empirical research effort in recent years has identified the varying ways students have appropriated these different technologies. On the face of it the overall claim that simply growing up with digital technologies leads to a general facility with future technologies is not supported by the evidence and it requires further clarification and research.

4.5 A Generational Fallacy?

Ellis and Goodyear (2010) argue that Prensky's analysis fails with regard to what they call a demographic fallacy, that is treating generations of people as if everyone in a generation shared common characteristics and that there were sharp breaks between generations. The idea a specific net generation composed of digital natives has a strong relationship to explicitly generational arguments. Howe and Strauss wrote *Millennials Rising* (2000) several years after the book *Generations: The History of America's Future and The Fourth Turning: An American Prophecy* (1991). They place the Millennial generation in cyclical view of history based on the history of the United States since the sixteenth century. In this generational account the Millennials are simply the most recent expression of an historical process. Indeed Millennials are the most recent form of the what is called the 'Civic' generational type which is said to have core values that include community and technology. For Howe and Strauss exposure to digital technology takes second place to a general historical cycle. The idea of a Millennial generation was introduced into the discussion of the net generation and education in the work of Oblinger and Oblinger (2005).

The authors who use the terms net generation and digital native do not generally advance this cyclical argument about generations but their arguments do have a strong generational component. Oblinger and Oblinger (2005), for example, are careful to state their claims cautiously and although they associate the new generation with the work of Howe and Strauss they define the net generation in terms of its exposure to technology (Jones 2011). As we noted earlier research has shown significant diversity when looking beyond the basic and entrenched technologies and patterns of access to, and use of other technologies varied considerably amongst students of a similar age. Thee empirical evidence suggests that the net generation age cohort is divided internally and while age is clearly a factor differentiating students, there is no generational gap and students of a similar age are diverse. Kennedy et al. (2010); Brown and Czerniewicz (2010) both found that those students displaying net generation characteristics were in a minority. Brown and Czerniewicz also draw attention to the character of student contexts in emerging economies that have different technological and arguably generational characteristics.

Thinyane (2010) who also reported on South African students portrayed a heterogeneous student population that had varied levels of access to a range of technologies and as with many other studies noted that students' use of web 2.0 technologies weren't actively used either in general daily life or for study. These results confirmed a more general picture of university students in South Africa (Brown and Czerniewicz 2008, 2010; Czerniewicz et al. 2009). South African research showed that mobile phones were the most accessible tools among students. Tasks involving the use of mobile phones ranked the top in both students' daily activities with technologies and use of technology particularly for their studies. The technological context of students in South Africa is clearly different to that envisaged in the digital native and net generation arguments, but the generational discussion also focuses on other factors. The end of apartheid and the 'born free' political generation arguably having more importance than technology.

Overall the net generation and the idea of digital natives seems to be very focused on a view of students based on North American experience in relatively wealthy and educated families. The South African case is a clear contrast to this but so is the example of China. There is a research that suggests variations in information searching (Li and Ranieri 2010; Li and Kirkup 2007). Shao's (2010) report on Chinese university students' use of technologies indicated that there was diversity in use of technology and the use of Web 2.0 technologies were relatively low. Shao (2010) also found a large number of students whose computer skills levels were far from what one might expect of digital natives and like Li and Ranieri (2010) found big disparities among participants in their digital competences. Jones and Shao (2011) report other relatively small scale surveys that showed variations from surveys in the USA, Australia and Europe but found that there was a similar lack of consistency in students in information searching and that much of the students' online experience was in activities such as watching news and movies and in playing games rather than for educational purposes. Overall these studies show that the context in China is different from the context assumed in the net generation and digital native thesis. Once again we should also note that the generational discussion in China is more related to national and social conditions than to technology (Chen 2008). Generation is discussed in relation to the single child policy and the emergence of the 'Little Emperors' and in terms of the year or decade of birth, in particular in this context the post-80 generation (Liu and Zhao 2008).

Apart from diversity in terms of national and regional variation there has been little discussion of variation of experience in relation to access and disabilities. Lewthwaite (2011) argues that:

> accessibility was frequently an afterthought or bolt-on within e-learning, rather than integral to new design. This is compounded by the normative views of an 'average' or proto-typical student expressed in much e-learning commentary [e.g., Prensky's (2001) 'Digital Natives']

Seale et al. (2010) comment on the way the digital native and net generation characterisation of students have rendered disabled students 'invisible'. Seale et al. noted the range of strategies that disabled students adopted and devised to make use of technologies in their learning.

> Students described on average about seven strategies each. The most common types of strategy adopted by students tended to be related to computer or information access, and ways of coping with written work. (Seale et al. 2010, p. 451)

These strategies involved both the use of specialist assistive technologies and generic technologies and encouragingly while these students do not fit the standard picture they do show a marked 'digital agility'.

> Digital inclusion in higher education, therefore, will not always be about practitioners opening the door and/or teaching disabled students how to step over the threshold. Sometimes, digital inclusion might be about disabled students using their considerable digital agility to 'break and enter' on their own terms. (Seale et al. 2010, pp. 458–459)

Overall Lewthwaite (2011) sums up an important lesson about generational stereotypes from the perspective of disability and access when she argues that a first step must be to abandon assumptions about who the learner is and engage with the uncertainties that abandoning generational descriptions give rise to.

4.6 Concluding Points

The main problem with the idea of a net generation of digital natives is that it encourages a way of understanding students that directs attention towards a divide that is not found in empirical work, and away from those divides that persist in education. In particular the idea that there is a single generational change related to digital technologies needs to be abandoned. There are age related changes but these are not generational in character and it is important to abandon generalized assumptions about the nature of a generational cohort of students and engage with the uncertainties that abandoning these simple generational descriptions give rise to. The argument that technologies have affected an entire age cohort obscures those age related changes that are taking place which give rise to a diverse student population exhibiting a variety of responses to the various digital and networked technologies in their environment. I have argued previously that there are potentially two different arguments about the changes taking place amongst young people (Jones 2011). The first argument is the one most associated with the idea of the Net Generation and Digital Natives which claims that:

- The ubiquitous nature of certain technologies, specifically gaming and the Web, has affected the outlook of an entire age cohort in advanced economies.

The second argument is that:

- The new technologies emerging with this generation have particular characteristics that afford certain types of social engagement.

It is this second argument that holds the most promise for understanding the future shape of the student.

In addition there is a problem in the view of causation found in digital native and net generation arguments. These arguments assume that at a general level there is something distinctive and already known about the new technologies; whereas empirical research in recent years has identified the variety of ways students have appropriated a range of digital technologies. Affordance suggests a more relational approach in which different technologies, although all digital in form, present different possibilities to students who can then interpret these possibilities in diverse ways. The ubiquitous nature of social network sites and the growth of mobile technologies including smartphones, tablet computers and e-book readers are all recent developments. However, it is not clear that there are common affordances to this variety of digital technologies, nor will the available possibilities be appropriated in the same ways by students in different contexts.

Students are active agents in the process as noted by Czerniewicz et al. (2009) and in relation to accessibility by Seale et al. (2010). One good reason why the net generation and digital native arguments have persisted is because they draw attention to real changes that are associated with age. The mistake is to believe that either we already know the nature of the digital native student or that the student population can be reduced to a proto-typical average—the net generation student. The task for educational researchers is to develop a rich picture of the range of student types emerging with new technologies and to be alert to all the factors that influence these, including age.

If the idea of the digital native and a net generation of students is to be replaced by a richer understanding of the changes that are taking place then the patterns of student engagement with technology will need to described in ways that are accessible to educators. There have been several attempts using cluster analysis of survey data to provide some further detail. In a recent study, Kennedy et al. (2010) found that within the population of young students there were disparities in how students used technologies. They identified four types of student users:

- power users,
- ordinary users,
- irregular users and
- basic users.

They indicated that power users made use of a wide range of technologies whilst ordinary users used mainly web and mobile technologies. Irregular users were similar to ordinary users but their frequency of using web and mobile technologies were lower and were less likely to use emerging technologies except for Web 2.0 publishing. Basic users were irregular users of new and emerging technologies but were regular users of standard mobile phones. Kennedy et al. (2010) suggested that the advanced user were a subset of students who might fit in with Prensky's idea of the digital native.

Jones and Hosein (2010) identified four groupings amongst English first year university students the composition of which was relatively stable over the period of one academic year. Van den Beemt et al. (2010a) showed a relationship between interactive media use and educational level, and between use and gender. Van den Beemt et al. (2010b) distinguished four factors of interactive media activities among a varied age range of students and labelled them: interacting, performing, interchanging and authoring. They distinguished four clusters of interactive media users labeling them; 'Traditionalists', 'Gamers', 'Networkers' and 'Producers'. An important outcome from this research was the complex relationship between behavioural dimensions. The factors grouped activities, but they did not relate in a straightforward way to clusters of users.

Despite these attempts to provide a more coherent and diverse description of students there is a need for methodological innovation. The distributed nature of mobile and networked technologies is a barrier to traditional forms of observation and new and innovative approaches to collecting in vivo data are required. As Staksrud et al. (2009) noted much of the early research work took the form of large and medium scale surveys. Recently there has been a development of a range of methods to research in contexts not appropriate for survey research. Judd and Kennedy (2011) used logs from computers in a large open-access computer laboratory to study a group of undergraduate medical students and their computer-based task switching and multitasking behavior. Hargittai et al. (2010) mixed interviews with stratified samples of students and observation of students' searching behavior. Jones and Healing (2010a) made use of a cultural probe in which students were issued with small video cameras and notebooks and responded to set questions when they received SMS text messages on their mobile phone. These methodological approaches take our understanding beyond the surface covered by surveys. However there is still a need for further innovation to gain a fuller picture of the shape of the student in the emerging technological conditions.

The implications for Higher Education are that the gap between students and their teachers is neither fixed nor is the gulf so large that it cannot be bridged. Universities should be confident that the provision of what might seem to be basic services (for example Learning Management Systems) often fulfills most if not all of their students' needs. The evidence shows that students appreciate and make use of basic elements of such infrastructures for learning that are often criticised for being out of date and unimaginative uses of new technology. Advice to government and policy makers derived from generational arguments should not be used to promote radical changes in university structures designed to accommodate a net generation of digital natives. The evidence indicates that young students do not express consistent or generationally organised demands and political choices should be made explicit and not disguised by arguments about generational change.

References

Bavelier D, Green CS, Dye MWG (2010) Children, wired: for better and for worse. Neuron 67(5):692–701

Bayne S, Ross J (2007) The 'digital native' and 'digital immigrant': a dangerous opposition. paper presented at the annual conference of the society for research into higher education, Brighton 11–13th Dec 2007. Retrieved from: http://www.malts.ed.ac.uk/staff/sian/natives_final.pdf

Bennett S, Maton K, Kervin L (2008) The 'digital natives' debate: a critical review of the evidence. British J Educ Technol 39(5):775–786

Brown C, Czerniewicz L (2010) Debunking the 'digital native': beyond digital apartheid, towards digital democracy. J Comput Assist Learn 26(5):357–369

Brown C, Czerniewicz L (2008) Trends in student use of ICTs in higher education in South Africa. Paper presented at the 10th annual conference of WWW Applications. Retrieved from: http://ahero.uwc.ac.za/index.php?module=csheandaction=downloadfileandfileid=94408130412238895743498

Buckingham D, Willett R (eds) (2006) Digital generations: Children, young people and new media. Erlbaum, Mahwah

Bullen M, Morgan T, Qayyum A (2011) Digital learners in higher education: generation is Not the issue. Can J Learn Technol 37(1). [Online]. Retrieved from: http://www.cjlt.ca/index.php/cjlt

Carstens A, Beck J (2005) Get ready for the gamer generation. Tech Trends 49(3):22–25

Caruso JB, Kvavik RB (2005) ECAR study of students and information technology 2005: convenience, connection, control and learning: EDUCAUSE. Retrieved from: http://www.educause.edu/ECAR/ECARStudyofStudentsandInformat/158586

Chen H (2008) Generation Y and the post 80s culture identity: a cross cultural perspective. Paper presented at the annual meeting of the association for education in journalism and mass communication, Marriott Downtown, Chicago, IL [Online]. 2011-06-07 from http://www.allacademic.com/meta/p271830_index.html

Corrin L, Lockyer L, Bennett S (2010) Technological diversity: an investigation of students' technology use in everyday life and academic study. Learn Media Technol 35(4):387–402

Czerniewicz L, Williams K, Brown C (2009) Students make a plan: understanding student agency in constraining conditions ALT-J. Assoc Learn Technol J 17(2):75–88

Dede C (2005) Planning for "Neomillennial" learning styles: implications for Investments in technology and faculty. In: Oblinger J, Oblinger D (eds) Educating the net generation. EDUCAUSE Publishers, Boulder, pp 226–247

Dede C, Dieterle E, Clarke J, Ketelhut D, Nelson B (2007) Media-based learning styles: implications for distance education. In: Moore MG (ed) Handbook of distance education, 2nd edn. Lawrence Erlbaum Associates, Mahwah

Ellis R, Goodyear P (2010) Students' experiences of e-learning in higher education: the ecology of sustainable innovation. Routledge, New York

Gabriel MA, Wiebe S, MacDonald RJ (2009) Net generation expectations for technology-mediated learning at the university level. Paper presented at the M-ICTE2009 conference, research, reflections and innovations in integrating ICT in education, Lisbon

Garcia P, Qin J (2007) Identifying the generation gap in higher education: where do the differences really lie? Innovate, 3(5). Retrieved from http://www.innovateonline.info

Harasim L (ed) (1990) Online education; perspectives on a new environment. Praeger, New York

Harasim L, Hiltz SR, Teles L, Turoff M (1995) Learning networks: a field guide to teaching and learning. MIT Press, Cambridge

Hargittai E (2010) Digital na(t)ives? variation in internet skills and uses among members of the ''net generation''. Sociol Inq 80(1):92–113

Hargittai E, Fullerton L, Menchen-Trevino E, Thomas KY (2010) Trust online: young adults' evaluation of web content. Int J Commun 4, 468–494. Retrieved from: http://ijoc.org/ojs/index.php/ijoc/article/download/636/423

Herring SC (2008) Questioning the generational divide: technological exoticism and adult construction of online youth identity. In: Buckingham D (ed) Youth, identity, and digital media. MIT Press, Cambridge, pp 71–94 [Online] Preprint: http://ella.slis.indiana.edu/~herring/macarthur.pdf

Hiltz SR, Turoff M (1978) The network nation—human communication via computer, 1st edn. Addison-Wesley, Reading

Hosein A, Ramanau R, Jones C (2010a) Are all net generation students the same? the frequency of technology use at university. Paper presented at the IADIS E-learning conference July 2010. Retrieved from: http://oro.open.ac.uk/24114/

Hosein A, Ramanau R, Jones C (2010b) Learning and living technologies: a longitudinal study of first-year students' frequency and competence in the use of ICT. Learn Media Technol 35(4): 403–418

Howe N, Strauss B (2000) Millennials rising: the next great generation. Vintage Books, New York

Jones C (2012) Networked learning, stepping beyond the net generation and digital natives. In: Dirckinck-Holmfeld L, Hodgson V, McConnell D (eds) Exploring the theory, pedagogy and practice of networked learning. Springer, New York

Jones C (2011) Students, the net generation and digital natives: accounting for educational change. In: Thomas M (ed) Deconstructing digital natives. Routledge, New York, pp 30–45

Jones C, Healing G (2010a) Networks and locations for student learning. Learn Media Technol 35(4):369–386

Jones C, Healing G (2010b) Net generation students: agency and choice and the new technologies. J Comput Assist Learn 26(5):344–356

Jones C, Hosein A (2010) Profiling university students' use of technology: where is the net generation divide? Int J Technol Knowl Soc 6(3):43–58

Jones C, Ramanau R, Cross SJ, Healing G (2010a) Net generation or digital natives: Is there a distinct new generation entering university? Comput Educ 54(3):722–732

Jones C, Ramanau R (2009) Collaboration and the net generation: the changing characteristics of first year university students. In: Malley O', Suthers CD, Reiman P, Dimitracopoulou A (eds) Proceedings of the 9th international conference on computer supported collaborative learning: CSCL2009: CSCL practices. University of the Aegean, Rhodes Greece, pp 237–241 Retrieved from: http://oro.open.ac.uk/18689/

Jones C, Shao B (2011) The net generation and digital natives: implications for higher education. Higher Education Academy, New York. [Online] http://www.heacademy.ac.uk/resources/detail/evidencenet/net-generation-and-digital-natives

Jones N, Blackey H, Fitzgibbon K, Chew E (2010b) Get out of myspace. Comput Educ 54(3):776–782

Jones S (2002) The Internet goes to college: how students are living in the future with today's technology. Pew Internet and American Life Project, Washington

Jorgensen B (2003) Baby boomers, generation X and generation Y? policy implications for defence forces in the modern era. Foresight 5(4):41–49

Judd T, Kennedy G (2011) Measurement and evidence of computer-based task switching and multitasking by 'net generation' students. Comput Educ 56(3):625–631

Kennedy G, Judd T, Dalgarno B, Waycott J (2010) Beyond natives and immigrants: exploring types of net generation students. J Comput Assist Learn 26(5):332–343

Kennedy G, Dalgarno B, Bennett S, Gray K, Waycott J, Judd T, Bishop A, Maton K, Krause KL, Chang R (2009) Educating the net generation: a handbook of findings for practice and policy. Melbourne University and Australian Learning and Teaching Council Ltd, Melbourne Retrieved from: www.netgen.unimelb.edu.au

Kennedy G, Dalgarno B, Bennett S, Judd T, Gray K, Chang R (2008) Immigrants and natives: investigating differences between staff and students' use of technology. In hello! where are you in the landscape of educational technology? Proceedings ascilite Melbourne 2008. Retrieved from: http://www.ascilite.org.au/conferences/melbourne08/procs/kennedy.pdf

Kennedy G, Dalgarno B, Gray K, Judd T, Waycott J, Bennett S, et al (2007) The net generation are not big users of Web 2.0 technologies: preliminary findings. In ICT: providing choices for learners and learning. Proceedings ascilite Singapore 2007. Retrieved from: http://www.ascilite.org.au/conferences/singapore07/procs/kennedy.pdf

Krause KL (2007) Who is the e-generation and how are they fairing in higher education. In: Lockard J, Pegrum M (eds) Brave new classrooms: democratic education and the Internet. Peter Lang, New York, pp 125–139

Kvavik R (2005) Convenience, communications, and control: how students use technology. In: Oblinger DG, Oblinger JL (eds) Educating the net generation pp 82–101. Retrieved from: http://www.educause.edu/ir/library/pdf/pub7101.pdf

Lenhart A, Rainie L, Lewis O (2001) Teenage life online: the rise of instant-message generation and the internet's impact on friendship and family relationships. Pew Internet and American Life Project, Washington

Lewthwaite (2011) Critical approaches to accessibility for technology-enhanced learning. Learn Media Technol 36(1):85–89

Li Y, Ranieri M (2010) Are 'digital natives' really digitally competent?—a study on Chinese teenagers. British J Educ Technol 41(6):1029–1042

Li N, Kirkup G (2007) Gender and cultural differences in Internet use: a study of China and the UK. Comput Educ 48(2):301–317

Liu L, Zhao E (2008) China's generation Y: new trend-setter in the workforce. Proceedings of the IEEE 4th international conference on wireless communications, networking and mobile computing, WiCOM, Dalian, pp 1–4

Livingstone S, Bober M, Helsper E (2005) Internet literacy among children and young people: findings from the UK children go online project. 4. OFCOM/ESRC, London [Online] http://eprints.lse.ac.uk/id/eprint/397

Lohnes S, Kinzer C (2007) Questioning assumptions about students' expectations for technology in college classrooms. Innovate 3(5) available at: http://innovateonline.info

Luckin R, Clark W, Logan K, Graber R, Oliver M, Mee A (2009) Do web 2.0 tools really open the door to learning: practices, perceptions and profiles of 11–16 year old learners. Learn Media Technol 34(2)

Margaryan A, Littlejohn A, Vojt G (2011) Are digital natives a myth or reality? university students' use of digital technologies. Comput Educ 2:429–440

McCrindle M (2006) New generations at work: attracting, recruiting, retraining and training 'generation Y'. McCrindle Research

McNaught C, Lam P, Ho A (2009) The digital divide between university students and teachers in Hong Kong. In: same places, different spaces. Proceedings of Ascilite, Auckland 2009. Retrieved 5th Dec 2011 from: http://www.ascilite.org.au/conferences/auckland09/procs/mcnaught.pdf

Nagler W, Ebner M (2009) Is your university ready for the Ne(x)t-generation?. In: Proceedings of 21st world conference on educational multimedia, hypermedia and telecommunications, June 22–26, (EDMEDIA), Honolulu, pp 4344–4351

Oblinger D (2003) Boomers, Gen-Xers and Millennials: understanding the new students. Educause Rev 38(4):37–47

Oblinger DG, Oblinger J (2005) Educating the net generation. EDUCAUSE Online book. Retrieved from: http://www.educause.edu/ir/library/pdf/pub7101.pdf

Oliver B, Goerke V (2007) Australian undergraduates' use and ownership of emerging technologies: Implications and opportunities for creating engaging learning experiences for the net generation. Australasian J Educ Technol 23(2):171–186

O'Reilly T (2005) What is web 2.0: design patterns and business models for the next generation of software. Retrieved 5th Dec 2011 from: http://www.oreillynet.com/pub/a/oreilly/tim/news/2005/09/30/what-is-web-20.html

Palfrey J, Gasser U (2011) Reclaiming an awkward term: what we might learn from 'digital natives'. In: Thomas M (ed) Deconstructing digital natives. Routledge, New York, pp 186–204

Palfrey J, Gasser U (2008) Born digital: understanding the first generation of digital natives. Basic Books, New York

Pedró F (2009) New millennium learners in higher education: evidence and policy implications. Centre for Educational Research and Innovation (CERI), Paris

Prensky M (2011) Digital wisdom and Homo Sapiens digital. In: Thomas M (ed) Deconstructing digital natives. Routledge, New York, pp 15–29

Prensky M (2010) Teaching digital natives: partnering for real learning. Sage Publishers, London

Prensky M (2009) H. Sapiens digital: from digital immigrants and digital natives to digital wisdom. J Online Educ 5(3)

Prensky M (2001a) Digital natives, digital immigrants. Horizon 9(5):1–6

Prensky M (2001b) Digital natives, digital immigrants, part 2: do they really think differently? Horizon 9(6):6

Rosen LD (2010) Rewired: understanding the i-generation and the way they Learn. Palgrave Macmillan, New York

Rowlands I, Nicholas D, Williams P, Huntington P, Fieldhouse M, Gunter B, Withey R, Jamali HR, Dobrowolski T, Tenopir C (2008) The google generation: the information behaviour of the researcher of the future. In: Aslib Proceedings, Vol 60 No 4, pp 290–310

Salajan FD, Schönwetter DJ, Cleghorn BM (2010) Student and faculty inter-generational digital divide: fact or fiction? Comput Educ 55(3):1393–1403

Salaway G, Caruso JB (2007) The ECAR Study of undergraduate students and information technology. EDUCAUSE Center for Applied Research, Boulder

Säljö R (2010) Digital tools and challenges to institutional traditions of learning: technologies, social memory and the performative nature of learning. J Comput Assist Learn 26(1):53–64

Schulmeister R (2010) Students, internet, eLearning and web 2.0. In: Ebner M, Schiefner M (eds) Looking toward the future of technology-enhanced education: ubiquitous learning and digital native. IGI Global, Hershey

Schulmeister R (2008) Is there a net gener in the house? dispelling a mystification. E-Learn Educ, 4(5)

Seale J, Draffan EA, Wald M (2010) Digital agility and digital decision making: conceptualising digital inclusion in the context of disabled learners in higher education. Stud High Educ 35(4):445–461

Selwyn N (2011) Schools and schooling in the digital age: a critical analysis. Routledge, London

Selwyn N (2009) The digital native—myth and reality. Aslib proceedings: new information perspectives, 61(4):364–379

Selwyn N (2008) An investigation of differences in undergraduates' academic use of the internet. Active Learn High Educ 9(1):11–22

Selwyn N (2003) Doing IT for the kids': re-examining children, computers and the 'information society. Media Cult Soc 25(3):351–378

Shao B (2010) University students' use of technologies in China. Paper presented at the European conference on educational research 2010: education and culture change. Helsinki 25–27th Aug 2010

Smith SD, Borreson Caruso J (2010) The ECAR Study of undergraduate students and information technology, 2010 research study, vol 6. EDUCAUSE center for applied research, Boulder 2010. Retrieved from http://www.educause.edu/ecar

Smith S, Salaway G, Borreson Caruso J (2009) The ECAR Study of undergraduate students and information technology, 2009 research study, vol 6. EDUCAUSE Center for Applied Research, Boulder 2009. Retrieved from http://www.educause.edu/ecar

Staksrud E, Livingstone S, Haddon L, Ólafsson K (2009) What do we know about children's use of online technologies? a report on data availability and research gaps in Europe, 2nd edn. Deliverable D1.1 data availability for the EC safer internet plus programme, EU Kids Online, London [Online] http://eprints.lse.ac.uk/id/eprint/24367

Stoerger S (2009) The digital melting pot: bridging the digital native-immigrant divide. First Monday 14(7)

Tapscott D (1997) Growing up digital: the rise of the net generation. McGraw-Hill, New York

Tapscott D (1999) Educating the net generation. Educ Leadersh 56(5):6–11

Tapscott D (2009) Grown up digital: how the net generation is changing your world. McGraw-Hill, New York

Tapscott D, Williams A (2010) Innovating the 21st century university: it's time. Educause Rev 45(1):16–29

Thinyane H (2010) Are digital natives a world-wide phenomenon? an investigation into South African first year students' use and experience with technology. Comput Educ 55(1):406–414

Van den Beemt A, Akkerman S, Simons PRJ (2010a) The use of interactive media among today's youth: results of a survey. Comput Hum Behav 26:1158–1165

van den Beemt A, Akkerman S, Simons PR-J (2010b) Patterns of interactive media use among contemporary youth. J Comput Assist Learn 27(2):103–118

Veen W (2003) A new force for change: homo sapiens. Learn Citizen 7:5–7

Weiler A (2005) Information seeking behavior in 'generation Y' students: motivation, critical thinking, and learning theory. J Acad Librarianship 31(1):46–53

Waycott J, Bennett S, Kennedy G, Dalgarno B, Gray K (2009) Digital divides? student and staff perceptions of information and communication technologies. Comput Educ 54(4):1202–1211

White DS, Cornu Le A (2011) Visitors and residents: a new typology for online engagement. First Monday 16(9). [Online] http://firstmonday.org/htbin/cgiwrap/bin/ojs/index.php/fm/article/viewArticle/3171/3049

Chapter 5
Digital Natives: Exploring the Diversity of Young People's Experience with Technology

Linda Corrin, Sue Bennett and Lori Lockyer

Abstract The concept of 'digital natives', based on assumptions of high technology literacy of the current generation of students, has triggered extensive discussion and debate in relation to technology use in higher education. Whilst several previous studies have demonstrated that generational views of technology literacy and engagement are not useful to the planning of future teaching and learning developments in higher education (Helsper and Eynon 2009; Kennedy et al. 2008; Bennett and Maton 2010), the digital natives discussion has eventually led to research offering a greater insight into the reality of students' engagement with technology. From the non-empirical foundations of the digital natives concept through initial quantitative studies and now towards new in-depth qualitative studies, a greater understanding is being developed of the diversity that exists around students' adopt and use of technology. This chapter reports on a study which aims to further the understanding of the motivations, attitudes and practices of young people in relation to technology. Eight student case studies are presented which provide an in-depth exploration of the stories behind students' choices and uses of technology across the contexts of their everyday life and academic study.

5.1 Introduction

As Turkle (2011, p. 19) observed "Technologies, in every generation, present opportunities to reflect on our values and direction". Based on the assumption that the current generation of young people who have grown up surrounded by technology have an innate ability with and preference for technology in all aspects of

L. Corrin (✉) · S. Bennett · L. Lockyer
Faculty of Education, University of Wollongong, Wollongong, Australia
e-mail: lcorrin@unimelb.edu.au

R. Huang et al. (eds.), *Reshaping Learning*, New Frontiers of Educational Research,
DOI: 10.1007/978-3-642-32301-0_5, © Springer-Verlag Berlin Heidelberg 2013

their lives, the concept of 'Digital Natives' (Prensky 2001) or the 'Net Generation' (Tapscott 1998) has prompted much discussion and debate about the role of technology in higher education. Whilst several research studies have since shown that these labels cannot be universally applied to the current generation of higher education students (Kennedy et al. 2006; Jones et al. 2010; Margaryan et al. 2011), the process of challenging the digital natives claims has identified the need for a more in-depth understanding of the motivations, attitudes and practices of young people in relation to technology.

This chapter presents the results of a study designed to provide a greater insight into young people's adoption and use of technologies across everyday life and academic contexts of their lives. Multiple methods of data collection were used to compile in-depth cases studies examining first-year higher education students' learning preferences and access, frequency of use, preferences, adoption, and adaption of technology. The unique profiles which resulted highlight the diversity of technology experience of young people and in some cases provide what may seem like counter-intuitive insights (Bennett and Maton 2011) into the motivations and attitudes towards technology. Such insights help to provide a better understanding of the nature of the diversity in students' technology engagement so that educators can make informed choices about when and how to integrate technology most effectively in the classroom.

5.2 What Do We Know About 'Digital Natives'?

When the concepts of 'digital natives' and the 'net generation' emerged ten or so years ago this prompted calls for radical changes to higher education in order to cope with this new generation of learners (Prensky 2001; Oblinger and Oblinger 2005). Initial claims focused on the identification of characteristics common to all students in this generation. These were said to include a high digital aptitude, a preference for multitasking, literacy across multiple media, a culture for sharing information, a need for speed of information delivery, and a desire to be constantly connected (Barnes et al. 2007; Prensky 2004; Oblinger and Oblinger 2005; Dede 2005). Further claims suggested that young people's constant use of technology had altered their learning preferences. Prensky (2001, p. 1) claimed that "today's students think and process information fundamentally differently from their predecessors".

For some time a 'certainty-complacency spiral' existed (Bennett and Maton 2011). Many in higher education, including educational administrators, accepted the digital natives notion, regardless of the lack of empirical evidence, due to the common sense nature of the generational claims. As empirical research emerged it was found that the alleged generational characteristics were not common to all young people. Instead significant diversity was discovered in relation to young people's access to, use and adoption of technology (Kennedy et al. 2006; Jones et al. 2010; Margaryan et al. 2011). Other studies searched for the existence of a digital generation of learners with radically different learning preferences but found no evidence to suggest that today's students' learning approaches are incompatible with traditional learning and teaching methods (Garcia and Qin 2007; Sanchez et al. 2011).

Although the diversity of students' engagement with technology had been established by several quantitative, survey-based studies, there is still a lack of qualitative research that provides an in-depth look at the motivations, attitudes and experiences behind technology adoption, adaption and use (Helsper and Eynon 2009; Kennedy et al. 2007). Recently a number of studies have emerged which employ multiple methods of data collection to explore this area in greater depth (Jones and Healing 2010; Czerniewicz and Brown 2010). However, these studies still use methods which rely primarily on self-reported data from participants in the form of surveys and interviews. In order to provide more in-depth and reliable accounts of students' technology engagement wider methods of data collection need to be employed.

The concept of digital natives, whilst having provided the impetus for much of the recent research into students' engagement with technology, is very technologically determinist in nature (Helsper and Eynon 2009). Suggestions for the future direction of this research area call for a move away from a focus on generational labels towards questions around the development of knowledge and experiences (Bennett and Maton 2011). This involves looking beyond the technology itself to other social and historical factors that may influence young people's technology use. To date, few studies have examined technology adoption and adaption within the various contexts of young people's lives. A greater understanding of the relationship between technology use across the contexts of everyday life and academic study has the potential to aid educators in making more informed decisions about the development and implementation of technology in learning and teaching (Kennedy et al. 2007; Bennett and Maton 2011).

5.3 Looking Closely at Digital Natives

The purpose of this study was to investigate young people's experiences with technology across the different contexts of their lives. The research was guided by the following questions:

1. To what extent do the patterns of technology use of first year university students reflect the notion of 'digital natives'?
2. How do first year students select and adapt technologies to suit their learning goals and strategies?
3. How do first year students use and preference for particular technologies relates to the identities they adopt in everyday and academic life contexts?

The theoretical framework for the study was informed by models of technology appropriation (Carroll et al. 2002) and theories of identity (Benson and

Makolichick 2007). Specifically, we took the view that people adopt and adapt technologies according to their perceptions and needs in ways that are not necessarily consistent with the original designers' intentions. Furthermore, these individualised patterns of technology use can relate to expressions of identity. This perspective views technology use as a broad array of social practices shaped by personal contexts and preferences, in tandem with technological change.

The study used a two phase mixed method design comprising: (1) a survey of first-year university students across a range of disciplines; and (2) case studies of individual students purposively sampled from survey respondents. The paper-based survey was administered during class time in first year courses across nine faculties at the University of Wollongong. Data was collected on access to technology, self-rated ability with technology, technology-supported activities spanning everyday and academic contexts, and demographic information. A total of 547 responses were received. Respondents born prior to 1980 were removed from the sample to focus only on individuals who fit the 'digital native' profile, leaving 470 responses for analysis. Descriptive statistics were used to characterise the sample and the key findings were compared with similar large scale surveys (Corrin et al. 2010).

Case study participants were selected from survey respondents to ensure a cross-section of individuals based on their technology adoption, ability and experience, ranging from those who rarely used technology to those who were heavily engaged. The 14 chosen participants were first interviewed to gain a detailed understanding of their technology-based activities. They were then tracked over a 3-week period during academic session using a modified experience sampling method (ESM) which prompted them to complete diary entries about their daily technology-based activities. Participants were sent three text messages each day asking them to provide a series of brief responses and reminding them to complete an end-of-day summary.

During this period, the researchers also conducted observations of online activities to which participants provided access as part of the study. These included activities such as social networking, blogging, and discussion forum posts. Participants were interviewed again at the end of the 3-week period and asked further questions about the activities recorded and observed. These data sources were analysed qualitatively to develop case study accounts for each of the participants. This then allowed for a cross case analysis to be conducted and connections with the theoretical framing to be made.

5.4 The REAL Lives of Digital Natives

This paper presents the learning and technology profiles of eight of the case study participants in the study. Each case explores the participants' experiences with technology in everyday life, learning goals and strategies, experiences with technology as part of academic study, and adoption and adaption of technology.

The participants ranged in age from 19 to 21 and were enrolled in a range of programs from Arts, Creative Arts, Education, Information Technology, Law, and Science.

5.5 Jessica

Jessica was an 18-year-old Bachelor of Primary Education student who lived at home with her family. She had a daily 1-h commute each way to university by train. Jessica felt that a degree in education would equip her with both the theoretical and practical knowledge to become a proficient teacher.

5.5.1 Everyday Life

A self-professed gamer and "photoshop-aholic", Jessica rated herself as an advanced user of technology. She owned (or had access to) a laptop and desktop computer, iPod, digital camera (still), mobile phone (not 3G-enabled), USB memory drive, games console and had broadband Internet at home. Jessica was an avid photographer who shared photos that she took at social events with her friends online. Before uploading the photos to Facebook (her preferred method of sharing), Jessica used Photoshop to edit the photos and add effects.

Jessica played games on 19 of the 21 days surveyed on her laptop or Nintendo DS console. She said she enjoyed games of skill and strategy over "button-mashing" games. The portability of Jessica's Nintendo DS meant she was able to play games in various locations, in particular, on the train during her commute to university when she connected wirelessly with her friends' consoles so they could play games together.

Jessica used of her mobile phone primarily to send text messages. Over the 3-week ESM period she sent 328 messages (average 15.6 messages per day) which she claimed represented her typical text message use. Jessica only used her phone for voice calls if she was trying to locate someone or needed an immediate answer to a question. Whilst Jessica owned a mobile phone with multimedia capabilities, she didn't use these features very often instead using it mainly as a communication device:

> my mobile phone has Internet and photographs and video recording, but I never actually use any of that because the quality is pretty shoddy, so when I have, you know, my actual camera, that I love, I use that instead. So usually it's just to communicate.

Jessica used her iPod to listen to music and podcasts on the train during her commute to university. She listened to radio show podcasts that she wasn't able to listen to live. She also used her iPod to watch television shows both on the train and in bed before going to sleep at night.

Jessica's main online activity was Facebook. She said her friends convinced her to set up an account which she said she checked only "every now and then". This was consistent with the data collected during the ESM period in which she logged onto Facebook on 9 of the 21 days. Jessica noted that she generally only visited Facebook when prompted by an email alert. When assessments were approaching, Jessica said her Facebook use would drop substantially.

Jessica used the Internet to research the answers to specific questions she had, but didn't generally browse. She used instant messaging occasionally, however she reported that her use was substantially less than before going to university. Jessica did not make use of the Internet to conduct banking or to pay bills. Security concerns and a lack of a credit card deterred her from buying and selling things online.

5.5.2 Academic Study

Jessica said she regularly attended classes and took an active role in classroom activities. She liked to be organised in advance for assignments and examinations. She studied by making handwritten notes from lecture slides and audio recordings of key terms and concepts for revision. Jessica felt that the process of writing out notes from the teaching materials helped her to remember the content.

Jessica made regular use of the university's learning management system to access course materials and communicate with other students via the discussion boards. She used lecture recordings to catch up on material she had missed or to revise certain content. When searching for resources to support her studies, Jessica first went to the library catalogues as she found this produced more relevant and scholarly sources than a general Internet search.

Jessica communicated with lecturers and tutors via email to ask questions about subject content and assessments. However, when communicating with peers she used text messages and instant messaging, unless files needed to be exchange in which case she used email. Jessica said she made extensive use of the online discussion boards for her subjects to seek help from or assist other students.

Jessica was satisfied with the current level of technology used in her subjects. However, she also appreciated opportunities to learn about new technologies that she may be able to use in her future teaching career.

5.5.3 Adoption and Adaption of Technology

Jessica demonstrated willingness to try and adopt new technologies. She attempted to understand how new technologies worked on her own, before seeking help from friends or a manual. Jessica explored the functionality of the technology before deciding which features she would use. She identified ease of use, relevance, appearance, price and durability as the factors that influence her decision to adopt new technologies. Jessica often consulted friends to see what they used before making her decision. She also referred to manufacturers' websites to check features. However, Jessica only investigated new technologies when she had identified a need, she did not upgrade just because a new technology was available.

5.6 Trent

Trent was a 22-year-old Bachelor of Health and Physical Education student. He lived between two houses, both approximately 1 h from campus. Trent aspired to a political career but felt he first needed to establish himself as "a valuable member of society". He chose education as he felt this was a career that would set him up with many transferable skills. Trent participated in several community organisations and during the ESM period was heavily involved in a political campaign.

5.6.1 Everyday Life

Trent identified his mobile phone and laptop computer as the technologies he used most frequently. He reported that he used his laptop mainly for word processing and accessing the Internet. Trent only had access to the Internet at one of the houses in which he lived and so had to work offline on his laptop when at the house without Internet. Trent also owned a desktop computer; however this was housed at the house without Internet so he primarily used this machine for working on video, music and photos which he transferred between laptop and desktop by USB drive. He was very keen to improve his video editing and website development skills which he was teaching himself using resources from the Internet. During the ESM period Trent also began to learn a language using online tools and free downloadable software.

Trent said that he was rarely without his mobile phone: "it doesn't leave my side and I use it all day". He used the phone to make calls, send messages, as a camera and an alarm clock. Trent wanted to use the Internet on his phone, but found it too expensive. During the ESM period he sent 337 text messages, an average of 16 messages a day, and made calls every day. Trent also occasionally used instant messaging to talk to his girlfriend.

Trent frequently used the Internet in order to keep up with the latest news and political developments. When he was at the home without Internet he accessed news via a Pay-TV service. He sometimes used the Internet to check prices on items he wanted to purchase, however he was wary of transferring money online and didn't have a credit card.

Trent used MySpace and Bebo accounts previously, but recently moved to Facebook for social networking. Trent commented that, whilst he had originally approached Facebook as a fun social network, he then changed his profile to make his online presence more business-like including a profile photo of him giving a speech at parliament house:

> suited up, notes in hand, at the lectern, mid sentence, and I've got the Australian and Aboriginal flags behind me… I specifically put that there because that's the look that I need.

Trent considered his use of status updates on Facebook as an alternative to a personal blog. He saw broadcasting his activities and following other people's status updates as a valuable networking opportunity, especially with acquaintances made through his community or political projects. Trent also maintained MySpace pages for two community groups.

Trent claimed that time pressures and the limitations of his laptop stopped him from playing games as much as he would like. When he did play games they tended to be online word games through Facebook which he played against friends (e.g., Scrabble, Word Twist) and strategy games like Nations. He owned a Playstation 2 but hadn't played it in a long time. Likewise, Trent owned an iPod but used it very rarely.

5.6.2 Academic Study

Trent's main study technique was to read. He also liked to reinforce concepts by talking about them with others in an informal way rather than a formal study group. He said he was active in classroom discussions and occasionally used the online discussion board. He thought the format of the online forums was difficult to follow a conversation and thus reduced student engagement. In preparing for exams, Trent made study notes in a question and answer format from textbooks, lecture notes and notes he took in class. He then got someone to ask him the questions to test his knowledge. For one anatomy exam he made a recording of important concepts and played it on his iPod as he drove to the exam.

Trent made use of numerous technologies as part of his studies. He regularly accessed the University's learning management system to download lecture notes and access discussion boards. A number of his recent assessments had involved using technology including the creation of a video, PowerPoint presentations, and the evaluation of online educational games. To support a group assignment Trent's group established an email address to which group members emailed relevant articles so everyone could access them.

Trent said that he would like to see more technology used to expand services to students who can't always get to the University campus. In particular, Trent wanted more lectures to be delivered via video conferencing to the University campus near his homes rather than having to drive to the main campus. He also expressed a preference for more learning activities that allowed him to use technology to be creative.

5.6.3 *Adoption and Adaption of Technology*

Trent was enthusiastic about adopting new technologies and tools that he could use to support his busy lifestyle. However, his adoption of technology was ruled by cost considerations causing him to justify each purchase in terms of a definite need. When using a new technology, Trent explored and learnt the tool's functions by orderly trialling each function rather than consulting other people or manuals.

5.7 Lucy

Lucy was a 20-year-old Bachelor of Biomedical Science student who travelled overseas for a year before starting university. Lucy's home was several hours away from the University in a small town so she lived in university residences during semester. Lucy was enrolled in an undergraduate degree in biomedical science as a stepping stone to a postgraduate medicine or forensic anthropology degree.

5.7.1 *Everyday Life*

In her everyday life, Lucy used a limited number of technologies in ways tailored to her needs. Lucy rated herself as intermediate in terms of her level of ability with technology. Lucy noted that there hadn't been a lot of technology around the house when she was growing up. She said she had only had exposure to more technologies in the last few years.

She owned a very old laptop which she claimed was only good enough to use to watch movies. For other computer functions she used computers in labs at university or her parents and brothers' desktop computers when she was back at home. She had broadband Internet access at her parents' house; her access to the Internet during the semester at university was metered so she was careful not to use it too much.

Lucy took photos on her digital camera which she often shared with her friends online via Facebook. However, Lucy didn't trust the university computers for doing this activity so waited until she was at her parents' house to upload photos. When at home, Lucy played role play games such as Diablo on her brothers' games console. She claimed to play games at home "all the time" as there wasn't much to do in a small town. When at university Lucy played a number of online games such as Nation States (a simulation game) and various Facebook games.

Lucy owned a mobile phone which she used to make calls although she didn't always keep her phone with her. Lucy reported that she had only ever sent one text message claiming that it took too long to type text messages. Generally Lucy kept her mobile usage to a minimum due to the cost of having to buy more credit. Instead she used email as that was a “free” alternative.

Lucy did not own a portable music player, a PDA or USB drive. When she needed to transfer files between computers Lucy emailed them to herself. Lucy was not familiar with technologies such as podcasts or RSS feeds She commented that she knew what she needed to know about technology to do the things she needed to do, but not much else.

The technology that Lucy claimed to use most frequently was the Internet. She used the Internet to play games, use Facebook, and visit online forums and favourite sites including Uncyclopedia. However, Lucy did not shop online or do banking or pay bills due to security concerns. Lucy originally set up her Facebook account to keep in contact with friends while she was overseas and then “was hooked on it” by the time she got back. She found it a very useful tool to keep up to date with what her friends were doing. Her profile displayed information about herself including a short bio, favourite music/movies/TV shows/quotes, and her contact details. During the experience sampling method period Lucy accessed Facebook on 8 of the 21 days. She reported that her Facebook usage could be sporadic and sometimes she would go for weeks without logging in.

For communication, Lucy also used email and phone to keep in contact with friends and family. During the 3-week ESM period Lucy sent 17 emails. She said she also used instant messaging via MSN, however not as much during semester due to the quota restrictions on her Internet use.

5.7.2 Academic Study

Lucy said she was committed to her studies and regularly attended classes, claiming that she “hadn’t missed a lecture yet”. Her study methods included reading textbooks, doing practice exercises/questions and reading over notes taken in lectures and tutorials. She preferred to study alone and prepared well in advance for assessments and examinations.

Lucy used the Internet to support her studies by looking up topics of interest or clarifying content. She regularly logged into the university’s learning management system to access lecture notes and complete the online quizzes required for her course. Lucy also used PowerPoint for some assessments, however not as much at university as she had at high school.

Lucy accessed her email on a regular basis as it was the University’s method of sending announcements. She also used email to communicate with other students for group assignments as she had found it difficult to arrange face-to-face groups meetings due to her group members’ different study timetables. A day prior to the first interview one of Lucy’s assignment groups had decided to set up a Facebook group to facilitate discussion.

5.7.3 *Adoption and Adaption of Technology*

Lucy said she adopted a technology primarily when prescribed as part of her degree. She initially learnt to use functions needed for her study and then played around to see if there were any additional functions she liked. Lucy identified utility, price and appearance as factors that influenced her adoption of new technologies. She said she looked to see that a technology had the basic functions that allowed her to do what she needed and didn't seek out models with extra features. When researching technology purchases Lucy's only method was to ask friends for their opinion and experience with the technology. Once she had purchased a technology she consulted the manual to work out how to use the main features she needed, then over time she explored additional capabilities of the technology sometimes adopting features if they served a useful purpose.

5.8 Michael

Michael was a 20-year-old Bachelor of Information Technology student. During semester Michael lived in university residences as his hometown was 3 h from campus. Although initially wanting to work in the field of sports management, Michael chose a degree in information technology as he felt the job prospects were better.

5.8.1 *Everyday Life*

Michael considered himself an advanced user of technology. The technologies he said that he used most were his laptop and mobile phone. He primarily used his laptop to access the Internet to keep up with news and sports, watch videos on YouTube and use social networking. Michael accessed certain news sites on a regular basis and also read blogs on soccer.

Michael used Facebook to keep in contact with friends. During the ESM period he accessed Facebook on 13 of the 21 days. He occasionally shared photos via Facebook—during the ESM period posted an album of 45 photos of a social event. Michael provided many personal details in his profile including his date of birth, email addresses and former schools. When asked about how he liked to portray himself online, Michael said he presented himself as he is, although he did say he was selective in the information he made available. In describing himself in the interview he identified primarily as a university student with an interest in sport. His love of sport was obvious in his Facebook profile:

Interests	sport!!! football, rugby league, rugby union, cricket everything! also love my music and computers… occasional drinker
Favorite Books	sport section in the newspaper…

For communication, Michael used his mobile to contact friends and family via calls and text messages. During the ESM period Michael sent 25 text messages and made calls on 9 of the 21 days. Michael also used his phone's calendar and calculator features. Email was Michael's other main form of communication—he sent 19 emails during the ESM period. Michael said that he previously used instant messaging but "grew out of it" when he came to university. However, he indicated that he made use of instant messaging on 3 of the ESM days via the chat tool in Facebook rather than a stand-alone instant message tool (e.g., MSN Messenger).

During semester Michael enjoyed playing games on his computer (e.g., Minesweeper and Solitaire). When working on assignments Michael said that he procrastinated by playing these and other games such as Call of Duty (a first-person and third-person shooter game). When at home during holiday breaks Michael played soccer on his games console.

Michael did not own a portable music player or listen to podcasts, he didn't maintain a blog or website, and didn't use tools such as RSS feeds. He used the Internet to do his banking and pay bills, but did very little shopping online.

5.8.2 Academic Study

Michael's main study technique was to read through his lecture notes and textbooks and take notes. Michael expressed a strong preference for practical activities as part of his studies. At exam time, Michael reviewed his notes and revisited diagrams and tables which provided summaries of important concepts. Whenever possible, Michael liked to study in a group with friends who worked on questions together.

Michael used his laptop for programming and other university work as part of his studies. He regularly accessed the University's learning management system to download lecture notes and read, but rarely contribute to, the discussion board. He made limited use of presentation software as his degree required very few presentations. Michael used email to communicate with peers for his studies and also used text messaging for some group assignments. Michael thought that the level of technology incorporated in his degree was appropriate. He had not considered making use of any of his everyday technologies as part of his studies, however indicated that he thought Facebook might be useful for group work.

5.8.3 Adoption and Adaption of Technology

Michael reported that his main motivation for adopting new technologies was to gain functionality. When choosing a new technology, Michael considered functionality, performance (e.g., speed, capacity), price and durability. He acknowledged that with the frequency of the emergence of new technologies he was interested in purchasing technology that would "do for a little while that is affordable" knowing it wouldn't be too long before he would replace the technology for greater functionality. When purchasing a new technology Michael sought advice from store salespeople, rather than consulting with friends or doing prior research online.

5.9 Toby

Toby was a 20-year-old Bachelor of Creative Arts (Performance) student. He lived in a share house 15 min away from the campus. Toby planned to enter the entertainment industry and wanted a degree in creative arts to prove he had studied professional acting techniques with recognised people in the field.

5.9.1 Everyday Life

Toby rated himself as an intermediate user of technology. He identified the Internet, mobile phone and MP3 player as his most frequently used technologies. He said he spent a lot of time on the Internet checking emails, chatting to people, reading fan fiction and web comics, and randomly surfing. He used his mobile phone for communication, but also as a camera and an alarm clock. He listened to his MP3 player when in transit: "*If I'm going somewhere and don't have anyone to speak to it is in my ears*".

Toby occasionally shared photos online via email or Facebook, but as he didn't take many photos himself, he was more likely to be the recipient of photos from friends. He didn't keep a blog but intended to start one when he spent time overseas as an exchange student. He didn't read blogs by others or subscribe to RSS feeds.

Toby liked to play role-play and strategy games on his computer. He also used online emulators of old games systems to play old games. Whilst he owned a game console, he used it only for playing DVDs as it was missing a memory card. He also owned a Nintendo DS but hadn't used it for a long time—he said he went through times when he used it a lot and then he would put it aside for several months. Toby conducted his banking, paid bills and bought items on eBay online.

Toby preferred to make calls on his mobile rather than send texts as he saw this as the quicker and cheaper option. He checked email frequently but did not send many emails as he saw his network of friends on a regular basis at university. Whenever he was on his computer, Toby logged into his MSN instant messaging tool, although he didn't use it much as he saw his friends every day.

Toby also used Facebook but again, as he saw his friends so often, his level of Facebook usage was quite low. During the ESM period he only accessed Facebook on 6 of the 21 days. He indicated that he only checked Facebook when he received an email notification to say there was something new online for him to check.

5.9.2 Academic Study

Toby had a preference for practical learning activities which matched well with his chosen degree. He claimed that he didn't 'study' as such, instead he said he 'absorbed' information through classes, reading and discussing concepts with classmates which he was able to 'regurgitate' during assessments and exams with little review. Toby said he was a very active participant in class discussions, usually being the first to express an opinion. He particularly liked classes when he could do something practical and receive immediate feedback (e.g., singing classes).

Toby used the Internet to access readings, explore topics and find journal articles to support assignments. He accessed the University's learning management system occasionally to get details of the readings for his course. Toby was encouraged by his lecturer to use the Sephonics learning tool to learn about the phonetic alphabet which he found very useful. He rarely made use of online communication tools as in his small faculty the teachers and students see each other every day. Occasionally he used email to distribute a script or notes from a class to his classmates. He also accessed videos on YouTube as reference material in order to prepare impersonations for dramaturgy classes. Toby indicated that he would like to see the use of more podcasts in his course, not recordings of the classes but external resources covering the theory of what they were learning in the classroom.

5.9.3 Adoption and Adaption of Technology

Toby liked to adopt technology that provided some 'quantum leap' from what was previously available. If a new technology was just an incremental upgrade on something already in existence then Toby delayed adopting it until the price had dropped to an affordable range. When adopting new technology his primary considerations were price and functionality, something that would make his life easier. He indicated that he wanted a number of new technologies including a laptop to replace his dying desktop computer, and a new MP3 player with a bigger capacity and ease of use. When purchasing a new technology he did not research it in advance beyond looking at advertising material, instead relying on the experience of the shop assistants to guide his purchases. He found learning to use a new technology simple and approached it by trial and error, eventually consulting the manual if he was unable to work something out.

5.10 Bree

Bree was a 19-year-old Bachelor of Information Systems student. She lived at home with her family 20 min away from the University. Bree wasn't sure of her career direction at the end of high school so decided to pick something that interested her at university. She chose Information Systems as she wanted to gain a better understanding of technology and how it can be used in business.

5.10.1 Everyday Life

Despite being enrolled in an IT-based course, Bree only considered herself an intermediate user of technology. She identified her computer and mobile phone as the technologies that she used most often. She was involved in church and community groups for which she produced audio and video presentations and shared photos online using Photobucket with her church friends. She surfed the Internet frequently for items relating to her interest groups, to keep up with the news, to pay bills and do banking, to buy clothes and to sell textbooks online.

Bree downloaded and listened to podcasts of local and national radio stations. She occasionally played computer games primarily using the games website www.hallpass.com. She also owned a Nintendo Gameboy which she had received as a gift, but commented that "I would rather read books than sit down and play my Gameboy for hours on end". During the ESM period Bree only played games on 3 of the 21 days.

Bree used Facebook almost daily to keep in contact with friends. During the ESM period Bree expanded her Facebook network by accepting 17 friend requests. She said she wasn't interested in using Facebook applications, but did join several groups. Bree made an effort when she logged into check the pages of friends who she hadn't been in contact with for a while.

For communications, Bree used her mobile phone to keep in contact with friends. Her phone was a very basic model which only allowed her to make calls and send text messages. She sent 99 text messages over the ESM period and made calls on 11 of the 21 days. Bree also communicated via instant messaging most nights, primarily with friends who she didn't see on a regular basis or who lived overseas.

5.10.2 Academic Study

Bree's main study technique consisted of making notes from lectures and textbooks and writing or typing them over and over. She left copies of her notes all over the house and would even write key points to memorise on windows using a special marker. In class and online Bree was keen to get involved in class discussions, but only when she was confident that she knew what she was talking about. Bree expressed a strong dislike of group work and also preferred to study alone. In preparation for exams, Bree listened to audio recordings of notes from her course that had been made by her friends.

Bree regularly used technology in her studies. She accessed the University's learning management system to download lecture notes, complete online quizzes, access assessment information and read the discussion forums. In some of her subjects the discussion forums were used extensively by students, but not always for study related matters, instead as a social network for sharing links and discussing favourite movies and TV shows. Bree used instant messaging and email to communicate with group members for assignments. Bree said she would like to see the introduction of audio recordings of lectures for review and the incorporation of more multimedia such as YouTube videos. Bree was enthusiastic about new technologies, but recognised that the time that it sometimes took to learn all the elements of a new technology made it difficult for them to be incorporated in subjects only taught over 13 weeks. She had been required to use a blog as part of one of her subjects which she had found frustrating and redundant. However, she commented that, if used well, a blog could be an interesting learning tool.

5.10.3 Adoption and Adaption of Technology

Bree extensively researched technologies before adopting anything new. She considered cost, purpose, features, capacity and performance when making decisions to purchase new technology. She found picking up new technologies easy and would try a few functions before reading the instruction booklet to learn the full range of features. Bree also subscribed to email newsletters and regularly browsed the Internet to learn about new technologies and keep up with the latest IT trends. She expressed a desire to purchase an iPhone which had just been released to the Australian market at the time of this study.

5.11 Bridget

Bridget was a 19-year-old Bachelor of Law and Bachelor of Arts (Communications) student. She lived in a share house approximately 25 min from the University campus. Bridget had always planned to come to university as all the careers she had considered required a university education. Whilst she had originally thought that she would use her law degree to practice law, she changed her mind in her first year to aim towards a career in journalism. Despite this, she still saw her law degree as important to this new career direction as it provided knowledge in another field to add credibility to her writing.

5.11.1 Everyday Life

Bridget considered herself to be an intermediate user of technology. She said she used her mobile phone the most, especially as she did not have access to a home phone in her shared accommodation. In addition to communication, Bridget also set reminders for events in her phone and saved important information she needed to regularly reference in text messages. She also made use of her laptop, which was handed down to her by her father, for accessing the Internet.

Bridget shared photos with friends and family via email and on Facebook. She kept a 'blog' on MySpace when she was at high school but no longer updated it. She occasionally read her friends' MySpace 'blogs', in particular two of her friends who had been using MySpace to blog about their upcoming weddings. Outside MySpace Bridget didn't regularly follow any blogs or RSS feeds.

Bridget primarily used her phone to keep in contact with friends and family by text messages. In the first interview Bridget estimated that she sent around 25 text messages a day. During the ESM period she sent 201 text messages, an average of 9.6 text messages a day, and no more than 20 messages in any one day. Bridget was not as enthusiastic about email and said that she tended only to reply when the reply could be short. For anything that required a long response she preferred to ring or visit. At high school Bridget used instant messaging a great deal, but by the time she reached university she only used it to communicate with her grandmother. Her communication preference was firmly face-to-face communication.

This preference was also observed in her use of social networking tools. She had recently moved from MySpace to Facebook. She claimed that the majority of her communication on Facebook was with people she saw on a regular basis, and primarily for the purpose of arranging face-to-face activities. She commented:

> Well the people I talk to are the people I'm catching up with if I go out. So I might as well just go and see them. It's so much more fun than just like typing away. It's not a means of catching up, it's just a means of organising your timetable.

Bridget accessed Facebook on 8 of the 21 days in the ESM period. During this time she received many wall posts from friends, however her only activity was to upload an album of photos from a camping trip, change her profile picture (to one of the new photos), to accept 5 friend requests and write on one friend's wall.

Bridget regularly used the Internet to buy items that either she had trouble finding locally (e.g., camping equipment) and/or wanted to get at a lower cost (e.g., books). She also did all of her banking and paid her bills online. Bridget listened to music on her iPod as she walked to and from university, but didn't listen to podcasts for pleasure.

5.11.2 Academic Study

Bridget's main study technique was to read her notes and materials over and over. She highlighted and made notes of important concepts and reviewed these prior to exams. When working on assignments she liked to prepare them well in advance and hated group work for the fact that others in the group were generally happy to leave things to the last minute. When working on assignments and studying for exams Bridget spent time in the library as she found this environment to have fewer distractions. She liked to participate in class discussions when she had done her readings in advance. Online she participated in discussions as her participation was assessed. She said that had participation not been assessable she may have read the discussion board postings but would have been unlikely to respond.

Bridget made some use of technology as part of her study. She accessed the University's learning management system for lecture notes if the lecture was cancelled (she would normally just take notes in class), to check announcements, to access assessment questions and to participate in compulsory online discussion activities. She used her laptop at home to work on assignments and study, but used the university computers when on campus. She researched assignments online using the law resources available through the library website as well as other blogs and/or related articles online. When asked if she would like to see more technology used as part of her studies she replied:

> I'm quite content to just stick to pens and paper. I had a typewriter in high school because my grandfather gave it to me. Cause I loved the idea of having a typewriter. I was in year 10 before we got our [family] computer.

As part of one of her law classes Bridget was required to listen to an ABC radio podcast and she indicated that she enjoyed that sort of activity. Bridget was also involved in the shooting of a video for a University student association.

5.11.3 Adoption and Adaption of Technology

Bridget felt that a number of technologies seemed forced upon her in both her everyday life and academic study due to the convenience they afford (e.g., microwaves, computers, printers, etc.). When adopting a new technology Bridget considered factors of convenience, aesthetics, functions, compatibility, durability, price and necessity. She was not interested in doubling up on technologies, for example, she already owned a digital camera so when shopping for a new mobile she was not interested in getting one with a good camera. She used a technology until it stopped working and then sought out a replacement that was advanced enough that it would last for a reasonable time. Bridget also indicated she was influenced by what type of technologies her friends owned. She didn't necessarily research her purchases in advance, instead relying on the expertise of shop assistants. When learning to use a new technology she preferred a demonstration by another person before she would try it on her own.

5.12 Jack

Jack was a 21-year-old Bachelor of Biological Science student. Initially, he didn't get the prerequisite marks to enter university directly from high school so waited until he could enter a degree as a mature age student. Jack was very career driven towards his goal of becoming a microbiologist. He was also interested in the technical aspects of audio-visual equipment and had completed a technical college course in this area prior to starting university.

5.12.1 Everyday Life

Jack identified himself as an advanced user of technology with a preference for online gaming. He used his desktop computer, mobile phone and video games console most frequently. He used his computer for playing games and accessing the Internet. He used his mobile phone for calls and messages as well as accessing the Internet, checking news, and as a personal organiser.

Jack had a very strong interest in gaming, especially World of Warcraft (WoW) and first person shooter and strategy games on various game consoles (e.g., xBox360, Playstation 3 and Nintendo Wii). During the ESM period he played games on 18 of the 21 days. His love of games formed the basis of many of this other online activities. He made blog postings on MySpace about game censorship. He regularly listened to podcasts about xBox360 releases and WoW updates. He had RSS feeds set up to deliver game-related news and would use eBay to buy and sell games (as well as movies and clothes). He previously managed a games forum online but found he didn't have the time to keep it maintained. Instead he now spent his time on game console forum sites (e.g., xBox360 Live Forum) where he reported his gaming achievements as well as contributing to discussions and reviewing games.

For social networking, Jack used MySpace which he accessed 7 of the 21 days of the ESM period. His MySpace profile strongly represented his interests in gaming, horror films and heavy metal music. He said that he shared photos and checked MySpace for messages and comments that he received regularly, but didn't update his profile or use it to communicate.

Whenever Jack was online he had his instant messaging client open (Windows Messenger). During the ESM period he used instant messaging on 20 of the 21 days. He also sent 107 text messages and 14 emails.

5.12.2 Academic Study

At the end of each day at university, Jack went home and reviewed the day's lecture notes, looking up online anything that was unclear. Only if he was unable to find helpful information on the Internet would he then refer to the textbook. Jack was part of a study group which met weekly and he said that the act of describing concepts to others helped him to concrete them in his own mind. Whilst Jack's preference was to work alone on assignments and study, he recognised the importance of having friends in his class and in the years above with whom he could discuss concepts in his course that were challenging him. In preparation for exams Jack reviewed the lecture notes and repeatedly completed practice quizzes until he had memorised the answers, albeit this was usually done at the last minute.

Jack used a number of technologies as part of his studies. He used his mobile phone to store copies of the lecture notes and to keep track of assignment due dates or if class times changed. He logged into the University's learning management system almost daily to download lecture notes, access practice quizzes and check assignment information. Jack suggested that students should be given more guidance towards useful online sites/resources to support their studies. He spent a lot of time looking for resources online which could clarify the concepts he was being taught in the classroom. He also expressed a wish to use games, even WoW, in his studies. At his own initiative he found some small science-based games online which he used, including a chemistry program which allowed students to put together molecules and see what they looked like in a 3D space.

5.12.3 Adoption and Adaption of Technology

When adopting new technologies Jack considered the price, function and longevity (how long he could use it before it would seem out-of-date). Before purchasing a new technology Jack researched it thoroughly online using technology review websites and user forums to see what other people thought of the technology. He indicated that he was considering purchasing a laptop for its portability as he was finding his phone screen too small to read lecture notes and the keyboard on his phone was not suitable for fast note taking. Jack said he found it easy to pick up new technologies and would do so by playing around and exploring the functions. During the ESM period he had adopted GPS navigation through his phone which he found very useful when riding on his motorbike.

5.13 Exploring Young Peoples' Technology Diversity

The main premise of the digital natives claim is that young students currently entering higher education have a universally high level of digital literacy and technology use. Contrary to these claims the cases in this study demonstrated diversity in students' technology access, usage, confidence and adoption. Each student presented a unique approach towards adoption and use of technology which they had customised over time to support their interests, social communication, employment, study and free-time. Whilst some students made extensive use of technology across all the contexts of their life, others made limited use of technology for very specific purposes. This is consistent with the findings of several other large scale studies (Kennedy et al. 2006; Jones et al. 2010; Margaryan et al. 2011) which also found significant diversity in technology use.

Overall technology access levels across the cases showed unanimous adoption of technologies such as computers, mobile phones and digital cameras as well as high levels of adoption of MP3 players, USB drives and game consoles. However, diversity was found in all other categories of ownership and usage. In some cases the diversity was quite distinct from high levels of use in some cases to no use at all. Consistent with the findings of Judd and Kennedy (2010), social networking and communication tools showed generally high levels of engagement by the students, yet adoption of other "Web 2.0" tools (blogs, RSS feeds, photo sharing, etc.) was much less. Yet, what this study has allowed is to move beyond examination of diversity through frequencies of access and broad categories of technology-based activities alone to explore the students' motivations, interests and attitudes to technology in more detail.

Primarily, the cases demonstrated that uses of technology in everyday life were firmly driven by the students' personal interests and social priorities. For example, Jack used technology predominantly to play games (computer, games consoles), talk about games (online forums), research new games (RSS feeds, Internet) or buy and sell games (eBay). Trent used technology to support and promote his political and community activities and to create a strong image for himself as part of his strategy towards a career in politics. Bridget was interested in maintaining an active social life and used technology as a tool to organise social activities rather than as a forum for the social activities themselves.

Beyond specific interests, other lifestyle factors influenced students' use of technology. It is common in Australia for students to travel significant distances to get to university each day. In this study, students with travel times of 20 min or more indicated that they used technology to fill in this time. Jessica played games with friends using her portable games console on the train. Toby, Bridget and Bree listened to their MP3 players as they walked to university. Trent took advantage of his hour-long car journey to listen to news on the radio or listen to recordings of study notes when exams were approaching.

The influence of peers was strong in relation to the choice and use of some technologies. Some students reported that the consulted their peers when making decisions about adopting new technologies. For all students in the study the use of social networking sites was influenced by their peers' activities and engagement, in particular the transition several of the students had made from MySpace to Facebook. A decrease in the use of instant messaging since leaving high school was observed which participants attributed to shifts in their friends' activities.

The students' attitudes towards adopting new technology also showed diversity, contrary to the digital natives' assumption that all young people are willing to take on new technologies. Jack, Trent and Bree actively followed the latest trends in technology and updated their technologies as quickly as their student budgets would allow. Toby's futurist view led him to virtually ignore incremental upgrades and wait until he saw a technology that offered something completely new. Jessica and Michael only sought out new technologies when they had a definite need and took advice from friends and salespeople to choose a new technology without any further research. Bridget said that she felt that many technologies were forced upon her by society's focus on convenience and only replaced technology that no longer worked. Lucy didn't actively seek out new technologies at all, instead she only adopted a technology when it became a requirement of something in which she was involved (e.g., university). Cost was the common consideration which influenced all the students' adoption habits especially as only some students had part-time incomes. This also led them to focus on the durability of the technology, as students didn't want new purchases to break down or be out of date too quickly. The ECAR study in the US found that students were most likely to adopt new technologies when the benefits and cost align (Salaway and Caruso 2008).

It has been suggested that the study of students' technology use needs to be move beyond a focus on the technology towards the contexts within which the technology is used (Bennett and Maton 2010). This study examined students' use of technology across the contexts of their everyday and academic lives and found little support for the claim that students actively seek to use everyday life technologies as part of their studies. The cases demonstrated that whilst students would identify and personalise technologies to support their everyday life activities, when it came to academic study students tended not to stray outside the technology requirements established by their teachers and their university's infrastructure offerings. Use of the University's learning management system was consistently high across the cases, with some students logging in almost daily to check for new materials and discussion postings. A generally high level of satisfaction with University learning management systems has also been observed in several previous studies (Salaway and Caruso 2008; Jones et al. 2010).

Throughout the research it became clear that most students had difficulty articulating their different technology use across contexts. This was even more pronounced when students were asked to identify how they used technology for academic study (technology used driven by institutional requirements) as opposed to technology use for personal study (technologies chosen by the students to support their individual study methods).

5.14 Technology Use in Academic Study

The cases demonstrated a limited transfer of everyday life technologies into academic study technologies. When students were asked if they would like to see any of their everyday life technologies incorporated into their academic context, few were able to offer any suggestions. An example of one suggestion came from Jack who wanted the use of games as part of the teaching in his course. At the other extreme, some students were very keen for their everyday technologies to remain everyday and not become study tools (e.g., social networking tools).

The digital native concept has prompted calls for changes to the way students are taught in higher education to accommodate this generation's technology preferences and literacy. Prensky (2001) claimed that today's students are radically different in their use of technology and have a different view of learning from that of their teachers. Yet, the cases in this study provided little support for these assertions. Students' motivations for studying, study methods and assessment approaches did not indicate a perspective different to those compatible with the traditional teaching and learning practices they were experiencing in the higher education classroom. Nor did the students claim that the teaching they were receiving wasn't meeting their learning needs. This is consistent with the research of Garcia and Qin (2007) who found that digitally literate students were still comfortable with traditional learning and teaching methods.

Traditional methods of study including making notes and reviewing textbooks were common to all students' study preferences. Some students used technology to support study methods, for example making audio recordings of study notes or typing notes repeatedly instead of writing them. However this technology was a support to traditional study methods rather than a radical new form of studying.

Additionally, the majority of students indicated that they were happy with the level of technology currently available in their university courses. Suggestions that students made for more technologies in their studies focused on alternative access to existing teaching methods such as audio recording of lectures (for review purposes) or video conferencing of lectures to reduce travel burdens. None of the students in these cases suggested the use of more technology as a replacement for classroom teaching activities; rather they suggested technology as a supplement to current methods. This was consistent with McWilliams (2002, p. 295) observation that "there is no clear evidence to date that any group of students, apart from those studying in distance mode, want to *replace* on-campus teaching and learning with web-based pedagogy".

The diversity of students' technology experiences also raises important consideration for support resources in the implementation of technology-based activities. The digital natives claims assume that students' informal use of technology has equip students with the digital literacy and skills necessary to tackle any technology offered in the classroom. In reality, a wide variance in technology confidence and ability has been found in this study as well as others (Caruso and Kvavik 2005; Kirkwood and Price 2005; Kennedy et al. 2007; Margaryan et al.

2011). As Ryberg et al. (2010) suggest, pedagogic support for the development of digital literacy skills needs to be made available to students to ensure all students are adequately prepared to use technologies for academic purposes. Whilst students may have experience using technology as part of their everyday life, the use of the same technology in an academic context may require a different approach to use which needs to be adequately supported.

The amount of time available for students to learn a new technology poses another challenge to using technology in the classroom (e.g., Bree's blog activity). Allowing students to develop better understandings of what certain technologies can do, as well as the other non-technical skills related to their use (e.g., the art of reflection for composing blog entries), may allow more engaging uses of the technology to occur. A solution to this problem would be the coordination of development activities across subjects within a course that incrementally built on students' technology skills.

5.15 Suggestions for Educators

The case studies in this research demonstrated that these young people are diverse in their motivations, attitudes and practices in using technology, providing a further challenge to generational assumptions. For educators and administrators in higher education, this means that it is necessary to look past the assumptions about what young people expect of the technology used in their academic environment. The diversity of technological experience and literacy of the students in this study indicates to teachers that methods in the classroom should not be designed for a single generation with mutual characteristics, but must cater for a variety of different learners. Students are different, with different learning styles and approaches to study. Technology diversity just adds another dimension to this consideration for curriculum design.

From an educational perspective these young people were generally satisfied with how technology was incorporated into their programs. Exploration of the adoption of technology across the cases found that these students were not necessarily interested in the 'bells and whistles' of technology. Rather they are discerning and purposeful in their technology practices and therefore may be sceptical of technology that was used for education without clear purpose. Limited transfer was found between the technologies students used in their everyday life and those they used for their academic study. It is therefore important that educators build in adequate support for different uses of technology in an academic context as students' informal use of technology may not adequately prepare them for such activities.

Overall, this study demonstrates the complexity inherent in understanding the technology practices of young people. Whilst the diversity of motivations, attitudes and experiences appears to complicate the patterns of technology use observed in large survey-based studies, the wealth of detail is crucial to developing a broad appreciation of the contexts, social factors, identities and influences on how technology is adopted and adapted by young people. As Bennett and Maton (2011) suggest, it is time now to move away from labels such as 'digital natives' and move towards a wider understanding of the factors influencing young people's use of technology so we can determine when and how to implement technology in the classroom in the most effective way possible.

References

Barnes K, Marateo RC, Ferris SP (2007) Teaching and learning with the net generation. Innovate 3(4). http://www.innovateonline.info/index.php?view=article&id=382. Accessed 1 April 2007

Bennett S, Maton K (2010) Beyond the 'digital natives' debate: towards a more nuanced understanding of students' technology experiences. J Comput Assist Learn 26(5):321–331

Bennett S, Maton K (2011) Intellectual field or faith-based religion: moving on from the idea of 'digital natives'. In: Thomas M (ed) Deconstructing digital natives: young people, technology and the new literacies. Routledge, New York, pp 169–185

Benson DE, Makolichick J (2007) Conceptions of self and the use of digital technologies in a learning environment. Education 127(4):498–510

Carroll J, Howard S, Vetere F, Peck J, Murphy J (2002) Just want do the youth of today want? Technology appropriation by young people. In: Proceedings of the 35th Hawaii international conference on system sciences (HICSS-35), Maui, Hawaii, Jan 2002

Caruso JB, Kvavik RB (2005) ECAR study of students and information technology, 2005: convenience, connection, control, and learning roadmap. EDUCAUSE Center for Applied Research. http://connect.educause.edu/library/abstract/ECARStudyofStudentsa/37610. Accessed 31 Dec 2011

Corrin L, Lockyer L, Bennett SJ (2010) Technological diversity: an investigation of students' technology use in everyday life and academic study. Learn Media Technol 35(4):387–401

Czerniewicz L, Brown C (2010) Born into the digital age in the south of Africa: the reconfiguration of the 'digital citizen'. In: Proceedings of the seventh international conference on networked learning 2010. Lancaster University, Aalborg, pp 859–65

Dede C (2005) Planning for neomillennial learning styles. EDUCAUSE Q 28(1):7–12

Garcia P, Qin J (2007) Identifying the generation gap in higher education. Innovate 3(4). http://innovateonline.info/index.php?view=article&id=379. Accessed 5 April 2007

Helsper E, Eynon R (2009) Digital natives: where is the evidence? British Educ Res J 36(3): 503–520

Jones C, Healing G (2010) Net generation students: agency and choice and the new technologies. J Comput Assist Learn 26:344–356

Jones C, Ramanau R, Cross S, Healing G (2010) Net generation or digital natives: is there a distinct new generation entering university? Comput Educ 54(3):722–732

Judd T, Kennedy G (2010) A five-year study of on-campus Internet use by undergraduate biomedical students. Comput Educ 55(4):1564–1571

Kennedy G, Krause K, Gray K, Judd T, Bennett S, Maton K, Dalgarno B, Bishop A (2006) Questioning the net generation: a collaborative project in Australian higher education. In: Proceedings of the 23rd annual ascilite conference: Who's learning? Whose technology? Sydney University Press, Sydney, pp 413–417

Kennedy G, Dalgarno B, Gray K, Judd T, Waycott J, Bennett S, Maton K, Krause K, Bishop A, Chang R, Churchward A (2007) The net generation are not big users of Web 2.0 technologies: preliminary findings from a large cross-institutional study. In: Atkinson R, McBeath C, Soong A, Cheers C (eds) Providing choices for learners and learning: proceedings of the 24th annual

conference of the Australasian Society for Computers In Learning In Tertiary Education. ASCILITE, Singapore, pp 517–525
Kennedy G, Judd TS, Churchward A, Gray K (2008) First year students' experiences with technology: are they really digital natives? Australas J Educ Technol 24(1):108–22
Kirkwood A, Price L (2005) Learners and learning in the twenty-first century: what do we know about students' attitudes towards and experiences of information and communication technologies that will help us design courses? Stud High Educ 30(3):257–274
Margaryan A, Littlejohn A, Vojt G (2011) Are digital natives a myth or reality? University students' use of digital technologies. Comput Educ 56(2):429–440
McWilliam EL (2002) Against professional development. Educ Philos Theory 34(3):289–300
Oblinger D, Oblinger J (2005) Is it age or IT: first steps toward understanding the net generation. In: Educating the net generation, EDUCAUSE, pp 2.1–2.20
Prensky M (2001) Digital natives, digital immigrants. On the Horizon 9(5):1–6
Prensky M (2004) The emerging online life of the digital native: what they do differently because of technology, and how they do it. http://www.marcprensky.com/writing/default.asp. Accessed 13 May 2007
Ryberg T, Dirckinck-Holmfeld L, Jones C (2010) Catering to the needs of the "digital natives" or educating the "net generation"? In: Lee MJW, McLoughlin C (eds) Web 2.0-based e-learning: applying social informatics for tertiary teaching. IGI Global, Hershey, pp 301–318
Salaway G, Caruso JB (2008) The ECAR study of undergraduate students and information technology, 2008. Educause Center for Applied Research. Educause, Boulder. http://www.educause.edu/ECAR/TheECARStudyofUndergraduateStu/163283. Accessed 12 July 2011
Sanchez J, Salinas A, Contrereas D, Meyer E (2011) Does the new digital generation of learners exist? A Qualitative Study. British J Educ Technol 42(4):543–556
Tapscott D (1998) Growing up digital: the rise of the net generation. McGraw-Hill, New York
Turkle S (2011) Alone together: why we expect more from technology and less from each other. Basic Books, New York

Chapter 6
Adapting for a Personalized Learning Experience

Margaret Martinez

Abstract The latest advances in technology are making it easier for educators to explore more innovative learning methods and environments for adaptive or more personalized learning. Most educators recognize that conventional classroom strategies will not always fit future types of learning, especially with all influences of social networking, mobile learning and 24/7 media availability. This can be especially true when an instructor is not around to stimulate interest, commitment, motivation, persistence or measure learning progress and achievement. How do you put personalized solutions similar to those that previously worked in the classroom into new online learning strategies to achieve similar or even better results? This chapter explores how to use adaptive learning technology, strategies and models, learning orientations, learner analytics, professional development and the neurobiology of learning research to find innovative ways to adapt and improve learning and enhance educational, workplace and career success for future generations.

Adaptive learning seeks to personalize the right kind of learning at the right time to motivate more successful learning continuously

6.1 Offering a Personalized Learning Experience

The Web, mobile learning devices and new wireless technology offer the perfect ubiquitous technology and environments for individualized learning because learners can be uniquely identified, content can be specifically personalized, and learner progress can be monitored, supported, and assessed at any time.

M. Martinez (✉)
The Training Place, Inc, 743 W. Bougainvillea, Oro valley, AZ 85755-1791, USA
e-mail: mmartinez@trainingplace.com

R. Huang et al. (eds.), *Reshaping Learning*, New Frontiers of Educational Research,
DOI: 10.1007/978-3-642-32301-0_6, © Springer-Verlag Berlin Heidelberg 2013

Technologically, researchers are increasingly making progress toward realizing the personalized learning dream with newer adaptive learning and measurement technology.

> Just as technology is at the core of virtually every aspect of our lives and work, we must leverage it to provide engaging and powerful learning experiences, content, and resources and assessments that measure student achievement in more complete, authentic, and meaningful ways. Technology-based learning and assessment systems will be pivotal in improving student learning and generating data that can be use to continuously improve the education system at all levels (US Department of Education 2010). (National Education Technology Plan 2010)

6.2 Foundational Considerations

However, two important considerations are being ignored or overlooked in accomplishing the personalization dream. One missing consideration concerns a whole-person understanding about key psychological sources that influence how individuals want and intend to learn online. Conventional, a primarily cognitive solution (which focuses on how a learner may process, build, and store knowledge) offers a restricted view of how people learn and too often leads to unstable or ineffective online learning solutions leading to drop outs, underachievement and barriers to learning.

A more whole-person perspective includes emotions and intentions and social factors in the learning process. Also missing is the integration of instructional purpose, values, and strategies based on individual differences in learning into the design, development, and presentation of content. Up to now, developments have focused on technology rather than more important learner-centric issues.

Adaptive learning research was actively pursued in the fifties, however, today's advances in the neurosciences and adaptive learning technology provide many more opportunities for more analytics, better models and the collection of data for more successful adaptive learning. In the fifties, Cronbach (1957) challenged the field to find "for each individual the treatment to which he can most easily adapt". He suggested that consideration of the treatments and individual together would determine the best payoff because we "can expect some attributes of person to have strong interactions with treatment variables. These attributes have far greater practical importance than the attributes which have little or no interaction (Cronbach 1957)".

6.2.1 Creating Systemic Change

High drop out rates show that too many students today lack interest and persistence that leads to unsophisticated cognitive ability and inability to use today's technology. However, rapid advances in many technologies are changing the way people learn and how people are able to develop their brain. What are the paradigm-shifting models and strategies that can increase student interest and help them achieve in today's more demanding world. Education and corporations can equally prosper by understanding these necessary changes and using emerging technologies to deliver personalized instruction matched to the increasingly complex learning needs.

The challenge of developing innovative adaptive technology is finding and supporting an equally sophisticated, lifelong learning audience that can embrace and keep pace with every new innovation and change. Failure means that new technologies may create cognitive overload, attrition, stress, lack of product use and student underachievement.

In creating systemic change for tomorrow's generation, we must deepen our knowledge about individual differences in learning. Increasingly, learners are getting used to personalization and want education customized to their individual needs. Personalization requires that we better understand why some individuals are more prepared to use their emotions and abilities to succeed. Neuroscience research advances make it vitally important that we tap into the dominant power of emotions on learning, memory, attention, values, and persistence to help those who are less emotionally and socially prepared to learn. We can no longer afford the luxury of overlooking the impact of emotions and need for personalization, technology can help us.

6.3 Exploring New Models and Theories

In this chapter, we will introduce an adult learning model to help you understand sources of the individual learning differences that are the basis for the blueprint presented later in the chapter. This learner-centric model focuses on the dominant psychological factors that impact self-motivation, self-directedness, and learning autonomy, three key factors that deeply impact learning.

It is based on research into the neurobiology of learning and memory, and incorporates the dominant impact of emotions, intentions, and social factors, and the more conventionally research cognitive considerations. The model explores designs for technology and online learning environment, online presentation of instruction, role of the instructor, expected outcomes, and student expertise, achievement and satisfaction. It also illustrates models and strategies to help learners improve learning ability as they become more self-motivated, self-managed, independent successful learners online.

In order to use adaptive learning more successfully, it is necessary to account for the many factors that facilitate or impede learning adaptively. Secondly, it is necessary to identify and match the theories, conceptual frameworks, processes, relationships, methodologies, treatments, and environments that best influence more successful learning for different types of learners. Finding the right research and evidence is essential to the creation of instructionally sound adaptive learning solutions.

What theories, strategies, and methodologies support sophisticated online learning needs? Snow (1987) suggested that sound learning theories require a whole-person view that integrates cognitive, conative, and affective aspects, "otherwise, explanations about learning differences will be ambiguous and isolated from reality". According to Snow (1989), the best instruction involves individualized treatments that differ in structure and completeness and high or low general ability measures. Highly structured treatments (e.g., high external control, explicit sequences and components) seem to help students with low ability but hinder those with high abilities (relative to low structure treatments).

Bereiter and Scardamalia (1989) also suggested that learners in supportive environments have high levels of self-efficacy and self-motivation and use learning as a primary transformative force. Despite an increased interest in emotions, intentions, and personalized learning in the past two decades, most of today's researchers still recognize cognitive factors as the dominant influence on learning and other key factors continue to be relegated to a secondary role. This research typically alludes to or at best discusses aspects of conation and affect without any evidence-based research. Nevertheless, personalized learning approaches remain largely dependent on unsubstantiated (no proven evidential research) cognitive formulations, such as cognitive learning styles.

6.3.1 Adaptive Learning and Professional Development

The goal of professional development is to ensure that learners have empowering, satisfying, and engaging learning experiences that help them to be active, innovative, skilled and productive members of a global educational community. Educators and students alike will need to learn how to master new technologies using effectively designed and engaging adaptive learning programs. Educators will need to support adaptive learning and assessment that help them use data, adaptive content, diverse resources and new kinds of achievement and experiences to inspire more successful learning. Educators will need to learn how to implement and evaluate adaptive learning programs to ensure that learners progress and emerge ready for innovative work in the global working community.

It will be difficult for educators to relinquish conventional models that do not adapt and inhibit learning in the Information Age. Adaptive learning will highlight the need for educators to adopt need definitions for assessment, productivity, and achievement in education. Educators will need to learn how to understand new measures, competencies, policies, practices and decision-making tools for improved learning outcomes.

6.3.2 Adaptive Learning and Infrastructure

The goal of infrastructure is to ensure that students have the environment and opportunity to improve creativity and achievement, find satisfaction and attain standards, instructional objectives and self-directed goals and expectations. Adaptive learning requires that all students have sufficient access to effective infrastructure, including fast access to the Internet, relevant wireless activity possible within and outside schools, access to adequate resources for searching, multimedia development, communication and support for community or team development. Because technology develops so rapidly, adaptive learning requires maintenance, support and the ability to innovate and evolve continuously.

6.3.3 Adaptive Learning and Assessment

Building effective adaptive e-learning environments require new methods of assessment. Adaptive assessment is an alternative to traditional approaches and a way to improve assessment methodologies. It is an additional way to personalize the adaptive learning process for each student.

Adaptive assessments use a personalized path to assess a student's progress and achievement and adapt providing questions to the student's tested ability level. Typical adaptive assessments use algorithms, more often based on item response theory, to search a pool of available questions. The questions in a pool differ in difficulty and content level. For example, initially adaptive assessments may select questions from a pool and estimate student progress. Eventually, questions may be selected based on what is known about what the student accomplished on a previous question or set of questions. If a student performed poorly on a question, the student might then be presented with an easier question. If a student performed well on a question, the student might then be presented with a more difficult question. This process is repeated until the goals and criteria of the assessment have been met. As a result, students receive different tests to meet the same goals and criteria.

The goal is to capture data that describes what learners do to progress as they are assessed. The student interactivity supported by adaptive learning and collected by adaptive assessment can provide detailed information about the students and offer new learning opportunities and improvements.

Adaptive assessments have several benefits. Well-designed and tested adaptive assessments are typically able to (1) improve test security, (2) improve measurement to be more precise about student competencies, especially if students have very wide range of abilities, (3) provide validity and reliability evidence, (4) collect data (e.g., item statistics) to manage, deliver the test and the pool of questions and interpret the results more effectively, (5) reduce guessing on too difficult questions (skewness), (6) reduce the number of questions that are too easy for those students that can handle more difficult questions, (7) provide scores immediately, (8) provide a wider source of item types, (9) individualize pace of testing and (10) address test anxiety issues, and (10) provide a comprehensive blueprint for instructional design (Way 2006).

Adaptive assessments are not fit for all subjects and skill. They also have several other limitations. Technology, e.g., influenced by software, bandwidth and hardware, can especially limit adaptive assessments. Special key issues are providing enough computers for students, test security, administration, supporting item types, cheating, perceptions and anxiety. The expense to develop, deliver and maintain a high-stake adaptive assessment program may also be a key limitation.

6.3.3.1 Computerized Adaptive Testing

Computerized adaptive testing (CAT) is a common form of adaptive assessment. It uses CAT technology to deliver assessment more precisely and efficiently, especially for students with a wide range of abilities (Wainer 2000).

> Computerized adaptive testing (CAT) is the redesign of psychological and educational measuring instruments for delivery by interactive computers. CAT can be used for tests of ability or achievement and for measures of personality and attitudinal variables. Its objective is to select, for each examinee, the set of test questions from a pre-calibrated item bank that simultaneously most effectively and efficiently measures that person on the trait (International Association for Computerized Adaptive Testing 2011).

An example of computerized adaptive testing is the GRE revised General Test. A list of operational CAT Testing programs is available at: http://www.psych.umn.edu/psylabs/catcentral/. More information about CAT is available from Wainer (Snow 1989), Way (Bereiter and Scardamalia 1989) and (Bunderson et al. 1989).

6.3.4 Adaptive Learning and Analytics

Davenport and Harris "argue that the frontier for using data has shifted dramatically. Leading companies are doing more than just collecting and storing information in large quantities. They're now building their competitive strategies around data-driven insights that are, in turn, generating impressive business results. Their secret weapon? Analytics: sophisticated quantitative and statistical analysis and predictive modeling supported by data-savvy senior leaders and powerful information technology (Davenport and Harris 2007)."

Amazon.com has long used customer analytics, algorithms and predictive modeling to succeed and offer the best customer experience. They have always been very relentless about analyzing its customers' activities and preferences and making modifications based on what data they collect.

Currently, data analytics is increasingly important in almost every industry, not just widely-used in education. While "data-driven education" is on the horizon, most educators are just recognizing how data, analytics and predictive modeling can positively impact education and student success. Certainly, it can have a disruptive impact on how schools are organized and administered. These "data-driven" advances in the past decade provide persuasive pressure for positive and measurable change in education. It should be useful to use appropriate assessments and learner analytics to assess a student's expertise and progress to compare to competencies and standards. Student learning data can be collected and used to predict and improve learning outcomes and productivity continuously (IBM 2011).

In addition, reporting tools provide information about historical results, trends, and progress.

> Predictive modeling—known commonly as predictive analysis—complements this historic view by using algorithms to find patterns and hidden associations within the data that may not be immediately apparent from a traditional report or without more in depth analysis. These "golden nuggets" provide much deeper insight into the historical trends by revealing the factors that drove a particular historic outcome—and then predicting what is likely to happen next (Black and Wiliam 1998).
>
> When combined with learning systems, technology -based assessments can be used formatively to diagnose and modify the conditions learning and instructional practices while at the same time determine what studies have learned for grading and accountability purposes. Both uses are important, but the former can improve student learning in the moment (Black and William 1998). Furthermore, systems can be designed to capture students' inputs and collect evidence of their knowledge and problem solving abilities as they work. Over time, the system "learns" more about students' abilities and can provide increasingly appropriate support (Black and Lynch 2003; Siemens 2012).

6.3.4.1 Adaptive Learning and Learners

Fortunately, learner analytics and student intelligence are rapidly evolving to improve adaptive learning systems, thus helping to maximize student success more efficiently. At the Learning Analytics Conference, 2011, Malcolm Brown, from EDUCAUSE, noted that learning analytics "are moving faster than any of us realize" (Siemens 2012). Increased business interest and investment in the educational technology sector are greatly impacting the rapid growth of learning analytics.

> Next-Generation Analytics. Analytics is growing along three key dimensions:
>
> 1. From traditional offline analytics to in-line embedded analytics. This has been the focus for many efforts in the past and will continue to be an important focus for analytics.
> 2. From analyzing historical data to explain what happened to analyzing historical and real-time data from multiple systems to simulate and predict the future.
> 3. Over the next three years, analytics will mature along a third dimension, from structured and simple data analyzed by individuals to analysis of complex information of many types (text, video, etc.…) from many systems supporting a collaborative decision process that brings multiple people together to analyze, brainstorm and make decisions.

> Analytics is also beginning to shift to the cloud and exploit cloud resources for high performance and grid computing.
>
> In 2011 and 2012, analytics will increasingly focus on decisions and collaboration. The new step is to provide simulation, prediction, optimization and other analytics, not simply information, to empower even more decision flexibility at the time and place of every business process action (Gartner Inc 2012).

Examples to explore learner analytics are available at Purdue's Signals, UBMC's "check my activity", and WCET's PAR. These examples provide analytics tools and concepts to provide real-time feedback and interventions to improve student achievement and satisfaction.

6.3.5 Adaptive Learning Supported by Social Media

Social media has had a profound effect on all things today, especially learning. We are in the infancy of understanding how to combine adaptive learning models and social medial interaction. How can we better understand how one can use social media to provide an individualized learning experience to support meaningful formal, informal or incidental learning relationships? How will social media best support adaptive learning situations with discussion, immersion, mentoring, shared, discovery, or other interactive experiences? Especially important is collecting and understanding the results and feedback that will improve any learning experience. Without a doubt, this aspect of adaptive learning will be important in motivating smarter and more self-directed, passionate and independent learners.

Research and common sense suggest that the most successful students are those who are more positive, mindful, and socially and educationally stimulated. Appropriate social media resources can nurture factors that are important to learning success, including commitment, resilience, discipline, reflection, mindfulness, creativity, and holistic and critical thinking. Appropriate social media resources can also influence factors that limit learning success, such as stress, anxiety, cynicism and lack of commitment.

While using social media resources may have many benefits there are also key limitations and important considerations. Attention is a key component of learning. While lack of focus and distraction is a common problem for learning, the surplus of computers, cell phones, other mobile devices, and constant stimuli, e.g., from social networking, create a complex challenge for learning.

> In "Growing Up Digital, Wired for Distraction", Matt Richtel examined this issue in detail. "(Kids') brains are rewarded not for staying on task but for jumping to the next thing", said Michael Rich, an associate professor at Harvard Medical School and the executive director of the Center on Media and Child Health. "The worry is we're raising a generation of kids in front of screens whose brains are going to be wired differently." While not reaching any single conclusion or method to address the problem, the article

cited research that showed that developing brains need some downtime to absorb the knowledge and information they are exposed to. Perhaps one more reason to tell your kids to step away from the screens for a while every night (Richtel 2012).

Researchers need to study the risk concerning developing brains that may be more easily accustomed to jumping to new tasks constantly or even getting addicted to the ubiquitous use of technology. Will these important concerns make it difficult for young learners less able to focus, sustain attention, meditate and reflect, i.e., key attributes of learning success?

In considering how technology is affecting young brains, a "2010 study by the Kaiser Family foundation (see: http://www.kff.org/entmedia/upload/8010.pdf) found that students 8 to 18 spend more than 7.5 h a day engaged with computers, cell phones, TV, music, or video games. Forty percent of kids in middle school and high school say that when they're on the computer, most of the time they're also plugged into other media. The effects this multitasking has on still-forming brains can be positive and negative. 'The prefrontal cortex, which is essential for social behavior, planning, reasoning, and impulse control, is not fully developed until the early 1920s,' says Jordan Graman of the Kessler Foundation Research Center (see: http://kesslerfoundation.org or http://www.kff.org/entmedia/upload/8010.pdf). 'Its development is largely dependent on what activities you do.' Studies have shown that multitasking can lead to faster response time, improved peripheral vision, and greater ability to sift through information quickly. But it also results in a diminished ability to focus on one thing for long. 'You get better at the physical and visual motor parameters of what you're doing, but not the deeper, thoughtful aspects,' Grafman says. How will the generation coming of age now—less accustomed to sustained concentration—be affected? No one's sure. Dr Gwenn O'Keeffe, (lead author of the American Academy of Pediatrics 2011) recently spoke to a group of college students. 'They said they feel real bombarded, they're not user they're learning effectively, and they're not sure how to turn it all off. We need to learn in from they're saying and help our current teenagers as well as younger kids learn to disconnect' For parents, that might entail modeling a bit of self-discipline, like refraining from making calls while you drive… (Listfield 2011)'"

6.4 Neurobiology of Learning

"One of the most important developments in neuroscience over the past few decades is the creation of methods for examining what parts of the brain are most active when we are doing different things (Zull 2002a)." By understanding the neurosciences and how humans learn, educators can help students improve their learning and development.

Knowing what enhances learning, or conversely, what hinders learning offers unique advantages that can help educators improve their design, delivery, development and presentation of instruction. In the future, this kind of brain research should also continue to provide evidence that supports using adaptive learning to predict an individual's existing knowledge, preferences and investment towards positive change, growth, and self-improvement.

6.4.1 Neuroplasticity

Brain research is a rapidly moving target with the introduction of the latest in medical measurement and brain imaging technology. Tracking today's neuroscientific research and using evidence to update and improve understanding, interpretation, use, and guidance is a helpful "bridge for understanding" and interpreting results towards self-improvement and efforts towards more successful brain activity and development. Nowadays, we can use the technology to see that the brain consists of billions of neurons (cells). "Neurons are sensitive and observant. They pick up signals and send them to other neurons. These signals can come from the outside world in the form of light or sound, for example, or from other neurons (Zull 2002b)". When people pay attention and engage in learning their neural networks get stronger. Conversely, neuronal networks can weaken with lack of use, disease or unhealthy living styles.

The research in brain plasticity shows that the brain's learning process impacts how the connections change between neurons and the influence the formation of neural networks. It is an individual's habits, abilities and unique response to change that differentiates one student from another. Some students may be enthusiastic about learning and others may become frustrated and resist change.

"The single most important factor in learning is the existing networks in the learner's brain (Zull 2002b)." Zull suggests that if educators ascertain what memory, knowledge and ability already exists and teaches to engage the pre-existing capability (stored in neuronal networks), then learning is more successful. The author of this chapter proposes a similar biology-based approach to pedagogy throughout the rest of this chapter.

6.4.2 Nuture Versus Nature

Researchers believe that we are a product of both "nature vs. nurture", a catch-phrase indicating the roles played by heredity and environment our neuronal networks and human development. However, we still do not know how much is determined by our DNA and how much by life experiences.

As our understanding about human genetics evolves, we can learn to identify human traits that are partially or mostly genetic and those that can be hypothetically improved. According to a long-standing theory, learning takes place and memories form when the same message travels repeatedly with feedback between specific cells in the brain.

Communication between cells grows stronger with repetition and multiple processing. The more we practice a skill, the more the automatic the skill or habit becomes. Eventually the cells no longer need to be stimulated by an outside source such as a teacher or input from the senses. A student's investment or commitment and lack of cynicism to learning the skill may prove to be an important mortar that attracts the attention and drives the effort towards more successful learning and self-improvement.

6.4.3 Brain Lateralization

The neuropsychological research of the 1970s focused on the left/right dichotomies, referring to the fact that the brain has two halves, and although similar looking, they do *not* exactly function alike. Looking at cross sections of the brain, you can see two right and left cerebral hemispheres connected by a thick layer of cells called the corpus callosum. The corpus callosum aids in the constant communication between the two bilateral hemispheres.

Today we know more about lateralization. Despite the apparent symmetrical similarities, research shows that from birth asymmetries, both functional and anatomical, do exist. The two brain hemispheres do have specialized functions for a majority of humans. For example, people with left-hemisphere language specializations may also have some or parts of language function (e.g., like *prosody*–the emotional content of speech) specialized in the right hemisphere. Or, as an another example, music appreciation may largely be located in the right hemisphere but the actual of learning music is more often active in the left hemisphere.

However, for a small percentage of humans, their brains may function differently, e.g., right-hemisphere language specialization. Additionally, if parts of the brain are damaged, certain functions that have been lost may sometimes be learned in a different part or hemisphere of the brain.

Today, researchers can show brain activity that is more iterative than specialized as it fires in very different parts of the brain–involving coordinated activity in both hemispheres. What is important is that research continues to show that left-brain functions typically include linear algorithmic processing, pattern perception, concrete-oriented detail, and grammar and word production. And, right-brain functions typically include spatial perception, holistic and algorithmic processing, and abstract-oriented mathematics. The research on lateralization of brain functioning is ongoing and in the future will be useful to show how adaptive learning can support brain lateralization and specialization more successfully.

6.4.4 The Emotional Brain

Emotions play a crucial role in memory and learning. "By the 1960s, research about the neural basis of emotions had all but come to a halt, or at least a slow crawl (Ledoux 2002a)". Like psychologists and educators, brain researchers were enamored with the emerging cognitive sciences fostered by the simultaneous emerging computer development (i.e., input, process, and output). Additionally, the technology did not yet exist to identify, measure, and understand the brain's emotional activity more reliably. Measures for states like motivation, persistence, commitment, and others were fuzzy.

> The wiring circuits for emotion in the brain turn out to be sitting directly next to—and are deeply connected to—the circuits that control heart rate, blood pressure and how much

> adrenaline one secretes. 'You can see the two circuits talking to each other on imaging machines,' says Dr. Harry Lodge, an internist in New York City and co-author of Younger Next Year. 'A bad emotional state makes needles jump (Ledoux 2002b).'"

In the 1970s, finding the neural basis of emotions was still not thought relevant and often ignored in cognitive research. Emotions were still "not part of the cognitive game plan (Sheehy 2006)." Emotions and feelings were subjugated or overlooked during the hegemony of the cognitive brain research. The limbic system was typically mentioned for its role in emotional processing, short-term memory, and short-term memory transition into long-term memory. It was not until the 1990s, that researchers began using more sophisticated medical measurement technology to discover and measure emotions. Emotions were found to be very relevant to learning and indeed have a more powerful impact on brain activity than previously understood.

6.4.4.1 The Emotional Center: Amygdala

Today, the limbic system theory fails when it attempts to "account for all emotions simultaneously, and in so doing, did not adequately account for any one emotion (Ledoux 2002a)." For example, current research suggests that emotional processing is an essential part of decision-making and planning (i.e., cognitive processing). After more than fifty years of debate, a generally accepted criteria or comprehensive theory about the limbic system still does not exist. "Perhaps the notion of the limbic system simply needs to be modernized by treating it as an emotional-processing network rather than the seat of conscious feelings"—where the brain makes emotions and feelings (Ledoux 2002b).

New research highlighting the amygdala, part of the limbic system, is providing explanations about how our emotions interact with conscious and unconscious thinking. Pathways that take information into the amygdala without first going via the neocortex (e.g., in an emergency or survival situation), show that we can unconsciously experience emotions. In contrast, other pathways go via the neocortex and show how we can consciously experience emotions.

Today's research suggests that the amygdala typically has a powerful impact on cognitive processes. The amygdalae, a part of the limbic system, sit on both sides of the brain and play a key role in emotional processing. From his primate research studies, David Amaral has shown that the amygdala typically projects back to the neo-cortex more strongly indicating the powerful ability of the amygdala to control the cortex (Ledoux 2002c).

> You might also notice that more connections run from the amygdala to the cortex than those that run the other way. LeDoux suggests that this explains why emotions tend to overpower cognition, rather than the reverse (Zull 2002c). (Synaptic Self)

In contrast, Richard Davidson, a neuroscientist at the University of Wisconsin, did a study (Davidson and Lutz 2008) using fMRI imaging to see the brain activity experienced by a group of monks' and novices' compassion meditation. As expected, their brains showed activity in the brain's emotional regions. More interesting was the fact that the more experienced monks showed stronger connections from the frontal regions to the emotion regions. This research shows that through mental or enlightenment training, the monks had developed pathways by which higher thought or cognitive processing could control their emotions. In other words, instead of being controlled by emotion, meditation helped the monks to use cognitive processing to manage emotion more effectively.

Future research should provide clearer evidence about how emotional and cognitive processing and the associated limbic structures play a custodial role in the management of the learning process and provide ample evidence supporting how adaptive learning can stimulate emotions more positively and effectively.

6.4.4.2 Latent Inhibition and Creativity

> Psychologists from the University of Toronto and Harvard University have identified one of the biological bases of creativity. The study in the September issue of the Journal of Personality and Social Psychology says the brains of creative people appear to be more open to incoming stimuli from the surrounding environment. Other people's brains might shut out this same information through a process called 'latent inhibition' - defined as an animal's unconscious capacity to ignore stimuli that experience has shown are irrelevant to its needs. Through psychological testing, the researchers showed that creative individuals are much more likely to have low levels of latent inhibition. 'This means that creative individuals remain in contact with the extra information constantly streaming in from the environment,

says co-author and U of T psychology professor Jordan Peterson. 'The normal person classifies an object, and then forgets about it, even though that object is much more complex and interesting than he or she thinks. The creative person, by contrast, is always open to new possibilities (University Of Toronto 2003).'

Peterson and his co-researchers—lead author and psychology lecturer Shelley Carson of Harvard University's Faculty of Arts and Sciences and Harvard PhD candidate Daniel Higgins hypothesized that latent inhibition might also contribute to original thinking, especially when combined with high IQ. They administered tests of latent inhibition to Harvard undergraduates. Those classified as eminent creative achievers—participants under age 21 who reported unusually high scores in a single area of creative achievement—were seven times more likely to have low latent inhibition scores. The authors hypothesize that latent inhibition may be positive when combined with high intelligence and good working memory—the capacity to think about many things at once—but negative otherwise. Peterson states: "If you are open to new information, new ideas, you better be able to intelligently and carefully edit and choose. If you have 50 ideas, only two or three are likely to be good. You have to be able to discriminate or you'll get swamped (University Of Toronto 2003)."

Future research should provide clearer evidence about how latent inhibition can play a custodial role in the management of the learning process and show how adaptive learning can stimulate learning more positively. Other important areas of brain research to follow are: Neuromodulation, Synapse Communication, Mirror Neurons, Cingulate Cortex or Gyrus, "Master Regulator", Chemoreception, Insular Cortex, Genomics, HDAC enzymes and other Genetics Research. It will be especially interesting to discover how this research can support adaptive learning more successfully.

As one example,

> Neuromodulators can have a strong effect on how organisms learn and compete for resources. Neuromodulators, such as dopamine (DA) and serotonin (5-HT), are known to be important in predicting rewards, costs, and punishments. To better understand the effect of neuromodulation on decision-making, a computational model of the dopaminergic and serotonergic systems was constructed and tested in games of conflict (Kirchner 2010).

> "In 2003 my colleague Jordan Peterson and I reported on research we conducted at Harvard and the University of Toronto, where we found that highly creative individuals are more likely to display cognitive disinhibition when compared with those who are less creative. In a series of studies, we tested several hundred subjects on a latent inhibition task (a measure of how easily subjects ignore stimuli to which they have already been exposed). We also measured creativity in several different ways, including divergent thinking tasks (which require a large number of responses or solutions to a problem), openness to experience (the personality trait most highly predictive of creativity), the Creative Personality Scale, and the Creative Achievement Questionnaire (a measure of lifetime creative achievement). When we looked at high scorers on each of these creative measures, we found that they were more likely to have lower scores on the latent inhibition task (indicating cognitive disinhibition) than were the less creative subjects. We think that the reduction in cognitive inhibition allows more material into conscious awareness that can then be reprocessed and recombined in novel and original ways, resulting in creative ideas (Carson 2011)." (The Unleashed Mind: Why Creative People Are Eccentric)

6.5 The Whole-Person Perspective

The overall failure of education in many situations (e.g., high drop-out rates, low achievement, and low completion rates) often highlights the limitations of the typical primarily cognitive approach. For example, online or virtual courses that lack adequate support for how people learn differently (from a whole-person perspective) too often end up being more informational than efficient or instructional. Often the learned information is quickly forgotten. It is especially important to remember that in traditional settings instructors have been in the classroom managing emotions, intentions, social, and cognitive issues on an individual or group basis (some more effectively than others).

Until the advent of online learning and rapidly changing more complex society requirements, it was seemingly enough to deliver primarily cognitive instructional solutions and rely on the instructor to deliver the personal approach. The reality is that many online learners (after years of instructor-managed learning) are simply not adequately prepared for self-managed online learning. Or, for the younger generation, it may be important for educators to be there to help students focus, keep on task to attain instructional goals and not be distracted. Too often students lack the self-motivation, intentions, independence, learning efficacy, or learning and time management skills to stay online learning continuously and successfully.

6.5.1 Passive Learning

Many criticize American education for fostering passive learning, the industrial learning paradigm. Berryman defines passive learning thus: Passive learning means that learners do not interact with problems and content and thus do not receive the experiential feedback so key to learning. Students need chances to engage in choice, judgment, control processes, and problem formulation; they need chances to make mistakes (Berryman 1993).

Berryman and others attribute passive learning practices to the system of industrial learning strategies in which each person's task is laid out carefully by the instructor. This is similar to how an industrial worker is told not only what to do but how to do it. Berryman claims that this industrial style of education places external "control over learning in the teacher's, not the learner's hands (Berryman 1993)."

These industrialized teaching and learning models are obsolete for today's more sophisticated need for educated, innovative, mobile learning knowledge workers. Adaptive learning can help improve passive, one-size-fits-all solutions. More active learning and personalized education models can help students tap into external emotional resources, master internal emotions, support the learning process, and achieve true potential, which is key for innovation. Innovation underpins the growth of nations and depends on education that fosters the achievement of a talented, continuously achieving and passionate workforce.

6.5.2 Innovative Learning

The National Science Board (National Science Board 2004) reports a troubling decline in the number of U.S. citizens who are studying in fields that require higher-order thinking skills and innovation. Today's challenge as a nation is to find solutions that encourage more active-thinking knowledge Information Age workers who want to make learning a rewarding part of everyday life. Unfortunately, if we are still using yesterday's industrial-age education models, we will continue to create a passive workforce that lacks higher order thinking and decision making abilities and lacks training for today's constantly changing, information-seeking world.

As we build and present solutions for successful more personalized adaptive learning, some educators are finding that conventional, primarily cognitive perspectives are flawed and restricted by a heavy emphasis on how individuals think (cognitive processes) without thorough consideration of other profound influences on learning (Martinez 2000). These perspectives particularly lack adequate consideration of how people want, intend or expect to learn online. Specifically, these explanations overlook the dominant impact of emotions, intentions, and social factors on learning. It is not enough to assume that if learning technology products are instructionally sound (from a cognitive perspective) and technologically sophisticated, that they will be widely adopted and uniformly appreciated, managed, and utilized. The typical lack of attention to emotions, intentions, and social factors and over reliance on technology often result in instructional products and other learning resources that are not actually useful or support successful or continuous learning.

6.6 Personalization

Missing from conventional approaches is the consideration of two important issues to support learning. The first is the close integration of learner-centric, more personalized learning that can help improve instructional value and student progress, expertise and achievement. Second, is a comprehensive understanding about individual learning differences and will be discussed in the next section.

The Web offers an excellent environment for personalized learning, especially using the latest adaptive learning technology (Martinez 2004). Personalized learning needs to use strategies that can address individual needs, states and effective steps towards individual success. It must also use technology to change the instruction presented to each learner based on their individual needs. As previously mentioned, computerized adaptive testing is just one approach. Personalization may take many forms as it adapts content, practice, feedback, or navigation to match individual progress and performance. For example, two individuals using the same instruction simultaneously may see, perceive and expect two completely different sets of instruction. These influences would affect how they approach the instructional goals.

The greatest benefit of personalized learning is the ability of instructional technology to make complex instruction easier by presenting only the specific information that a particular learner wants, expects or needs in the appropriate manner and at the appropriate time. Another wonderful benefit of personalization is that each time you personalize, you can learn and store a little more about a learner's unique set of needs and set them up for more successful and satisfying learning. Most educators know that engagement, enjoyment and satisfaction are key ingredients to learning success and continuous achievement.

6.6.1 Personalization Types

There are many ways to personalize learning. Nevertheless, like the terms learning styles and motivation, personalization is another ill-defined term. In order to be more specific in this chapter, personalization is described here with five levels with increasing sophistication, each level describing a specific personalization strategy. From the simplest to most complex, the five strategies are: (a) name-recognized; (b) self-described; (c) segmented; (d) cognitive-based; and (e) whole-person-based. Each type has a specific purpose, influence, and resulting impact. These strategies can work separately but to be most effective they should work together to create a comprehensive or hybrid learning experience.

It is necessary to note that many of these strategies have been used by advertising and marketing companies for many years under the guise of mass customization. Enabled by technology, companies can personalize products or services to meet customers' needs.

The concept of mass customization is attributed to Stan Davis in *Future Perfect* (Davis 1996) and was defined by Tseng and Jiao (2001, p. 685) as 'producing goods and services to meet individual customer's needs with near mass production efficiency'. Kaplan and Haenlein (2006) concurred, calling it 'a strategy that creates value by some form of company-customer interaction at the fabrication and assembly stage of the operations level to create customized products with production cost and monetary price similar to those of mass-produced products'. (*Mass Customization* –Wikipedia)

6.6.1.1 Name-Recognized Personalization

Name-recognized personalization is simple and easy to implement. This strategy is useful and powerful because most people value being acknowledged as an individual. For example, the learner's name can appear in the instruction or with each activity. The name can be stored and used whenever it is appropriate. Using a name acknowledges the learner as an individual.

6.6.1.2 Self-Described Personalization

Self-described personalization enables learners, (using questionnaires, surveys, registration forms, and comments) to describe preferences and common attributes. For example, learners may take a pre-course quiz to identify existing skills, preferences, or past experiences. Afterwards, options and instructional experiences, resources and activities may appear based on the learners' self-described answers.

6.6.1.3 Segmented Personalization

Segmented personalization uses demographics, common attributes, or surveys to group or segment learning populations into smaller, identifiable and manageable groups. For example, learners that share a common job title, class, or work in a certain department would receive content based on prescriptive rules that would support the learning and performance requirements for the segmented group.

6.6.1.4 Cognitive-Based Personalization

Cognitive-based personalization uses information about cognitive processes, strategies, and ability to deliver content specifically targeted to specific types (defined cognitively) of learners. For example, learners may choose to use an audio option because they indicated that they prefer hearing text rather than reading it. Or, a learner may indicate preference for presentation of content or activities in a linear fashion, rather than an unsequenced presentation with hyperlinks. This type of personalization may operate using more complex algorithms than the previous types and is able to factor more learner attributes into each interaction. This strategy works by collecting data, monitoring learning activity, comparing activity with other learner behavior, and predicting what the user would like to do or see next.

6.6.1.5 Whole-Person Personalization

Whole-person personalization uses learning orientation theory (Martinez 2004). This personalization strategy supports the complex set of deep-seated psychological sources (in addition to the conventional cognitive-based prescriptions) impacting differences in learning and performance. This type of personalization strategy makes predictions about delivering content from a whole-person perspective, i.e., based on identified individual differences in learning. This strategy not only delivers content to help learners achieve learning objectives but, more importantly, it also attempts to improve overall learning ability and satisfaction and enhance online learning relationships.

As the individual learns, the adaptive system can also learn as it collects data, tracks progress, and compares responses and common patterns to improve responses (i.e., it becomes more precise over time). In its most sophisticated form, whole-person personalization requires real-time personalization using inferential technology and algorithms to modify responses to a learner based on a dynamic learner model that is changing throughout the learning experience, when it occurs, just as it occurs.

6.7 Whole-Brain Learning Orientation Theory

Can technology and educators better support student learning by identifying individual differences in learning and raising self-awareness? Can individuals that have a better understanding of themselves and their learning see opportunities to optimize their approach to planning, goal setting, decision making, and creativity? To consider these questions, this chapter will next examine (a) the often overlooked dominant impact of emotions and intentions on learning, (b) critical human relationships between learning environments and key psychological factors (e.g., conative, affective, social, and cognitive) that influence learning, and (c) design guidelines for supportive learning solutions and environments that adapt to how people learn best. These insights suggest multiple ways to personalize by also addressing how individuals learn, perform, and achieve differently. As previously mentioned, this theory embraces a neurobiology-based approach to pedagogy.

6.7.1 Learning Orientations

This chapter introduces Learning Orientations for personalized adaptive learning. Learning orientations use the whole-person perspective (as an alternative to primarily cognitive-based theories) and recognize the impact of emotions, intentions and social factors on learning.

Learning Orientations, uses the neurosciences to explore how individuals have different learning experiences and mature as learners. Learning orientations offer strategies and guidelines for designing, developing, and delivering more personalized learning to help students gradually become more confident, sophisticated, and adept at understanding and managing an increasingly complex interplay of personally relevant affective, conative, social, and cognitive learning factors.

Thus, the significant contrast in how individuals approach learning, their "learning orientation," lies in the unique, personal way that they understand, assess, and manage their learning to achieve or accomplish goals. For example, an understanding of the extent and depth of fundamental desires, values, and beliefs about why, when, and how to use learning and how it can accomplish personal goals or change events is fundamental to understanding how successfully an individual wants or intends to experience learning. Likewise, the degree to which educators understand learning orientations is the degree to which they can better support the adaptive learning process.

Learning Orientations (1) highlight the influence of emotions, intentions, social, and cognitive factors on learning (how the brain supports learning), (2) identify and address the higher-order psychological dimension that can differentiate learning audiences, and (3) guide analysis, design, development, and evaluation of learning objects and environments. Learning orientations describe an individual's complex intrinsic managing and use of key psychological factors (to varying degrees) as they approach and experience learning.

Learning orientations are not learning styles. The key distinction is that by definition learning styles typically consider the dominant influence of cognitive factors (and typically demote other factors to a secondary or no role), learning orientations recognize the often dominant influence of emotions, intentions and social factors. This perspective reflects recent neurological research that provides evidence for the dominant influence of the brain's emotional center (Martinez 2004) on learning and memory. "After decades of speculation and experiments, researchers have discovered brain changes that may underlie learning and memory (Cromie 2002)." As another example, highlighting the importance of intentions, Philips and Gully (1997) also provide evidence describing the important use of goal orientation (intentions) for learning. Bandura (1977) offered his social learning theory in the seventies. His work has added considerably to the research for more successful learning.

6.7.2 Learning Orientation Construct

In Fig. 6.1, learning orientations has a three factor construct that describes key learner-difference factors, including: (a) conative and affective learning focus, (b) committed strategic planning and learning effort, and (c) learning independence or autonomy (Martinez 2001).

Conative and Affective Learning Focus describes the individual's will, commitment, intent, drive, or passion for improving, transforming, setting and achieving goals, and meeting expected and unexpected challenges.

Committed Strategic Planning and Learning Effort refers to the degree that learners plan and commit deliberate, strategic planning and effort to accomplish learning and goals.

Learning Independence or Autonomy refers to the individual's desire and ability to take responsibility, make choices, and control, self-assess, self-motivate, and manage or improve their learning.

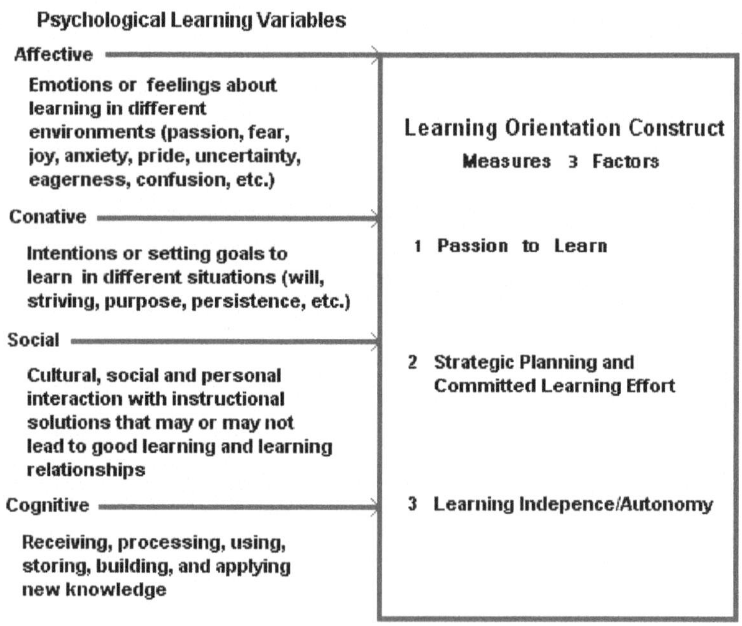

Fig. 6.1 Three construct factors in the learning orientation construct

As shown in Fig. 6.1, a number of factors (left column) play a role in determining an individual's orientation to learn. What is most notable about this model is the suggestion that emotions and intentions, not just cognitive ability or technological superiority of an innovation, play key roles in determining learning success.

The interplay between the deep-seated psychological sources of emotional reactions, learning differences, responses, and outcomes suggests that a complex conceptual structure exists with a qualitative order of influence. A clearer definition of the brain activity that can support such a complex, conceptual structure would help explain or predict how learning orientation strongly influences outcomes in differentiated learning audiences. Figure 6.1 suggests that emotions and intentions can stimulate responses that cultivate and manage subordinate differences in learning. In turn, emotional responses can influence our cognitive assessments, choices, and use of cognitive strategies and skills or vice versus.

6.7.3 Learning Orientation Model

The Learning Orientations Model (Table 6.1) describes four groups that broadly represent the existing diversity of learning orientations, enable us to explain key sources of learning differences, and describe specific strategies to mass customize learning (in terms of instruction, assessment, presentation and environments): they are, *Transforming*, *Performing*, *Conforming*, and *Resistant* learners (Martinez 2001).

Learning Orientations specifically highlight how learners expect to control their learning to accomplish personal goals. As Zull explains, "one important rule for helping people learn is to help the learner feel she is in control (Zull 2002d)."

6.7.3.1 Transforming Learners

Transforming Learners are generally highly-motivated, passionate, highly-committed learners. They place great importance on learning and use it as an important intrinsic resource to bring about and manage change (innovate) and transform. They rely on their visionary, creative, holistic thinking, sophisticated learning, problem solving and strategic planning ability and capacity to commit great effort and endure stressful challenges.

They use independence, personal strengths, persistence, constant desire for challenges and exploration, high standards, learning efficacy, risk-taking, and positive expectations to self-motivate and self-direct learning successfully. However, these learners may become demotivated, bored, frustrated, or even resistant in environments or conditions that mismatch their assertive, exploratory, self-directed learning needs.

Table 6.1 Four learning orientation profiles (Martinez 1999a)

Orientation	Conative/affective aspects	Strategic planning and committed learning effort	Learning autonomy
Transforming learners (Innovators)	Focus strong passions and intentions on learning. Are assertive, expert, self-motivated, and goal-oriented learners. Use exploratory learning to transform to high, personal standards	Set and accomplish personal short- and long-term challenging goals that may not always align with goals set by others; maximize effort to reach personal goals. Commit great effort to discover, elaborate, and build new knowledge and meaning. Know how to like to commit great effort to succeed	Assume learning responsibility and self-manage goals, learning, progress, and outcomes independently. Experience frustration if restricted or given little learning autonomy and prevented from accomplishment of personal goals
Performing learners (Implementers)	Focus emotions/intentions on learning towards personal benefits or situationally. More goal-oriented and self-motivated learners when the content appeals. Meet above-average group standards, only when the benefits or opportunity especially appeals	Set and achieve short-term, task-oriented, process/procedure-oriented goals that meet average-to-high standards; situationally minimize efforts and standards to reach assigned or negotiated standards. Selectively commit measured effort to assimilate and use relevant knowledge and meaning. Satisfaction arises from successful planning and implementation of proven designs and projects	Situationally assume learning responsibility in areas of interest but willingly give up control in areas of less interest. Prefer coaching and interaction for achieving goals. Experience frustration if asked to do tasks that do not meet self-accepted proven ideas and designs
Conforming learners (Sustainers)	Focus intentions and emotions cautiously and routinely as supported. Low-risk, modestly effective, more cynical, and extrinsically motivated learners. Use learning to conform to achieve group standards more easily	Follow and try to accomplish simple task-oriented goals that are assigned and guided by others. Try to please and conform and maximize efforts in supportive environments with safe, attainable standards. Commit careful, measured effort to accept and reproduce knowledge to meet external requirements and attainable goals	Assume little responsibility for learning. Comply and use continual guidance and expect scaffolded reinforcement for achieving short-term goals. Experiences anxiety if asked to changed from self-accepted norm

(continued)

Table 6.1 (continued)

Orientation	Conative/affective aspects	Strategic planning and committed learning effort	Learning autonomy
Resistant learners (Resistance)	Focus on not cooperating. Be cynical and perceive non-benefits. Actively or passively resist learning goals set by others. Chronically avoid learning (be apathetic, frustrated, bored, discouraged, or "disobedient")	Use personal needs to set goals in other directions. Often avoid using learning to achieve academic goals assigned or expected by others. Consider lower standards, fewer academic goals, conflicting personal goals, or no goals. Maximize or minimize efforts to resist assigned or expected goals either assertively or passively	Assume responsibility for not meeting goals set by others and set own personal goals that avoid meeting formal learning requirements or expectations

Situational Performance or Resistance: In diverse, negative situations learners may situationally improve, perform, or resist in response to positive or negative learning conditions or situations

Contrasts: These learners believe they hard work and commitment not luck that leads to success. In contrast to other learning orientations, transforming learners know that they can plan and strategically commit great effort to accomplish important, long-term, transformational goals. They seldom solely rely on deadlines, structured environments, short-term projects, normative performance standards, expected social or instructional compliance, extrinsic rewards, or others for learning efficacy or self-motivation. Instead they rely on themselves or prefer mentoring relationships to learn and use learning as a valuable resource to innovate or transform.

6.7.3.2 Performing Learners

Performing Learners are generally self-motivated in learning situations (task-oriented, project-oriented, hands-on applications) that interest them. Otherwise, they seek extrinsic rewards for accomplishing objectives that appear to have less value and perhaps require more effort then they are initially willing to commit. They may clearly acknowledge meeting only the stated objectives, getting the grade, streamlining learning efforts, and avoiding exploratory steps beyond the requirements of the situation and learning task, commiserate with their degree of interest in the stated goal.

These learners take some control and responsibility for their learning but often rely on others for motivation, goal setting, coaching, schedules, and direction. However, they may self-motivate and exert greater effort and excellence in situations that greatly interest or benefit them. They most often are detailed-oriented, lower risk, skilled learners that systematically and capably get the project done as they achieve average to above average learning objectives and tasks, according to their own personal goals. These learners lose motivation or may even get angry if too much effort is required and the rewards are not enough to compensate the perceived effort.

Contrasts: In contrast to transforming learners, performing learners are short-term, detail, task-oriented learners (less holistic or big-picture thinkers). They like to use proven processes, procedures, designs, steps and theories and do not appreciated challenges to their effectiveness. They take fewer risks with challenging or difficult goals, focus more on grades and rewards, and may cheerfully achieve less whenever standards are set below their expectations or capabilities. They are most comfortable with interpersonal, coaching relationships, and rely on or like external support, resources, and interaction to accomplish a task.

In contrast to conforming learners, these learners have more sophisticated skills, commit greater effort to achieve higher standard goals, and prefer more sophisticated learning and performance environments with entertaining interaction that creates progressive effort, interest, competition, fun, and attainable goals. These learners are not afraid to change, they just need to see the long-term benefit or opportunity.

6.7.3.3 Conforming Learners

Conforming Learners are generally more compliant and may passively accept knowledge, store it, and reproduce it to conform, complete routine or assigned tasks (if they can), and please others. They prefer learning in groups with explicit guidance and feedback. These learners do not typically think holistically, critically, or analytically, synthesize feedback, solve complex problems, monitor and review or reflect upon progress independently, or accomplish challenging goals.

These learners are typically less skilled, uncomfortable with decision-making, and may have little desire to control or manage their learning, take risks, or initiate change in their jobs or environment. Learning in open learning environments, which focus on high learner control, discovery or exploratory learning, complex problem solving, challenging goals, and inferential direction, may frustrate, demoralize, or demotivate these learners. These learners need scaffolded, structured solutions, guiding direction, simple problems, linear sequencing, and explicit feedback. They depend on scaffolded, linear learning events. These learners do not know that it is hard work and commitment (not luck) that leads to success.

Contrasts: In contrast to other learning orientations, conforming learners learn best in well-structured, directive environments using explicit, step-by-step procedures. Unlike transforming and performing learners, who have stronger, more positive beliefs about learning and greater learning efficacy, these learners believe that learning is most useful when it helps them avoid risk and meet the basic requirements in their job. They are comfortable with minimum effort on simple goals that others set for them and help them achieve.

6.7.3.4 Resistant Learners

Resistant Learners lack a fundamental belief that academic learning and achievement can help them achieve personal goals or initiate positive change. Too often they have suffered repeated, long-term frustration from inappropriate or ineffective learning situations. A series of unskilled, imperceptive instructors, unfortunate learning experiences, or missed opportunities have deterred resistant learners from enjoying and using learning to progress or improve. These learners do not believe in or use formal education or academic institutions as positive or enjoyable resources in their life. Formal or institutional learning has been too often a negative experience.

Resistant learners are resistant for many reasons. Ironically, some resistant learners may actually be eager learners on their own outside of formal learning institutions. For example, they may be frustrated transforming learners who aggressively resisted the strictures of too structured or restrictive goals and environments and chose to learn on their own, often quite successfully. These learners may have learned to dislike school but they may also have learned how to succeed using their own strategies outside of school.

Contrasts: In contrast to other learning orientations, resistant learners focus their energy on resistance within the formal system, whether it is passive or aggressive. Their need to progress or improve lies in directions other than the established norm. Some of these learners will progress and succeed on their own, while others will fall along the way.

6.7.4 Learning Orientation Dynamics

Learning orientations are generalizable to all learning situations and are not domain or environment specific. However, despite a general learning orientation, individuals may, depending on the situation, manage their approaches to learning differently (not change learning orientation) in response to a topic, delivery method, environment, condition, or teacher (Martinez 2001).

For example, a transforming learner may prefer learning more cautiously with less learner control if the topic is unfamiliar or complicated. However, once they reach their comfort level they might gradually push themselves to greater independence (a more typical approach). Although learners' reactions and processes naturally vary depending on the learning task and situation, a conforming learner is unlikely to become a performing learner (change learning orientation) very quickly or at all.

To change learning orientation is to change the deep-seated psychological sources that influence learning and memory. However, it is very possible with extraordinary effort. For example, a conforming learner that intentionally experiences (with structured support) more risk, independence, holistic thinking, and complex problem-solving may over time push themselves into a performing orientation. These considerations about how individuals approach learning differently raise important questions about presenting adaptive learning in environments that identify and match these individuals' situational approaches, needs and expectations.

Another important consideration is that learning orientations are not arranged in a value hierarchy with transforming learners valued highest at the top. In terms of human value and importance, it is commonly accepted that morals and ethics play a great role in humanity. However, each learning orientation has strengths and possible areas for individual intentional improvement. For example, a transforming learner, who wants to learn more intentionally, may focus sometimes on less passion and exploration and attend to accomplishment, e.g., short-term details and task- and project-completion. In contrast, a performing learner may want to focus on more holistic, long-term or lateral thinking and more challenging goals.

6.8 Designing Adaptive Learning

Good adaptive learning requires standard-based designs based on good personalization strategies and learner centric models. However, there are few implementations addressing the adaptive learning problem as a whole successfully. We need much more research, evidence, data collection and analytics showing what works and what does not work. Design models from previous adaptive learning efforts, e.g., intelligent tutoring or hypermedia, do not meet current critical instructional design issues, probably because standards, strategies, and guidelines for personalized or adaptive learning are still fuzzy concepts for many. Fortunately, more research is becoming available (Martinez 1999b).

> Neuromodulators can have a strong effect on how organisms learn and compete for resources. Neuromodulators, such as dopamine (DA) and serotonin (5-HT), are known to be important in predicting rewards, costs, and punishments. To better understand the effect of neuromodulation on decision-making, a computational model of the dopaminergic and serotonergic systems was constructed and tested in games of conflict. This neural model was based on the assumptions that dopaminergic activity increases as expected reward increases, and serotonergic activity increases as the expected cost of an action increases. Specifically, the neural model guided the learning of an agent that played a series of Hawk-Dove games against an opponent. The model responded appropriately to changes in environmental conditions or to changes in its opponent's strategy. The neural agent became Dove-like in its behavior when its dopaminergic system was compromised, and became Hawk-like in its behavior when its serotonergic system was compromised. Our model suggests how neuromodulatory systems can shape decision-making and adaptive learning in competitive situations (Asher et al. 2010). (Effect of neuromodulation on performance in game playing: A modeling study)

As a result, the need for an instructional framework or blueprint showing how to present adaptive learning to achieve instructional objectives is still being researched and documented. This situation is comparable to building a house without a blueprint or even developing assessments without a blueprint. Two questions have to be asked. How can adaptive learning be presented in an instructionally sound manner if the presentation is not guided by the appropriate planning, learning, and instructional information, e.g., a blueprint? More importantly, how can one conceivably design and develop adaptive learning without the larger picture and criteria of how they should be instructionally used, presented, measured or assessed?

6.8.1 Adaptive Learning Environments Models

Technology is changing the way we learn and is forcing us to rethink next generation instructional design (ID) issues for e-learning. Blended learning, e-learning, m-learning, informal learning, Web 2.0—learning is increasingly complicated and solutions may becoming too complex for less sophisticated learners. While traditional ID models were designed for the classroom, professionals need to rethink next generation ID issues for the new types of learning, especially to support the shift from:

- trainer-centered to learner-centered training
- linear to hypermedia, virtual and discovery learning

- instruction to measured outcomes and performance
- passive to active, self-directed and collaborative learning
- one-size-fits-all to personalized or adaptive learning
- traditional assessment to adaptive assessment
- simple to complex learning systems
- from trainer as sage to trainer as facilitator, coach, or mentor

Using adaptive learning models to create supportive, personalized learning environments is an additional challenge. To be effective, adaptive learning should be designed to exist in environments that address the unique sources of learning differences, influence success, measure process and collect data for analysis. More specifically, they should emulate the instructor's experienced, intuitive ability to recognize and respond to how individuals learn differently and creatively foster interest, value, enjoyable, and more successful, independent learning.

6.8.2 Adaptive Learning Environments: Strategies

If we are to meet Cronbach's (1957) challenge for better learning environments, then we need to learn how to present instruction that provides "for each individual the treatment (personalized adaptive learning environment) which he can most easily adapt" for the best payoff. Below are simple guidelines for presenting instruction to create personalized learning environments for three learning orientations.

6.8.2.1 Transforming Learners

For *Transforming Learners* design discovery-oriented, unsequenced, and mentoring environments. These environments are for learners who want to be passionate, assertive, and challenged by complex problem solving and lateral thinking and are able to self-motivate, self-manage, and self-monitor learning and progress to attain high standard, long-term goals. Additional design guidelines appear in Table 6.2.

6.8.2.2 Performing Learners

For *Performing Learners* design task- or project-oriented, competitive, and interactive (hands-on) environments. Focus on process, procedures and meaning. These environments should use coaching, practice, and feedback to encourage and support self-motivation, task solving, self-monitoring progress, and task sequencing, while minimizing the need for extra effort, risk, and difficult standards. Additional design guidelines appear in Table 6.2.

Table 6.2 Strategies and guidelines for three learning orientations

Learning issues	Transforming learners	Performing learners	Conforming learners
General relationship	Prefers loosely structured, mentoring relationships that promote challenging goals, discovery, reflection and self-managed learning	Prefers semi-complex, semi-structured, coaching relationships that stimulate personal value and provide creative interaction (hands-on). Highlight meaning	Prefers safe, structured, guiding relationships that help them avoid mistakes and achieve easy learning goals in a simple fashion
Goal-setting and standards	Sets and achieves personal challenging short- and long-term goals that may exceed goals set by others. Maximizes effort to reach own high-standard personal goals	Sets and achieves more short-term, task-oriented, meaningful goals that meet average-to-high standards. May situationally minimize commitment and efforts and standards to reach assigned or negotiated standards	Follows and tries to achieve simple, task-oriented goals assigned by others. Tries to please and conform. May maximize efforts in supportive relationships with safe, simple standards
Learner autonomy and responsibility	They are self-motivated to assign meaning, assume learning responsibility and self-direct goals, learning, progress, reflection and outcomes. They experience frustration if restricted or given little learning autonomy	They are situationally self-motivated to find meaning and assume learning responsibility in areas of interest. They willingly give up control and extend less effort in areas of less interest or in restrictive relationships	They are cautiously motivated, prefer less responsibility and self-directed learning, like to be more compliant, and are ready to follow others
Knowledge building	Commit great effort to discover, elaborate, and build new knowledge and meaning intentionally	Selectively commit measured effort to assimilate and use relevant knowledge and meaning sometimes intentionally	Commit careful, measured effort to accept and reproduce knowledge to meet simple, external requirements
Problem solving	They prefer case studies and complex, whole-to-part, problem-solving opportunities	They prefer competitive part-to-whole problem solving	They prefer scaffolded support for simple problem solving.
User interface	Recommendation: Open learning interface for high stimulation and multitasking capability	Recommendation: Hands-on learning interface for medium stimulation and multitasking capability	Recommendation: Consistent and simple interface for minimal stimulation and multitasking capability.

(continued)

Table 6.2 (continued)

Learning issues	Transforming learners	Performing learners	Conforming learners
Adapted presentation	They prefer occasional mentoring and interaction for achieving goals (MENTORING)	They prefer continual coaching and interaction for achieving goals (COACHING)	They prefer continual guidance and reinforcement for achieving short-term goals (GUIDING)
Strategies to achieve objectives	Support high-standard, strategic goal-setting and planning, support realistic personal goals, lateral thinking and ability to put theory into practice	Foster personal value (intrinsic benefits) and more holistic thinking, and hands-on, practical support to encourage planning and effort for continuous improvements	Provide time and comprehensive, structured, scaffolded support for adapting training and transitioning skills for improved performance
Feedback	They prefer inferential feedback	They prefer concise feedback	They prefer explicit feedback
Motivational feedback	Discovery	Coached discovery	Guided achievement
Learning module size	Short, concise, big picture, with links to more detail if necessary	Medium, brief overview with focus on practical application	Longer, detailed guidance, in simple, linear steps
Information need	Holistic, probable information needed to solve a problem	General interests, practice, short-term, task-completion focus	Guidance to fulfill a requirement
Content structuring	Prefers freedom to construct own content structure	Prefers general, hands-on instruction identifying process and procedure, e.g., maps, diagrams and charts	They prefer to let others decide the content structure
Sequencing methods	Hypermedia, adaptive, multiple access. Avoid step-by-step instruction and heavy emphasis on process and procedures.	Semi-linear, logical branching, access by subtopic. Minimize high discovery and exploration	Linear, page-turner representations, general access. Avoid learner control and exploration
Inquiry	Asks probing, in-depth questions about content. Expect inferential, theoretical challenges	Asks questions to complete assignments. Expect specific, practical directions	Asks mechanistic questions about assignments. Expects explicit guidance

6.8.2.3 Conforming Learners

For *Conforming Learners* design simple, scaffolded, structured, facilitated, low-risk environments that use explicit, careful guidance to help individuals learn comfortably in an easy, step-wise fashion. Focus on minimizing the nemesis of change. Additional design guidelines appear in Table 6.2.

6.9 Summary

The dream to deliver personalized adaptive learning that fits the real-time, anywhere, anytime, just-enough 24/7 needs of the learner is already becoming a reality. As a result, along with many important developments in instructional psychology, learner-centric models, algorithms, structured markup languages for interoperable data representation, and the shift of instructional flow control from the client to the server-side, an entirely new foundation is making truly personalized online learning possible. The most obvious benefit of these innovations is the creation of a learning ecology that shares resources from large reservoirs of content where learning content can be shared individually, widely, and more effectively and economically.

6.9.1 Paradigm Shift

It is time to acknowledge that our public education system must experiences a huge paradigm shift. The answer is to use adaptive learning technology to offer an alternative, flexible model that fits the needs of groups of learners with common learning patterns, expectations and capabilities. This approach is particularly helpful for those students at both the high end and low end of the "bell curve", whose needs are unmet by the typical classroom model. However, we must constantly be vigilant to ensure that the ubiquitous nature of 24/7 technology does not negatively impact learners, especially young minds.

6.9.2 Diverse Abilities

Of particular importance to the adaptive and assessment learning model is the solution for improving the learning ability of those students in the middle of the curve. The adaptive and assessment learning model can address the continuing gaps and increasing failure rates in our educational programs. The good news is that research shows that everyone can improve their brain with learning. We just need to get better at showing students how to get passionate about finding meaning, committing great effort and being the best that they can be.

6.9.3 Individual Difference in Learning

Technologically, researchers are making rapid progress toward realizing the personalized learning dream with adaptive technology. However, two key elements still need to be addressed in the development and use of more personalized learning. The first is a whole-person understanding of how individuals want and intend to learn. Primarily cognitive learning solutions (i.e., those whose primary focus is on how learners process and build knowledge) are no longer enough as we move away from the classroom. When we design learning with only a universal type of learner in mind or without guiding their higher-level instructional use we unintentionally set learners up for frustration and possible failure. If we are serious about providing good adaptive instruction for learners, we must plan multiple, cost-effective ways to provide instruction and environments so that all learners have opportunities for success.

The second key element is the lack of consideration for instructional issues in the dynamic supported how people learn differently. We need to collect the student data and measure and provide evidence to understand outcomes showing what works most successfully. Learning orientations may be a first step in recognizing, accommodating and measuring individual learning differences from a whole-person perspective. They may also be an important step in recognizing the expanded, dominant role and impact of emotions and intentions on learning, especially since online learners need to become more independent, self-motivated, and self-directed learners. Additionally, we can use learner analytics to design better learner-centric instructional models which can guide more personalized instruction, assessment, and learning environments.

6.9.4 Professional Development for Adaptive Learning

Contemporary professional development should help designers and educators understand how learning differences allows us to tap into key psychological factors that help learning success. Recognizing a learning ability gap and providing interventions, environments and solutions that consider the whole-person perspective are two key steps toward helping students become successful, self-directed, independent and passionate learners. As educators, designers and developers decide on new directions and next-generation personalized learning alternatives, it is important that they also learn to identify, understand, and harness the dominant power of emotions, intentions and social factors.

It is also important for educators, designers and developers to learn more about collecting data and using learner analysis to improve their learning, teaching and assessment models to make better decisions.

6.9.5 Adaptive Technology

Adaptive learning is expanding the supportive learning role that technology can rightfully play in enhancing learning and correcting learning problems that have continually perplexed training markets in the past. Adaptive learning and assessment technology is important because it supports flexible solutions that dynamically adapt content to fit instructional objectives. For sophisticated learners it also enables them to select components to customize their learner-centric environment. For all learners, it enables them to gain more sophisticated online learning ability over time. How else can learners keep up with the rapid pace of change and need for more creativity and more sophisticated ability?

As learners move online, adaptive learning and assessment is a more sophisticated solution for learning and performance improvement and meaningful online relationships. Hopefully, these suggestions will contribute to more successful learning via the Internet and a greater understanding about fundamental learning differences and online instructional issues.

We often automatically expect online learners to take on more responsibility for their own learning, raise their online learning achievement, and improve their ability over time. In contrast, often times in the classroom, passive learning was acceptable and less autonomy, strategic planning and self-directed effort was expected. We will begin to see which groups of learners will need more or less support for adaptive learning. At the same time, key success attributes, patterns and capabilities will emerge that identify gaps in people's readiness to engage in adaptive learning.

6.9.6 Brain Research

The good news is that there many researchers who are getting involved with making sense of the brain research for the classroom, education and future learning in the twenty-first Century. An example is the annual conferences supported by Learning & the Brain (http://www.learningandthebrain.com/). This and other similar conferences highlight how the neurosciences are discovering where intelligence resides in the brain, how schools, emotions and environment shape achievement and how abilities and success can be improved. They explore how to use the neurosciences to improve attention and motivation skills and ways to increase student motivation and mental focus for learning.

Most research suggests that learners in supportive environments have high levels of self-efficacy and self-motivation and use learning as a primary transformative force. Translating this kind of research, the neurosciences and other psychological information into learning, teaching, design and technology strategies can help designers and developers create personalized learning situations, resources and environments that work best for the intended audience and identified needs and objectives. The need to understand how the brain works rapidly increases as we put more and more learners online.

6.10 Future Research and Directions

Our future demands a creative global workforce managed by high-performing, successful leaders who have the key competencies for managing change and innovation, developing global, multicultural strategies, solving problems, and collecting and analyzing the data to achieve global agility. An essential component of future adaptive learning strategies should support these core competencies, embrace the brain's incredible ability to adapt and mature continuously and show students how to commit, create, produce, reflect and persist to achieve their fullest potential.

> The development of our nation's human capital through our education system is an essential building block for future innovation. Currently, the abilities of far too many of America's young men and women go unrecognized and underdeveloped, and, thus, they fail to reach their full potential. This represents a loss for both the individual and society. There are students with high potential from every demographic and from every part of our country, who with hard work and the proper educational opportunities, will form the next generation of science, technology, engineering, and mathematics (STEM) innovators (National Science Board 2010). (Preparing the Next Generation of STEM Innovators: Identifying and Developing Our Nation's Human Capital)

References

Asher DE, Zaldivar A, Krichmar JL (2010) Effect of neuromodulation on performance in game playing: a modeling study. Retrieved 1 Dec 2011, from http://ieeexplore.ieee.org/xpl/freeabs_all.jsp?arnumber=5578851

Bandura A (1977) Social learning theory. General Learning Press, New York

Bereiter C, Scardamalia M (1989) Intentional learning as a goal of instruction. In: Resnick LB (ed) Knowing, learning, and instruction: essays in honor of Robert Glaser. Erlbaum Associates, Hillsdale, pp 361–392

Berryman SE (1993) Learning for the workplace. Rev Res Educ 19:343–401

Black SE, Lynch LM (2003) The new economy and the organization of work. In: Jones DC (ed) The handbook of the new economy. Academic, New York

Black P, Wiliam D (1998) Inside the black box: raising standards through classroom assessment. King's College, London

Bunderson CV, Inouye DK, Olsen JB (1989) The four generations of computerized educational measurement. In: Linn RL (ed) Educational measurement, 3rd edn. American Council on Education and Macmillan, New York, pp 367–407
Carson S (2011) The unleashed mind: why creative people are eccentric. Retrieved 1 Dec 2011, from http://pastebin.com/4WnGpCx4
Cromie WJ (2002) Brain changes in learning measured: results could aid those with mental illness. Retrieved 1 Dec 2011, from http://news.harvard.edu/gazette/2002/05.30/01-fear.html
Cronbach L (1957) The two disciplines of scientific psychology. Amer Psy 12:671–684
Davenport TH, Harris JG (2007) Competing on analytics: the new science of winning. Harvard Business School Press, On the Book Flap
Davidson R, Lutz A (2008) Buddha's brain: neuroplasticity and meditation (In the Spotlight). IEEE Signal Process Mag 25(1):174–176
Davis S (1996) Future perfect, Harlow, England, Addison-Wesley Pub Co. Retrieved 1 Dec 2011, from http://www.managingchange.com/masscust/overview.htm
Gartner Inc (2012) Gartner identifies the top 10 strategic technologies for 2012. Presented at Gartner Symposium/ITxpo, Oct 16–20, in Orlando. Retrieved 1 Dec 2011 from http://www.gartner.com/it/page.jsp?id=1826214
IBM (2011) Predicting the outcome: business analytics for education. The Jour. (White Paper). Retrieved 1 Dec 2011 from http://thejournal.com/whitepapers/2011/11/ibm_predicting-business-analytics-education.aspx?tc=page0
International Association for Computerized Adaptive Testing (2011) What is cat? Retrieved 1 Dec 2011 from http://iacat.org/?q=node/441
Kaplan AM, Haenlein M (2006) Toward a parsimonious definition of traditional and electronic mass customization. J Prod Innov Manage 23:2
Kirchner J (2010) Effect of neuromodulation on human–robot interactions and game playing. Presentation at electrical engineering and computer sciences. Retrieved 1 Dec 2011, from https://eecs.ucmerced.edu/public/seminars/copy_of_2010-10-15
Ledoux J (2002a) Synaptic self. Viking, New York, p 201
Ledoux J (2002b) Synaptic self. Viking, New York, p 212
Ledoux J (2002c) Synaptic self. Viking, New York, p 227
Listfield E (2011) Generation wired. Parade.com, pp. 14+ Retrieved 1 Dec 2011 from http://www.parade.com/health/2011/10/generation-wired.html?index=1
Martinez M (1999a) Using learning orientations to investigate how individuals learn successfully on the web. Tech Commun 46(4):471–487
Martinez M (1999b) Mass customization: a paradigm shift for the 21st century. ASTD Tech Training Mag 10(4):24–26
Martinez M (2000) Intentional learning in an intentional world: audience analysis and instructional system design for successful learning and performance. ACM J Comput Documentation 24:3
Martinez M (2001) Building interactive Web learning environments to match and support individual learning differences. J Interact Learn Res 11(2):2000
Martinez M (2004a) Adaptive learning. In: Stein S, Farmer S (eds) Connotative learning. Kendall/Hunt Publishing, Dubuque, pp 11–26
Martinez M (2004b) Adaptive learning. In: Stein S, Farmer S (eds) Connotative learning. Kendall/Hunt Publishing, Dubuque, pp 14–17
National Science Board (2004) An emerging and critical problem of the science and engineering labor force. Retrieved 1 Dec 2011, from http://www.nsf.gov/statistics/nsb0407/
National Science Board (2010) Preparing the next generation of STEM innovators: identifying and developing our nation's human capital. Retrieved 1 Dec 2011, from http://www.nsf.gov/nsb/stem/innovators.jsp
Phillips J, Gully S (1997) Role of goal orientation, ability, need for achievement, and locus of control in the self-efficacy and goal–setting process. J Appl Psychol 82(5):792–802

Richtel M (2012) Rich M (ed) In Growing up digital, wired for distraction. Retrieved 1 Dec 2011 from http://orderoochaos.com/index.php?option=com_content&view=article&id=72:wired-for-distraction&catid=36:new-a-noteworthy&Itemid=58

Sheehy G (2006) Lodge H (ed) In: Why marriage is good medicine for men. Retrieved 1 Dec 2011, from http://www.marriagemattersjackson.com/Resources/Documents/Why%20Marriage%20is%20good%20medicene%20for%20men%20HEALTH.pdf

Siemens G (2012) Learning and analytics blog. Retrieved 1 Dec 2011 from http://www.learninganalytics.net/

Snow R (1987) Aptitude complexes. In: Snow R, Farr M (eds) Conative and affective process analysis, vol 3. Erlbaum Associates, Hillsdale, pp 11–34

Snow R (1989) Toward assessment of cognitive and conative structures in learning. Educ Researcher 18(9):8–14

Tseng MM, Jiao J (2001) Mass customization. In: Handbook of industrial engineering, technology and operation management (3rd edn). Wiley, NY

University Of Toronto (2003) Biological basis for creativity linked to mental illness. ScienceDaily. Retrieved 1 Dec 2011, from http://www.sciencedaily.com-/releases/2003/10/031001061055.htm

US Department of Education (2010) Transforming American education: learning powered by technology, p 3. Retrieved 1 Dec 2011 from http://www.ed.gov/technology/netp-2010

Wainer H (ed) (2000) Computerized adaptive testing: a primer, 2nd edn. Erlbaum, Hillsdale

Way W (2006) Practical questions in introducing computerized adaptive testing for K-12 assessments. Pearson Educational Measurement Research Report

Zull JE (2002a) Art of changing the brain. Stylus, Sterling, p 23

Zull JE (2002b) Art of changing the brain. Stylus, Sterling, p 96

Zull JE (2002c) Art of changing the brain. Stylus, Sterling, p 74

Zull JE (2002d) Art of changing the brain. Stylus, Sterling, p 52

Part III
The Future of Learning Content

Chapter 7
The Changing Nature of E-Learning Content

Robby Robson

In 1996 Bill Gates wrote an essay entitled "Content is King" (Gates 1996). The title has persisted as a meme, but the nature of content and how it is created has changed significantly 1996. At that time, content was static and the Internet was just beginning to take hold as a channel that everyman could use to access and distribute content. Fifteen years later, in 2011, digital world is brimming with content, including increasing quantities user-generated content, mobile content, and dynamically changing content such as social media, news sites, and online games. Studies show that E-learning is to somewhat behind the curve in adopting new forms of content but it is nonetheless clear that the next generation of E-learning content will be more dynamic, context aware, immersive and mobile. A new set of standards and formats will be relevant and, at least in the short run, different and more technical skills will be required to produce it. More importantly, perhaps, E-learning content is experiencing a shift in underlying pedagogical theories from cognitive, instructivist, and behaviorist to social, constructivist and connectivist. In these theories, it is context that is king. This chapter examines the characteristics of the first generation of E-learning content and discusses what might be expected from the next generation of E-learning content and how this will affect the processes used to create it.

7.1 The Nature of Content

The word "content" is overused and under-defined. In the context of learning, education and training, the content of a lesson consists of words, images, sounds, movements and other stimuli intended to effect a change in cognitive, affective or

R. Robson (✉)
Eduworks Corporation, Corvallis, OR, USA
e-mail: robby.robson@eduworks.com

R. Huang et al. (eds.), *Reshaping Learning*, New Frontiers of Educational Research,
DOI: 10.1007/978-3-642-32301-0_7,

psychomotor state. In this sense, content is abstract and exists independently of any medium. In practice, however, it is common to refer to documents, web sites, presentations, videos and other digital objects as content even though strictly speaking they are only containers for content. As Mr. Gates pointed out in 1996, "when it comes to an interactive network such as the Internet, the definition of 'content' becomes very wide" (Gates 1996).

7.1.1 Implicit Assumptions About Content

Intertwined with the notion of content are the processes of creation, dissemination and curation. Legally, creation takes place when content is expressed in a specific format, and the common view of content-oriented business is that content should be monetized when it is distributed. In US Copyright law, for example, copyright protection subsists when a work is "fixed in any medium of expression" and the law protects the right to reproduce, distribute or perform a work (US copyright office 2011).

Two important assumptions are buried in copyright law and in the business practices related to producing and disseminating content.

Assumption 7.1 The first assumption of copyright law and business practices is that the channel from author to consumer can be controlled, usually by a third party such as a publisher or educational institution.

Desktop publishing and the Internet have disrupted this. As Mr. Gates observed in 1996, "one of the exciting things about the Internet is that anyone with a PC and a modem can publish whatever content they can create" (Gates 1996). Today, everyman can create and publish documents, web pages, music, and video, and the cost of copying and dissemination is very small. To maintain control over distribution channels and to protect their business models, publishers have implemented digital rights management (DRM) and advocated for laws such as the digital millennium copyright act (DMCA). While academic and educational communities champion open access journals and open educational resources (OER) (ISKME 2011; Atkins and Brown 2007), they monetize their distribution channels by charging for credits and degrees. Schools and colleges charge tuition (or are publically supported) largely for the services of ensuring that content is valid, adding value through instruction, and certifying that students have comprehended the content.

Assumption 7.2 The second assumption of copyright law and business practices is that content is immutable once it is "fixed in any medium".

In legal terminology, substantial alterations constitute derivative works that are differentiated from the original work. This view is less and less valid. In the emerging world of social media, mash-ups, serious games, and web-service based applications, content is dynamic and is continually generated and altered by end users and computer programs long after it has been published. Even ignoring user- and computer-generated content, web sites such are not static. Erik W. Black has described Wikipedia as a "content-malleable" system (Black 2008). Malleability is forced upon sources such as Wikipedia because knowledge is not static, and the same applies to learning content.

7.1.2 The Change to Dynamic and Malleable Content

Dynamism and malleability are fundamental changes in the underlying nature of all digital content. Paradoxically, they may serve to undo some of the changes that self-publishing and the Internet have triggered by (at least temporarily) re-inserting the role of publisher as a necessity. Although everyman may be able to write a blog or create a video and publish it on YouTube™, creating a game or interactive learning environment integrated with external sources via multiple web services requires technical expertise, teamwork and tools beyond everyman's reach. As data discussed later in this chapter shows, the effort involved in producing interactive E-learning content is on the order of five times that of producing standard self-paced learning.

Dynamic and malleable content does more than change the nature of content. It also challenges notions of ownership, authorship, and validation. Who is the owner of user-generated content, who deserves credit for it, and how is it demonstrated to be accurate? These are important questions, especially for educational and academic applications. One way to look at these questions is that attribution and validation are services associated with content and that validation of content, at least, is possibly as valuable as the content itself.

This perspective is crucial for understanding how content is evolving in the emerging information environment. In fact, one can argue that the value of content has always been small compared to the value of the services based on it. In the case of traditional publishing, these services included editing, printing, marketing and dissemination, and in the case of education and training these services include validation, interpretation, and certification of skills, knowledge and abilities. We now live in an environment where static content has become an abundant resource and where search engines and open content are lowering barriers to access. In this environment the value of information and data is even less compared to the value of the services that organize and interpret it. As we will see, this is reflected in new learning theories as well as in technical standards that increase the likelihood of significant changes in the nature of learning content.

7.1.3 Changes in Learner Behavior

This chapter considers technological and economic predictors of change in the development and dissemination of learning content. It does not, however, consider changes in the learners themselves. As stated in the journal *Pediatrics,* "a large part of this generation's social and emotional development is occurring while on the Internet and on cell phones" (O'Keeffe and Clarke-Pearson 2011). The effects of this phenomenon on learning and learning content are beyond the scope of this chapter other than to the extent it is embedded in pedagogical models and learning theories. What is clear, however, is that the ubiquity of content is causing learners to learn differently. For example, in a 2010 study Head and Eisenberg reported that the majority of college students use Wikipedia but that they tend to use it for background research and while relying on what they perceived as more validated sources for in depth research (Head and Eisenberg 2010). These results are hardly surprising but do serve to reinforce the view that the services around content are more valuable than the raw content itself—Wikipedia has become a service used to get an initial grasp on a subject and provide citations and search terms rather than an authoritative source of information itself.

7.2 First Generation E-learning Content

Before talking about how content is changing, it is useful to baseline what E-learning content looks like today, i.e. in 2011. Most of it is first generation content that can be described as "variants of books on computers" (Robson and McElroy 2008) that do little more than transfer existing content and pedagogies to a new medium. A convenient framework for describing first generation content consists of the levels used for describing and procuring E-learning content in corporate and military settings.

7.2.1 Levels Used in Corporate Training

Level one: The common picture of a corporate E-learning module is a series of pages with text and multimedia interspersed with multiple choice quizzes used for knowledge checks or normative assessment. E-learning of this type is called level one content or, in industry slang, a "page turner" because the majority of learner interactions consist of clicking the "next" button to get to the next page. Page turners are easily produced using rapid E-learning tools (Ganci 2011) that convert PowerPoint™ to online formats such as HTLM and Flash™ or that provide their own authoring canvases into which text, multimedia and quizzes can be inserted.

Level two: Some tools, including rapid E-learning tools, can produce moderately adaptive content that enables students to skip or remediate sections based on assessment results. Another set of tools and prepackaged content allows authors to configure games and puzzles (often modeled after television game shows or popular board games) with specific subject matter. Programmers can also create additional interactive elements such a virtual workbench. Content that includes higher degrees of interactivity and more sophisticated branching is called level two. It usually requires some programming to produce and also usually sticks with a didactic approach to instruction—the content informs the learner and may let the learner try some things out, but it is not immersive or experiential learning.

Level three: The most sophisticated E-learning content contains models and simulations of machinery or laboratories that students can manipulate and may include game dynamics such as (player) levels, point rewards and punishments, bonus content, etc. This is called level three and requires significant effort to produce. In addition to higher levels of interaction, level three is typified by discovery and problem-based learning and creates a more immersive experience for the learner.

Levels describe the general nature of E-learning content and are used in corporate training to get a rough estimate of development effort and procurement costs. A survey of almost 250 organizations across all industry sectors conducted by the Chapman Alliance in 2010 indicates that the time required to produce one hour of content (an industry standard measure) varies from 80 h of development effort at a cost of $10,000 for level one content to 500 or more hours at a cost of $50,000 for level three content (Chapman 2010). For reference, the definitions used in that survey are given in the Table 7.1.

The survey conducted by the Chapman Alliance asked for time spent and various activities in development of content, starting with front end analysis and continuing through review of the completed product. The survey found that production (graphics, audio, video, and authoring/programming) accounts for only 40 % of the total effort with approximately one-third of the total effort going into design and analysis and the remainder to quality assurance, project management, reviews, and testing (Chapman 2010). Interestingly, these percentages did not change significantly with the level of the content. In other words, each of these

Table 7.1 Levels of E-learning as defined by the chapman alliance

Level one content	Level two content	Level three content
Content pages, text, graphics, perhaps simple audio, perhaps simple video, test questions. Note: PowerPoint-to-E-learning often falls into this category. Basically, pages with assessment	Level one plus 25 % (or more) interactive exercises (allowing learners to perform virtual "try it" exercises), liberal use of multimedia (audio, video, animations)	Highly interactive, possibly simulation or serious game based, use of avatars, custom interactions, award winning caliber courseware

Table 7.2 Levels of interactive multimedia instruction as defined by the US department of defense

Level one IMI	Level two IMI	Level three IMI	Level four IMI
Passive. The student acts solely as a receiver of information	Limited participation. The student makes simple responses to instructional cues	Complex participation. The student makes a variety of responses using varied techniques in response to instructional cues	Real-time participation. The student is directly involved in a life-like set of complex cues and responses

aspects becomes uniformly more challenging as the level of the content increases. Thus even if tools and technology could reduce the time required to produce highly interactive and immersive content, significant investment would still be required in the remaining 60 % of the development process.

7.2.2 Levels Used in the U.S. Military

A slightly different take on levels of E-learning content is that used by the U.S. military to categorize interactive multimedia instruction (IMI). Four levels of IMI are defined in a lengthy handbook (MIL-HDBK-29612-3A) that discusses procurement procedures, development processes, media formats, and instructional design (US department of defense 2001). Superficially, the military IMI classification (Table 7.2) is more concerned with student interaction and pedagogy than the levels used by the corporate training industry, but in practice it is used in much the same way as a tool for estimating costs and for identifying the requirements a content developer will be expected to meet (Table 7.3).

7.2.3 How Much Content is Corporate Level three?

It is difficult to know how much existing online training content is highly interactive and is in the (corporate) level three category, but observationally most of it is not. Data on tools used to develop E-learning content corroborate this observation. Studies such as those published by the E-learning Guild (Wexler 2008) the American Society for Training and Development (Robyn A Defelice 2009) indicate that the most common tools used to produce E-learning content are:

- Screen capture tools that enable annotations to be added
- PowerPoint™ and PowerPoint-to-Flash converters that can be used to add basic assessment and branching logic (these are in the category of Rapid E-learning Tools
- Microsoft Word™ (and Adobe Acrobat™)

Table 7.3 Ambient insight taxonomy (Adkins 2012)

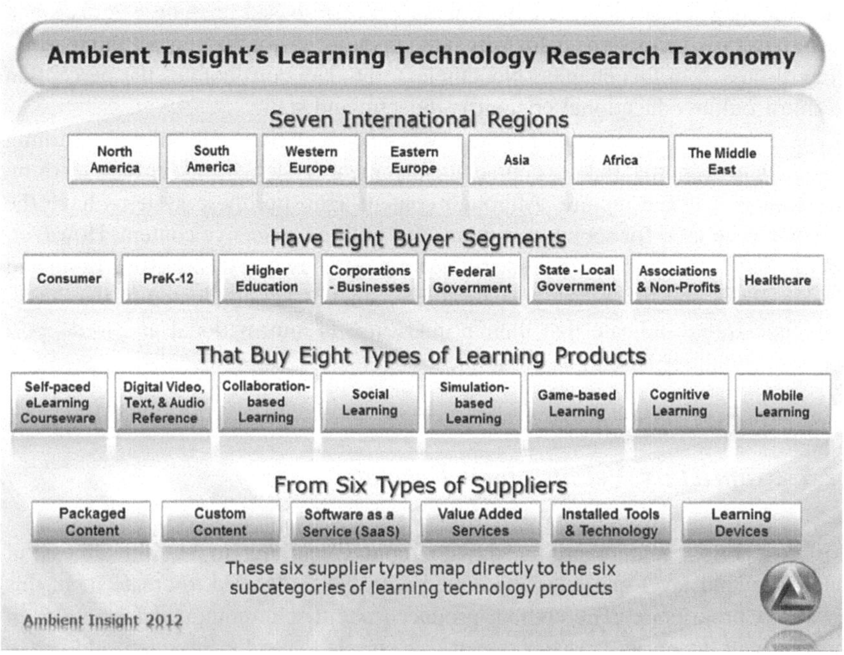

- Webinar recording tools, and
- HTML editors.

Towards the bottom of the list are E-learning authoring tools that can go a bit further in terms of adding multimedia and varieties of assessments, but even these are not easily used to produce level three content.

7.2.4 What Does Educational Content Look Like?

As with corporate content, today's educational content is largely static and not very interactive. Statistics gathered on 20 Dec 2011 from MERLOT (MERLOT 2011) indicated that of the 32,026 materials in MERLOT, only 2,967 (9.26 %) were labeled as simulations while 11,225 (35.05 %) had format type HTML/Text Of the 6,048 materials added in 2011, only 78 (1.29 %) were labeled as simulations and 2,220 (36.71 %) had format type HTML/Text. On the same day, the OER Commons (ISKME 2011) had 39,924 resources of which 1,309 (3.55 %) were labeled as games or simulations, only 306 (0.83 %) had format "interactive" and 31,351 (84.91 %) had format "HTML/Text".

Considering the diversity of resources in MERLOT and OER Commons, these figures should not be over-interpreted. These collections contain lesson plans and static web pages that describe experiments, problem-based learning exercises and other educational experiences for which the resource is not the content in the sense being discussed in this chapter. Nonetheless, the data corroborates the perception that most online educational content is didactic and static.

The same conclusion is reached when considering educational learning management systems (a.k.a. course management systems and virtual learning environments) in the picture. Although content-agnostic, these systems have the potential to be used for social learning and to pull in immersive content. However, several studies of their use in higher education (Hamuy and Galaz 2010; Lonn and Teasley 2009) and secondary education (De Smet 2011) conducted in the 2008–2010 time frame indicate that their primary use is informational and to support learning modalities based on communication.

7.2.5 Proprietary Versus Open Formats

Most E-learning content produced with rapid E-learning tools, and almost all content beyond level one, must be edited with the tools used to create it. In this sense it is proprietary. The content produced is either in compiled formats or in open formats (such as HTML) that uses compiled, vendor-provided add-ins to enable key functionality such as scoring of assessments. Once published, the content is fixed.

Lock-in caused by the use of proprietary formats is an issue for first generation content. Authoring tools and content developers use such formats for many reasons, including providing customers with desired specialized functionality, but their use forces content owners to go back to content developers for updates. Proprietary tools and formats also cause longer term problems. The most advanced first generation E-learning content was created with products such as Author ware™ and Tool Book™. As these products evolve or disappear, and as the content can no longer be used with modern browsers and on mobile platforms, organizations that own the content are faced with the challenge of converting it to newer formats (e.g. Flash or HTML5) or re-developing it from scratch. Conversion is usually less expensive than re-development but is made more costly if the original content is proprietary.

7.3 The Expanding Horizon of E-learning

The picture of E-learning painted in the previous sessions is that of page turners, webinars, and online assessment, possibly organized and delivered using learning management systems. This picture is changing due to many factors, including increased malleability and dynamism in all types of online content, the rise of social media and mobile computing, and the proliferation of high bandwidth access needed for online simulation and gaming. But the most fundamental factor may still be the natural and inevitable transition from using a new medium to deliver old material to using the new medium to create new forms. The american society for training and development (ASTD) defines E-learning as "the use of electronic technologies to deliver information and facilitate the development of skills and knowledge" (Michael Green 2011). This is a broad definition that, significantly, includes both delivery and facilitation. Whereas delivery fits into traditional publishing and pedagogical models, facilitation goes beyond them.

7.3.1 Facilitation Versus Delivery

Facilitation is different than delivery in many ways. Pedagogically, it represents a move from behaviorist and cognivist to humanist, social and situational theories of learning (Smith 1999) or, as put by Anderson and Dron, from cognitive-behaviorist design to designs based on social constructivism and connectivism (Anderson and Dron 2010). Connectivism is a learning theory proposed by Siemen (2004) and Downes (2006) that emphasizes the ability to process and derive knowledge from an abundance of networked information (See also Siemens and Conole 2011). In business terms, thinking of E-learning as facilitation emphasizes value-added services rather than content.

Facilitation uses different technologies than delivery. Authoring tools produce content meant for delivery and consumption while learning management systems (both corporate and academic) have primarily been used to organize, deliver and track static content. They are controlled by authors and administrators, consistent with a top-down view of content creation and dissemination. Even if they have social and collaborative learning aspects and can technically integrate with immersive learning tools, they have not been extensively used for these purposes.

Facilitative technologies, in contrast, tend to be steered by users and more dynamic. These include:

- Discussion boards and forums, which are a traditional part of educational learning management systems but are not among the most used features.
- Webinars and similar technologies that enable an instructor or mentor to interact with students in real time. These are called "collaboration-based learning" by Ambient Insight. Ambient predicts they will "have the largest reach of all technology-based learning products" in the 2011–2015 timeframe (Adkins 2011).
- Wikis, Twitter™, and other social media that are increasingly being considered as learning tools (Reid and Ostashewski 2011; Lenoue et al. 2011; Foroughi 2011; Kelly 2011). A significant aspect of social media is that content is generated by users, which breaks the model of the author as the sole source of authority.

- Intelligent agents that retrieve information and present it to the learner (Giotopoulos et al. 2011; Axita and Sonal 2011). Source of data could include personalized search results (Axita and Sonal 2011), Census data (Finzer 2007), environmental data (Kotzinos et al. 2005), and data from real or virtual laboratories (Goodwin et al. 2011; Von Borstel and Gordillo 2010; Wolf 2010; Gomes and Bogosyan 2009).
- Intelligent tutoring systems (Graesser et al. 2012) that monitor and adapt content based on the learner's cognitive state and demonstrated knowledge (Axita and Sonal 2011; Graesser et al. 1999; Stillson and Alsup 2003).
- Recommender systems that track trends across broader populations and integrate that data with personal histories and assessment outcomes for the purpose of steering learners to relevant or interesting content.
- Serious games (Barnes et al. 2009) and simulations which engage learners in guided discovery and problem-based learning. Facilitation in these environments includes interactions with other players and with non-player characters managed by the game or by other people.

7.3.2 Content is Mobile, Personal and Contextual

Content used for E-learning is also being affected by the form factors used to deliver it, in particular mobile computing. Mobile computing is experiencing rapid growth (Matt Murphy 2011; Pettey and Stevens 2011; Kim et al. 2012) and is increasingly being used in learning (Pace 2011; Meister et al. 2011). As such mobile learning (or M-learning) is a significant change agent in learning technology.

M-learning is not new (Peng et al. 2009). The International Association for Mobile Learning (2011) has been holding conferences since 2002 and research groups at SRI and elsewhere were studying applications of ubiquitous computing to learning in the 1990s (Tinker and Vahey 2002). However, the meaning of m-learning is changing.

The first challenge faced by practitioners of m-learning mobile platforms was the lack of device capabilities compared to laptop and desktop computers. As pointed out by Goh and Kinshuk (Goh and Kinshuk 2006) and others, adapting to device capabilities is part of the more general problem of adapting content to the of the learner. The capability gap between mobile and older platforms may not be as significant anymore, but the notion of adapting to *and leveraging* device capabilities has taken on new meaning. M-learning is starting to differentiate itself from traditional E-learning by exploiting location and context-awareness (Glahn and Specht 2011; Traxler 2010; Godwin-Jones 2011) and is moving towards a vision of dynamic personal learning environments that adapt to the capabilities and needs of the learner and of the learning platform (Kalloo and Mohan 2010; Chen and Li 2010; Su 2011).

The proliferation of m-learning changes the paradigm of E-learning from mass-produced to personalized, contextualized and location-based. This has the potential to accelerate change in the way content is developed and disseminated. At the same time, the underlying technologies associated with mobile delivery are not mature and enterprises are struggling with issues caused by the "bring your own device" (BYOD) phenomenon (Oppliger 2011). Typically, only early adopters are willing to invest in new technology in this state of flux.

7.3.3 The Ambient Insight Taxonomy and Reported Trends

A more refined approach to classifying E-learning content than the traditional levels approach is taken by the research firm Ambient Insight (Adkins 2011) for the purposes of market analysis. This is shown in Table 7.4, reproduced with permission from the 2012 version of the cited work. The row that relates the most to content is the row showing eight types of learning products. First generation content falls into the first two boxes (self-paced courseware and what Ambient calls "reference ware"). This type of learning is static and based on an instructivist theory of learning. The next box, collaboration-based learning, includes screen sharing, webinars, virtual labs, and other technologies used to facilitate collaboration. Content in these categories could be static or malleable and could be instructivist or constructivist: a didactic lecture delivered via a webinar is still a didactic lecture and is static in nature. The next three boxes—social, simulation-based and game-based learning—tend to be more malleable and dynamic and based on instructivist and behaviorist learning theories. These move away from first generation content and, in the case of social learning, towards the socio-constructivist and connectivist theories of learning. As stated by Ambient, social learning represents "a shift from top-down centralized sources of learning to bottom-up widely distributed peer-to-peer learning communities" (Adkins 2011) (see Table 7.5).

The cognitive learning category includes products designed to improve cognition and brain fitness as well as intelligent tutoring systems. These are not content in the usual sense but they represent attempts to bring cognitive science to bear on the design of learning systems. Systems such as Auto tutor (Graesser et al. 1999; Graesser 2005) use sophisticated techniques including semantic analysis and domain ontologies to track learner progress and sequence the delivery of content. This is an important trend that, like m-learning (the last box) represents an approach that genuinely diverges from first generation content.

The market analyses provided by Ambient show a clear trend away from first generation content. In North America, a mature E-learning market, self-paced and collaborative learning are predicted to grow at a steady but modest rate (about 4 and 6 % per year) and authoring tools are predicted to have a negative growth rate

Table 7.4 First generation and next generation content, 2008 version (Robson and McElroy 2008)

First gen content	Next gen content
Monolithic and linear	Granular and adaptive
Web 1.0 content is static	Web 2.0 content is dynamic and changeable
Developed by technically skilled staff	Developed by community and able to evolve
Often untagged on hard-to-find servers	Tagged and searchable by entire organization
Single purpose and context	Adaptable to multiple contexts
Integrated component packaging	Constructed in multiple, separable layers
Proprietary delivery platforms	Open standards/interoperability

Table 7.5 Next generation content (2011 version)

	First generation E-learning content	Next generation E-learning content
Content is king	Raw content is a valuable resource. There is value in the expression of information, facts and data	Raw content is an abundant resource. There is value in the assembly and interpretation of information, facts and data
Granularity	Content is self-contained and tends to be monolithic	Content is a mash-up and increasingly granular, but granularity itself is a fuzzy concept when discussing dynamic content
Production	Standard E-learning is easy to produce with readily available tools	Technical skills are required to create games, simulations, and content that harvests real time data or invokes multiple services
Pedagogy	Cognitive, behaviorist, instructivist	Social, constructivist, connectivist
Metadata	Metadata is an aid to discovery. Adding metadata to resources helps find them in digital libraries and other collections	Paradata is replacing metadata. Search has improved, so understanding the context, use and interpretation of an object is more important than labeling it
Open educational resources	Educators want OER to avoid lock-in. Publishers are struggling with the consequences	Most OERs are first generation content. This is not as valuable as it once was, and next generation content that is valuable is too complex to produce as OERs
Standards	Standards facilitate content portability	Standards facilitate context portability
E-learning	E-learning is primarily a means of delivering learning content	E-learning is a primarily a means of facilitating learning
Platforms	E-learning is web-based	E-learning is mobile, but the lines between web-based and mobile are not clear
Context is king	First generation content is not context-aware	Next generation content is context-aware. M-learning is a proxy for this and includes location-awareness and the ability to adapt to learner traits and history

(Adkins 2011), whereas the growth rates of other types of content is much higher. Ambient concludes that "there is clear evidence now that newer learning technologies such as Mobile Learning and Social Learning are cannibalizing Self-paced E-learning revenues in a classic product substitution pattern" (Adkins 2011).

7.3.4 The Education Market

In identifying differences between education and training, it is often stated or implied that self-paced E-learning is used in corporate training but not in education. According to Ambient Insight data, this is not the case. Education sales of self-paced learning exceed corporate sales in every region other than North America where the margin is small and where educational sales are predicted to overtake corporate sales by 2015 (Adkins 2011). There is also a perception that within education, E-learning is primarily used in higher education but not in K-12. Ambient Insight's latest findings (at the time of this publication) are that PreK-12 is experiencing massive migration to learning technology and the most dynamic market segment listed in Table 7.4. Other reports corroborate this conclusion (Picciano 2002; Speak up 2011). Moreover, there is significant evidence that online education is more effective than face-to-face instruction: A 2010 US Department of Education meta-analysis of 99 studies (nine from K-12) famously concluded that "on average, online learning produced better student learning outcomes than face-to-face instruction in those studies with random-assignment experimental designs ($p < 0.001$) and in those studies with the largest sample sizes ($p < 0.01$)" (Means 2010).

7.4 Standards that Address E-learning Content Interoperability

Technical standards are enabling technologies for learning management systems, open content, and the social and mobile technologies that are shaping the future of E-learning content. In learning technology they have served as a platform for innovation, policy and debate. It is therefore worthwhile looking at the directions being taken by some of the relevant standards development organizations.

In the 1997–2004 timeframe, standards focused on content portability. The most widely adopted standards developed during that period were (Robson 2006).

- IMS Content Packaging (Consortium 2004)
- The Shareable Content Object Reference Model (SCORM) (2004)
- The Aviation Industry CBT Committee Computer Managed Instruction (AICC) (McDonald 2004)

- IMS Question and Test Interoperability (IMS QTI) (Easterby-Smith 2003)
- IEEE Learning Object Metadata (LOM) (IEEE 2002).

SCORM and AICC addressed the problem of "develop once, play in any LMS" for corporate and military training. IMS Content Packaging, which was included as part of SCORM, and IMS QTI handled portability for the educational sector. These standards were key industry enablers: Because of them, content is no longer married to delivery systems.

The standards developed 10 years ago predictably are tailored to first generation E-learning. SCORM and AICC standards explicitly assume that a single learner is interacting with a self-contained unit of content via a web browser. Multi-user content and communication among content objects are not supported. Test scores, objectives, and metadata about content are reported by content and recorded by an LMS. In this sense, content is indeed king!

The first set of learning technology interoperability standards did not anticipate collaborative work, content delivered from multiple systems, or adaptive learner models. They assumed that each learning object was a self-contained experience crafted by an author or instructional designer who was the sole authority on how the experience should be described and evaluated. This is the traditional view of instructional design.

In the 2005–2010 timeframe the learning technology standards community addressed some of the limitations inherent in the original content-related standards. Standards committees embraced web services, service oriented architectures and mashed-up content. The IMS Global Learning Consortium published standards intended to enable tools and services to be more easily integrated into educational platforms (Paulsson and Berglund 2008; Severance et al. 2010; Alario-Hoyos and Wilson 2010) and finalized the Common Cartridge specification (Consortium 2011) in October of 2011. Common Cartridge expands the definition of content to include external services, discussion boards, and authentication.

Newer content standards may accommodate more malleable and dynamic content, but a more interesting story is developing out of two very different initiatives: Project Tin Can (Rustici Software 2011) (supported by the U.S. Department of Defense Advanced Distributed Learning Initiative) and the Federal Learning Registry (Jesukiewicz and Rehak 2011; US Department of Education 2011) (managed by the U.S. Department of Education). The common thread of these two projects is an emphasis on statements about activities (in the form actor—verb—object) as the basic unit of information that learning systems should exchange. In Tin Can, these are learning records. In the Learning Registry, these are statements about an object, such as a rating, correlation with a curriculum standard, or an indication of how an object was used in teaching.

Statements about an object and how it is used and interpreted are called "paradata" (Beacham et al. 2009; Gundy 2011), a term that apparently comes from (and is used slightly differently in) the survey world (Kreuter and Paradata 2010). Communities that have been focused for fifteen years on exchanging test scores and student names are now developing standards to exchange para data. This radical move supports the view that the value of content lies in how it is used and interpreted rather than in the content itself.

7.4.1 Standards and Open Content

Content portability standards such as IMS Content Packaging, SCORM, AICC CMI and IMS Common Cartridge operate at the module or course level. With the exception of QTI, commonly used learning content standards do not define how to represent underlying content objects themselves. Since this is where lock-in occurs, it is worth asking why.

Although there are no widely adopted learning content standards, it is not for lack of choices or efforts. Many commercial products use internal XML formats to represent learning content and t in some cases these are publicly available. Projects such as Connexions (Connexions 2011) and the DITA subcommittee on learning and training content (Hunt 2011) have proposed standards, and standards have been adopted for specialized content types such as test questions (QTI) and mathematics formulas (MathML) (Carlisle et al. 2010). A more plausible explanation is that learning content is too heterogeneous to be standardized. This may be true for level three and next generation content, but it is contradicted by the uniformity of level one and two content. Most likely, the lack of standardization is a statement by the market that there is no compelling business case for standards for first generation content.

7.5 Next Generation E-learning Content

A white paper written in 2008 by the author and Patrick McElroy for Adobe Systems (Robson and McElroy 2008) included the following table summarizing the transformation from first generation to next generation content:

The table below is an updated version based on the developments and observations in this chapter.

As discussed earlier, most existing E-learning content is still first generation. However, there are reasons to believe the transition will accelerate. Technological drivers such as tablets, mobile operating systems, a new browsers (Google Chrome became the most popular browser in Nov, 2011) (w3schools.com 2011; Claburn 2011), and cloud computing are obsoleting first generation content at a higher rate. Poor economic conditions have had a dampening effect on the procurement of new content and the conversion of existing content, but regardless of economic outlook, there comes a point where extending the life of outdated proprietary content is no longer a viable option. As stated in the 2011 "State of the Industry" report published by the American Society for Training and Development (Michael Green 2011), "many organizations are investing in technology-based delivery systems and methods, and the growing use of technology to deliver content—especially through social media tools—will continue to shape the future of the learning field." According to reports, the K-12 sector is about to experience rapid growth in the use of online educational technology. While newly developed content may not be leading edge, it will at least embrace web 2.0 technology which is now the previous generation.

7.5.1 Next Generation Design and Development

If the future of E-learning content lies in dynamic mobile content driven by socio-constructivist and connectivist learning theories, what does this mean for those who design and develop it?

In corporate environments, rapid E-learning tools have put authoring back in the hands of subject matter experts and diminished the role of designers. In a 2009 Driscoll and Caroliner went as far as to say that "if instructional designers do not find a critical role for themselves, promote it, and gain acceptance of that need, they might find themselves bypassed and looking for alternative employment" (Driscoll and Carliner 2009). At the same time, data from the Chapman Alliance indicates that planning and design is an important and constant aspect of developing E-learning at any interaction level. Designing immersive learning environments with simulations and game dynamics is at least as complex as designing first generation E-learning content, and the same is true for mobile and context aware applications. If one views the role of an instructional designer as designing first generation content, then this role must indeed diminish as content becomes abundant and its value decreases. But if one views the role of an instructional designer as designing the experience and environment in which the content is used and in which learners interact, the role may be different but is no less critical.

The predicted explosion of the use of online technologies in the K-12 sector will also have significant impact because the culture of content creation and dissemination in K-12 is different than in post-secondary education. In the United States at least, K-12 content is generally not created by teachers and is purchased at the institutional level. At the end of 2010, 38 states had state virtual schools or state-led online initiatives, including 27 with fulltime online schools serving students statewide (Wicks 2010). When content is procured at the state level, the stakes are higher and more can be invested in design and development. The logical trend is for widely used next generation resources to become more highly produced (and not free) while didactic content becomes more open and freely available.

7.6 Conclusion

Content carried over from the print era is still dominant among content used for learning, but the future lies elsewhere. It remains to be seen how quickly the transformation takes place, but instructional designers and educational technologists must clearly familiarize themselves with new tools that produce new formats (e.g. HTML5) and learn to design experiences rather than author content or build technology. In the world of personalized, mobile learning, it is context, not content, that is king.

References

Gates B (1996) Content is King. 3rd Jan, Available from http://www.craigbailey.net/content-is-king-by-bill-gates/

US Copyright Office (2011) Copyright law of the united states and related laws contained in title 17 of the united states code

ISKME (2011) OER Commons: open educational resources 20 Dec, Available from http://www.oercommons.org/

Atkins D, Brown JS, Hammond A (2007) A review of the open educational resources (OER) movement: Achievements, challenges, and new opportunities. The William and Flora Hewlett Foundation

Black EW (2008) Wikipedia and academic peer review: wikipedia as a recognised medium for scholarly publication? Online Info Rev 32(1):73–88

O'Keeffe GS, Clarke-Pearson K (2011) The impact of social media on children, adolescents, and families. Pediatrics 127(4):800

Head AJ, Eisenberg MB (2010) How today's college students use wikipedia for course-related research. First Monday 15(3)

Robson R, McElroy P (2008) Transforming to next generation digital learning content. 28 Dec Available from http://www.adobe.com/resources/E-learning/pdfs/95010540_digitallearning_wp_ue.pdf

Ganci J (2011) Rapid E-learning authoring: top tools. E-learning guild research 2011, Santa Rosa, CA

Chapman B (2010) How long does it take to create learning

US Department of defense (2001) Development of interactive multimedia instruction (IMI)

Wexler S et al (2008) Authoring and development tools. 360 degree reports

Robyn A Defelice KMK (2009) Time to develop one hour of training learning circuits

MERLOT (2011) 20 Dec Available from http://www.merlot.org/merlot/index.htm

Hamuy E, Galaz M (2010) Information versus communication in course management system participation. Comput Educ 54(1):169–177

Lonn S, Teasley SD (2009) Saving time or innovating practice: investigating perceptions and uses of learning management systems. Comput Educ 53(3):686–694

De Smet C et al (2011) Researching instructional use and the technology acceptation of learning management systems by secondary school teachers. Comput Educ

Michael Green EM (2011) State of the industry 2011: ASTD's annual review of workplace learning and development data

Smith MK (1999) Learning theory. The encyclopedia of informal education

Anderson T, Dron J (2010) Three generations of distance education pedagogy. Int Rev Res Open and Distance Learn 12(3):80–97

Siemens G (2004) Connectivism: a learning theory for the digital age

Downes S (2006) Learning networks and connective knowledge

Siemens G, Conole G (2011) Special issue–connectivism: design and delivery of social networked learning. Int Rev Res Open and Distance Learn 12(3)
Adkins S (2011) The US collaboration-based learning market: 2010–2015 forecast and analysis
Reid D, Ostashewski N (2011) Social media tools supporting your professional learning
Lenoue BM, Hall T, Eighmy MA (2011) Adult education and the social media revolution. Adult Learn
Foroughi A (2011) A research framework for evaluating the effectiveness of implementations of social media in higher education. Online J Workforce Educ Dev 5(1):5
Kelly P (2011) Web 2.0-based E-learning: applying social informatics for tertiary teaching. J Open Distance E-learn 26(3):280–283
Giotopoulos K et al (2011) Bringing AI to E-learning: the case of advancing education with information communication technologies. Facilitating New Trends, , p 126
Axita S, Sonal J (2011) An agent based personalized intelligent E-learning. Int J Comput Appl 20(3):40–45
Finzer W et al (2007) On getting more and better data into the classroom. Technol Innov Stat Educ 1(1)
Kotzinos D, Konstantinou G, Chrysoulakis N (2005) Servicing environmental E-learning (E 2-learning): using geographic information and remote sensing web services to support E 2-learning
Goodwin GC et al (2011) Emulation-based virtual laboratories: a low-cost alternative to physical experiments in control engineering education. IEEE Trans 99:1–1
Von Borstel FD, Gordillo JL (2010) Model-based development of virtual laboratories for robotics over the internet systems, man and cybernetics, part A: systems and humans. IEEE Trans 40(3):623–634
Wolf T (2010) Assessing student learning in a virtual laboratory environment. IEEE Trans 53(2):216–222
Gomes L, Bogosyan S (2009) Current trends in remote laboratories industrial electronics. IEEE Trans 56(12):4744–4756
Graesser AC, Conley MW, Olney A (2012) Intelligent tutoring systems, in APA educational psychology handbook, vol 3. Application to teaching and learning. In: Karen R SU, Tim G, Adriana GB, Sonya M, Lee SH (eds) Washington, pp 451–473
Graesser AC et al (1999) Auto tutor: a simulation of a human tutor. Cognitive Syst Res 1(1):35–51
Stillson H, Alsup J (2003) Smart ALEKS or not? Teaching basic algebra using an online interactive learning system. Math Comput Educ 37(3):329–340
Barnes T, Encarnação LM, Shaw CD (2009) Serious games. Comput Graph Appl 29(2):18–19
Matt Murphy MM (2011) Top mobile internet trends
Pettey C, Stevens H (2011) Gartner lowers pc forecast as consumers diversify computing needs across devices
Kim P et al (2012) A comparative analysis of a game-based mobile learning model in low-socioeconomic communities of India. Int J Educ Devel 32(2):329–340
Pace A (2011) At last: m-learning going mainstream. Training Devel 65(6):1
Meister J, Kaganer E, Feldt RV (2011) The year of the media tablet as a learning tool. Training Devel 65(4):3
Peng H et al (2009) Ubiquitous knowledge construction: mobile learning re-defined and a conceptual framework. Innov Educ Teach Int 46(2):171–183
International association for mobile learning (2011) 26 Dec, available from http://www.iamlearn.org/
Tinker R, Vahey P (2002) CILT2000: ubiquitous computing—spanning the digital divide. J Sci Educ Technol 11(3):301–304
Goh T, Kinshuk D (2006) Getting ready for mobile learning–adaptation perspective. Int J Educ Multimedia Hypermedia 15(2):175–198
Glahn C, Specht M (2011) Structuring mobile and contextual learning
Traxler J (2010) Distance education and mobile learning: catching up, taking stock. Distance Educ 31(2):129–138

Godwin-Jones R (2011) Emerging technologies: mobile apps for language learning. Language Learn Technol 15(2):2–11
Kalloo V, Mohan P (2010) Personalized game based mobile learning to assist high school students with mathematics. IEEE
Chen CM, Li YL (2010) Personalised context-aware ubiquitous learning system for supporting effective english vocabulary learning. Interact Learn Environ 18(4):341–364
Su JM et al (2011) A personalized learning content adaptation mechanism to meet diverse user needs in mobile learning environments. User modeling and user-adapted interaction, pp 1–45
Oppliger R (2011) Security and privacy in an online world. Comput 44(9):21–22
Adkins S (2011) Ambient insight's 2011 learning technology research taxonomy
Graesser A et al (2005) Auto tutor: an intelligent tutoring system with mixed-initiative dialogue, IEEE Trans Educ. p 612–618
Adkins S (2011) The worldwide market for self-paced E-learning products and services: 2010–2015 forecast
Adkins S (2011) The US market for self-paced E-learning products and services: 2010–2015 forecast and analysis. Ambient Insight
Picciano AG et al (2002) Examining the extent and nature of online learning in American K-12 education: the research initiatives of the Alfred P. Sloan foundation. The internet and higher education
Speak up (2011) Congressional briefing: national release of speak up 2010 k-12 students and parents data. 31 Dec available from http://www.tomorrow.org/speakup/speakup_congress.html
Means B et al (2010) Evaluation of evidence-based practices in online learning: a meta-analysis and review of online learning studies
Robson R (2006) The future of standards (Slide 32)
IMS Global Consortium (2004) IMS content packaging specification, Version 1.1.4 final specification
Advanced distributed learning initiative (2004) SCORM 2004 3rd edn. US Department of Defense
McDonald WA, Hyde J, Montgomery A (2004) AICC–CMI guidelines for inter operability rev. 4.0. Aviation Industry CBT Committee
Easter by-Smith S et al (2003) IMS question and test interoperability specification v 1.2.1. IMS Global Learning Consortium
IEEE computer society learning technology standards committee , IEEE standard for learning object metadata, in IEEE Std 1484.12.1-20022002, IEEE Standards Association
Paulsson F, Berglund M (2008) Suggesting an SOA framework for modular virtual learning environments: comparing two implementation approaches. Int J Web-Based Learn Teach Technol (IJWLTT) 3(1):43–57
Severance C, Hanss T, Hardin J (2010) IMS learning tools interoperability: enabling a mash-up approach to teaching and learning tools
Alario-Hoyos C, Wilson S (2010) Comparison of the main alternatives to the integration of external tools in different platforms
IMS global learning consortium (2011) IMS Common Cartridge Specification. 27 Dec, available from http://www.imsglobal.org/cc/index.html
Rustici Software (2011) Project tin can phase 3: overview. 27 Dec, available from http://scorm.com/tincanoverview/
Jesukiewicz P, Rehak DR (2011) The learning registry: sharing federal learning resources, in interservice/industry training, simulation, and education conference 2011, National Training and Simulation Association, Florida
US Department of Education (2011) The learning registry. 27 Dec, available from http://www.learningregistry.org/
Beacham R, Denard H, Niccolucci F (2009) London charter for the computer-based visualisation of cultural heritage: glossary. 27 Dec, available from http://www.londoncharter.org/glossary.html
Gundy SV (2011) Progress report–Apr. Summary of STEM exchange initiative
Kreuter F, Paradata (2010) Previous developments and recent discussions

Connexions (2011) Connexions Tutorial and Reference 29 Dec, available from http://cnx.org/content/col10151/latest/
Hunt J (2011) DITA learning and training content specialization SC. 29 Dec, available from http://www.oasis-open.org/committees/tc_home.php?wg_abbrev=dita-learningspec
Carlisle D, Ion P, Miner R (2010) Mathematical markup language (MathML) ver 3.0 , 3rd edn. In: Ausbrooks R et al (eds) W3C recommendation
w3schools.com (2011) Browser statistics, 31 Dec, available from http://www.w3schools.com/browsers/browsers_stats.asp
Claburn T (2011) Google chrome overtakes Firefox, Information week 2011, UBM techweb
Driscoll M, Carliner S (2009) Who's creating the E-learning? Michael Allen's 2009 E-Learning Annual 44:43
Wicks M (2010) A national primer on k-12 online learning. International association for K-12 online learning
Adkins S (2012) Ambient insight's 2012 learning technology research taxonomy, research methodology, product definitions, and licensing model

Chapter 8
The Open Future of Course Content Development and Dissemination

M. S. Vijay Kumar

Abstract An emergent Open Education (OE) movement characterized by an abundance of information and interaction opportunities, as well as new connections between content, curriculum and community, presents the potential of profound impact on educational access and quality. Fueled by the affordance of networks and technology tools, OE presents the ability to overcome traditional assumptions about the development and delivery of educational resources and the opportunity to radically alter the economics and ecology of education. While the open education movement points to promising opportunities, there is clearly a need for a fresh perspective on how we think about resources and the relationships available to education to constructively leverage this new ecology blending technology and open education resources in powerful ways. This chapter builds on recent efforts at Massachusetts Institute of Technology and elsewhere illuminating some of the transformative possibilities. It also highlights some of the technological, organization, and cultural dimensions of "readiness" needing to be addressed for the promise of the open education movement to be realized.

8.1 A Prelude to Open Content

In 2001, MIT implemented research into action, making the contents of its courses open, accessible by colleagues and industry practitioners though Open Course Ware (OCW). Its bold announcement signaled the transformative possibilities of

M. S. Vijay Kumar (✉)
Office of Educational Innovation and Technology, Office of the Dean of Undergraduate Education, MIT, Cambridge, MA, USA
e-mail: vkumar@mit.edu

R. Huang et al. (eds.), *Reshaping Learning*, New Frontiers of Educational Research,
DOI: 10.1007/978-3-642-32301-0_8, © Springer-Verlag Berlin Heidelberg 2013

"open"; one of OCW's goals was to create a platform to universally raise the quality of university teaching (UNESCOPRESS 2002, para 6). Since then, the contents of over 2,000 courses have been published online and made freely available, and used by 127 million people, annually, worldwide. Over the years, OCW has demonstrated its successful impact: 32 % of MIT professors believe OCW increased the quality or organization of their own materials (Program Evaluation Findings Summary 2006). OCW is a visible and voluble signal of MIT's intent to extend open technology-enabled opportunities for expanding educational access and quality.

OCW is the most mature of the Open Educational Resources (OER) initiatives; it inspired an Open Education movement made evident by the founding of the OCW Consortium (www.ocwconsortium.org). More than 250 major institutions worldwide are now members of this consortium which includes important initiatives such as the Connexions Project from Rice Carnegie-Mellon's Open Learning Initiative and the NPTEL (http://nptel.iitm.ac.in/) initiative in India along with institutions such as Johns Hopkins, University of Notre Dame, schools in Japan, China, and Europe as well as leading institutions of open and distance learning such as UK's Open University. Collectively, the Consortium has published over 13,000 courses.

8.2 OCW: Setting the stage for OER

These growing number of open education initiatives serve as a foundation of the Open Education movement, and lead to the broad definition UNESCO introduced of Open Education Resources (OER) as "digitalized educational materials and tools freely offered for educators, students, and self-learners to use and reuse for the purposes of teaching, learning, and research-2002" . It would take the next few years for this new concept to harden with institutions—to truly understand what OER meant.

By 2007, with the Internet's progression to Web 2.0 and the growing number of openly available educational resources, the time was ripe to build the open education movement to better understand and harness its potential. However, educators were not taking full advantage of shared knowledge about how these open resources were being used, what local innovations were emerging, and how to learn from and build on the experiences of others.

In response, The Carnegie Foundation for the Advancement of Teaching and The MIT Press published *Opening Up Education: The Collective Advancement of Education through Open Technology, Open Content, and Open Knowledge,* edited by Toru Iiyoshi and M. S. Vijay Kumar. In the book's 30 essays, 40 prominent leaders and thinkers in the open education movement reflect on current and past open education initiatives, offer critical analyses, share the strategic underpinnings of their own work, and delve into open education's implications in three areas: technology, content, and knowledge. They approach–from both macro and micro perspectives–the central question of how open education tools, resources, and knowledge can improve the quality of education. The contributors also discuss the impact of their projects and strategies for sustaining open education. *Opening Up Education* argues that we must develop not only the technical capability but also the intellectual capacity for transforming tacit pedagogical knowledge into commonly usable and visible knowledge: by providing incentives for faculty to use (and contribute to) open education goods, and by looking beyond institutional boundaries to connect a variety of settings and open source entrepreneurs.

A key recommendation from the book is to explore the "transformative potential and ecological transitions of the movement-2008". A variety of recent initiatives–from small course related to large-scale national movements–illuminate the value proposition and transformative potential.

8.3 Value Proposition and Transformative Potential

Open Education initiatives and OER are changing the landscape of education, allowing new potential for the practice, implementation, and dissemination of education. It is important for institutions to investigate the implications of these initiatives for their goals of quality and scale along several dimensions, some of which are described below:

8.3.1 Curriculum Planning Models for Educators

OER initiatives such as MIT's OCW present a powerful model for educators to plan and develop curriculum. For example, OCW makes course planning materials such as syllabi and pedagogical statements, subject matter content such as lecture notes, reading lists, full-text readings, video/audio lectures, as well as problem sets, essay assignments, labs, and projects openly available and accessible. Faculty from other educational institutions including even high school instructors point to the benefit of these resources for guiding the planning and improvement of their courses. Educators and industry practitioners use OCW to better their own teaching curriculum, incorporate new resources, learn new teaching methods, or simply to improve self-knowledge (Sudan 2012 p 28, para 3).

Arguably, even more significant is the potential for the Open Education movement to advance the overall quality of educational resources by making innovative teaching transparent—much like OCW is making the structure and content of MIT courses transparent. Pedagogical innovations, often remain in isolated and in closed domains and are rarely shared across classrooms, institutions, or disciplines. The Open movement in education is revolutionizing the way that educational resources, practice, and pedagogical experience and knowledge are shared, peer-reviewed, reused, and continuously improved. OERs can also serve to provide quality benchmarks for course-content while supporting faculty development programs for capacity building in institutions and nations.

Lastly, OERs offer a new dimension to distance education, enabling extensive access to globally created educational resources that serve the knowledge needs of diverse communities. These resources, combined with distance education technologies, offer new possibilities for delivering interactive educational experiences in flexible formats and fostering communities of engagement in learning. In fact, OERs bring us closer to the vision of lifelong learning than ever before. Universities are constantly adding quality open course materials allowing more choice, which means that distance education, which has typically been treated in the formal education structure as a second-class citizen, can be as good as or even better than what we expect of a traditional, face-to-face education experience.

8.3.2 Customization and Localization through R*4

The four main attributes of open content that make OERs different and significantly more valuable than other online resources, are that OERs can be ***R***eused, ***R***evised, ***R***emixed, and ***R***edistributed. The first three of the "Rs" promote using and localizing pre-existing OERs, while the last "R" promotes the sharing within and among learning communities (David Wiley 2010). Reusing, revising, and remixing resources, as well as connecting communities of content exploration presents the opportunity for innovative activities at the intersections of domains.

Consider the following examples:

- A University of Michigan School of Information professor remixed an existing Computer Science Python textbook, licensed under an open license in only 11 days. Michigan's espresso book machine printed copies for $10.[1]
- CK-12 has produced several open textbooks called "flexbooks". Their Physics Flexbook is being used in Virginia high schools, being developed and delivered within 6 months.
- At the Open High School of Utah teachers build their customized curriculum from the ground up using OER. This innovative approach results in dynamic, courses that can be easily modified to meet the individual needs of the student. Open High not only creates curriculum from open educational resources, it even shares its curriculum with anyone worldwide, for free. The school reports that it's approach to curriculum development, coupled with its personalized teaching methods, have produced superior results as evidenced by their students' criterion-reference test (CRT) scores which were over ten points above the state average in both Science and English (Open High School of Utah 2011).

[1] Professor Charles Severance remixed an existing textbook and released it under a CC BY-SA license, to support his course using open content: http://creativecommons.org/weblog/entry/20559

8.4 Community-Based Learning

Community-based learning builds on technologies that provide intellectual and cognitive support for individuals and groups through community-based peer learning: two well-known models illuminating such opportunities are Peer 2 Peer (P2P) University[2] and Open Study.[3] The use of OER facilities alternative opportunities for structured learning because it makes high-quality content available, enabling data-driven discussions that were once only available in the framework of traditional institutions.

8.4.1 Augmented Learning

> Last semester, I had a course in metallurgical engineering. I didn't have notes, so I went to OCW. I downloaded a course outline on this, and also some review questions, and these helped me gain a deeper understanding of the material.
>
> Kunle Adejumo, Engineering student at Ahmadu Bello University, Zaria, Nigeria (MIT OCW 2012, para 7).

Through the years, the testimonies of countless students illustrate how OER is used globally to supplement classroom learning or to reinforce specific concepts. Emerging applications such as *Recommenders* (www.ocwfinder.org) and the *Spoken Media Browser* (spokenmedia.mit.edu) are increasing the capacities for learners to harvest relevant resources by enabling learners to more effectively find supplemental learning resources, or even find alternative pathways to learning.

8.4.2 Adaptive Learning Opportunities: the Long Tail Effect

The "long tail effect" describes the possibility of creating tailored, niche communities of education. By making use of openly available high quality digitized educational content and tools, we can develop customized learning experiences capable of shaping learning experiences for different contexts and for different kinds of learners—instead of the standardized "one-size-fits-all" teaching models.

---

[2] P2P University: P2P is a grassroots open education project that uses OER to make possible high-quality yet low-cost education possibilities. Essentially, it makes possible the teaching and learning by peers for peers, enabling life-long learners to give back to a community of eager learners, or learn more openly. (www.p2p.org).

[3] OpenStudy: An online social learning network, OpenStudy allows students to seek answers to questions, or to give help and connect with others. Many resources connect directly with institutions to provide online study groups for courses, such as those from MIT's OCW (. www.openstudy.com).

The OE movement creates the space and the vehicle to deliver interactive educational experiences in flexible formats—both formal and non-formal—supporting alternate ways to learn and to engage deeper learning.

8.4.3 Blended and Boundary-Less Education

OE extends education beyond the typical lines of geography and politics to cross-disciplinary lines, linking researching and teaching. Beyond the implications for scaling and localizing, this presents the promise of *blended learning environments* involving optimal combinations of the physical and virtual, integrating conventional pedagogical methods with innovative network-based learning to deliver quality educational opportunities. This can include bringing "experts" in contact with learners or even situated learning experiences, such as laboratories, real and virtual, to supplement online access to content in distance education situations. OER includes a variety of resources supporting learning, incorporating interactive content, simulations as well as hands-on activities. For instance, MIT's iLab initiative enables access to real labs without concern of distance. Labs located at MIT or elsewhere are available to learners anywhere—students in Singapore or South America, for example, are now allowed a more enriching science and engineering education experience by greatly expanding the range of experiments that students are exposed to in the course of their education. It has the potential to add new practical dimensions to on-line vocational education.

Openness also facilitates the transcending of traditional institutional as well as disciplinary boundaries to advance thematic education (e.g., directing education toward an understanding of big problems) and integrative learning (pursuing learning in more intentional, connected ways across subjects).

The implications of blended and boundary-less education for scaling excellence are particularly noteworthy in that they present the opportunity to transform and improve the notion of distance education including through blended education (US Department of Education 2010)—typically treated in the formal education structure as a second-class citizen—to be as good as or even better than traditional, situated formal education.

8.5 Real Transformation

Disruptive change happens when existing structural assumptions and relationships are dislodged. The OE and OER movement is already demonstrating their abilities to dislodge conventional and hitherto immutable relationships among factors associated with the value chain of education.

8.5.1 The Iron Triangle

Perhaps the most notable example regarding the classic assumptions between access, cost, and quality of education, is that of the *Iron Triangle*, eloquently articulated by Sir John Daniels. Simply put, we used to believe that increased access leads to diminished quality, or that an increase in high-quality resources leads to increased costs. However, through the agency of OER and community, we see these assumptions being challenged. And he paints a brilliant picture of the promise of open education: "Open education broke open the iron triangle of access, cost and quality that had constrained education throughout history and had created the insidious assumption, still prevalent today, that in education you cannot have quality without exclusivity. Each subsequent technology has made those economies of scale even more impressive and recast even more radically the iron triangle. Web distribution of learning materials is almost cost free. Electronic communication between students and institutions means that feedback, a vital part of learning, is faster and cheaper. The result is that today the major obstacle to open education, because it is the major cost factor, is the creation of good learning materials. Here there are fewer technological short cuts, because the design of courses that are academically current, intellectually attractive and pedagogically efficient will always require serious investment of human brainpower. The answer is not to skimp on the brainpower, but to make the products of that brainpower more widely available (Ahrash Bissell 2008, para 3)".

8.5.2 Distributed Learning Opportunities

OER shifts the attention from teaching to learning as the dominant vehicle for delivering educational opportunities. A variety of distributed learning opportunities are breaking the traditional, strict provider-consumer relationship between learner and intuition and challenges past notions of who learns, how they learn, and when they're learning. Just-in-time and flexible self-learning opportunities for individuals and for self-organized communities—such as P2P U—are made possible by the abundance of content and relationships; network-enabled learning illustrates this.

8.5.3 Disaggregation and Diversity of Credentialing Models

A significant, even if subtle, traditional education relationship being disrupted is the role institutions historically have had with respect to "credentialing". We are beginning to witness new models of affirming and certifying knowledge, including both a separation of institutions that deliver education opportunities from those that provide credentials—as well as the emergence of differentiated credentials, such as badges and certificates reflecting varieties of learning opportunities available.

The recent launch of several initiatives is illustrative of the shifts in alternative delivery and credentialing models. In addition to P2P University using badges, the following examples use new ways to certify knowledge:

- Khan Academy, a popular open, online video-based lessons resource for everything from mathematics to physics, rewards learners for watching instructional videos. Students are even provided opportunities to complete online, standardized tests to earn master or challenge patches.
- Recently, MIT and Harvard announced their partnership to create edX, developing an open-source platform to deliver online courses. Such collaborative efforts provide high-quality, online self-learning systems where students can earn certificates by taking tests based on free OCW is a glimpse to what the OE movement can provide. edX builds on MITx, which was announced a few months prior.
- OpenStudy, which also partners with MIT OCW, awards online badges for students that support others, providing useful answers and insights.

The increased agency of the online community afforded by open resources is becoming an important factor in the changing relationship between learners and institutions.

8.5.4 Large Scale Transformation

The emerging educational landscape is characterized by several demand factors that render it ripe for taking advantage of the transformational potential of open education. These factors include the following:

- An aggressive development agenda of nations requiring radical solutions to address the needs of educational access and quality,
- The unaffordable and unmanageable cost of education,
- Agility needed for rapidly changing knowledge and skills,
- A new generation of diverse learners.

The recognition that OE potentially addresses these and that OE delivers large scale change is reflected not only through the institutional initiatives mentioned above but also through the national and global initiatives such as those of the Commonwealth of Learning, UNESCO, the US Department of Labor and India's National Knowledge Commission (2012) for whom the use of OER is a key strategy to meet important educational challenges.

8.5.4.1 Readiness

Several "readiness" considerations, e.g., technical and cultural challenges that affect adoption, need to be addressed for us to realize the value proposition of OER including open course content.

For instance, despite the extensive availability of content, the challenge remains of effectively finding, assessing and making the best use of these resources in one's own educational context, whether from the perspective of a teacher or a learner.

Even if potentially useful content were to be located, it is not always easy to *get* them or *use* them either due to intellectual property (IP) restrictions or technical barriers.

Technical design aspects often limit the portability and interoperability of learning resources even if they are openly accessible, and consequently inhibit the kind of flexibility that leads to support of diverse pedagogy and sharing of learning materials. Learning resources created in one setting cannot be easily used in different contexts or to address different learning goals. Recommendation Systems as well as the "wisdom of the crowds" can help address this to some extent.[4] There is more work that needs to be done to map content to Learning Outcomes.

There are some illustrative areas of technical development that show promise in support curricular communities of practice and more effective use of open educational content:

i. OER Harvesting: there has been exciting work in the use of "intelligent" crawlers, semantic technologies and other means of automatically investigating and tagging educational content. Integrating this work would relieve the burdensome aspects of marking up and classifying materials.
ii. Collective Intelligence Systems[5]: social tagging and social networking tools offer new opportunities for collecting information about content to help teachers and student more quickly find useful materials. Such systems, if appropriately linked with the repositories that host OER content, can allow curricular communities to come together to share content and also information about the quality and use of content to meet educational objects of common interest.
iii. Content Federation and Re-aggregation: once data and services are in place to make identification of content for use in teaching and learning easier it is critical that we also make it easier for faculty and students to incorporate this content with the software tools and online environments that educators find useful in their everyday work. Ongoing work within MIT's Office of

---

[4] See OCW Finder (www.ocwfinder.org), OCW Consortium (www.ocwconsortium.org/use/use-dynamic.html), OER Recommender (www.oerrecommender.org).

[5] Examples of Collective Intelligence System include OER Commons (www.oercommons.org) and Folksemantic (www.folksemantic.com).

Educational Innovation and Technology (OEIT), stemming from the O.K.I. project among others, focuses on the problem of federated searching for content and aggregation of content from multiple sources within content authoring, visualization and course management tools.

iv. Advancing Concept-Content Linkages: the recently launched MIT Core Concept Catalog (MC3) project (http://oeit.mit.edu/gallery/projects/core-concept-catalog-mc3) is designed to explore and enhance re-use of OER like OCW and other online educational content or activities, from the perspective of core curricular concepts and learning objectives/outcomes. The end goal of current MC3 efforts is the ability for a teacher or learner to search, browse and/or otherwise navigate educational resources based on the criteria of educational objectives for a particular class, discipline or field of study. From a teacher's perspective it is designed to facilitate the re-use of cross-disciplinary content in the preparation of course materials. For students it is designed to allow for efficient navigation of the vast and growing collection of OER content to help augment and deepen understanding. This initial MC3 project is producing a proof-of-concept application to create and manage a set of curricular concepts and learning objectives for a subject or field of study and facilitate mapping of these objectives to OER content.

There are other more subtle but significant challenges in converting OER to productive educational experiences. An important consideration is determining how can we make good practice and useful knowledge of teaching and learning visible and shareable? Furthermore, how can we openly share the tacit knowledge that underlies educational resources?

A significant factor that militates against realizing the potent opportunities of open education is the inertia of our current culture and practice of education. Our instructional practices and even business models for education are based on a "scarcity paradigm"—they assume that resources available to education—content, contact, labs and so forth—will be scarce. The Open movement shifts this notion by making quality resources, relationships and community extensively available suggests an "abundance paradigm" and requires that we recast our approaches accordingly.

8.6 Conclusion

Clearly the Open Education movement and the implications for open course content demand a fresh perspective on resources and relationships and a recasting of traditional roles available to education. More importantly we must understand that Open Education is an opportunity towards broadening and deepening our collective understanding of teaching and learning. Difficult and uncharted as the terrain appears, we anticipate at least three dramatic improvements over time: increased quality of tools and resources, more effective use, and greater individual and collective pedagogical knowledge. Ideally, all will occur concurrently, combining local innovations and learned lessons through global knowledge sharing (2008).

References

About National Knowledge Commission (2012) Retrieved May 21, 2012, from http://www.knowledgecommission.gov.in/about/default.asp

Learning Studies (2010) *US Department of Education*. Retrieved May 1, 2012, from http://www2.ed.gov/rschstat/eval/tech/evidence-based-practices/finalreport.pdf

Bissell A (2008) *Sir John Daniel Comments on Open Education*. Retrieved April 22, 2012, from http://creativecommons.org/weblog/entry/8139

Kunle A (2012) *MIT OCW*. Retrieved April 21, 2012, from http://ocw.mit.edu/about/ocw-stories/kunle-adejumo/

Program Evaluation Findings Summary (2006) *MIT OCW*. Retrieved April 23, 2012,from http://ocw.mit.edu/ans7870/global/05_Eval_Summary.pdf

Open High School of Utah (2011) Retrieved April 21, 2012, from http://www.openhighschool.org/open-high-school-of-utah-wins-best-of-state-award-for-curriculum-development/

Sudan SA (2012) Opening up Education: a Case for School Leaders. Unpublished senior thesis, Harvard University, Cambridge, MA

Wiley D (2010) Openness as a Catalyst for an Educational Reform. EDUCASE Review 45(4): 14–20

UNESCOPRESS (2002) Retrieved March 24, 2012, from http://portal.unesco.org/en/ev.php-URL_ID=4316&URL_DO=DO_PRINTPAGE&RL_SECTION=201.html

Author Biography

Dr. M.S. Vijay Kumar Senior Associate Dean, Director, Office of Educational Innovation and Technology, Office of the Dean of Undergraduate Education, MIT. (Cambridge, MA, USA).http://web.mit.edu/~vkumar/www/

Doctorate, Education (Future Studies), University of Massachusetts, Amherst. (Massachusetts).

MS, Industrial Management, Indian Institute of Technology (IIT), Madras. (India).

B. Tech. in Chemical Engineering, Indian Institute of Technology (IIT), Madras. (India).

Alek Sudan

Research Associate; Bachelor of Liberal Arts, Educational Technologies Minor, Extension Studies, Harvard University. (Cambridge, MA, USA).

Chapter 9
Pilot Curriculum in China: The Practice of Promoting the Quality of Higher Education

Yanyan Li, Yue Zhou and Lanfang Zeng

Abstract The issue of quality has drawn great attention of the nations around the world in the process of the popularization of higher education. China has launched the construction and assessment of National Pilot Curriculum (NPC) as one of the measures to solve the quality issue of higher education. This chapter first introduces the initiative background of the construction of NPC in China and analyzes the challenges of higher education in the process of popularization in China. Then it presents the quality assessment framework to identify a curriculum as NPC, and summarizes the supporting role of the construction of NPC in promoting the quality of higher education in China. In order to further reveal the impact of the construction of NPC on the quality of Chinese higher education, this chapter also briefly reports two studies that adopt content analysis and survey investigation separately to study the changes of the instructional methods in universities and the ways of resource sharing in the construction of NPC. It can be concluded that the construction of NPC is an innovative movement implemented in China to solve the quality issue of higher education, which has certain values for reference to the policy efforts, faculty development activities in universities, open courseware movement, and other related work in the perspective of quality assurance system.

Y. Li (✉)
School of Educational Technology, Beijing Normal University, Beijing, People's Republic of China
e-mail: Liyy1114@gmail.com

Y. Zhou
Media College, Inner Mongolia Normal University, Huhhot, Inner Mongolia, People's Republic of China
e-mail: zhouyue715@qq.com

L. Zeng
Faculaty of Education, Beijing Normal University, Beijing, People's Republic of China
e-mail: zenglf@bnu.edu.cn

R. Huang et al. (eds.), *Reshaping Learning*, New Frontiers of Educational Research,
DOI: 10.1007/978-3-642-32301-0_9,

Keywords National pilot curriculum · Higher education · Quality · Quality assessment framework

9.1 Introduction

In face of the development trend of higher education all over the world, Martin Trow, the American educational sociologist proposed the 'Theory of Stages in the Development of Higher Education' based on the development law of higher education in Europe and the U.S. In his view, when the gross enrollment rate of higher education is between 15 and 50 %, the development of higher education is at the stage of popularization, but when it is over 50 %, it indicates that higher education in that country has entered the stage of dissemination (Trow 1972). In 1940, the gross enrollment rate of higher education in U.S. was over 15 % and rose up to 50 % in 1971. By 2002, the development of higher education in 33 member countries of UNESCO in Asia–Pacific region had been generally divided into three conditions. A few countries, mainly developed countries such as Australia, Japan, New Zealand, South Korea are close to or moving forward to the goal of the dissemination of higher education. A considerable proportion of developing countries have entered the threshold of the popularization stage of higher education. Most countries are facing serious challenges of realizing the popularization of higher education, such as China, India, Pakistan, and Bangladesh (Wang 2002).

As a populous country, the gross enrollment rate of higher education in China in 1998 was only 9.7 %. In 1999, the Ministry of Education (MOE) of China began to expand the enrollment scale of higher education to guide higher education in China to the path of popularization. In the next ten years, the gross enrollment rate of higher education in China has developed rapidly. In 2002, the gross enrollment rate of higher education in China reached 15 %, and in 2008, it reached 23.3 %. In 2010, the number of on-campus students in all kinds of higher education institutions in China reached 31.05 million, with the gross enrollment rate at 26.5 %. By that time, China had entered the popularization stage of higher education (China Education 2011).

In the popularization of higher education, along with the growth of the number of on-campus students in higher education institutions, the quality issues of higher education gradually emerge. Many countries including the U.S. have faced the criticism in the public opinion because of the quality of higher education. UNESCO puts forward in the "Policy Document on the Reform and Development of Higher Education" that "the quality issues involve all major functions and activities of higher education, which ultimately depend on the quality of the faculty, curriculum and students, as well as that of the infrastructure and academic environment".

In developing countries like China, due to the relatively low level of economic, higher education in the process of popularization have to face more challenges. For instance, the number of students increases rapidly in the short term, which causes the decrease of the indicators of infrastructure such as the ratio of teachers and students in universities, and the number of teaching equipment for each student and so on to some extents. Especially, the popularization of higher education put forwards new challenges for the quality of teachers (such as knowledge, abilities and skills). It is a requirement for the capability of the teachers today that how to change the teacher-centered and impartation-and-acceptance-based teaching mode to the student-centered and inquiry-and-collaboration-based teaching mode. It is well known that the characteristics of the students are also undergoing changes in the process of the popularization of higher education. Most present college students are "digital natives" or "net generation" (Bennett and Maton 2008), who have strong personalities, are able to quickly receive information and like to deal with a variety of tasks at the same time (Prensky and Hu Zhibiao 2009). In many cases, they have received more information and learned more knowledge on the Internet than their teachers. Therefore, how to adapt to the new learners to improve the quality of teaching becomes an important issue.

Accompanied with the development of the scale of higher education, the countries around the world actively promote the reform in the field of higher education. In the national reform of higher education, curriculum quality assurance has always been a top priority, which is the core element in the quality assurance system of higher education. Massachusetts Institute of Technology started Open Course Ware (OCW) Program in 2000, while the UK started OU-OCI Programme in 2006 and France, Japan, Vietnam and other countries also launched the OCW courses.

In order to effectively solve the problems emerged in the process of the popularization of higher education, China has made great efforts in a number of ways, such as carrying out assessments of universities, increasing funding, changing the concept of quality and constructing quality assurance system and so on. In 2003, the MOE of China formulated "Action Plan for the Revitalization of Education 2003–2007", pointing out that we should vigorously implement "the project on instructional quality and instructional reform of higher education". In the same year, the MOE of China has started the construction of pilot curriculum as one of the important part of the above project, aiming to realize the sharing of excellent learning resources and improving the quality of teaching in higher education institutions and talent education by the construction and assessment of pilot curricula available for free.

The project requires the provinces, autonomous regions and municipal cities and even universities to formulate curriculum construction plan and execute the implementation so as to constitute a three-level assessment system. The curricula construction and assessment at the university level and provincial or municipal level are considered as the pre-selection of the assessment of NPC. There are three types of pilot curricula, which are regular undergraduate, vocational college and online education, and the pilot curricula of regular undergraduate take a larger part of the total number. The NPC focus on seven aspects: set scientific construction plan, strengthen the construction of teaching team, emphasize teaching content and

Table 9.1 The annual number of national pilot curricula from 2003 to 2010

Years	2003	2004	2005	2006	2007	2008	2009	2010
The number of national pilot curricula	151	299	298	360	660	649	648	725
The number of national pilot curricula for undergraduates	127	248	239	254	411	400	404	442

curriculum system reform, emphasize the utilization of advanced teaching methods and means, emphasize the construction of teaching materials, attach importance to both theoretical teaching and practical teaching as well as establish an effective incentive and assessment mechanism.

During the eight years from 2003 to 2010, China has developed 3790 NPC, among which 2525 NPC are for regular undergraduates, and 1265 NPC are for vocational colleges and online education. The annual number of NPC is shown in Table 9.1. In addition, pilot curricula are developed in terms of the university level and provincial or municipal level, and the total number of pilot curricula is 10 times far more than NPC.

9.2 How to Identify a Curriculum as a NPC

In the wave of the construction and reform of the curriculum and instruction, how to assure the quality of the curriculum becomes an important issue. Curriculum assessment is an important method of examining the curriculum quality. What kind of curriculum assessment can be used to examine and screen out pilot curriculum from a large number of candidate curricula becomes an important issue.

In the process of rapid development of OCW movement, the quality of OCW are mainly assessed from the perspectives of project impact and its application via project assessment, with less focus on the assessment of the quality of contents, such as the report of OCW assessment results by MIT (2005, 2009), the report of the assessment of AAIUAAIC project team in Beijing (2005), etc. Those curriculum assessments are mostly done by themselves, without the involvement of a third party. For instance, the assessment of MIT is mainly organized by OCW themselves. In addition, the foreign countries have carried out a large number of analysis and studies on the quality of curriculum for higher education. For instance, based on the framework of TQM and ISO 9000, the 90-Day Work Group Report submitted by the Course Quality Assurance Group of the University of Alaska Steering Board in March 2005,[1] discusses the quality policy of the university, analyzes the quality system of the university and formulates the criteria for the curriculum assessment in UAA, including institutional support services,

[1] 90-Day Work Group Report of Course Quality Assurance Group, University of Alaska Steering Board, [EB/OL] www.alaska.edu, March 28–29, 2005.

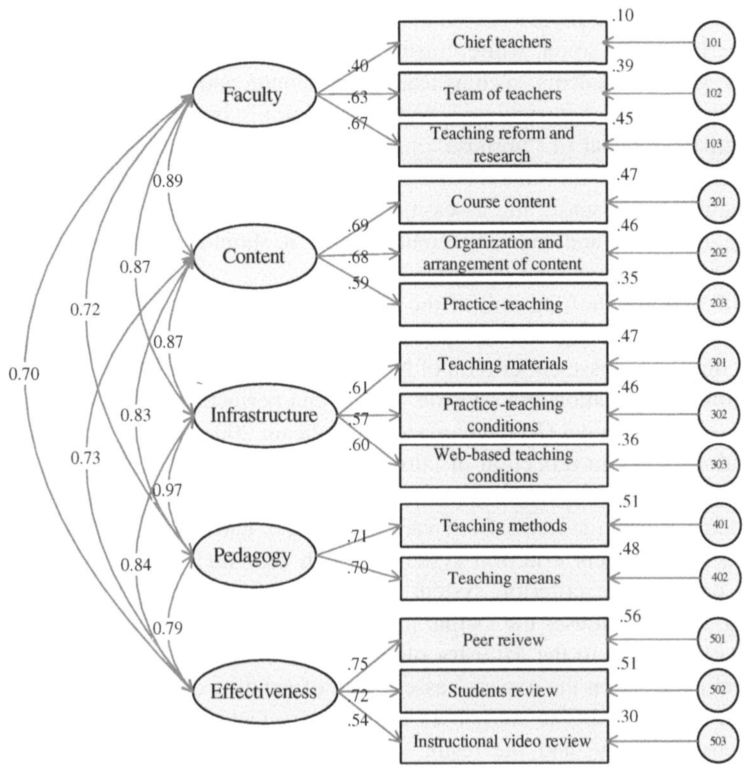

Fig. 9.1 FCIPEs quality assessment framework

student support services, faculty support services, course content & course delivery, and students participation and so on. QUT has developed guidelines for course quality assurance, which intends to examine the curriculum quality from the following aspects, such as individual course performance reports, faculty academic program reports, the faculty review process and so on.[2]

The proper understanding of the concept of "curriculum" is the basis of the formulation of curriculum assessment indicator system that is the key to effective assessment. However, there is not a unified definition of curriculum. By summarizing the various viewpoints, Connelly and Lantz point out that there are at least nine different definitions of curriculum (Connelly and Lantz 1985). Bingde defines curriculum as "the content outline and objective system of classroom instruction, extra-curricular learning and self-study activities, which is the overall plan and its process of all kinds of learning activities of instruction and students" (Bingde 1991). Compared with the concept of "instruction", "curriculum" emphasizes

[2] Guidelines for Course Quality Assurance, Academic Quality Officer of QUT, [EB/OL] www.appu.qut.edu.au, Last Updated: March 2007.

more on the learning objectives, contents and scopes, such as knowledge, activity and experience and so on, while "instruction" mainly focuses on the behavior of teachers' guiding students, such as teaching, dialogue and guidance and so on, so the relationship of "curriculum" and "instruction" is more in line with the characteristics of that of "purpose" and "means". Therefore, curriculum assessment cannot ignore the characteristics of instructional process included in the curriculum. In this sense, the assessment of pilot courses cannot be confined to teaching materials and teaching contents, but it should include the important features of the instructional process.

In 2003, as the drafting unit of the criterion formulation, Research Center for Knowledge Engineering of Beijing Normal University with other parties finished the first draft of assessment criteria of NPC in three stages, which are investigation and drafting, verification and revision, testing and perfection with reference to the CIPP assessment model (Kellaghan and Stufflebeam 2003). The study extracts 10 observation points in reflection of curriculum quality, such as the faculty, infrastructure, and teaching management, by analyzing more than 20 curriculum assessment criterion systems from various colleges and universities in China. It establishes assessment criterion system through the Analytic Hierarchy Process (AHP), presents the criterion system in the form of descriptive level criterion (Kedong 2003), then uses the Delphi method to constantly modify and refine, and finally is submitted to the Ministry of Education in China. Zhang (2007) makes statistical analysis on the experts' assessment of submitted curriculum during the period of 2003–2006. The study uses confirmatory factor analysis to examine the constructive validity, and the result show that the constructive validity of the assessment indicator system is good. Figure 9.1 shows the FCIPEs Quality Assessment Framework.

The FCIPEs is the core quality characteristics of NPC, which is released as the assessment indicators of NPC after the revision by MOE of China. Table 9.2 lists the assessment indicators of NPC for undergraduates,[3] and detailed contents are listed in Appendix 1.

9.3 The Support of Pilot Curriculum Construction to the Enhancement of the Quality of Higher Education

The project of NPC construction plays an active role in the solution to the quality issues of higher education in China. In order to have more curriculum be selected as NPC, universities pay more attention to the instruction with support of policy,

[3] The assessment index system of pilot curriculum and exquisite curricula network education in higher vocational and professional college is enacted separately. National quality course evaluation index of network education (2010) http://www.cwnu.edu.cn/jpkc/15.doc, national quality course evaluation index of higher vocational education (2010) http://www.zztrc.edu.cn/kyws/wenzhang/Upfiles/20103594013720.doc.

Table 9.2 Assessment indicators of national pilot curriculum (Undergraduate 2010)

Class-A Indicators	The Scores of Class-B Indicators
Faculty 20%	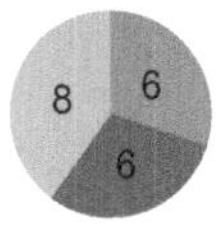 Curriculum manager and teacher Structure and quality of teaching team Teaching reform and research
Content 20%	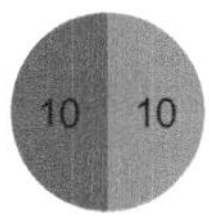 Curriculum content Organization of content
Infrastructure 20%	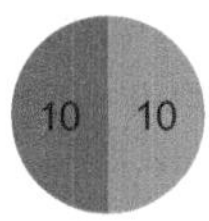 Teaching materials, references, and experimental condition Web-based learning environment
Pedagogy 20%	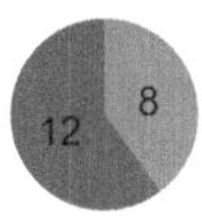 Instructional design Teaching methods
Effectiveness 20%	 Peer review Students' review Instructional video review

funding and personnel, etc. They have invested more and more funding in the curriculum construction so as to significantly improve the basic infrastructure like the number of instructional equipment per student, and to inspire some professors who focus on research but ignore teaching to undertake teaching undergraduates. From 2003 to 2010, a total of 20,000 professors and associate professors participate in the construction and instruction of more than 2,000 NPC for more than once, and the number of professors in the teaching team of each NPC on average rise from 4 in 2003 to 5 in 2010 (Yue 2011). A great number of university teachers constitute teaching teams and devote more time and energy to the instruction. They study on the instructional reform and apply the research results in the practical teaching, which greatly promotes the instructional reform and informatization construction in the universities. NPC provides the demonstration of instructional process for teachers in many subjects. In order to give a good lesson, many teachers refer to similar NPC. According to the investigation of the project team of "Research on the Sharing and Application Mechanism of NPC", the resources that teachers most want to refer to are courseware, followed by lesson plans, syllabus, experiment guidance, instructional videos, examination and test, and the list of references and so on (Lanfang et al. 2010). In this way, the holistic faculty structure changed. Besides, the content, pedagogy and instructional administration gain more attentions and get improved.

Many organizations carry out corresponding trainings. The Network Training Center for Teachers of National Higher Education affiliated to China Higher Education Press carries out 130 cycles of trainings on nationwide network teacher trainings, with a total of over 35,000 trainees, and organizes over 50 online discussions on the experience sharing and exchange of the construction of pilot curriculum resources with satisfactory effects.[4] The Steering Committee of the Instruction of Various Disciplines affiliated to MOE of China plays a positive role in the process of construction and sharing of pilot curriculum. They organize face-to-face trainings of pilot curriculum many times in a number of cities including Hangzhou, Changsha and Jinan, involving curriculum in the majors of computers and medical sciences with almost one thousand trainees. They also organize or participate in a number of teacher trainings and experience exchange meetings of pilot curriculum and are invited to give reports on the experience on the pilot curriculum construction all over China for dozens of times. The teachers who participate in the trainings or the meetings generally reflect that such kind of trainings and exchanges are very helpful to broaden their horizons and enhance their instructional capability.

On the other hand, diverse websites have been built for large-scale sharing of NPC instructional resources. Department of Higher Education of MOE of China build the website of "Construction of National Pilot Curriculum of Higher Education" for the assessment and publication of curriculum (http://www.jpkcnet.com), establishes the Resource Center for NPC and sets up NPC Resource Network (http://www.jingpinke.com). China Open Resources of Education (CORE) also take the pilot curriculum resources as an important part of open educational resources and designs corresponding column on the website. Universities and colleges also open the column of "pilot curriculum" on the university website, among which nearly half of NPC have independent curriculum websites. These specialized websites or columns become an important platform for sharing instructional resources of pilot curriculum. According to the statistics, by July 2008, the Construction Network of National Pilot Curriculum of Higher Education" (www.jpkcnet.com) and the sharing system of NPC resources (http://www.jingpinke.com, http://166.111.229.73/courses/) have been visited for a total of more than 300 million times (Aihua et al. 2008). With the constant increase of the average daily visits, a growing number of students, teachers and other off-campus learners will benefit from pilot curriculum.

---

[4] The sub-project of national pilot curriculum "national pilot curriculum shared service and sustainable development" concluding report.

Online sharing and the above-mentioned trainings play an important role in the development of teacher profession and the elevation of their instruction, especially for the fostering of young teachers. The instructional level of young teachers who participate in the construction of NPC is significantly enhanced through funding academic exchanges, organizing the interaction of listening and assessing lessons and arranging relevant research projects. The young teachers who refer to the instructional resources of NPC consciously study each part of the curriculum for reflection and comparison, which is very helpful for them to become reflective teachers and to develop their professions.

Furthermore, university students often visit the websites of pilot curriculum of various types and levels due to their personal interests, recommendation of their teachers and reference to curriculum selection. According to the investigation of the project team of "Research on the Sharing and Application Mechanism of NPC", the curriculum resources in which students have great interests are lecture scripts, followed by exercises, recommended extra-curricular books, instructional videos, and syllabus and so on. The person in charge of the "Electronic Technology Foundation" of NPC, Peng Rongxiu from Central China University of Science and Technology says, "the pilot is featured with the five most, among which advanced pedagogy is most popular in carrying out inspiring instructional activities and helping students to develop their independent learning capability". The construction of NPC facilitates the fostering of talents in universities. Students can deepen their systematic understandings of curriculum contents by self-selection of the instructional resources of NPC, and it is most important to foster their capability of web-based self-learning.

9.4 NPC Motivate the Changes of Pedagogy in Universities

The construction of pilot curriculum motivates the changes of the pedagogy in universities. The studies indicate that in the construction of pilot curriculum, university teachers devote more and more time and energy to the instruction. Besides basic instruction and contents updating, they are more committed to the innovation and exploration of pedagogy and pay more attention to the active role of digital learning resources in the instruction, so that the pedagogy, instructional resource sharing and promotion modes are changed, which may have greater significance.

9.4.1 The Change of Pedagogy in Universities

Research Center for Knowledge Engineering of Beijing Normal University finds out that in the process of pilot curriculum construction, the instructional philosophy and pedagogy for undergraduates increasingly concerns the trend of student learning, which facilitates rapid development of self-learning pedagogy, and the application of the network has profound impact on the changes of the pedagogy for the undergraduates. The construction of pilot curriculum also has important influence on the ways in which university teachers construct, share and promote instructional resources.

In 2008, Research Center for Knowledge Engineering of Beijing Normal University take a sampling strategy of every two years to carry out the content analysis of 339 applications of pilot curriculum in the years of 2004, 2006 and 2008. Each content is analyzed by three persons and then tested reliability on the computers, which results in the reliability of all items greater than 0.8. Based on the classification of pedagogy in universities, the study extracts corresponding descriptions in the applications of pilot curriculum for labeling and encoding in order to acquire the data of different types of pedagogy distributed in different years to reflect the changing trends of the pedagogy of pilot curriculum (Ronghuai et al. 2010).

The study divides the university pedagogy into imparting teaching method, visualization teaching method, experience-enhancing teaching method and practical teaching method according to the effective access to learning experience and the learning methods of students (as shown in Fig. 9.2). Besides, instructional scenarios can be divided into abstract scenarios and concrete scenarios based on the degree of abstraction of instructional scenarios required by the pedagogy, in consideration of the focus on student learning in specific pedagogy, so the pedagogy can be divided into four types, which are abstract-acceptance teaching method, abstract-inquiry teaching method, concrete-acceptance teaching method and concrete-inquiry teaching method (as shown in Fig. 9.3).

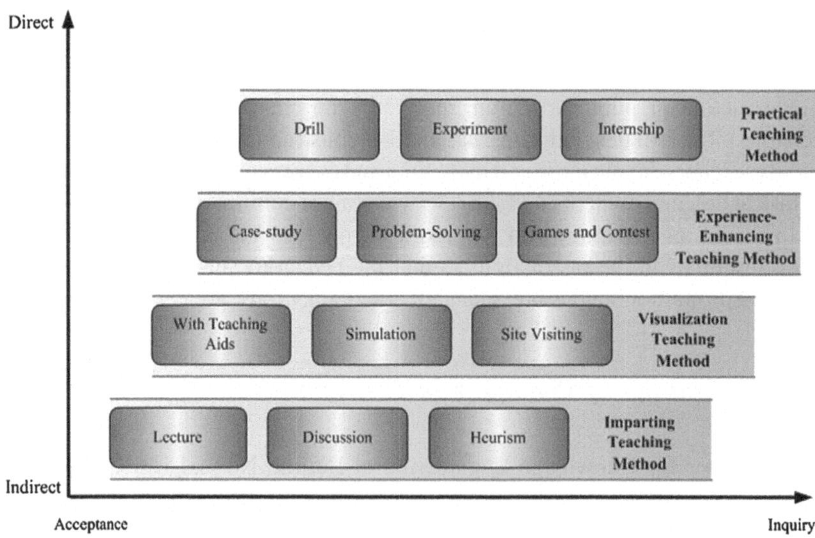

Fig. 9.2 Categories of teaching methods based on the sources of learning experience and learning styles of students

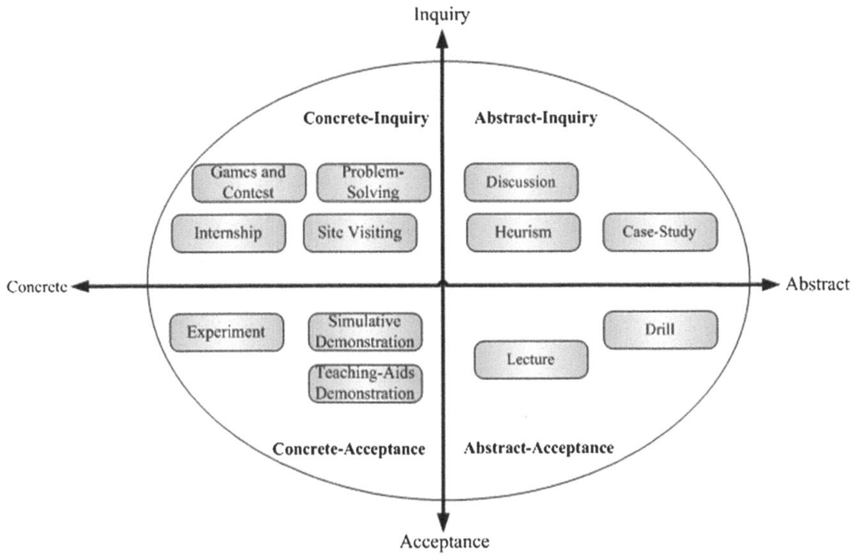

Fig. 9.3 Categories of teaching methods based on the learning scenarios and learning styles of students

The analysis shows that there is a tendency of changes in the pedagogy for Chinese undergraduates, which can be seen in the following three aspects.

First of all, as shown in Table 9.3, regarding the aspect of the changes in pedagogy, in the period of 2004 to 2008, the proportion of curriculum using discussion, site visiting, case study and problem solving for undergraduate rises significantly, especially shown in the comparison of that in 2004 and in 2008 (MD = 0.19, $p = 0.002$;MD = 0.18, $p = 0.000$; MD = 0.15; $p = 0.023$; MD = 0.19, $p = 0.000$). From the annual changes of different types of pedagogy, experience-enhancing teaching method in 2008 increases significantly compared with that in 2004 (MD = 0.25, $p = 0.000$), and practical teaching method in 2008 increases significantly compared with that in 2006 (MD = 0.15, $p = 0.02$). Besides, the site visiting of visualization teaching method and discussion of imparting teaching method shows significant growth in every two years. All the above shows the instruction of Chinese universities focuses more and more on teacher-student interaction, students' experience and practice. On the other hand, the growth of pedagogy in universities mainly occurs in the concrete-inquiry teaching method and abstract-inquiry teaching method, which indicates that the pedagogy used in Chinese universities emphasizes more on students' independent inquiry learning.

Secondly, as shown in Table 9.4, concerning the changes in the organizational forms, the proportion of curriculum that use social practice, involving students in scientific research and outdoor class appears gradually increasing trend. The proportion of curriculum that use social practice and outdoor class increases

Table 9.3 Annual changes of pedagogy

Type of pedagogy	Pedagogy	Percentage (%)		
		2004	2006	2008
Imparting teaching method	Lecture	100	100	100
	Discussion	56.3	77.2	75.2
	Heurism	25	71.9	40.2
Visualization teaching method	Simulation	68.5	91.2	58.1
	Site visiting	0.9	6.1	18.8
Experience enhancing teaching method	Case-study	29.6	41.2	44.4
	Problem-solving	6.5	28.1	25.6
	Games and contest	2.8	1.8	7.7
Practical teaching method	Drill	12	12.3	20.5
	Experiment	13.9	7.0	12.0
	Internship	2.8	6.1	6.8

Table 9.4 Annual changes of the forms of teaching organization

Years	Outdoor class (%)	Group learning (%)	Social practice (%)	Scientific research (%)
2004	3.7	9.3	5.6	2.8
2006	7.0	29.8	13.2	6.1
2008	23.1	25.6	17.9	6.8

significantly in 2008 compared with that in 2004 (MD = 0.12, $p = 0.005$; MD = 0.19, $p = 0.000$), which indicates that the organizational form of Chinese universities pay more attention to the development tendency of the curricular and extracurricular combination and on-campus and off-campus linkage.

Thirdly, as shown in Table 9.5, in the aspect of the changes of assessment method, the proportion of NPC that use assignments, tests, products, curriculum papers as the means of assessment shows a gradual increasing tendency from 2004 to 2008, which indicates that the assessment methods in Chinese universities are developing towards the diversification. Therefore, teaching methods emphasizing students' participation and experience are more frequently applied in NPC. In recent years, the uses of teaching methods, teaching organization forms and assessment methods in the instructional process emphasize more and more on the teacher-student interaction and students' dominant position, which is developing in the direction of students' self-learning.

The study also finds out that the application of the network has profound impact on the changes of the pedagogy for undergraduates. Table 9.6 shows the annual changes of the network application. Compared with that in 2004, the proportion of network application in pilot curriculum in 2008 with the purpose of interaction, tests and assessment and practice all increases, especially significantly in interaction, test and assessment, which indicates that the network is more and more widely applied in promoting teacher-student interaction and students' self-learning

Table 9.5 Annual changes of assessment methods

Years	Assignments (%)	Tests (%)	Products (%)	Curriculum papers (%)
2004	10.2	3.7	2.8	14.8
2006	56.1	31.6	16.7	25.4
2008	47.0	35.9	29.9	26.5

Table 9.6 Annual changes of the network application

Years	Delivering resources		Interaction		Tests and assessment		Practice	
	Frequency	Percentage (%)	Frequency	Percentage (%)	Frequency	Percentage (%)	Frequency	Percentage (%)
2004	105	97.2	44	40.7	27	25.0	6	5.6
2006	105	92.1	71	62.3	32	28.1	6	5.3
2008	116	99.1	82	70.1	43	36.8	8	6.8

and becomes an important prerequisite for "the instruction of Chinese universities focus more and more on teacher-student interaction and allowing students to take initiative in learning".

National pilot curriculum is a demonstration course with top-ranking teacher teams, teaching contents, teaching methods, teaching materials as well as teaching management in higher education. It can be found that, in recent years, Chinese university courses pay more attention on students' participation, experiential pedagogy, and interaction between teachers and students. In addition, Web application has made objective influence on the pedagogy reform, just as the first World Conference on Higher Education in the late twentieth century reports that the rapid development of the new information and communication technology has not only changed the knowledge development, knowledge accessing and delivery channel but also provided opportunities for curriculum innovation and pedagogy as well as expanding higher education opportunities (Zhao 1998). Therefore, how to use web-based learning platform and digital resources for teachers and students is an important task of the universities to promote the undergraduate teaching reform.

9.4.2 The Changes of Instructional Resource Construction, and the Approaches of Sharing and Promotion

The researchers believe that the development of Chinese higher education informalization has passed from infrastructure construction to the digital resources construction and IT application stage (Li 2008; Zhenzhong 2006; Huang et al. 2007)

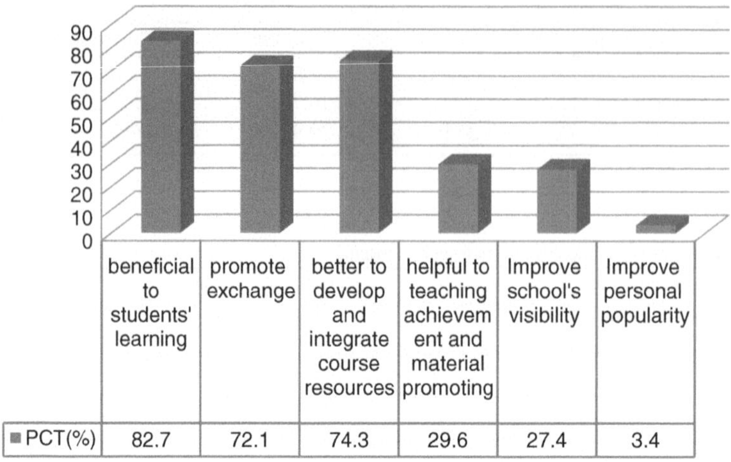

Fig. 9.4 The recognition of NPC teachers about effect of NPC resource sharing

During June and September 2008, Research Center for Knowledge Engineering of Beijing Normal University carried out a questionnaire survey among the NPC faculty,[5] expecting to acquire their opinions on the development requirement and sharing wishes. The questionnaire involves their feedbacks on three aspects, which are the sharing effectiveness of curriculum resources, the construction and update of curriculum resources, and the application and promotion of curriculum resources. Teachers of NPC from 12 universities complete the questionnaire, with a total of 184 valid questionnaires received. The study finds out that (Zeng et al. 2010):

1. The teachers of NPC recognize that the sharing of pilot curriculum resources has positive impact on teaching. They think that the sharing of pilot curriculum resources is helpful for students' learning (82.7 %), followed by the development and integration of instructional resources (74.3 %), and the promotion of exchanges among fellow teachers (72.1 %). At the same time, 90.8 % of them consider that the construction of NPC has largely promoted their instruction. Figure 9.4 shows the statistics results of NPC teachers' recognition about effect of NPC resource sharing.
2. The NPC teachers are willing to share curriculum resources, but they have different opinions on the degree of the permission of open resources. They basically agree with the display and download of curriculum resources, but they disagree with the modification of the contents by the other users. As shown in Fig. 9.5, 45.1 % of them welcome the sharing ways of browsing and downloading without modification, 31.5 % tend to agree with browsing without downloading and 18.5 % agree with browsing, downloading and modification.

[5] Chief teachers in pilot curriculum.

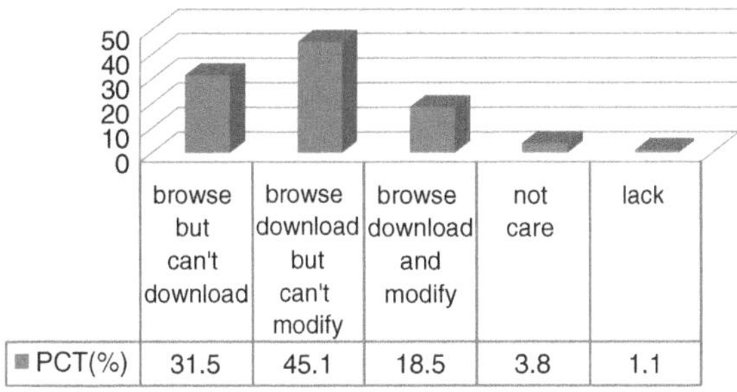

Fig. 9.5 Teachers' tendency of sharing modes

3. The NPC teachers often use pilot curriculum resources to support teaching and learning, but their concerns and application of the curriculum resources vary to the types and sources. They use their own websites of pilot curriculum more frequently, 67.9 % of whom often and 26.6 % occasionally do so. Nearly 80 % often encourage their students to use their websites to facilitate their learning, while 16.8 % do so occasionally.

   The teachers mainly concern about the resources closely related to their instruction, such as courseware, lesson plans, syllabus, etc. In contrast, they pay less attention to the resources closely related to students' learning, such as assignments, thinking questions, examinations and tests, answers to questions and so on. Furthermore, as shown in Fig. 9.6, science teachers have more expectations on the update of exercises and thinking questions, pictures or animation, answers to exercises or tests and experimental instruction than liberal arts teachers, while liberal arts teachers have more requirements on PPT

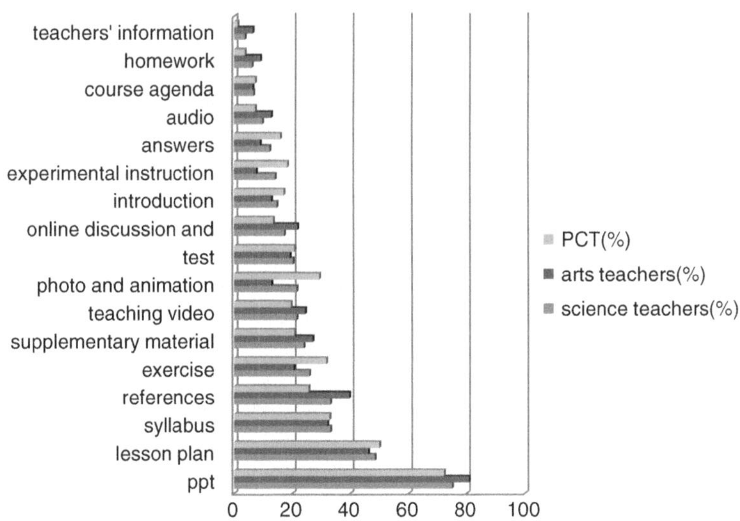

Fig. 9.6 Preferred type of resources

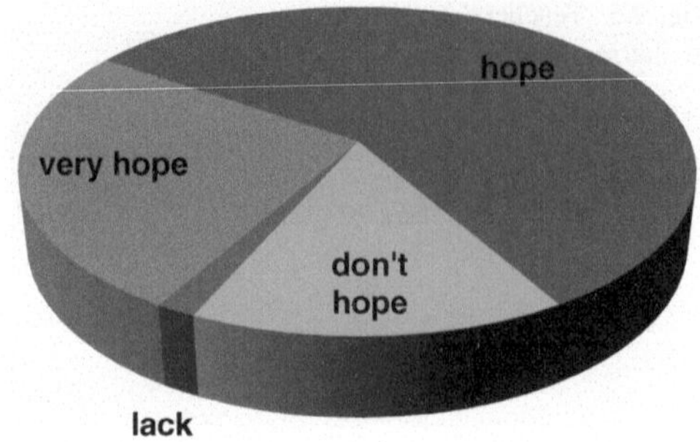

Fig. 9.7 The NPC teachers' willing about connections with other teachers

scripts or courseware, reading materials or references, online discussions and interaction than science teachers.

4) The NPC teachers welcome other users of their curriculum resources to contact them, but they have diverse attitudes towards the necessity of providing advice, as shown in Fig. 9.7. The survey results show that 83.2 % of them hope the other teachers who use their curriculum resources to contact them. Further analysis reveals that the attitude about whether to provide advice or not is significant difference ($F = 6.419$, $p < 0.05$). As shown in Fig. 9.8, 25 % of NPC teachers think it is very necessary to provide advice for teachers in other school, and 53.3 % of them think it is necessary.

In summary, the NPC teachers have already realized NPC resource sharing can support and facilitate the course teaching. The tangible resources, such as the syllabus, lecture notes and exercises, can be easily shared through the Internet and other means, but intangible resources like teaching concepts and ideas, has to be shared through communication and exchange (Shi and Xue 2011). Thus, it is

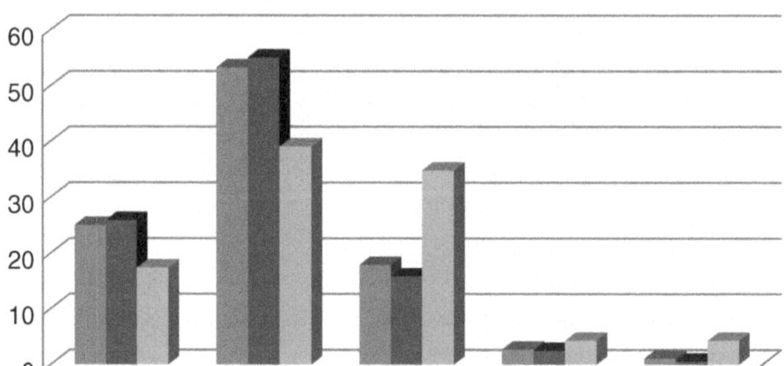

	very necessary	necessary	a little necessary	don't necessary	lack
PCT(%)	25	53.3	17.9	2.7	1.1
985	25.9	55.1	15.8	2.5	0.6
211	17.4	39.1	34.8	4.3	4.3

Fig. 9.8 NPC teachers' attitude about consulting service

necessary to establish the mechanisms or channels to support effective communication between pilot curriculum teachers and users to achieve the full range resources sharing. How to expand the beneficial group and explore the effective promotion and utilization mechanism are the practical needs of instructional reform of Chinese higher education (Liu and Xu 2011). The promotion of pilot curriculum not only realize the extensive sharing of teaching resources and facilitate the application of ICT in teaching, but further lead to the overall reform of higher education's pedagogy and eventually improve the education quality (Qin 2011).

9.5 Conclusions

NPC is an innovative action to solve the quality issues of higher education in China. In terms of the quality issues of higher education, the studies and efforts that have been carried out in the countries all over the world mainly focus on two aspects: the studies and practice on the policies and regulations related to quality assurance system, the construction of mechanism and corresponding activities related to faculty development in universities. As well, the construction of instructional resources represented by OCW also has reference value to solving quality issues. Accordingly, the construction of NPC in China integrates different approaches of solving problems of higher education quality in an effective way by connecting the work of different aspects, such as policies and regulations, faculty, teaching contents and teaching materials, teaching methods and management, teaching approaches and resources, so as to significantly reflect the overall advantage.

Concerning the studies and practice on the policies and regulations related to the quality assurance system, the construction of NPC has a positive impact on the investment of instructional funds in universities and the teacher-and-student ratio, etc. on the level of policy. Also, by focusing on curriculum instruction evaluation, the process of curriculum instruction, the improvement and updating of teaching methods, and the implementation of student-centered learning philosophy in teaching, the construction of NPC has a direct impact on the curricular and extracurricular instructional activities in Chinese universities so as to make sure that the quality assurance work can really lie on the crucial "teaching activities".

Concerning the mechanism construction and corresponding activities related to faculty development, such as "Center for Faculty Development", etc., the construction of NPC further highlights the special status of the "teaching" development in the faculty development. It guides the faculty to set up teaching team per curriculum, to carry out researches on curriculum teaching, and to take the construction of teaching resources as the main form of research products so as to innovate the mode of "the research and development of teaching resources" for faculty development. Therefore, the construction of NPC breaks through the discussion-based situation as the main activity form of faculty development such as workshops, connects the conception of the faculty development and teaching theories to the practical work of the development of teaching resources for supporting the faculty development with more meaningful activities.

The construction of NPC in China is initiated and coordinated by the Department of Higher Education of MOE. Compared with OCW, which is the resource construction movement initiated by universities and responded by the community, it helps more with the advancement of work in a large scale. In the process of construction, the issues of intellectual property gradually draw enough attention, so the top-level design is continuously strengthened and the construction mechanism is gradually more and more systematic. OCW comparatively concentrates on the practice of resource construction, while the construction of NPC can better integrate resource instruction and teaching activities as a whole, which helps with the overall improvement in the aspects of teachers' devotion of time and energy so as to improve teaching quality. In terms of evaluation methods, OCW uses project-based evaluation methods, while NPC uses comprehensive evaluation index system that examines various actual situations of curriculum teaching, which is more conducive to the support of NPC to the teaching quality. In August 2011, MOE of China issued "On the Implementation of 'Project of the Instructional Quality and Instructional Reform for Undergraduates in Universities in the Twelfth Five-year Period". In November 2011, MOE of China issued "On the Implementation of the Construction of National Pilot Open Curriculum", which makes important adjustments to the construction of NPC and promotes it onto a new starting point.

Therefore, as the practice of promoting the quality of higher education with large depth and scale, NPC in China has shown innovative features in the aspects of the project organization, faculty development, pedagogy reform, infrastructure, course content, and evaluation methods. It has referential value for the nations that have quality issues in the popularization process of higher education.

Appendix

A.1 Assessment Indicators of National Pilot Curriculum (For Undergraduates, 2010)

A.1.1 Description of Assessment Indicators

(1) The assessment indicators are formulated according to the spirit of On the Implementation of Instructional Quality and Instructional Reform Project for Undergraduates released by the Ministry of Education and the Ministry of Finance (JG[2007]No.1), On Further Deepening Instructional Reform for Undergraduates to Improve Overall Instructional Quality released by the Ministry of Education (JG[2007]No.2) and the Announcement of Initiating the Construction of Pilot Curriculum in Project of Instructional Quality of

Class-A indicators	Class-B indicator	Main assessment points	Assessment standards	Score (M_i) (%)	Scoring class (K_i)				
					A 1.0	B 0.8	C 0.6	D 0.4	E 0.2
Faculty (20 %)	1-1 Chief teachers	The teaching style, academic level and instructional level of the teachers	Chief teachers have good morality of teachers, with high academic attainments, excellent instructional capability, rich instructional experience and distinctive instructional features, who are in charge of teaching this curriculum for no less than 2 cycles in the recent 3 years	6					
	1-2 Team of teachers	Knowledge structure, age structure, personnel allocation and the cultivation of young teacher	The teachers in the team have strong responsibility, good spirit of teamwork and collaboration, with reasonable knowledge structure, age structure and academic geographical structure. The tutors are allocated according to the requirement of the curriculum. The training plan for young teachers is scientific and rational with practical effectiveness. The experts with professional background should be encouraged to participate in the team	6					
	1-3 Instructional reform and research	Instructional and research activities and instructional outcomes	Active instructional ideas and innovative instructional reform are required. Instructional research activities promote the instructional reform with significant effectiveness, such as the instructional achievements, planned teaching materials or instructional reform projects at or above the level of province or ministry. Academic papers of instructional research of high quality are published.	8					

(continued)

(continued)

Class-A indicators	Class-B indicator	Main assessment points	Assessment standards	Score (M_i) (%)	Scoring class (K_i)				
					A 1.0	B 0.8	C 0.6	D 0.4	E 0.2
Content (20 %)	2-1 Curriculum Content[1]	Design of curriculum content	The design of curriculum content should embody modern educational philosophy according to the objectives of talent training, in accordance with scientific nature, advancement and the law of education and instruction.	10					
			The relationship of classical and modern contents of theoretical curriculum is properly dealt with. The theoretical contents are fundamental, investigative and pilot, which can bring the latest development outcomes and instructional reform and research outcomes of the disciplines to the instruction						
			The relationship of technology, comprehensiveness and exploratory of experimental content (including independent experimental content) is properly treated, which can effectively develop the practice capability and innovative capability of the students						
	2-2 Organization of content	Organization and arrangement of content	Put the theory into practice with the curricular and extracurricular combination, integrate knowledge imparting and capability fostering to quality education and encourage related internship, social investigations or other practical activities with remarkable results	10					

(continued)

(continued)

Class-A indicators	Class-B indicator	Main assessment points	Assessment standards	Score (M_i) (%)	Scoring class (K_i) A 1.0	B 0.8	C 0.6	D 0.4	E 0.2
Infrastructure (20 %)	3-1 Teaching materials	The construction of teaching materials and relevant materials	Select excellent materials (including national pilot teaching materials and those in the national plan, foreign original materials of high level or those composed by the faculty themselves). Have rich relevant materials such as courseware, case studies, and exercises and so on, and provide effective literature and references for the inquiry learning and self-learning of students. The experimental teaching materials are complete to meet the requirements of instruction	10					
	3-2 Practice teaching conditions	The advancement and openness of practice teaching environment	Practice teaching conditions can satisfy the requirements of the instruction. Open instruction is allowed with significant effectiveness (curriculum of science and engineering can provide experiments of high level for choice)						
	3-3 Web-based teaching conditions	Web-based instructional resources and hardware environment	The hardware environment of the campus network is good enough to run the websites of curriculum, with rich instructional resources, with complete functions of assisting instruction and learning for effective sharing	10					

(continued)

(continued)

Class-A indicators	Class-B indicator	Main assessment points	Assessment standards	Score (M_i) (%)	Scoring class (K_i)				
					A 1.0	B 0.8	C 0.6	D 0.4	E 0.2
Pedagogy (20 %)	4-1 Instructional design	Instructional philosophy and instructional design	Emphasize inquiry learning and research learning, reflecting the student-centered and teacher-mentored educational philosophy. Make reasonable instructional design according to the curriculum content and students' characteristics (including teaching methods, teaching means, assessment methods, etc.)	8					
	4-2 Teaching methods	The application of various teaching methods and their effectiveness	Emphasize pedagogy reform, flexibly use a variety of appropriate teaching methods to effectively motivate the learning enthusiasm of students and enhance the development of their learning capability	12					
	4-3b Teaching means	The application of information technology	Make appropriate and full use of modern educational technology to carry out instructional activities with visible effectiveness in the aspects of stimulating students' interests in learning and improving instructional effects						

(continued)

(continued)

Class-A indicators	Class-B indicator	Main assessment points	Assessment standards	Score (M_i) (%)	Scoring class (K_i)				
					A 1.0	B 0.8	C 0.6	D 0.4	E 0.2
Effectiveness (20 %)	5-1 Peer review	The assessment of external experts and internal supervisor group and the fame	The evidence materials are authentic and reliable with excellent assessment and good reputation	4					
	5-2 Students' review	Students' assessment and suggestions	The original materials of students' assessment are authentic and reliable with excellent results. The curriculum should have supporting materials of the students' assessment data in recent three years provided by the instructional administrative office of universities	8					
	5-3 Instructional video review	Video of classroom teaching	Effectively use a variety of instructional media, give thorough interpretation of the issues with enthusiasm and appeal with outstanding focuses, clear thinking, mature contents and numerous information. The contents taught in the classroom can reflect or link to the new ideas, new concepts and new achievements of the development of the disciplines, which can inspire the thinking, association and innovative thinking of students	8					
Features, policy support and radiation sharing	Experts give scores in accordance with the features and innovation written in the application form of National Pilot Curriculum in 2010			40					
	Effective policy and measurements for supporting and encouraging the construction of pilot curriculum in the applied universities			30					
	Strong radiation-sharing measurements with promising future construction plan			30					

[1] According to the types of curriculum, give scores in the part of "content design" in reference to corresponding standards

Class-A indicators	Class-B indicators	Score (%)	Proportion of total score	
			Class-B indicators	Class-A indicators
Faculty 20 %	1-1 Chief teachers	6		
	1-2 Team of teachers	6		
	1-3 Teaching reform and research	8		
Content 20 %	2-1 Course content	10		
	2-2 Organization and arrangement of content	10		
Infrastructure 20 %	3-1 Teaching materials	10		
	3-2 Practice-teaching conditions			
	3-3 Web-based teaching conditions	10		
Pedagogy 20 %	4-1 Instructional design	8		
	4-2 Teaching methods	12		
	4-3 Teaching means			
Effectiveness 20 %	5-1 Peer review	4		
	5-2 Student review	8		
	5-3 Instructional video review	8		

Universities and Instructional Reform release by the Ministry of Education (JG[2003]No.3), we established the assessment indicators.

(2) Pilot curriculum refers to the excellent curriculum with features and first-class instructional level. The construction of pilot curriculum has to embody modern educational philosophy in accordance with talent fostering goals, meets the universal law of scientific nature, advancement and education and instruction, and also has distinct features as well as properly utilizing modern educational technology and methods with obvious effectiveness as a demonstration and radiation for popularization.

(3) The assessment of pilot curriculum should embody the direction of educational and instructional reform, guide the teachers to innovate the methods of education and instruction, ensure students' benefit and the improvement of instructional quality and pay attention to the following questions: ① The contents should balance the relationship between the classic and the modern and that between theory and practice, attach importance to cultivating students' practical and innovative capability in the practical instruction. ② The infrastructure should pay attention to the construction and improvement of high-quality instructional resources and strengthen the assistant instructional function of curriculum websites. ③ The pedagogy should flexibly utilize various instructional methods to arouse the students' enthusiasm in teaching and to promote the development of their learning capability. It should coordinate the application of traditional instructional approaches and modern educational technology for better integration with the curriculum. ④ The construction of faculty should pay attention to the leading and demonstrative role of the teachers in charge of pilot curriculum so as to promote the structural perfection and the improvement of the faculty.

(4) The criteria combine qualitative assessment with quantitative assessment to improve the reliability and comparability of assessment results. The assessment indicators are divided into two parts, which are comprehensive assessment and feature as well as policy support and radiation sharing. In the centesimal grade, the comprehensive assessment accounts for 80 % and the feature, policy support and radiation sharing accounts for 20 %.

(5) Calculation formula of total score: $M = \sum K_i M_i$, K_i is the coefficient of scoring class, the coefficients of A, B, C, D and E are 1.0, 0.8, 0.6, 0.4 and 0.2 respectively, and Mi refers to the scores of each Class-B indicator.

References

Aihua W, Yongsong Z, Jinjiang C (2008) Thinking about promoting national pilot curriculum construction. China Edu Info 13:4–6

Beijing (2005) http://jpkc.bjedu.cn/aaic/repport/Executive_Summary.pdf

Bennett S, Maton K, Kervin L (2008) The digital natives debate: a critical review of the evidence. British J Edu Tech 5:775–786

Bingde L (1991) Pedagogy. People Education Press, vol 1, p 159

China Education (2011) version 2, 6 July

Connelly FM, Lantz O (1985) Definition of curriculum. In: Husén T, Neville Postlethwaite T (eds) The international encyclopedia of education. Pergamon Press, Oxford, pp 1160–1163
Huang R, Jiang X, Zhang J (2007) Innovation and change: the core value of education informatization, Science Press
Kedong L (2003) researching method of educational technology. Beijing Normal University Press, Beijing, vol 4, p 281
Kellaghan T, Stufflebeam DL (2003) International handbook of educational evaluation. Kluwer Academic publishers
Lanfang Z, Jin F, Ronghuai H (2010) The survey and analysis of national pilot curriculum development and sharing demand, open education research, vol 10(3), pp 88–93
Li H (2008) Several hot issues in the development of information technology of higher education. E-education Res 5:19–22
Liu D, Xu W (2011) The study about promotion and using pattern of pilot curriculum. Jiangsu Higher Educ 2:89–90
MIT (2005) http://ocw.mit.edu/ans7870/global/05_Eval_Summary.pdf
MIT (2009) http://ocw.mit.edu/ans7870/global/09_Eval_Summary.pdf
Prensky M, Zhibiao H, Kai W (2009) Digital natives digital immigrants. J Distance Edu 2:48–50
Qin L (2011) Study about national pilot curriculum promotion mode. China Educ Technol 266(3):50–54
Ronghuai H, Lanfang Z, Lanqin Z (2010) The research of the undergraduate's teaching method reform trend in China. E-Education Res 5:84–90
Shi X, Xue W (2011) Problems and countermeasures about pilot curriculum resources sharing. China's High Res 1:90–91
Trow M (1972) The expansion and transformation of higher education, international review of education, no 1, pp 61–63
Wang Y (2002) The popularization of high education—the bottleneck and strategic choice faced by developing countries in Asia-Pacific region, southeast education
Zhou Y (2011) Teaching research status analysis in pilot curriculum construction. PhD thesis, Beijing Normal University, vol 12, p 93
Zeng L, Fang J, Huang R (2010) The survey and analysis of national pilot curriculum development and sharing demand. Open Educ Res 10(3):88–93
Zhang Y (2007) The quality and characteristics of university programs in China—the characteristics of "national pilot curriculum" and its computer-aided analysis. PhD thesis, Beijing normal university, vol 6
Zhao J (1998) The outlook and framework of higher education in 21st century—the overview of 98 world conference on higher education. Shanghai Higher Educ Res 12:1–8
Zhenzhong D (2006) Higher education informatization research at home and abroad. Vocat Educ Explor Res 4:63–65

Part IV
New Dimensions of Learning Technologies

Chapter 10
Mobile Learning: Shaping the Frontiers of Learning Technologies in Global Context

John Traxler

Abstract Learning with mobiles will undoubtedly shape the frontiers of learning technologies in every global context. Looking back over the past 10 years of mobile learning we can see increasing evidence and experience of mobiles driving the agenda for other established learning technologies and either taking learning to people and communities who were previously too distant or expensive to reach or enhancing, enriching and challenging the conceptions of learning itself. This has taken place in an increasingly global context gradually achieving international visibility and recognition but has not been wholly benign as the medium for specific agendas. This chapter reviews this previous decade and then looks forwards to a world where increasingly the notion of learning technology is itself problematic as technology, especially mobile technology, becomes a pervasive, universal, ubiquitous and defining characteristic, taken-for-granted and not-worth-mentioning. The world is no longer a world with technology and mobile technology added in, somehow separate, additional and optional, but is becoming a world unthinkable without technology, particularly mobile technology. This transforms knowledge and knowing and challenges education to stay credible. Learning with mobiles is no longer learning as we knew it somehow delivered or enriched by mobile technology, it becomes learning defined by societies defined by mobile technology. This chapter explores these issues.

J. Traxler (✉)
School of Technology, University of Wolverhampton, London, UK
e-mail: John.Traxler@wlv.ac.uk

R. Huang et al. (eds.), *Reshaping Learning*, New Frontiers of Educational Research,
DOI: 10.1007/978-3-642-32301-0_10, © Springer-Verlag Berlin Heidelberg 2013

10.1 Introduction

This chapter addresses two issues, firstly the history and development of mobile learning and secondly the opportunities that mobile learning provides for teachers and learners. These are both highly contextualised issues, with a variety of different perspectives and relationships. The chapter does this against the wider challenge of looking at the trends and future development of learning processes, at innovative pedagogic changes, at the effects of new technologies on education and at future learning content. Lastly, the chapter attempts to predict the changes and identify positive and active reactions to help the trend go smoothly and in a beneficial way.

This is an ambitious agenda for any account of learning with technology but most especially for an account of learning with mobile technology. This technology is not only becoming increasingly more powerful and widespread but also increasingly appropriated and co-opted across society. From the perspective of someone at the heart of European mobile learning research, development, policy and organisation, the past decade or so has seen a gradual transformation but one that is reaching a major milestone, one that is crucial to our account and to this chapter.

The mobile learning research community is about ten years old. In this time, the community has persuasively demonstrated that mobile devices can deliver learning to people, communities and countries where other educational interventions have been too expensive, difficult or demanding. The community has also demonstrated that mobile devices can extend, enhance, enrich, challenge and disrupt existing ideas and assumptions about learning. The community has also challenged existing conceptualisations and theories of learning itself and has shown that mobiles can raise motivation for learning amongst disenfranchised and disengaged learners.

As we have just said, the community now seems to be at a tipping point, when the work of the community of researchers, practitioners and activists will bear fruit, when we will move on and finally address the challenges of scale, sustainability, equity, blending and embedding. This may be illusory. The community has hitherto worked largely within institutional contexts, positioned at the vanguard of e-learning, buying into the rhetoric of *innovation*—and ironically innovation in any formal sense always in reality seemed to fail—and working from the top-down. The community has also however worked mainly in small-scale, fixed-term subsidised projects staffed by enthusiasts, growing out of the conceptions, foundations, aspirations and limitations of *e-learning*. These developments took place when technology was scarce, difficult and expensive; now technology is ubiquitous, cheap and reliable. Everyone now has mobile technology, they own it, choose it, understand it; they may now have (limited) opinions and ideas about its educational value and its education use, and about its place within the economy of knowledge but they know little about the mission of *e-learning*. What we will see in the next 10 years will not be a continuation of the trajectory defined by the previous 10 years and may not even be informed by these previous 10 years.

We now see dramatic changes and increases globally in the personal, domestic and social use of personal connected mobile devices. These devices potentially redefine how communities and individuals understand learning as a consequence of the way they redefine the nature and significance of knowledge. They provide increasing *anywhere/anytime* access to images, ideas and information; they also provide *just-in-time/just-for-me/just-here* access to them and they turn undifferentiated knowledge consumers into highly differentiated knowledge producers. Furthermore, they redefine how we can think about discourse, identity and community and they have led to new forms of commerce, employment, crime, artistic expression, political organisation and to new artefacts, commodities, businesses, resources, organisations and economic assets, at an individual level, a corporate level and at a national level. These developments are a challenge to the mobile learning community globally and are significant factors in the future development of mobile learning (Traxler 2010a, b).

We also see a growing shift in the global balance and focus within the mobile learning community itself as US practitioners, developers, researchers, funders and corporations make their interests, their perceptions and their perspectives felt within the established community. These might take mobile learning away from its European roots in highly theorised ideas about informal and contextual learning towards mobile training, downloadable *apps* and the connected classroom.

A side-effect of these global changes might be that mobile learning researchers become an optional, no longer necessary, component of the eco-systems of mobile learning; if experiences of (a limited range of) learning with mobile devices become common-place and apparently common-sense amongst developers, practitioners, policy-makers, publishers and managers, are researchers and their evidence still necessary?

10.2 The History and Development of Mobile Learning

We will start by reviewing the achievements of the mobile learning community and then explore the factors shaping its frontiers and its global context. There are already attempts to document the history, evolution and development of mobile learning (Kukulska-Hulme et al. 2011; Pachler et al. 2010). These are excellent accounts from early key players in European mobile learning research and are valuable for their scholarly and critical readings of events and concerns in the first decade of mobile learning. There are also sources that give a more US or global perspective (Herrington et al. 2009; Ally 2009; Cobcroft 2006; Metcalf 2006; Schuler 2009; Quinn 2000). Our focus now is to move onward and outward from these accounts and to explore an ever-widening picture. This book and this chapter aspire to address learning in a global context. This is by no means easy when that global context is now shaped by mobile technologies—mobile technologies *are* the global context not just the contextual container. There are however, regional and historical contexts, and perhaps the most obvious historical and regional context is the evolution of mobile research in Europe.

As we said, the mobile learning research community has demonstrated that it can enhance, extend and enrich the concept and activity of learning itself, beyond earlier conceptions of learning. This includes ideas of

- Contingent learning and teaching, where learners and/or teachers can react and respond to their environment and their changing experiences, for example with real-time data collection and analysis on geography field trips; where teachers can change their teaching in response to the changing affordances of the environment or the learners, for example using pico-projectors and improvised interactive whiteboards (Traxler and Griffiths 2009) or using personal response systems with groups of students (Draper and Brown 2004)
- Situated learning, where learning takes place in surroundings that make learning relevant and meaningful. This includes learning about religions whilst visiting temples, mosques, churches and synagogues (Burke 2010); language learning (Thorton and Houser 2005) and natural history, for example butterfly spotting (Chen et al. 2003), and the work of Wild Knowledge (http://www.wildknowledge.co.uk/).
- Authentic learning, where meaningful learning tasks are related to immediate learning goals, for example basic literacy or numeracy in work-based learning on the job or learning on placement for junior doctors in surgeries, student vets in consultations, nursing trainees in the wards and trainee teachers in schools (Kneebone et al. 2003; Smordal and Gregory 2003; White et al. 2005; Kneebone and Brenton 2005; Kenny et al. 2009)
- Context-aware learning, where learning is informed by the history, surroundings and environment of the learner, for example learning in botanical gardens, museums, game parks or heritage sights. Until recently, this has been episodic, individual and isolated but the increased functionality of mainstream retail devices opens up enormous possibilities for developing more intelligence and using more history behind the learner experience (Lonsdale et al. 2004).
- Augmented reality mobile learning, where learning builds on local physical context supplemented by an audio and/or video overlay (Smith 2008; Jarvis and Priestnall 2008)
- Personalised learning, where learning is customised for the preferences and abilities of individual learners or groups of learners (Kukulska-Hulme and Traxler 2005a)
- Learning support, currently exemplified in the UK by the publicly-funded open-source Mobile Oxford (http://m.ox.ac.uk/desktop/) and the proprietary CampusM (http://www.ombiel.com/). Both provide information from across city and university, providing a guide to help students with day-to-day tasks, including finding for example, a library book, checking the next bus, the next lecture and finding what time the nearest post box is collected. The systems can be accessed by any mobile phone with a web browser and GPS both systems giving

university students location-specific guidance to academic resources and urban venues.
- Pastoral support, enabling students to access non-academic services and support (Vuorinen and Sampson 2003), and organisational support for students (Corlett et al. 2005). Increasingly this can be context and location-aware, allowing personalised and timely support.
- Game-based learning, not always mobile but now increasingly so (Facer et al. 2004; Giles 2009; Kato et al. 2008; Pulman 2008)
- Assessment techniques that are aligned to these new affordances, for example physiotherapy (Dearnley et al. 2008)

All of these represent or facilitate a trend to take learning away from the classroom and the lecture theatre, in fact away from the institution, and at a practical level to support courses and programmes that engage with the world outside the institution, either exploring that world or training students to take their places in it. They do however represent a specific set of pedagogic assumptions about relations between the institution, experience, learning and education that are not necessarily universal. Not all cultures or countries would share these assumptions.

The mobile learning research and development community has also demonstrated that it can take learning to individuals, communities and countries that were previously too remote or sparse, economically, socially or geographically, for other external educational initiatives to reach. This second category has included addressing

- Geographical, geometric or spatial distance, for example reaching into deeply rural areas. This is also becoming educationally richer as networks drive out greater bandwidth and coverage but is still held back by shortage of more modern handsets and support. An example is the Janala project in Bangla Desh (BBC 2010)
- Sparsity, connecting thinly spread and perhaps nomadic learners to create viable communities of learners, sometimes held back lack of experience in supporting communities of distance learners and sometimes by the ways that the most widespread network tariffs restrict access to services.
- Infrastructural or technical barriers, for example, areas of in South or Central Asia or sub Saharan Africa, supporting those communities lacking mains electricity, secure clean buildings or land-line connectivity, for example the SEMA project in Kenya (Traxler 2007)
- Social exclusion, for example reaching students unfamiliar with and lacking confidence in formal learning, for example the homeless, gypsies, marginal groups, nomads, those not-in-education-employment-or-training (NEETs) (Collett and Stead 2002; Attewell and Savill-Smith 2004), lower socio-cultural groups (Unterfrauner et al. 2010) and township youth (Botha et al. 2008)
- Physiological or cognitive differences, for example supporting learning access and opportunities for people with impaired hearing or mobility, or scheduling and organisational support for people with dyslexia (Rainger 2005, and also the work of TechDis in the UK (http://www.techdis.ac.uk/index.php?p=9_5_32)

- Privacy and connection, for example, helping chaperoned or secluded women and girls in some cultures to access informal and social learning. Cultural sensitivities may however inhibit the reporting of this aspect.
- Dead-time, small bursts of otherwise unused time, such as waiting in elevators, cafes, buses, queues; sometimes used as an example of *bite-sized* learning; although possibly educationally limited in this form, mobile phones will always be carried by learners whereas books or laptops might not be (Levy and Kennedy 2005).
- Corporate training, delivering training to dispersed and peripatetic workforces (Pasanen 2003; Gayeski 2002)

For any activities of this category but especially those where learning is being extended into communities that are somehow remote, we have to recognise that technology always has some ideology or perhaps pedagogy embedded in it. This includes mobile technologies. These technologies project the pedagogies, strictly speaking perhaps the epistemologies, of *outsiders* into communities that already have their own learning. There is a risk that mobile technologies delivering learning in this way represent both a Trojan horse and also a cargo cult (Lindstrom 1993; Worsley 1957) that threatens or undermines a fragile educational ecosystem. The issue is not one of developing regions but of any small and fragile cultures (and sub-cultures and even counter cultures) and their capacity to negotiate an optimal balance between the preservation of language, heritage and culture on the one hand and engagement with the wider world and the global knowledge economy, on the other.

The mobile learning research community has also challenged and extended theories of learning (for example, Laurillard 2002 in extensions to her own *conversational framework*) and engaged with wider theories (for example, Engeström with his *activity theory* (1987) and wildfire learning (2009), and for example, Beddall-Hill and Raper (2010) and Wright and Parchoma (2011) both engaging with *actor network theory*). This has taken place across both formal learning, including the university sector and the schools sector, and informal learning, including adult learners and visitors in art galleries and heritage sites. No society is monolithic in terms of culture, specifically in terms of pedagogy and epistemology; perhaps what people know, how they know it, how they come to know it and how they pass it on are some of the defining features of different cultures. The global knowledge economy and the common ethos and practices of university education might tend homogenise or harmonise higher level formal learning, and global techniques and technologies might tend to standardise vocational and technical education but these effects are likely to be less apparent within informal, family and community learning, within communities with an oral culture rather than a literate culture. This must necessarily create a very diverse epistemological and pedagogic ecology, one that has not been adequately explored or documented. This is clearly part of the much larger issue of the interaction and the dynamic between technology, learning and culture. "Some see technology as supporting modernisation, economic growth and improved lifestyles. Others look upon it as an imperial force, mono-cultural, invasive, eroding traditional cultures." (Latchem and Jung 2010, p. 14) expresses this very clearly. The trends and future development of learning processes, as well as every other aspect of pedagogy, are, on the one hand, shaped by the ability of the mobile learning community to enrich and extend learning, but, on the other hand, shaped by the dynamic between society and mobile technologies changing the nature and significance of learning. Any discussion of innovative pedagogic changes must inevitably be grounded in ideas about whether educational change is driven from inside the academy or outside the academy. Mobile technologies, unlike desktop technologies, empower and legitimise voices outside the academy.

In a more general sense, mobile learning is now sufficiently mature and varied to have at least one major textbook (Kukulska-Hulme and Traxler 2005a, b), some practical resources (JISC 2005, 2010), some peer reviewed academic journals including an International Journal of Mobile and Blended Learning, a number of prestigious international conference series (most obviously, IADIS Mobile Learning in Europe, *mLearn* the global leader in its tenth year in 2012, the IEEE's WMTE workshop in Asia Pacific), greater clarity about the significant issues (see for example Sharples 2006, defining the *big issues*), a more sharply defined research agenda (see for example, Arnedillo-Sánchez et al. 2007). Other signs of growing consolidation have been the first mobile learning MOOC, *MobiMOOC*, which attracted 600 students in its first six-week run in 2011 and is scheduled to run again in September 2012, and an attempt, sponsored by the South African Department of Basic Education and endorsed by the International Association of Mobile Learning, to draw up a generic mobile learning curriculum framework, the template for universities and colleges that train teachers and hope to introduce a module or an option into their programmes. There have also been workshops, specifically building capacity amongst mobile learning early-career researchers.

There has also been increasing clarity about the definition of mobile learning, and a continual but not coherent movement away from definitions based on technology and devices, through definitions based on learners and there movement through space and context to definitions that see movement and connectedness as the defining features of the early twentieth-first century and mobile learning defined as merely any and every learning that is aligned to those realities (Traxler 2008).

What has characterised the years since about 2009 has been an increased awareness of mobile learning as potentially a financially sustainable or at least financially justifiable project within national and international education, social and development policies, amongst corporate and government stakeholders. There has been a discernible increase and a discernible shift in interest in using mobiles to support and deliver learning in development amongst the wider world of agencies, corporates and ministries. In October 2010, for example, the UNESCO Chair in e-Learning in Barcelona sponsored an international seminar that focussed on *mobiles, learning and development*. At about the same time the GSMA Development Fund published its *mLearning: A Platform for Educational Opportunities at the Base of the Pyramid* (GSMA 2010) intended to give the mobile network operators (MNOs) a sense of the possible business case. In February 2011, the *World Mobile Congress* in Barcelona sponsored its first awards for learning and attracted an impressive field from organisations working in development. In August 2011, USAID convened the first *m4Ed4Dev* symposium in Washington DC as a prelude to launching the *mEducation Alliance* in early 2012. In November 2011, the WISE debate in Qatar focussed on *mobiles, education and the hard-to-reach*. In December 2011, UNESCO in Paris organised its first *Mobile Learning Week* as the opening of a 3 year collaboration with Nokia, with a programme of outputs including policy guidelines and support for teacher development. UNESCO will jointly host an International Symposium in Washington DC in March 2012. The World Economic Forum Annual Meeting in January 2012 will be reviewing a report on mobile learning. The apparent focus of these events on the Global South belies the fact that much of the debates have addressed wider concerns of educational disadvantage and exclusion, and digital divides defined across a range of dimensions. Looking for a global sense of mobile learning, we see a fragmented and complex picture not easily characterised as developed vs. developing. The regional surveys undertaken by UNESCO reveal mobile learning projects and pilots have been limited to a small number of countries; initially South Africa and the United Kingdom were pre-eminent with contributions from elsewhere, joined latterly by the United States, and to a small number of centres and individuals who had pursued every available funding opportunity and created pockets of continuity of expertise and experience. These are all components of the frontiers of mobile learning in the coming global context.

The final claim is often made, most often in funding proposals, that learning with mobile devices increases learners' enthusiasm and motivation (there is considerable impressionistic soft evidence for this claim) and consequently retention and progression, key educational performance indicators, are improved (a very dubious proposition).

The nature of the research infrastructure and research funding has often meant that these achievements, especially those in the first category, the category of enrich and enhancing learning, have occurred in the developed regions of the world. The achievements in the second category, a category where mobile learning is essentially solving a problem or remedying a deficit, have been spread more haphazardly across both the developed and developing regions of the world. They too have still mostly been driven by funding but funding for a variety of social and economic objectives ranging from capacity building, economic regeneration, greater inclusion, increased social capital or wider participation. One of the key challenges facing the mobile learning community is ensuring that their achievements and outputs are not limited to rich individuals, rich communities, rich institutions and rich countries. The frontiers of learning technologies, and the technologies of mobile learning, in a global context will depend on the capacity of economies around the global to continue to sustain these kinds of activities.

10.3 The Challenges and Hurdles to Mobile Learning

The near universality, increasing functionality and decreasing real cost of mobile devices does mean that all of these educational opportunities are becoming much more accessible and sustainable in all the regions of the world and across all social classes and economic groups. Different cultures will however respond differently, for example, to the perceived frivolity of game-based mobile learning or the apparently individualistic nature of personalised mobile learning. The dominant perspectives of the mobile learning community will not necessarily align with formal or informal ideas about learning in every culture in the world and the global context is not stable and homogeneous in spite of mobile technology seeming to be infinitely scalable.

As we have said, development of mobile learning, based around pilots and projects, has so far often been driven by pedagogic necessity, technological innovation, funding opportunity and the perceived inadequacies of conventional e-learning and/or the perceived inadequacies of the ODL (Open and Distance Learning) infrastructure. Furthermore, this development has worked within relatively narrow educational discourses (see Kukulska-Hulme and Traxler 2007, for analyses of a sample of these developments). There are a variety of challenges still to be addressed. These are mostly in the periphery of the research community itself, beyond the core issues of technology and pedagogy. As we outlined earlier, these challenges include:

Scale and generality, that is, developing an understanding of how specific pilots, projects and trials can be safely enlarged, how test sites and samples can be best deployed, to what extent are outcomes contingent on specific and possibly insignificant local factors or submerged factors; understanding how to abstract or generalise (see Lee and Baskerville 2003). This is complemented by the challenge of transferability and relevance, that is, the need to develop an understanding of how the lessons, mechanics or principles of projects, pilots and trials can be applied elsewhere with confidence.

Sustainability, or perhaps a business case or just an exit strategy, that is developing an understanding of mobile learning projects in terms of their ability to generate revenue or meet their costs and an understanding of their impact on human, economic and social capital in relation to their various costs. Sustainability is clearly a complex and important issue; in countries where *big* government supports education, it is dependent on the capacity of the project to influence policy. In other countries, those of *small* government or perhaps bad government, the sustainability of an intervention depends on some complex interplay between markets, either mature or emerging, and social entrepreneurs and social enterprises. In South Africa, for example, the Meraka Institute uses Living Labs such as the one at Sekhukhune (Schaffers et al. 2007) to explore suitable strategies. In many parts of the developing world, however, national educational priorities may be quite stark, concentrated on literacy, primary teacher training, Millennium Development Goals and little else. Developing frameworks, for what might be called sustainable and appropriate mobile learning ecosystems of private, public and local players, is increasingly the obvious priority.

Embedding, that is, the integration with other institutional technology enhanced learning systems and with institutional and organisational processes, for example in colleges, schools and universities. This has proved difficult owing to funders, researchers and developers analysing and prioritising projects rather than the environment of the host institutions or systems, of perhaps also due to cultural and psychological differences between innovators especially those who are outsiders and regulators and administrators within institutions.

Evidence, that is, data demonstrating relevance, significance and impact. Mobile learning researchers and developers have not always had the time, resources and expertise (Traxler and Kukulska-Hulme 2006) to generate credible and appropriate evidence; the evaluation of mobile learning has been inherently challenging compared to e-learning because the context and the environment act as confounding variables, attenuating the signal-to-noise ratio; methods are epistemologically inappropriate (Buscher and Urry 2009); because the Hawthorne effect comes into play (Mayo 1933); because the evaluations focus inappropriately on hard objective outcomes (Dewson et al. 2002) and because short-term projects do not give time for the technology to bed in reliably and for the novelty to wear off. Furthermore because projects, for ease of experimental design and deployment, invariably used project-supplied devices not *learner devices*, outcomes if good educationally are still nevertheless unsustainable for financial reasons. Projects are also likely to work with enthusiastic innovative teaching staff alongside, not within, compulsory curricular thus undermining the credibility or transferability of outcomes to the core curriculum with mainstream teachers. In the light of our earlier remarks about the familiarity with mobile technologies amongst policy-makers, managers and practitioners—and learners—this is perhaps not the problem it once was. Practice no longer needs to be research-informed; it has passed out of the domain of specialists.

Many of these challenges are shared with other types of intervention, for example those of mainstream e-learning. There are however wider contextual challenges, those of recognising the profound societal and philosophical changes catalysed by these technologies (and documented in the growing literature of mobilities, for example Sheller and Urry 2006), and of recognising their local echoes and implications within mobile learning. This is the global context of education, the globalisation of technology and the global impact of the technology.

10.4 The Future of Mobile Learning

As we have said already, mobile learning is at a turning point and many of the features that constitute its rapidly changing environment have already been identified. Most people live in societies where the norm or the default is to be connected and moving, where the mobile phone is ubiquitous and pervasive.

Mobile phone technology is no longer something bolted on to our daily experiences; it is built into our daily experiences.

A decade ago it might have been reasonable to question the value and the role of mobile technology in the class room (especially when implicitly compared to the technical superiority of the desk top computer). Now, given the impact of these technologies on economic practices, social practices, political practices, cultural practices even religious practices, we should question anyone seeking to inhibit their impact on educational practices. To put in another way, the frequent question about whether mobile technologies are good—in whatever sense—for education, is the now the wrong question. If education has any relationship at all to servicing the economy or the epistemology of society, the question should be about the education response to the outside world of mobility and connection. As we said earlier, mobile technologies *are* the global context and education should reflect that context. Learning processes will need to reflect that shift and so will teaching.

There is a view that *e-learning* in some university institutions in some countries are merely the industrialisation of learning—the logical consequence of the *massification*, out-sourcing, privatisation and globalisation of higher education; implicitly the consequence of cost-effective mass production educational capital (to use a rather Marxist turn of phrase) is the need to automate and industrialise, to introduce machinery into learning in order to survive and compete (Traxler 2010b). Seen in this light, mobile learning might be merely a means of greater competitive advantages and increased student satisfaction, part of a move from first generation mass production to a more responsive post-Fordist approach. This is perhaps a rather dystopian analysis.

A more optimistic but still fundamentally challenging account is based on *learner devices* (Traxler 2010c) or *BYOD*, bring-your-own-device, to use the increasingly preferred term. This phrase refers to those devices owned by learners rather than by schools, colleges and universities and exploited by educators in order to underpin an economically viable and institution-wide vision of mobile learning in formal education. Whilst adopting a learner devices strategy would seem financially attractive and would free institutions from the responsibility of providing the hardware for learning, it brings a host of technical and tactical challenges, for example, network infrastructure, quality assurance, staff development. The big challenges, especially when learner devices are seen as part of a wider strategy of learner-owned technologies that includes social networks, immersive worlds and blogging are however around teacher perceptions, often quite justifiable, about the locus of control within the classroom and the institution shifting towards the learners and away from teachers. This is another aspect of our assertion that technologies in education are no longer a *top-down* innovation but an *outside-in* token of continued credibility.

10.5 Personal Reflections and Conclusions

Much of this chapter has stood back from the specifics and details of the past decade of mobile learning and has attempted to discern general trends and deeper issues. Mobile learning, but obviously learning too in its broadest sense, is not necessarily straightforward, benign or equal and the reach and familiarity of mobile technologies can both mask and accentuate these dilemmas. There is perhaps a sense that the early ownership of the ideas and ideals of the pioneer mobile learning research community have now passed on to and into a more diffuse, complex and fragmented set of stakeholders. The second decade will be different from the first.

So in conclusion we can return to the two themes of this chapter, namely the history and development of mobile learning and the opportunities that mobile learning provides for teachers and learners. Within the narrow contexts of the (various) mobile learning research and practitioner communities, these are both, as we have described, fairly straightforward narratives, ones that in many senses mimic the trajectories of other educational technology and could continue to do so. We have however attempted to place these within a wider context of social change and social appropriation, where the opportunities are more challenging and uncertain, and where the education system as whole, not just e-learning specialists or mobile learning researchers, must come to terms with learning, knowledge and education having rapidly changing and fragmenting meanings in a world and in a future where mobility and connection are the defining characteristics.

References

Ally M (ed) (2009) Mobile learning: transforming the delivery of education and training. University of Athabasca Press, Athabasca

Arnedillo-Sánchez I, Sharples M, Vavoula G (eds) (2007) Beyond mobile learning workshop. Trinity College Dublin Press, Dublin

Attewell J, Savill-Smith C (2004) Learning with mobile devices. Learning and Skills Network, London

BBC (2010) Online http://www.bbc.co.uk/worldservice/trust/whatwedo/where/asia/bangladesh/2010/01/100115_bangaldesh_janala_project_overview.shtml

Beddall-Hill N, Raper J (2010) Mobile devices as 'boundary objects' on field trips. J Res Cent Educ Technol 6(1)

Botha A, Vosloo S, Kuner J, van den Berg M (2008) Improving cross-cultural awareness and communication through mobile technologies. In: Traxler J, Riordan B, Dennett C (eds) Proceedings of mLearn, Telford, UK

Burke D (2010) Using mobile devices to enhance fieldwork. In: Law P, Wankel C (eds) Streaming media in higher education

Buscher M, Urry J (2009) Mobile methods and the empirical. European J Soc Theor 12(1):99–116

Chen YS, Kao TC et al (2003) A mobile learning system for scaffolding bird watching learning. J Comput Assist Learn 19(3):347–359

Cobcroft RS et al. (2006) Literature review into mobile learning in the university context. Queensland University of Technology: Creative Industries Faculty, Queensland

Collett M, Stead G (2002) Meeting the challenge: producing m-learning materials for young adults with numeracy and literacy needs. In: Proceedings of mLearn, Birmingham, UK, The University of Birmingham, UK

Corlett D, Sharples M et al (2005) Evaluation of a mobile learning organiser for university students. J Comput Assist Learn 21(3):162–170

Dearnley CJ, Haigh J, Fairhall J (2008) Using mobile technologies for assessment and learning in practice settings: a case study. Nurse Education in Practice: Elsevier

Dewson S, Eccles J, Tackey ND, Jackson A (2002) Measuring soft outcomes and distance travelled: a review of current practice. Institute for Employment Studies for DfEE

Draper SW, Brown MI (2004) Increasing interactivity in lectures using an electronic voting system. J Comput Assist Learn 20(2):81–94

Engeström Y (1987) Learning by expanding: an activity-theoretical approach to developmental research. Orienta-Konsultit, Helsinki

Engeström Y (2009) Wildfire activities: new patterns of mobility and learning. Int J Mob Blended Learn 1(2)

Facer K, Joiner R, Stanton D, Reidt J, Hull R, Kirk D (2004) Savannah: mobile gaming and learning? J Comput Assist Learn 20:399–409

Gayeski D (2002) Learning unplugged—using mobile technologies for organisational and performance improvement. AMACON—American Management Association, New York

Giles J (2009) Physios recommend a healthy dose of gaming. New scientist. At www.newscientist.com/article/mg20227145.700-physios-recommend-a-healthy-dose-of-gaming.html

GSMA (2010) mLearning: a platform for educational opportunities at the base of the pyramid. GSMA Development Fund, London. Available from http://www.gsmworld.com/documents/mLearning_Report_Final_Dec2010.pdf

Herrington J, Herrington A, Mantei J, Olney I, Ferry B (eds) (2009) New technologies, new pedagogies: Mobile learning in higher education. Faculty of Education, University of Wollongong, Wollongong

Jarvis CH, Priestnall G (2008) Visualisation futures: a teaching and learning perspective. Horizon scanning for GIS and visualisation, Salford, 1 Apr 2008

JISC (2005) Innovative practice with e-Learning: a good practice guide to embedding mobile and wireless technologies into everyday practice. Joint Information Services Committee, Bristol

JISC (2010) JISC mobile and wireless technologies review. Available at http://mobilereview.jiscpress.org, also http://mobilereview.jiscpress.org/mobile-version/

Kato PM, Cole SW, Bradlyn AS, Pollock BH (2008) A video game improves behavioural outcomes in adolescents and young adults with cancer: a randomised trial. Paediatrics 122(2):305–317

Kenny RF, Park CL, Van Neste-Kenny JMC, Burton PA, Meiers PA (2009) Using mobile learning to enhance the quality of nursing practice education. In: Ally M (ed) Mobile learning: transforming the delivery of education and training. Athabasca University Press, Athabasca

Kneebone R, Brenton H (2005) Training perioperative specialist practitioners. In: Kukulska-Hulme A, Traxler J (eds) Mobile learning: a handbook for educators and trainers. Routledge, London

Kneebone R, Nestel D et al (2003) The use of handheld computers in scenario-based procedural assessments. Med Teach Med Teach J1—Med Teach 25(6):632–642

Kukulska-Hulme A, Traxler J (2005a) Mobile learning: a handbook for educators and trainers. Routledge, London

Kukulska-Hulme A, Traxler J (2005a) Making the case for personalisation through mobile learning. In: Proceedings of CAL'05, Bristol

Kukulska-Hulme A, Traxler J (2007) Design for mobile and wireless technologies. In: Beetham H, Sharpe R (eds) Rethinking pedagogy for the digital age. Routledge, London

Kukulska-Hulme A, Sharples M, Milrad M, Arnedillo-Sánchez I, Vavoula G (2011) The genesis and development of mobile learning in Europe. In: Parsons D (ed) Combining E-learning and M-learning: new applications of blended educational resources. Information Science Reference (an imprint of IGI Global), Hershey, pp 151–177

Latchem C, Jung I (2010) Distance and blended learning in Asia. Routledge, Abingdon

Laurillard D (2002) Rethinking university teaching—a conversational framework for the effective use of learning technology, 2nd edn. Routledge, London

Lee AS, Baskerville RL (2003) Generalizing generalizability in information systems research 14(3):pp 221–243

Levy M, Kennedy C (2005) Learning Italian via mobile SMS. In: Kukulska-Hulme A, Traxler J (ed) Mobile learning: a handbook for educators and trainers. Routledge, London

Lindstrom L (1993) Cargo cult: strange stories of desire from melanesia and beyond. University of Hawaii Press, Honolulu

Lonsdale P, Barber C, Sharples M, Byrne W, Arvanitis T, Brundell P et al (2004) Context awareness for MOBIlearn: creating an engaging learning experience in an art museum. In: Murelli E, Da Bormida G, Alborghetti C (eds) Proceedings of MLEARN. CRATOS, Odescalchi Castle

Mayo E (1933) The human problems of an industrial civilization. MacMillan, New York, Chap. 3. or Roethlisberger FJ, Dickson WJ (1939) Management and the worker. Harvard University Press, Cambridge

Metcalf DS (2006) mLearning: mobile learning and performance in the palm of your hand. HRD Press, Amherst

Pachler N, Bachmair B, Cook J, Kress G (eds) (2010) Mobile learning—structures, agency, practices. Springer, London

Pasanen J (2003) Corporate mobile learning. In: Kynaslahti H, Seppala P (eds) Mobile learning. IT Press, Helsinki, pp 115–123

Pulman A (2008) Mobile assistance—the nintendo DS lite as an assistive tool for health and social care students. Online at www.swap.ac.uk/docs/casestudies/pulman.pdf

Quinn C (2000) mLearning: mobile, wireless and in-your-pocket learning. Line Zine Magazine

Rainger P (2005) Accessibility and mobile learning. In: Kukulska-Hulme A, Traxler J (eds) Mobile learning: a handbook for educators and trainers. Routledge, London

Schaffers H, Cordoba MG, Hongisto P, Kallai T, Merz C, van Rensburg J (2007) Exploring business models for open innovation in rural living labs. In: Proceedings of the 13th international conference on concurrent enterprising, pp 49–56

Sharples M (ed) (2006) Big issues in mobile learning. nottingham: kaleidoscope network of excellence. Mobile Learning Initiative

Sheller M, Urry J (2006) The new mobilities paradigm. Environ Plann A 38:207–226

Shuler C (2009) Pockets of potential: using mobile technologies to promote children's learning. The Joan Ganz Cooney Center at Sesame Workshop, New York

Smith C (2008) Simulation as an aid to archaeological drawing, teaching and learning in archaeology 2008 conference. University of Liverpool, 25–26 June, organised by the HEA subject centre for history, classics and archaeology

Smordal O, Gregory J (2003) Personal digital assistants in medical education and practice. J Comput Assist Learn 19(3):320–329

Thornton P, Houser C (2005) Using mobile phones in English education in Japan. J Comput Assist Learn 21:217–228

Traxler J (2007) IS4DEV—IS development and development issues. In: Barry C, Lang M, Wojtkowski W, Wojtkowski G, Wrycza S, Zupancic J (eds) (2008) The inter-networked world: ISD theory, practice, and education. Springer-Verlag, New York, ISBN 978-0387304038

Traxler J (2008) Learning in a mobile age. Int J Mob Blended Learn 1(1):1–12

Traxler J (2010a) Sustaining mobile learning and its institutions. Int J Mob Blended Learn 2(4):129–138

Traxler J (2010b) e-Learning—the next wave. In: Proceedings of ALT-C, Association for Learning Technology, Oxford

Traxler J (2010c) Will student devices deliver innovation, inclusion and transformation? J Res Cent Educ Technol at Kent State University, Spring 2010

Traxler J, Griffiths L (2009) IWB4D—interactive whiteboards for development. In: Proceedings of ICTD2009 doha, Qatar: IEEE

Traxler J, Kukulska-Hulme A (2006) The evaluation of next generation learning technologies: the case of mobile learning. In: Research proceedings of ALT-C2006. Association for Learning Technology, Oxford

Unterfrauner E, Marschalek I, Fabian C (2010) Mobile learning with marginalized young people. In: Arnedillo Sánchez I, Isaias P (eds) Proceedings of the IADIS international conference mobile learning, pp 28–35

Vuorinen R, Sampson JP (2003) Using mobile Information technology to enhance counselling and guidance. In: Kynaslahti H, Seppala P (eds) Mobile learning. IT Press, Helsinki, pp 63–70

White A et al (2005) Infusing PDA technology into nursing education. Nurse Educator 30(4):150–154

Worsley P (1957) The trumpet shall sound: a study of "cargo" cults in Melanesia. MacGibbon and Kee, London

Wright S, Parchoma G (2011) Technologies for learning? An actor-network theory critique of 'affordances' in research on mobile learning. Res Learn Technol 19(3)

Chapter 11
Paradigm Shifts in E-Learning: From Web-Based Learning to Context-Aware Ubiquitous Learning

Gwo-Jen Hwang

Abstract Although digital learning, such as web-based learning and computer-assisted learning, has been recognized as being an effective learning channel that provides rich and diverse content, educators have emphasized the importance and necessity of conducting "authentic activities" in which students can work with problems from the real world. Recent progress in computer, wireless communication and sensing technologies has provided opportunities to conduct authentic learning activities in the real world with supports from digital systems. Such a new development of technology-enhanced learning has been called context-aware ubiquitous learning by researchers, and shifts the learning paradigm from virtual to authentic contexts. In such an innovative learning environment, the learning system is able to sense the real-world situation of the learners, interact with them and provide them with adaptive supports accordingly. In this chapter, we shall address how the e-learning has been affected by these emerging technologies via reviewing several studies and applications; moreover, the strategies of applying the new approach as well as the potential research issues are discussed.

11.1 Paradigm Shifts in Technology-Enhanced Learning

In the past decade, researchers have developed various digital learning systems to provide a more adaptive learning environment with rich learning resources. Much attention has been focused on new learning strategies with appropriate software

G.-J. Hwang (✉)
Graduate Institute of Digital Learning and Education, National Taiwan University of Science and Technology, 43, Sec.4, Keelung Rd, Taipei 106, Taiwan
e-mail: gjhwang.academic@gmail.com

R. Huang et al. (eds.), *Reshaping Learning*, New Frontiers of Educational Research,
DOI: 10.1007/978-3-642-32301-0_11, © Springer-Verlag Berlin Heidelberg 2013

tools and environments (Fabos and Young 1999), such as computer scaffolding (Williams van Rooij 2009), the activity-theoretical approach (Liaw et al. 2007), and computer-supported assessment and learning diagnosis (Panjaburee et al. 2010). These learning strategies have been applied in classroom teaching with Internet access.

Earlier studies of educational computer tools focused on the development of Computer-Assisted Instruction (CAI) systems. A CAI system can be perceived as a tutorial system, which is a guided system to provide well-constructed information. For example, Burks (1996) presented computer-based tutorials and a virtual classroom to teach circuit analysis; Gang et al. (1996) proposed a tutorial system by using artificial intelligence technology. Some researchers utilized auxiliary software to enhance their tutorial systems (Robert 1996; William and Marion 1996), while some provided interactive tutorials for manuals with graphical user interfaces (Sally 1996) or with rich multimedia formats (Pui and William 1996). The study of Barrett and Lally (1999) showed the effectiveness of such computer-assisted instruction systems based on empirical evaluation. Davidovic et al. (2003) also concluded that greater efficiency can be achieved by basing the system development on the theoretical background of cognitive knowledge acquisition.

Recently, the efficiency and popularity of the Internet has received much attention that has motivated efforts towards integrating web-based learning activities into the curriculum (Khan 1997). Considerable work has been conducted on the use of the Internet as a distance-learning tool (Apkarian and Dawer 2000), and the use of web-based simulation tools for education (Sreenivasan et al. 2000). Moreover, some practical usages of web-based information-searching systems in schools have been reported Hwang and Kuo(2010b), Hwang et al. (2008b). In addition to their obvious use in a distance-learning scenario, those educational tools can also be utilized to enrich classroom experience through the use of a data projector (Ringwood and Galvin 2002).

Although several studies have demonstrated the benefits of computer and web-based learning (e.g., Hill 1999; Hill and Hannafin 1997; Pena-Shaffa and Nichollsb 2004; Yakimovicz and Murphy 1995), educators have emphasized the importance and necessity of "authentic activities" in which students can work with problems from the real world (Brown et al. 1989; Wenger 1997; Minami et al. 2004). In order to situate students in authentic learning environments, it is important to place them in a series of designed lessons that combine both real and virtual learning environments (Hwang et al. 2008a).

The advance and popularity of wireless communication and mobile technologies has provided unprecedented opportunities to implement new learning strategies by integrating real-world learning environments and the resources of the digital world (Hwang and Chang 2011; Norris et al. 2011). With the help of these new technologies, individual students are able to learn in an authentic context with support or instructions from computer systems via a mobile device with wireless communications to access the digital content. Recently, the advancement of sensing technologies, such as Radio Frequency Identification (RFID), Global Position System (GPS), Quick Response (QR) code and Sensor Networks, has further brought us a new form of technology-enhanced learning, that is, *context-aware ubiquitous learning* (context-aware u-learning), which has been indicated by Hwang et al. (2008a) as being a more specific definition of broad-sense ubiquitous learning. A context-aware u-learning system is able to detect and record the learning behaviors of the students in both the real world and the digital world with the help of the sensing technology (Hwang et al. 2008a; Ogata and Yano 2004; Yang et al. 2008). It not only supports learners with an alternative way to deal with problems in the real world, but also enables the learning system to more actively interact with the learners.

While a context-aware u-learning environment refers to the use of mobile, wireless communication and sensing technologies in learning, broad-sense ubiquitous learning has been viewed as "anywhere and anytime learning". With this broad-sense definition, any learning environment that allows students to access learning content in any location at any time can be called a ubiquitous learning environment, no matter whether wireless communications, mobile devices, sensing technologies or even ubiquitous computing technologies are employed or not. From this viewpoint, a learning environment which allows students to access learning content via mobile devices with wireless communications is a kind of broad-sense ubiquitous learning Hwang et al. (2008a).

Figure 11.1 summarizes how these technologies foster such paradigm shifts in technology-enhanced learning (Liu and Hwang 2010). In the first stage, computer, communication and web technologies enabled students to access digital content and interact with learning systems, teachers or peers on the Internet, thus providing a virtual environment with a digital learning context. Later, the advancement of wireless communication and mobile technologies enabled students to access the

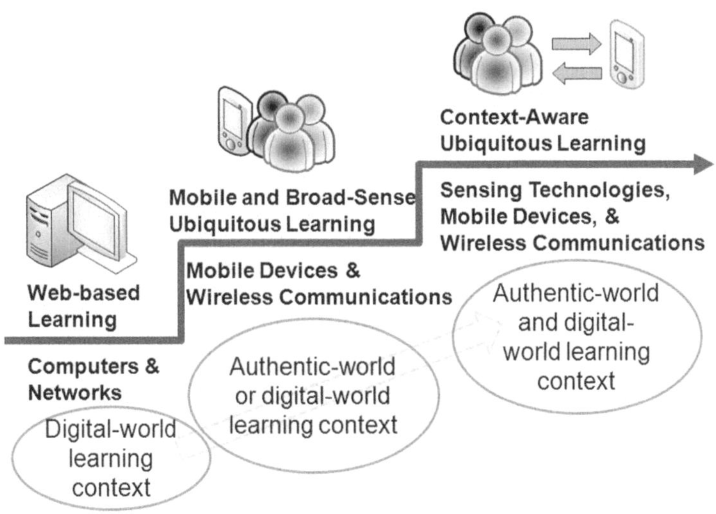

Fig. 11.1 Paradigm shifts in technology-enhanced learning

digital content anywhere and at anytime. In this stage, the learning context could be virtual or authentic, depending on the course content and learning design. For example, students can access English course content via mobile devices with wireless networks. The learning content could be irrelevant to the authentic environment in which the students are situated. On the other hand, the students might be located in an ecology park to observe some learning targets; in the meantime, they need to search for supplementary materials from the Internet. In the second case, the learning context is highly related to the authentic environment.

By employing mobile, wireless communication and sensing technologies in a context-aware u-learning environment, the learning system can immediately detect and collect students' learning status as well as environmental parameters in the authentic world, such that learning supports or guidance can be actively provided. In the English or the ecology learning activity mentioned above, a context-aware u-learning system can actively provide authentic context-related supplementary materials to individual students after detecting their location, or even guide them to complete learning missions in the authentic environment. For example, Ogata and Yano (2004) presented a context-aware u-learning system which has been used to help students to learn Japanese in real-world situations. Such systems can provide students with appropriate expressions via mobile devices by detecting the contexts (e.g., occasions or locations) in which they are situated. Chu et al. (2010) developed a context-aware u-learning system for guiding students to learn to identify the plants on a school campus. With the help of RFID devices, the learning system is able to guide the students to find the locations of the target plants and the comparative plants for making observations and comparisons; in addition, the learning system helps the students complete their learning missions by providing relevant supplementary materials and hints based on their locations and their observation records during the learning missions.

11.2 Emerging Technologies to Support Authentic Learning

The rapid advance of broadband and wireless Internet technologies has promoted the utilization of wireless applications in our daily lives. A variety of invisible embedded devices and corresponding software components have also been developed and connected to the Internet. *Ubiquitous computing* (u-computing) is one such new technology that enables users to seamlessly utilize huge amounts and various kinds of "functional objects" anytime and anywhere through network connections (Rodríguez and Favela 2003; Minami et al. 2004). Another feature of ubiquitous computing is the use of wireless communication objects embedded with sensors to detect users and environment information for the provision of personalized learning supports.

It should be noted that "context-aware u-learning," as defined by Hwang et al. (2008a), is not necessarily accomplished by "using the u-computing technologies in learning". In fact, most existing context-aware u-learning environments do not contain the full characteristics of a u-computing environment. In an ideal u-computing environment, computing, communication, and sensing devices are embedded and integrated into learners' daily life to make learning immersive. However, most existing context-aware u-learning environments are developed by employing conventional mobile devices and wireless communication equipment with popular sensing technologies, such as RFID, GPS or QR-code.

From the system designer's point of view, physical integration and spontaneous interoperation are the two main characteristics of ubiquitous computing systems (Kindberg and Fox 2002). Physical integration means that a ubiquitous computing system involves some integration between computing nodes and the physical world. For example, a smart coffee cup, such as a Media-Cup (Beigl et al. 2001), serves as a coffee cup in the usual way, but also contains sensing, processing and networking elements that let it communicate its state (full or empty, held or put down), enabling the cup to give hints about its state, as well as that of its owner. Moreover, consider a smart meeting room that senses the presence of users in meetings, records their actions (Abowd 1999), and provides services as they sit at a table or talk in front of a whiteboard (Ponnekanti et al. 2001). The room contains digital furniture such as chairs with sensors, whiteboards that record what is written on them, and projectors that can be activated from anywhere in the room, using a Personal Digital Assistant (PDA).

In the meantime, a ubiquitous computing system must spontaneously interoperate in changing environments. A component interoperates spontaneously if it interacts with a set of communicating components that can change both identity and functionality over time as its circumstances change (Kindberg and Fox 2002). A spontaneously interacting component changes partners during its normal operation, as it moves or as other components enter its environment; it changes partners without needing new software or parameters (Feeney et al. 2001). For example, to seamlessly hold a video conference, the system needs to immediately locate the nearest functional objects, such as a CCD camera and display equipment, for each attendee. If the attendee moves toward another room, the system will change devices according to the user's context, so that the video conference can be seamlessly continued. If the attendee switches his or her device from a notebook with a 100 Mbps local area network to a PDA with a lower-speed wireless network, the system will locate additional translation coders or drivers accordingly.

From the user's point of view, in a ubiquitous computing environment, anyone can make use of computers that are embedded everywhere in a public environment, at any time. A user equipped with a mobile device can connect to any of them, and access the network by using wireless communication technologies (Uemukai et al. 2004). Moreover, not only can a user access the network actively, but computers around the user can recognize the user's behavior and offer various services according to the user's situation, the mobile terminal's capability, the network bandwidth, and so on (Cheng and Marsic 2002). User assistance via ubiquitous computing technologies is realized by providing users with proper decisions or decision alternatives. That is, a ubiquitous computing technology-equipped system supplies users with timely information and relevant services by automatically sensing users' various context data, and smartly generating proper results (Kwon et al. 2005). Therefore, by employing this new technology in education, the learning system is not only adapted to the individual's needs, but is also actively involved in his or her learning activity.

It is expected that, in the near future, more u-computing technologies can be applied to the development of ideal context-aware u-learning environments, in which the learning systems can be highly adaptive based on the student's prior knowledge and real-world learning performance to provide seamless guidance or apprenticeship for them without being limited by time and locations, or even the forms of learning devices.

11.3 Characteristics of Context-Aware U-Learning

No matter what kinds of sensing technologies are employed, the context-aware feature of a context-aware u-learning environment allows the learning system to better understand the learner's behavior and the timely environmental parameters in the real world, such as the locations and behavior of the learner, and the temperature and humidity of the learning environment (Kawahara et al. 2003). Lonsdale et al. (2003) indicated that, among various contexts that can be sensed, "time" and "location" could be the most important and fundamental parameters for recognizing and describing a learner's context. For example, Rogers et al. (2005) integrated the learning experiences of indoor and outdoor activities by observation in a workplace. Learners are not only capable of getting data, voice and images from the scene by observation, but also of gathering related information from learning activities via wireless networks. Hwang et al. (2009) developed a context-aware u-learning environment for guiding inexperienced researchers to practice the single-crystal x-ray diffraction procedure. The learners were guided by a mobile device with an RFID reader, while the three laboratories that contain the target equipment were provided with RFID tags; moreover, an expert system was developed for providing corresponding advice to the learners during the operational procedure of individual equipment.

In addition to developing context-aware u-learning systems or conducting learning activities, researchers have attempted to figure out principles and methods for designing learning activities in authentic contexts (Yang et al. 2007). For example, Chu et al. (2010) demonstrated how a grid-based Mindtool can be used to help students organize the knowledge for differentiating real-world learning targets in a context-aware u-learning activity; Chiou et al. (2010) proposed an adaptive navigation support mechanism for guiding students to learn with optimal learning routes by taking the authentic context of a museum into account. Hwang et al. (2008a) further proposed the criteria of a context-aware u-learning environment as follows:

1. A context-aware u-learning environment is context-aware; that is, the learner's situation or the situation of the real-world environment in which the learner is located can be sensed, implying that the system is able to conduct the learning activities in the real world.
2. A context-aware u-learning environment is able to offer more adaptive supports to the learners by taking into account their learning behaviors and contexts in both the cyber world and the real world.
3. A context-aware u-learning environment can actively provide personalized supports or hints to the learners in the right way, in the right place, and at the right time, based on the personal and environmental contexts in the real world, as well as the profile and learning portfolio of the learner.
4. A context-aware ubiquitous learning environment enables seamless learning from place to place within the predefined area.
5. A context-aware ubiquitous learning environment is able to adapt the subject content to meet the functions of various mobile devices.

They further indicated that five types of situation parameters could be considered for a learning activity conducted in the authentic context (Hwang et al. 2008a).

1. Personal contexts sensed by the system: includes the learner's location and time of arrival, temperature, level of perspiration, heartbeat, blood pressure, etc.
2. Environmental contexts sensed by the system: includes the sensor's ID and location, the temperature, humidity, air ingredients, and other parameters of the environment around the sensor, and the objects that are approaching the sensor.
3. Feedback from the learner via the mobile learning device: includes the observed or sensed data of the target items (such as environmental temperature and the acid value of water, air pollution, shape and color of a tree, machine status after performing an operation, etc.), and acquired photos or interactions with the learning system (e.g., the answers to the test items or the log for operating the system).
4. Personal data retrieved from databases: includes the learner's profile and learning portfolio, such as the pre-defined schedule of the learner, expected starting time of a learning activity, the longest and shortest acceptable time period of a learning activity, the learning place, the learning paths or sequences of a course, the constraints or prohibitions of a course of learning activity, etc.
5. Environmental data retrieved from databases: includes the detailed information of the learning site, such as the schedule of learning activities arranged at the site, the constraints or management rules of the site, notes for using the site, the equipment located at the site, the persons who use or manage the site, etc.

Figure 11.2 shows the learning scenario of a context-aware u-learning activity conducted in a butterfly ecology garden in southern Taiwan. The aim of the activity was to guide the students to observe the butterfly ecology. Each student

Fig. 11.2 Illustrative example of a context-aware u-learning activity

had a PDA equipped with the wireless communication facility and an RFID reader, and each learning target (i.e., ecology area) was labeled with an RFID tag. With the help of the RFID technology, the learning system was able to detect the location of the students, guide them to find the target ecology areas, and show them the corresponding learning tasks or related learning materials.

11.4 Learning Supports for Context-Aware U-Learning

In the past decade, a variety of context-aware u-learning activities have been conducted with various learning strategies, tools, or assistance mechanisms. Although most of the activities are in the form of pilot studies, it can be foreseen that the popularity of mobile, wireless communication and sensing technologies will soon foster the development and application of context-aware ubiquitous learning. Currently, there are three categories of learning supports provided in the context-aware u-learning activities, that is, provision of location-based guidance with supplementary materials, provision of location-based guidance with learning advice, and provision of Mindtools or knowledge organization tools for exploring in the authentic context.

11.4.1 Provision of Location-Based Guidance with Supplementary Materials

The most straightforward way for providing context-aware learning supports is to guide the students to find the learning targets in the real world, and to provide them with the corresponding supplementary materials. Such an approach has been widely adopted in various practical applications, such as the u-learning activities conducted in museums (Chiou et al. 2010), cultural buildings (Shih et al. 2010), school campuses (Chen et al. 2008; Hwang et al. 2010b), or ecology parks (Chen et al. 2003). It engages students in extensive thinking by providing rich-resources that link what they are observing to relevant learning targets in the real-world environment or supplementary content in the database of the learning system. Such an approach enables students to know more details about learning targets, and hence the learning motivation of the students could be promoted. For example, when visiting an ancient building, the students' learning interests could be significantly promoted if the background stories of the building can be provided.

It should be noted that the supplementary materials provided via the mobile devices ought to be complementary to what can be observed or collected in the real-world environment. For example, when the students are observing an artifact in a museum, the information provided by the learning system could be the introduction to the artifact, or the other artifacts created by the same artist. It would be better to avoid showing the photo of the artifact and the information that has already been given on the instructional sign of the museum, unless parts of the artifact need to be noted and further explained.

11.4.2 Provision of Location-Based Guidance with Learning Advice

A further learning support for context-aware u-learning activities is to provide learning advice or suggestions to individual students based on their real-world learning status or learning performance. In recent years, most of the u-learning studies have adopted this approach. For example, Hwang et al. (2010a) proposed a decision-tree-oriented approach for providing learning advice to the students who were guided to learn to identify the characteristics of butterflies in a museum.

A remarkable example of providing learning advice for context-aware u-learning is the study of Hwang et al. (2009), who developed an expert system to advise the learners how to operate a set of devices for a complex chemical experiment procedure "single-crystal X-ray structure determination," which provides the most convincing evidence to elucidate the three-dimensional structure of crystalline solids such as porous materials. Such a technique is very useful to researchers in analyzing the features and potentials of the materials, and has become a must-learn technique which assists researchers in obtaining the atomic coordinates, bond lengths, bond angles and arrangement of atoms in nano-scale from single-crystal X-ray data. In traditional instruction, a three-to-six month training period is usually needed for a new researcher, since an experienced researcher is asked to accompany the novice. To provide a more efficient and effective learning environment, Hwang et al. (2009) developed a context-aware u-learning environment by installing RFID tags in the building to detect the locations of the learners. Each learner is equipped with a PDA with an RFID reader. Via sensing the learner's contexts (e.g., locations) and the environmental contexts (e.g., room temperature), the learning system is able to actively present instructional content retrieved from the server via the wireless network. Moreover, an expert system was developed for advising the novices during the training process based on the domain knowledge and practical experience provided by those experienced researchers.

In the first stage of the experimental procedure, the learner is guided toward the lab equipped with microscopes. The expert system will identify the status of the learner as "Crystal selecting", and hence the procedure for instructing the learner to select a crystal of good quality and suitable size through the optical microscope will be presented, as shown in Fig. 11.3.

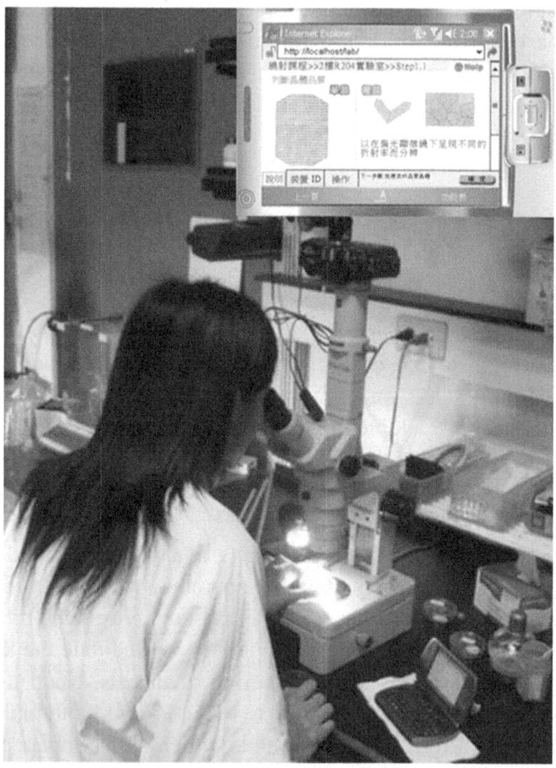

Fig. 11.3 Illustrative example of guiding the learner in the "crystal selecting" stage

In the second stage, the learner is guided to operate the X-ray diffractometer, as shown in Fig. 11.4. When the expert system confirms that the "operating the X-ray diffractometer" stage is completed, it will guide the student to another lab to proceed with the structural determination phase via operating analytical software on a computer connected to the X-ray diffractometer. Hwang et al. (2009) have shown that such an approach not only improves the efficiency and effectiveness of training the single-crystal X-ray structure determination procedure, but also reduces the manpower cost.

Most of the studies employed the "question-based" learning approach; that is, a series of questions were presented to the students via the mobile devices, and the students were required to find the answers based on their in-field observations and explorations. Some studies further encouraged the students to search for more data from the Internet during the learning process. If the students submitted an incorrect answer, the learning system would try to guide them to find the answer in the field. For example, in the study of Chu et al. (2010b), the students were asked to observe a set of target plants on the school campus and learn to identify the plants based on their appearance. The students were then asked to observe the "leaf point" of "Liquidambar" and answer the question prepared by the teacher, as shown in Fig. 11.5a.

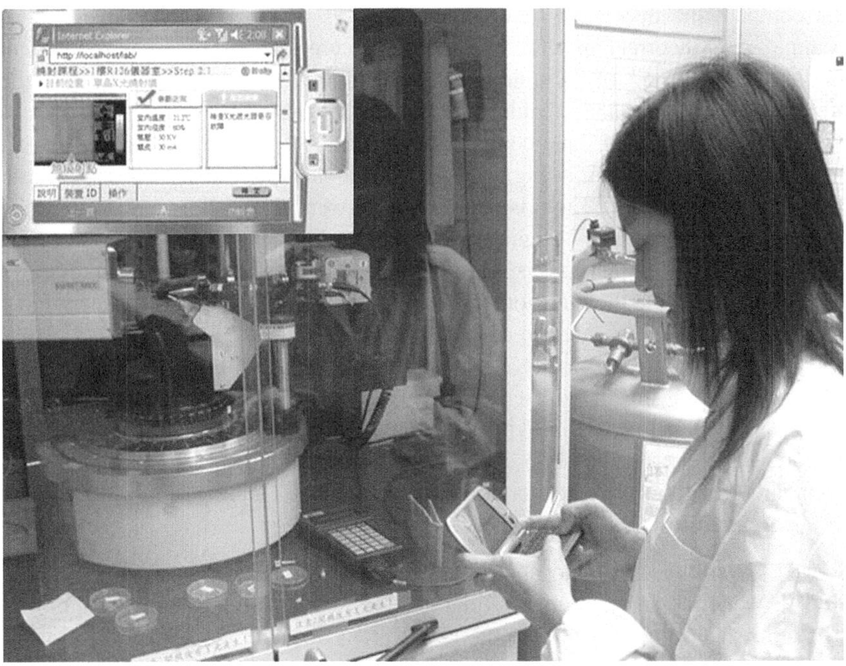

Fig. 11.4 Illustrative example of guiding the learner to operate the X-ray diffractometer

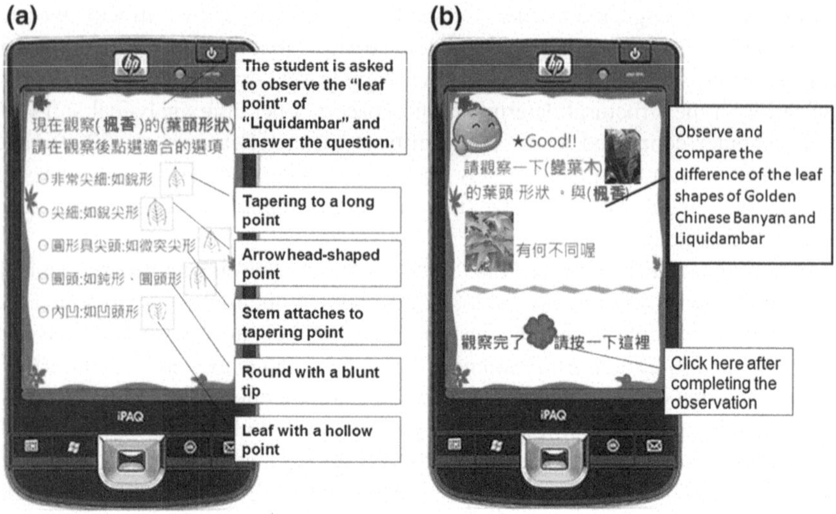

Fig. 11.5 Example of guiding the student to find and observe the target plant (Chu et al. 2010b)

If the student failed to correctly identify the plant feature, the learning system would guide the student to observe another plant exhibiting the incorrect answer, and compare the difference between the features of the two target plants. For example, if an incorrect answer "Round with a blunt tip" was given by the student for the "leaf shape" of "Liquidambar", the learning system would guide the student to find the plant "Golden Leaves" that really has a leaf point that is "Round with a blunt tip" and compare it with the leaf point of the original target "Liquidambar", as shown in Fig. 11.5b. The student would then be asked to walk back to the target plant "Liquidambar", and answer the question concerning "the leaf shape of Liquidambar" again. If the student submitted the correct answer (i.e., "long and thin"), the learning system would guide him/her to investigate the in-depth issue related to the question, such as "Why is the leaf shape of Liquidambar long and thin? Is this related to its growing environment?"

Chu et al. (2010b) further formulated such location-based guidance with learning advice as the "Two-Tier Test Guiding" (T^3G) mechanism, which is able to detect the location of individual students and provide them with adaptive supports via the use of mobile devices, sensing technologies and wireless communication facilities. The details of the Two-Tier Test Guiding (T^3G) Mechanism are given as follows:

Step 1: Guide the student to find the location of the target plant.
Step 2: Conduct first-tier observations on the target plant: Present the first-tier question concerning a feature of the target plant to guide the student to observe that feature.

Step 2.1: If the student fails to recognize the feature of that plant by giving an incorrect description:

Step 2.1.1 Guide the student to a comparative plant to show the difference in that feature between the two plants.
Step 2.1.2: Ask the student to answer the question again. If the student fails to correctly recognize the feature again, present the corresponding supplementary materials to the student.

Step 2.2: If the student correctly recognizes the feature of the plant:

Step 2.2.2: If the student fails to correctly answer the second-tier question, present some hints or supplementary materials to the student and go to Step 2.2.1.

Step 3: Repeat Step 2 until the student has correctly recognized all of the features of the plant and has been confirmed to be well equipped with the relevant knowledge.
Step 4: Guide the student to visit the next target plant and repeat Steps 2 to 5 until all of the target plants are observed.

11.4.3 Provision of Mindtools or Knowledge Organization Tools for Exploring in the Authentic Context

Jonassen et al. (1998) indicated that "technologies should not support learning by attempting to instruct the learners, but rather should be used as knowledge construction tools that students learn with, not from." Mindtools are such an effective computer system for helping learners interpret and organize their personal knowledge (Jonassen 1994, 1999; Jonassen and Carr 2000). Jonassen et al. (1998, p. 1) formally defined Mindtools as "Computer applications that, when used by learners to represent what they know, necessarily engage them in critical thinking about the content they are studying."

Recently, researchers have attempted to develop Mindtools to assist learners in interpreting and organizing knowledge in a context-aware u-learning environment, and have achieved satisfactory results. For example, Hwang et al. (2011b) reported a concept map-oriented context-aware u-learning approach for helping students organize their knowledge about butterfly ecology based on their in-field observations and the prior knowledge learned from the textbooks. Hwang et al. (2011c) further developed an interactive concept map approach to supporting knowledge organization for in-field learning activities. Hwang et al. (2011a) indicated that "concept maps would be a good choice if the learning objective is to find the relationships between the learning targets (or concepts) instead of finding their similarities and differences…"

Another form of Mindtool, that is, grid-based knowledge organizing tools, has been reported by researchers for supporting context-aware u-learning activities that aim to foster students' differentiating knowledge (Chu et al. 2010a; Chu et al. 2010; Hwang et al. 2011a). In such a learning activity, the students are asked to collect data from a set of learning targets (e.g., plants, ecology areas, or cultural relics) and record the data in a grid based on their observations and explorations in the field. Cragun and Steudel (1987) have indicated that representing knowledge in grids makes it easy to inspect and analyze the organization and logic of the knowledge; Ford et al. (1991) further indicated that the visual metaphor of grids amplifies individuals' ability to recognize the distinctions between the targets.

11.5 Potential Research Issues

It can be seen that, owing to the context-awareness features, a context-aware u-learning environment is able to conduct more active and more adaptive learning activities in the real world with learning supports from the digital world, which makes it quite different from traditional in-class learning, e-learning or even the broad sense u-learning environment (Hwang et al. 2008a). Therefore, various research issues arise in this new learning environment, including the usage of personal and environmental contexts in improving the learning effectiveness of students, the learning strategies for fostering the real-world problem-solving abilities of students, the methods for evaluating real-world problem-solving abilities, and the potential applications of such an innovative approach. Accordingly, several issues concerning context-aware u-learning are summarized as follows:

1. Re-examine and revise pedagogical theories for context-aware u-learning. As context-aware u-learning is still in its developmental stage, researchers with educational backgrounds may propose some innovative thoughts about its pedagogy by modifying some existing theories, in particular, those related to cognitive processing.
2. Reconsider existing learning strategies or tools for context-aware u-learning. Although context-aware u-learning seems to be a new way of learning, the nature and objective of the cognitive and learning processes remain the same. Consequently, more research can be conducted to investigate the learning effectiveness of applying existing learning strategies and tools to u-learning activities after making proper adjustments.
3. Develop new assessment strategies and measuring tools for context-aware u-learning. As the learning scenarios of a context-aware u-learning environment are quite different from those of other learning environments, new assessment strategies and measuring tools for evaluating the students' learning performance as well as measuring their perceptions of the learning activities need to be developed.

4. Apply the context-aware u-learning approach to new applications, and analyze the learning portfolios in depth. It is expected that more innovative use of context-aware u-learning can be conducted and reported, in particular, large-scale and long-term studies. Moreover, as context-aware u-learning environments have the capacity to record a variety of each individual learner's personal information, related behaviors and environmental parameters (as a personal electronic portfolio), it is expected that researchers can properly utilize these data to analyze student learning processes and related factors which may facilitate learning (Hsieh et al. 2011; Peng et al. 2009; Shih et al. 2011).
5. Applying the context-aware u-learning approach to enterprise training and professional development. As has been demonstrated by the study of Hwang et al. (2009), context-aware u-learning has the potential of providing one-to-one training for complex operational procedures, implying the potential of applying such an approach to enterprise training programs, in particular, for those programs that require step-by-step guidance and hints. In addition, a review of research trends in mobile and ubiquitous learning by Hwang and Tsai (2011) further indicated that "it is worth paying more attention to investigations of teachers and working adults' mobile and ubiquitous learning in the future" since these issues are important but have been rarely investigated in the past decade.
6. Developing more Mindtools for context-aware u-learning. In addition to the concept map and the grid-based approach, there are several computer systems that can serve as Mindtools, such as databases, spreadsheets, computer conferencing, hypermedia construction, simulation programs, dynamic modeling tools and expert systems (Jonassen et al. 1998). It is expected that the use of more Mindtools will be taken into account by researchers when designing context-aware u-learning activities.

11.6 Conclusions

Combining digital and real-world resources to provide an authentic and supportive learning environment to learners has been considered as a promising approach. In this chapter, we have attempted to present the current progress of context-aware u-learning and the relevant research issues. It can be recognized that such a learning approach has great potential in providing an authentic learning environment in a more active and adaptive manner. Moreover, the future advancements and popularity of sensing and u-computing technologies could even amplify the effectiveness of this approach.

Before ending this chapter, I would like to remind the readers that technologies are not the most important consideration for establishing an authentic learning environment with access to digital resources, although they do enable the opportunities of providing a more powerful learning system with rich resources. The key factor of the success of a learning activity is the learning design, including the learning content and learning strategies that guide students to achieve the learning objectives. Therefore, in some situations, not all of the technologies need to be included in developing the learning environments. The adoption of technologies should depend on the learning objective requirements. For example, Nussbaum et al. (2009) demonstrated an effective use of mobile technologies in a mathematics course. In their study, mobile devices were used in a face-to-face collaborative learning activity to encourage the students to solve mathematics problems in small groups; therefore, sensing technologies were not necessary in this case. Another study reported by Hung et al. (2010) aimed to foster the students' exploration ability in an ecology park; consequently, sensing technologies were not used for guiding the students in the designed activity; instead, the students were equipped with a mobile device, a telescope and a digital camera for observing the learning targets and collecting data during the exploration process. It can be seen that broad-sense u-learning activities were designed in these two studies.

To sum up, it can be foreseen that the number of context-aware u-learning applications will increase at a fast pace, and the effectiveness of this type of learning will be more significantly revealed owing to the popularity and advancements of technologies; in the meantime, more attention needs to be paid to the development of relevant strategies and tools as well as to the teachers' professional competences in the future.

11.7 Gwo-Jen Hwang, PhD

Chair Professor, Graduate Institute of Digital Learning and Education
National Taiwan University of Science and Technology
43, Sec.4, Keelung Rd., Taipei, 106, Taiwan
E-mail: gjhwang.academic@gmail.com

Gwo-Jen Hwang is a Chair Professor at National Taiwan University of Science and Technology, Taipei, Taiwan. His research interests include mobile and ubiquitous learning, adaptive learning, and knowledge engineering. Dr. Hwang has published more than 400 academic papers. Owing to the good reputation in academic research and innovative inventions of e-learning, in 2007 and 2011, he received the annual Most Outstanding Researcher Award from the National Science Council in Taiwan.

References

Abowd GD (1999) Classroom 2000: an experiment with the instrumentation of a living educational environment. IBM Syst J 38(4):508–530

Apkarian J, and Dawer A (2000) Interactive control education with virtual presence on the web. In: proceedings of American Control Conference June 2000, Chicago, 3985–3990

Barrett E, Lally V (1999) Gender differences in an on-line learning environment. J Comput Assist Learn 15:48–60
Beigl M, Gellersen HW, Schmidt A (2001) Mediacups: experience with design and use of computer-augmented everyday objects. Comput Netw 35(4):401–409
Brown JS, Collins A, Duguid P (1989) Situated cognition and the culture of learning. Educ Researcher 18(1):32–42
Burks O (1996) A virtual classroom approach to teaching circuit analysis. IEEE Trans Educ 39:287–296
Chen GD, Chang CK, Wang CY (2008) Ubiquitous learning website: scaffold learners by mobile devices with information-aware techniques. Comput Educ 50(1):77–90
Chen YS, Kao TC, Sheu JP (2003) A mobile learning system for scaffolding bird watching learning. J Comput Assist Learn 19(1):347–359
Cheng L, Marsic I (2002) Piecewise network awareness service for wireless/mobile pervasive computing. Mobile Netw Appli (MONET) 7(4):269–278
Chiou CK, Tseng JCR, Hwang GJ, Heller S (2010) An adaptive navigation support system for conducting context-aware ubiquitous learning in museums. Comput Educ 55(2):834–845
Chu HC, Hwang GJ, Tsai CC (2010a) A knowledge engineering approach to developing mindtools for context-aware ubiquitous learning. Comput Educ 54(1):289–297
Chu HC, Hwang GJ, Tseng JCR (2010) An innovative approach for developing and employing electronic libraries to support context-aware ubiquitous learning. The Electronic Library 28(6):873–890
Chu HC, Hwang GJ, Tsai CC, Tseng JCR (2010) A two-tier test approach to developing location-aware mobile learning systems for natural science courses. Comput Educ 55(4):1618–1627
Cragun BJ, Steudel HJ (1987) A decision-table-based processor for checking completeness and consistency in rule-based expert systems. Int J Man Mach Stud 26:633–648
Davidovic A, Warren J, Trichina E (2003) Learning benefits of structural example-based adaptive tutoring systems. IEEE Trans Educ 46:241–251
Fabos B, Young MD (1999) Telecommunication in the classroom: rhetoric versus reality. Rev Educ Res 69(3):217–259
Feeney LM, Ahlgren B, Westerlund A (2001) Spontaneous networking: an application-oriented approach to ad hoc networking. IEEE Commun Mag 39(6):176–181
Ford KM, Petry FE, Adams-Webber JR, Chang PJ (1991) An approach to knowledge acquisition based on the structure of personal construct systems. IEEE Trans Knowl Data Eng 3:78–87
Gang Z, Jason TL, Peter AN (1996) Curriculum knowledge representation and manipulation in knowledge-based tutoring systems. IEEE Trans Knowl Data Eng 8:679–689
Hill B (1999) A conceptual framework for understanding information seeking in open-ended information system. Educ Tech Res Dev 47(1):5–27
Hill JR, Hannafin MJ (1997) Cognitive strategies and learning from the world wide web. Educ Tech Res Dev 45(4):37–64
Hsieh SW, Jang YR, Hwang GJ, Chen NS (2011) Effects of teaching and learning styles on students' reflection levels for ubiquitous learning. Comput Educ 57(1):1194–1201
Hung PH, Lin YF, Hwang GJ (2010) Formative assessment design for PDA integrated ecology observation. Educ Tech Soc 13(3):33–42
Hwang GJ, Chang HF (2011) A formative assessment-based mobile learning approach to improving the learning attitudes and achievements of students. Comput Educ 56(1):1023–1031
Hwang GJ, Tsai CC (2011) Research trends in mobile and ubiquitous learning: A review of publications in selected journals from 2001 to 2010. British J Educ Tech 42(4):E65–E70
Hwang GJ, Chu HC, Lin YS, Tsai CC (2011a) A knowledge acquisition approach to developing mindtools for organizing and sharing differentiating knowledge in a ubiquitous learning environment. Comput Educ 57(1):1368–1377
Hwang GJ, Chu HC, Shih JL, Huang SH, Tsai CC (2010a) A decision-tree-oriented guidance mechanism for conducting nature science observation activities in a context-aware ubiquitous learning environment. Educ Tech Soc 13(2):53–64

Hwang GJ, Kuo FR, Yin PY, Chuang KH (2010b) A heuristic algorithm for planning personalized learning paths for context-aware ubiquitous learning. Comput Educ 54(2):404–415

Hwang GJ, Shi YR, Chu HC (2011b) A concept map approach to developing collaborative mindtools for context-aware ubiquitous learning. British J Educ Tech 42(5):778–789

Hwang GJ, Tsai CC, Yang SJH (2008) Criteria, strategies and research issues of context-aware ubiquitous learning. J Educ Tech Soc 11(2):81–91

Hwang GJ, Tsai PS, Tsai CC, Tseng JCR (2008) A novel approach for assisting teachers in analyzing student web-searching behaviors. Comput Educ 51(2):926–938

Hwang GJ, Wu PH, Ke HR (2011c) An interactive concept map approach to supporting mobile learning activities for natural science courses. Comput Educ 57(4):2272–2280

Hwang GJ, Yang TC, Tsai CC, Yang SJH (2009) A context-aware ubiquitous learning environment for conducting complex experimental procedures. Comput Educ 53(2):402–413

Jonassen DH (1994, 1999). Computers as mindtools for schools, engaging critical thinking. Prentice-Hall, NJ

Jonassen DH, Carr CS (2000) Mindtools: affording multiple knowledge representations for learning. In: Lajoie SP (ed) Computers as cognitive tools. No more walls. Lawlence Erlbaum Associates, Inc vol 2. Hillsdale, NJ, pp 165–196

Jonassen DH, Carr C, Yueh HP (1998) Computers as mindtools for engaging learners in critical thinking. TechTrends 43(2):24–32

Kawahara Y, Minami M, Morikawa H, Aoyama T (2003) A real-world oriented networking for ubiquitous computing environment. IPSJ SIG Technical Reports (UBI-1-1), 39:1–6

Khan B (1997) Web-Based Instruction. Educational Technology Publication, NJ

Kindberg T, Fox A (2002) System software for ubiquitous computing. IEEE Pervasive Comput 1(1):70–81

Kwon O, Yoo K, Suh E (2005) ubiES: An intelligent expert system for proactive services deploying ubiquitous computing technologies. Paper presented at the 38th hawaii international conference on system sciences (HICSS'05). Hilton Waikoloa Village, Big Island, Hawaii

Liaw SS, Huang HM, Chen GD (2007) An activity-theoretical approach to investigate learners' factors toward e-learning systems. Comput Hum Behav 23:1906–1920

Liu GZ, Hwang GJ (2010) A key step to understanding paradigm shifts in e-learning: towards context-aware ubiquitous learning. British J Educ Tech 41(2):E1–E9

Lonsdale P, Baber C, Sharples M, Arvanitis T (2003) A context awareness architecture for facilitating mobile learning. Paper presented at the meeting of the second European conference on learning with mobile devices (MLEARN), UK

Minami M, Morikawa H, Aoyama T (2004) The design of naming-based service composition system for ubiquitous computing applications. In: the proceedings of the 2004 international symposium on applications and the internet workshops (saintw'04 IEEE Comput Soc, DC, pp 304–312

Norris C, Hossain A, Soloway E (2011) Using smartphones as essential tools for learning- a call to place schools on the right side of the 21st century. Educ Tech May-June, 18–25

Nussbaum M, Alvarez C, McFarlane A, Gomez F, Claro S, Radovic D (2009) Technology as small group face-to-face collaborative scaffolding. Comput Educ 52(1):147–153

Ogata H, Yano Y (2004) Context-aware support for computer-supported ubiquitous learning. Paper presented at the 2nd IEEE international workshop on wireless and mobile technologies in education, Taiwan, Mar

Panjaburee P, Hwang GJ, Triampo W, Shih BY (2010) A multi-expert approach for developing testing and diagnostic systems based on the concept-effect model. Comput Educ 55(2):527–540

Pena-Shaffa JB, Nichollsb C (2004) Analyzing student interactions and meaning construction in computer bulletin board discussions. Comput Educ 42(3):243–265

Peng HY, Chuang PY, Hwang GJ, Chu HC, Wu TT, Huang SA (2009) Ubiquitous performance-support system as Mindtool: A case study of instructional decision making and learning assistant. Educ Tech Soc 12(1):107–120
Ponnekanti SR, Lee B, Fox A, Hanrahan P, Winograd T (2001) ICrafter: a service framework for ubiquitous computing environments. In: the Proceedings of the 3rd international conference on ubiquitous computing (Ubicomp), lecture notes in computer science, Springer, Georgia, 2201 56–75
Pui ML, William GS (1996) Developing and implementing interactive multimedia in education. IEEE Trans Educ 39:430–435
Ringwood JV, Galvin G (2002) Computer-aided Learning in artificial neural networks. IEEE Trans Educ 45(4):380–387
Robert OH (1996) Teaching in a computer classroom with a hyperlinked, interactive book. IEEE Trans Educ 39:327–335
Rodríguez M, Favela J (2003) A framework for supporting autonomous agents in ubiquitous computing environments. Paper presented at the meeting of system support for ubiquitous computing workshop. workshop conducted at the fifth annual conference on ubiquitous computing (UbiComp), Washington
Rogers Y, Price S, Randell C, Fraser DS, Weal M, Fitzpatrick G (2005) Ubi-learning integrating indoor and outdoor learning experiences. Commun ACM 48(1):55–59
Sally WL (1996) A new approach to interactive tutorial software for engineering education. IEEE Trans Educ 39:399–408
Shih JL, Chu H. C, Hwang GJ, Kinshuk (2011) An investigation of attitudes of students and teachers about participating in a context-aware ubiquitous learning activity. British J Educ Tech 42(3):373–394
Shih JL, Chuang CW, Hwang GJ (2010) An inquiry-based mobile learning approach to enhancing social science learning effectiveness. Educ Tech Soc 13(4):50–62
Sreenivasan R, Levine WS, Rubloff GW (2000) Some dynamic-simulator-based control education models. In: proceedings of ACC'00, Chicago, pp 3458–3462
Uemukai T, Hara T, Nishio S (2004) A method for selecting output data from ubiquitous terminals in a ubiquitous computing environment. In: the proceedings of the 24th international conference on distributed computing systems workshops (ICDCSW) IEEE Comput Soc Japan, pp 562–567
Wenger E (1997) Communities of practice: learning, meaning, and identity. Cambridge University Press, UK
William MM, Marion OH (1996) Implementation issues in SIMPLE learning environments. IEEE Trans Educ 39:423–429
Williams van Rooij S (2009) Scaffolding project-based learning with the project management body of knowledge (PMBOK®). Comput Educ 52(1):210–219
Yakimovicz AD, Murphy KL (1995) Constructivism and collaboration on the Internet case study of a graduate class experience. Comput Educ 24(3):203–209
Yang SJH, Zhang J, Chen IYL (2007) Ubiquitous provision of context-aware web services. Int J Web Serv Res 4(4):83–103
Yang SJH, Okamoto T, Tseng SS (2008) A matter of context-aware ubiquitous learning. J Educ Technol Soc 11(2):1–2

Chapter 12
Reusable Authentic Learning Scenario Creation in Ubiquitous Learning Environments

Kinshuk and Ryan Jesse

Traditional classroom learning paradigm has been criticized for being too artificial, rigid and unresponsive to the needs of today's society. Researchers argue that learning is largely a situated phenomenon and real-life experiences in authentic settings are a primary requirement for successful and effective learning. Ubiquitous learning environment are touted and look forward to provide such settings of authentic learning, by making virtual and electronic resources available through mobile devices to help learners during their interactions with physical objects in their surroundings. Ubiquitous learning no longer restricts learning process to be inside the classroom or formal learning environments. Rather, the learning involves situating learners in both the real world and the virtual world to extend learners' learning experiences.

Technology has also enabled mobile devices to make use of various multimedia objects. Recently, mobile devices equipped with input and sensor options have allowed for user generated content, which can be used to create examples of real life learning situations, or authentic learning examples. However, existing research and implementations display a gap between the creation of authentic learning examples and their subsequent reuse as learning objects (LOs). Therefore, this chapter will discuss an implementation of an application for a mobile device to author authentic learning examples for ubiquitous learning environments, with ability to be reused.

Kinshuk · R. Jesse
Athabasca University, Athabasca, Canada
e-mail: kinshuk@ieee.org

R. Huang et al. (eds.), *Reshaping Learning*, New Frontiers of Educational Research,
DOI: 10.1007/978-3-642-32301-0_12, © Springer-Verlag Berlin Heidelberg 2013

12.1 Introduction

The extremely rapid growth of wireless technology in recent years, increasing availability of high bandwidth network infrastructures, advances in mobile technologies and the popularity of handheld devices have opened up new accessibility opportunities for citizens. The true potential of e-learning as "anytime, anywhere" has finally begun to be realized.

Research is now becoming mainstream in exploring and developing different applications and content delivery systems, extending our understanding of ubiquitous learning to provide rich learning experiences. For example, mobile device users can capture and upload photos from their smartphones directly into social platforms, wherein they tag subjects in the photos with their names; ostensibly adding metadata to a multimedia sample. The content can then be shared amongst other users who may consume the media in any number of contexts, mobile or otherwise. Frequently, the media captured with modern mobile devices includes location data like GPS coordinates. Many mobile applications also allow users to query and share their current location.

This phenomenon creates new possibilities for these concepts (capturing multimedia with mobile sensors and sharing across multiple users via a centralized store) in concert, when applied to ubiquitous learning. With a mobile device and appropriate mobile application, a learner could capture multimedia, such as photos or videos in any location. Within the same integrated application, the learner could add descriptive metadata to describe the multimedia content for assisting others in finding the resource. Furthermore, the location of each media sample, representing where a learning situation occurred, can be added. This is a prime example of ubiquitous learning which permits learners to participate in educational activities without the constraint of location by focusing on the mobility of the user, thereby enabling learning outside the classroom with portable technologies, what Traxler and Kukulska-Hulme (2005) also described as essential ingredients of mobile learning.

Moreover, learner generated content can be shared via learning experiences and activities in a well justified shift in learning theory to the social constructionism paradigm. To further the goal of sharing learning content, a repository can be leveraged as a distribution platform. Therefore, a tool is required, for learners and instructional designers alike, to easily create learning content and activities and in turn, deposit in the aforementioned repository.

Research has shown that large efforts have been made in developing interoperable tools for editing and running IMS Content Packages and IMS Learning Designs. However, to take advantage of these existing tools, content must be available in a format that is widely implemented. This enables the use of existing platforms such as learning management systems (LMSs) and learning design players in which to deliver content. Authoring content in an interoperable format precludes the need for development of specialized tools to permit reuse and allows for distribution beyond the context in which the content was authored.

Creating learning content and activities in a standardized format is critical. Without encapsulating learning content within well-defined formats, content captured in a ubiquitous setting would be difficult to import into other contexts. Most implementations of ubiquitous learning environments lack interoperability with learning management systems, playback environments, and other authoring and editing tools, representing a contextual boundary. Nor do these environments provide the capacity for authoring learning designs, specifically using authentically captured learning objects. These issues represent a major research problem. The research presented in this chapter seeks to enable reuse of authored learning content and activities in ubiquitous learning environments via standardization to promote interoperability.

The aim is to develop a methodology and associated implementation to create standardized learning resources and activities from authentic learning examples in ubiquitous learning environments to address the following research questions:

1. Can mobile device functionality be utilized to create, in context, authentic ubiquitous learning examples contained in reusable learning objects?
2. Can these learning objects be utilized in context to create learning designs conforming to IMS standards?
3. Can these learning designs permit authentically authored ubiquitous learning content and learning activities to be shared across contextual boundaries?

12.2 Background

The research addressed in this chapter is centered on using mobile functionality to capture authentic learning examples for use in authoring of learning objects or learning designs in ubiquitous learning environments.

While the concept of learning objects remains ill-defined in the literature, McGreal (2004) classified LOs into four categories, from broad to contextual (McGreal 2004). The first learning object definition defines it as any asset, component, or learning resource. McGreal (2004) points to definitions that stipulate that a learning object, in this classification, can be 'anything' and 'everything.' Examples could be a person, or a tree; meaning learning can be garnered from any context. This definition is prohibitively broad and Sosteric and Hesemeier (2002) argue that it would be too general "to be of any use in identifying, developing, or criticizing learning objects."

Secondly, the learning objects could be any digital resource, such as a content object, media object, or information object. Wiley (2000) argues that anything digital qualifies as a learning object, regardless of an educational purpose, such as a video, electronic text, or an MP3 audio file. Downs (2004) argues that learning objects must be digital to enable online use; physical entities cannot be readily shared.

The third classification of the term 'learning object' is a digital resource with an explicit learning purpose or goal. Definitions by Koper (2003), Churchill (2008), and Sosteric and Hesemeier (2002) state that the meaning of learning object must have a pedagogical purpose such as a learning outcome.

The last and most specific meaning of a learning object stipulates its use in a specific learning environment. In this classification, the LO would be referred to as a reusable learning object (McGreal 2004). A specific learning environment, such as a learning management system or a learning object standardization such as IMS Content Packaging or SCORM, are requirements to apply this classification. Due to the degree of variation in those definitions, the practical approach is to present the selected aggregation of learning object definitions from those explored in Churchill (2008), and McGreal (2004, 2006):

- digital resource in support of learning (Wiley 2000);
- reusable instructional component (McGreal 2004);
- possessing intrinsic instructional value (Higgs et al. 2003);
- learning units consisting of learning resources such as multimedia or text (McGreal 2006); and,
- a module demonstrating concept(s) (Cochrane 2005).

Given this aggregation, a learning object in the context of this chapter is referred as digital, reusable, and designed for an educational purpose in a learning environment. The selected definition aligns with the fourth and most specific terminology classification previously outlined, as supported by (Ally 2004). Thus, learning object, under the selected definition, is synonymous with reusable learning object. Reusability in an LO is a necessary attribute of learning objects; learning content authored in one context must be executable in another context (Higgs et al. 2003).

Functionally, as Wiley (2000) states, learning objects serve as an instructional design component in e-learning for the development and delivery of educational content. LOs are small digital entities containing instructional media for electronic delivery. Electronic courseware developed for a learning management system, such as Moodle, contain standardized learning objects which may contain digital text, video, audio, and assessment tasks (McGreal 2004). Furthermore, McGreal (2004) submits that learning objects serve an educational purpose or learning outcome by being components "in a lesson or assemblage of lessons grouped in units, modules, courses, and even programmes" (McGreal 2004). This assertion is supported by Downs (2004) who stipulates that learning objects must be modular and able to be combined and packaged into larger units. For the aggregation of learning objects into larger units to be possible, the property of granularity must be maintained in a learning object (Koper 2003). Granularity is the "size" of a learning object and can be measured in the time it takes to use a learning object, the value of the learning presented, or the number of concepts covered. Optimum granularity is a debated topic, and ranges from a single concept, to a larger educational objective, to a specific allotment of time (Moisey et al. 2006; Wiley 1999).

The notion of modularity implies that LOs must be independent. Learning objects are self-contained and do not rely on other learning objects or resources to make sense. They can entirely encapsulate "coherent chunks of information, activities or assessment" (Higgs et al. 2003).

For learning objects to be organized into larger entities, they must be interoperable (Downs 2004; Higgs et al. 2003). Objects produced by different authors may be combined to produce a learning module given this degree of compatibility. LO standardization is critical to this endeavour.

The benefits of learning objects are extolled by Wiley (2000) and Downs (2004) as:

- accessible and affordable;
- reusable and able to be reassembled and combined to support instructional needs, learning scenarios, and goals; and,
- ability to be accessed by many simultaneous users (unlike traditional educational media).

Critics of learning objects contend that they are too rigid, standards are not being leveraged, and that despite the interest initially expressed in the literature, reusability concerns remain (McGreal 2008). The mechanism proposed in this chapter includes a flexible authoring environment, which helps address reusability via standards based output.

Extending learning objects, to incorporate support for mobile technologies, creates mobile learning objects (MLO) (Cruz-Flores and López-Morteo 2008). This approach extends the learning objects to the mobile devices and provides an additional context of interaction between students and educational resources (Cruz-Flores and López-Morteo 2008). The MLO paradigm is directly inherited from LO theory whereby an MLO entity is self-contained, interoperable, and reusable. MLOs additionally include adaptation in their definition so that learning activities can utilize mobile technology (Cruz-Flores and López-Morteo 2008).

Castillo and Ayala (2008) propose two types of interaction with mloS that particularly support ubiquitous learning. A learner can move to the learning situation which allows interaction with learning resources when and where the authentic activity occurs. This type of interaction requires location aware mobile learning objects, which could be authored using the proposed mechanism for later sharing and reuse.

Secondly, MLO can simulate a learning situation in order to enable the learners to engage with an authentic ubiquitous activity, anytime and anywhere. Authentic learning situations are captured in authentic learning examples, and simulation activities could be created using learning design.

Svensson et al. (2010) expand on learning object theory by defining emerging learning objects (ELOs). They present a case of convergence, wherein mobile devices, such as modern smart phones, host multiple functionality such as media players, cameras, GPS and communication tools. They propose that mobile devices can, as a result of convergence, support digital content creation for a wide range of learning activities which can be augmented with metadata from sensors like GPS. Emerging learning objects refer to learning content representing a learning situation, augmented with sensor metadata, created in an ubiquitous context, with limited formal control over the capture process.

A strict ELO definition states that sensor data, like GPS location, is captured as metadata. However, IMS Metadata (IMS GLC 2001) does not provide an element or data definition in the information model for contextual metadata. In order to maintain compliance with the IMS Metadata standard, the contextual metadata was included within the learning object, rather than in the metadata. When deviating from schemas, like IMS Metadata, there is difficulty in maintaining the semantics across systems and contexts which are left to resolve possible ambiguity or incomplete data (Svensson et al. 2010). This would curtail interoperability, thus, this issue was avoided in the proposed implementation. It would be a trivial programming effort to augment the existing metadata to include contextual (location based) metadata; the difficulty would be in ensuring reuse and standard compliance.

This raises the problem regarding how to represent "complexity of representing contextual characteristics as metadata" and requires research into the interoperability of ELO metadata (Svensson et al. 2010). Svensson et al. (2010) present a linked data approach to depicting ELOs with contextual metadata. Other approaches include utilizing the Web Ontology Language (OWL) and Resource Description Framework (RDF) to form ontologies for defining authentic learning examples (Svensson et al. 2010). Specifically, the Learning Object Context Ontology (LOCO) and the mobile-LOCO projects provide a framework to elicit context-specific metadata garnered from learning objects and learning designs (Jovanovic et al. 2007; Siadaty et al. 2008).

The literature shows an absence of a tool that extends the authoring context in ubiquitous learning environments. Such a ubiquitous authoring tool is necessary as asserted by Yang et al. (2004) "that the value of authentic activity is not constrained to learning in real-life locations and practice" and that authentic activities can enhance learning online. Hence, this tool will permit capturing of these authentic activities and then re-using them in different modes of learning. Furthermore, Griffiths et al. (2005) state that specialized tools to provide user friendly methods to author learning designs used within a specific pedagogy may be required. In this case, the tool provides a method of authoring in an authentic learning or social constructionism pedagogy.

The IMS LD based ubiquitous authoring tool presented in this chapter can arguably be classified as a general purpose tool rather than a specific purpose tool. "Not all users need access to the whole specification" and that tool complexity can be reduced by presenting only the required functionality (Griffiths et al. 2005). This is useful if the tool is used for authoring in a well defined pedagogic approach, however, the proposed tool implements the breadth of the IMS LD Level A standard. Thus, it should be considered as a general purpose tool and is not limited to any particular pedagogy.

12.2.1 Mobile Sensors

The inclusion of integrated hardware sensors in mobile devices provides the possibility of augmenting learning activities with sensor data. Technology enhanced learning activities, such as created with the ubiquitous authoring tool in this project, capture spatially distributed physical sensory data, such as video, photos, audio recordings, and GPS locations. Vogel et al. (2010) state that there are ongoing research challenges related to integrating this collected data to support learning. Thus, the proposed tool must promote capturing contextual experiences via multimedia examples of the environment and their locations. Context is defined as "any information illustrating the situation of a learner" such as location, time, activities, and surrounding environmental characteristics (Vogel et al. 2010). As a result, the proposed tool is intended to capture a representation of all of these contextual attributes.

A number of systems are available in the literature that create authentic learning and demonstrate mobile learning via sensor data. Examples include the HyCon framework wherein mobile devices can be used to browse, search, and create new learning materials in a mobile context (Hansen and Bouvin 2009); Mobile Butterfly-Watching Learning System where mobile learners capture photos in the field using a PDA (Ogata et al. 2010); Learning Environment for Mobile Network-Able Devices (LEMONADE) providing an interface to author learning activities for student fieldwork (Giemza et al. 2010); Linking of RFID and Movie System (LORAMS) in which users can record experiential videos on a mobile device and tag the location or physical object in the video with an RFID (Ogata 2008); and, Advanced Mobile and Ubiquitous Learning Environments for Teachers and Students (AMULETS) seeking to structure user generated content (photos, videos, audio), and contextual content (GPS) for use as guides during authentic learning scenarios (Pettersson and Gil 2010). However, reuse of content in multiple contexts is limited in these systems. Typically, the contextual and authentic learning examples created within these systems appear to be shared only within the system they were authored for.

To this point, all mobile sensor projects provide for capturing or authoring of learning content using sensor data. However, an array of projects uses sensor data to present or dynamically create an appropriate learning object for playback in a given environment. For example, Mitchell and Race (2005) describe a system which accesses learning objects related to physical entities or locations via QR codes. Li et al. (2009) adapt learning objects to form ubiquitous learning objects (ULO) suitable for use in a mobile environment based on learners' environmental contexts such as screen size, network speeds, and device storage capacity. These ubiquitous learning use cases fit within run tool or player context, while the tool in our research is primarily concerned with sensor data at design time.

12.2.2 Authentic Learning

Authentic learning is an instructional theory focused on learning in context, or real life application of knowledge (Rule 2006). Rule states that authentic tasks are used to integrate knowledge and skills into life or work setting, via complex activities. Instructional approaches that utilize authentic learning tasks include problem based learning, situated learning, constructive learning environments, and collaborative learning environments (Rule 2006).

Lombardi (2007) asserts that authentic learning can be implemented with role-playing exercises, participation in a community of practise, or case studies. Thus, authentic learning can be viewed as learning by doing, rather than an instructionalist pedagogy; learner motivation is increased as a result.

In the past, learning by doing may have been difficult to implement; but technological tools, such as simulations, observation using remote instruments, field work with mobile devices as data collection platforms, and connecting with mentors and research communities enables authentic learning experiences in ubiquitous learning environments (Lombardi 2007).

Lombardi (2007) and Herrington et al. (2003) put forth ten design elements for authentic learning experiences, namely, real-world relevance, ill-defined problems, sustained investigation, multiple sources and perspectives, collaboration, reflection, interdisciplinary perspective, integrated assessment, productivity, and multiple outcomes.

Rule (2006) underscores the importance of inquiry based learning as a component of authentic learning—wherein students "engage in asking questions, conducting studies, drawing conclusions, revising theories, and communicating results to others."

Collectively, these elements describe authentic learning as a constructivist pedagogical method. The authentic learning examples created with the proposed authoring tool in this chapter attempts to engage these elements.

12.3 Implementation

This aim of this research is to develop methodology to create IMS Content Packages and IMS Learning Design, in ubiquitous learning context. Authoring in a ubiquitous context provides the opportunity to capture authentic learning examples, as they happen and where they happen. These authentic learning examples are used as components of IMS Content Packages and IMS Learning Designs; all created while in a ubiquitous context. The implementation seeks to provide a bridge between authentic learning example creation, and their subsequent reuse in online or ubiquitous learning environments. The standardization provided by the IMS specifications enables the output of implementation to be imported into a variety of learning environments. This desired interoperability enables authentic learning examples to be shared beyond the context in which they were created and the specific learning instance in which they were captured.

The resulting solution is a ubiquitous application, called Mobile Authentic Authoring in IMS (MAAIMS), which runs on smart phones. The mobile device component of MAAIMS connects to the server component via an internet connection.

The component running on the mobile device is a compiled and installed executable which uses the Blackberry WebWorks Development Platform. The mobile component presents the user interface and interacts with the hardware mobile device sensors and IO channels, such as the touch screen, keyboard, the global positioning sensor, the embedded camera, and the microphone.

This portion of the application could be considered as the client in a client–server model of a distributed application, or as the presentation tier in a multi-tier architecture. The mobile client connects to a server for uploading metadata and authentic learning content, and subsequently for downloading the assembled content package to the local storage of the mobile device. By default, this ensures that learning content is stored on the server, which acts as a repository. However, it necessitates that the mobile device is connected to the internet for the duration of the application execution.

Given the rapid proliferation of 3G and 4G mobile data networks, along with Wi-Fi coverage in most educational institutions, the connectivity requirement of this application has been deemed acceptable. This application is designed to run on a smart phone, and therefore an assumption of Wi-Fi or mobile broadband access capability is made.

The server component accepts the data provided from the client, stores it in a database, and then assembles XML according to the IMS standards, and bundles it into a package interchange file. The server component resides on an internet connected Linux machine, which hosts a web server (Apache), a relational database management system (MySQL), and a scripting language for dynamic XML and HTML generation, and business logic (PHP). This is a typical Linux, Apache, MySQL, and PHP (LAMP) server configuration used in many web applications.

12.3.1 System Architecture

The MAAIMS application utilizes BlackBerry WebWorks development platform which allows mobile applications to access APIs which interface with the device features, such as the camera and video recorder, and GPS via the WebWorks Software Development Kit. It also uses web standards like HTML5, CSS, JavaScript, and AJAX running inside the WebKit browser engine. The WebKit browser engine resides inside the WebWorks Platform, which in turn runs on top of the operating system (GitHub 2011).

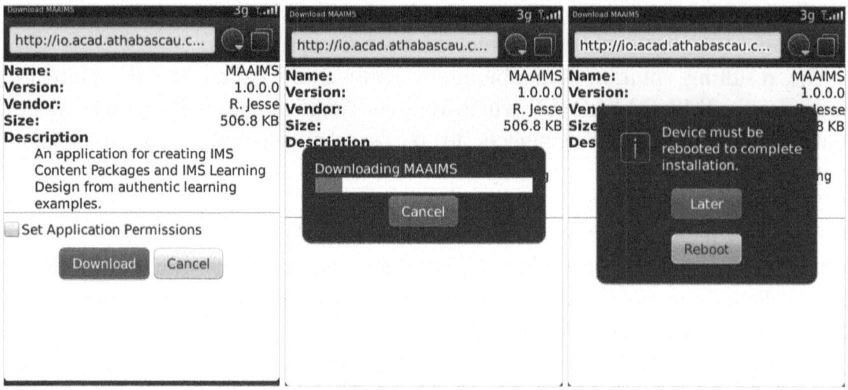

Fig. 12.1 The OTA installation of MAAIMS

MAAIMS is distributed to the users with the Over-the-air (OTA) deployment method. OTA allows a user to download and install the application to their device by visiting a specified URL in the mobile device browser. The compiled application is hosted on a web server, and a link to the application's.jad file is supplied to the end user. Figure 12.1 displays the OTA installation process for MAAIMS.

The WebWorks platform is open, extensible and permits third party APIs. These extensions are written in Java which are then included in the WebWorks project. These extensions can access any of the native BlackBerry API features and provide their own JavaScript interface to the WebWorks application (Tyberg et al. 2011). MAAIMS uses one such third party API, namely PhoneGap. This framework allows a common API across multiple mobile platforms, such as BlackBerry, Android, and iPhone. This means that an application written on one platform can easily be ported to run on another platform because PhoneGap provides a common set of APIs. MAAIMS was developed on a BlackBerry platform. However plans are in place to port the application to an Android platform. The PhoneGap API is called when accessing the native BlackBerry video recording application, the camera application, and the audio recording application for capturing authentic learning examples.

The mobile client interface of MAAIMS utilizes standard web technologies such as HTML5, CSS, JavaScript, AJAX. This simplifies user interface development over that of a full Java Mobile application.

The WebKit browser engine implements the WC3 Geolocation API, which allows a standardized interface to query current geographical location through GPS functionality of the device. This client side location data is used to tag authentic learning objects. MAAIMS is designed to capture real-life learning examples, such as fieldwork demonstrations. Thus, outdoor examples which are location dependant can be geo-tagged. Learners could thereby visit a location of a learning example, or location data could enable adaptive location based learning. An authentic learning example could be presented to learners depending on their location and context.

Each authentic learning example queries for the location of its capture. This means that each example is independently geo-tagged because the user can change locations between capturing each example. The user must opt to include the location of each authentic learning example by means of a checkbox. This ensures that only examples where location is relevant are geo-tagged.

AJAX is used to dynamically display fields and field data via the Document Object Model (DOM). For example, when creating a learning design, any number of activities can be added within an act. This is achieved without reloading the page; rather fields appear dynamically.

HTML5 is used along with Cascading Style Sheets for most of the MAAIMS user interface. Standard forms and form elements are used to author the metadata and learning design. The collected data is submitted to a PHP script hosted on the MAAIMS server.

The authentic learning examples are uploaded by the mobile device to the server. The server interfaces with the mobile client over standard HTTP and TCP/IP. The server hosts an Apache HTTP Server, a common web server platform.

12.3.2 Design of the MAAIMS Application

Figure 12.2 displays the conceptual design of MAAIMS which is elaborated.

The MAAIMS conceptual design aligns with the research questions mentioned in the introduction section of this chapter. The three boxes in the Fig. 12.2, from top to bottom, represent one of the research questions. The authentic learning example box represents the first question: if authentic learning examples can be captured with mobile device sensors. The middle box, or unit of learning, represents the research question which asks whether IMS Content Packages or IMS Learning Design can be authored in a mobile context. Lastly, the lowermost box, containing a repository and LMS, seeks to verify whether the results of MAAMS permit authentically authored learning designs to be shared across traditional boundaries.

12.3.2.1 Step 1: Collect Learning Object Metadata

Two mobile client screens collect metadata. The metadata fields collected follow the IMS Metadata specifications based on the IEEE Metadata Elements and Structure.

Figure 12.3 displays the metadata collection screen. This screen collects metadata which will apply to all of the authentic learning examples collected. The metadata collected corresponds to several sets of metadata elements specified by IMS Meta-data Best Practice Guide such as general, lifecycle, and metametadata (IMS GLC 2006). The generated imsmanifest.xml file will have the corresponding elements.

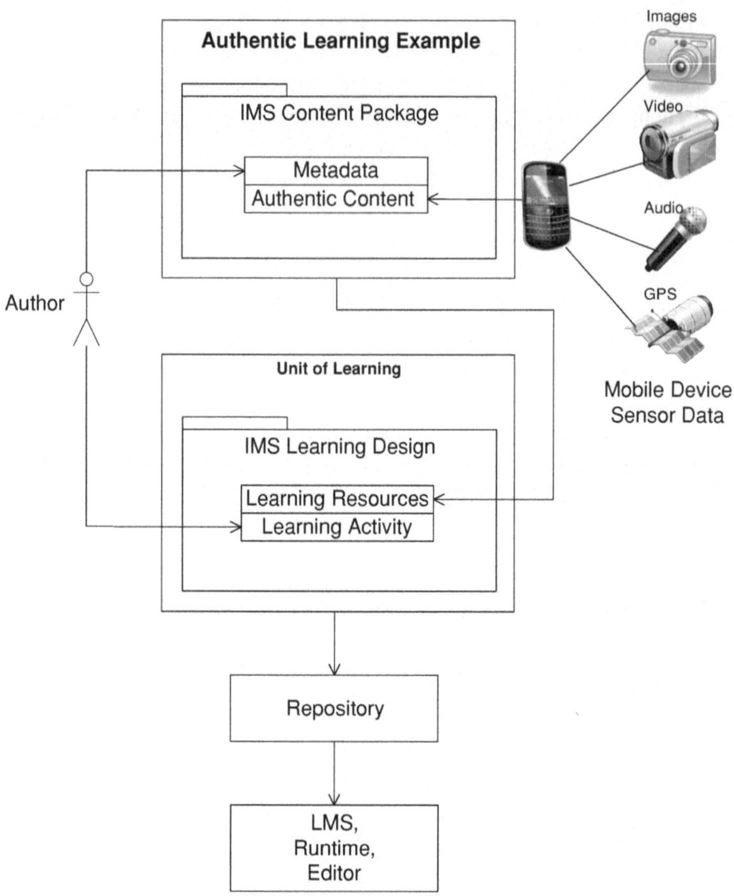

Fig. 12.2 MAAIMS conceptual design

Within these metadata elements, values are either application generated, or input by the user. Where a field is present in the user interface, it is assumed to be user input. However, other fields such as datetimestamp and identifier are generated within the application. Fields such as catalogue type ("MAAIMS"), language ("en" for English), and version ("1.0") are all hardcoded within the application as they are assumed to be constants. Upon submitting user authored data from each screen to the server, the metadata resides in the database. Near the end of the application execution, the database is queries and the XML code is assembled. The XML is a combination of the user entered fields, and values generated by the application.

The general element "groups information describing learning object as a whole" (IMS GLC 2001). Lifecycle provides information on the resource, such as version, contributors, and date. Metametadata element set "features of the description rather than the resource" (IMS GLC 2001) such as catalogue type and identifier.

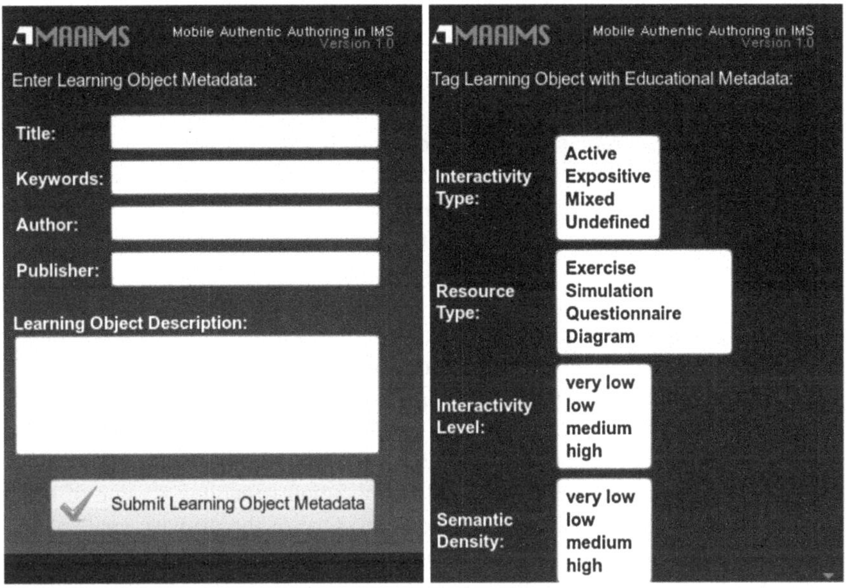

Fig. 12.3 Metadata collection in MAAIMS

The general section can have multiple entities representing keywords. Consequently, the keywords field in the user interface can have multiple comma delimited entries, which are parsed by the application so that each entry will be a separate keyword element.

The technical section of the metadata is entirely application generated. This section describes the technical contents of the resources in the content package. This includes requirements to view the content at runtime, file types included in the package, and the location at which the content package is available.

The educational Metadata collection screen is presented to the user after the collection of authentic learning examples as the responses to fields such as typical learning time will depend on the content, number, and type of the learning examples collected. This metadata represents the "educational or pedagogic features of the learning object" (IMS GLC 2001). The fields primarily have a defined vocabulary for responses or have short responses that could be selected from a small list of options. Some fields, such as interactivity type allow for only a single response, in which case the interface only permits the selection of one response from the list of responses. Other fields permit a maximum number of responses that are greater than one. The context field allows the user to select multiple items from the list of responses, and the user interface accepts multiple selections to conform to the metadata schema.

The educational element contains entities which describe the target end user (age, language, typical learning environment such as primary, secondary, or undergraduate school) as well as the pedagogical characteristics of the learning object (interactivity type, learning resource type, interactivity level, semantic density, difficulty and usage description) (IMS GLC 2001). Of special note is the taxonomy field. This field collects increasingly specific, comma separated, classification of the objects captured. For example, "Biology, microbiology, bacteriology, soil microbes" represents a taxonomic path.

Although metadata is optional, the MAAIMS application requires some key fields. Learning object title metadata cannot be left blank because it is also used later in the application as the title of the content package in the organizations section. Other fields are set as required fields because additional metadata availability means increased searchability and reusability, such as author, and learning object description. When an optional field is permitted, and its value is left blank, the manifest file will not include the corresponding element in the XML.

The rights section of IMS Metadata specifies the conditions of use of content package (IMS GLC 2001). This section specifies if a cost is associated with the usage of the content package, and whether copyrights or other intellectually property restrictions apply. The MAAIMS application generates a value of no to both the cost and copyright restriction elements. One of the primary goals of this project is to maximize content reuse. Implementing restrictions would be a barrier to this goal. It is assumed that all content produced with MAAIMS is free of cost and copyright or other restrictions; thus these XML element values are hardcoded.

12.3.2.2 Step 2: Collect Authentic Learning Examples

Key to this project is the use of mobile sensors to capture authentic learning examples. The MAAIMS application achieves this task by integrating with the built-in applications of the mobile device for three mediums of media capture. GPS location and learning example description are also independently obtained for each example.

MAAIMS novelty is due in part to the tight integration between metadata collection, authentic learning example collection, and learning design authoring. Alternatively, capturing authentic learning examples using native applications, saving the multimedia file to local storage, and manually uploading to a hosted website, then tagging with metadata would result in a disjointed user experience with decidedly less efficacy in meeting the research goals.

Figure 12.4a shows the screen that is presented after the initial learning object metadata has been submitted. It presents options for each type of authentic learning examples. The users can select, using the touch screen, one of the options of their choice. If the user selects "Capture Audio", the application will launch the audio recording application, as seen in Fig. 12.4b. Similarly, the camera application will launch if the "Capture Picture" option is selected and the video camera application will launch if "Capture Video" is selected.

The user can then capture the authentic learning example by recording an authentic learning scenario. The user interfaces directly with native capture application where the resolution of the video or photo can be changed by selecting

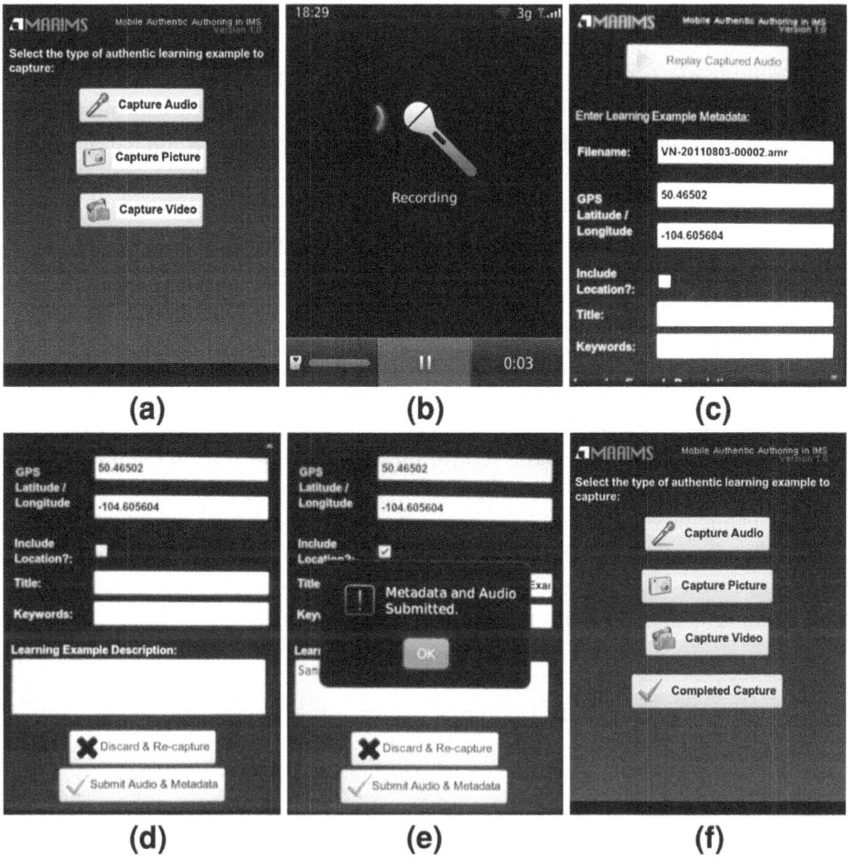

Fig. 12.4 The process of selecting, capturing, adding metadata, and submitting an authentic learning example with MAAIMS

"options". To record the audio or video, record is pressed to begin, and pause to end. A photo can be taken by pressing the snapshot button. Once each capture is complete, the multimedia will be saved to local storage, and pressing the hardware "Back" button returns the user to the screen in which metadata about the captured example is input.

The GPS coordinates are queried for each authentic learning example captured. Upon loading of the mobile client capture page, the geolocation process begins. It is important to begin the query as soon as each sample type is selected, as the GPS location can take several seconds or even minutes to receive a longitude and latitude, depending on sky visibility.

Figure 12.4c displays the metadata collection for each authentic learning example. The filename field and latitude/longitude fields are auto-filled by the application, and cannot be overwritten by the user. The location fields are only available if the mobile device was able to receive GPS coordinates. The "Include

Location?" checkbox should be selected if the author wishes to include the location of capture in the resource file.

Each authentic learning example can be replayed from within the MAAIMS application. This functionality lets the user decide if the capture was of sufficient quality or educational value before tagging with metadata or including in the content package. "Replay Captured Audio" will replay the previously captured audio sample from within the application by calling the native audio playback tool included with the operating system. The same playback process occurs for video, and pictures, whereby an integrated full screen player automatically loads and plays the media. The media player automatically closes and returns to the metadata capture screen when playback is complete.

If the user does not wish to keep the media recording, he/she can press "Discard and Re-Capture" button, as seen in Fig. 12.4d, which will discard the first media file and metadata, and re-launch the recording application. This process can be repeated as many times as is required for the user to achieve an authentic learning example to his/her liking.

Once a suitable capture has been completed and the required metadata has been entered, the user can press the "Submit Audio and Metadata" button. This uploads the media to the web server, and the metadata to the MAAIMS database. The application will notify when the upload is complete, as seen in Fig. 12.4e.

12.3.2.3 Step 3A: Complete Content Package

Once the completed capture option has been pressed, the application collects educational metadata as previously discussed in Step 1. Prior to submitting the educational metadata, the user is presented with two options, as seen in Fig. 12.5a. "Add Learning Design" will create learning activity within the content package, and "Complete Content Package" will complete the content package without embedded learning design. This step covers the program flow when complete content package option is selected. The add learning design functionality is detailed in the next step.

The screen in Fig. 12.5b is shown when the complete content package option is selected. This screen presents two options to the user. The first option, "Save Content Package" allows the user to download the package interchange file. At this point, the physical files (actual media representing authentic learning objects), and the manifest (containing the metadata, resources, and organizations sections) are compiled into a standalone package.

12.3.2.4 Step 3B: Add Learning Design

Step 3A displays the method to create a content package without embedded learning design. Alternatively, this step displays how to create a content package including learning design. Figure 12.5a shows the educational metadata collection

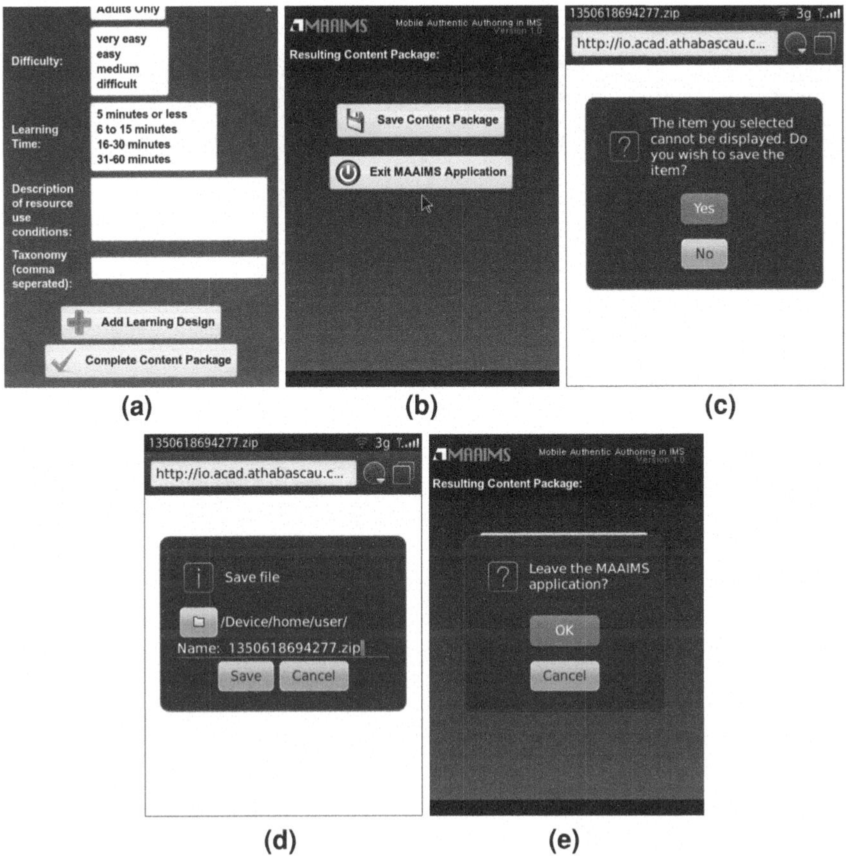

Fig. 12.5 The process of completing MAAIMS without adding learning design

screen's options. Pressing the "Add Learning Design" button will direct the program flow as this step details.

IMS Learning Design "includes the core set of elements added by the Learning Design Specification to the existing Content Packaging Specification" (IMS GLC 2003a). The organizations section of the IMS manifest file will include the Learning Design element at its root. Figure 12.6 presents title, learning objectives, prerequisites, components and methods as core elements within the Learning Design root element.

The learning design root element contains several mandatory attributes. MAAIMS specifies these attributes on behalf of the user. These attributes are the learning design level (A), the URI where the learning design resides, and a unique learning design identifier which is derived from the MAAIMS generated content package unique identifier.

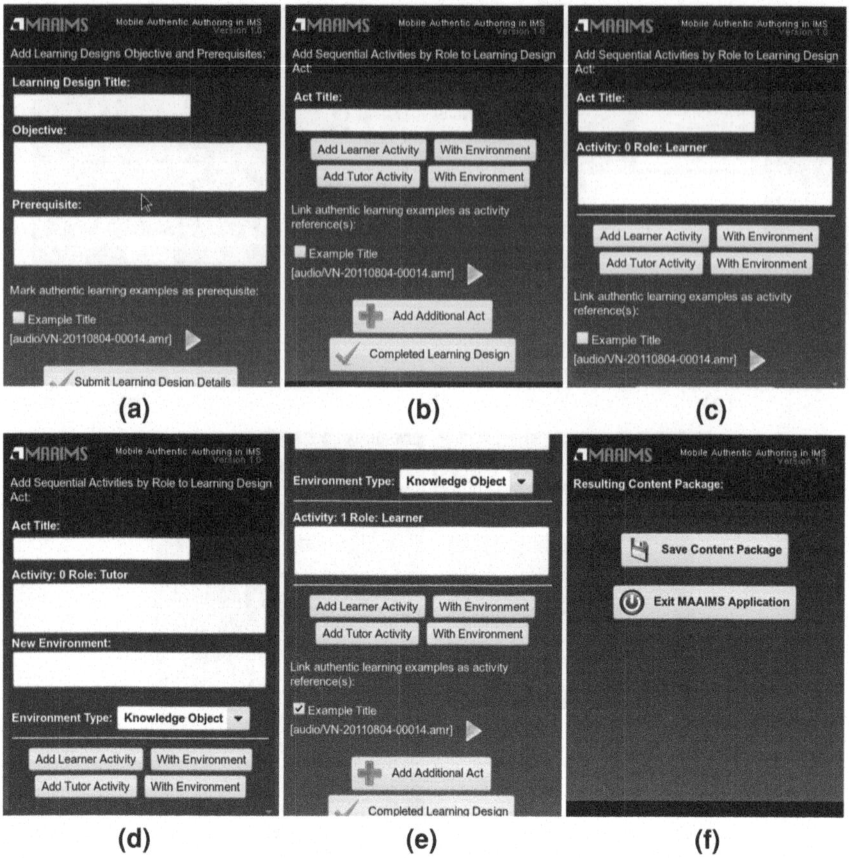

Fig. 12.6 MAAIMS implementation of IMS learning design authoring

Adding Learning Design Objectives and Prerequistes

Figure 12.6a is the user interface where the learning design title, objectives and prerequisites are collected.

The learning objective field in Fig. 12.6a represents the overall goals to be met by learners who complete the activities in the learning design and the authentic learning examples contained in the content package. There are two levels of detail the learning objectives can be specified. "First, it is possible to define the learning objectives at the global level of the unit of learning. Second, it is possible to specify learning objectives for every single activity in the learning design" (IMS GLC 2003a). MAAIMS defines the learning objective at the global level. The objectives apply to the learning design as a whole, as objectives are not collected on each activity. Creating an individual objective for each learning activity would require additional time and text input which may be burdensome while using mobile device in ubiquitous environment. Effort is made to minimize the amount of input to ensure the application remains suitable for a mobile device.

The learning-objectives section within the learning design root element contains a pointer to the source of the defined objective for the learning design. Next, the user input prerequisites is requested. Prerequisites are entered as text in the similarly labelled field. Previously captured authentic learning objects can also be tagged as a prerequisite to the unit of learning. The check box representing each of the previously captured learning examples can be selected if the example specifies on of the entry requirements for interacting with the learning design. The title, type, and filename of each learning example is displayed to aid in tagging the correct examples, as none or all can be tagged as prerequisites. Figure 12.6a only displays one authentic learning example, but all examples captured in the same instance will be listed for referencing as prerequisites. Additionally, the authentic learning examples can be viewed by pressing the play button to the right of each example. This will launch playback of the video, audio, or picture. After viewing, the player closes and the application resumes. This functionality aims to assist in tagging the correct examples as multiple samples can be collected. If many authentic learning examples are captured, it would be difficult to recall which examples represent prerequisites, or which will be related to learning activities.

Adding Acts

Shown at the bottom of the initial learning design authoring screen in Fig. 12.6a is the submission button. Pressing "Submit Learning Design Details" will upload the learning design title, objective, and prerequisites to the server. The mobile application will then proceed to add acts as shown in Fig. 12.6b, c, d. The majority of the learning design elements are created as a result of this screen, which may be executed multiple times. Each time the screen is run, an additional act is created. Each act contains one or more activity, which is assigned to either the learner run-time participant, or tutor run-time participant, known as role. Each activity may optionally be created with an environment, with a selected environment type. Furthermore, any previously captured authentic learning examples can be referenced by the activities created in the act.

Plays

Each learning design has a sequence of activities or a learning process. The main element containing this process description is a method. MAAIMS creates a single method, which contains a single play. The play subelement is the root element for learning design interpretation.

> It represents the flow of activities during the learning process (the 'workflow' or better: the 'learningflow'). A play consists of a series of acts and an act consists of a series of role-

parts. There is always at least one play in every learning design (and every unit-of-learning). In runtime the play is interpreted to show and hide activities, (other) units-of-learning, environments and resources to the users (IMS GLC 2003a).

Although the information model specifies that multiple plays can be created within a method, MAAIMS creates a single play. Multiple plays, at learning design runtime, create independently and concurrently run activities, which may be assigned to the same user. The multiple layers of abstraction caused by creating multiple activities for multiple roles for concurrent execution creates several interface challenges; within the constraints of a mobile authoring tool user interface, multiple plays have potential to present a confusing authoring environment. A single play element eliminates these issues. Moreover, multiple plays "can only be done when the activities are independent of each other" (IMS GLC 2003a). MAAIMS does not provide any assurance that activities are fully independent; thus a single play element is further justified.

A play has a title element which is equal to the title of the content package as specified in step 1. The reuse of the information previously provided avoids having to query the user again. The title of the learning design play and the title of the content package are likely to be substantially similar.

An act consists of one or more role-part elements. These elements assign activities to specific roles. In MAAIMS, these roles are represented by either learner or tutor. Each role-part corresponds to an activity which is linked via a referenced activity structure.

The titles of each role-part element are generated by MAAIMS to represent their act and sequential creation order. The first role-part is assigned to a learner and the second role-part is assigned to the tutor role. Activities are referenced by linking to an activity-structure in the case of a learner role, or a support-activity in the case of a tutor role. Tutor activities are assigned to a support activity as they are not linked to authentic learning examples; learner assigned activities may reference authentic learning objects which is done in an activity structure. Such activity structures will contain a reference to the resource HTML file linking to the authentic learning example if tagged as a reference.

Accordingly, the activities element, nested within the components element, will have a learning-activity element created for each learner assigned activity. These activities are referenced in the activity-structure. The components element also contains the support-activity activity elements for tutor activities.

An activity-structure has an attribute of structure-type which dictates how the activities will be presented to the user. MAAIMS sets this attribute to "sequence" which displays learning activities to the learner in the order they were created. The alternative setting is "selection" which allows the user to carry out activities in any order they wish. However, this requires that "activities must be presented as some kind of menu or navigation aid for the user to select" (IMS GLC 2003b). Authoring such a menu would require another set of user input, further extending the authoring process.

An act contains a complete-act element which defines which role-parts must be completed to consider the act complete. MAAIMS defines that all role-parts (which represent activities) must be completed for the act to be complete.

The IMS Learning Design Best Practice and Implementation Guide states that "the most common use is for different activities to be given to learners and teachers" (IMS GLC 2003b). Therefore, the MAAIMS application provides only these two roles, with tutor role representing the teacher. Creating more pre-defined roles or allowing the user to create additional roles was deemed unnecessary since it overly complicated the smaller user interface.

Adding Activities

Pressing the "Add Learner Activity" button will create a new activity, assigned to the learner role, in the current act. Figure 12.6c displays the results of adding a learner activity. The "Add Tutor Activity" button will perform the same function, but the tutor role will be assigned. These buttons will dynamically display a new text field for entering the activity description.

Learning-activity and support-activity contain a complete-activity declaration which specifies when the activity has been completed. Rather than specify a defined time limit, MAAIMS lets the user decide when the activity is complete via the "user-choice" element.

The Add Learner Activity "With Environment" button and Add Tutor Activity "With Environment" create an activity within the current act which will include an environment. The activity created will be identical to the previously described "Add Learner Activity" function, but will present an activity text box, in addition to the "New Environment" text box, and environment type selection, as seen in Fig 12.6d. Creating an activity with an environment creates a relationship between the activity and an environment within which the activity is executed. An environment is a learning object, service, or tool which is available to the learner at runtime. For instance, an activity stating "Use the microscope to count the amount of bacterial growth," refers to an environment, the microscope tool. The microscope must be available to the actor completing the activity. Other examples may include "web pages, text books, productivity tools (text processors, editors, calculators,…), instruments (microscope, etc.), test items" (IMS GLC 2003a), or an "exercise, simulation, questionnaire, diagram, figure, graph, index, slide, table, narrative text, exam, experiment, problem statement, self assessment, and lecture" (IMS GLC 2003a). The environment required for the activity can thus be entered into the environment text box. Strictly applied, "every noun mentioned in the description refers to a resource in the environment. It is up to the author to have a strict representation of the nouns in the environment or a more open one (leaving nouns implicit)" (IMS GLC 2003a). MAAIMS adopts the latter approach by permitting only a single environment to be created for each activity. Again, this decision was driven in part to ensure a simple authoring tool suitable for a mobile device.

The environment will be one of three types: knowledge-object, tool-object and test-object. A knowledge object would be selected when the environment consisted of a text or diagram. A tool object would be selected if the environment references a software tool such as a spreadsheet, or hardware tool such as a microscope. The test object environment type is selected when referring to an exam or questionnaire.

Referencing Authentic Learning Examples

Previously created authentic learning examples can be referenced within an act in a similar manner to how they are referenced as a prerequisite in the previous screen. These references from the LD reuse content package resources. If an authentic learning example is referenced within an act, it would be considered a relevant learning object to the activities contained within the act. It would be treated as reference material for completing the activities defined.

If a resource is tagged as a resource, as shown in Fig. 12.6e, the learning-activity elements have a reference created to the resource. This means that only learner activities are related to authentic learning examples. Tutor activities are not related to the tagged resources as it is assumed that the tutor role has knowledge of each resource and acts as in a support role of the learner. Each authentic learning example can be tagged in any or all of the acts. Rather than tagging each individual activity with reference resources in the form of authentic learning examples, the tagged resources are applied on an act level. That is, each learner activity within an act will have related resources applied if tagged within the act. This serves to streamline the interface. Each content package may consist of one to possibly dozens of authentic learning examples and querying the user to create relations between each activity and each learning example would be too complex.

After all activities have been entered into the current act, two options are given to the user: "Add Additional Act" and "Completed Learning Design." The add additional act option will insert another act into the learning design, and will repeat the process of adding activities, environments, and referencing authentic learning examples. As many acts can be added as the author deems necessary to meet the defined learning objective.

12.4 Using MAAIMS with Learning Platforms

MAAIMS content reuse has been demonstrated using some of the most widely used IMS compliant learning platforms. IMS Content Packaging repository content created through MAAIMS has been imported into Moodle LMS (Moodle 2011) and OLAT LMS (University of Zurich 2011) for testing playback, and the Reload Editor (Reload Project 2004) for augmentation or editing. The latter also demonstrated that MAAIMS authored IMS Metadata is imported and consistent with the IMS LRM profile. In addition, XML validation of the manifest file against the IMS Content Packaging schema has been completed with XML validation tools.

The LD authored in MAAIMS has been exhibited in a multitude of platforms. Editors and authoring tools such as the Reload Learning Design Editor and ReCourse Learning Design Editor TEN Competence Foundation (2010) successfully imported, validated and/or modified MAAIMS IMS LD content. Similarly, CopperCore (Open Universiteit Nederland 2009) successfully validated MAAIMS LD content and acted as a runtime engine for LD players such as Reload Learning Design Player, SLeD, and CopperCore Learning Design Player. MAAIMS authored IMS Metadata is also accessible and compliant within both editing and runtime tools. From within an LMS platform, dotLRN was also able to import and play the IMS LD authored in MAAIMS.

Testing revealed opportunities for further exploration of MAAIMS content in third party repositories, application of MAAIMS metadata in agents and ontologies, and further testing into mobile runtime environments with MAAIMS authored content.

Overall, MAAIMS has been demonstrated to produce valid IMS Metadata, Content Packages, and Learning Design which incorporates authentic learning examples in ubiquitous learning environments. The MAAIMS repository provides a platform for sharing and reuse of MAAIMS content across the most predominate authoring and editing tools, learning design players, LMSs and runtime environments.

12.5 Limitations

The MAAIMS tool is still in its infancy and despite the obvious benefits it provides for reusable authentic learning scenario creation in ubiquitous learning environments, it has several notable limitations.

The IMS LD roles in MAAIMS are predefined and are limited to learner and tutor. The IMS specification permits additional roles, which could be defined during authoring rather than being limited to predefined roles. For example, evaluator, facilitator, coordinator and chairperson, are all examples of additional staff roles which could exist in addition to the tutor role. Similarly, multiple roles for the learners could be defined.

While the scenarios created by MAAIMS themselves are reusable, the MAAIMS environments are not reusable in different activities. For example, if a tool-object environment of microscope is defined in one activity, it cannot be reused in subsequent activities requiring a microscope tool. If an activity references an environment, it must be defined as a new environment for each activity. While this limitation does not hinder reuse beyond the authoring tool, it hinders reuse of LD elements within the authoring tool. MAAIMS is also limited to a single environment per activity although the IMS LD specification permits more than one environment per activity.

Each authoring session can produce only a single method element in the learning design whereas tools like Reload can produce multiple method elements each containing a nested structure of play, act, and role-part elements. MAAIMS content is limited to one learning design per content package.

It is possible to create an authentic learning example and never reference it as either a prerequisite or as a required learning object for a learning activity while authoring the learning design. This has the risk of orphaning the authentic learning example within the content package so that it is never seen by the learner at runtime. Conversely, this provides the learning design author the flexibility to reference only the most relevant and highest quality of the authentic learning examples captured during the authoring session.

Finally, the time needed to acquire a standalone GPS position (relying strictly on satellites) is approximately 30 s to a minute, and is often limited to outdoor applications. Most modern mobile devices also employ assisted GPS, or A-GPS, which utilizes mobile network such as 3G to download approximate positions from the network provider to decrease the time it takes to acquire coordinates to just a few seconds and improve indoor sensitivity. However, testing has revealed that the use of A-GPS relies on subscribing to a mobile data plan or mobile voice plan (in the case of a smartphone) with this feature provided as an option from the network carrier. Thus, using MAAIMS on Wi-Fi or without a network carrier's A-GPS feature enabled will limit geo-location to a standalone operation with longer query times.

12.6 Conclusions

The purpose of this research has been to develop a mechanism to create standardized learning resources and activities from authentic learning examples for ubiquitous learning environments. The outcome of this research has important advantages in terms of enabling learners and educators alike to benefit from ubiquitous learning environments, using mobile devices. This work serves to bridge ubiquitous, mobile and e-learning contextual boundaries and extends authoring of learning content and activities to mobile devices while identifying areas for future study.

References

Ally M (2004) Designing effective learning objects for distance education. In: McGreal R (ed) Online education using learning objects. Routledge, London, pp 87–97

Castillo S, Ayala G (2008) ARMOLEO: an architecture for mobile learning objects. In: 18th international conference on electronics, communications and computers, IEEE Computer Society, Washington, pp 53–58

Churchill D (2008) Learning objects for educational applications via PDA technology. J Interact Learn Res 19(1):5

Cochrane T (2005) Interactive quicktime: developing and evaluating multimedia learning objects to enhance both face-to-face and distance e-learning environments. Interdisc J Knowl Learn Objects 1(1):33–54

Cruz-Flores R, López-Morteo G (2008) A Model for collaborative learning objects based on mobile devices. In: Mexican international conference on computer science, IEEE Computer Society, Los Alamitos, pp 89–95

Downs S (2004) Learning objects: Resources for learning worldwide. Online education using learning objects. Routledge, London

Giemza A, Bollen L, Seydel P, Overhagen A, Hoppe HU (2010) LEMONADE: a flexible authoring tool for integrated mobile learning scenarios. In: IEEE international conference on wireless, mobile, and ubiqutious technologies in education, IEEE Computer Society, Los Alamitos, pp 73–80

GitHub (2011) BlackBerry WebWorks—GitHub. https://github.com/blackberry/WebWorks/wiki. Retrieved 19 July 2011

Griffiths D, Blat J, Garcia R, Vogten H, Kwong K (2005) Learning design tools. Learning design: modelling and implementing network-based education and training. Springer, Heidelberg, pp 109–135

Hansen FA, Bouvin NO (2009) Mobile learning in context–context-aware hypermedia in the wild. Int J Interact Mob Technol (iJIM) 3(1):6–21

Herrington J, Oliver R, Reeves TC (2003) Patterns of engagement in authentic online learning environments. Aust J Educ Technol 19(1):59–71

Higgs P, Meredith S, Hand T (2003) Technology for sharing: researching learning object and digital rights management. Flexible learning leader report, Australian National Training Authority

IMS GLC (2001) IMS Learning resource meta-data information model. http://www.imsglobal.org/metadata/imsmdv1p2p1/imsmd_infov1p2p1.html. Retrieved 24 July 2011

IMS GLC (2003a) IMS learning design information model. http://www.imsglobal.org/learningdesign/ldv1p0/imsld_infov1p0.html. Retrieved 30 July 2011

IMS GLC (2003b) IMS learning design best practice and implementation guide. http://www.imsglobal.org/learningdesign/ldv1p0/imsld_bestv1p0.html. Retrieved 23 July 2011

IMS GLC (2006) IMS Meta-data best practice guide for IEEE 1484.12.1-2002 standard for learning object metadata. http://www.imsglobal.org/metadata/mdv1p3/imsmd_bestv1p3.html. Retrieved 24 July 2011

Jovanovic J, Gasevic D, Knight C, Richards G (2007) Ontologies for effective use of context in e-learning settings. Educ Technol Soc 10(3):13

Koper R (2003) Combining reusable learning resources and services with pedagogical purposeful units of learning. In: Littlejohn A (ed) Reusing online resources a sustainable approach to e-learning. Kogan Page, london, pp 46–59

Li Y, Guo H, Gao G, Huang R, Cheng X (2009) Ubiquitous e-learning system for dynamic mini-courseware assembling and delivering to mobile terminals. In: Proceedings of 5th international joint conference on INC, IMS and IDC, pp 1081–1086

Lombardi MM (2007) Authentic learning for the 21st century: an overview. Educause Learn Initiative 1:1–7

McGreal R (2004) Learning objects: a practical definition. Int J Instr Technol Distance Learn 1(9):21

McGreal R (2006) Implementing learning object metadata for mobile devices using CanCore. In: Presented at the advanced international conference on telecommunications and international conference on internet and web applications and services, Guadeloupe, French Caribbean

McGreal R (2008) A typology of learning object repositories. In: Adelsberger HH, Kinshuk Pawlowski JM, Sampson D (eds) Handbook on information technologies for education and training, 2nd edn. Springer, Heidelberg, pp 5–28

Mitchell K, Race NJP (2005) uLearn: facilitating ubiquitous learning through camera equipped mobile phones. In: IEEE international workshop on wireless and mobile technologies in education, IEEE Computer Society, Los Alamitos, pp 274–281
Moisey SD, Ally M, Spencer B (2006) Factors affecting the development and use of learning objects. American J Distance Educ 20(3):143–161
Moodle (2011) IMS content package. http://docs.moodle.org/20/en/IMS_content_package. Retrieved 23 Aug 2011
Ogata H (2008) Computer supported ubiquitous learning: augmenting learning experiences in the real world. In: 5th IEEE international conference on wireless, mobile, and ubiquitous technology in education WMUTE, pp 3–10)
Open Universiteit Nederland (2009) Copper core technical documentation. http://coppercore.sourceforge.net/documentation/technical_documentation.shtml. Retrieved 12 Sep 2011
Pettersson O, Gil D (2010) On the issue of reusability and adaptability in m-learning Systems. In: IEEE international conference on wireless, mobile, and ubiquitous technologies in education, IEEE Computer Society, Los Alamitos, pp 161–165
Reload Project (2004) Reload editor introductory manual. http://www.reload.ac.uk/ex/editor_v1_3_manual.pdf. Retrieved 18 Aug 2011
Rule A (2006) The components of authentic learning. J Authentic Learn 3(1):1–10
Siadaty M, Torniai C, Gasevic D, Jovanovic J, Eap TM, Hatala M (2008) LOCO: an ontology-based framework for context-aware mobile learning. In: Proceeding of the 6th international workshop on ontologies and semantic web for intelligent educational systems, presented at the 9th international conference on intelligent tutoring systems, Montreal, Canada
Sosteric M, Hesemeier S (2002) When is a learning object not an object: a first step towards a theory of learning objects. Int Rev Res Open Distance Learn 3(2):1–15
Svensson M, Kurti A, Milrad M (2010) Enhancing emerging learning objects with contextual metadata using the linked data approach. In: The 6th IEEE international conference on wireless, mobile, and ubiquitous technologies in education, pp 50–56
TENCompetence Foundation (2010) ReCourse learning design editor. http://tencompetence-project.bolton.ac.uk/ldauthor/index.html. Retrieved 11 Sep 2011
Traxler J, Kukulska-Hulme A (2005) Mobile technologies and systems. Routledge, London
Tyberg J, Brooks M, Verner J, Gill S (2011) PhoneGap—getting started with PhoneGap blackberry WebWorks. http://wiki.phonegap.com/w/page/31930982/Getting-Started-with-PhoneGap-BlackBerry-WebWorks. Retrieved 20 July 2011
University of Zurich (2011) More information about OLAT. http://www.olat.org/website/en/html/unit_about.html. Retrieved 23 Aug 2011
Vogel B, Spikol D, Kurti A, Milrad M (2010) Integrating mobile, web and sensory technologies to support inquiry-based science learning. In: IEEE presented at the wireless, mobile, and ubiquitous technologies in education, pp 65–72. doi:10.1109/WMUTE.2010.41
Wiley DA (1999) The post-LEGO learning object. http://cmap.upb.edu.co/rid=1146063082796_1162237027_9479/The%20Post-LEGO%20Learning%20Object_wiley.pdf. Retrieved 1999
Wiley DA (2000) Connecting learning objects to instructional design theory: a definition, a metaphor, and a taxonomy. Learn Technol 2830(435):1–35
Yang, JTD, Chiu CH, Tsai, CY, Wu TH (2004) Visualized online simple sequencing authoring tool for SCORM-compliant content package. In: Proceedings of IEEE international conference on advanced learning technologies, pp 609–613)
Ogata H, Misumi T, Hou B, Li M, El-Bishouty M, Yano, Y (2010) LORAMS: sharing learning experiences with social and ubiquitous media. In: IEEE presented at the wireless, mobile, and ubiquitious technologies in education, pp 151–155. doi:10.1109/WMUTE.2010.18

Chapter 13
Educational Use of Computer Games: Where We Are, and What's Next

Morris S. Y. Jong, Jimmy H. M. Lee and Junjie Shang

13.1 Introduction

The activities that games are associated with are "play" (Games and Squire 2011). Piaget (1964, 1970) regarded curiosity as the best driving force for learning. He advocated that keeping learners curious by engaging them in play-like activities is the best approach to education, and thus games are an important avenue toward learning. Papert (1980, 1993), a proponent of Piaget, observed that gaming can foster students' deep learning. He highlighted that, in gaming, students are more conscious of the objects that surround them. When students interact with what goes on around them in a game, they begin to understand "what things are and how things work", and thus become more willing to spend time and effort on it. Shulman and Keislar (1966) realized that gaming can help students develop their skills of learning. Students will feel better about what they learn in games, and try to apply the acquired knowledge and skills in the future.

The early educational use of computer games, which treated computer games as "a content transmission platform" as opposed to "a tool to think with", was less contributive to education (Provenzo 1991). Along with the advancement of technology and the advocacy of student-centredness in education, the contemporary educational use of computer games has become more connected with learning

M. S. Y. Jong (✉)
Department of Curriculum and Instruction, The Chinese University of Hong Kong, Hong Kong, China
e-mail: mjong@cuhk.edu.hk

J. H. M. Lee
Department of Computer Science and Engineering, The Chinese University of Hong Kong, Hong Kong, China

J. Shang
Department of Education Technology, Peking University, Beijing, China

R. Huang et al. (eds.), *Reshaping Learning*, New Frontiers of Educational Research, DOI: 10.1007/978-3-642-32301-0_13,

models that promote learning as experience (Dede 2011). It is believed that "good" computer games have the potential to provide learners with authentic and engaging experiences that enhance their learning and retention (Cannon-Bowers 2010; Tobias and Fletcher 2011).

This chapter aims at providing readers with a contextual view on educational use of games, particularly, computer games. In Sect. 13.2, before elaborating on the intrinsic educational traits of computer games and some early instances of computer game-based learning, we will start from discussing games "in general", and some examples of "non-computer" games for learning. In Sect. 13.3, we will introduce two recent initiatives of educational use of computer games, namely, "education in games" and "games in education", and discuss a number of representative instances in each initiative. In Sect. 13.4, we will delineate the challenges of computer game-based learning that we are facing currently, and discuss the areas which are worth investing further research effort. Section 13.5 is a conclusion of the chapter.

13.2 Games and Education

Heinich et al. (1982) described "game" as an activity in which players follow prescribed rules for attaining some challenging goals. They highlighted that the rules in games are different from those in real life and thus make gaming fantastic and entertaining. Although Heinich et al.'s argument is applicable to some non-computer games (e.g., *Tic-tac-toe*, *Bingo*, *Chess*, etc.) and also some computer games (e.g., *Pan Man*, *Tetris*, *Mario Brothers*, etc.), it has yet to be comprehensive enough to cover all games in the past and today. For example, *Rift Raft* (Leigh and Kinder 1999), a non-computer role-play game, replicates authentic happenings arising when people are engaging in negotiation. *Journalism.net* (Shaffer 2006), a computer simulation game, lets people gain first-hand experience of how journalists think and behave in real life.

Giving a definition to "game" is a difficult and complex task (Livingstone 1972; Sandford and Williamson 2005). Different games, no matter non-computer-based or computer-based, can have a very different "technical" design therein. Some games have scoring, but some do not. Some games have real win and lose stages, but some do not. Some games are in a purely competitive manner, but some require players to work collaboratively. Some games focus on providing players with fantasy experience, but some advocate for offering players authentic experience. Instead of proposing a universal definition of "game", Mayer (2011) generalized four key structural characteristics of games that make a game a "game;" they are (1) *rule-based*, (2) *responsive*, (3) *challenging*, and (4) *cumulative*. Rules in games enable players to play. Responses of games make players feel their actions are reacted. Challenges in games pose goals for players to achieve. Cumulative features of games aggregate players' past gaming successes.

13.2.1 Learning Through Gaming

The earliest utilization of games for learning purposes can be traced back to the use of war games in the 1600s for improving the strategic planning of armies and navies (Gibbs 1974; Gredler 2004; Lederman 1992; Peters and Vissers 2004; Wolfe and Crookall 1998). Parallel to the spread of the ideas of "learning through playing" to education by a number of constructivist learning theorists in the early 1960s (e.g., Bruner 1960; Piaget 1964; Shulman and Keislar 1966), there have been more educators, school teachers, and vocational trainers endeavouring to infuse games (non-computer ones) into classroom teaching or skill-based training (e.g., Barton 1970; Bredemeier and Greenblat 1981; Heinich et al. 1982; Leigh and Kinder 1999; Smith and Avedon 1971; Thiagarajan and Stolovitch 1978; van Ments 1999). Cruickshank and Telfer (1980) categorized those non-computer games for education into *non-simulation games* and *simulation games.*

Non-simulation games (Cruickshank and Telfer 1980) are those in which players solve problems such as spelling and mathematics by making use of principles of a subject or discipline. For example, in *Acrostics*, students have to find words of equal length, the number of words being the same as the number of letters in each word. Afterward, the words are arranged so that each can be read vertically and horizontally. *Scrabble*, *Sudoku*, etc. are other well-known examples of non-simulation games and still popular to date. Prensky (2001, 2006), however, argued that non-simulation games are only attractive to pre-schoolers or lower-grade students, but not higher-grade students—particularly the youngsters of *digital native*—"the new 'native speakers' of today's digital language of computers, computer games, and the Internet" (p. 28).

Simulation games (Cruickshank and Telfer 1980), another category of non-computer games for education, aim at providing students with insights into the processes or events from the real world that are simulated. Games in this category usually involve students in making decisions and communicating with one another in a role-playing manner. For example, in *Prisoner's Dilemma* (Barton 1970), two players are placed in the role of captured criminals presented singly with the opportunity to confess to the crime and thereby promised a shortened sentence for themselves and a longer one for the accomplice. If only one confesses, he wins a shorter sentence. If both confess, they both receive longer sentences. This game lets players experience and understand phenomena of competition and cooperation.

Simulation games are considered suitable for simulating interaction between humans, as well as the functions performed by humans under various social circumstances (Leigh and Kinder 1999; van Ments and Hearnden 1985; van Ments 1999). This kind of games are, however, less capable for simulating scientific models and systems (composed of mathematical variables and equations) in some disciplines such as Geography, Physics, Economics, etc. On top of that, simulation games are usually subjected to a limit on the number of participants, allowing only a few students to participate simultaneously (Heinich et al. 1982).

13.2.2 Computer Game-Based Learning

Apart from the introduction of non-computer games to education, the discussion of harnessing computer games for learning and teaching has been launched since the widespread popularity of *Pac-Man* in the early 1980s (Squire 2003), and catalyzed by video-game consoles and personal computers entering households. Undoubtedly, the games discussed in most of today's computer game-based learning (GBL) research are different from the ones that were used in the last few decades. The differences do not lie solely on the technical enhancement brought by the advancement of technology, but also their underpinning educational paradigm, shifting from behaviourism to constructivism.

13.2.2.1 Computer Games for Behaviourist Learning

The behaviourist conception in education advocates a human's mind can be treated as a black box (Skinner 1938). The inner-workings inside this black box need not be uncovered. The study of learning should focus only on observable events (i.e., stimuli and responses). Through practice students will learn the correct response to a stimulus; learning can be imposed by conditioning and reinforcement. Behaviourism was the dominating learning paradigm adopted in the design of "educational games" (or "edutainment") when computer games were introduced initially to education (Egenfeldt-Nielsen 2007; Gredler 1996; Squire 2003). These games are composed of fantasy themes wrapped around drill-and-practice activities, and thus so-called "drill-and-practice games".

Drill-and-practice games usually consist of a clear reward structure for pushing students' learning forward, but have weak or even no relationship between learning content and game context (Egenfeldt-Nielsen 2007). For example, in *Math Blaster!*, students have to shoot down the right answer to a mathematics question shown on the screen. On each success, their balloon will move towards a needle. A student who can pop his/her balloon eventually will win the game. Tying closely in-game rewards to in-game actions, drill-and-practice games, to a certain extent, can provide attractive frameworks for learning activities, and foster pleasant and relaxed classroom atmosphere which is helpful especially for low academic achieving students who unlike conventional types of learning and teaching (Heinich et al. 1996). However, it has been criticized that the movement design of these games is usually too fast and leaves no room for students to think and reflect; students may just play with their spontaneous responses or trial-and-error strategies (see Wong 2003).

A game that is fun to play but does not help students acquire the intended knowledge, skills, or attitudes has little value for instructional purposes (Tobias and Fletcher 2011, p. 535). Kirriemuir and McFarlane (2004) argued that the "sugared" and "parrot-like" activities in drill-and-practice games should not occupy a significant part of a school day or during students' independent study time. Gee (2011) criticized further that decontextualized drill-and-practice experience in these games can never facilitate human to learn deeply and meaningfully.

13.2.2.2 Computer Games for Constructivist Learning

Drawing from Dewey's (1938, 1958) and Piaget's (1964, 1970) notions of constructivist play, some educators and game researchers in the early days tried to develop their computer games to facilitate constructivist learning. For example, in the early 1970s, three teachers in Minnesota created *Oregon Trail*, a computer game for helping students understand the historical complexities of American pioneers' lives during nineteenth century migrations (cited in Games and Squire 2011). Students in this game can interact with a virtual world by typing text-based commands, engaging in activities like hunting for food, and protecting caravan members from disease, poisonous animals, and other possible dangers. In the early 1980s, Papert (1980) developed *Microworlds*, a computer game encompassing self-contained interactive worlds for modeling real-life systems. The worlds therein are able to react to students' commands in accordance with, for example, Newton's model of the laws of motion. This game let students explore phenomena that are difficult to access either in the real world or school settings due to physical constraints or disciplinary prerequisites. The publication of *Multiple Use Labor Element* (M.U.L.E) in 1983 was another milestone of constructivist use of computer games in education (cited in Games and Squire 2011). This game involves mechanics of strategic resource management, allowing one to four players to contest resources as prospectors on a fictional planet. Players can choose various traits and skills for their colonists, tying them to various strategies. Players should not only compete but also work cooperatively in order to survive in the planet.

In the recent years, along with the advancement of computers, multimedia, and the Internet (such as sophisticated computer simulations, 3D user-interfaces, dynamic synchronous players' interactions, etc.), as well as the pervasive promotion of student-centric pedagogy, the discussion of drill-and-practice games has become in the minority in the domain. On the other hand, the focus of educational use of computer games has been place significantly on the issue of how to harness their motivational, cognitive, and social abilities to facilitate constructivist learning. The following will discuss the traits of todays' computer games that support constructivist learning, in terms of *promoting learners' motivation*, *offering learners situated cognitive experiences*, as well as *exploiting learning communities*. For writing convenience, unless otherwise specified, hereafter the terms *game(s)*, *gaming*, and *game-based learning* (GBL) denote "computer game(s)", "computer gaming", and "computer game-based learning" respectively.

Promoting learners' motivation

Fun and enjoyment are essential elements in the process of learning as students can be more relaxed and motivated to learn (Bisson and Luncker 1996; Cordova and Lepper 1996). Gamers always undergo hard but engaging, challenging but pleasurable, and risk-taking but rewarding experiences in gaming (Prensky 2001). All these are the experiences of fun and enjoyment.

There have been a number of GBL studies focusing on investigating what, why, and how gaming can make students more motivated during the process of learning. For example, based on a series of surveys, observations and interviews with gamers, Malone (1980, 1981) put forward a motivation theory, which asserts that *challenge*, *fantasy*, *control*, *curiosity*, *cooperation*, *recognition*, and *competition* are the most significant elements that make gaming fun and engaging, and sustain gamers' continual motives. Malone advocated that schools should try to integrate similar gaming elements into education so as to arouse students' intrinsic motives in learning. Bowman (1982) tied his study on learning through gaming with Csikszentmihalyi's (1975, 1990) psychological conception of "flow". Flow is a state of experience of "intense concentration and enjoyment". Under the flow state, a person will engage in a complex, goal-directed challenge not for external rewards, but simply for the exhilaration of dealing with the challenge. Bowman observed that learning through gaming is a spontaneous way to bring students to the flow state of learning.

Although the studies of Malone (1980, 1981) and Bowman (1982) were done a few decades ago, recent empirical evidence (e.g., Cordova and Lepper 1996; Mayer et al. 2002; DeLisi and Wolford 2002) still accords with their assertions. From both theoretical and empirical points of view, it is expected that students will be more motivated to participate in educational activities if these activities take place in a form of gaming.

Offering learners situated cognitive experiences

Jonassen and Howland (2003, p. 8) argued the "greatest intellectual sin" that educators have committed is to oversimplify knowledge and skills taught at school in order to make them more "transmissible" to students. The learning contents at school are often fragmented into small and unconnected pieces (Papert 1993). The original intention is for making learning easier, but this usually ends up neglecting the rationale behind the knowledge itself, creating unrealistic learning contexts, and rendering the whole learning process boring. Without chunking or turning learning content into a series of "split-screens", with the advancement of multimedia and simulation technology, today's games do well in presenting near real-life contexts for students to acquire knowledge and skills in a more spontaneous manner (Shaffer 2006). This sort of learning experience coincides with Lave and Wenger's (1991) conception of "situated learning".

Gee (2003, 2005, 2007) believed that gaming is a new cognitive way for learners to acquire knowledge and skills in a constructivist fashion. Today's games offer the prospect of user-defined learning environments (Halverson 2005) in which individuals can try out and get feedback on their assumptions and strategies. Most gaming tasks are generative and open-ended without prescribed gaming strategies. Gamers engaged in gaming cannot be passive (Antonacci and Modaress 2008). They need to interact (compete, cooperate, or collaborate) with other human gamers or non-player characters (NPCs) inside games (Mason and

Moutahir 2006). They also have to analyze and evaluate the perceived information and context in games proactively, and to create new gaming strategies based on their knowledge and skills.

Exploiting learning communities

Scardamalia and Bereiter (1993, 1996, 2003) observed that, focusing on individual students' abilities and learning, schools inhibit rather than support collaborative knowledge building. In fact, knowledge itself arises from social needs, fulfills social functions, and is tied inherently with cultural conditions (Cole 1996; Collins et al. 1989). In other words, how to educate students is not seen as how to build representations in each of their heads, but how to engage them in socio-cultural activities (Lave and Wenger 1991). Learning is not just a process of mastering facts, or even conducting complex tasks, but rather, participating in socio-cultural practices. This requires learners to develop their own identity in relation to others.

Today's games are considered as "cultural artefacts situated within socio-technical system" (Games and Squire 2011, p. 28) in which entwine practice, participation, community, and identity (Wenger 1998). The gamer generation prefers human competitors and/or collaborators rather than purely artificial intelligence (AI) (Prensky 2001). Gamers meet online and form teams to discuss challenges, complete quests, and solve puzzles in games. Moreover, nearly every prevalent game does not simply appear alone as a game itself, but exists logically as a *game system* (Prensky 2006). In each of these systems, besides the game concatenating with a built-in real-time chat console, it also entails gamers' self-initiated components, such as online discussion forums, fan sites, blogs, etc. All these components enable and encourage individuals to share, discuss, evaluate, and apply the collective knowledge co-constructed by gamers/learner communities (Antonacci and Modaress 2008).

13.3 Contemporary Initiatives of GBL

In this section, we will discuss a number of recent instances of constructivist educational use of games in the domain. We categorize these instances into two initiatives, namely, (1) *education in games* (i.e., adopting existing *recreational games*[1] from the commercial market for educational use, and (2) *games in*

[1] Researchers and commentators sometimes use the terms "mainstream games" (e.g., Kirriemuir and McFarlane 2004; Sandford and Williamson 2005), "off-the-shelf games" (e.g., Prensky 2001, 2006; Squire2003), and "serious games" (e.g., Gee 2003, 2005; Mishra and Foster 2007) to mean *recreational games*.

education (i.e., developing *educational games*[2] that are designed with specific educational purposes).

13.3.1 Education in Games

In Richter and Livingstone's (2011) recent publication, they discussed a person, who works in a major global Internet firm, credits his experience in running a large guild in *World of Warcraft* as an important factor in his subsequent success securing a senior management position his company. Gee (2003, 2005, 2007), an active education-in-game proponent, realizes that nowadays recreational games in the commercial market are not only extending the creative boundaries of interactive media, but also suggesting powerful models of next-generation interactive learning environments. He observes that many bestselling recreational games are already state-of-the-art learning games since they are hard but fun, time-consuming but enjoyable, and complex but "learnable". In his recent publication (Gee 2011), he went on arguing that—

> In my view, no one has made such [an educational] game that is as good as, say, the commercial game Portal, which allows players to experience and use principles like the conservation of momentum ...... no one, in my view, has made such [an educational] game that is as good as the commercial game Civilization, a game that lets players experience and use principles about historical change and the clash of civilizations ...... (p. 231).

Besides Gee (2003, 2005, 2007, 2011), there have been a number of education-in-game proponents (e.g., Cameron 2008; Huh 2008; Johnson 2005; Marquis 2008; Prensky 2001, 2006; Salen 2007, 2008) advocating for the potential of recreational games for promoting youngsters' high-order thinking skills (Anderson et al. 2001) and/or so-called "twenty-first century literacy" (Jenkins et al. 2006). However, it has been argued that this advocacy is just a kind of "theoretical argument", without empirical evidence (DiPietro et al. 2007; Mayer 2011; Mishra and Foster 2007). Instead of staying in theoretical discussions, some education-in-game initiators have conducted empirical studies on adopting recreational games in educational settings (e.g., Adams 1998; Betz 1995; Kemp and Livingstone 2006; Rankin and Shute 2010; Squire 2004, 2005).

In fact, the educational use of recreational games coming to larger public attention was in 1989—the time that *SimCity* was first released. This game is a city-building game where players play the role of a city mayor, planning and executing changes to the infrastructure of a city, and managing the consequences

---

[2] In contrast to recreational games which are designed originally for entertainment purposes, the term *educational game(s)* refers to the game(s) that are designed deliberately for education purposes. Some researchers and commentators (e.g., Kirriemuir and McFarlane 2004; Gee 2003, 2005) use the term "learning games" to mean *educational games*.

of their design decisions (see Games and Squire 2011). *SimCity* was a commercial hit upon its release. In education, this game and its newer versions released in 1990s were a common interest for many educators who had been exploring the use of computer simulations for learning and teaching in the areas such as government and urban planning in that decade (Kirremuir and McFarlane 2004). For example, Adams (1998) adopted *SimCity* in a university-level introductory Urban Geography course for his own students to acquire urban planning concepts in a self-directed manner. Adam realized that the game could not only approximate to near real-world conditions and phenomena of designing and building a city, but also demonstrate the potentially successful or disastrous consequences of complex decision making in urban planning. Prior to the adoption, Adam analyzed *SimCity*, and set up a number of learning objectives related to urban planning that he expected the students could achieve after playing the game. Further, he conducted a learning experiment to verify quantitatively whether the gaming would yield the expected learning outcomes. The research results were positive, in terms of the students' knowledge acquisition and their perceptions of "learning through gaming". These findings also accorded with those in a similar study conducted by Betz (1995) who had adopted *SimCity* in teaching his college-level Architecture course.

Civilization (first released in 1991) is another popular recreational game which has aroused the interest of educators and GBL researchers. *Civilization* is a turn-based game. In each turn players must choose from a multitude of possible actions ranging from studying the map of the world surrounding their tribe, to creating new cities, to exploring new technologies or making war against other civilizations. The game provides opportunities for players to learn how to micromanage the resources that they own (such as gold, food, building materials, etc.), and the consequences of policy decisions (such as raising or lowing taxes, changing the form of government, etc.). In the recent versions of *Civilization*, the ability to customize game scenarios and move students from players to designers of scenarios (creating their own versions of historical simulations) has been compelling more educators to bring this game to education (see Games and Squire 2011). As an empirical study, Squire (2004, 2005) integrated *Civilization* into a US high-school classroom for teaching of a formal school curriculum of world-history. In his study, Squire concluded the students could develop more understanding and interest in historical knowledge to a certain extent; on the other hand, he found that it was difficult to align the "educative" content in the game with what was required in the curriculum concerned.

The empirical adoptions of *SimCity* and *Civilization* in educational settings have led to further discussions of educational potential of some technically-similar recreational games such as *Sim Earth* for learning of ecology, *Zoo Tycoon* for learning of zoology, etc. (see Prensky 2006). Kemp and Livingstone's work (2006) is another representative education-in-game instance. They utilized *Second Life*, an massively multiplayer online role-playing game (MMORPG), as an online "socio-cultural" learning management system (LMS) to facilitate learning and teaching activities (lectures, tutorials, discussions, student presentations, etc.) in university courses. More recently, Rankin and Shute (2010) have also re-purposed *EverQuest*

II, another MMORPG to promote learning in the context of second language acquisition. In their experimental study, they observed that the in-game social interactions between native speakers and non-native speakers could provide greater learning engagement among the participants. In contrast to traditional classroom teaching, this game-based approach facilitated an enhancement of the non-native speakers' second language vocabulary acquisition and reading comprehension.

Notwithstanding some positive education-in-game instances discussed above, there have been critiques on this initiative. For example, the authenticity and accuracy of the "educative" contents in recreational games have been arousing concern from educators, teachers, and also learners (Kirriemuir and McFarlane 2004; Klabbers 2006). For example, *SimCity* distorts the mayor's authority in public planning, simplifies the historical vitality of race and ethnicities in the evaluation of cities, and overestimates the appeal of public transportation to most Americans (Kolson 1994). A large percentage of players doubt the historical accuracy of *Civilization* (Squire 2004, 2005). Moreover, designed originally for entertainment purpose rather than education purpose, recreational games are difficult to be adopted in normal curriculum teaching by school teachers (McFarlane et al. 2002; Halverson 2005; Rice 2007). Without a GBL expert [like Squire (2004, 2005) in his study] in schools, it is unrealistic to ask a teacher (who is usually a non-gamer) to identify what and how a particular recreational game is relevant to a particular part of a subject curriculum, and design according learning activities based on the game, and then implement the activities in his/her teaching practice.

13.3.2 Games in Education

Instead of adopting existing recreational games from the commercial market, game-in-education researchers design and implement their educational games based upon explicit pedagogical paradigms or/and articulated with specific learning contents. The following are some selected instances upon this initiative.

Emergent narrative is the underlying pedagogy of Aylett's (2005) "narrative games". This paradigm suggests learning through role-playing in an improvised, rather than scripted digital story. The plot of the story in a narrative game emerges from the interactions between players' avatar and NPCs therein. *FearNot!* (Aylett et al. 2006), which is an example of narrative games, was developed specifically for an anti-bullying campaign for child education. Children in this game act as counselors to give advice to victims (the NPCs in the game) who are being bullied. Their advice will influence the proceedings about the victims in the next gaming episode. The children can then observe the consequence of the actions taken by the victims in accordance with their prior advice.

Progressive inquiry (Muukkonen et al. 1999) is the underlying learning paradigm of Jong et al.'s (2010) *Learning Villages (LV)*—a computer supported collaborative learning (CSCL) game. *LV* operates in a form of MMORPG, in which each student can design his/her own avatar to participate collaboratively in "two-tier" inquiry in a progressive manner. In the "virtual world" of *LV*, each "village" represents an inquiry issue. A student can initiate an issue for inquiry by creating a village (he/she becomes the "chieftain" of this village). Other students can enter this village and build "houses" to elaborate on their views, arguments or questions with respect to the issue (and hence they become the "villagers" of the village). Further, both chieftain and villagers can construct different types of "roads" to interconnect the houses for delineating their in-between relationships. This is the first-tier inquiry, so-called "village-level discussion". Apart from that, every house in the village is "enterable", functioning as an individual forum to facilitate discussion of a particular view, argument or question raised at the village-level. This is the second-tier inquiry, so called "house-level discussion". When the number of quality houses reaches a certain amount, the village will be upgraded by their learning facilitator (usually their teacher). Benefits brought to the students by the upgrade include higher social status conferment for enjoying extra privileges in the virtual world, such as pet keeping, mini-game playing, etc. The two-tier inquiry approach in *LV* visualizes, in the process of learning, students' collective views, arguments and questions, as well as their in-between relationships in the form of mind map (at the village level), while the discussion of a particular view, argument, or question can be recorded in and recalled from a single access point systemically (at the house level). *LV* has been adopted in facilitating cross-region inter-school collaborative inquiry learning projects among Hong Kong students and other students from China, Singapore, and USA, in the areas of personal, social and humanity studies.

Distributed authentic professionalism, which refers to the distribution of authentic professional expertise between NPCs and players' avatars, is the underlying educational belief of Shaffer's (2006) "epistemic games". Shaffer realized that members of a profession have an epistemic frame—a particular way of thinking and working. From the learning perspective, epistemic frames are the conventions of participation to which learners become internalized and acculturated. Thus, developing people to be members of a particular profession is a matter of equipping them with a right epistemic frame. To accomplish this, Shaffer and his team developed a number of epistemic games as extra-curriculum programmes for middle-school-aged students (outside school hours) to participate in simulations of various professional communities (which they might someday inhabit). These communities include, for example, biomechanical engineers in *Digital Zoo*, and ecological thinkers in *Urban Science*. More recently, a number of epistemic games have been adopted as a testing tool for assessing students' higher order thinking (see Shaffer and Gee 2010).

Based on the theoretical foundations of *Situated learning* (Lave and Wenger 1991), *scaffolding* (Vygotsky 1978), and *reflection* (Dewey 1958), Jong et al.'s (2010a) proposed Virtual Interactive Student-Oriented Learning Environment (VISOLE)—a teacher-facilitated pedagogical approach to GBL. It encompasses the creation of a near real-life online interactive world modeled upon a set of multi-disciplinary domains, in which each student plays a role in this "virtual world" and shapes its development. It aims at providing students with opportunities not only to acquire subject knowledge in a multi-disciplinary fashion, but also sharpen their higher-order thinking skills. VISOLE is composed of three pedagogical phases. In Phase 1 (*Multi-disciplinary Scaffolding*), a teacher assists students in gaining some preliminary high-level abstract knowledge (as their prior knowledge to the next learning phase) based upon a selected multi-disciplinary framework. Phase 2 (*Game-based Situated Learning*) and Phase 3 (*Reflection and Debriefing*) take place in an interlacing fashion. Phase 2 deploys an online multi-player interactive game portraying a virtual world in which the students play a role to shape the development of this world by accomplishing generative and open-ended tasks. In order to finish the tasks, they have to acquire new knowledge and skills on their own not only from the designated learning resources but also the Internet. In Phase 3, the students are required to write a piece of gaming journal to reflect on their learning experience in the virtual world after each bout of gaming. Also, in this phase the teacher will monitor the students' development of the virtual world at the backend, and extract scenarios arising in the game to debrief the students through case studies. *Farmtasia* (Cheung et al. 2008), the first game for enabling Phase 2 of VISOLE, was developed based on a multi-disciplinary topic, Agriculture, in the formal senior secondary Geography curriculum in Hong Kong. It is a bout-based game, deploying interacting farming systems of cultivation, horticulture, and pasturage. Teachers can review students' performance and extract gaming scenarios for conducting case studies through a dedicated teacher console. In this game, each student acts as a farm manager to run a farm and competes for financial gain and reputation. They have to optimize their investment and operational strategies in order to yield both quality and abundant farm products for profit making. Moreover, they have to be conscious of their practice in sustainable development and environmental protection which determine their reputation in the virtual world. Jong et al. (2010b), in an evaluation study of VISOLE with 254 Grade 10 students from 16 secondary schools, obtained positive results in terms of the students' advancement in the knowledge and higher-order thinking skills concerned.

Upon the game-in-education initiative, so-called "serious games" [or "non-entertainment-based learning games" in Gee's (2011) terms] has become another focus in the recent years. Serious games, which refer to the games implemented with the state-of-art gaming technologies, are designed for instruction purpose (either education or training) rather than entertainment purpose (Cannon-Bowers 2010; Sawyer and Smith 2008), consisting of meaningful and near-real life contextualization to engage learners for achieving specific "serious" instructional goals (Games and Squire 2011). These games can not only provide learners with relatively safe and non-threatening environments to conduct more "risk-taking" tasks in the course of learning, but also protect them from the severe consequences of their mistakes made therein (Garris et al. 2002). *River City* (Dede et al. 2008) and *Guardian Angel* (Andrews et al. 2010) are two recent examples of serious games. *River City* encompasses a 3D multi-player "virtual world", placing learners in the role of scientists to research an outbreak of diseases in a virtual town. In this game, they have to make observations, collect data, as well as conduct analysis for investigating the cause of the diseases. *Guardian Angel* is for mental health education, particularly in the area of addiction recovery and prevention. In this game, each player plays the role of an angel to "watch over and guide" a NPC (a virtual patient) in a full year of sobriety. This game aims at equipping players with relapse prevention (RP) craving-management techniques, including drink refusal, identification of high-risk situations, lifestyle-balancing, cognitive restructuring, assertiveness training, cognitive restructuring, and stimulus control.

13.4 GBL: Next Challenges

Tobias and Fletcher (2011) argued that—

> It is difficult to be specific about the place of games in schools of the future. At one extreme are traditional schools pursuing the required curriculum and ignoring games entirely. At the other extreme are experimental schools where games essentially are the curriculum ...... Games may gradually be infused into the curriculum. The pace of such infusion is likely to depend on research findings demonstrating that games improve student learning ... (pp. 539–541).

Although most of today's youngsters regard games as a "must-have" item at school (Kamil and Taitague 2011), we are indeed hard to predict the extent of the use of games in education in the coming decades. Mayer (2011, p. 281) argued that, "many strong claims are made for the educational value of computer games, but there is little strong empirical evidence to back up those claims". Regardless a considerable number of education-in-game and game-in-education instances in the current domain (as discussed in Sect. 13.3), the learning effectiveness of GBL has still been a large concern from the public (see DiPietro et al. 2007; Hannifin and Vermillion 2008; Mishra and Foster 2007; O'Neil and Perez 2008).

In (Tobias et al. 2011) recent literature review of the GBL studies carried out between 1992 and 2009, they observed that the evidence regarding learning from games has been less robust than what educators and other educational stakeholder are expecting. Most of those studies were summative evaluations, each looking at if there is a significant difference between the advocating GBL approach and an ordinary educational practice. Dede (2011) argued the scholarly focus of GBL should expand beyond the narrow concern of whether a recreational or educational game can yield so called "learning outcomes" at "a significance level of 0.05". The future of GBL depends on the researchers' ability in the field to show how games can be applied in education successfully (Cannon-Bowers 2010). The following four aspects, we believe, need further attention in the GBL domain. We urge more research effort should be put into these aspects in the coming years.

For "whom" GBL works

Learning is quite diverse in its manifestations among humans (Bransford et al. 2005). There are always different kinds of learners in an educational setting (Biggs and Moore 1993). So is in a GBL environment. There has been no consensus on the categories of "players" in gaming. Gee (2011) divided game-players in general into *not-at-all gamers*, *causal gamers*, and *regular gamers*. Bartle (2003) classified MMORPG players into *killers*, *socializers*, *achievers*, and *explorers*. However, it should be noted that the "players" described by Gee and Bartle are "gamers," not equivalent exactly to "players in GBL". Gamers play (or do not play) games in accordance with their own personal preference and choices (e.g., interest, experiences, as well as what games, when, where, etc.). On the other hand, "players in GBL" are actually learners in ordinary educational settings. We should always remember that not every learner enthuses about gaming. Besides, not every game is appealing to learners even if they love gaming. Some non-gamer students (who are not interested in gaming) may see GBL is a sort of "unpleasant" homework which they are "subjected" to do it (Jong et al. 2010c). Some academic achieving students (who are examination-oriented) may realize participation in GBL is wasting their time and impeding them to get good results in school exams (Jong et al. 2011a). Some gamer-students (who possess rich experiences in gaming) may criticize that the games used in GBL at school are too boring, in comparing with the ones they are playing during their leisure time (Jong et al. 2011b).

We argue that, when one claims a particular GBL approach or a game is good (or effective or bad/ineffective, etc.) for learners, it is important for the one to specify clearly what kinds of learners whom are in his/her claim. Gee (2011) and Dede (2011) in their recent publications have also shared a similar view with us—

> Showing that a game, a type of game, or games as a whole work or don't work for one category of gamer or learner does not show they work or don't work for other categories of gamers and learners … (Gee 2011, p. 225).
>
> Educational research strongly suggests that individual learning is as diverse …yet theories of learning and philosophies about how to use interactive media for education tend to treat learning as an activity relatively invariant across people … (Dede 2011, p. 236).

In most of past evaluation studies of GBL approaches, in fact, there has been little discussion of categorizing different kinds of GBL learners and then studying in-depth the learner's GBL process in each category. We believe, however, this is crucial work for answering the "whom" question if a researcher want to conclude a particular GBL approach is contributive to education. In our previous study of VISOLE [as discussed in Sect. 13.3.2, see also Jong et al. (2010b)], we observed a number of the students' personal factors affecting their participation in the GBL process. These personal factors were *gaming interest*, *prior gaming experiences, emotions generated during gaming*, and *conceptions of learning*. These findings can provide some insights into the issue of how to categorize learners in a GBL setting.

Significance of meta-gaming in GBL

Most of today's GBL advocators (e.g., Barab et al. 2007; Gee 2003, 2005, 2007; Jong et al. 2010a; Shaffer 2006) argue games are good for education because they observe games are not just pieces of computer software, but "game systems" (as discussed in Sect. 13.2.2.2, and see also Prensky 2006) involving abundant in-game and off-game interactivities among players. In-game interactivities are apparent in many nowadays multi-player recreational and educational games in which players interact (compete or/and collaborate) with one another simultaneously. Off-game interactivities usually involve players' self-initiated social interactions, such as discussing and sharing gaming strategies and experiences, as well as learning how to modify ("mod") games through discussion forums, blogs, social networking systems, fan websites, etc. These players' interactivities are termed "meta-gaming" (Gee 2011).

GBL, in today's context, is a combination of gaming and meta-gaming (Gee 2003, 2005, 2007, 2011; Prensky 2001, 2006). The learning outcomes of a particular GBL approach stem not only from gaming but also meta-gaming. The latter, however, has been receiving little attention in empirical research in the domain. We urge more research effort should be placed on investigating (1) *the significance of meta-gaming in the process of GBL*, (2) *the inner-workings between gaming and meta-gaming*, and (3) *how gaming and meta-gaming are articulated best for maximizing the effectiveness of GBL.*

Teachers' roles in GBL

The games in nowadays GBL instances are usually composed of near-real life simulations for providing learners with learning contexts as similar as those in the real world (Cannon-Bowers 2010). Nevertheless, even high-fidelity simulations can never be exact reflections of the reality (Thiagarajan 1992, 1998). On top of that, learners often have difficulties in making connections between the simulated situations in a game and the referring real-world systems (Clegg 1991; Crookall 1992). Although learners are sometimes requested to reflect on their own experience in the process of GBL, not everyone is able to do it well equally (Bransford et al. 2005).

Despite the promotion of constructivist learning paradigms in GBL that emphasizes a more active student role, teachers are still the best at seeing when, what and why students are confronted with puzzles arising in the process of the learning, and scaffolding them to solve the puzzles constructivistly (Brush and Saye 2002; Howard 2002; Johnston and Cooper 1997; Jonassen 1988; Peters and Vissers 2004). Regrettably, there has been little discussion of the significance of teachers and their specific roles in the process of GBL. Our proposal of VISOLE (a teacher-facilitated pedagogical approach to GBL, as discussed in Sect. 13.3.2) has been in the minority in the field.

VISOLE (Jong et al. 2010a) specifies a number of teacher scaffolding and debriefing tasks in GBL for helping students transform their gaming experience into learning experience. VISOLE, however, has yet to be "perfect". For example, in our empirical study (Jong et al. 2010b), we found that teachers' emotional support to students is indeed a very important element in the process of GBL, but we had not considered this aspect in the design of VISOLE. We believe, nevertheless, the pedagogical paradigm of VISOLE, and its empirical findings regarding teacher facilitation in GBL can shed light on the further discussion of teachers' roles in both education-in-game and game-in-education initiatives in the domain.

GBL works best in "what"

There has been literature (e.g., Bransford et al. 2005; Shulman 1986) documenting no optimal pedagogical approach is effective across different subject areas. Dede (2011) also argued that—

> No learning medium is a technology like fire, where one only has to stand near to get a benefit from it ...... the nature of the content and skills to be learned shape the type of instruction to use ...(p. 237).

Learning is an activity variant across different curricula. Similar to other constructivist learning approaches such as WebQuest (Dodge 1995), Problem-based Learning (Barrows 1996), and Project-based Learning (Krajcik and Blumenfeld 2006), GBL does not work universally. Apart from students' personal factors and teachers' facilitation, the success of a GBL instance depends largely on whether the learning content concerned is suitable to be embedded in a game-based context. We realize that further research on what kinds of educational aims, objectives, topics, and subjects are delivered best through GBL is important.

13.5 Conclusion

In this chapter, we have discussed the educational use of games, starting from its early purpose of "sugaring the pill" (making learning more interesting) to its recent focus of facilitating constructivist learning in terms of games' abilities to sustain spontaneous players' engagement, offer players near real-life simulation-based experiences, and exploit proactive players' communities. We also categorize the contemporary constructivist GBL instances into two initiatives, *education in games* and *games in education*, as well as discuss a number of representative instances among each initiative.

Similar to other educational innovations (either technology-based or non-technology-based), GBL holds a number of promises for education. It is expected that educational use of games will continue to be prominent for the foreseeable future (Games and Squire 2011; Kamil and Taitague 2011). However, the proof for games as a tool for learning has yet to be deep so far (Gee 2011; Mayer 2011; Tobias and Fletcher 2011); further research has to be done before we can provide the public with convincing evidence for supporting GBL. We realize a good research model for educational innovation is not only to answer "whether" an innovation works in general, but also understand how it works and explain why it works. Instead of proposing a full research agenda for GBL researchers (it is complicated work that absolutely needs collective effort in the field), we aim at adding some items into this agenda, or at least initiating a "dialogue" about some directions for evolving this agenda. We have suggested four areas which are worth investing additional research effort. They are (1) *for "whom" GBL works*, (2) *significance of meta-gaming in GBL*, (3) *teachers' roles in GBL*, as well as (4) *GBL works best in "what"*. We believe gaining an in-depth understanding of each of these aspects will certainly provide new insights into the future development (both design and implementation) of games for educational use.

References

Adams PC (1998) Teaching and learning with SimCity 2000. J Geogr 97:47–55

Anderson LW, Krathwohl DR, Airasian PW, Cruikshank KA, Mayer RE, Pintrich PR, Raths J, Wittrock MC (2001) A taxonomy for learning, teaching, and assessing: a revision of bloom's taxonomy of educational objectives. Longman, New York

Andrew A, Joyce R, Bowers C (2010) Using serious games for mental health education. In: Cannon-Bowers J, Bowers C (eds) Serious game design and development: technologies for training and learning. IGI Global, New York, pp 246–259

Antonacci D, Modaress N (2008) Envisioning educational possibilities of user-created virtual worlds. AACE Journal 16(2):115–126

Aylett R (2005) And they both lived happily ever after? Digital stories and learning. In: Dettori G, Giannetti T, Paiva A, Vaz A(eds) Technology-mediated narrative environments for learning. Sense Publishers, Amsterdam. Retrieve July 28, 2008, from http://www.macs.hw.ac.uk/~ruth/Papers/narrative/Kal-Lisbon.pdf

Aylett R, Figuieredo R, Louchart S, Dias J, Paiva A (2006) Making it up as you go along—improvising stories for pedagogical purposes. In: Gratch J, Young M, Aylett R, Ballin D, Olivier P (eds) Proceedings of the 6th international conference IVA 2006 (pp 307–315)

Barab SA, Sadler TD, Heiselt C, Hickey D, Zuiker S (2007) Relating narrative, inquiry, and inscriptions: supporting consequential play. J Sci Educ Technol 16(1):59–82

Barrows HS (1996) Problem-based learning in medicine and beyond: A brief overview. New Dir Teach Learn 68:3–12

Barton RI (1970) A primer on simulations and gaming. Prentice Hall, Englewood Cliffs

Bartle R (2003) Designing virtual worlds. New Riders Games, Indianapolis

Betz JA (1995) Computer games: increase learning in an interactive multidisciplinary environment. J Educ Technol Syst 24(2):195–205

Biggs JB, Moore P (1993) *The process of learning*, 3rd edn. Prentice Hall, New York

Bisson C, Lunckner J (1996) Fun in learning: the pedagogical role of fun in adventure education. J Exp Educ 9(2):109–110

Bowman RF (1982) A Pac-Man theory of motivation: tactical implications for classroom instruction. Educ Technol 22(9):14–17

Bransford J, Derry D, Berliner S, Hammerness D, Beckett (2005) Theories of learning and their roles in teaching. In: Darling-Hammond L, Bransford J (eds) Preparing teachers for a changing world, Jossey-Bass, San Francisco (pp 40–87)

Bredemeier ME, Greenblat CS (1981) The educational effectiveness of simulation games. Simul Games 12(3):307–332

Bruner JS (1960) The process of education. Harvard University Press, Cambridge

Brush TA, Saye JW (2002) A summary of research exploring hard and soft scaffolding for teachers and students using a multimedia supported learning environment. J Interact Online Learn 2(1):1–11

Cameron B (2008) Gamingpig, cognitive style, and feedback in the achievement of learning objectives. In: Kidd TT, Song H (eds) Handbook of research on instructional systems and technology. Information Science Reference, Hershey, pp 416–448

Cannon-Bowers J (2010) The way ahead for serious games. In: Cannon-Bowers J, Bowers C (eds) Serious game design and development: technologies for training and learning. IGI Global, New York, pp 305–310

Cheung KKF, Jong MSY, Lee FL, Lee JHM, Luk ETH, Shang JJ, Wong MKH (2008) FARMTASIA: an online game-based learning environment based on the VISOLE pedagogy. Virtual Reality 12(1):17–25

Clegg AA (1991) Games and simulations in social studies education. In: Shaver JP (ed) Handbook of research on social studies teaching and learning. Macmillan, New York, pp 523–528

Cole M (1996) Cultural psychology: a once and future discipline. The Harvard University Press, Cambridge

Collins A, Brown JS, Newman SE (1989) Cognitive apprenticeship: teaching the crafts of reading, writing, and mathematics. In: Resnick LB (ed) Knowing, learning and instruction: essays in honour of Robert Glaser. LEA, Hillsdale, pp 453–494

Cordova DI, Lepper MR (1996) Intrinsic motivation and the process of learning: beneficial effects of contextualization, personalization, and choice. J Educ Psychol 88:715–730

Crookall D (1992) Debriefing. Simul Gaming 23(2):141–142

Cruickshank DR, Telfer R (1980) Classroom games and simulations. Theor Into Pract 19(1):75–80

Csikszentmihalyi M (1975) Beyond boredom and anxiety. Jossey-Bass, San Francisco

Csikszentmihalyi M (1990) Flow: the psychology of optimal experience. Harper & Row, New York

Dede C (2011) Developing a research agenda for educational games and stimulations. In: Tobias S, Fletcher JD (eds) Computer games and instruction. Information Age Publishing, Charlotte, pp 233–250

Dede C, Garduno E, Smith J (2008) River City, Retrieved from December 20, 2011, from http://muve.gse.harvard.edu/rivercityproject/

DeLisi R, Wolford JL (2002) Improving children's mental rotation accuracy with computer game playing. J Genet Psychol 163(3):272–282

Dewey J (1938) Experience and education. Macmullan, New York

Dewey J (1958) Art as experience. Capricorn Books, New York

DiPietro M, Ferdig RE, Boyer J, Black EW (2007) Towards a framework for understanding electronic educational gaming. J Educ Multimedia Hypermedia 16(3):225–248

Dodge B (1995) WebQuests: a technique for Internet-based learning. Distance Educator 1(2): 10–13

Egenfeldt-Nielsen S (2007) Third generation educational use of computer games. J Educ Multimedia Hypermedia 16(3):263–281

Games A, Squire K (2011) Searching for the fun: a historical perspective on the evolution of educational video games. In: Tobias S, Fletcher JD (eds) Computer games and instruction. Information Age Publishing, Charlotte, pp 17–46

Garris R, Ahlers R, Driskell JE (2002) Games, motivation, and learning: A research and practice model. Simul Gaming 33(4):441–467

Gee JP (2003) What video games have to teach us about learning. Palgrave, New York

Gee JP (2005) What would be a state of the art instructional video game look like?, Retrieved July 28, 2008, from http://www.innovateonline.info/index.php?view=article&id=80

Gee JP (2007) What video games have to teach us about learning and literacy, 2nd edn. Palgrave, New York

Gee J (2011) Reflections on empirical evidence on games and learning. In: Tobias S, Fletcher JD (eds) Computer games and instruction. Information Age Publishing, Charlotte, pp 223–232

Gibbs GI (1974) Handbook of games and simulation exercises. Spon, London

Gredler M (1996) Educational game and simulations: a technology in search of a research paradigm. In: Jonassen D (ed) Handbook of research on educational communications and technology. MacMillan, New York, pp 521–539

Gredler M (2004) Game and simulations and their relationships to learning. In: Jonassen D (ed) Handbook of research on educational communications and technology, 2nd edn. Lawrence Erlbaum Associates, New Jersey, pp 571–581

Hannifin RD, Vermillion JR (2008) Technology in the classroom. In: Good TL (ed) 21st century education: a reference handbook, vol 2. Sage, Thousand Oaks, pp 209–218

Halverson R (2005) What can K-12 school leaders learn from video games and gaming? Innovate, 1(6). Retrieved Jan 15, 2009, from http://www.innovateonline.info/index.php?view=article&id=81

Heinich R, Molenda M, Russell JD, Smaldino SE (1982) Instructional media and new technologies of instruction. John Wiley & Sons, New York

Heinich R, Molenda M, Russell JD, Smaldino SE (1996) Instructional media and technologies for learning, 6th edn. Merrill, Upper Saddle River

Howard J (2002) Technology-enhanced project-based learning in teacher education: Addressing the goals of transfer. J Technol Teach Educ 10(3):343–364

Huh J (2008) Adoption and dissemination of digital game-based learning. In: Kidd TT, Song H (eds) Handbook of research on instructional systems and technology. Information Science Reference, Hershey, pp 409–415

Jenkins H, Purushotma R, Clinton K, Weigel M, Robison AJ (2006) Confronting the challenges of participatory culture: media education for the 21st century. MacArthur Foundation, Chicago

Johnson S (2005) Everything bad is good for you. Penguin, New York

Johnston S, Cooper J (1997) Supporting student success through scaffolding. Coop Learn Coll Teach 9(3):

Jonassen DH (1988) Integrating learning strategies into courseware to facilitate deeper processing. In: Jonassen DH (ed) Instructional designs for microcomputer courseware. Erlbaum, Hillsdale, pp 151–181

Jonassen DH, Howland J (2003) Learning to solve problems with technology: a constructivist perspective. Merrill Prentice Hall, Upper Saddle River

Jong MSY, Shang JJ, Lee FL, Lee JHM (2010a) VISOLE—A constructivist pedagogical approach to game-based learning. In: Yang H, Yuen S (eds) Collective intelligence and e-learning 2.0: Implications of web-based communities and networking. Information Science Reference, New York, pp 185–206

Jong MSY, Shang JJ, Lee FL, Lee JHM (2010b) An evaluative study on VISOLE—virtual interactive student-oriented learning environment. IEEE Trans Learn Technol 3(4):307–318

Jong MSY, Shang JJ, Lee FL, Lee JHM (2010c) A case study of a non-gamer student's learning process in VISOLE. In: Proceedings of the 3rd IEEE International Conference on Digital Game and Intelligent Toy Enhanced Learning (DIGITEL 2010). Kaohsiung, Taiwan, pp 77–84

Jong MSY, Chen WQ, Tse AWC, Lee FL, Lee JHM (2010e) Using posting templates for enhancing students' argumentative elaborations in computer-supported collaborative inquiry learning. Res Pract Technol Enhanced Learn 5(3):275–294

Jong MSY, Shang JJ, Lee FL, Lee JHM (2011a) A case study of an academic achievement-oriented student in game-based learning. In: Proceedings of the 11th IEEE international conference on advanced learning technologies, Athens, Georgia, USA, pp 7–11

Jong MSY, Shang JJ, Lee FL, Lee JHM (2011b) A case study of a gamer-student in game-based learning. In: Proceedings of the 19th international conference on computers in education (ICCE 2011), Chiangmai, Thailand, pp 508–512

Kamil M, Taitague C (2011) Developing an electronic game for vocabulary learning: a case study. In: Tobias S, Fletcher JD (eds) Computer games and instruction. Information Age Publishing, Charlotte, pp 331–354

Kemp J, Livingstone D (2006) Putting a second life "metaverse" skin on learning management systems. In: Proceedings of the second life workshop at the second life community convention, San Francisco, pp 13–18, Aug 20 2006
Kirriemuir J, McFarlane A (2004) Literature review in games and learning (No. 8). Futurelab, UK
Kolson K (1994) The politics of city planning simulations. Paper presented at the annual meeting of the American political science association, New York
Klabbers J (2006) The magic circle: principal of gaming and simulations. Sense Publishers, Rotterdam
Krajcik JS, Blumenfeld P (2006) Project-based learning. In: Sawyer RK (ed) The Cambridge handbook of the learning sciences. Cambridge University Press, Cambridge, pp 317–334
Lave J, Wenger E (1991) Situated learning: legitimate peripheral participation. Cambridge University Press, Cambridge
Lederman LC (1992) Debriefing: toward a systematic assessment of theory and practice. Simul Gaming 23(2):145–160
Leigh E, Kinder J (1999) Learning through fun and games NSW. McGraw Hill, Australia
Livingstone SA (1972) Games. In: Inbar M, Stoll C (eds) Simulations and gaming in the social sciences. Free Press, New York, pp 299–306
Malone TW (1980) What makes things fun to learn? a study of intrinsically motivating computer games. Xerox, Palo Alto
Malone TW (1981) Toward a theory of intrinsically motivating instruction. Cogn Sci 4:333–369
Marquis J (2008) Computer game as a new arena for IST research. In: Kidd TT, Song H (eds) Handbook of research on instructional systems and technology. Information Science Reference, Hershey, pp 395–407
Mason H, Moutahir M (2006) Multidisciplinary experiential education in Second Life: A global approach. In: Kemp J, Livingstone D(eds) Proceedings of the second life education workshop at the second life community convention, San Francisco, pp 30–34
Mayer RE, Mautone P, Prothero W (2002) Pictorial aids for learning by doing in multimedia geology game. J Educ Psychol 94:171–185
Mayer RE (2011) Multimedia learning and games. In: Tobias S, Fletcher JD (eds) Computer games and instruction. Information Age Publishing, Charlotte, pp 283–305
McFarlane A, Sparrowhawk A, Heald Y (2002) Report on the educational use of games. TEEM, Cambridge
Mishra P, Foster AN (2007) The claims of games: a comprehensive review and directions for future research. In: Proceedings of society for information technology and teacher education interactional conference 2007, Texas, pp 2227–2232
Muukkonen H, Hakkarainen K, Lakkala M (1999) Collaborative technology for facilitating progressive inquiry: the future learning environment tools. In: Proceedings of the CSCL'99 conference, Lawrence Erlbaum and Associates, Palo Alto, pp 406–415, December, 12–15
O'Neil HF, Perez RS (eds) (2008) Computer games and team and individual learning. Elsevier, Oxford
Papert S (1980) Mindstorms. Basic Book, New York
Papert S (1993) The children's machine: rethinking school in the age of the computers. Basis Books, New York
Peters V, Vissers G (2004) A simple classification model for debriefing simulation games. Simul Gaming 35(1):70–84
Piaget J (1964) Development and learning. J Res Sci Teach 2:176–186
Piaget J (1970) Science of education and psychology of the child. Oxford University Press, New York
Prensky M (2001) Digital game-based learning. McGraw Hill, New York
Prensky M (2006) Don't bother me mom—I'm learning. Paragon House, St. Paul
Provenzo EF (1991) Video kids: making sense of Nintendo. Harvard, Cambridge

Rankin YA, Shute MW (2010) Re-purposing a recreational video game as a serious game for second language acquisition. In: Cannon-Bowers J, Bowers C (eds) Serious game design and development: technologies for training and learning. IGI Global, New York, pp 178–195
Rice JW (2007) New media resistance: Barriers to implementation of computer video games in the classroom. J Educ Multimedia Hypermedia 16(3):249–261
Richter J, Livingstone D (2011) Multi-user games and learning. In: Tobias S, Fletcher JD (eds) Computer games and instruction. Information Age Publishing, Charlotte, pp 101–124
Salen K (2007) Gaming literacies: a game design study in action. J Educ Multimedia Hypermedia 16(3):301–322
Salen K (ed) (2008) The ecology of games: connecting youth, games, and learning. The MIT press, London
Sandford R, Williamson B (2005) Games and learning: a handbook. Futurelab, Bristol
Sawyer B, Smith PA (2008) Serious games taxonomy. Paper presented at the game developers conference, San Francisco
Scardamalia M, Bereiter C (1993) Technologies for knowledge-building discourse. Commun ACM 36:37–41
Scardamalia M, Bereiter C (1996) Adaptation and understanding: a case for new cultures of schooling. In: Vosniadou S, DeCorte E, Glaser R, Mandl H (eds) International perspectives on the design of technology-supported learning environments. Lawrence Erlbaum Associates, Hillsdale, pp 149–163
Scardamalia M, Bereiter C (2003) Knowledge building: encyclopedia of education. Macmillan Reference, New York, pp 1370–1373
Shaffer DW (2006) *How computer games help children to learn*. Palgrave Macmillan, New York
Shaffer DW, Gee JP (2010) Looking where the light is bad: video games and the future of assessment. Phi Delta Kappa International EDge 6(1):3–19
Shulman LS (1986) Those who understand: knowledge growth in teaching. Educ Researchers 15(2):4–14
Shulman LS, Keislar ER (1966) Learning by discovery: a critical appraisal. Rand McNally, Chicago
Skinner BF (1938) The behavior of organisms. Appleton-Century-Crofts, New York
Smith BS, Avedon EM (1971) The study of games. Wiley, New York
Squire KR (2003) Video games in education. Int J Intell Games Simul, 2(1). Retrieved July 30, 2008, from www.cyberfest.us/Education/Video_Games_in_Education-MIT_Study.pdf
Squire KR (2004) Replaying history: learning world history through playing civilization III. Dissertation, Indiana University
Squire KR (2005) Changing the game: what happens when video games enter the classroom? Innovate, 1(6). Retrieved July 28, 2008, from http://www.innovateonline.info/index.php?view=article&id=82
Thiagarajan S (1992) Using games for debriefing. Simul Gaming 23(2):141–142
Thiagarajan S (1998) The myths and realities of simulations in performance technology. Educ Technol 38(5):35–41
Thiagarajan S, Stolovitch HD (1978) Instructional simulation games. Educational Technology Publications, Englewood Cliffs
Tobias S, Fletcher JD (2011) Computer games, present and future. In: Tobias S, Fletcher JD (eds) Computer games and instruction. Information Age Publishing, Charlotte, pp 525–545
Tobias S, Fletcher JD, Dai DY, Wind AP (2011) Review of research on computer games. In: Tobias S, Fletcher JD (eds) Computer games and instruction. Information Age Publishing, Charlotte, pp 127–221
van Ments M (1999) The effective use of role-play, 2nd edn. Kogan Page, London
van Ments M, Hearnden K (1985) Effective use of games and simulation. Sagset, Leicestershire
Vygotsky L (1978) Mind and society. MIT Press, Cambridge
Wenger E (1998) Communities of practice: learning, meaning, and identity. Cambridge University Press, Cambridge

Wolf J, Crookall D (1998) Developing a scientific knowledge of simulation/gaming. Simul Gaming 29(1):7–19

Wong NY (2003) The influence of technology on the mathematics curriculum. In: Bishop AJ, Clements MA, Keitel C, Kilpatrick J, Leung FKS (eds) Second international handbook of mathematics education, vol 1. Kluwer Academic Publishers, Dordrecht, pp 271–321

Chapter 14
Supplemental Versus Essential Use of Computing Devices in the Classroom: An Analysis

Cathie Norris, Akhlaq Hossain and Elliot Soloway

Abstract Increases in student achievement can be observed in classrooms where computers are used as essential tools in the curriculum. In contrast, when computers are used as supplemental to the curriculum—even in classrooms that are 1:1 (one laptop per student)—no increase in student achievement is observed. These claims are based on the analyses of a number of empirical studies of classroom computer use. We draw on the work of Project RED, a nationwide survey of classroom computer use, to identify the characteristics that distinguish between essential and supplemental use. This distinction is not an empty one; it could and should guide the next wave of 1:1 classrooms as mobile computing devices experience increased adoption. Indeed, the reality of every student having a computing device in the palm of his or her hand is within reach in the near term. However, if those computing devices are used as supplements to the curriculum then a great opportunity will be lost. In contrast, with a change in pedagogy and curriculum, K-12 education is poised to experience a dramatic increase in student achievement.

C. Norris (✉) · A. Hossain
Department of Learning Technologies, University of North Texas, Denton, USA
e-mail: cathie.norris@gmail.com

A. Hossain
e-mail: akhlaqhossain@yahoo.com

E. Soloway
Department of Computer Science and Engineering, University of Michigan, Ann Arbor, USA
e-mail: soloway@umich.edu

R. Huang et al. (eds.), *Reshaping Learning*, New Frontiers of Educational Research, DOI: 10.1007/978-3-642-32301-0_14, © Springer-Verlag Berlin Heidelberg 2013

14.1 Introduction

1:1(a computing device for each learner) is set to make a major sweep across America's K–12 land scape. Why? Two reasons: (1) Students and their parents are demanding that schools be on the right side of the twentyfirst century—pencil and paper simply is no longer good enough—and (2) the cost of going 1:1 has dramatically been reduced. But, in this second wave of 1:1, we had better learn from them is takes K–12 made during the first wave of 1:1, lest more money be spent with the same limited impacts.

Briefly, during those 1:1 laptop days, while each and every student had access to a computer, the predominant use of computers was supplemental to the existing and relatively unchanged curriculum. That is, the same instructionalist/direct instruction/didactic pedagogy used before computers were introduced was still being used, but now computers were employed as glorified typewriters and front-ends for Google searches.

In contrast, in this second wave of 1:1—a wave that will gain momentum over the decade—where schools are reporting upwards of 30 % improvement in standardized test scores, computing devices are being used as essential to the curriculum, i.e., the students use the devices from 40 to 70 % of the school day and for periods after school as well (Norris et al. 2011b), and the "active-learning" pedagogy emphasizes student constructive and collaborative activities (Bransford, Brown and Cocking 2000).

The second wave of 1:1 will not be based on laptops, but rather the computing device of choice will be a mobile device, such as a smartphone, a tablet, or a netbook. The cost of the device + network is dropping and, sooner than expected, schools will be able to make use of student-provided devices, and thus schools will not even need to provide computing devices perse—all that schools will need to provide is the Internet access and educational software.

Under what circumstances, then, does computer use lead to increased student achievement? In what follows, we make an argument for the notions of "supplemental tool use" vs. "essential tool use" to explain how computer use can lead to student achievement gains. First we look at how initial laptop use was, by and large an example of supplemental tool use—and thus gains in student achievement were not observed. In the next section, we use data and analyses from Project RED to illustrate essential use of the computer—that is correlated with gains in student achievement. Next, we apply a Project RED-style analysis to "first wave" studies of laptop use in order to both confirm Project RED's analysis and also to question it, at the same time. Then we give an example of how a mobile device is being used as an essential tool for learning in an elementary school in Singapore, where we are seeing significant increases in student achievement. We close with yet another conjecture, i.e., we speculate as to why mobile devices elicit such a positive response from students about learning, and we close with a prediction.

14.2 The First Wave of 1:1 Implementations: The Computer as Supplement

In about 2002, K–12 schools started to implement 1:1 laptop programs. Typically, a student would be issued a laptop computer for use 24/7. Maine funded the first 1:1 state wide program in the country. Michigan followed suit, as did schools and districts all around the U.S. While the costs were high, to say the least, the access problem was finally being addressed (Donovan et al. 2007).

On May 4th, 2007, a day that will live in infamy for educational technologists, The New York Times (Hu 2007) published an article entitled: "Seeing No Progress, Some Schools Drop Laptops". The article said that schools were not seeing increases in test scores that could be attributed to the use of the 1:1 computers, and thus schools were rethinking their expensive, 1:1 programs.

The NYT article (Hu 2007) pointed to two reasons to explain the lack of impact: (1) There was no educational software—the laptops came with Microsoft Office and a Web browser—and (2) the teachers were not provided with sufficient professional development support, i.e., the teachers were taught how to use the computers, but they weren't taught how to transform their existing paper-and-pencil curriculum into curriculum that took advantage of the affordances of the networked laptops.

Stepping back from the specifics of any particular school's 1:1 implementation, in reviewing the 1:1 studies, (Livingston 2009; Penuel 2005) we came to see that the news article (Hu 2007) was indeed insightful. Oftentimes, the lessons the teachers implemented used the computers as typewriters and encyclopedias; students used their word processors to write reports and used search engines to find information on the Internet. While the teachers did integrate the computers into their lessons, the lessons were, by and large, pencil-and-paper lessons with computers tacked on as a supplement. The computer-based activities took up a very small percentage of time in the total lesson.

Particularly telling was the following sort of question that teachers reported their students asking: "Do we need to bring our computers to class tomorrow?" Inasmuch as the students were issued seven-pound transportable computers, aka laptops, plus bulky text- books, such a question was perfectly reasonable, since the laptops were not used on a daily basis.

Given the lack of professional development and given the lack of educational software, it is not surprising that the teachers created lessons that were generally paper-and-pencil lessons with a little computer activity thrown in. With respect to educational software, for students there has been a dearth of provocative applications. Besides the drill-and-kill programs—Math Blasters was definitely more fun than math worksheets—the only dominant educational app was a concept mapping program called Inspiration, which spawned Kidspiration, a version for the younger crowd. Still further, educational software was not low-cost, let alone free, e.g., Civilization, SimEarth, etc., were $19.95–39.95 per copy. Buying a copy of each educational application for each student was prohibitively expensive.

For teachers, there has been an even greater dearth of support software. While there were electronic grade books, there has been precious little support for the teaching and learning processes. In contrast, 2000–2010 has been the golden era for software support for professionals—outside of K–12. Could a professional accountant do a professional job with just a spreadsheet? Could a travel agent do his or her job with just a database? Indeed, today essentially every professional employs a layer of professional software that has been designed to make that professional's job more efficient and more effective: Sales people use CRM systems—customer relationship management systems; journalists use media management systems, etc.

In sum, then, the early 1:1 laptop initiatives showed little impact on student achievement. Data did suggest that attendance was up and behavior problems were down (Silvernail and Lane 2004). Motivation and engagement in 1:1 classrooms definitely showed an uptick—working with computers for the digital generation was much more pleasurable than working with pencil and paper!

14.3 The Second Wave of 1:1 Implementations: Computer as Essential

Project Revolutionizing Education (RED), as reported in eSchool News, has surveyed "nearly a thousand schools with diverse student populations and varying levels of technology integration" (Devaney 2010). Table 14.1 summarizes a key finding: Using 1:1 when not "properly implemented" has no more effect than using computers on wheels (COWS), computer labs, etc. Frankly, this is a huge finding, since the cost of going 1:1 is significantly greater than the cost of simply using COWS and labs. Given the Project RED findings, the cost/benefit ratio does not justify moving to 1:1—unless the school does it "properly".

What does "properly implemented" mean? In Table 14.2, we list, in "rank order", the "Key Implementation Factors" directly from the Project RED press release (Greaves and Hayes 2010).

If we step back from the specifics of Project RED's findings, we see how important the daily use of computers (i.e., use various pieces of software) "in the core subjects" is. In other words, increased time on task is one of the factors that leads to increased student achievement (Stallings 1980). We do hasten to point out that factor #4 includes "... in core subject classes". The factor doesn't just say more time using the computer; indeed, there have been studies that show that more

Table 14.1 Key finding from project RED

How use technology?	Use technology but not 1:1	1:1	1:1 Properly implemented
Report increased student achievement	69 %	70 %	85 %

Table 14.2 Project RED factors: rank order of key implementation factors

1	Technology is integrated in every class
2	Principal leads change management
3	Students use technology daily
4	Technology is integrated into daily curriculum
5	Online assessments
6	Student to computer ratio (1:1)
7	Virtual field trips
8	Daily use of search engines
9	Best practices and tech training for teachers

computer use leads to poorer student performance (Stross 2010). The key is that the pedagogy driving the students' use of the computer has changed from an instructionalist/direct instruction/didactic pedagogy to one where the students are more active in their learning.

While there are doctrinaire pedagogical approaches that emphasize social-constructivism, and while Project RED is indeed mute on the exact pedagogy employed in classrooms where there were reports of significant gains in student achievement, it is our conjecture that the teachers were not doctrinaire, but opportunistic: The teachers were comfortable letting loose their reins and allowing their students to be active learners. Clearly, more research is needed to identify the pedagogies that are being used in classrooms where student achievement gains are seen in conjunction with significant amounts of time spent using computing devices.

Using the "supplemental versus essential" terminology, then, we would argue that the Project RED data support the argument that when computers are used as essential tools in the curriculum, e.g., daily use with active learning pedagogies, that is when computers "move the needle", that is when students experience increases in achievement.

Most interestingly, Project RED points out that not one school reported using all of the top six factors! The "daily use" mentioned in factors 3 and 4 continues to be a challenge. In order to use the 1:1 infrastructure daily, the teachers would need to rethink their curriculum, since their existing paper-and-pencil curriculum is based on a didactic, instructionalist pedagogy that does not lend itself to students working independently of the teacher. And, inasmuch as teachers and schools/districts have already invested in developing their existing curriculum, they are loathe to throw it out and start again. Rather, it has been our experience in dozens of schools all around the country that teachers take their existing curriculum and simply add activities that incorporate the computer, which they feel does accomplish the goal set forth by their administrators, i.e., "integrate the computer into your curriculum".

Candidly, it is not just the non-trivial cost involved in rewriting the curriculum that stops districts from doing the rewrite—and stops districts from using their 1:1 infrastructure on a continuous, daily basis. The issue goes to the heart of school change: The nature of the curriculum and the nature of the instruction will need to change if the school is going to use the computers on a daily basis (Bain and Weston 2011). Those teachers who are already using a more project-based/problem-based/inquiry-based pedagogy, where the emphasis is on student-centered exploration, tend to find it easier to transform their existing curriculum into one that takes full advantage of the affordances of a networked environment.

In sum, then, in order to move the needle and increase student achievement, 1:1 implementations must be "proper", according to Project RED, which means that the computing devices must be seen as essential, not supplemental.

14.4 First Wave Revisited

After combing the research literature, we found nine studies of 1:1 computer use that reported student achievement impact. Interestingly, it was not easy to find studies that actually reported what we feel are critical "details", e.g., what subjects were the computers used in, how long did the students use the computers for that subject, what was the impact on student achievement of that computer use, etc.

Unlike many educational research studies, six of the nine studies were methodologically rigorous. For example, each of the six studies had a control group and an experimental group; in each of the studies, one major factor that was varied was the "use—or not—of a computer 1:1". The curriculum in the six studies was the same for the control group as it was for the computer-using group; and the instructional strategies were more or less the same in both conditions. While methodologically different, the Fried (2008) and Zucker and Hug (2007, 2008) studies did provide enough detailed information so that we were able to include these studies in our categorization scheme.

Although these "first wave" of 1:1 SBR-level studies were carried out before Project RED introduced their criteria into the community's discourse, we decided to use the Project RED criteria to re-analyze these first –wave studies with the hope that we might be able to better understand the findings in these studies.

14.5 Supplemental Use is Linked to No Increase in Student Achievement

In studies of 1:1 laptop programs by Fried (2008), Grimes and Warschauer (2008), and (Wurst et al. 2008) there were a number of key commonalities: in each study, the curriculum and the instructional practices used in both the laptop and the non-laptop classes were traditional lecture and textbook-based curriculum and instruction. Moreover, the laptops were primarily used as typewriters for a couple hours per week by each student. Neither the curriculum nor the instruction took advantage of the affordances of a 1:1 laptop setting. In effect the culture in the laptop-using classrooms was the same culture as the non-laptop-using classrooms;

Table 14.3 Factors in play in the first wave 1:1 laptop studies

Project RED factors	Total factors in play	Student achievement	1	2	3	4	5	6	7	8	9
(Fried 2008)	2	–	–	–	–	–	–	E	–	1	–
(Grimes and Warschauer 2008)	2	–	–	–	E	–	–	E	–	–	–
(Wurst et al. 2008)	2	–	–	I	–	–	–	E	–	–	–
(Bebell and Kay 2010)	6	+Increase	E	–	I	E	–	E	–	E	E
(Brown 2009)	3	+Increase	–	–	E	E	–	E	–	–	–
(Gulek and Demirtas 2005)	4	+Increase	–	–	E	E	–	E	–	I	–
(Lowther et al. 2003)	3	+Increase	–	–	–	I	–	E	–	–	E
(Zucker and Hug 2007, 2008)	9	+Increase	E	I	E	E	E	E	I	E	I

E explicitly mentioned that factor was in play, *I* inferred that factor was in play, *+increase* study observed increase in student achievement

in effect the laptops were used as supplements to the existing curriculum and instruction. And, most importantly, in these three studies the laptop-using students show no increase in student achievement when compared with their non-laptop-using colleagues (Table 14.3).

Here are some observations that were made about the laptop-using students:

- "Laptop use interfered with student's ability to pay attention to and understand the lecture material, which in turn resulted in lower test scores" (Fried 2008).
- "98 % of students used laptops to write papers at school…. Language Arts classes averaged 2.8 h. per week (of laptop use in school)…" (Grimes and Warschauer 2008).
- "Students too easily got distracted using the laptop for internet activities instead of being attentive to the professor" (Wurst et al. 2008).

These three studies affirm a perception actually voiced by some faculty in the Fried 2008 study: "[the laptops] distract students and detract from learning". Indeed, this comment speaks volumes about the faculty's view of instruction: the teacher is the fount of knowledge and students need to pay attention to the teacher in order to learn. While computers are powerful enabling devices, their enabling power is effectively blocked when used by educators with attitudes like those in these studies.

14.6 Essential Use is Linked to Increased Student Achievement

In six of the studies of 1:1 laptop use, significant increases in student achievement were noted. What then was different in these six studies in comparison to the three studies where no increases were observed? Using the Project RED criteria

(Table 14.2), the difference is easiest to see in the studies by Zucker and Hug (2007, 2008).

- In the Zucker studies, the instructional practices of the teachers were fundamentally changed. 90 % of the teachers in these two studies agreed with the statement: "I have changed the way I organize classroom activities".
- Students used a number of different software applications (Sketchpad, LoggerPro, Inspiration, etc.)
- And, while the amount of computer use varied by subject matter, students did use their computers for significant amounts of time.

It is interesting to note that the Project RED factors (Table 14.2) did not include a factor about "teacher change". But, the observation that how the teachers taught changed—from didactic to more project/inquiry-based jumps out of the study. Thus, it would be interesting to go back into the Project RED data to explore how a factor "teacher practices were significantly changed; they practiced didactic instruction less or much less".

The teacher factor, in fact, grows in importance when we look at four studies in this "first-wave". In the four studies listed in italics in the chart, we show the Project RED factors in play in the classrooms. While the studies report increases in student achievement, the number of Project RED factors in play was mixed—more than in the study where student achievement was not observed but less than in the study where it was clear that the computers were used as essential tools. But, in those four studies, there were reports of changes in teacher pedagogy, for example:

- (Babell and Kay 2010): Fundamental change in teaching was noted; "particularly teaching strategies, curriculum delivery, and classroom management". Technical and curricular professional development and support was provided to teachers to integrate the new technology into their curriculum.
- (Brown 2009): Three reading strategies were implemented via the mobile devices; to accommodate visual learners, visual and kinesthetic learners and auditory learners. Specific reading material was designed to teach vocabulary, using mobile phones.
- (Lowther et al. 2003): Participation teachers received computer integration training. Laptop class teachers placed greater emphasis on "research and project oriented tasks" and "laptop students had greater accessibility to and better skills at using application software geared to solving open-ended learning problems". Also Laptop classes "used more student-centered instructional strategies".

In sum, then, using the Project RED lingo, we would say that in the Fried (2008), Grimes and Warschauer (2008) and Wurst et al. (2008) studies where increases in student achievement were not observed, this was due to the lack of the presence of at least three factors, while in our terms, we would argue that the reason was due to the use of the computers as supplements and not as essential tools. Similarly, using Project RED lingo, we would say that the increases in student achievement observed in the Zucker studies were due to the presence of all the Project RED factors—a situation that Project RED did not observe at any school that reported their data to the project. (Project RED 2010)!

Now, using Project RED lingo, the six studies where student achievement was observed were due to at least 3 but not more than 6 factors—except in the Zucker studies. However, given the variability in the number of factors in play and the specific factors in play, frankly, the Project RED argument feels weak. Interestingly, though, one factor that Project RED didn't include in their list—the change in teacher's pedagogy—did seem to play a role in the studies where student achievement was observed to increase. And, there is some rationale for why the "teacher" factor is relevant: as the classroom moved from a didactic to a more project oriented classroom, students typically take on more responsibility for their learning and that in turn typically results in greater engagement, and greater time on task. It is those actions on the students' part that typically are associated with increases in student achievement (Bransford et al. 2000).

We draw two conclusions from this retrospective application of Project RED-style analysis to the First-Wave of 1:1 laptop-using schools:

- Given the critically important role that the teacher apparently played in 6 of the studies—in essentially all the studies where student achievement was observed to increase, we wonder at the completeness of the list of factors put out by Project RED.
- The notions of supplemental and essential do seem to have some explanatory power; when computers are used by the students as essential tools—as represented by having a large number of Project RED factors in play and/or by teachers changing their pedagogy from didactic instruction to a more project-oriented pedagogy. In so doing this gives the students more opportunity and more responsibility for their own learning—which in turn is significantly enhanced by each student having his or her own computer to use.

14.7 Using Smartphones as Essential Tools: A Case Study

In the section, we illustrate what a classroom looks like that uses computing devices as essential tools by describing how a P3 (3rd grade) class in Singapore's Nan Chiau Primary School (NCPS) has used mobile computing devices in helping students increase their achievement—their already high achievement, in fact.

While Singaporean students tend to score quite high on international tests, Singapore's Ministry of Education (Ministry of Education 2010) is encouraging schools to prepare Singaporean students for positions in the global, knowledge-work economy by helping them develop twentyfirst century skills, e.g., self-directed learning and collaborative learning. One needs twentyfirst century tools to truly teach twentyfirst century skills, and that means 1:1. Now, the choice of device was clear: Laptops are not sustainable. But smartphones are sustainable, cost-wise, and smartphones are more in concert with the emergence of mobile technologies as a dominant technology in the coming decade.

Dr. Chee-Kit Looi and his associates from the National Institute of Education in Singapore (Looi et al., in press) are working with Mr. Chun Ming Tan, principal of Nan Chiau Primary School and his teachers to (1) rewrite the P3 science curriculum to take full advantage of mobile smartphones, (2) implement inquiry-based pedagogical instructional strategies that support the Ministry's goals, and (3) track the impact of this changeon student achievement at NCPS.

During the 2008 school year, students in P3 (3rd grade) at Nan Chiau Primary School used HTC 68000 smart- phones with software that enabled the entire lesson to be presented and enacted on the smartphone, i.e., all the activities that a student undertakes during the lesson would be specified in the software on his or her smart- phone. That support software was provided by GoKnow, Inc., and is called the Mobile Learning Environment (MLE); see Fig. 14.1. Some of the tiles (rectangles on the screen) are learning resources identified by the teacher for the students, and some of the tiles are learning activities that the students enact. Not all the resources and assigned learning activities are displayed on the screen; a student would scroll down to find more tiles. Tapping on a tile "opens" the tile, e.g., invokes a program such as a concept mapping program, or links to a Website.

In Fig. 14.2, we present an image from the classroom that shows how the students use their MLE-equipped smartphone (Zhang et al. 2010). Various learning activities supported by software applications are shown in Fig. 14.3. For example, in the Plant Systems lesson, students are asked to create a concept map, a KWL chart, an animation, a spreadsheet, etc. The entire, multi-day lesson is represented in the MLE.

The students spent approximately 30 min a day, three times a week for three weeks on the plant systems unit for a total of 4.5 h. The students were also allowed to do science when they had free time; virtually all the students took advantage of this extra time to work on their science. In addition to class time, students worked

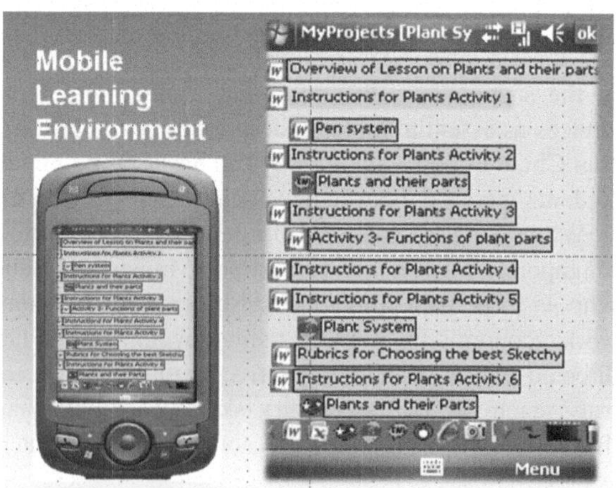

Fig. 14.1 Plant lesson in MLE

Fig. 14.2 Students using MLE in classroom

on their plant systems lesson at home. The following list gives examples of some of the activities done by students on the plant unit at home:

- complete KWL chart;
- watch videos on functions of plant parts; record the functions of roots, root hair, stems, and leaves in a table;
- take pictures of different kinds of plant parts in their neighborhoods (each group took one part of the use of Sketchy to illustrate the transport systems in a plant; and
- complete a PicoMap to summarize what they had learned for plants and plant parts.

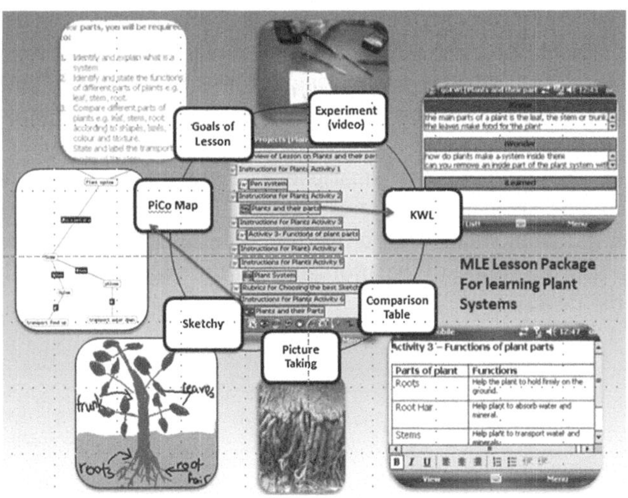

Fig. 14.3 Sample screens from plant lesson in MLE

Two issues to note about the above list:

1. Camera: Students were constantly using the camera on the smartphone to take pictures that enabled them to relate the abstract ideas in the lesson to the concrete things in the world. We have seen math teachers, for example, asking students to take pictures of things in their world outside the classroom that illustrate, say, obtuse angles. The students bring the pictures into class the next day and discuss them—why is that an obtuse angle?
2. Homework is schoolwork: What the students do outside of class is very much the same as the work they do inside of class. This observation is relevant to the issue raised below about the role of the smartphone outside of school.

Notice that because of the ease with which the students can carry their smartphone, the smartphone is available to them for their school work essentially 100 % of the time during the lesson. In as much as all the writ- ten (e.g., concept maps, animations, etc.) activities were enacted on the smartphone; students spent a considerable percentage of the 4.5 lesson hours using the smart- phone. Now, collaboration is a key twentyfirst century skill that Singapore's teachers are trying to help their students learn. So, in addition to working on their smartphone, the students are engaged in dialogue and other collaborative activities, as illustrated in Fig. 14.2. While Fig. 14.4 is a picture from a middle school in Ohio, it is an excellent illustration of how the smallness of the smartphone facilitates conversation and sharing.

The students in P3 at NCPS experienced a total of 21 weeks of lessons that had been redesigned from the ground up to be inquiry-based, focused on self-directed learning and collaborative learning skills, but still contained the high degree of content that is typical of Singaporean lessons. It was a challenge, quite frankly, to pack all that required content together with the focus on process skills that are supported by the use of the smart- phone (Bransford, Brown and Cocking 2000).

Even though the students were not exposed to all of required content, the results nonetheless indicate that among the six mixed-ability classes[1] in Primary (Grade) 3 in the school, the smartphone-using class performed significantly better than the other five classes, as measured by traditional assessments in the science subject (Looi et al., in press).

In sum, for the P3 class, their smartphone was definitely an essential tool to engage in learning about plant systems—and, using Project RED's terminology, the P3 class did implement 1:1 "properly." The lesson was created from the ground up to take advantage of the affordances of the smartphone and the software running on the device:

[1] In Singapore, the top and lowest performing students are grouped into special classes; the middle students—mixed ability—are then organized evenly into classes. Our comparison groups are the other mixed-ability classes.

Fig. 14.4 Students collaborating using smartphones

- from the Mobile Learning Environment, which supported the teacher in the process of creating a complete and comprehensive lesson and supported the student in enacting the lesson; and
- to the individual applications like Sketchy, PicoMap, Mobile Word, etc., which supported the teacher in creating engaging and effective learning activities and which supported the students by enabling them to engage in a broad range of inter- active learning activities.

The students had access to the device essentially 100 % of the time they were working on the lesson, and they used the smartphone for every artifact in the lesson. The students used the smartphone at school and outside of school. In effect, both the teacher and the students used the smartphone like a twentyfirst century knowledge-worker— as a tool that is critical to getting their job done—where the job of a teacher is to create lessons and support students enacting those lessons, and where the job of the student is to enact the lessons provided by the teacher.

In the next section, we go beyond the Project RED framework and discuss the impact of the particular realization of 1:1. That is, while RED is neutral on what computing device is used to implement 1:1, we, for the past nine years, have been exploring the use of low-cost, handheld, mobile devices. While we started with the Palm Pilot many years ago, today we are using standard- issue smartphones—since they are low-cost, handheld, and very mobile. In what follows, we identify a specific contribution that we are seeing mobile devices make above and beyond the contributions identified by RED.

14.8 The Medium Does Matter: A Conjecture

In the early 1990s there was a debate between Richard Clark and Robert Kozma (Materi 2001) about the role of the media in learning. It boiled down to this: Whether lettuce is delivered by a truck or a car, it is still lettuce. The media—be it a computer or a book—do not matter, as long as they both deliver the same content.

While there may well have been a bit of murkiness with respect to trucks and cars, there really does seem to be a considerable difference between students using laptops and even netbooks and students using smartphones. Although laptops, netbooks, and smartphones may all have the same basic functionality, e.g., one can use Microsoft Word on all three devices, there are two proper- ties that separate smartphones from laptops and netbooks.

Portability and always-available: Since the weight and size of a smartphone is negligible, it literally fits in the palm of an individual's hand, and since toting it requires almost no conscious effort, students tend to carry them around constantly. In addition, since smartphones are relatively instant-on devices—booting up and shutting down are not painful, time-consuming procedures—the effort involved in accessing the device is for all intents and purposes zero: Essentially no effort is needed to physically take command of the device, and essentially no effort is needed to navigate to where a question can be posed.[2]

In contrast, toting a 2.1 + pound netbook takes a conscious act, and there is definitely a boot-up and shut-down procedure. Anderson (Tischler 2008) has called netbooks "carry alongs"—as contrasted with laptops, which are transportable computers, and smartphones, which are truly portable devices.

Since the smartphone is omnipresent, its pattern of use is different from that of a netbook. In our classroom in NCPS in Singapore, we see children taking advantage of the fact that they always have the device in their possession to ask questions and explore other concepts in the lesson. In interviews with teachers where smart-phones are being used, we hear the teachers commenting that they see the students using their devices all the time—because they can, because they are right there in the palms of the students' hands.

Respect and vindication: We feel that portability/availability isn't the only reason why students are spending more time doing their schoolwork on the smart- phones. We make the following conjecture:

- Students use mobile devices outside of the class- room all the time; indeed the "kids these days" are the mobile technology generation. But schools, by and large, ban the use of mobile technologies from the classroom. Clearly, they are of the opinion that mobile technologies in classrooms are bad ("distracting, disruptive"). On the other hand, the students know that using mobile technologies outside the classroom is in fact a very good strategy for coming to understand, finding entertainment, communicating with friends, etc. The value of using mobile technologies is something the students experience firsthand—outside the classroom.

---

[2] Individuals report enjoying the activity of making use of their smartphone (personal communications from various individuals).

- So when schools finally say: Ok, you can use the same technology inside the classroom as you are already using outside the classroom, the students feel respected—finally—and vindicated: YES, we, the students, were right after all; mobile technology use in classrooms is indeed a good idea.
- The respect and vindication the students now feel, i.e., the acknowledgment by adults, is a strong motivator. The students are effective at using mobile technologies outside of school, and thus they can now use those same skills inside the classroom effectively on their school work. As well, the students may well feel that they need to demonstrate—to further prove—that mobile technologies are valuable, so the school won't change their mind and re-ban the devices.
- One might conjecture that this sort of emotional element would be ephemeral and wear off. Empirically, that's not what we see; we see students expending as much—if not more—time on school tasks at the end of the semester as at the beginning of the semester. The effect of using the mobile technologies is not a Hawthorne Effect.

Clearly, this is a conjecture; and while the anecdotes below are supportive, but provocative, our conjecture is definitely in need of substantiating evidence:

- Toms River, NJ: 150 fifth-graders used smartphones from February to June, 2010. The teachers and the Director of Technology claim that all 150 students did every homework assignment on time.
- Garnerville, NY: Every one of the 30 fifth-graders in the pilot class did all their homework—on a snow day at home!
- Toms River, NJ: A teacher tells the story of a parent driving his son and a friend to a Giants football game on Sunday. The boys were both in the back seat, quiet—too quiet. So the father asked: "What are you guys doing back there?" And they responded: "Doing our homework". (And they were!)
- Watkins Glen, NY: After an hour of 30 students showing 100+ IT directors from neighboring school districts how to use the smartphones, a 12-year- old boy asked to address the group and was given permission to do so. In front of the 100+ adults, who were virtually strangers, the lad said: "I want to thank all of the adults here for bringing smartphones into our school and giving us this opportunity to help us learn".
- Saratoga Springs, NY: At the rollout of the 30 smartphones to his class, a fifth-grade boy hugged the Verizon salesperson and said: "This is the way schools should be".
- Katy, TX: A teacher was showing parents the paragraph that their fifth-grade boy had written. The parents said: "Our boy is autistic; he doesn't write". The teacher responded: "He doesn't write with pencil-and-paper, but he does write if he is using his smartphone".
- Garnerville, NY: Sue Tomko, Director of Technology, paid $5,000 for insurance on the 80 phones for 2009–2010. She said she wouldn't buy insurance again since she lost just two styluses the entire school year. The loss and breakage rate of the smartphones by the students, across the dozen or more projects during

2009–2010, was phenomenally low; on the level of a few styluses typically and a few damaged screens.
- Katy Intermediate School District (Katy, TX) is on record as claiming an increase in test scores in the 20–30 point range for those using the devices. Comparable increases in test scores were claimed in St Marys, OH, and Toms River, NJ.[3]

Indeed, the stories, frankly, are endless and at the same time provocative and implausible! All 150 students do every lick of homework for five months? On time? While there is prima facie evidence that smartphone use does appear to make a difference in the learning of K–12 students, it will take considerably more evidence to substantiate that claim.

There are real implications of our conjecture on the Clark-Kozma debate. Assume our conjecture is correct—that smartphone use, for the reasons identified above, engenders a substantial emotional pull on a student so that the use of the smartphone actually makes a difference to a student's understanding and final level of achievement. Then, those students would not perform as well in a classroom that uses laptops or a classroom that uses no technology. Laptops are not today's students' mobile technologies; rather, laptops are their parents' technologies. And, a curriculum change alone, e.g., bringing into the classroom a more active learning, constructivist pedagogy without the use of smartphones, would not engender the gains in achievement seen in classrooms using smartphones. The method of learning does matter; the instrument of learning does matter. Using a device—mobile technologies such as smartphones—in which students have a substantive emotional investment, does make a difference in learning outcomes—if our conjecture is true. Given how much is at stake, then, it certainly makes sense for the research community to explore this issue.

14.9 Concluding Remarks

Schools all over the world are being challenged to prepare their students for a new world— a global, knowledge-work marketplace (Partnership for twentyfirst Century Skills 2008). Countries, such as Singapore, which have traditionally scored very high on tests—tests of content, tests of "what"—are realizing that in this new world order a different set of skills is needed (Ministry of Education 2008). Here in the U.S., where the same tests of "what" have ruled the land in K–12, recognition is dawning that we must prepare—and test—our children differently (ATC21S 2010). That is, while there are items that must be memorized, we need to prepare students to understand how systems work and, most importantly, we need to prepare students to work both independently and in a team. In order to

[3] Norris and Soloway are in the process of documenting these scores.

teach those twentyfirst century skills and that twentyfirst century content—the "how"—we can't be using tools based on eighteenth century pencil-and-paper.

Project RED (2010) is leading the way towards providing the proof that school districts appear to want to justify the significant effort that is going to be needed to make the shift to twentyfirst century teaching and learning. Integral to that shift is the realization that if schools are going to move the needle—make an impact on student achievement—then using computing devices as supplemental to the existing curriculum is not enough. As long as computing is only supplemental, it will have limited impact on teaching and learning (Norris and Soloway 2010c; Bain and Weston 2011). Moving the needle requires education to use the twentyfirst century technology as other twentyfirst century knowledge-workers are doing, as essential tools. State Education Technology Directors Association (SETDA) in their "Class of 2020: Action Plan for Education" (2008) report suggests that: "computers need to be used continuously and seamlessly..." in the classroom. "Continuously and seamlessly" is more than "integrated into the curriculum" and more even than RED's "use daily".

But, as RED is seeing and as we are seeing (Norris and Soloway 2011a) on a more anecdotal level, there is real benefit to be gained from going 1:1 using smartphones—not only, as RED observes, do test scores go up but we see students engaging in school at a level that is unprecedented. Given that level of impact, we fully realize that much more research needs to be done before substantiated claims can truly be made. However, we feel that there is ample prima facie evidence to warrant the expenditure of funds to more systematically explore the conjectures raised here.

We have gone on record publically (Norris and Soloway 2010a) with the following prediction: By 2015 every child in every grade in every K–12 classroom in America will be using a mobile learning device. Research can contribute by informing and shaping the implementation of these mobile technologies. RED (2010) has observed that 1:1, if not properly implemented, offers little benefit over traditional uses of technology. Research can help schools use mobile technologies effectively—and not waste resources. But, regardless of what research does, the rollout will proceed. Mobile technologies are bigger than the Internet. The Internet is a roadway; without a car, a roadway is useless. Mobile technologies are the cars for the Internet. Mobile technologies are giving voice to individuals who otherwise would have none. The momentum behind mobile technologies is unprecedented (Murphy and Meeker 2011). Mobile technologies are insinuating themselves into every crevice of the consumer world as well as pushing into the business enterprise. They will even invade K–12, which has staunchly resisted change for hundreds of years. Mobile technologies are moving at bullet-train speeds!

Full Disclosure: Norris and Soloway are co-founders of and consultants for GoKnow, Inc. The software used at Nan Chiau Primary School in Singapore was provided by GoKnow. Schools in Toms River, NJ, Watkins Glen, NY, St. Marys, OH, Garnerville, NY, Katy, TX, and Saratoga Springs, NY used GoKnow's software in their mobile learning projects.

Acknowledgments This work is based on the efforts of Dr. Chee- Kit Looi and his colleagues at the National Institute of Education, Singapore, and on the vision and cooperation of Chun Ming Tan, Principal of Nan Chiau Primary School, and Gene Lim, head of department and teacher at Nan Chiau. Two of Dr. Looi's associates, Gean Chia and Peter Seow, in particular, have played major roles in the creation and enactment of the mobilized curriculum used at Nan Chiau. And we wish to acknowledge Jenny Lee and Shirlyn Cheng, teachers at Nan Chiau for their leadership in being early adopters of the mobilized curriculum. We (Norris and Soloway) proudly work with all the above as members of CERA—Center for Education Research and Action. CERA is a unique collaboration, housed at Nan Chiau Primary School, among academics, administrators, teachers, researchers, and commercial concerns. In a conversation with us at his home in Atlanta, Mark Weston (Rivero 2010) used the term "essential" in reference to the computer's role in learning. Thank you, Mark, for sharing and for that pivotal conversation.

Portions of this book chapter appeared earlier in Education Technology Magazine in an article entitled: Using Smartphones as Essential Tools for Learning: A Call to Place Schools on the Right Side of the 21st Century, Norris, C., Hossain, A. & Soloway, E., Educational Technology Magazine, May/June 2011.

Portions of this book chapter appeared earlier in a Conference paper entitled: Under What Conditions Does Computer Use Positively Impact Student Achievement? Supplemental vs. Essential Use, Norris, C., Hossain, A. & Soloway, E. Proceedings of the SITE 2012 Conference, Society for Information Technology and Teacher Education, Austin, TX.

References

ATC21S (2010) Status report as of January 2010, Assessment and teaching of 21st century skills, http://atc21s.org/wp-content/uploads/2011/11/1-Defining-21st-Century-Skills.pdf

Bain A, Weston M (2011) The learning edge: what technology can do to educate all children. Teachers College Press, New York

Bebell D, Kay R (2010) One to one computing: a summary of the quantitative results from the Berkshire wireless learning initiative. J Technol, Learn Assess 9(2):5–59

Bransford JD, Brown AL, Cocking RR (eds) (2000) How people learn: brain, mind, experience and school. National Academy Press, Washington, DC

Brown L (2009) Using mobile learning to teach reading to ninth-grade students. Learning 5(1):105–123

Devaney L (2010) Study reveals factors in ed-tech success, Jun 28th, 2010, *eSchool News*, http://projectred.org/uploads/eSchoolNews_ProjectRed.pdf

Donovan L, Hartley K, Strudler N (2007) Teacher concerns during initial implementation of a one-to-one laptop initiative at the middle school level. J Res Technol Educ 39(3):269–283

Fried BC (2008) In-class laptop use and its effects on student learning. Comput Educ 50(2008):906–914

Greaves T, Hayes J (2010) Study shows which technology factors improve learning, June 28, 2010, http://www.projectred.org/uploads/Press%20Release%20062710%20v2.pdf

Grimes D, Warschauer M (2008) Learning with laptops: s multi-method case study. J Educ Comput Res 38(3):305–332

Gulek CJ, Demirtas H (2005) Learning with technology: the impact of laptop use on student achievement. J Technol Learn Assess 3(2):4–35

Hu W (2007) Seeing no progress, some schools drop laptops, May 4, 2007. New York Times, http://www.nytimes.com/2007/05/04/education/04laptop.html?pagewanted=1

Livingston P (2009) 1-to-1 learning laptop programs that work, 2nd edn. International society for technology in education (ISTE), Eugene

Looi CK, Zhang BH, Chen W, Seow P, Chia G, Norris C, Soloway E (2011) 1:1 mobile inquiry learning experience for primary science students: A study of learning effectiveness. J Comput Assist Learn 27:269–283

Lowther DL, Ross SM, Morrison GM (2003) When each one has one: the influences on teaching strategies and student achievement of using laptops in the classroom. ETR&D 51(3):23–44

Materi R (2001) Media and learning: a review of the debate, ingenia training, http://www.ingenia-consulting.com/files/Media-and-Learning-Debate.htm

Ministry of Education (2008) MOE launches third Masterplan for ICT in education, http://www.moe.gov.sg/media/press/2008/08/moe-launches-third-masterplan.php, Singapore

Ministry of Education (2010) Primary education-the way forward, Singapore, http://www.moe.gov.sg/initiatives/peri/

Murphy M, Meeker M (2011) Top mobile internet trends, http://www.businessinsider.com/mary-meeker-matt-murphy-2011-2#-1, Feb

Norris C, Soloway E (2010a) Why is mobile technology different from other technology? Among many other reasons, students will be using their own devices. District Administration Magazine, Feb. http://www.districtadministration.com/article/why-mobile-technology-different-other-technology

Norris C, Soloway E (2010c) What will move the needle? Only one technology has the potential to make an authentic impact on student achievement. District Administration Magazine, July. http://www.districtadministration.com/article/what-will-move-needle

Norris C, Soloway E (2011a) Mobile devices as essential tools: carts of laptops haven't raised student achievement—and neither will carts of iPads. District Administration Magazine, April, http://www.districtadministration.com/article/mobile-devices-essential-tools

Norris C, Hossain A, Soloway E (2011b) Using smartphones as essential tools for learning: a call to place schools on the right side of the 21st century. Educ Technol 51(3):18–25

Partnership for 21st century skills (2008) 21st Century skills, education and competitiveness: a resource and policy guide, http://www.p21.org/storage/documents/21st_century_skills_education_and_competitiveness_guide.pdf

Penuel WR (2005) Research: what it says about 1-to-1 learning. Cupertino: Apple Computer Inc. Available online at: http://www.ubiqcomputing.org/Apple_1-to-1_Research.pdf

Project RED Reports (2010) The technology factor: nine keys to student achievement and cost-effectiveness, http://www.projectred.org/uploads/PREP11/ProjectREDPreview.pdf

Rivero V (2010) Interview: Mark Weston, Edtech Digest; http://edtechdigest.wordpress.com/2010/07/26/interview- mark-weston-2/

SETDA (2008) Class of 2020: action plan for education, state educational technology directors association, http://www.setda.org/c/document_library/get_file?folderId=270&name=DLFE-296.pdf

Silvernail DL, Lane DMM (2004) The impact of Maine's one-to-one laptop program on middle school teachers and students: Phase one summary evidence. Maine Education Policy Research Institute, University of Southern Maine, Portland

Stallings J (1980) Allocated academic learning time revisited, or beyond time on task. Educ Researcher 9(11):11–16

Stross R (2010) Computers at home: educational hope vs. teenage reality; http://www.nytimes.com/2010/07/11/ business/11digi.html?_r = 1&pagewanted = print

Tischler L (2008) MarkAnderson's 10 predictions for 2009; http://www.fastcompany.com/blog/lindatischler/ design-times/mark-andersons-10-predictions-2009

Wurst C, Smarkola C, Gaffney MA (2008) Ubiquitous laptop usage in higher education: effects on student achievement, student satisfaction, and constructive measures in honors and traditional classrooms. Comput Educ 51(4):1766–1783

Zhang B, Looi C-K, Seow P, Chia G, Wong L-H, Chen W, So H-J, Soloway E, Norris C (2010) Deconstructing and reconstructing: Transforming primary science learning via a mobilized curriculum. Comput Educ 55:1504–1523

Zucker AA, Hug ST (2007) A study of the 1:1 laptop program at the Denver School of Science and Technology

Zucker AA, Hug ST (2008) Teaching and learning physics in a 1:1 laptop school. J Sci Educ Technol 17:586–594

Part V
Emerging Trends in Learning Technologies

Chapter 15
Application of Cloud Technology, Social Networking Sites and Sensing Technology to E-Learning

Yueh-Min Huang, Hsin-Chin Chen, Jan-Pan Hwang and Yong-Ming Huang

Abstract With the development of information technology, Cloud computing looks promising in support of e-learning, it could provide a variety of learning services and resources to facilitate a ubiquitous learning environment to preview and review the course content. Meanwhile, the Cloud technology supports the social networking sites (SNSs) that provide a virtual interactive learning platform to communicate with each other and enhance online cooperative learning. In addition, recently the sensor technology-based applications for e-learning has become a popular research issue, which includes context awareness, augmented reality, motion learning, data acquisition. Therefore, this chapter tends to highlight the possible application of Cloud technology, SNSs and sensing technology on e-learning, and explore the pedagogical development with these technologies. By the objective above, it is hoped the content addressed in this chapter can inspire readers reshaping the relationship between education and latest information technology so as to broaden their horizon on forthcoming development of e-learning.

15.1 Introduction

Over the recent years, the application of information technology to educational learning has become an important subject in social science domains. As the computer network develops rapidly, the teaching environment has evolved from

Y.-M. Huang (✉) · H.-C. Chen · J.-P. Hwang · Y.-M. Huang
Department of Engineering Science, National Cheng Kung University,
No. 1, University Road, Tainan City 701, Taiwan (R.O.C.)
e-mail: huang@mail.ncku.edu.tw

R. Huang et al. (eds.), *Reshaping Learning*, New Frontiers of Educational Research,
DOI: 10.1007/978-3-642-32301-0_15,

traditional classrooms into the present network multimedia, the life and learning behaviors of learners have changed greatly. Nowadays, the application of network-based learning Web is developed from Web 1.0 into Web 2.0. As the concept and technology of Web 2.0 are popularized in different domains, the research and discussion related to network-based teaching are widespread. Related studies indicate that the interactive network-based learning introduced into Web 2.0 has successfully improved the learning effectiveness of learners. Meanwhile, with the popularization of wireless network and the advancement of mobile computing technology, the functions hand-held devices have improved, and the application becomes increasingly extensive. The mobile learning combining the hand-held devices with digital teaching materials will be the main stream of learning styles in the future, thus, the network-based teaching is no longer limited to locations and learning carriers, and the teaching environment becomes ubiquitous depending on this technology. Some studies suggest that most of learners evaluate mobile learning positively, and the learning outcomes and efficiency can be improved with the assistance of mobile technology.

However, the Cloud technology plays a very important part in merging next generation information technology into teaching. Cloud computing is another new revolution following the switchover from large-scale computer to client-side--server in the 1980's. At present, Cloud computing has been regarded as the most potential technology; it can be used to realize different kinds of innovative application. Many studies suggest that Cloud computing has great potential in promoting innovative applications of education. With the support of Cloud computing technology, the social networking sites (SNSs) have been widely accepted and applied by the public, such as Facebook, MySpace, Plurk and Twitter, providing a virtual interactive platform for users to communicate and cooperate with each other in a social group. The application of SNSs to education has attracted wide attention, especially in cooperative learning; the SNSs provide a favorable environment for group interaction, sharing and cooperation.

At present, e-learning has evolved beyond the application of information equipments and Internet in early stages, and has been merged with other different technologies and elements. The sensor technology-based application and learning style have thus emerged, such as context awareness, augmented reality, motion learning, data acquisition, etc. The data collected by sensors and information equipments can be provided for teachers to master the learning state of students and to give proper feedback.

This chapter aims to introduce the application of Cloud technology, SNSs and sensing technology to e-learning, in order to explore the development situations of these technologies and their applications to teaching. It also discusses the relationship between education and technology, and provides suggestions and opinions on forthcoming development of merging information technology into teaching.

15.2 Cloudalized Learning (C-Learning)

Cloud computing is a computing mode of networks, it provides software and hardware resources as a type of service on the network, and these software and hardware resources are placed in a data center to provide services (Armbrust et al. 2010; Weiss 2007). The software and hardware resources in the data center are called Cloud. If this Cloud is accessible to the public, it is called public cloud; on the contrary, if it is for an internal organization, it is called private cloud (Armbrust et al. 2010). As Cloud computing is applicable to massive storage and massive calculation (Foster et al. 2008), users can enjoy the convenience of Cloud computing.

Many studies have discussed the influences Cloud computing on education. Sultan (2010) and Weber (2011) suggested that some educational services under financial pressure could use Cloud computing to provide various information services, as the payment mode of Cloud computing is pay-as-you-go. Therefore, these educational services can increase or decrease software and hardware resources at any time as required, and ensure the efficient use of the resources, thus to save cost. Wheeler, Waggener (2009) and Ercan (2010) suggested that many services of Cloud computing could be used in education directly, such as Google Apps for Education and Google Docs, thus, the educational services do not need to develop their own information technology services. They can use the existing information technology services for teaching directly (Wen 2011). Calvo et al. (2011) used Google Docs service to develop a Cloud computing-based learning tool, and applied it to cooperative writing. This tool assists teachers in managing large-scale cooperative writing.

Based on the above, the influence of Cloud computing on education has been widely discussed. However, the effect of Cloudalized learning is seldom mentioned. This study attempted to explore the effect of Cloudalized learning, including its advantages and disadvantages as reference for future research.

15.2.1 Characteristics of Cloud Computing

Many scholars have proposed their definitions for Cloud computing (Foster et al. 2008; Gong et al. 2010; Vaquero 2011). There are four major definitions: (1) it is applicable to massive storage and massive calculation; (2) its payment mode is pay-as-you-go, the users only need to pay for actually used resources; (3) it is a computing mode providing services according to requirements, the required resources may not be allocated beforehand; (4) it is a service-oriented architecture, the service scale can be set and provided dynamically according to requirements (Foster et al. 2008; Gong et al. 2010; Vaquero 2011). Basically, Cloud computing provides three levels of service: IaaS (Infrastructure as a Service), PaaS (Platform as a Service) and SaaS (Software as a Service).

15.2.2 Impact of Cloudalized Learning

The Cloudalized learning is extensively defined as "Cloud Computing-based E-learning". According to this definition, e-learning in any case can be advanced to Cloudalized learning. Specifically, the three elements, services, contents and learners of e-learning will be influenced, as shown in Fig. 15.1. This study thus proposes the impact of Cloud Computing on the three elements, the details are described below.

15.2.3 Impact of Cloud Computing on Service

Service is defined as different kinds of application programs for education based on Cloud computing, it can be application programs of webpage or application programs for windows. In Cloudalized learning, it is in charge of providing various services for learners to assist learners with learning. With the assistance of Cloud computing, these services have five major characteristics: instant, intelligent, multi-sensory, seamless and social, as described below.

Instant: it refers to instant services, such as Google Instant (Google 2011b) and Google Scribe (Google 2011c). Google Instant provides an instant searching engine, while Google Scribe provides a real-time aid for writing. As shown in Fig. 15.2, the common characteristic of the two examples is using Cloud

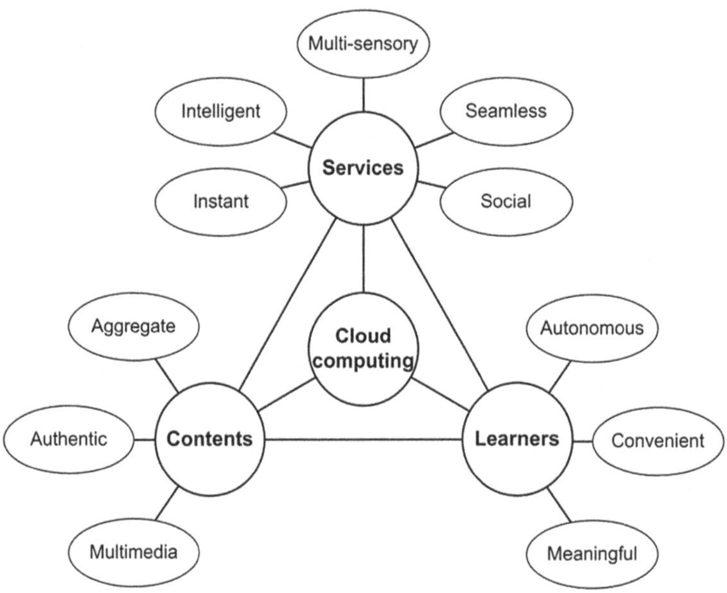

Fig. 15.1 The impact of c-learning

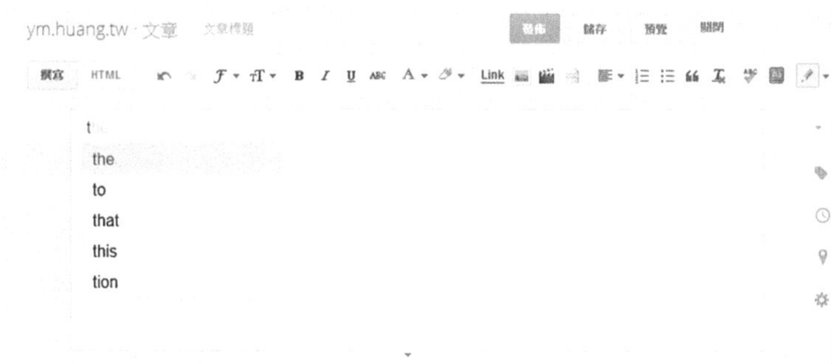

Fig. 15.2 The Google scribe

computing to guess the text that the users want to enter timely, so as to provide the search result or suggested words for the user to reduce the user's input load to increase the input efficiency.

Intelligent: it refers to intelligent services. For example, Google Goggles (Google 2011a) is an intelligent image searching engine, running in mobile devices. Google Goggles searches the photos taken by users. Up to now, Google Goggles can identify letters, landmarks, books and signs automatically, as shown in Fig. 15.3. Google Goggles is an artificial intelligence technology for image recognition, but it realizes AI technology by Cloud computing, and sends back the result to the user side. Therefore, Cloud computing is helpful to realizing different kinds of AI technology.

Multi-sensory: it refers to the service that provides the users with multi-sensory user experience. For example, Qwiki (2011) provides users with network-based knowledge service of multi-sensory experience. Qwiki captures different data from Cloud automatically based on AI and collects, edits and dubs them into a slide with sound and light automatically, as shown in Fig. 15.4. In Cloud computing, the information presentation of service develops towards the presentation with

Fig. 15.3 The Google Goggles (Google 2011a)

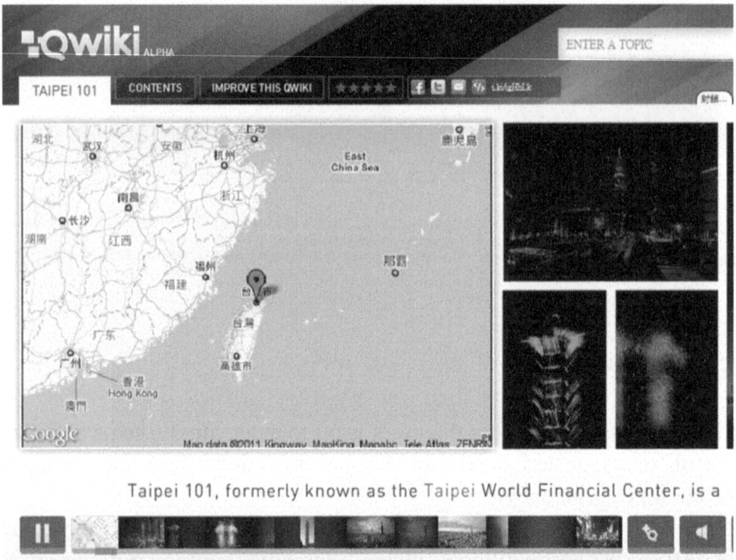

Fig. 15.4 Qwiki

multi-sensory experience, so that the users can receive information more efficiently.

Seamless: it refers to seamless use of service. For example, Google Docs is a text editing service, and it allows users to use this service via browsers of general computers or App of mobile devices. Users can create and edit files, electronic forms or briefing on Cloud directly by using Google Docs, and invite others to review or edit his files or briefing. The original single version App can be Cloudalized by Cloud computing, and the data are stored in Cloud, so that the users can use the App seamlessly in the network.

Social: it refers to the service provides users with social interaction. For example, Facebook is the most famous social networking site at present, providing users with many services for social interaction, including message boards, chat rooms, blogging and games. Moreover, the users can use Facebook to find their friends, and even know their friends' friends, so as to expand their circles.

15.2.4 Impact of Cloud Computing on Content

Content is defined as various teaching materials. In Cloudalized learning, it provides learners with different knowledge sources, so that the learners can learn different kinds of knowledge effectively. As Cloud computing is involved, the content is influenced accordingly, it will be mainly characterized by aggregate, authentic and multimedia, described below.

Aggregate refers to collect various data on the Cloud automatically and technologically and reorganize them into a meaningful content. For example, Qwiki (2011) and Wikihood (2011) use technology to capture various data on the Cloud automatically, and reorganize them into meaningful information for users to use. Flipboard (2011) and Zite (2011) allow the users to aggregate various data on the Cloud, and even aggregate the information of Facebook, Twitter or blog, so that the users can receive real-time and useful information conveniently.

Authentic refers to a part of the contents is derived from the real world. The examples are Qwiki, Wikihood and Google Goggles. These services allow the users to use the knowledge in the virtual environment to further know the characters, sites, and articles in the real world. The users can learn knowledge in the virtual environment, and experience the real environment. In Cloud computing, the technology will provide more intelligent and real-time assistance.

Multimedia means that the form of contents tends to be multimedia form, such as Qwiki and Youtube. Qwiki uses AI technology to integrate various data on the Cloud, and reorganizes them into a dynamic slide. Youtube is a video sharing platform as well as a video blog. In Cloud computing, the information content grows very rapidly, the users must face a huge data volume, including text, pictures, sound, movies, etc. Therefore, the information in multimedia form is absorbed by users most efficiently.

15.2.5 Impact of Cloud Computing on Learners

In Cloudalized learning, the learners' learning becomes more autonomous, convenient and meaningful with the assistance of Cloud computing.

Autonomous is defined as autonomous learning of learners without teachers' intervention. In the past, the learners usually learn a subject under the teachers' instruction, and the learning process is passive. However, as the technology develops, the learners can learn more autonomously than ever. For example, the ubiquitous learning makes the learners' learning more autonomous (Huang et al. 2012). However, this type of learning is usually limited to a certain situation. As Cloud contains enormous data, and these data can be rearranged or organized into meaningful learning materials, these instant and intelligent learning services and various data on the Cloud enable the learners to learn more autonomously. For example, on Google Goggles, the learners can understand relevant information of the scenery even without teachers' assistance.

Convenient means that the learners can learn conveniently. The Cloud computing provides instant learning assistance (e.g., Google Scribe), intelligent learning assistance (e.g., Google Goggles), multi-sensory service experience (e.g., Qwiki), seamless service (e.g., Google Docs), and service for social interaction (e.g., Facebook). In general, as Cloud computing can create many more convenient technologies, the learners will learn more conveniently.

Meaningful refers to the learners' learning is meaningful. Huang et al. (2011) indicated that meaningful learning has five characteristics: active, authentic, construction, cooperation and personalization. Active means the learners play an active role in learning activities; authentic means the learners learn knowledge in a real situation; construction means the learners learn new knowledge based on their previous knowledge; cooperation means the learners learn knowledge cooperatively; personalization means the learners' learning is personal. Cloud computing provides the learners with personal learning, so that the learners play an active role in the real environment to construct knowledge cooperatively through cooperative learning.

15.2.6 Potential Risks in Cloudalized Learning

Although Cloudalized learning brings many advantages, it has some shortcoming, such as privacy, security and reliability. In Cloud computing, the data are mostly stored in Cloud, which means that the privacy of data is not held by the users, thus, the privacy should be protected more carefully. In addition, as the Cloud can store a great amount of information, if the Cloud administrator finds out the correlation among the seemingly meaningless or incomplete data, he can change the seemingly harmless data into menacing data. Therefore, in Cloud computing, the users must select the Cloud supplier cautiously. In addition, the security of data is one of important subjects, in Cloud computing, the data are stored in Cloud. Therefore, the security of data is very important. Similarly, the reliability of service is important because in Cloud computing, the original App will be Cloudalized gradually, the services on the Cloud should be more reliable, and various factors should be reduced to avoid them influencing the services. Moreover, besides the aforesaid potential risks in the technology aspect, the potential risks in the content aspect need to be careful consideration. As cloud computing is involved, the content in part can be originated from the cloud. For example, various online encyclopedias, such as Wikipedia, provide learners with the opportunity to access a wide variety of contents. However, these contents may not undergo a rigorous review. Accordingly, the quality of the contents may be inconsistent. Even some contents are fake and wrong. Similarly, such problems may be raised in other content production services, such as blog and micro-blogging. Therefore, in Cloudalized learning, the learners must cautiously notice the quality of contents that includes objectivity, reliability, and validity. Finally, the potential risks in the education aspect of Cloudalized learning are inevitable. Therefore, whether there is an education theory or a learning theory corresponding to the Cloudalized learning should be further discussed.

15.3 Impact of SNSs on E-Learning

In recent years, the SNSs have become a popular trend in the world, for promoting the relationships among users, and helping the users to share their ideas, events and interests with friends through networks (Lampe et al. 2006). On the Internet, Web App provides a virtual interactive platform for users to have more chances to communicate or cooperate with people of the same generation or friends in social intercourse (O'Reilly 2005, 2007). There are many SNSs in the market, the most popular SNSs at present include Facebook, Twitter, MySpace, Plurk, Google+, Micro Blogging, etc. Most of social networking services provide users with e-mail service and instant message service, so that users can interact with each other on the Internet. The SNSs can record users' personal profile, such as users' background, interest, and enable the users to see other users' profile (Lampe et al. 2006; Rau et al. 2008). Figure 15.5 shows the types and functions of SNSs.

Many studies have discussed the impact of SNSs (Cuéllar et al. 2011; Liu and Lee 2010). The SNSs have the following three characteristics (Boyd and Ellison 2007): (1) in one web system, the users can create an open or semi-open profile; (2) in this network community, the users can share their messages with other members; (3) the users can read friends' profile and their information on the Wall. For example, Facebook is the most popular social networking site at present, according to the statistical information on the official website of Facebook, there are more than 0.8 billion registered users, each member has 130 friends on average, and posts 90 messages on average per month (Facebook 2011).

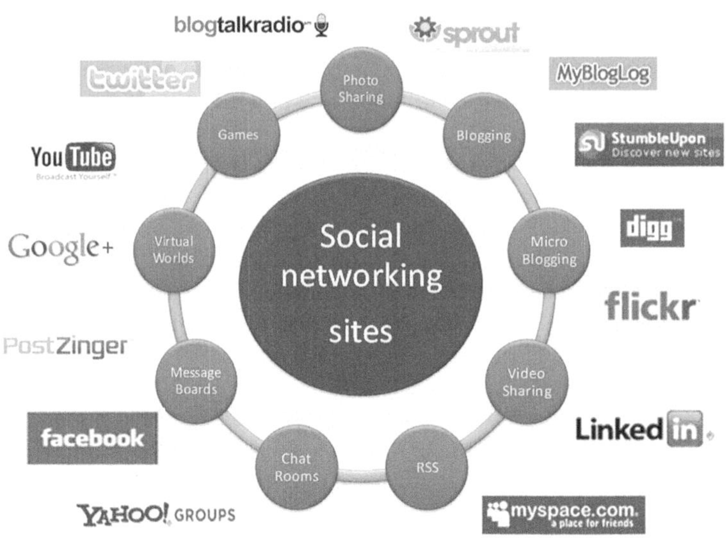

Fig. 15.5 Functions of social networking sites

Facebook has four common social networking services (Ellison et al. 2007; Ophus and Abbitt 2009; Sheldon 2008; Stern and Taylor 2007; Urista et al. 2009; Zhao et al. 2008): (1) profile: the website allows users to create personal file, including personal basic information, such as user name; the system informs the friends of the user's current state automatically; (2) communication function: the system supports multiple communication functions, such as e-mail, chat room and the Wall shared; the users can publish their personal messages on the Wall to tell their friends, and their friends can return comments and opinions; the users can also create an activity, and the system will invite friends automatically to join in this activity; (3) data uploading function: the system allows the users to upload photos to personal photo album to share with others, and can mark the photos; (4) good friends forms: the system searches the user's friends from the user's email and recommends an appropriate list of good friends to the user. Therefore, Facebook provides the users and their friends with a diversified and complete contact channel.

15.3.1 Network-Based Cooperative Learning

The cooperative learning in education has been paid much attention to, many studies have discussed the application of cooperative learning to different educational environments (Huang and Liu 2009; Su et al. 2010; Uzunboylu et al. 2011). The learning construction theory indicates that the cooperative learning can promote the building of knowledge effectively based on the discussions among people (Schunk 1996). In the cooperative learning environment, the learners can easily share their ideas and opinions, and make discussions to understand the learning contents effectively (Wegerif 1998). In the course of cooperative learning, the learners use cooperative interaction among members to inspire more creative ideas, it becomes the major contributor to knowledge building (Sawyer and DeZutter 2009).

As the computer and network technologies develop rapidly, more and more studies begin to discuss the effect of CSCL (Koschmann 1996; Light et al. 1994). Dori and Herscovitz (1999) indicated that in the Web version CSCL system, the students can ask their partners questions about learning contents, and then these questions are collected and integrated into an appropriate examination for learners. Liaw (2008) suggested that if the Web version cooperative learning system is applied to the knowledge management, the learners can participate in discussion and knowledge exchange, they work together to solve problems. Su et al. (2010) proposed a Web 2.0 cooperative annotation system, the learners can share personal annotations with cooperators to help them in understanding the learning contents.

15.3.2 Application of SNSs to Educational Environment

The SNSs such as Facebook, MySpace and Plurk have become indispensable contact tools for numerous users in daily life; meanwhile, they are applied to educational situation. These websites allow individuals to create personal webpage, to introduce their background and interest, and share them with other friends (Cheung et al. 2011; Rau et al. 2008). Besides the SNS provides a platform for knowledge transfer in online learning environment, SNS can also be used in traditional classroom. With the development of Tablet PC, it is regarded as a popular learning device to replace the textbooks and provide a multimedia learning environment to strengthen the reading effect. Therefore, SNS can provide powerful interaction and assists learners in building the relationship of cooperative learning by using Tablet PCs, and becomes a learning platform for mutual communication between teachers and students.

For instance, Facebook is one of most popular SNSs at present; it has been extensively applied to educational environment. Many studies have discussed the use of Facebook in education, and some studies indicate that the learners can build knowledge, gain meaningful learning experience and enhance their elaborative faculty through the network community-based learning (Garrison and Kanuka 2004). The building of an effective group should consider the requirements of the course, the learners' benefit and individual abilities, so as to improve the students' performance in cooperative learning. Blattner and Fiori (2009) used Facebook to build an environment for learning foreign language, and led the learners and partners, teachers and foreign students to conduct group discussion. The results showed that Facebook increased the chances for speech interaction among learners and improved the ability in communication in foreign language. Kabilan et al. (2010) found that Facebook could improve the students' language skills and learning motivation and confidence, and has positive impact on the attitude towards English learning. The online community-based learning is advantageous to the learners' opinion exchange and interrelationship, enhancing the comprehension of contents and building common understanding (Mazman and Usluel 2010). Bosch (2009) established communities in Facebook, where learners can share their interests and ideas in the communities, and participate in cooperation and discussion to improve both teaching and learning. For these reasons, Facebook can improve the effect of cooperative learning, and can let learners build knowledge together more effectively.

15.3.3 Negative Influence of SNSs

On the other hand, the SNSs have some problems, such as: (1) social network dependence: the community depends on the relationship in the network community; the virtual presentation makes people believe this is a normal social relationship, so that they lose more chances for obtaining real social experience and drilling, and cannot build deep human relation human relations with others (Manago et al. 2008); (2) change in thinking model: young people are more likely to be attracted by network technology, so that the life style and cognitive mode of students incline to be discussed on network (Pfeil et al. 2009), they believe the network world is the real life, resulting in the difference between thinking model and traditional life style; (3) waste of time: due to the popular network communities, the users can discuss with friends longer and longer through social network more conveniently. The young students with curiosity may be immersed in social network for a long time, their school work or real interpersonal interaction may be influenced (Jones et al. 2010; Rosen et al. 2008).

The characteristics of famous SNSs also have their problems, as described below. Facebook has security and privacy problems (Christofides et al. 2009; Khe Foon 2011). Once a user is registered in Facebook, Facebook obtains the user password, as well as the users' e-mail passwords easily by the friend searching tool. Mostly users have no idea of whether these passwords are secured properly or not. In addition, Facebook requires users to use real name, otherwise, the account will be suspended, the authenticity of name should be authenticated by notary units, and the problem of user privacy may be caused.

15.3.4 Combination of SNSs and Mobile Learning

As the mobile equipments, such as intelligent mobile phones and tablet PC, will be the main stream of development of future computers, and the wireless network technology develops rapidly. Past studies have focused on the mobile learning field. In addition to traditional classroom-based learning, distance learning and mobile learning can extend the learning time, so that learners have more learning opportunities as served with mobile learning. At present, there have been numerous studies providing strategy process for mobile learning activities to assist learners to obtain better learning effect (Huang et al. 2010, 2011). In addition, some studies have discussed cooperative learning in mobile environment, and built a new learning pattern, so that learners can implement cooperative learning everywhere at any time. The mobile technology in cooperative learning is known as Mobile CSCL (MCSCL) (Huang et al. 2010; Zurita et al. 2005).

At present, the intelligent mobile phones or tablet PC's with Android operating system or Windows operating system support SNSs, such as Facebook, Twitter, MySpace, Plurk, Google+, etc. The application of SNSs to educational environment has matured gradually, however, as the mobile equipments develop, the services of SNSs become mobile. The SNSs-based mobile learning will be a trend in the future, and the cooperative learning, community interaction and discussion are implemented to build knowledge and share information, to develop the learners' critical thinking, comprehension and learning performance, as well as to further improve their learning motivation and social skills to realize ubiquitous learning.

15.4 Application of Sensing Technology to E-Learning

The rapid development of information technology and network technology in the 1990's brought e-learning a chance for rapid development, meanwhile developed a new learning style. The sensor technology-based applications to education and learning include context awareness, augmented reality, motion learning, data acquisition, etc. The concepts and meanings of the aforesaid sensor applications can be described by the Iceberg model proposed by Psychologist Satir et al. (1991). According to Fig. 15.6, most of the data collected by sensors and information equipments are apparent user behaviors and environmental events, only a corner of iceberg. It is observed below the horizontal line that a lot of hidden meaningful information related to situation and user are not completely obtained and used. According to this conceptual graph, there is still a long way to go before the sensing technology is deeply applied to learning and education. This chapter mainly introduces and describes the sensor technology presently applied to learning.

15.4.1 Types of Sensor Technology

With the aid of sensor technology, the vital functions are improved effectively and various problems are solved, its assistance and application are the most extensive and practical key technology (Mukhopadhyay et al. 2009; Mukhopadhyay and Huang 2008). The sensor technology is used in medical treatment, chemistry, aids, life situation and environmental monitoring; the sensors can be approximately classified into three major types, namely physical, chemical and physiological

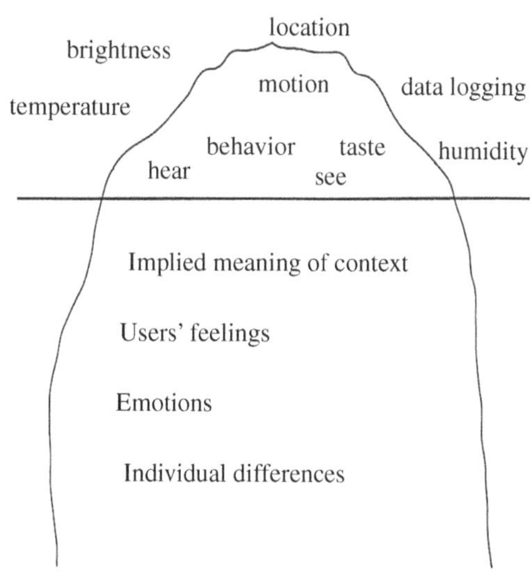

Fig. 15.6 Iceberg model

types (Bloss 2011; Burleson 2006; De Wied et al. 2009; Matte et al. 1990; Woolf et al. 2009). The physical sensors include sensors for pressure measurement, sensing distance, curvature detection and illumination induction; the chemical sensors are detection devices for pH value and oxygen content; and the physiological sensors are usually applied to biomedicine, such as electroencephalograph, blood oxygen and pulse sensors.

15.4.2 The Existing Circumstance of Development of Sensor Application to E-Learning

This section introduces the existing circumstance of the application of sensing technology in three aspects, classified by the degree of interaction between sensing technology and learners. First, the application of multiple sensors for observing and recording learners to scientific education is of low interaction; secondly, using the sensing technology to detect the learners' learning situation to provide the learners with environment related information and auxiliary functions is of moderate interaction; finally, the interaction relying on learners integrated with intuitive and real-time motion learning is of high interaction.

(1) Data-logging

As early as in the 1990's, there were studies related to the application of data logger to scientific education in the United States (Newton 2000; Rogers 1997; Rogers and Wild 1994, 1996), completely combining virtual digital signals with scientific phenomena of physical world, as well as fully reflecting the educational meaning and process emphasized by scientific exploration. For example, the users could comprehend the transition of physical and chemical phenomena profoundly and instantly during implementation through the procedure of "Predict-Observe-Explain" (White and Gunstone 1992). In addition, the data logger has advantages of portability, accuracy and multiple display modes. There were practical cases and related study cases of using data logger in geology teaching, velocity and time variation, three-state change in water, and conversion of thermal energy for scientific education (Deaney et al. 2006). Figure 15.7 shows the photo of Data-logging System, this system is applied to chemistry of senior high school, the data are captured by the sensor, and displayed by the computer instantly, it can enhance the users' comprehension of chemical concepts in the experiment (Deng et al. 2011).

(2) Context awareness

Situation refers to the physical location of the user and various information of the environment. The context awareness can be combined with different types of sensing technology according to the purpose, such as location, temperature, humidity, gravity, and social interaction situation, multiple different sensing technologies must be used together with high-speed analytic calculation to obtain

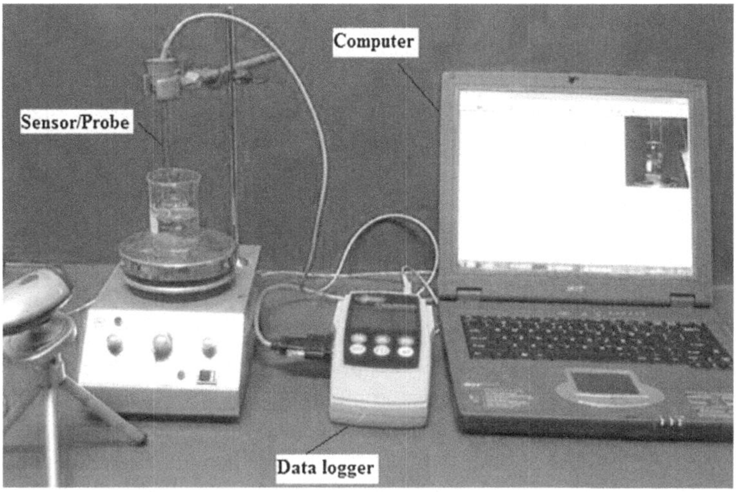

Fig. 15.7 The data-logging system (Deng et al. 2011)

the corresponding result. As the information communication technology develops, the context awareness learning and ubiquitous learning become mature, merging the concept of combining sensors with context awareness into learning situation is the trend of E-learning at present (Huang et al. 2012). With the sensing technology, various information in learning situation can be merged into teaching materials, so as to provide the users with personal learning service at proper sites and time, and to instantly and actively present the teaching materials required by the users in the real environment for outdoor learning activities, so as to build a learning pattern for high interaction between users and learning situation.

The information provided by context awareness is derived from four steps. First, the situation information is recognized to obtain the location, temperature, etc., of the physical environment; and then to obtain the sensor data, such as face recognition, gravitational sensor and direction sensor; thirdly, the obtained information is collected and analyzed; finally, the analytic result is fed back to the user. At present, the sensor technologies extensively used in context awareness, besides common GPS, RFID, pressure, temperature, humidity and luminance, the Cloud technology, social network and other elements begin to be combined, thus, the context awareness can widely augment interpersonal interaction and can be combined with the advantages of Cloud to bring more innovative and abundant applications.

(3) Motion Learning

With the release of SONY® PlayStation 3 and Microsoft® Xbox 360 Kinect, the motion-sensing technology has become a technology noticed by game, reading, advertising and medical domains, and the E-learning puts study and application development in children's learning.

The motion-sensing technology is used very extensively, such as control and interaction of computer games, medical simulation training, and physical fitness test (Lai and Tsay 2010; Tainchi et al. 2011). As for its application to learning, the learning activities can be carried out by simple and intuitive body interaction; multiple sense organs of body strengthen memory and attention to improve the learning effect.

15.4.3 Examples of Applying Sensors to Various Domains

This section introduces the examples of application of current sensors. Prof. Picard put forward the concept of "affective computing" in 1995, meanwhile the new type of design concept of human–machine interface was derived, and the research team under his leadership built a multi-sensor-based multivariate model as the base of human–machine interaction, behavior detection and affective computing, including sitting position analysis sensing chair, video equipment, pressure sensing mouse and bracelet sensor (Burleson 2006; Woolf et al. 2009). The purpose was to use sensor technology to know the correlation between the user's behavioral model and emotion, and to detect the user's state dynamically for further adaptive and personal assistance. The sensor equipments used are shown in Fig. 15.8.

Ark et al. (1999) proposed the concept of Emotion Mouse, the Sensor was affixed to the mouse to measure the user's heart rate, skin temperature and myo-electric reaction, as shown in Fig. 15.9, so that the computer could induce the user's physiological conditions, and proper response was expected. Picard et al. published several algorithms for characteristic-based recognition methods, and collected four physiological characteristics based on electromyogram, blood stream pulse, skin conductivity and breath, so as to observe daily changes for a long time. The aforesaid emotion sensing system can use many sensors as information sources, including video, audio, external behavior and physiological

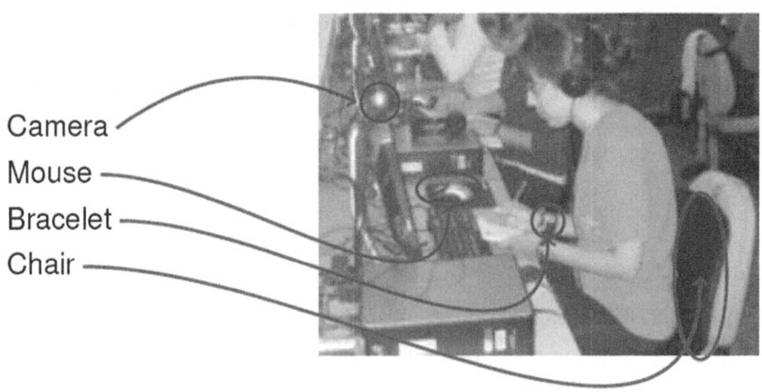

Fig. 15.8 The four sensors

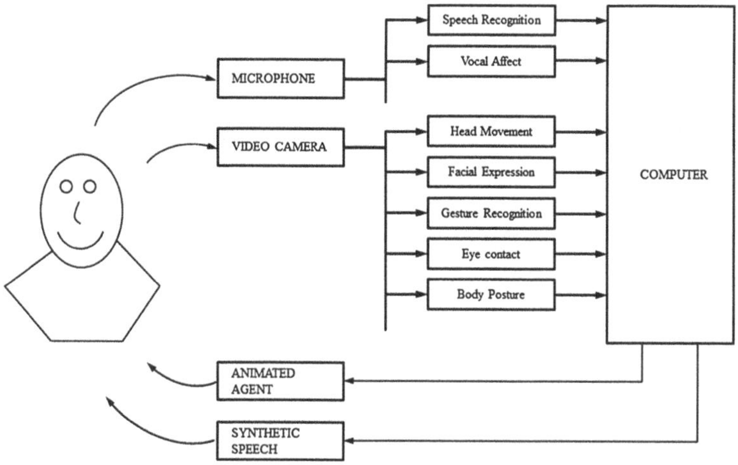

Fig. 15.9 The interface of multimode human–machine interaction

signals. Sebe et al. (2005) mentioned integrated the information from multiple sources to propose a conceptual structure of multimode human–machine interaction interface after comprehensive analysis and identification, as shown in Fig. 15.9.

University of Georgia has concentrated on studying a game for deaf children to learn sign language since 2005, known as CopyCat (Brashear et al. 2006; Zafrulla et al. 2011). It is based on image recognition and the information collected by glove sensors for identifying the deaf children's gestures and giving response; it enhances the memory and vocabulary of sign language of deaf children, and enables them to learn fast and enhances their learning motivation. As shown in Fig. 15.10, the gloves contain acceleration sensors which work with a camera to identify the deaf children's gestures accurately, so as to proceed with the tasks and games on the screen.

15.4.4 Conclusions and Future Prospects

Cloud computing brings an unprecedented revolution and it makes the use of technology more convenient, so as to change the e-learning mode into Cloudalized learning. Based on Cloud computing, the services of e-learning will develop towards five major characteristics including instant, intelligent, multi-sensory, seamless and social. In addition, the form of contents will develop towards aggregate, authentic and multimedia gradually. Meanwhile, the development of SNSs promotes the interpersonal relationships among learners, improves the interpersonal information exchange, and realizes instant and interactive functions.

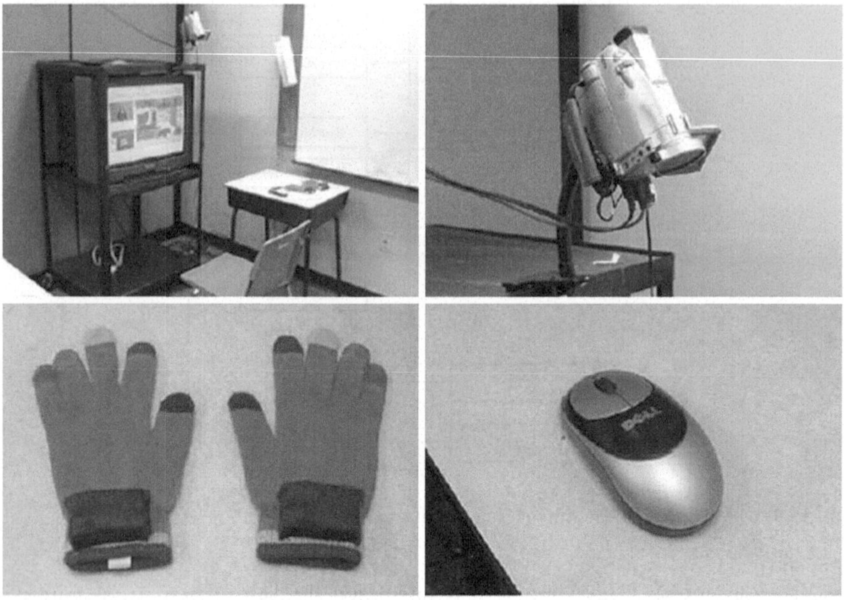

Fig. 15.10 The four sensors (Brashear et al. 2006)

The instant and interactive network has replaced labor and time consuming physical activities, and the SNSs and network real-time tools maintain and tighten the relationship between teachers and students. The diversified interaction in SNSs can enhance cooperative learning. Therefore, the learners can undertake meaningful learning more autonomously and conveniently. However, the Cloudalization also has problems, including the learners' privacy, data security and reliability, and the education theory or learning theory required for Cloudalized learning has not yet been developed completely. In other words, the potential risks in Cloudalized learning are one of future research subjects though we have enjoyed the benefit of Cloudalized learning.

In addition, with the assistance of sensing technology, the life quality is improved effectively and various problems are solved, its assistance and application are one of the most extensive and practical key technologies. The module integrated with multiple sensors is used in medical treatment, chemistry, aids, learning situation and environmental monitoring as the sensor technology develops, and there are good results, it has been able to be used in many domains as the sensor technology becomes mature gradually. The applications to E-learning are mostly apparent sensing technology applications, such as context awareness, ubiquitous learning, and there are few studies of physiological sensing technology, this is one of chances for development of e-learning in the future. Facing the development and advancement of future technology, the strong advantage of combination of sensor technology and Cloud computing as well as high interpersonal interaction of social network, the e-learning can develop towards five major characteristics such as instant, intelligent, multi-sensory, seamless and social interaction.

References

Ark WS, Dryer DC, Lu DJ (1999) The Emotion Mouse. Paper presented at the proceedings of HCI international (the 8th International Conference on Human-Computer Interaction) on human-computer interaction: Ergonomics and user interfaces-volume I

Armbrust M, Stoica I, Zaharia M, Fox A, Griffith R, Joseph AD et al (2010) A view of cloud computing. Commun ACM 53(4):50

Blattner G, Fiori M (2009) Facebook in the language classroom: promises and possibilities. Int J Instr Technol Distance Learn 6(1):1–13

Bloss R (2011) Real-time pressure mapping system. Sens Rev 31(2):101–105

Bosch TE (2009) Using online social networking for teaching and learning: facebook use at the university of Cape Town. Communicatio 35(2):185–200

Boyd D, Ellison N (2007) Social network sites: definition, history, and scholarship. J Comput Mediat Commun 13(1):210–230

Brashear H, Henderson V, Park KH, Hamilton H, Lee S, Starner T (2006) American sign language recognition in game development for deaf children. Paper presented at the proceedings of the 8th international ACM SIGACCESS conference on computers and accessibility

Burleson W (2006) Affective learning companions: strategies for empathetic agents with real-time multimodal affective sensing to foster meta-cognitive and meta-affective approaches to learning, motivation, and perseverance. Massachusetts Institute of Technology, Cambridge

Calvo RA, Rourke STO, Jones J, Yacef K, Reimann P (2011) Collaborative writing support tools on the cloud. IEEE Trans Learn Technol 4(1):88–97

Cheung CMK, Chiu P-Y, Lee MKO (2011) Online social networks: why do students use facebook? Comput Hum Behav 27(4):1337–1343

Christofides E, Muise A, Desmarais S (2009) Information disclosure and control on facebook: Are they two sides of the same coin or two different processes? Cyber Psychol Behav 12(3):341–345

Cuéllar MP, Delgado M, Pegalajar MC (2011) Improving learning management through semantic web and social networks in e-learning environments. Expert Syst Appl 38(4):4181–4189

De Wied M, Boxtel AV, Posthumus JA, Goudena PP, Matthys W (2009) Facial EMG and heart rate responses to emotion-inducing film clips in boys with disruptive behavior disorders. Psychophysiology 46(5):996–1004

Deaney R, Hennessy S, Ruthven K (2006) Teachers' strategies for making effective use of datalogging. Sch Sci Rev 88(323):103–110

Deng F, Chen W, Chai CS, Qian Y (2011) Constructivist-oriented data-logging activities in Chinese chemistry classroom: enhancing students' conceptual understanding and their metacognition. Asia-Pac Educ Res 20(2):207–221

Dori YJ, Herscovitz O (1999) Question-posing capability as an alternative evaluation method: Analysis of an environmental case study. J Res Sci Teach 36(4):411–430

Ellison NB, Steinfield C, Lampe C (2007) The benefits of facebook "friends:" social capital and college students' use of online social network sites. J Comput Mediat Commun 12(4):1143–1168

Ercan T (2010) Effective use of cloud computing in educational institutions. Procedia Soc Behav Sci 2(2):938–942

Facebook (2011) Statistics of facebook. http://www.facebook.com/press/info.php?statistics

Flipboard. (2011). Flipboard. from http://flipboard.com/
Foster I, Zhao Y, Raicu I, Lu S (2008) Cloud computing and grid computing 360-degree compared. Paper presented at the grid computing environments workshop, Austin, Texas
Garrison DR, Kanuka H (2004) Blended learning: uncovering its transformative potential in higher education. Int High Educ 7(2):95–105
Gong C, Liu J, Zhang Q, Chen H, Gong Z (2010) The Characteristics of Cloud Computing. Paper presented at the 2010 39th international conference on parallel processing workshops, San Diego, California
Google (2011a) Google Goggles. http://www.google.com/mobile/goggles/
Google (2011b) Google Instant. http://www.google.com/insidesearch/instant-about.html
Google (2011c) Google Scribe http://scribe.googlelabs.com/
Huang Y-M, Liu C-H (2009) Applying adaptive swarm intelligence technology with structuration in web-based collaborative learning. Comput Educ 52(4):789–799
Huang JJS, Yang SJH, Huang Y-M, Hsiao IYT (2010a) Social learning networks: build mobile learning networks based on collaborative services. Educ Technol Soc 13(3):78–92
Huang Y-M, Lin Y-T, Cheng S-C (2010b) Effectiveness of a mobile plant learning system in a science curriculum in Taiwanese elementary education. Comput Educ 54(1):47–58
Huang Y-M, Chiu P-S, Liu T-C, Chen T-S (2011) The design and implementation of a meaningful learning-based evaluation method for ubiquitous learning. Comput Educ 57(4):2291–2302
Huang Y-M, Huang Y-M, Huang S-H, Lin Y-T (2012) A ubiquitous english vocabulary learning system: evidence of active/passive attitudes vs. usefulness/ease-of-use. Comput Educ 58(1):273–282
Jones N, Blackey H, Fitzgibbon K, Chew E (2010) Get out of my space! Comput Educ 54(3):776–782
Kabilan MK, Ahmad N, Abidin MJZ (2010) Facebook: an online environment for learning of English in institutions of higher education? Int High Educ 13(4):179–187
Khe Foon H (2011) Students' and teachers' use of facebook. Comput Hum Behav 27(2):662–676
Koschmann T (1996) CSCL: theory and practice of an emerging paradigm. Lawrence Erlbaum Associates, Mahwah
Lai CH, Tsay TIJ (2010) Stroke motion learning for a humanoid robotic ping-pong player using a novel motion capture system. J Comput Sci 6(8):946–954
Lampe C, Ellison N, Steinfield C (2006) A face(book) in the crowd: social searching vs. social browsing. Paper presented at the CSCW '06: proceedings of the 2006 20th anniversary conference on computer supported cooperative work, Banff, Alberta
Liaw S–S (2008) Investigating students' perceived satisfaction, behavioral intention, and effectiveness of e-learning: A case study of the blackboard system. Comput Educ 51(2):864–873
Light P, Littleton K, Messer D, Joiner R (1994) Social and communicative processes in computer-based problem solving. Eur J Psychol Educ 9(2):93–109
Liu F, Lee HJ (2010) Use of social network information to enhance collaborative filtering performance. Expert Syst Appl 37(7):4772–4778
Manago AM, Graham MB, Greenfield PM, Salimkhan G (2008) Self-presentation and gender on my space. J Appl Dev Psychol 29(6):446–458
Matte TD, Hoffman RE, Rosenman KD, Stanbury M (1990) Surveillance of occupational asthma under the SENSOR model. Chest 98(5 Supplement):173S–178S
Mazman SG, Usluel YK (2010) Modeling educational usage of facebook. Comput Educ 55(2):444–453
Mukhopadhyay SC, Huang Y-M (2008) Sensors: advancements in modeling, design issues, fabrication and practical applications. Springer, Berlin
Mukhopadhyay SC, Gupta GS, Huang RY-M (2009) Recent advances in sensing technology. Springer, Berlin
Newton LR (2000) Data-logging in practical science: research and reality. Int J Sci Educ 22(12):1247–1259

Ophus DJ, Abbitt TJ (2009) Exploring the potential perceptions of social networking systems in university courses. J Online Learn Teach 5(4):639–648
O'Reilly T (2005) What is Web 2.0: design patterns and business models for the next generation of software. www.oreillynet.com/pub/a/oreilly/tim/news/2005/09/30/what-is-web-20.html
O'Reilly T (2007) What is web 2.0: design patterns and business models for the next generation of software. Int J Digital Econ 65:17–37
Pfeil U, Arjan R, Zaphiris P (2009) Age differences in online social networking—a study of user profiles and the social capital divide among teenagers and older users in myspace. Comput Hum Behav 25(3):643–654
Qwiki (2011) Qwiki. http://www.qwiki.com/
Rau P-LP, Gao Q, Ding Y (2008) Relationship between the level of intimacy and lurking in online social network services. Comput Hum Behav 24(6):2757–2770
Rogers L (1997) New data-logging tools: new investigations. Sch Sci Rev 79(287):61–68
Rogers L, Wild P (1994) The use of IT in practical science: a practical study in three schools. Sch Sci Rev 75(276):21–28
Rogers L, Wild P (1996) Data-logging: effects on practical science. J Comput Assist Learn 12(3):130–145
Rosen LD, Cheever NA, Carrier LM (2008) The association of parenting style and child age with parental limit setting and adolescent MySpace behavior. J Appl Develop Psychol 29(6):459–471
Satir V, Gomori M, Gerber J (1991) The Satir model: family therapy and beyond. Science and Behavior Books, Palo Alto
Sawyer RK, DeZutter S (2009) Distributed creativity: how collective creations emerge from collaboration. Psychol Aesthetic, Creativity Arts 3(2):81–92
Schunk DH (1996) Goal and self-evaluative influences during children's cognitive skill learning. Am Educ Res J 33(2):359–382
Sebe N, Lew MS, Huang TS (2005) Computer vision in human-computer interaction. Paper presented at the ICCV 2005 workshop on HCI, Beijing
Sheldon P (2008) Student student favorite: facebook and motives for its use. Southwestern J Mass Commun 23(2):39–53
Stern LA, Taylor K (2007) Social networking on facebook. J Commun, Speech Theatr Assoc North Dakota 20:9–20
Su AYS, Yang SJH, Hwang W-Y, Zhang J (2010) A web 2.0-based collaborative annotation system for enhancing knowledge sharing in collaborative learning environments. Comput Educ 55(2):752–766
Sultan N (2010) Cloud computing for education: a new dawn? Int J Inf Manage 30(2):109–116
Tainchi L, Chinhung K, Chochih L, Yitung L (2011). Applying motion sensing technology to interact with 3D virtual characters. Paper presented at the defense science research conference and expo (DSR), 3–5 Aug 2011
Urista MA, Dong Q, Day KD (2009) Explaining why young adults use MySpace and facebook through uses and gratifications theory. Hum Commun 12(2):215–229
Uzunboylu H, Bicen H, Cavus N (2011) The efficient virtual learning environment: a case study of web 2.0 tools and windows live spaces. Comput Educ 56(3):720–726
Vaquero LM (2011) Educloud: Paas versus Iaas cloud usage for an advanced computer science course. IEEE Trans Educ 54(4):
Weber AS (2011) Cloud computing in education in the Middle East and North Africa (Mena) region: can barriers be overcome? Paper presented at the proceedings of the 7th international scientific conference Else: eLearning and software for education. Bucuresti, Romania
Wegerif R (1998) The social dimension of asynchronous learning networks. J Asynchronous Learn Netw 2(1):34–49
Weiss A (2007) Computing in the clouds. Commun ACM 11(4):16–25
Wen JR, Chen CP (2011) The strategy of implementing the internet and cloud computing in teaching. Int J Res Rev Comput Sci 2(1):83–87
Wheeler B, Waggener S (2009) Above-campus services: shaping the promise of cloud computing for higher education. Educ Rev 44(6):52–67

White R, Gunstone R (1992) Probing understanding. Falmer, London

Wikihood (2011) Wikihood. http://www.qwiki.com/

Woolf B, Burleson W, Arroyo I, Dragon T, Cooper D, Picard R (2009) Affect-aware tutors: recognising and responding to student affect. Int J Learn Technol 4(¾):129–164

Zafrulla Z, Brashear H, Presti P, Hamilton H, Starner T (2011) CopyCat: an American sign language game for deaf children. Paper presented at the automatic face and gesture recognition and workshops (FG 2011), 2011 IEEE international conference on, 21–25 Mar 2011

Zhao S, Grasmuck S, Martin J (2008) Identity construction on facebook: digital empowerment in anchored relationships. Comput Hum Behav 24(5):1816–1836

Zite (2011) Zite. http://www.zite.com/

Zurita G, Nussbaum M, Salinas R (2005) Dynamic grouping in collaborative learning supported by wireless handhelds. Educ Technol Soc 8(3):149–161

Chapter 16
Immersive Environments for Learning: Towards Holistic Curricula

Longkai Wu, Chee-Kit Looi, Beaumie Kim and Chunyan Miao

Abstract The design and implementation of innovative pedagogical practices is an echo to the social needs for educational change in the twenty-first century. It has emerged to meet the request for unlocking the inventiveness of the learner's potential, and the need to take into account new possibilities for learning in a highly technology-mediated world. With the goal of illustrating the value of holistic curricula embodied with immersion technology, we propose a holistic pedagogical model and elaborate on the design of a curriculum to establish engaging scenarios where learners could experience three holistic learning dimensions in classroom: virtual reality immersion, agent mediation, and teacher moderation. Finally, we describe a vision of how immersive environments could offer a possible solution to the requirement of holistic curricula that schools are seeking for.

16.1 Introduction

Countries and education systems round the world are viewing education as geared not only to the teaching of academic subjects, but also towards a holistic education, i.e., preparing students for well-roundness to live and work in the interconnected world. Indeed, the Education Minister of Singapore (Minister outlines MOE's plans for holistic education 2012) says that "[Holistic Education] is more about how to process information, discern truths from untruths, connect seemingly disparate dots, and creates knowledge even as the context changes. It is about developing an enduring core of competencies, values and character to anchor our

L. Wu · C.-K. Looi (✉) · B. Kim · C. Miao
Nanyang Technological University, Singapore, Singapore
e-mail: cheekit.looi@nie.edu.sg

R. Huang et al. (eds.), *Reshaping Learning*, New Frontiers of Educational Research,
DOI: 10.1007/978-3-642-32301-0_16,

young and ensure they have the resilience to succeed". There is also quite a strong holistic education attempt or movement in USA, UK and Canada (Mayne, Holistic Education). Educationists have observed that 'the failure of education in the twentieth century is not the failure to teach humankind science, language or mathematics, but the failure to teach humankind to live together in peace and to harness the potentials in individuals and societies for full and equitable development' (Ordóñez 1998). A holistic reform—not of "pieces of curriculum" but in the ways teaching is conducted daily—is to help students prepare for their future life and work. To succeed in the twenty-first century, students need to acquire the ability to create, design, innovate, and think critically to solve complex challenges that will face them. They need deep knowledge and strong skills, become literate in science in very broad sense of science literacies, and remain excited and ready to apply that knowledge in authentic context.

A key feature of this approach to curriculum is that capability is understood as 'holistic … the essential integration of personal qualities, skills and specialist knowledge which enables students to be effective' (Stephenson and Weil 1992). Harding (2011) regards that holistic science concerns itself with the rigorous and integrated deployment of the full capacities of the human psyche in order to develop a deeply and truly participative relationship with nature. In this respect it differs from mainstream science, which believes that we can gain reliable knowledge of the world only through analytical mathematical reasoning in order to achieve the ideal of complete dominance and control of nature one day. For Stephenson and Weil (1992), the holistic curriculum integrates personal, social and work dimensions of capability development. In total, the holistic process is one of discovery—for oneself and through one's own life work– of wholeness through the exploration of elements of science, philosophy, curiosity and memories of wholeness or fragmentation and their meaning. However, a critical look at current curriculum research on science learning suggests that such considerations have rarely been given to such a holistic approach in real classroom practices (Miller 2007).

The past two decades have also seen a surge of interest in Multi-User Virtual Environments (MUVEs) and virtual worlds—such as *Active Worlds* and *Second Life*—especially in terms of the unique affordances these worlds potentially offer to education. For example, Dickey (Dickey 2003) provides one of the earliest analysis account of the pedagogical affordances of communication and movement tools in *Active Worlds* that emerge through implementation of a constructivist activity. Studies (Kemp and Livingstone 2006; Minocha and Roberts 2008) also note that the three-dimensional representation of avatars and environments in which the avatars can move and interact with each other through communication tools can afford a sense of self and presence, which may result in immersion and support socialization and collaborative learning. Meanwhile, innovative pedagogies or pedagogical models are strongly explored for such virtual worlds to be really applied in the context of formal education (Keskitalo et al. 2011). Girvan and Savage (2010) try to identify communal constructivism as one potential pedagogy for use in the virtual world *Second Life*. But the lack of appropriate and universal pedagogies has been one of major obstacles to introduce virtual worlds into formal education.

As part of an investigation to address the challenges as well as the opportunities emerging from the use of MUVEs for education, this chapter advocates a program of research that explores innovative pedagogical practices for designing a holistic curriculum that is embodied into an immersive environment for learning.[1] The chapter first discusses issues in the literature related to holistic education, holistic learning and holistic curriculum, as well as immersive environments. Then, a pedagogical model for holistic curriculum with immersive environment is proposed. We provide an instantiation of such a curriculum by describing the *Chronicles of Virtual Singapura* (VS2) which is an immersive environment for learning biological knowledge in secondary science education. The discussion of the curricula and learning environment will be focused on virtual reality presence, behaviors of the intelligent agents assuming mediation roles for learning, and the associated teacher moderation for guidance. Finally, we ponder on a future research agenda for immersive environments and holistic curriculum.

16.2 Review of Literature

16.2.1 Holistic Education and Holistic Learning

There has been no universal definition of holistic education yet. It is even argued that such a concept should not be defined or contained in one definition. One possible and acceptable definition comes from (What is holistic education 2012), which states that holistic education is a multi-leveled experiential journey of discovery, expression and mastery where all students and teachers learn and grow together in an expedition for understanding and meaning. From this definition, the objective of holistic education is to cultivate whole persons with curiosities who can learn whatever they need to know in any new context. (What is holistic education 2012) further proposed that by introducing students to a holistic view of the planet, life on earth, and the emerging world community, holistic strategies enable students to perceive and understand the various contexts that shape and give meaning to life, with recognition of the innate potential of every student for intelligent, creative, systemic thinking.

The term ‘holistic learning’ signifies an methodology to learning to foster holistic education which is predominantly ‘whole person’, i.e. it seeks to engage fully all aspects of the learner—mind, body and spirit (Holistic learning 2012). The

[1] Various terms are used to describe virtual environments for use in learning contexts. We prefer the use of *immersive environment for learning* in this chapter to stress the purpose of these systems in educational contexts in contrast to implicit views of “games” as an entertainment outlet.

underlying principle, as stated, is that a complex organism functions most effectively when all its component parts are themselves functioning and co-operating effectively. And this idea relates very closely to the concept of synergy, with the whole being greater than the sum of its parts. In terms of mainstream education a 'whole person' approach to learning is much more likely to be observed within the sensory-rich nursery or primary school activity room than in the intellect-dominated university lecture theatre (Holistic learning 2012).

John Heron (1992) proposes a multi-modal up-hierarchy model of holistic learning, based on four modes of psychological being: practical, conceptual, imaginal and affective. As signalized by (Holistic learning 2012), most significantly, according to this model human learning is firmly grounded on feeling, rather than thinking. These are illustratively represented in the form of a pyramid (Fig. 16.1) with feeling at the base and practical at the top. So, what is particularly unusual about the model is that feeling is presented as learner's fundamental mode, rather than thinking. This contrasts sharply with much of mainstream traditional education, where cognitive thinking and the pursuit of intellectual competence have the pre-eminent role. The significance of this alternative orientation is that the crucial requirement for each learner is to establish a relationship with their total learning situation which is intimate, resonant and positive (i.e. in the feeling mode). Only when this is firmly in place is it considered that the learner will be free to tap fully into the other three modes of the learning model, viz. imaginal, thinking and practical (Holistic learning 2012).

Holistic learning is organized around relationships within and between learners and their environment while empowering learners to live fully in the present and to co-create preferred futures. It is concerned with the growth of every person's intellectual, emotional, social, physical, artistic, creative and spiritual potential. It actively engages students in the teaching/learning process and encourages personal and collective discernment and responsibility. It seeks to open the mind, warm the heart and awaken the spirit (What is holistic education 2012).

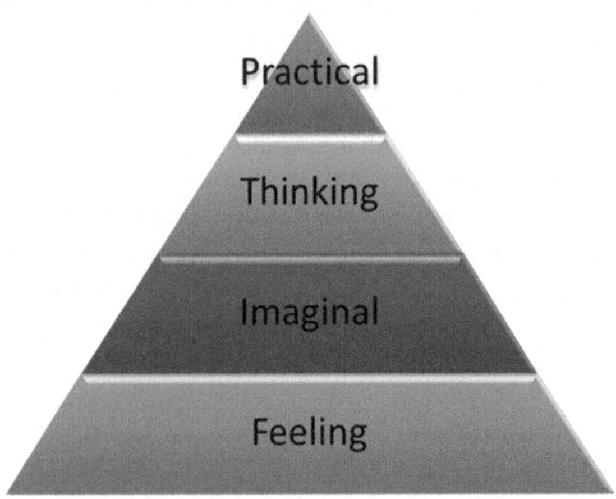

Fig. 16.1 Model of holistic learning (Harding 2011)

16.2.2 Holistic Curriculum

Holistic curriculum is inquiry driven, interdisciplinary and integrated, and is based on explicit assumptions of interconnectedness, wholeness and multi-dimensional being. It recognizes that all knowledge is created within a cultural context and that the "facts" are seldom more than shared points of view. It encourages the transfer of learning across academic disciplines. An holistic curriculum encourages learners to critically approach the cultural, moral and political contexts of their lives (What is holistic education 2012).

A holistic approach enables the interrelationships and interconnectivity between the cognitive and learner values that underpin the learning process. The double helix of learning power developed by McGettrick (2002) is a useful metaphor for holistic learning (Fig. 16.2), which, by borrowing from the DNA double helix model, provides a visual conceptualization of this interconnectivity. In a double helix, there are two strands which are joined together by bars that cross the helix. One strand of the double helix is thought of as the knowledge, skills and understanding of the curriculum. The other strand is the attitudes, feelings, dispositions and motivations of the learner. In any classroom, students learn two things. They learn a subject and they learn to love or to hate that subject.

The bars that hold the learner to the curriculum can be described by the seven dimensions of learning or the energy to learn [adapted from Cricka et.al. (2004)]:

- Critical curiosity refers to an orientation to 'get beneath the surface', as contrasted to being 'passive'.

  With critical curiosity, learners become energetic and desire to be insightful about the underlying issues or principles of something. They are curious about seeking the driving

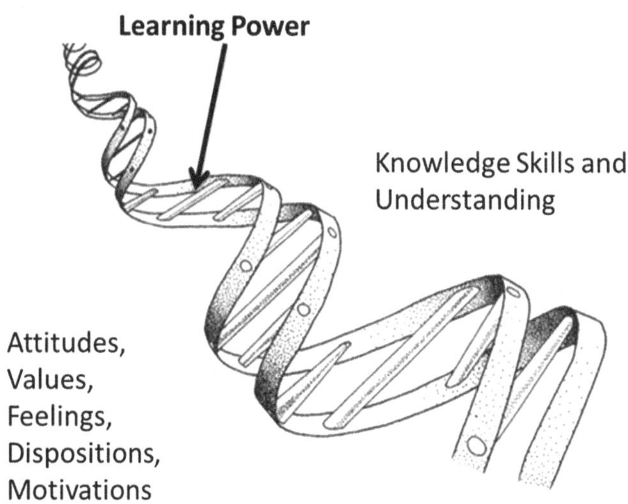

Fig. 16.2 Holistic curriculum in double helix model (Keskitalo et al. 2011)

forces or finding out working mechanisms. Easily being told or superficial understanding is far from being sufficient to meet their requirement. Instead, they are more than enthusiastic to excavate by themselves to get in-depth knowledge. During the excavation process in an inquiry, they are equipped with an inquisitive mindset to ask questions and look for possible answers or solutions. As active learners, they take the ownership of their own learning process to cope with various difficulties and challenges. In stark contrast, passive learners tend to take a subordinate role in the learning process by consenting to what is told without critical thoughts. It is not necessary they are less smart than their curious peers. They just lack the impetus to find things out by themselves in active speculation or exploration.

- Changing and learning refer to a sense of oneself as someone who learns and changes over time, as contrasted to being 'stuck and static'.

Learners with the power of changing and learning perceive learning as dynamic process as they grow. Learning does not only happen during the school years. It is a lifelong process that will never stop in one's lifetime. Change is always the core part of life, so learning to adapt is a key theme. The settled past can be instructive to cope with the changeable current and future. Comparatively, learners being "stuck and static" have a fixed view of learning. To them, one is always fixed with the "learning power" that will never being changed. Thus, they are stuck to their limitations or weaknesses. Challenging situations are more burdensome to them rather than serve as opportunities to learn.

- Meaning making refers to making connections and seeing that learning 'matters to me', as contrasted to simply 'accumulating data'.

Learners possessing the power in meaning-making are to make connections between what they are learning and what they have known. Such connections help them to make sense of what is happening and make judgments about what matters to them and what does not. They tend to ask questions to eventually get a coherent understanding of the big picture by weaving their web of knowledge. In contrast, learners who simply "accumulate data" tend to perceive what they are learning without much reflection.

- Creativity refers to risk-taking, playfulness, imagination and intuition, as contrasted to being 'rule-bound'.

Creative learners are always looking for possible solutions and alternatives to solve challenging problems. They have different perspectives to look at one issue and various ideas to play with. They are usually relying on their hunches and imagination to conceive new ideas. Learning, to them, is rather playing than purposeful and systematic thinking. They are inclined to create pictures or diagrams to contribute vividness to their ideas. Comparatively, less creative learners take a stiffer position to cope with complex issues. They need clear instructions to get things done. Otherwise, they will be uncertain or puzzled on how to proceed. Thus, they tend to be comfortable in solving routine problems and are bounded to certain rules.

- Learning relationships or interdependence refers to learning with and from others and also being able to learn alone, as contrasted to being 'isolated' or 'over-dependent'.

Empowered with the ability to collaborate, learners take a balance between learning collaboratively and independently. They regard others, whether peers, teachers and parent, as learning partners that can learn from and with, as well as to share knowledge and thoughts. They intend to perceive learning as a social process that can happen in group sharing or discussions. Other people are not just information resources, but also creators of new knowledge and reliable companions to conquer difficulties in the learning journey. By contrast, learners who are "isolated" lack engagement with other people, and learners who are "over-dependent" are exhibiting over-dependency in seeking excessive guidance from other people.

- Strategic awareness refers to being aware of one's thoughts, feelings and actions as a learner and being able to use that awareness to plan and manage learning processes, as opposed to being 'robotic'.

  Learners with strategic awareness are more self-directed learners, who are well aware of own objectives and available methods. They can employ different strategies or approaches in learning to check out what has happened and make corresponding adjustments. Reflection is important for them to conduct self-evaluation and make decisions in allocating time, resources or effort on a specified learning talk. They are willing to take responsibility to plan and organize for their learning. They are also able to pacify their emotion when being frustrated or repair gap when encountering errors. Otherwise, 'robotic' learners develop less self-awareness of self-directness of their learning process. They do not have a clear roadmap in their mind of how to plan and proceed with their learning activities.

- Resilience refers to the orientation to persevere in the development of one's own learning power and to relish challenges, as contrasted to being 'fragile and dependent'.

  Resilient learners are not afraid of challenges and uncertainties in learning. They are aware that learning is always not easily to achieve and difficulty is indeed the pathway leading to robust learning. Confusion, frustration or even anxiety is often accompanied with us in the learning process. They know how to live with the negative emotions and recover from them. They also do not fear to make mistakes or admit failure. They learn from them. In the contrast, dependent or fragile learners easily give up or collapse when they are stuck with difficulties. They are not willing to take risks to achieve a certain goal even it is achievable. They are always staying in their comfort zone without attempt to challenge their limit. They also count on other people or external forces to solve the problems for them.

The holistic approach of curriculum design is about to synthesize, by integrating and connecting, the seven dimensions of learning power. It is about looking at learners as 'whole people' of thinking, feeling, and doing, and not just about cognition or behaviour or skills. By balancing attention to include both the 'person' as the learner and the 'curriculum' that is being learnt, we see each of them as inseparably associated with the seven dimensions that are inter-connected aspects of a complex but single concept.

The holistic curriculum is intended to unleash the learning power, so that learners can use the ones that are their strengths to help strengthen the others. For example, the learning power of 'meaning making' and 'learning relationships' could depend upon linking up and relating to other people and new ideas. Learning power is also developmental in the sense that every learner is always on a learning journey. The assumption underlying the design of holistic curriculum is that the higher level of learning power could be achieved by effective organization of teaching and learning that lead learners in personal development in terms of the seven dimensions of learning power.

16.2.3 Immersive Environments for Learning

Recent research has emphasized creating virtual learning worlds that provide students with a sense of immersion into the content, with the ability to both manipulate the content and change the content to derive new understanding (Coffman 2007). Claims have been made that some of these immersive worlds for education, such as Active Worlds (Dickey 2005) and Second Life (Rymaszewski et al. 2006), have significant potential to foster students' learning in several aspects, such as learning outcomes (Virvou et al. 2005), transformations of social interactions (Bailenso et al. 2008) and argument-based negotiations (Jamaludin et al. 2007). Dede and Barab (2009) note that immersive designs in virtual world (e.g., immersive interfaces (Dede 2009)) offer promising vistas for improving science education, whereas emerging technologies, such as agent technology (Chase and Chin 2009) can be incorporated to address core issues of student's engagement, mastery of sophisticated knowledge and skills, transfer of learning, and attaining scale.

Dede (2009) further points out that immersion in the virtual world involves the willing suspension of disbelief, and the design of immersive learning experiences that induce this disbelief draws on sensory, actional, and symbolic factors, which enhance science education in at least three ways: multiple perspectives, situated learning, and transfer. However, Trindade et al. (2002) find that not all students' sense of immersion can contribute to their conceptual understanding of science even as they provide substance to abstract concepts. Coffman and Klinger (2007) argue that students need scaffolding or moderation to solve problems in immersive environments. Meanwhile, other studies show that pedagogical agents, which are life-like personas, can execute behaviors that involve emotive responses, interactive communication, and effective pedagogy, to mediate and optimize students' learning by exploiting their characteristics (Person and Graesser 2003).

Although instances of immersive environments for learning are prevalent during the years, pedagogical models are not staying abreast of the development work to introduce them in the context of formal education. Such a gap motivate us in exploring possibilities by developing and deploying innovative pedagogical practices enabled by immersive environment for holistic learning, such as the augmentation of learners' immersion in virtual reality context; the personalization of mediation as well as the enhancement of scaffolding or moderation inside and outside the immersive presence, for the purpose of enhancing engagement and thus promoting holistic learning.

16.3 The Proposed Holistic Pedagogical Model

Barab and Dodge (2008) suggest that an emphasis of supporting meaningful participation within experientially rich contexts at the core of design embodied curriculum, which is a shift as a move away from the acquisition metaphor that has guided much of the practice in K–12 schools, toward a participation metaphor in which knowledge is considered fundamentally situated in practice. Comparatively, "learning to be" is a holistic and integrated approach to values education for human development: Core values and the valuing process for developing innovative practices for values education toward international understanding and a culture of peace. The pillar 'learning to be' implies a new vision of education that goes beyond an instrumental view of education (Learning to be: a holistic and integrated approach to values education for Human Development 2002).

The guiding principle of our designing a holistic pedagogical model is a gradual progression from the concrete levels of the curriculum towards its more abstract components (Orion 2007), which can be used for designing a whole curriculum, a course, or a small set of learning activities. Building on related work that connects person, content, and context (Brown et al. 1989; Barab et al. 2010) we have developed a holistic pedagogical model to account for the experiences that we wish to foster through our designs and the elements to which we must attend in creating a new curriculum embodied with an immersive space. Merely being immersed in a virtual world does not ensure that one is engaged in holistic learning. Similar to the transformational learning/playing proposed by Barab et al. (2010) holistic learning involves (1) taking on the leading role in the learning journey (2) employing conceptual understandings (3) making choices (4) having the potential to transform herself (5) having a problem-based fictional context and ultimately (6) understanding the content as well as of (7) herself as someone who has used academic content to address a socially significant problem. Such a holistic perspective integrates person, content, and context as part of a system in which each type of positioning motivates and is motivated by the other types.

Figure 16.3 shows pedagogical model enabled by the immersive environment for learning. A holistic pedagogical model, based on the guiding principle and an

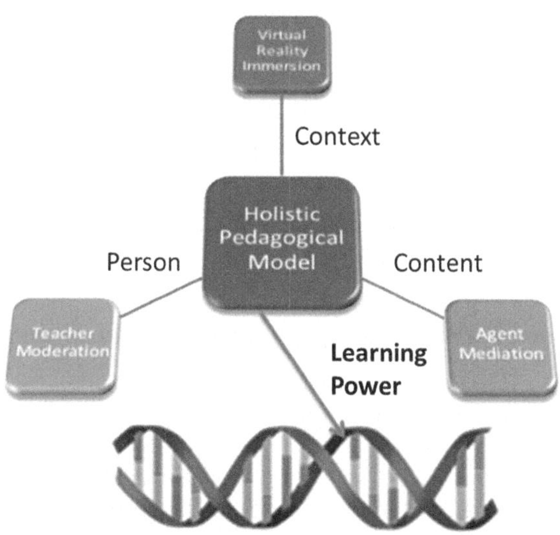

Fig. 16.3 Holistic pedagogical model

Table 16.1 Seven dimensions of holistic pedagogical model

Dimension	Description
Changing and learning	A sense of myself as someone who learns and changes over time
Critical curiosity	An orientation to want to "get beneath the surface"
Meaning making	Making connections and seeing that learning "matters to me"
Creativity	Risk-taking, playfulness, imagination and intuition
Interdependence	Learning with and from others and also able to manage without them
Strategic awareness	Being aware of my thoughts, feelings and actions as a learner, and able to use that awareness to manage learning processes
Resilience	The readiness to persevere in the development of my own learning power

Adapted from ELLI (Cricka et al. 2004)

Effective Lifelong Learning Inventory (Cricka et al. 2004), set out to identify the characteristics and dispositions of the "learning power" in the double helix model. It is about emancipation and empowerment, enhancing life through effective learning, It goes beyond just about cognition, behavior or skills, but helps learners to think, feel and do as whole person, and achieve the balanced attention to both the person as the learner and the curriculum that is being learnt.

As holistic pedagogical model plays the role of "learning power" that holds the learner to the curriculum, it also has seven dimensions of learning power that mentioned before, each with elements of 'thinking, feeling and doing' (Table 16.1).

One of the main goals of the ongoing research reported in this chapter is to explore ways in which students may learn challenging knowledge and skills in a virtual world in ways that they may develop in the seven dimensions of the holistic pedagogical model. Undertaking research of this type, however, requires attention to a number of design issues that span different areas of specialization. In next section, we use the *Chronicles of Virtual Singapura* (VS2) project as an embodiment to discuss designing for three orientations to support such a holistic pedagogical model: (1) Virtual Reality Immersion, (2) Agent Immersion, and (3) Teacher Moderation.

16.4 Design of Holistic Curriculum with an Immersive Environment

16.4.1 Overview of Immersive Environment

Chronicles of Virtual Singapura (*VS2*) represents one of Singapore's latest attempts to explore the next generation virtual learning environments (VLEs), which is a combination of virtual worlds and modeled according to early nineteenth century Singapore. A variety of artificial intelligent entities are designed to act as the

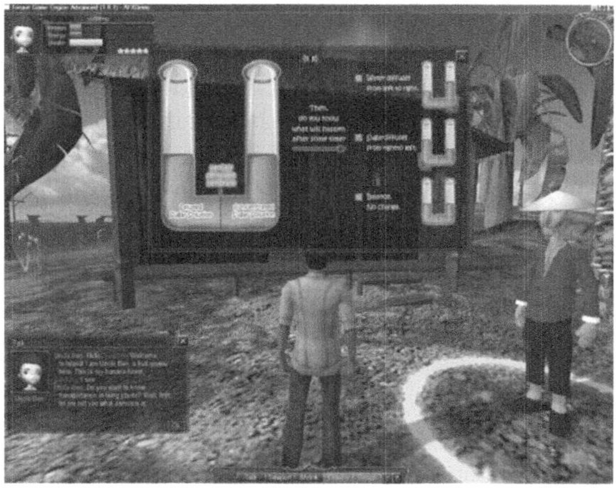

Fig. 16.4 Overview of chronicles of virtual Singapura: help uncle Ben to save the tree

learning companions for the learners. It empowers students to enjoy a virtual immersive experience and to be actively engaged in formal or informal learning as an individual or as a group.

As shown in Fig. 16.4, the student manipulates the avatar to interact and gets a quest from Uncle Ben, a peasant living on a rainforest island in Singapura during the early eighteenth century, to save a dying banana tree. Subsequently, she will learn basic knowledge about transport systems in plants by performing experiments in virtual labs on the island. The student avatar will enter inside a banana tree with water and mineral salts. During the trip inside the tree, food would be generated by photosynthesis and then distributed to save the tree. In such an adventure, the student will learn biological knowledge in a situated way. The whole curriculum activities accompanied with our immersive environment is presented in Table 16.2, with four sessions needed for students and teachers involved to complete the thorough adventure.

16.4.2 Design of Virtual Reality Immersion

The basic scenario for VS2 was inspired by the fictional nineteenth century River City MUVE research (Dede 2005) and the first generation of Virtual Singapura (Jacobson et al. 2009). As both VS and VS2 were initially intended for use in

Table 16.2 Curriculum activities

Phases	Activities	Description
Session 1	Join orientation	Get familiar with the virtual environment
Session 2	Conduct virtual experiments	Experiment with osmosis and diffusion
Session 3	Save the banana tree	Adventure with transport in plant
Session 4	Review for future learning	Teach the teachable agents

Singapore secondary science classrooms, the teachers who collaborated with the research teams suggested that a Singapore context for science learning might be more interesting to their students than the American centered River City MUVE. The design team elected to base the VS2 scenario more tightly on historical research information about disease epidemics in nineteenth century Singapore and about cultural practices and conditions of the period, in contrast to the more fictitious scenarios of River City or Quest Atlantis. The scenario for VS2 is to have twenty-first century Singapore students go back in time to help Uncle Ben, a peasant on the ancient island of Singapura, to figure out what is causing the dying of banana tree and to propose viable solutions to save the banana tree.

When students teleport back to nineteenth century Singapore, they arrive at the Boat Quay on the Singapore River and then use their avatars (computer generated characters on the screen that they control and communicate through) to explore investigate the local phenomenon of and learn about the basic relevant knowledge. They will visit various locations on the island, meet computer-generated residents (i.e., avatars), inspect evaporation and leakage of water to obtain information; and obtain air, water, and salt samples at selected data collection stations. The students communicate with team members using the group-chat function, as well as chatting with the various nineteenth century avatars they meet, such as the store sellers, coolies or peddlers. After the traveling around the island, they can conduct "modern" authentic experiments in the lab to understand diffusion and osmosis (Fig. 16.5).

Comparing to the authentic investigations, a more intriguing immersion design to learner is fictional actional immersion, which is incorporated as novel modes of interactions in the virtual environment and is not possible achieved in real world. For example, by allowing the learner to shrink his/her avatar down to microscopic sizes, the learner can "participate" in the osmosis/diffusion process as a tiny carrier of water or salt molecules. Learner avatar can also enact the process of photosynthesis at the molecule level (e.g., $CO_2 + H_2O \rightarrow \text{Glucose} + O_2$) in

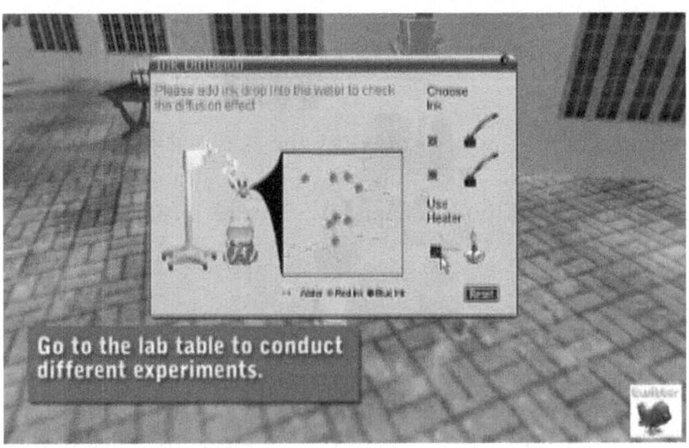

Fig. 16.5 Diffusion and osmosis experiment in virtual lab (authentic actional immersion)

Fig. 16.6 Generate food for the tree (fictional actional immersion)

active experiment (Fig. 16.6), by practicing shooting the molecules to produce food for the banana tree. The combination of authentic and fictional immersion designs enable learners to try out things from different perspectives on the problem at hand.

Additionally, student could refer to anchors, rationales, rubrics, curriculum documents, and various support materials during the exploration in VS2. Students were conferred with group members as their work were assessed and assigned to share experiences with the class. They were also engaged in a dialogue with a group of students to develop a common understanding of the levels of achievement. Collective discussions were allowed to unleash students' strengths, meet learning gaps and determine trends for the next steps.

16.4.3 Design of Agent Mediation

Several forms of agents, such as remembrance agents and teachable agents, are designed as learning companions to scaffold the student's execution of these actionable immersion tasks and consolidate their learning in the virtual environment. For example, a remembrance agent (Fig. 16.7) is designed to remember the

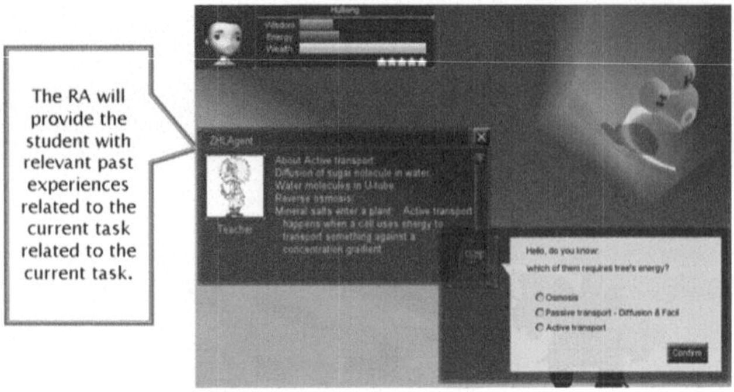

Fig. 16.7 Remembrance agent

scenes that the student experienced. In a new scene, the remembrance agent will find out the past game scenes with related knowledge and display the hints to the player to help him engage with tasks in the current scene. At the same time, the related knowledge is also reviewed.

Meanwhile, the teachable agent (Fig. 16.8) requires students to teach what they have learnt using rules (i.e. if…then…else… clauses) as a follow-up of their learning adventures. During the teaching process, the teachable agent (e.g., "The little banana tree"), based on a fuzzy rule inference, will check the acquired rules for potential conflicts and pose questions, e.g. "does more sunshine lead to higher temperature?", to prompt students to reflect upon how these conflicting rules may arise and correct their error and bias (Dickey 2005). The banana tree will thrive as a consequence of teaching the teachable agents correctly.

Fig. 16.8 Teachable agent

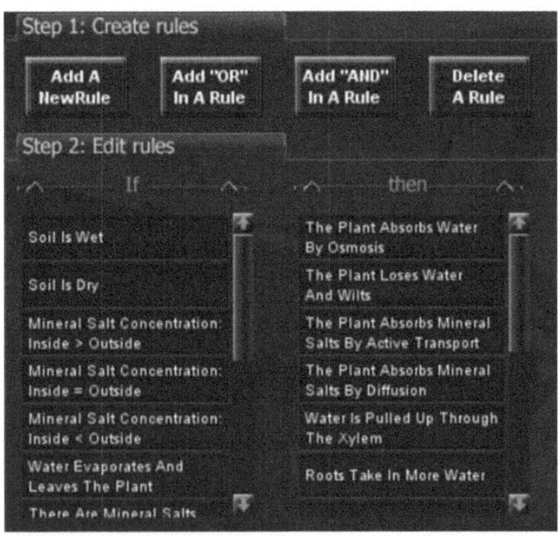

16.4.4 Design of Teacher Moderation

A holistic pedagogical model should not exclude the role of teachers in the classroom. As described in (Holistic education for the responsibility of freedom as self-empowerment: a scientific rationale 2012), in the new holistic paradigm for teaching, the teacher's function is described in terms of the facilitation of learning. The function of the teacher is to enhance the learner's intrinsic motivation. The effective teacher is a facilitator of learning. Effective teaching methods place the emphasis on the facilitation of self-directed learning. Facilitative teaching methods are effective because they comply with the natural holistic functioning of the brain. Teaching for effective learning is teaching to the brain's natural functioning while engaging the learner's personal development. In the paradigm of 'holistic education' the function of the effective teacher or 'soul educator' is defined in terms of the 'facilitation of learning'. Facilitative teaching is effective because it coincides with the natural holistic functioning of the brain. Brain development is functional in the development of natural intelligence or 'creative intelligence'. Teaching to the brain's natural intelligence functioning engages the learner in their personal development and their capacity for adaptation to changing environmental conditions.

There is also considerable evidence that teacher moderation, when conducted effectively to link assessment to improve instructional practice, can improve student learning (Black and Wiliam 1998). This process involves educators in a collaborative discussion of student work based on predetermined assessment criteria.

Little (2003) found that teachers who engaged consistently in the moderation process were able to:

- assess student performance more consistently, effectively, confidently, and fairly;
- build common knowledge about curriculum expectations and levels of achievement;
- identify strengths and areas for growth based on evidence of student learning;
- adjust and acquire new learning by comparing one's thinking to that of another student or teacher;
- share effective practices to meet the needs of all students, monitor progress, and celebrate growth.
- The most powerful aspect of teacher moderation is the discussion involved in assessing student work and the collective sharing of effective strategies in planning next steps for instruction.

In the proposed holistic curriculum, before the sessions, the teacher will make decisions collaboratively with researchers on the curriculum task based on identified curricular expectations that will identify students' strengths and learning gaps. She will also establish assessment tools and resources that will support assessment (e.g., rubrics, checklists, workbooks) and chose members in students groups. Multiple copies of student workbooks are to be prepared to distribute to group members, together with papers, books, and computers installed with VS2. During the sessions, the teacher will set goals for student progress based on curriculum expectations and achievement. She will also investigate and share key instructional strategies. After the Sessions, the teacher will assess the class progress, analyze to determine the effectiveness of current strategies and set new goals for class improvement.

16.5 The Future of Immersive Environment and Holistic Curriculum

In this chapter, we have sought to highlight issues relevant to the design of holistic curricula enabled by immersive learning environments. Developing our students, helping them to achieve a sense of holistic learning has always been a fundamental but often neglected goal of education. Twenty-first century educational goals together with the technology of immersive environment for learning suggest ways to develop innovative pedagogies that address this need in the context of schooling. We argued that three characteristics of learning in immersive game environments in a holistic pedagogical model—virtual reality immersion, agent mediation and teacher moderation—lend themselves naturally to forms of learning that value process skills, performance, and behaviors: demonstrations of learning power in contrast to traditional content acquisition goals. We hope that the perspectives discussed in this chapter might inform these design and development efforts both for the virtual world technologies themselves and for the overall holistic education in which they will be used.

Generally, it is our belief that agent-mediated immersive environments provide new technologies and possibilities for creating curriculum in which the learner experiences are experientially immersed, interactively mediated and reflectively moderated. Our central argument is that a holistic curriculum embodied in an immersive environment has the potential to liberate learners from the stigma of assessment and to encourage a disposition for innovation and a desire to challenge oneself as a natural part of the learning process.

Barab et al. (2004) have advanced a transactive perspective that involves positioning concepts and learners within rich, interactive systems that elevate concepts from abstracted facts to conceptual tools that operate and transform those very same narratives that imbued the concepts with worth. As they have argued, a transactive experience, as a goal for designing curriculum, offers much in terms of curing the crises of meaning currently ailing the educational system. Similarly, our holistic perspective to design curriculum embodied into an immersive environment is also not just simply in making the abstract concrete (that is, providing a perceptual instantiation of an academic concept), but making the abstract meaningful and stimulating a passion for schooling. Furthermore, in our case, by integrating up disciplinary context within holistic contexts, there is potential to not only change learner understanding of the use value of the content, but also offer learners the opportunity to regard themselves as ones who can meaningfully apply disciplinary content, be transformed into taking fullness of life (Roth and Eijck 2010) as the minimum unit to learn science.

Designing experiences to support personal engagement and transformation requires balancing a number of tensions (Barab et al. 2010; Barab and Roth 2006, which are raised between providing a contextually rich curricular environment and ensuring that learners attend to the particular content that the environment is designed to teach. As discussed by Barab and Roth (2006), a balancing process can happen in terms of the quality of content (explicit versus implicit) and the quality of context (noisy versus tailored)—to quality of person (detached versus engaged). Noisy contexts containing rich contextual detail and mostly implicit enlistment of disciplinary content can foster mystery, realness, discovery, and an appreciation of why the content matters. In our research, one tension lies in the balance of "inside" and "outside" experience of the virtual environment in classroom settings. It is interesting to notice the important role of teacher moderation in classroom when it is actually "outside" of the virtual environment, and thus shows the potential anchoring value of such classroom experiences to help foster learning through collaboration and reflection about the experiences students had been involved with "inside" the virtual world. Thus one future research might explore the potential value of nexus between experiential learning inside virtual worlds and reflective learning "outside" of the virtual world to foster deeper learning experiences. We argue that a sense of both attachment and detachment, regarding one learner, for the immersive environment can allow for more objective participation and reflection for him to be embedded in the curriculum. Although the detachment may breed apathy and disengagement to the virtual environment, it could generate engagement and reflection to the whole lesson.

Designing holistic curriculum to support pedagogical transformation also involves balancing tensions across students, teachers, content and context and call for innovative ways of assessment. For students, the assessment of their performance is oriented to analyze their experiences and outcomes "inside" and "outside" of the immersive environment. The first orientation is on analysis of activity-oriented learning experiences include whether the curriculum has functioned as intended in terms of task structure and action dynamics (e.g., log files of actions happened inside the immersive environment), the level of learner's engagement in the storyline (e.g., the data include interviews, surveys, and evidence of after-school activities), and learner's learning performance inside the environment (e.g., in-game tests, whole-class discussions, and submitted graphs). The second orientation is on evaluating curriculum-oriented outcomes which include teacher-created tests designed to test learning of the core concepts. The third orientation, as suggested by Barab et al. (2007), is on standards-oriented outcomes that involve primarily far-transfer assessment consisting of standardized items drawn at random from larger pools of items aligned to the targeted standards as well as other external measures not intentionally designed to test the particular unit. In our scheduled assessment of students' performance, we are intended to mainly attend to the first two orientations, but we are also looking forward to the third orientation of assessment when more consistent high-level performance data is collected.

16.6 Closing Thoughts

A holistic approach, as proposed in this chapter, allows researchers and teachers to understand what learners bring to each situation, whether "inside" or "outside" of the immersive environment, and how the resources, including immersion designs, agent mediation and teacher moderation, provide possibilities that are mobilized in metabolic ways, giving rise in the process to interest, emotional engagement, or motivation. With the dialectic of continuities and discontinuities that learners experience in real and virtual lives, such a holistic perspective will allow researchers and teachers to understand how learners can come to be engaged in as effective learners in holistic ways.

References

Bailenso JN, Yee N, Blascovich J, Beal d AC, Lundblad N, Jin M (2008) The use of immersive virtual reality in the learning sciences: digital transformations of teachers, students, and social context. J Learning Sci 17(1): 102–141

Barab SA, Dodge T (2008) Strategies for designing embodied curriculum. In: Spector JM, Merrill MD, Merrienboer JV, Driscoll MP (eds) Handbook of research on educational communications and technology. Lawrence Erlbaum associates, New York, pp 97–110

Barab SA, Roth W-M (2006) Curriculum-based ecosystems: supporting knowing from an ecological perspective. Educ Res 35(5):3–13

Barab Sa, Gresalfi M, Ingram-Goble A (2010) Transformational play: using games to position person, content, and context. Educ Res 39(7): 525–536. doi:10.3102/0013189X10386593

Barab SA, Ingram-Goble A, Gresalfi M (2004) Virtual worlds as transactive curricula: why games can seriously change schools. In: Thomas D (ed) Virtual worlds, vol 1. MIT Press, Boston, pp 1829–1841

Barab SA, Zuiker S, Warren S et al (2007) Situationally embodied curriculum: relating formalisms and contexts. Sci Educ 91(5):750–782

Black P, Wiliam D (1998) Inside the black box: raising standards through classroom assessment. Phi Delta Kappan 80(2):139–148

Brown JS, Collins A, Duguid P (1989) Situated cognition and the culture of learning. Educ Res 18(1):32–42

Chase C, Chin DB, Oppezzo M, Schwartz DL (2009) Teachable agents and the protégé effect: increasing the effort towards Learning. J Sci Educ Technol 18(4):334–352

Coffman T, Klinger MB (2007) Utilizing virtual worlds in education: the implications for practice. Int J Human Social Sci 2(1):29–33

Cricka RD, Broadfoota P, Claxtona G (2004) Developing an effective lifelong learning inventory: the elli project. Assess Educ Principles Policy Pract 11(3):247–272

Dede C (2005) Planning for neomillennial learning styles. Educause Q 28(1):7–12

Dede C (2009) Immersive interfaces for engagement and learning. Science 323:66–69
Dede C, Barab S (2009) Emerging technologies for learning science: a time of rapid advances. J Sci Educ Technol 18(4):301–304. doi:10.1007/s10956-009-9172-4
Dickey MD (2003) Teaching in 3D: pedagogical affordances and constraints of 3D virtual worlds for synchronous distance learning. Distance Educ 24(1):105–121
Dickey MD (2005) Teaching in 3D: pedagogical affordances and constraints of 3D virtual worlds for synchronous distance learning. Distance Educ 36(3):439–451
Girvan C, Savage T (2010) Identifying an appropriate pedagogy for virtual worlds: a communal constructivism case study. Comput Educ 55(1):342–349. doi:10.1016/j.compedu.2010.01.020
Harding S (2011) Holistic science. Holistic Sci J 1(1):1–4
Heron J (1992) Feeling and personhood: psychology in another key. SAGE Publications Ltd, Beverly Hills, p 272
Holistic education for the responsibility of freedom as self-empowerment: a scientific rationale. Retrieved 11 May 2012, from http://www.holisticeducator.com/INTRODUCTION.htm
Holistic learning. Retrieved 8 May 2012, from http://www.jwelford.demon.co.uk/brainwaremap/holist.html
Jacobson MJ, Kim B, Miao C, Shen Z, Chavez M (2009) Design perspectives for learning in virtual worlds. In: Jacobson MJ, Reiman P (eds) Designs for learning environments of the future: international perspectives from the learning sciences. Springer, New York
Jamaludin A, Mei C, Ho L, Chee YS (2007) Argument-based negotiation and conflict resolution through enactive role play in Second Life. In: Hirashima T, Hoppe U, Young SSC (eds) Proceedings of the 15th international conference on computers in education. IOS Press, Amsterdam, pp 561–568
Kemp J, Livingstone D (2006) Putting a second life "metaverse" skin on learning management systems. In: Second Life Education Workshop 2006
Keskitalo T, Pyykkö E, Ruokamo H (2011) Exploring the meaningful learning of students in second life. Subscription Prices Ordering Inf 14:16
Learning to be: a holistic and integrated approach to values education for human development (2002) UNESCO Asia and Pacific Regional Bureau for Education, p 183
Little JW (2003) Looking at student work for teacher learning, teacher community and school reform. Phi Delta Kappan 85(3):185–192
Mayne A (2012) Holistic education. Retrieved from http://www.scimednet.org/holistic-education
McGettrick B (2002) Transforming school ethos: transforming learning citizenship education in action. Bristol University Graduate School of Education
Miller JP (2007) The holistic curriculum. University of Toronto Press, Scholarly Publishing Division, p 208
Minister outlines MOE's plans for holistic education. Retrieved 20 Mar 2012, from http://www.channelnewsasia.com/stories/singaporelocalnews/view/1187853/1/.html
Minocha S, Roberts D (2008) Laying the groundwork for socialisation and knowledge construction within 3D virtual worlds. ALT-J 16(3):181–196
Ordóñez JAG (1998) The education of a schoolmaster: my years at St. Paul's School. Francis Press, Washington
Orion N (2007) A holistic approach for science education for all. Science 3(2):111–118
Person NK, Graesser AC (2003) Pedagogical agents and tutors. In: Guthrie JW (ed) Encyclopedia of education. Macmillan, New York, pp 586–589
Roth W-M, Eijck MV (2010) Fullness of life as minimal unit: science, technology, engineering, and mathematics (STEM) learning across the life span. Sci Educ 94(6):1027–1048. doi:10.1002/sce.20401
Rymaszewski M, Au WJ, Ondrejka C, Platel R (2006) Second life: the official guide. Wiley & Sons, Inc, Hoboken, New Jersey
Stephenson J, Weil S (1992) Quality in learning: a capability approach in higher education. Kogan Page, London

Trindade J, Fiolhais C, Almeida L (2002) Science learning in virtual environments: a descriptive study. Br J Educ Technol 33(4): 471–488

Virvou M, Katsionis G, Manos K (2005) Combining software games with education: evaluation of its educational effectiveness. Educ Technol Soc 8:54–65

What is holistic education? Retrieved 24 Mar 2012, from http://www.hent.org/intro2.htm

Chapter 17
Augmented Reality and Education: Applications and Potentials

Steve Chi-Yin Yuen, Gallayanee Yaoyuneyong and Erik Johnson

Abstract Over the last decade, development of mixed-reality technologies has leapt forward. With the popularity of ever-more-powerful mobile devices, such as Smartphone's and tablets, mixed-reality applications now see widespread use. Additionally, mixed-reality glasses have now become affordable for average consumers. Many researchers and educators have explored the potential of mixed-reality technologies, collectively branded as Augmented Reality (AR) applications, to improve aspects of teaching and learning. This chapter closely examines the spectrum of mobile and stationary AR applications and delivery systems, and proposes new definitions of AR inclusive of current technologies. Additionally, AR applications designed for education are discussed, as well as projects and pedagogical approaches suitable for use with AR technologies. In particular, the potentials of mobile AR for promoting ubiquitous learning, immersive learning experiences, and constructivist, discovery-based learning are discussed.

A Book Chapter Submitted to: Reshaping Learning—The Frontiers of Learning Technologies in Global Context, Published by Springer, January 2, 2012.

S. C.-Y. Yuen (✉)
National Kaohsiung Normal University, Kaohsiung, Taiwan
e-mail: steve@yuen.us

G. Yaoyuneyong
Department of Marketing and Fashion Merchandising, The University of Southern Mississippi, Hattiesburg, MS, USA

E. Johnson
The University of Southern Mississippi, Hattiesburg, MS, USA

R. Huang et al. (eds.), *Reshaping Learning*, New Frontiers of Educational Research,
DOI: 10.1007/978-3-642-32301-0_17, © Springer-Verlag Berlin Heidelberg 2013

17.1 Introduction

As world culture continues to ride a technological wave, demonstrated in part by the rapid spread and adoption of Smartphone's, smartpads, and other ever-more-powerful mobile devices, Augmented Reality (AR) is on the verge of becoming a ubiquitous component of people's daily lives. In simple terms, AR refers to the use of technology to superimpose virtual content into users' perceptions of the real world, in real-time. AR can also refer to technologies for interacting with superimposed digital content.

Each year, the Emerging Technology Initiative of the New Media Consortium (NMC) seeks to identify and explore emerging technologies within society that demonstrate the potential to positively impact creative inquiry, learning, and education (NMC 2011). In both the most recent Horizon Reports (NMC 2010, 2011), Augmented Reality was highlighted as a technology that would soon be adopted on a large scale in universities around the world. Even earlier, in 2008, the IT research and advisory firm, Gartner, Inc., predicted that AR would be one of the top 10 disruptive technologies for 2008 to 2012, causing sweeping and disruptive changes in the accepted ways things are done, across fields and industries, and throughout society (Gartner Inc. 2008). For those who are not in the habit of routinely reading 'top-10' reviews and downloading the newest 'most popular' or 'most useful' smartphone apps, a quick search of YouTube for 'AR apps' will reveal that the future, in the form of Augmented Reality, is already here.

Numerous startups companies are unveiling Augmented Reality Web-browsers, capable of displaying extra information linked to places, images, objects, or even people who are viewed through the phone's camera. More impressive, though perhaps not yet as useful, some mobile apps are able to superimpose almost photorealistic 3D images, which are often animated and sometimes even interactive, over and around flat pictures or physical objects. A perusal of YouTube will also provide searchers with footage showcasing incredibly realistic AR installation pieces; these take the form of 'virtual mirrors' in which pedestrians can see themselves, 'reflected' in large projection screens. People are surprised to see themselves sharing reality with animated and interactive leopards, dolphins, or more fantastic creatures, such as huge dinosaurs or winged angels. At the same time, though somewhat more quietly, both the medical field and militaries around the world have been employing AR training programs for many years now. Additionally, sports fans will have noticed that their televised professional league games have long since been augmented by superimposed lines, markers, and informational graphics to help spectators more fully appreciate the events as they unfold. These and many more Augmented Reality applications are already well-established in society.

Today the number of available AR experiences continues to grow at an accelerating rate. Augmented Reality technologies offer an unparalleled opportunity to change the way we live with, perceive, and work with information. However, due to the 'magic' of AR technologies, and a perception that they require extreme confidence and knowledge of technology to utilize for instruction, many teachers may feel intimidated and unwilling to explore the possibilities offered by AR. For this reason, this chapter will begin with a brief discussion of the history and development of AR, and then continue with an exploration of the Mediated Reality and the Mixed Reality Continuum, arriving at a working definition of AR. We will then examine key concepts in AR, stationary and mobile AR display systems, and AR applications specifically designed for teaching and learning.

17.2 Understanding Augmented Reality

Currently, the term Augmented Reality (AR) is used by researchers and developers to refer to a wide spectrum of technologies which integrate computer generated content, including text, video, 2D virtual images, and 3D virtual objects, into users' perceptions of the real world. Early on, researchers tended to define AR in reference to specific facilitating devices, such as head mounted displays (HMDs). Eventually Azuma (1997), as well as other researchers (Kaufmann 2003; Zhou et al. 2008) presented a definition of AR involving three criteria: (a) the combination of virtual and real-world elements, (b) which are interactive in real-time, and which (c) are registered in 3D (i.e., the display of information or virtual content is intrinsically tied to real-world loci and orientation). A similar definition is proposed by Höllerer and Feiner (2004), who define AR systems as those which combine "real and computer-generated information in a real environment, interactively and in real time, and [which align] virtual objects with physical ones" (p. 2). A less inclusive definition is provided by Ludwig and Reimann (2005) who define AR as "human–computer-interaction, which adds virtual objects to real senses that are provided by a video camera in real time" (p. 4). More broadly, Zhou et al. (2008) define AR as any technology "which allows computer generated virtual imagery to exactly overlay physical objects in real time" (p. 193). However, though similar, these definitions differ in emphasis on details such as interaction, specific display methods, the necessity for visual or 3D content, or the criteria for precise real-world registration and orientation of content.

17.2.1 The Development of AR: A Brief History

One starting point for both Augmented Reality (AR) and Virtual Reality (VR) came in a paper titled "The Ultimate Display", in which Ivan Sutherland (1965) described a room, cabable of creating matter as output, which would allow the user to completely control their surrounding environment, thus simulating (or creating) any environment, situation, or scenario with perfect realism. This display, Sutherland wrote, "could literally be the Wonderland into which Alice walked" (Sutherland 1965, pp. 507–508). Later, in 1968, Sutherland developed the first

Head-Mounted Display (HMD), an array that was so heavy it was nicknamed "The Sword of Damocles" (Sutherland 1968). Recognizing the limitations of this first device, Sutherland continued to work on improving the technology.

For many reasons, researchers continued to pursue the creation of computer displays which can supplement, overlay, or replace users' perceptions of the real world. Azuma et al. (2001) argue that Augmented Reality (AR) systems are particularly desirable because they allow for the enhancement of users' perceptions of, knowledge about, and interactions with the real world. Schmalstieg (2001) argues that AR technologies have the potential to improve users' productivity in performing real world tasks. While development of the necessary technologies has been going on for several decades (Billinghurst and Henrysson 2009), progress in AR has only become significant in the past decade (Phan and Choo 2010). Figure 17.1 shows a brief timeline of the development of AR.

Zhou et al. (2008) gave a useful review of research in AR presented in Augmented Reality conferences over the last 10 years (e.g., ISMAR, ISAR, ISMR, and IWAR). In general, AR research has focused on (1) development of new technologies and devices for the input and tracking of real world content and the display of virtual content, or (2) development of new applications which utilize existing technologies and devices (Billinghurst and Henrysson 2009). According to Zhou et al. (2008), AR falls primarilly into five core areas: (a) techniques for tracking (20.1 %), (b) techniques for real-virtual interaction (14.7 %), (c) registration and calibration issues (14.1 %), (d) development of new AR applications (14.4 %), and (e) display techniques (11.8 %); while other research has examined: (a) evaluation and testing, (b) mobile and wearable AR platforms, (c) AR authoring, (d) visualization, (e) multimodal AR, and (f) rendering.

In the present day, in conjunction with a surge in deployed AR-capable smartphones and tablets, AR development is booming, particularly in entertainment and marketing (Hamilton 2011). In 2010, just over 11 million AR mobile applications were downloaded; however, by 2015, 1.4 billion AR apps will be

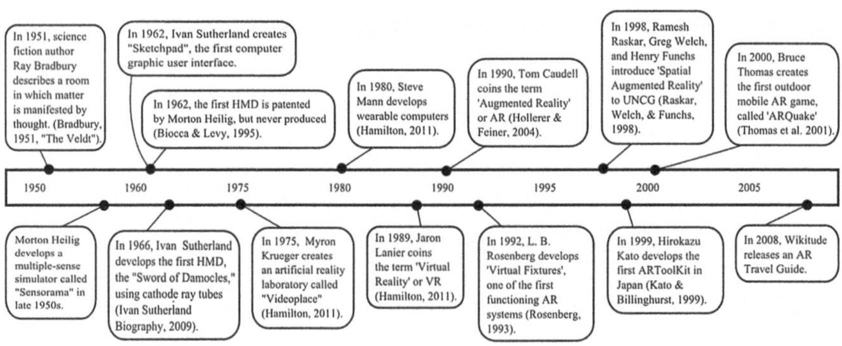

Source: Yuen, S., Yaoyuneyong, G., & Johnson, E. (2011). Augmented reality: An overview and five directions for AR in education. *Journal of Educational Technology Development and Exchange*, *4*(1), 119-140.

Fig. 17.1 The development of AR: an abbreviated timeline

downloaded annually (Juniper Research 2011). In addition, AR capable apps have diversified beyond location-based search apps to include AR games and AR apps centered on social networking, lifestyle, and personal healthcare (Grabham 2009).

For the moment, the general public may be more aware of AR applications in fields such as marketing (Zhu et al. 2004) and tourism/edutainment (Choubassi et al. 2010; Jihyun et al. 2008; Noh et al. 2009), in part because many of those applications involve mobile devices. However, AR systems are also currently deployed in other fields, including agriculture (Santana-Fernández et al. 2010; Vidal and Vidal 2010), architecture (Khan and Hornbæk 2011), urban and landscape planning (Graf et al. 2011; Portalés et al. 2010), construction (Kirchbach and Runde 2011), medicine (Ewers et al. 2005; Harders et al. 2007; Sielhorst et al. 2008), manufacturing (De Crescenzio et al. 2011; Shin and Dunston 2008), defense (Henderson and Feiner 2009), aeronautical maintenance (Hincapie et al. 2011), and education (Kaufmann and Schmalstieg 2003; Mejías Borrero and Andújar Márquez 2011; Núñez et al. 2008; Omolola et al. 2011).

17.2.2 Exploring Mediated Reality

Since the invention of computer graphics, researchers have worked on developing an array of interface technologies seeking to modify, interface with, augment, or even replace our perceptions of reality. On one extreme, devices such as human-sized VR spheres allow a user to enter into an immersive virtual world where everything they see, hear, and touch has been artificially created. Other interfaces involve mobile computers, which, combined with sophisticated glasses, project laser displays directly onto the wearer's retina. Like the rise of computing itself, various fields researching human–machine interfaces (HMIs) are emerging and evolving rapidly. This state of dynamic technological development has led to a multitude of semi-overlapping, but occasionally contradictory definitions for various display paradigms, with Augmented Reality being no exception.

To address this, Milgram and Kishino (1994) proposed a Mixed Reality spectrum categorizing technologies by the proportion of real-world content and virtual content users experience. On one side is the real world, in which everything experienced is part of our shared physical reality. On the far side are virtual worlds, where all content perceived is artificially generated and has no connection to real-world objects or locations. Between these two extremes are two conceptualized mixed reality environments: Augmented Reality (AR) in which computer-generated content is inserted into users' perceptions of the real world environment; and Augmented Virtuality (AV), in which the perceived world is mostly computer-generated with real-world content blended in or superimposed.

Figure 17.2 depicts the Mixed Reality (MR) Spectrum, or the Reality-Virtuality (RV) Continuum, as proposed by Milgram and Kishino (1994). Many students and instructors today will be familiar with applications from the entire range the Mixed Reality Spectrum.

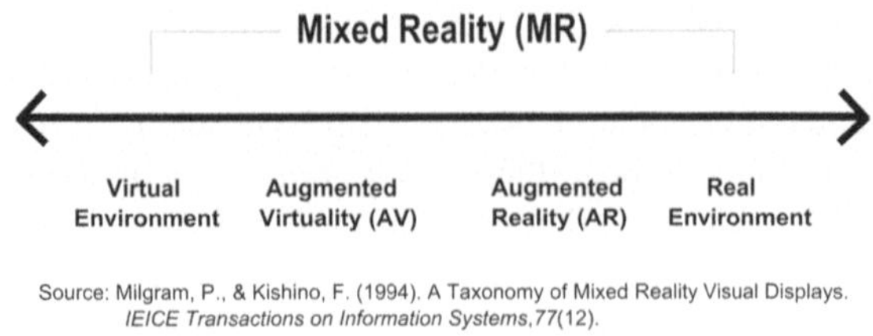

Fig. 17.2 The mixed reality (MR) spectrum

Virtual Environment (VE), or Virtual Reality (VR), applications present users with environments that are completely simulated and have no relation to the physical world. Virtual Reality is probably most familiar to students in the form of Massively Multiplayer Online Role-Playing Games, or MMORPGs (e.g., *Ultima Online*, *Everquest*, *Nexus: The Kingdom of the Winds*, *World of Warcraft*), in which users guide their characters (virtual avatars) through entirely virtual worlds, usually viewed through a computer monitor. Educators may be more familiar with *Second Life*, by Linden Lab, which functions as a more social/academic virtual world.

Augmented Virtuality (AV) applications are closer to the virtual end of the mixed reality spectrum, allowing users to experience environments that are mostly computer generated, but which incorporate real world elements. Numerous popular game consoles (e.g., *Nintendo Wii*, *PlayStation 3*, *Xbox 360*) have released sport-themed and other games in which users' real-world movements serve to direct avatars within virtual environments. For most users, these will be the most familiar examples of Augmented Virtuality (AV) applications.

Because it evolved as an extension of Virtual Reality (VR), Augmented Reality utilizes many of the same principles and technologies as VR (Milgram et al. 1994). Both VR and AR are characterized by interactivity, immersiveness, and information sensitivity. However, with AR applications, users' predominant source of input is the real world, with their perceptions of their surroundings improved by the addition of digital content (Azuma 1997). Many people will be most familiar with AR through smart phone or tablet virtual window applications which utilize GPS information to superimpose floating info-tags, or 3D hyperlinks, tied to real-world locations, over the user's view of the world through their mobile device webcam. Additionally, a growing number of games are being released both for mobile devices and stationary console systems in which 3D animated content seems to share space with users in the real world.

While the definition of VR remains more-or-less uncontested, it is somewhat harder to arrive at a definition which perfectly encompasses the applications and areas of research currently described as AR. The concept of Mediated Reality (Mann 2001; Mann and Fung 2002) can be used to describe a wide range of devices, including glasses, goggles, or Head-Mounted Displays (HMDs), which allow users to visually perceive the real world after the displayed information has been altered, either by adding, subtracting, or altering content (see Fig. 17.3). Some Modulated Reality (MR) applications include: (a) eyewear which distorts

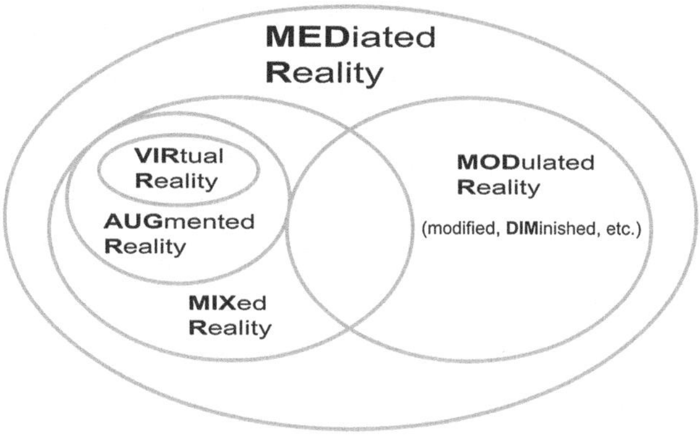

Source: Mann, S. (2002). Mediated reality with implementations for everyday life. *Presence: Teleoperators and Virtual Environments*. Retrieved from http://wearcam.org/presence-connect/

Fig. 17.3 Venn diagram illustrating mediated reality

the presented image around a blind-spot in the wearer's vision, (b) eyewear which magnifies the center of the user's field-of-view while leaving the rest of the scene unaltered, or (c) eyewear which heightens the contrast of the perceived scene, (i.e., making cracks and other obstacles in the terrain clearer without superimposing digital content). These applications all utilize optical displays and computers to alter the presented image; however, no virtual content is *added* to the user's experience, making these applications examples of Modulated Reality, rather than Augmented Reality (Mann 2001; Mann and Fung 2002).

Other mixed reality applications are actually Diminished Reality (DR) devices, with sunglasses serving as a low-tech example. A more complex DR device would be an interface which identifies billboards and other advertisements and removes them from the user's perception by overlaying them with other content (Mann and Niedzviecki 2001). While this example shows users' perceptions of reality being diminished, since real-world data is being deleted, it could also be considered an example of AR, in that the user's experience is being *improved* by the overlaying/addition of virtual content.

17.2.3 Defining Augmented Reality

One difficulty in defining AR has to do with the fact that most complex mixed reality or mediated reality applications utilize hardware that is similar, if not identical, such as glasses, goggles, or HMDs. Essentially, when considering worn devices, the determination of whether an application is AR, VR, AV, MR, or even DR, has more to do with intentions rather than the physical capabilities of the device.

AR applications currently represent the cutting edge of our culture's socio-technological development. Despite the definitions referenced earlier, there is currently no solid consensus as to what constitutes AR technologies, devices, or applications, or as to how possible AR applications should be conceptually organized. Initial definitions which define AR as technologies which superimpose virtual objects seamlessly in users' perceptions of the real world, are not sufficiently broad to cover the current devices branded as AR. Additionally, the availability of AR which utilizes multiple sensory channels (e.g., auditory, olfactory, haptic) renders merely visual definitions insufficient to deal with future developments in the field of AR (Hughes et al. 2005).

For this discussion, after careful consideration of devices and applications currently branded as AR technologies, the following definitions are proposed (see Table 17.1).

The proposed definitions recognize that research currently branded as AR fall into two categories: Sensory AR, which integrates virtual content into users' perceptions of the real World, and Manipulative AR, which implements intuitive motion- or gesture-based interaction with virtual content. AR content can be displayed through Overlay Devices, which present an image of the real world with superimposed virtual content, and through Projection Devices, which project virtual content into the physical world. Lastly, AR can be implemented through a Personal Interface, such that only one user perceives augmented content, or through a Shared Interface, such that multiple users simultaneously perceive the virtual content. While most AR and VR applications appeal primarily to the sense of sight, other senses may be engaged as well, through supplemental technologies.

In addition to applications which display virtual content through mobile devices, webcams, or HMDs, applications which project virtual content into the physical world (e.g., holographic projection televisions) are included, as are Human Machine Interfaces (HMIs), such as Wearable Projection Interfaces

Table 17.1 Conceptualizing augmented reality

Augmented reality (AR)	The use of overlay or projection devices to integrate virtual content into users' perceptions of the real world in real time; and/or the use of human machine Interface (HMI) technologies to implement intuitive movement based interaction with virtual content
Sensory AR	The use of overlay or projection devices to integrate virtual content into users' perceptions of the real world in real time
Manipulative AR	The use of human-machine interface (HMI) technologies to implement intuitive movement based interaction with virtual content
Overlay devices	Devices designed to integrate virtual content into users' perceptions of the real world
Projection devices	Devices designed to project virtual content into the real world environment
Personal AR	Mobile devices designed to privately integrate virtual content or information into users' perceptions of the real world
Shared AR	Devices designed to project virtual content or information into the shared real world environment such that the virtual content is perceived as being part of the unmediated reality of multiple users

(WPIs), which project digital content onto real world surfaces surrounding the user. Currently, Overlay Devices, Projection Devices, and various Manipulative AR interface devices are all branded as AR applications. However, as research continues and fields develop, these domains may disentangle themselves and become separate areas of inquiry.

17.3 The Mechanics of Augmented Reality

AR content can be displayed through an interface that is either mobile, or stationary. AR can also be conceptualized by the product, or experience, being delivered. This ranges from very simple AR experiences such as code-linked or image-linked media files, to far more complex AR experiences, such as virtual books, augmented object games, or intricate and interactive installation pieces.

17.3.1 Stationary AR Display Interfaces

Most stationary AR displays are Virtual Mirrors (see Table 17.2). A virtual mirror consists of any device or system which displays a 'reflection' of the real world, with virtual information or content superimposed such that it seems to exist in the real world. The most common stationary AR display system is a webcam equipped computer or game console running an AR application (program). The monitor/screen displays the user or space, along with added virtual content.

AR Installation Pieces, or AR Billboards, showing in public places (e.g., Times Square billboards, museum lobbies) utilize giant display screens, such as projection screens or digital billboards, to display very high quality, almost photo-realistic 3D animations interacting with pedestrians in real-time. In some cases possible interactions are pre-programmed, whereas in other cases human actors control 3D virtual characters, in order to create a realistic and unscripted interactive experience.

VR Workbenches, or AR Tables, are a stationary AR system with a long history of use for surgical training. Users wear HMDs, which are synced to a horizontal display surface, and use a haptic wand or glove for interaction. Highly detailed and interactive 'holographic' models are possible.

17.3.2 Mobile AR Display Interfaces

With the current proliferation and the ever-growing popularity of Smartphone, tablets, and other AR-capable mobile devices, many people's first experience with AR will be through downloadable apps, or software. Mobile AR apps can all be considered Virtual Windows, in that a camera and display screen allow the user to peer through the device to view the world marked up with AR content.

Table 17.2 Stationary AR (virtual mirrors and virtual tables)

Stationary AR overlay applications and display systems

Type	Common systems	Linking method	Content display	Example AR products	Implementation
Virtual mirrors	• Computer (Desktop/Laptop) • Display (Monitor/Tv/Projection Screen) • Webcam/Camera(s)	Code-linked (2D)	Non-anchored	Hyperlinked media	Easy
		Image-linked (2D)	Non-anchored	Hyperlinked media	Easy
		Surface-linked (3D)	Surface-tracking	3D Virtual books	Hard
		Object linked (3D)	Object-tracking	Augmented-object AR games	Professional
		Manually triggered	Non-anchored	Overlay mirror (2D)	Easy
		Non-linked	Object-tracking	Virtual dressing rooms (3D)	Professional
		Surface-linked (3D)	Human-tracking	AR installation pieces/AR billboards	Professional
	• Gaming Console • Display (Monitor/TV/Projection Screen) • Webcam/Camera(s) • Controller/Wand	Manually triggered	Controller-tracking Human-tracking	3D Virtual games	Professional
Virtual tables	• VR Workbench/AR Table • HMD • Wand/Smartglove	Manually triggered	Non-tracking	AR Surgery training tables	Professional

Mobile AR operates via two paradigms, either through location-recognition using GPS data, or through some form of image recognition using the mobile device's camera (see Table 17.3). Mobile AR apps are often subscription- or channel-based, allowing users, who are all utilizing the same application, to decide what content they perceive by signing up for a specific channel, or layer, of augmented content.

Unmanned Ariel Vehicles (UAVs), or Mobile Drones, offer another mobile platform for viewing AR content. Currently, AR Drones are in their infancy and offer limited AR experiences. For the most part, current drone-based AR focuses on implementing Virtual race-tracks and virtual dog-fighting, allowing users to race and to fire virtual weapons at other drones. While Drone AR currently focuses on interactions between drones, future developments will probably enable geo-tag and image-recognition apps similar to those available for smartphones and tablets.

17.3.3 Interacting with Virtual Content

Display technologies, which allow users to perceive virtual content, make up half of an AR system; the second half consists of the interface technologies which allow users to interact with virtual content. Table 17.4 presents an array of Human–Machine Interface (HMI) technologies ranging from simple input devices (e.g. keyboards), to high-tech mechanisms which detect and interpret neural impulses. Intermediate input strategies exist on a loose continuum of complexity. Motion-Sensing devices utilize an array of internal sensors, such as a GPS, a digital compass, and sensors to track and interpret their own movements. Motion-Tracking systems utilize computer vision to track human motions and gestures. Smartgear devices utilize both Motion-Sensing and Motion-Tracking to detect specific articulations, gestures, or movements of their wearer/user, as well as their own movements.

17.3.4 Adding Virtual Content to the Real World

Visual Capture describes the tendency of the human brain to believe what it sees in preference over other available senses (Welch 1978). It is this phenomenon that causes individuals, when watching television, to perceive actors' voices coming from their mouths, rather from the speakers (Welch 1978). Visual Capture leads to the Registration Problem, one of the fundamental difficulties in creating believable and immersive AR and VR experiences. Essentially, it is critical that real and virtual objects be correctly aligned and maintain their alignment. Even minor errors in tracking (the maintenance of real-virtual alignment), serve to impair users' sense of immersion when viewing AR content (Azuma 1997).

Understanding tracking is important for educators considering the use AR in education. Each type of tracking shapes the ultimate capabilities of the tool in

Table 17.3 Mobile AR (virtual windows)

Mobile AR overlay applications and display systems

Type	Common systems	Linking method	Content display	Example AR Products	Implementation
Geotag Apps	• Mobile Device (Smartphone/ Tablet/HMD) • GPS • Compass • Internal sensors • Camera	Point-linked (1D)	Point-tracking	Geo-referenced hyperlinked media	Easy
QR-Code Apps	Smartphone/Tablet/Mobile HMD	Code-linked (2D)	Non-anchored	Code-referenced hyperlinked media	Easy
Image-link Apps	• Camera	Image-linked (2D)	Non-anchored	Image-referenced Hyperlinked media	Easy
Augmented surface apps	• nternal sensors	Surface-linked (3D)	Surface-tracking	Augmented surface 3D content/games	Hard/ Professional
Augmented object Apps		Object-linked (3D)	Object-tracking	Augmented object 3D content/Games	Professional
Virtual costume apps		Human-linked (3D)	Human-tracking	3D Social networking links	Professional
Augmented environment games	Smartphone/Tablet/UAV (Drone) • Compass • Internal sensors • Camera	Object-linked (3D)	Object-tracking	Drone racing games, Drone combat games	Hard/ Professional

Table 17.4 Augmented reality input technologies

	Virtual content manipulation technologies			
Simple input You press/ touch/toggle it…	Motion-sensing You wave it around…	Motion-tracking It watches you…	Smartgear It knows where you are…	Bio-sensors It knows what you're thinking…
Keyboard Mouse Joystick Controller Trackpad Touchscreen	Controllers/Wands GPS equipped devices	Motion-tracking cameras	Spartphones/Tablets Headsets (Helmets, HMDs, HUDs, Goggles, Glasses, Contacts) WPIs Smartsuits/Datasuits Smartgloves/Datagloves/ Powergloves	HMI headbands HMI Inplants

question. It should be noted that there is a distinction between *recognition* of a code, image, or object, and *tracking* a code, image, or object. Recognition allows an application to trigger the display of content, whereas tracking refers to the ability to keep 2D or 3D content aligned with physical elements.

Mobile overlay apps which do not use GPS data, instead recognize and track images, from square fiducial markers (black-and-white AR markers) to more complex, but still sharp-edged images, such as magazine covers. The term, Markerless Tracking, generally refers to systems which do not require the use of overtly obvious markers. Figure 17.4 depicts various recognition (linking) techniques, while Tables 17.2 and 17.3 illustrate different combinations of Linking and Tracking.

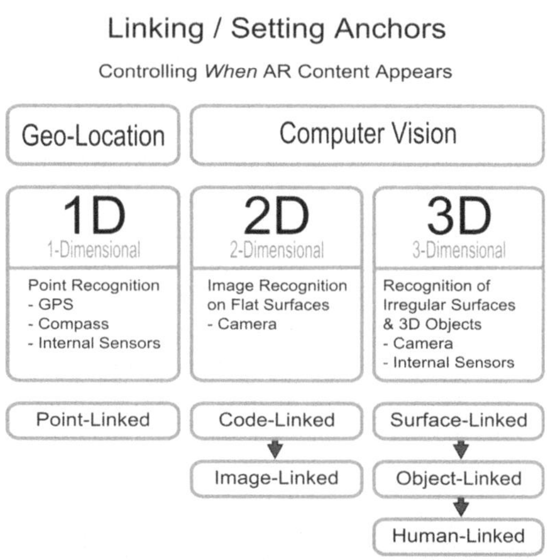

Fig. 17.4 Recognition of real-world content

17.4 AR Applications in Education

Ludwig and Reimann (2005) categorize AR applications as falling primarily into three categories: (1) presentation and visualization, (2) industry, and (3) edutainment. A later analysis by Hamilton (2011) examines numerous AR applications designed for education, as well as those developed for a variety of industries, including: gaming, media and entertainment, tourism and travel, marketing, social networking, and for the enhancement or augmentation of everyday life.

A discerning critic may note that numerous current AR applications, particularly those designed for mobile devices, currently seem transient, or gimmicky (Hamilton 2011). Despite this, many early AR applications, such as those discussed by Azuma (1997), have continued to be used and refined, and seem destined to play important roles in our evolving society. With this in mind, we will examine a number of AR applications that have been applied with some success to education, or which seem eminently suitable for use in teaching and learning.

17.4.1 AR Books

One way to bridge the gap between the digital and physical world is through AR books. Essentially, an AR book is an Augmented Object which combines 3D animations with image-linked video and/or audio files. A person reading an AR book, with the help of a virtual mirror (a desktop and a webcam), or AR glasses, will see 3D animations linked to the pictures and pages of a physical book. Additionally, some pictures in the book can cause the computer to display videos or other media related to the topic being presented on that page. Augmented books have tremendous potential to provide students with topic-relevant interactive experiences and 3D presentations, all very likely to appeal to digital native learners.

An excellent example is an AR book titled, "*The Future is Wild: The Living Book*" (developed by Metaio), which contains 42 integrated AR features (Yuen 2010, Nov 19). Other examples include the AR popup books (Digilog Books) designed by the Gwangju Institute of Science and Technology (GIST), in South Korea, or the AR textbooks designed by the Institute for the Promotion of Teaching Science and Technology, in Thailand (Yuen 2010, Nov 19). MagicBook, an interface system for creating AR books, allows users to create animated and even interactive 3D models using the text or illustrations on the pages of a conventional book (Billingurst 2002).

Other AR applications, such as LearnAR (www.learnar.org), function similarly to AR books, using a monitor, a webcam, and printable markers to let students explore interactive 3D learning materials designed to supplement various academic topics. One advantage of interactive AR learning materials is flexibility, since they can be used both in-class by students and teachers, and at home, so that students can explore topics at their own pace.

As constructivist learning tools, interactive AR storybooks can provide a pathway allowing learners to experience multiple levels of reality (Billinghurst et al. 2001). On one level, learners can interact and cooperate while holding and using the physical, real-world book. On another level, the popup, animated, 3D content of AR books can be simultaneously viewed by multiple users. On a third level, with AR gear, users can switch to a AV mode, virtually flying or teleporting 'down' into the 3D landscape created by the book, where they can interact with virtual objects, characters, and the other readers, as the story unfolds. In this process, learners have transitioned, in their perceptions, from the real world, to a virtually augmented physical world, and finally to a completely immersive, interactive, and completely virtual setting.

17.4.2 AR Gaming

Games have long been appreciated by educators as a way to engage students in learning. With AR technology, AR code markers can be utilized to make conventional flat boards into 3D animated settings when viewed through a webcam or mobile device. Another approach to AR educational gaming, modeled after the "quests" presented in popular computer games in the RPG (Role-Playing Game) genre, is to create group problem-solving, mystery, or exploration Augmented Environment games. In Augmented Environment games, students use mobile devices to explore their real-world school or surroundings, all while interacting with scripted 3D 'actors', or Non-Player Characters (NPCs), who play parts in a scenario which the students must solve or complete. In this type of game the 3D content, including objects and NPCs, can be geo-referenced and/or triggered by images or AR codes. Some AR games that have been tested in the academic setting with some success include *River City* and *Alien Contact* (Hough 2007).

Through AR games, educators have the chance to let students experience a form of highly interactive, collaborative, problem-based learning that holds students' attention while teaching a variety of highly transferable skills. So far, AR games tested in an academic setting have received very positive responses from both students and educators (Hough 2007). However, some new problems may arise, such as the need for teachers to be able to troubleshoot technical glitches, and the hazard that students may become so engaged in the game that they become oblivious to their real-world surroundings, which may pose a safety risk (Dunleavy et al. 2009).

Similar to the Augmented Environment games, AR applications which attach information to environments, objects, animals, plants, and people (e.g., Argon, Junaio, Layar, Wikitude,) open the door for discovery-based learning. Collectively, these apps are known as AR Web Browsers. Directly relevant to education in history, art, archaeology, and other fields, Virtual Buildings, or large Augmented Environments, supply an exciting new learning resource made possible by AR mobile browsers. While historic sites have often supplied maps and supplementary materials, such as informational pamphlets, AR browsers allow for historic tours of real-world locations which include 3D overlay maps, virtual structures, and linked media content.

Another exciting example of an Augmented Environment project is the iTacitus AR project (www.itacitus.org), funded by the EU, which will let visitors see and hear historic events play out as they view the real-world location through a mobile device. Rather than marking up locations, another tool, SREngine (Scene Recognition Engine), uses image recognition to give users information about everyday objects in the real world. In addition to letting shoppers compare product prices, SREngine will be able to help students learn to identify plants, animals, and other real-world content.

AR games offer a particularly useful tool for constructivist teachers. Dede (2008) argues that participation in immersive and interactive AR games can help students acquire skills such as: noticing and identifying patterns, creating and using sophisticated tools, models, and representations, communicating reasonably with individuals who hold different perspectives, and learning to dispassionately judge the value of different viewpoints (Dede 2008). Steinkuehler and Williams (2006) explain that the process of learning to adopt virtual personas while participating virtual tasks, problems, and games, can help learners disassociate themselves from blocks and negative self-conceptions that could otherwise act as barriers to their learning. Another advantage offered by immersive AR games is that, in the process of virtually shifting their identity, learners are able to gain greater awareness of multiple perspectives (Dede 2008). A last significant bonus of AR games is that the problem solving implicit in scenario-based AR learning experiences creates a situated learning environment, increasing the likelihood that students will be able to transfer their knowledge to deal with future problems and tasks, both in other games and in later real-life experiences (Dede 2008). For the future, researchers are experimenting with games as a medium to build users' interest in factual data, such as regional socio-economic statistical data (Diakopoulos et al. 2011). If this is successful, AR gaming could become a powerful tool promoting social reform.

17.4.3 Object Modeling

One capability of AR that makes it ideal for learning inquiry-driven, exploratory learning is the capacity for students to rapidly model virtual objects, in real-time, through intuitive interfaces. For example, the University of Canterbury Human Interface Technology Laboratory has created an AR tool that transforms sketches into 3D objects. Through image-capture Manipulative AR technology, students can draw on slips of paper to manipulate the physical properties of their created objects. This technology is currently being explored by architecture students at Mauricio De Nassau College, in Brazil, to create 3D scale models of student work, vastly speeding up the architectural proposal process.

17.4.4 Skills Training

One of the longest-standing applications for AR as an educational tool is in the area of skills training. Both the military and medical industries have been driving forces behind the initial development of AR technology, with the express purpose of giving users powerful in situ learning experiences and step-by-step contextual guides for tasks such as vehicle or aircraft repair maintenance, and numerous surgical operations. For skills training applications AR HMDs, goggles, or glasses, are used to visually demonstrate each step in a task, in 3D, while identifying necessary tools, and augmenting each step with supplementary text and audio instruction. Example applications include printer repair (Azuma 1997), 3D overlay ultrasound display (University of North Carolina at Chapel Hill), and repair and maintenance of armored military vehicles (ARMAR, Columbia University's Computer Graphics and User Interface Lab). Generally, users, such as mechanics utilizing the ARMAR system, find AR skills training or guidance tools to be intuitive and satisfying (Saenz 2010, Jan 11).

17.5 Research on AR in Education

Due to the rapidly developing functionality of Augmented Reality applications, and considering AR's manifest ability to serve as an improved user interface, researchers believe that Augmented Reality has potential to vastly transform teaching and learning (Billinghurst 2002; Cooperstock 2001; Klopfer and Squire 2008; Shelton and Hedley 2002). Through Augmented Reality, educators gain access to a powerful tool to: (1) engage, stimulate, and motivate learners to explore class materials from different perspectives (Kerawalla et al. 2006); (2) facilitate subjects where students are unlikely to have access to first-hand real-world experience (e.g. geography, astronomy, history) (Shelton and Hedley 2002); (3) enhance peer-to-peer and student–teacher collaboration (Billinghurst 2002); (4) help foster students' imagination and creativity (Klopfer and Yoon 2004); (5) allow students to control the path and pace of their own learning (Hamilton and Olenewa 2010), and (6) support authentic learning environments appropriate for various learning styles (Classroom Learning with AR 2010).

The educational potential of AR has been examined by researchers from multiple fields and disciplines. In medicine, Sielhorst et al. (2004) have examined AR as a tool enabling medical training simulations. Similarly, Liu et al. (2010) have examined applications of AR in general anesthesia education. A review of research into AR as a tool for medical display is provided by Sielhorst et al. (2008). Liarokapis et al. (2004) examined AR as a means of allowing students to explore concepts in mechanical engineering. Other research has focused on the use of AR as a means of promoting learning in mathematics and geometry (Kaufmann 2003; Kaufmann and Dünser 2007; Kaufmann and Schmalstieg 2003).

Additionally, reaserchers have explored the efficacy of AR applications for within fields such as: architecture (Billinghurst and Henrysson 2009; Thomas et al. 2001), interior design (Phan and Choo 2010), e-learning systems (Cho et al. 2007; Liarokapis et al. 2002), e-commerce (Zhu et al. 2004), and science education (Kerawalla et al. 2006; Shelton and Hedley 2002).

17.6 Pedagogical Perspectives on AR

With a working knowledge of AR display and interface technologies, as well as of methods of triggering virtual content (e.g., by location, code, image, or object), and methods of tracking (i.e., of orienting and aligning 2D or 3D content with codes, images, surfaces, objects, faces, arms, hands, fingers, etc.), it becomes possible for educators to seriously consider the options made available through any given AR system. While educators may adapt a given AR application to serve educational purposes, some applications, due to their inherent nature, easily serve to promote teaching and learning, especially when used in conjunction with a particular pedagogical approach, while other AR applications may be very difficult for teachers to utilize effectively. In the following section, we discuss three ways in which Augmented Reality ties in well with constructivist approaches to teaching and learning.

17.6.1 Ubiquitous Learning

One of the most immediate advantages of the transition to AR-enabled mobile technology is the possibility of increasingly useful ways to access information. Through developments in digital media systems and mobile devices, all of which are currently beginning to integrate AR interfaces and services, the paradigm of ubiquitous learning, a long-held goal for many educators, can become a reality (Cope and Kalantzis 2008).

Ubiquitous learning has developed as an extension of the concept of ubiquitous computing, whereby computers are seamlessly integrated into the physical world (Jones and Jo 2004). While early 'wearable' computer interfaces often included cumbersome equipment, modern mobile devices, including smartphones, smartpads (and, now, AR googles), make it possible for an ever larger portion of the population to live such that they are never without access to computers and online information. In this sense, current and future generations of learners now dwell in a ubiquitous computing environment.

Educators focusing on pedagogical theory and curricular design have wrestled with the possibilities, advantages, and disadvantages of e-learning, wherein students' learning is facilitated by computers, both with supervision, and in ways that are quasi-independent, or self-guided. However, even as awareness of the need to integrate computers into education spread through the teaching world, mobile devices rose to prominence, allowing cutting-edge educators to create mobile-learning (m-learning) environments (Cope and Kalantzis 2008).

It is through a combination of e-learning and m-learning that ubiquitous learning (u-learning) becomes possible (Cope and Kalantzis 2008). Through any laptop or desktop computer, or through smartphones, smartpads, or tablets, learners are able to receive or access class information, at any time, in any place, without constraints. Additionally, learners are able to synchronously or asynchronously communicate with, collaborate with, and receive on-demand support from classmates, peers, parents, instructors, tutors, other mentors, or experts on various topics who are willing to share their knowledge.

A well-designed u-learning environment can provide "an interoperable, pervasive, and seamless learning architecture to connect, integrate, and share three major dimensions of learning resources: learning collaborators, learning contents, and learning services" (Yang 2006, p. 188). Recent research in ubiquitous learning explores the importance of context-aware u-learning, "an innovative approach that integrates wireless, mobile, and context-awareness technologies to detect the situation of learners in the real world" in order to provide personalized, adaptive guidance, or support (Hwang et al. 2009, p. 402).

U-learning can empower students, giving them complete control of when and where they study, and allowing themselves to become immersed in the learning process (Zhao and Okamoto 2011). The challenge for educators designing u-learning environments and activities is to find intuitive ways to identify the correct learning collaborators, the necessary learning contents, and the useful learning services, and to create a system whereby students may access them at the right places and times (Yang 2006).

Through mechanisms such as schedule reminders, mentor recommendations, and the monitoring of students' learning status, u-learning environments have been shown to enhance students' achievement and accomplishment of tasks and learning goals, as well as their overall academic performance (Chen et al. 2008). However, while studies have indicated considerable support and interest in m-learning, little research has addressed ways to integrate mobile devices with web-based e-learning systems in order to fully-functional u-learning environments (Chen et al. 2008). The current lack of practical context-aware u-learning applications may be explained by most educators' lack of experience developing contextually-aware u-learning environments, or designing appropriate learning activities (Hwang et al. 2009).

The difficulty in implementing contextually-aware u-learning environments is understandable, because ideally they should fulfill a number of requirements: Accessability and Immediacy (learners should be able to access their work and relevant information from anywhere, at any time, such that their learning can be self-guided and they can solve problems more quickly), Permanency (learners' work and learning processes should be automatically recorded until deliberately deleted), Interactivity (learners should be able to synchronously and asynchronously interact with peers, teachers, or experts, such that knowledge, guidance, and support are readily available), and finally, Situated Learning (the learning should be integrated and embedded in daily life and activities) (Ogata and Yano 2004).

The last requirement, situated learning, has been shown to be extremely important; students have been shown to prefer 'authentic activities' in which they can work on problems from and within the real world (Hwang et al. 2009). The desire for their learning to be 'real' is perhaps one of the ways in which AR may be most helpful in creating contextually-aware u-learning environments. Through AR, online services and the information available through the internet are transforming from a Web located under reality, moving in wires beneath the floor or over our heads, to a all-encompasing field, surrounding us and filling our environment. Through mobile AR, learners will be able to instantly access location-specific information, compiled and made available by numberous organizations and individuals. Users will be able to visually scan their vicinity for Tweets from users who are physically nearby, or for location-specific trivia and historical information (wikitude.org), or even for the location of their own parked car (Raju 2009).

17.6.2 Discovery-Based Learning

Constructivist approaches to teaching and learning tend to focus on learning that is active, problem-based, and inquiry-based driven. Teachers are envisioned as facilitators, guiding students to explore, experiment, make inferences, draw conclusions, and collaborate. Just as mobile AR makes ubiquitous learning possible, it tremendously facilitates discovery-driven learning. Field trips can become virtual scavenger hunts in which students seek out AR codes, images, or specific information from different locations of interest. Additionally, AR Web Browsers enable teachers to create just-in-time quizzes, activated via GPS coordinates or image-recognition, whenever students encounter items of significance. As they explore, AR browsers can provide learners with up-to-the minute information regarding concepts, objects, and locations.

Other tenets of constructivist learning include the idea that knowledge is generated by the individual, as well as through collaboration, and that learning by teaching adds significance and engages students. Using AR Web browsers (e.g., Argon, Junaio, Layar, Wikitude) and 3D content platforms (e.g., daqri, Farrago), students can collaborate to create their own real-world Webquests, puzzles, and learning games, as well as informative content pertinent to concepts, areas, or events being studied. As an added bonus, student-generated content can then be made available publically, so everyone else using the same mobile application could then access the content when they visit the site in question. In this manner, AR Web Browsers will allow students to create and distribute knowledge as they learn (De Lorenzo 2009). Through learning by creating content, students' confidence in their own capacity, both for learning and for teaching, can go up, further sustaining their motivation for learning.

17.6.3 Immersive Learning

The concept of immersion exists in multiple contexts. For instance, it is common for those who love to read, to forget their surroundings for a while, tuning them out, while they are deeply engaged in a book. When something from the 'outside' world, such as multiple repetitions of the reader's name, finally penetrates, the world comes rushing back into their awareness, like a wave of sound and sensation. Immersion extends to other areas of aesthetic experience as well. People can be absorbed by music, cinema, art, performances, a view, or even by their own thoughts. These experiences are described by a mélange of words, including immersion. However, in the context of e-learning, m-learning, or u-learning, immersion has a more specific set of meanings tied to educational theory, to theories of game design and analysis, and to the physical and visual nature of VR and AR experiences.

Game designers deliberately target four categories of immersion, in order to make their products as engaging as possible: Sensory-Motoric Immersion, Cognitive Immersion, Emotional Immersion, and Spatial Immersion (Björk and Holopainen 2004). Sensory Motoric Immersion refers to the sense of focus, often referred to as 'being in the zone', felt by those engaged in activities that involve physical skill, timing, or dexterity, both in virtual games and in the physical world. Cognitive Immersion refers to the cerebral pleasure felt when making correct choices while solving difficult problems. Emotional Immersion refers to the feelings of attachment and investment felt by those experiencing or participating in stories, such as through books, movies, theatre, role-playing games, and story-driven video games. Spatial Immersion, which is of particular importance in VR and AR applications, refers to the feelings of enjoyment and fascination a user experiences when surrounded by simulated or augmented environments that are particularly complete, engrossing, and 'convincing' (Nechvatal 1999).

Educators should consider all of the four above-mentioned categories of immersion, noting that, regardless of media format, feelings of immersion relate to participants' subjective impression that what they are experiencing is comprehensive, realistic, valid, and meaningful (Lessiter et al. 2001; Sadowski and Stanney 2002). For students, participation in a digital immersive learning experience involves the willing suspension of disbelief, which is achievable when the educator designing the experience makes use of sensory, actional, and symbolic factors (Dede et al. 2000), thus promoting sensory-motoric, cognitive, and emotional immersion. When educators successfully create immersive digital experiences, students' learning can be enhanced in multiple ways, including: enabling multiple perspectives (which help clarify complex phenomenon), enabling situated learning (in which the learning activities directly mirror authentic, real-world problem-solving), and by facilitating transfer (the students' ability to apply what they have learned to other real-world problems or contexts) (Dede 2009).

In terms of learning theory, the premise of immersive learning is that students, as members of an active learning community, work together to explore complex situations related to realistic problem scenarios tied to the topic or curriculum, which makes immersive learning both compatible with and akin to principles of learner-centered design and situated learning (Blashki et al. 2007; Savin-Baden 2000). Within learner-centered immersive learning environments, learners participate in, direct, create, and implement engaging learning activities, both for themselves and for successive groups of students (Blashki et al. 2007).

Because many current immersive learning environments focus on resource-intensive VR and AR simulations it is easy to presuppose that immersive learning requires highly advanced technology; however, researchers argue that it is not the technology that makes learning environments immersive, rather it is the degree to which the included tasks and activities require realistic, real-world problem-solving (Herrington et al. 2007).

With this being said, technologically intensive AR technology, focused on Mediated Immersion, allows for teaching and learning within immersive participatory simulations wherein the physical world is supplemented with virtual objects, environments, and people (Herrington et al. 2007). In addition to increasing the fidelity of the world through the addition of richly sensory objects and environments, Mediated Immersion AR can allow learners to engage in non-proximal face-to-face communication, and can promote kinesthetic learning through physical movement (Dunleavy et al. 2009). Current research demonstrates that use of emerging AR interfaces for the creation of collaborative, mediated, immersive educational environments, which by their nature enable multiple learning modalities, can dramatically shape users' learning styles, preferences, characteristics, strengths, skills, and perceptions of knowledge (Clark et al. 2008; Dede 2005; Dunleavy et al. 2009).

Educators concerned with understanding currently existing AR applications, as well as with integrating AR into their own curricular design, should be familiar with the different types of immersion and the ways in which they can promote students' engagement and learning success. In a Mixed Reality Environment, including those presented by Virtual Reality systems and both Overlay (Personal) Augmented Reality (AR) systems and Projection (Shared) AR systems, users are able to perceive both the physical world and virtual content. Within the context of Mixed Reality systems, Spatial Immersion, or the degree to which an interface allows the user to forget the presence of the interface, can be particularly important. Display interface devices which are highly noticeable, and thus distract the user from the Virtual Content they are displaying, are low-immersion interfaces, while display devices which are less-noticeable, or very easy to forget, allow for high-immersion experiences (see Table 17.5).

When considering Augmented Reality, devices such as Virtual Mirrors, which present virtual content as mixed with reality in a 'reflection', spatial immersion, which affects overall impact, can be less than with mobile Virtual Windows, which allow users to see virtual content as they 'look through' their mobile device at the physical world surrounding them. Spatial immersion in AR is highest with devices which are worn (smartgear, smartwear), such as AR glasses, which allow the user to forget that they are actually using a device to perceive the virtual content

Table 17.5 Spatial immersion in mixed reality content display interfaces

	Mixed reality virtual content display interfaces		
	VR Devices Virtual reality	Overlay Devices Augmented reality	Projection Devices The real world (Shared AR)
Low immersion	*Shallow VR* (Desktop VR) • Second Life • 1st Person POV Games • MMORPGS	*Stationary AR* • Virtual mirrors (Camera + Video Display) • Virtual Screens (Augmented Televised Content)	*Standard projection Screens* • Slide Projectors/Video Projectors *Glass single-pane hologram projection* *Unidirectional holographic projection*
High immersion	*Deep VR* (Cave/Headset VR) • VR BOOMs • VR Caves (Projection Screen + Accessories) • VR Spheres (Headsets + Accessories) • VR Suspension Rigs (Headsets + Accessories)	*Moble AR (Personal AR)* • Mobile virtual windows (Smartphones, Tablets) • Vechicle mounted virtual windows (Vehicle HUDs)	*Multi-surface interface projection* • Stationary multi-Surface projection (Desktop projection interface system) • Mobile multi-surface projection (Mobile projection interface gear) *Particle-vapor hologram projection* *Glass multi-pane hologram projection* *Multidirectional Holographic projection* *VR CAVEs*
Total immersion	*Seamless VR* • Multi-sensory projection holodecks • VR implants • VR BCI headbands	*Seamless AR* • HMDs, Goggles, Glasses, Contacts • AR implants • AR BCI headbands	*Omnidirectional holographic projection* *Multi-sensory projection systems* • Audio spotlights (Tight Beam Sound) • Tactile holography

intermixed in the physical world around them. In the future, AR interfaces which allow for total immersion, or completely seamless intermixing of real and virtual content, may be possible through advances in neural interface implants and possibly through non-invasive Brain-Control Interfaces (BCIs) such as headbands, which utilize electromagnetic induction to stimulate various sensory centers of the brain.

For educators, awareness of the degree to which an AR experience is spatially immersive is important because studies have demonstrated that immersion in a digital or mixed reality environment can enhance learning in multiple ways (Dede 2009). For example, increased spatial immersion facilitates students' experience of multiple perspectives by allowing them to shift between exocentric (external to an object) and egocentric (internal to an object) frames of reference (Dede 2009). Each frame of reference has been shown to have different advantages for learning, such as increasing motivation, facilitating concrete, embodied learning, and fostering abstract and symbolic insights (Dede 2009).

Spatial Immersion, particularly through AR distance learning, can also facilitate situated learning (Dede 2009). In a situated learning environment, students experience authentic activities, context, and assesment in conjunction with mentoring, guidance, modeling, and peripheral participation from experts in a field (Dede 2009). In other words, through AR, students can engage in virtual field trips, or virtual laboratory learning, actually working to help solve real-world problems, with the guidance of practitioners in a field. Through activities of this sort, students can gain experience interacting with their peers, and can be inspired to pursue more advanced scholarship through observation of and interaction with more knowleadgeable mentors. Virtual real-world experience can also facilitate transfer, or the ability of students to apply knowledge learned in one situation to tasks encountered in another situation, and more pointedly to other problems encountered in the real world (Dede 2009).

Additionally, through the use of immersive AR technologies, students can utilize otherwise impossible physical models of abstract concepts in order to make sense of difficult scientific concepts (Dede et al. 1999). For example, working with AR visualization tools, students could perceive individual cells, and make decisions affecting them, in a displayed virtual scenario, all while within their classroom environment (O'Leary and Sherman 2008). The use of manipulatable AR models of this sort can facilitate a constructivist learning environment which can, in turn, help students memory and ability to construct more accurate mental models (Dede et al. 1999).

Dede (2008) argues that education situated in immersive activities, such as those which can be facilitated by AR, can supply modern learners with a critically needed twenty-first century education, preparing students for the challenges inherent in our technologically-advancing, rapidly-changing world. Modern learners, for example, need skills and experience in order to work on problems as part of a distributed but interactive team. In this way students can be prepared for future career challenges which may be too big to be handled, or even understood, by individuals working alone. In order to make meaning out of an ever-more-complex reality, learners must acquire the skills associated with both group reflection and self-guided reflection (Dede 2008).

17.7 The Future of Augmented Reality and Education

As information technologies transform, educators adapt and develop new methods of teaching and learning (Dede 2008). Simultaneous to this development, however, the characteristics of learners are constantly evolving; as are society's expectations regarding the areas of knowledge, expertise, and skill sets that are necessary for success (Dede 2008).

Today Augmented Reality applications are moving from the new into the commonplace. The affordability and increasing power of mobile devices, in terms of processing, display, and available bandwidth, are making the widespread use of AR feasible. Experts in industry have already predicted that the evolution and dispersal of AR-capable mobile devices will continue to escalate (Dede 2008). Before very much longer, both students and members of the general public will consider intuitive AR displays and interfaces to be a standard by which both technological and educational quality should be measured. Whether or not educators are prepared, the 2011 Horizon Report and other indicators predict the widespread use of AR technology in US colleges within the next 2 to 3 years (NMC 2011).

This is an exciting time. In many fields AR has demonstrated the potential to bring about sweeping improvements in teaching and learning. Training utilizing AR simulation, sometimes augmented by haptic feedback devices, has been linked to improved performance in multiple physical skills and tasks (Dede 2009; Saenz 2010), from the repair of armored vehicles to delicate surgical operations. Educators may be taken aback by the degree of specialized skill necessary to create AR educational tools for high-level tasks, such as medical or surgical procedures. However, each AR resource, once created, can become a permanent resource, indefinitely available to future learners.

Even more exciting, a growing array of AR Web-browsers, including Argon, Junaio, Layar, and Wikitude allow educators, with no background in programming or graphics, to create AR learning tools ranging from study guides augmented with linked media, to exploratory problem-solving and puzzle games where 3D content and other media are tied to real-world locations. Tools such as the Farrago AR app (Hololabs), which is branded as a user-friendly AR creation tool, allow users to create image and code-linked 3D AR content on-the-fly, using a smartphone or smartpad. This means that individual instructors, with no special training, can create dynamic, engaging, multimedia AR experiences for teaching and learning. As educators begin to explore the capabilities of the tools now available to them, new and exciting ways of teaching, learning, and guiding learner exploration will be devised.

Current trends are towards increasing focus on improved distance education, through both AR and VR interfaces, as well as through traditional web channels. This technological push is one that many educators have grown used to riding. Numerous instructors are in fact on the forefront of the technological wave, continuously pushing forward with new innovations and uses for emerging technologies. As AR becomes an ever-more-central aspect of society, researchers and educators should continue to monitor the changes AR makes possible, evaluate the ramifications of AR for education, and continuously experiment with ways in which AR can be used to improve teaching and learning.

References

Azuma RT (1997) A survey of augmented reality. Presence Teleoperators Virtual Environ 6(4):355–385

Azuma R, Baillot Y, Behringer R, Feiner S, Julier S, MacIntyre B (2001) Recent advances in augmented reality. Comput Graph 21(6):1–15

Billinghurst M (2002) Augmented reality in education. New Horizons for learning. http://www.newhorizons.org/strategies/technology/billinghurst.htm

Billinghurst M, Kato H, Poupyrev I (2001). The magic book: a transitional AR interface. Comput Graph 25:745–753

Billinghurst M, Henrysson A (2009) Mobile architectural augmented reality. In: Wang X, Schnabel M, (eds) Mixed reality in architecture, design and construction, vol 3, pp 93–104

Björk S, Holopainen J (2004) Patterns in game design. Independence. Charles River Media, Florence

Blashki K, Nichol S, Jia D, Prompramote S (2007) 'The future is old': Immersive learning with generation Y engineering students. Eur J Eng Educ 32(4):409–420

Chen GD, Chang CK, Wang CY (2008) Ubiquitous learning website: scaffold learners by mobile devices with information-aware techniques. Comput Educ 50:77–90

Cho K, Lee J, Soh J, Lee J, Yang HS (2007) A realisitc e-learning system based on mixed reality. In: Proceedings from 13th international conference on virtual system and multimedia (VSMM), pp 57–64

Choubassi ME, Nestares O, Wu Y, Kozintsev I, Haussecker H (2010) An augmented reality tourist guide on your mobile devices. Adv Multimed Model 5916:588–602. doi:10.1007/978-3-642-11301-7_58

Clarke J, Dede C, Dieterle E (2008) Emerging technologies for collaborative, mediated, immersive learning. In: Voogt J, Knezek G (eds) The international handbook of technology in primary and secondary education. Springer, New York, pp 901–910

Classroom Learning with AR (2010) Trends in EdTech wiki. http://augreality.pbworks.com/Classroom-Learning-with-AR. Accessed 25 July 2010

Cooperstock JR (2001) The classroom of the future: enhancing education through augmented reality. In: Proceedings from HCI international, pp 688–692

Cope B, Kalantzis M (2008) Ubiquitous learning: an agenda for educational transformation. In; Proceedings of the 6th international conference on networked learning, Halkidiki, greece. www.networkedlearningconference.org.uk/past/nlc2008/abstracts/PDFs/Cope_576-582.pdf

De Crescenzio F, Fantini M, Persiani F, Di Stefano L, Azzari P, Salti S (2011) Augmented reality for aircraft maintenance training and operations support. Comput Graph Appl, IEEE 31(1):90–101. doi:10.1109/MCG.2011.4

Dede C (2005) Planning for neomillennial learning styles. EDUCASE Q 28(1):7–12

Dede C (Speaker) (2008) Immersive interfaces for learning: opportunities and perils [Motion picture]. (Available from The President and Fellows of Harvard College). http://cyber.law.harvard.edu/interactive/events/luncheon/2008/12/dede

Dede C (2009) Immersive interfaces for engagement and learning. Science 323:66–68. doi:10.1126/science.1167311

Dede C, Salzman M, Loftin RB, Ash K (2000) The design of immersive virtual learning environments: fostering deep understandings of complex scientific knowledge. In: Jacobson MJ, Kozma RB (eds) Innovations in science and mathematics education: advanced designs for technologies of learning. Lawrence Erlbaum Associates, New Jersey, pp 361–413

Dede C, Salzman M, Loftin B, Sprague D (1999) Multisensory immersion as a modeling environment for learning complex scientific concepts. In: Feurzeig W, Roberts N (eds) Computer modeling and simulation in science education. Springer, New York, pp 282–319

De Lorenzo R (2009) Augmented reality and on-demand learning. The mobile learner. http://themobilelearner.wordpress.com/2009/10/17/augmented-reality-and-on-demand-learning/

Diakopoulos N, Kivran-Swaine F, Naaman M (2011) Playable data: characterizing the design space of game-y infographics. In: Proceedings from CHI 2011. Vancouver, BC, Canada

Dunleavy M, Dede C, Mitchell R (2009) Affordances and limitations of immersive participatory augmented reality simulations for teaching and learning. J Sci Educ Technol 18(1):7–22

Ewers R, Schicho K, Undt G, Wanschitz F, Truppe M, Seemann R, Wagner A (2005) Basic research and 12 years of clinical experience in computer-assisted navigation technology: a review. Int J Oral Maxillofac Surg 34:1–8

Gartner Inc (2008). Gartner identifies top ten disruptive technologies for 2008 to 2012. http://www.gartner.com/it/page.jsp?id=681107

Grabham D (2009) 8 awesome augmented reality apps for iPhone. Tech Radar. http://www.techradar.com/news/phone-and-communications/mobile-phones/8-awesome-augmented-reality-apps-for-iphone-639263

Graf H, Soubra S, Picinbono G, Keough I, Tessier A, Khan A (2011) Lifecycle building card: Toward paperless and visual lifecycle management Tools. In: Proceedings from the 11th symposium on simulation for architecture and urban design Boston, pp 135–142

Hamilton K (2011) The Augmented Reality in Education Wiki. http://wik.ed.uiuc.edu/index.php/Augmented_Reality_in_Education. Accessed 19 July 2011

Hamilton K, Olenewa J (2010) Augmented reality in education [PowerPoint slides]. Retrieved from Lecture Notes Online Web site: http://www.authorstream.com/Presentation/k3hamilton-478823-augmented-reality-in-education/

Harders M, Bianchi G, Knoerlein B (2007) In: Stephanidis (ed) Multimodal augmented reality in medicine. In: Proceedings from the 4th international conference on universal access in human-computer interaction, pp 652–658

Henderson SJ, Feiner S (2009) Evaluating the benefits of augmented reality for task localization in maintenance of an armored personnel carrier turret. In: Proceedings from ISMAR 2009: the 8th IEEE international symposium on mixed and augmented reality, Orlando, FL, USA, pp 135–144

Herrington J, Reeves TC, Oliver R (2007) Immersive learning technologies: realism and online authentic learning. J Comput High Educ 19(1):80–99. doi:10.1007/BF03033421

Hincapie M, Caponio A, Rios H, Mendivil EG (2011) An introduction to augmented reality with applications in aeronautical maintenance. In: Proceedings from ICTON 2011: 13th international conference on transparent optical networks, pp 1–4. DOI: 10.1109/ICTON.2011.5970856

Hough L (2007) Handhelds, avatars, and virtual aliens: how learning in the classroom is changing and why Professor Chris Dede and his team are on a non-crusade to figure out how all of the pieces fit together. http://www.gse.harvard.edu/news_events/ed/2007/fall/features/handhelds.html

Höllerer TH, Feiner SK (2004) Mobile augmented reality. In: Karimi HA, Hammad A (eds) Telegeoinformatics: location-based computing and services. CRC Press, pp 392–421

Hughes CE, Stapleton CB, Hughes DE, Smith EM (2005) Mixed reality in education, entertainment, and training. IEEE Comput Graph Appl 26(6):24–30

Hwang GJ, Yang TC, Tsai CC, Yang SJ-H (2009) A context-aware ubiquitous learning environment for conducting complex science experiments. Comput Educ 53(2):402–413

Jihyun O, Moon-Hyun L, Hanhoon P, Jong IIP, Jong-Sung K, Wookho S (2008) Efficient mobile museum guidance system using augmented reality. In: Proceedings from ISCE 2008: the 12th IEEE international symposium on consumer electronics. Algarve, Portugal, pp 1–4. DOI: 10.1109/ISCE.2008.4559482

Jones V, Jo JH (2004) Ubiquitous learning environment: an adaptive teaching system using ubiquitous technology. In: Proceedings from ASCILITE 2004 Conference Perth, Australia, pp 468–474

Juniper Research (2011) Mobile Augmented Reality. http://juniperresearch.com/reports/mobile_augmented_reality

Kaufmann H (2003) Collaborative augmented reality in education. In: Proceedings from Imagina 2003, pp 1–4

Kaufmann H, Dünser A (2007) Summary of usability evaluations of an educational augmented reality application. Lect Notes Comput Sci 4563:660–669

Kaufmann H, Schmalstieg D (2003) Mathematics and geometry education with collaborative augmented reality. Comput Graph-UK 27:339–345

Kerawalla L, Luckin R, Selijefot S, Woolard A (2006) Making it real: exploring the potential of augmented reality for teaching primary school science. Virtual Real 10(3–4):163–174

Khan A, Hornbæk K (2011) Big data from the built environment. In: Proceedings from UbiComp' 11. Beijing, China. ACM: 978-1-60558-843-8/10/0

Kirchbach K, Runde C (2011) Optimized work flow through VR and AR technology on construction sites. In: Proceedings from IV: the 15th international conference on information visualisation London, UK, pp 549–551. DOI: 10.1109/IV.2011.11

Klopfer E, Squire K (2008) Environmental detectives—the development of an augmented reality platform for environmental simulations. Educ Tech Res Dev 56(2):203–228

Klopfer E, Yoon S (2004) Developing games and simulations for today and tomorrow's tech savvy youth. TechTrends 49(3):41–49

Lessiter J, Freeman J, Keogh E, Davidoff J (2001) A cross-media presence questionnaire: the ITC-sense of presence inventory. Presence: Teleoperators, Virtual Environ 10(3):282–297

Liarokapis F, Mourkoussis N, White M, Darcy J, Sifniotis M, Petridis P et al (2004) Web 3D and augmented reality to support engineering education. World Trans Eng Technol Educ 3(1):11–14

Liarokapis F, Petridis P, Lister P, White M (2002) Multimedia augmented reality interface for e-learning (MARIE). World Trans Eng Technol Educ 1(2):173–176

Liu D, Jenkins SA, Sanderson PM, Fabian P, Russell WJ (2010) Monitoring with head-mounted displays in general anesthesia: A clinical evaluation in the operating room. Soc Technol Anesth 110(4):1032–1038

Ludwig C, Reimann C (2005) Augmented reality: information at focus. Cooperative computing & communication laboratory (Volume 4. No. 1). Universität Paderborn

Mann S (2001) Fundamental issues in mediated reality, WearComp, and camera-based augmented reality. In: Barfield W, Caudell T (eds) Fundamentals of wearable computers and augmented reality. Lawrence Erlbaum Associates, Inc, New Jersey, pp 295–328

Mann S, Fung J (2002) EyeTap devices for augmented, deliberately diminished, or otherwise altered visual perception of rigid planar patches of real world scenes. Presence: Teleoperators Virtual Environ, Mixed Real 11(2):158–175

Mann S, Niedzviecki H (2001) Cyborg: digital destiny and human possibility in the age of the wearable computer. Randomhouse (Doubleday)

Mejías Borrero A, Andújar Márquez JM (2011) A pilot study of the effectiveness of augmented reality to enhance the use of remote labs in electrical engineering education. J Sci Educ Technol. DOI: 10.1007/s10956-011-9345-9

Milgram P, Kishino F (1994) A taxonomy of mixed reality visual displays. IEICE Trans Inf Syst 77(12). http://etclab.mie.utoronto.ca/people/paul_dir/IEICE94/ieice.html
Milgram P, Takemura H, Utsumi A, Kishino F (1994) Augmented reality: a class of displays on the reality-virtuality continuum. Telemanipulator Telepresence Technol 2351:282–292
Nechvatal J (1999) Immersive ideals/Critical distances (Unpublished Doctoral Dissertation)
New Media Consortium (NMC) (2010) The 2010 horizontal report. http://wp.nmc.org/horizon2010/
New Media Consortium (NMC) (2011) The 2011 horizontal report. http://wp.nmc.org/horizon2011/
Noh Z, Sunar MS, Pan Z (2009) A review on augmented reality for virtual heritage system. In: Chang M et al. (eds) Edutainment, LNCS, 5670:50–61
Núñez M, Quiró R, Núñez I, Carda JB, Camahort E (2008) Collaborative augmented reality for inorganic chemistry education. In: Proceedings from EE'08: the 5th WSEAS/IASME international conference on engineering education. Heraklion, Greece, pp 271–277
O'Leary P, Sherman W (2008) Immersive interfaces for improving the scientific inquiry process [PowerPoint slides]. http://vis.cs.ucdavis.edu/Ultravis08/
Ogata H, Yano Y (2004) Context-aware support for computer-supported ubiquitous learning. In: Proceedings of the 2nd IEEE international workshop on wireless and mobile technologies in education (WMTE'04). Washington, DC, USA, pp 27–34
Omolola AA, Hetzel K, Parker LC, Loizzo J, Burgess WD, Robinson JP (2011) Using virtual field trips to connect students with university scientists: core elements and Evaluation of zipTripsTM. J Sci Educ Technol. doi:10.1007/s10956-011-9350-z
Phan VT, Choo S (2010) Interior design in augmented reality in environment. Int J Comput Appl 5(5):16–21
Portalés C, Lerma JL, Navarro S (2010) Augmented reality and photogrammetry: a synergy to visualize physical and virtual city environments. ISPRS J Photogramm Remote Sens 65:134–142
Raju (2009) 15 Stunning augmented reality apps for iPhone. Technically Personal. http://techpp.com/2009/10/21/15-stunning-augmented-reality-iphone-apps/
Sadowski W, Stanney K (2002) Presence in virtual environments. In: Stanney K (ed) Handbook of virtual environment. Lawrence Erlbaum Associates, New Jersey, pp 791–806
Saenz S (2010) Augmented reality to help military mechanics fix vehicles (Video). http://singularityhub.com/2010/01/11/augmented-reality-to-help-military-mechanics-fix-vehicles-video/
Santana-Fernández J, Gómez-Gil J, del-Pozo-San-Cirilo L (2010) Design and implementation of a GPS guidance system for agricultural tractors using augmented reality technology. Sensors, 10:10435–10447. DOI: 10.3390/s101110435
Savin-Banden M (2000) Problem-based Learning in higher education: Untold stories. The Society for Research into Higher Education & Open University Press, Buckingham
Schmalstieg D (2001) An introduction to augmented reality [PowerPoint slides]. Lecture Notes Online Web site: http://www.iswc.ethz.ch/events/tutorials/slides_schmalstieg.pdf
Shelton BE, Hedley NR (2002) Using augmented reality for teaching earth-sun relationship to undergraduate geography students. The First IEEE international augmented reality toolkit workshop. Darmstadt, Germany: IEEE, pp 1–8
Shin DH, Dunston PS (2008) Identification of application areas for augmented reality in industrial construction based on technology suitability. Autom Constr 17:882–894
Sielhorst T, Feuerstein M, Navab N (2008) Advanced medical displays: a literature review of augment reality. J Disp Disp Technol 4(4):451–467
Sielhorst T, Obst T, Burgkart R, Riener R, Navab N (2004) An augmented reality delivery simulator for medical training. In: International workshop on augmented environments for medical imaging—MICCAI Satellite Workshop AMI-ARCS, pp 11–20
Steinkuehler C, Williams D (2006) Where everybody knows your (screen) name: online games as "third places." J Comput-Med Commun, 11(4), article 1. http://jcmc.indiana.edu/vol11/issue4/steinkuehler.html

Sutherland IE (1965) The ultimate display. In: Proceedings from IFIP Congress. http://www.informatik.umu.se/~jwworth/TheUltimateDisplay.pdf. pp 506–508

Sutherland IE (1968) A head-mounted three-dimensional display. In: Proceedings from the AFIPS fall joint computer conference. Thompson Books, Washington, pp 757–764 http://www.cise.ufl.edu/research/lok/teaching/ve-s09/papers/sutherland-headmount.pdf. Accessed 14 Dec 2011

Thomas B, Close B, Donoghue J, Squires J, Bondi PD, Piekarski W (2001) First person indoor/outdoor augmented reality application. ARquake Pers Ubiquit Comput 6:75–86

Yang SJ-H (2006) Context aware ubiquitous learning environments for peer-to-peer collborative learning. Educ Technol Soc 9(1):188–201

Yuen SC-Y (2010) 3D Augmented reality books. http://steveyuen.org/blog/?p=754

Vidal NR, Vidal RA (2010) Augmented reality systems for weed economic thresholds applications. Planta Daninha 28(2):449–454

Welch RB (1978) Perceptual modification: adapting to altered sensory environments. Academic Press. ISBN 0-12-741850-4

Zhao X, Okamoto T (2011) Adaptive multimedia content delivery for context-aware u-learning. Int J Mob Learn Organ 5(1):46–63

Zhou F, Duh H-L, Billinghurst M (2008) Trends in augmented reality traching, interaction and display: A review of ten years in ISMAR. In: Proceedings from ISMAR 7th IEE/ACM international symposium: Mixed and Augmented Reality. Cambridge: IEEE, pp 193–202

Zhu W, Owen C, Li H, Lee J-H (2004) Personalized in-store e-commerce with PromoPad: an augmented reality shopping assistant. Electron J E-comm Tools Appl 1(3):1–19. doi:10.1.1.83.8198

Chapter 18
Facilitating Complex Learning by Mobile Augmented Reality Learning Environments

Dirk Ifenthaler and Deniz Eseryel

Abstract The widespread ownership of mobile devices has lead to an increased interest to ubiquitous learning that is supported by a wide range of mobile devices. Mobile learning (m-learning) is referred to as when the process of learning and teaching occurs with the use of mobile devices anywhere and anytime. These developments have led to new research challenges in integrating formal and informal learning opportunities in technological supported environments. Therefore, this chapter is intended to provide an overview on how complex learning may be facilitated by mobile augmented reality learning environments and discuss technological, theoretical, and assessment challenges that must be addressed by future research for mobile augmented reality learning environments to fulfill its potential.

18.1 Introduction

An increasing number of researchers in the fields of instructional design, learning sciences, and educational psychology argue that complex knowledge domains present the most challenges, both for designing effective learning environments and for determining factors which contribute to learning (see, for instance, Dörner 1987, 1996; Funke 1991; Jacobson 2000; Sabelli 2006; Spector et al. 2001).

D. Ifenthaler (✉) · D. Eseryel
University of Oklahoma, Oklahoma, USA
e-mail: dirk@ifenthaler.info

D. Eseryel
e-mail: eseryel@ou.edu

R. Huang et al. (eds.), *Reshaping Learning*, New Frontiers of Educational Research,
DOI: 10.1007/978-3-642-32301-0_18,

Challenges involved in learning in complex knowledge domains, such as Science, Engineering, Mathematics, Technology (STEM) domains, are two folds. First, learning in complex knowledge domains requires understanding complex systems. The heart and the brain are two examples of complex physiological systems. Such systems are complex in both their composition—typically many different kinds of components interacting simultaneously and nonlinearly with each other and their environments on multiple levels—and in the rich diversity of behavior of which they are capable. Future scientific and technological developments in many complex knowledge domains depend upon coming to grips with complex systems (Sabelli 2006; Kelso 2009). Recent years has witnessed an increasing emphasis towards this direction. The international workshop on complex dynamics of physiological systems is a recent example. It brought together more than 100 researchers from various fields including physics, mathematics, biology, and medicine to model the complex functions of the brain and the heart by using computer-based simulation systems to advance the fields of medical science and physiology (Dana et al. 2009). Hence, learning in complex knowledge domains is challenging; yet it is a continuous, life-long enterprise as these fields evolve and redefine themselves.

A second challenge of learning in complex knowledge domains, i.e., complex learning, is due to its situativity (cf. Greeno 1998) in real-life contexts. Complex knowledge domains are characterized by large numbers of non-recurrent skills, that is, skills that have to be applied differently and flexibly from situation to situation (van Merriënboer 1997). In contrast, simpler domains are characterized by large numbers of recurrent skills, which are performed similarly from situation to situation, thus, can be automated. This ability to flexibly apply previously learned knowledge and skills to solving new problems under novel situations requires that learners should be able to recognize the situational conditions and far-transfer their learning (Mayer and Wittrock 1996). Thus, complex learning involves the integration and coordination of qualitatively different knowledge, skills, and attitudes that constitute real-life task performance (van Merriënboer et al. 2002). Hence, rather than teaching relevant domain knowledge and skills in isolation, effective teaching in complex knowledge domains should simulate real-life, authentic practices. Yet, creating educational activities that allow students to engage in authentic practices is challenging within the boundaries of a classroom (Chinn and Malhotra 2002). For example, medical students have to learn about forensic medicine in order to differentiate between everyday injuries and wound patterns of trauma due to assault. However, ethical problems may arise when integrating real-life cases into the classroom. Additionally, the quality of available real-life cases may differ and not all relevant findings during a demonstration may be presented (Albrecht et al. 2011). As a possible solution, mobile augmented reality learning environments (MARLE) combine the benefits of mobile learning, virtual learning environments, as well as augmented reality and allows a realistic presentation of various forensic findings (Albrecht et al. 2011).

The widespread ownership of mobile devices has lead to an increased interest to ubiquitous learning that is supported by a wide range of mobile devices (e.g., Tablet-PC, smart phones). Mobile learning (m-learning) is referred to as when the process of learning and teaching occurs with the use of mobile devices anywhere and anytime (Traxler 2009). A virtual learning environment (VLE) models phenomena of the real world by integrating a set of equivalent virtual learning objects and instructional components such as materials, tests, and multimedia objects (Winn 2003). Augmented reality learning environments (ARLE) are considered as an extension of VLE. Generally, ARLE bring virtual learning objects into the real world and allow learners to virtually interact with the combined (real and virtual) world (Haller et al. 2007). MARLE integrates the instructional potential of mobile learning, virtual environments and augmented reality.

These developments have led to new research challenges in integrating formal and informal learning opportunities in technological supported environments. Therefore, this chapter is intended to provide an overview on how complex learning may be facilitated by mobile augmented reality learning environments and discuss technological, theoretical, and assessment challenges that must be addressed by future research for MARLE to fulfill its potential.

18.2 Complex Learning

Consider two medical doctors who are asked to diagnose two patients with the same illness. Now imagine that time travel is possible and one of these doctors and the patient are in 1600s; while the other one is in 2011. For the doctor in 1600s, diagnosing this patient's illness would be a simple problem of determining which of the four humors (blood, phlegm, black bile, and yellow bile) is imbalanced and the treatment options would include interventions like bleeding the patient or inducing vomiting to restore the balance of the four humors; and the required surgical skills would include using very basic instruments like drill, saw, or forceps. Fortunately, as our understanding of the human anatomy and physiology increased medical professionals moved away from defining human body based on the ancient Greek view of the four humors. Due to the technological advancements in the field of medicine, competent doctors of today have a better understanding of the complex physiological systems governing human physiology and the dynamic interactions among various system elements. Hence, they are better equipped to diagnose and treat a variety of illnesses. On the other hand, it is also due to these technological advancements that medical diagnosis in today's world would constitute a very complex and ill-structured problem that require an in-depth understanding the interrelationships among very complex physiological systems and finding the optimum treatment option among a number of possible treatment options, each with pros and cons. So, choosing the optimum solution would highly depend on situational factors. As new discoveries are made in the field of medicine, new drugs, new treatment options, new surgical techniques require competent doctors to adapt to the ever-changing requirements of their field.

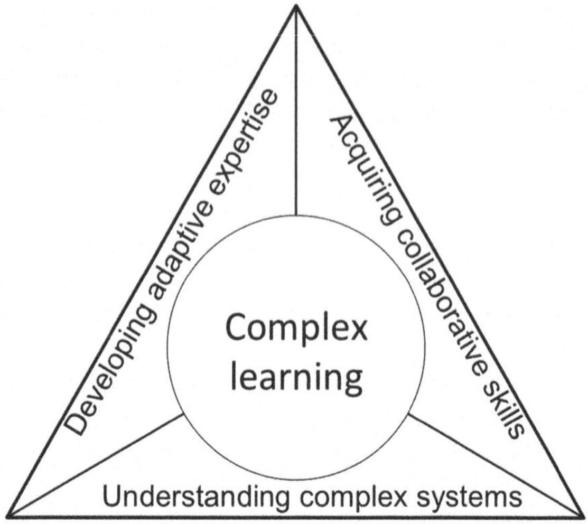

Fig. 1 Conceptual framework for complex learning

Similarly, the knowledge and skills required for the competent professionals in many scientific domains has increased in their complexity. As a result, the fields of education, training, instructional design, and learning sciences have become more conscious of the demand to prepare individuals to be competent professionals in complex knowledge domains. Hence, a core research agenda of interest shifted their attention to designing learning environments to facilitate complex learning.

As depicted in the example from the field of medicine, complex learning involves (1) in its knowledge base, the requirement of understanding complex systems; (2) in its hard-skills base, the requirement to flexibly apply large numbers of non-recurrent skills that call for adaptive expertise; and (3) in its soft-skills base, the requirement for collaboration, communication, task coordination with others, and other profession-specific attitudes (see Fig. 18.1). In the remainder of this section, we briefly discuss each of these requirements.

18.2.1 Understanding Complex Systems

An important attribute of complex learning is that it calls for understanding complex systems. Complex systems are best characterized by interconnected components whose behavior is not explained exclusively by the properties of their components. Rather the behavior emerges from the interconnectedness of the components. Complex systems depend on feedback, respond to multiple causes and effects, involve multiple interconnected levels, and operate at multiple time scales.

Understanding complex systems is fundamental to learning in many complex knowledge domains such as physics, physiology, environmental biology, and ecology. For example, to develop a proper conceptual understanding in ecology, students must be able to understand the dynamic interrelationships among different organisms within and across species. However, prior research suggests that humans have difficulty in understanding and monitoring complex systems, which calls for complex, and sometimes also ill-structured, problem solving (Dörner 1996). Dörner and Wearing (1995) and Funke (1991) identify a number of reasons for this difficulty. First of all, any given complex problem solving situation may involve multiple goals and it is very difficult to define goals operationally. Often, this requires decomposing the global goal into many subgoals but this leads to another difficulty: As time is always limited it is necessary, not only for one action to serve more than one goal, but also to order the priority of these goals. However, as the most important and urgent goal is being addressed the variables in the system may interact in such a way that lead to the requirement of reconsidering the overall system goal (MacKinnon and Wearing 1980). Nevertheless, in some cases, it may not be necessary to act at all to reach one's goals as the system's development may produce the goal state independently. If, however, the system does not move autonomously in the desired direction, it is necessary to act, taking into account the autonomous developmental tendencies of the system (Frensch and Funke 1995). In any event it is necessary but challenging to predict what will happen to the system as some of the goals may be contradictory which require reasonable trade-offs.

Rumelhart et al. (1986) argue that this type of complex problem solving calls for the interplay between *schemata* and *mental models*, which fulfill the basic cognitive functions of *assimilation* and *accommodation* as described in Piaget's epistemology (Fig. 18.2). Schemata assimilate new information into cognitive structures and constitute the fundamental basis for constructing mental models that aid in the process of accommodation (Ifenthaler and Seel 2011; Seel 2001). During complex problem solving, the solver's mental model takes as input "the specifications of the actions intended to be carried out and produces an interpretation of what would happen if the solver did that" (Rumelhart et al. 1986, p. 41). Part of

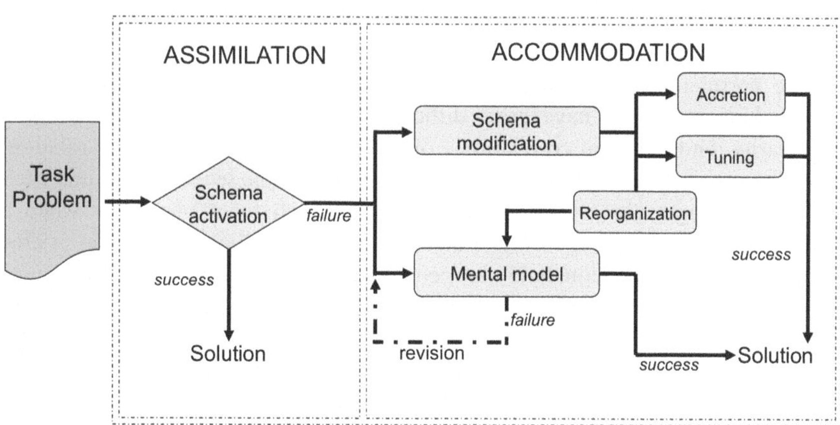

Fig. 2 Cognitive processes during complex problem solving (Ifenthaler and Seel 2011)

this specification might be a specification of what the new stimulus conditions would be like. Thus, the activated schemata takes input from the phenomena to be explained and produces relevant reactions, whereas the mental model help predict how the input would change in response to these reactions. In other words, during complex problem solving, a *mental simulation* "runs in the mind's eye" (Seel 2001, p. 407) to imagine the events that would take place if a particular action were to be performed. In this way, mental models allow one to perform entire actions internally and to judge the consequences of actions, interpret them, and draw appropriate conclusions. Accordingly, the learner makes a mental effort to understand complex systems and in doing so constructs appropriate mental representations to model and comprehend these systems.

This kind of learning involves the construction of causal explanations with the help of appropriate mental models (i.e., causal reasoning skills), hence, it aids in accumulation of domain-specific knowledge (i.e., structural knowledge). Stated in the terminology of Piaget's epistemology, it is a mode of accommodation rather than assimilation. Consequently, the construction of a mental model in the course of learning often necessitates both a restructuring of the underlying representations and a reconceptualization of the related concepts (Seel 2006).

Prior research point out a number of learning difficulties due to the challenges associated with constructing a mental model of the complex system to be managed (Hogan and Thomas 2001; Putz-Osterloh and Lemme 1987). In large part, these challenges are due to the intransparency of the complex systems. Complex systems typically involve large number of variables with high-degree of connectivity. Changes in one variable may affect a number of other variables, making it very difficult to anticipate all possible consequences of a given situation. Therefore, it is not possible to directly observe all of the variables involved or the relationships between them. Furthermore, not every action shows immediate consequences. Some of the effects may occur with time delay. All of these factors cause excessive demands on working memory and make it very challenging for building the mental model of the complex systems necessary for complex problem-solving and effective decision-making.

Studies by Brehmer (1980) show that people can generally detect linear, positive correlations given enough trials if the outcome feedback is accurate enough. However, they have great difficulty in the presence of random error, nonlinearity, and negative correlations, often never discovering the true relation. Similarly, experiments of Plous (1993) showed that people tended to assume each effect has a single cause and often cease their search for explanations when a sufficient cause is found ignoring situational factors. Studies by Axelrod (1976) and Dörner (1980) also conclude that people tend to think in single strand causal series and have difficulty in systems with side effects and multiple causal pathways. It is possible to argue that part of this inadequacy lies in the assumptions and practices of current educational system: Classroom problems are usually well-structured story problems, in which the problem given and problem goal are well-defined and there is only a single solution path to reach the goal. Therefore, students are trained to view all problems in a similar vain and look for a single solution (see, for a discussion, Jonassen 1997; Frederiksen and White 1992). On the other hand, complex ill-structured problem solving calls for causal reasoning skills that would allow the solver to view the complex problem space in its entirety as a complex system of interrelated components. This would allow the solver to *visualize* the outcome of all possible solution alternatives by mental simulation and choose the most appropriate solution approach while being able to justify the decision.

18.2.2 Developing Adaptive Expertise

A second important attribute of complex learning is that it requires mastery and coordination of a range of qualitatively different constituent skills. Van Merriënboer (1997) distinguishes between two types of constituent skills that make up the skill base in complex knowledge domains: (1) *recurrent skills*, which are performed similarly from situation to situation, thus, can be easily automated via repetitive exercises; and (2) *non-recurrent skills*, which have to be applied differently and flexibly from situation to situation. Furthermore, he argues that constituent skills are not merely subskills, which can be added together to make up the *Big Skill; hence,* teaching subskills separately does not guarantee that the learner would transfer the performance of the *Big Skill* in real life professional environment (van Merriënboer 1997).

Recent research also confirms that in complex knowledge domains, traditional instructional design approach of breaking down the overall complex skill into a cluster of subskills (that are easy to teach and assess) and training learners for mastering each subskill separately is ineffective and does not result with transfer of what is learned to real-life performance settings (Perkins and Grotzer 1997; Spector and Anderson 2000; van Merriënboer et al. 2002; Wightman and Lintern 1985). This approach is only effective if little or no coordination is required among the different skills during the real-life performance of the whole skill (Naylor and Briggs 1963). In contrast, real-life performance in complex knowledge domains are characterized by numerous interactions between the different aspects of overall task performance with very high demands on the coordination of non-recurrent skills (van Merriënboer et al. 2002).

A recent evidence of this realization comes from medical education research, which showed that 86 % of the medical students, who passed the standardized medical licensing examination by correctly answering questions regarding indicators of a certain illness, were not able to correctly *diagnose* the same illness when presented by patient in a real-life simulation (Jonassen 1997). So, being a *doctor* who can correctly diagnose a patient's illness (which is a complex problem solving task) is more than the sum of its subtasks (e.g., 'which illness cause which symptoms' + 'what type of scans are required to check for possible symptoms' etc.). Thus, an important aspect of complex learning is developing the ability to flexibly apply previously-learned knowledge and skills to solving new problems under novel situations in a way to recognize the situational conditions and far-transfer learning (Mayer and Wittrock 1996).

In their study of the expertise in complex knowledge domains, Hatano and Inagaki (1986) distinguished between the experts who can effectively and efficiently solve typical professional problems that are routinely faced in the workplace (i.e., *routine expertise*) and those who can develop innovative solutions to novel professional problems and adapt easily to the changes that occur in professional practice (i.e., *adaptive expertise*). They further argued that an important aspect of preparing professionals for complex knowledge domains should be to place them on a trajectory to develop adaptive expertise (Harris and Cullen 2007; Hatano and Oura 2003; Schwartz et al. 2005). This idea highlights that complex learning involves more than the integration and coordination of non-recurrent skills. Complex learning also involves (1) complex problem solving skills so that learners can flexibly adapt existing knowledge and skills to novel goals; (2) metacognitive and self-regulation skills so that learners can successfully monitor their understanding, thinking, and problem-solving; and (3) epistemological beliefs so that learners conceive of domain knowledge as dynamic in nature and that it will change as the field evolves so they continuously inquire for new learning in their domain expertise.

18.2.3 Acquisition of Collaboration, Communication, and Task Coordination Skills

The third important attribute of complex learning is that it calls for mastery of collaboration, communication, and task coordination skills. In complex knowledge domains, the complexity and expertise needed accomplish real-life professional tasks typically requires a team of individuals. In some cases, the team may comprise of individuals with similar expertise; in others the team may comprise of individuals who possess different but complementary expertise and roles. For example, in one project, the design of the nuclear power plant structure alone required about 200 civil engineers to collaborate together while the whole nuclear power plant project required collaboration among approximately 2,500 engineers with different specializations (Bechtel Power Corporation, n.d. 2011).

Hence, successful execution of real-life professional tasks in complex knowledge domains heavily relies on the collaboration, communication, and task coordination skills of the team members (cf. Hung 2011). In the cases where the collaboration requires individuals with different expertise and roles, communication and task coordination skills become even more crucial since different roles and expertise may bring with themselves different sets of vocabulary, protocols, requirements, and way of working, and so on. For instance, the professionals in the built environment disciplines often have to work together on design projects. For architects and interior designers, the design problem may be simply stated as:

Design a general office building with 65,000 square feet, three stories high, with green systems and materials for a location in downtown Dallas, Texas. Constraints may include such things as the building orientation allowed on the site, budget, or the desired level of sustainability. To solve this problem, architects and designers begin by executing their spatial perceptions about typical activities in the building and visualization techniques. Mental images form then from the spatial visualizations as room locations and features are represented. From this point the architects and designers begin the visual reasoning process as they ask questions about alternatives. Alternatives, for instance, about the design features that meet green building criteria. The architect may ask, "What are the options available for reducing heat gain anticipated by the building's orientation to the west?" Visual reasoning provides the architect with multiple possibilities to solve this complex problem. On the other hand, the process of design problem solving for engineers and engineers and constructors are quite different than that of the building architectural and space designers. They typically receive a set of 2–dimensional drawings for a building. The first task for engineers and constructors involves interpreting the symbols and graphical representations to develop some perception about the interior and exterior building space and their relationships. Once that is complete and they have their 'bearings', they can begin to mentally rotate the representation from a flat 2–dimensional representation (X,Y coordinates) to a 3-dimensional representation in which the Z–axis adds mass by adding volume to the form. It is at this point a clear mental image of the overall building and individual rooms is formed. Once the engineers and constructors have a valid mental image they can begin to process of reasoning about the optimal means and methods for transforming the building from paper and model to a real structure. Selecting the optimal means and methods by which to construct a building requires professionals ask questions about alternatives, such as: What happens if another pipe is added to a vertical chase in one area of the building? To answer this question, the engineer and constructor must consider the enclosure materials and impact on the space. They must understand more than just the functional aspects but also the changes to the horizontal and vertical space. Given the differences in the way these different professionals—who have to work together—approach the same design problem solving, building effective cross-communication would be more challenging and require an in-depth understanding of the *ways* of the others to develop a common vocabulary and an effective communication using multiple channels (written, verbal, visual, and so on).

The crucial importance of requirement of complex learning to include effective collaboration and communication skills is evident in the Institute of Medicine's 1999 publication, *To Err is Human: Building a Safer Health System,* which exposed troubles with the quality and safety of patient care in the United States, including the determination that between 44,000 and 98,000 lives were lost each year due to medical errors, most of which were attributed to collaboration and communication problems among doctors, nurses, ancillary staff, medical students, and other health care team members, who are integral components of the health care environment (Kohn et al. 1999).

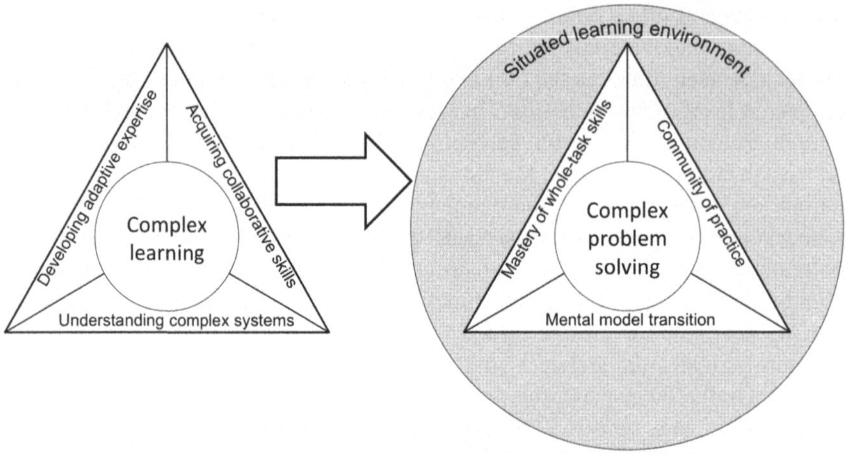

Fig. 3 Requirements for learning environments to facilitate complex learning

18.3 Designing Learning Environments to Facilitate Complex Learning

In previous section, we discussed three attributes of complex learning that should be targeted in an effective learning environment for complex knowledge domains: (1) understanding complex systems; (2) developing adaptive expertise; and (3) acquisition of collaboration, communication, and task coordination skills. Each of these attributes lead to the specification of different requirements for designing learning environments (see Fig. 18.3).

A common denominator underlying all three attributes is the requirement for situating the learning experience in a complex, ill-structured problem that is representative of the authentic, real-life professional work in the targeted complex knowledge domain. In Greeno's (1998) terminology, it is the *situativity* that affects learners' problem space, which he described as, "the understanding of a problem by a problem solver, including a representation of the situation, the main goal, and operators for changing situations, and strategies, plans, and knowledge of general properties and relations in the domain" (p. 7). Hence, situated learning theorists argue that there is no such thing as context-independent thought and behavior. Learning is always fundamentally about *doing* something for some purpose in a social context (Wertsch 1998). Thus, it is argued that the environment plays an important role during learning; effective action is always situated within environmental constraints and affordances (Dewey 1938; Peirce 1992; Salomon 1993). From this perspective, learning is understood as the ongoing transformation of identity (cf. Wenger 1998) and mark of developing domain expertise is one's ability to *see* the environment in particular *ways* ordained by the profession (cf. Glenberg 1997; Goodwin 1994).

Instructional approaches that emphasize situated learning include cognitive apprenticeship, problem-based learning, project-based learning, inquiry learning, guided discovery learning, case method, learning by design, anchored instruction, and so on. Regardless of the variances among the interpretations and applications of these approaches in the literature, we argue that the design of the situated learning environment should fulfill three requirements in order to facilitate complex learning as suggested in Fig. 18.3.

First, learning environments to facilitate complex learning should support learners in their understanding of complex systems. In the earlier section, we contended that learning in many complex knowledge domains, like science, calls for understanding complex systems. Self-organizing and adaptive biological systems such as cell biology; physiological systems such as those based on various multifunction organs including the brain and the immune system; ecological systems such as a lake ecosystem are all examples of complex systems. Understanding complex systems require students to build an accurate mental model of the complex system depicting the causal interrelationships among system components. The proponents of inquiry learning and guided discovery learning argue that these instructional approaches effectively assist students in their construction of accurate mental models of the complex systems and learn the deep principles that govern them (Bransford et al. 2000; Cavalli-Sforza et al. 1994; Eisenhart et al. 1996; McGinn and Roth 1999; Palincsar and Magnusson 2001). In inquiry or guided discovery methods, students were asked to solve a complex problem situated in an authentic activity. Students often start their inquiry or guided discovery learning investigations with an incomplete or incorrect mental model, which dictates the construction of their very first hypothesis to test the causality between the variables. Through multiple cycles of investigations, they are expected to infer from their findings the dynamic interrelationships among components of the complex system. The desired process of mental model transition is depicted in Fig. 18.4. Scaffolding is an critical aspect of designing such learning environments

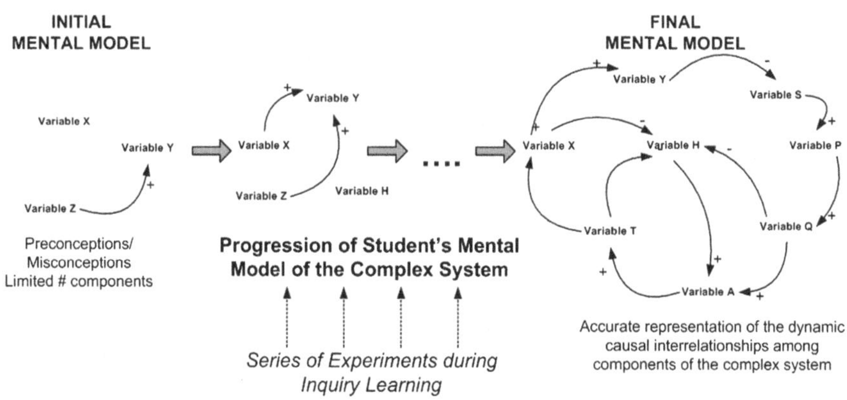

Fig. 4 Mental model transition

(de Jong and van Joolingen 1998; Kirschner et al. 2006); especially when the system under investigation is a complex system. Students are then required to conduct a multivariable analysis, which is very challenging since they have to simulate in their mind's eye a large number of system components and dynamic interrelationships among them (Eseryel and Law 2010). Given the limited information processing capacity (Miller 1956), this places an extraneous cognitive burden on students. Based on their findings Law and Eseryel (2011) further argue that unless students possess strong cognitive regulation skills, they would not be able to conduct the kind of multivariable analysis required for successful mental model transition. Hence, scaffolding cognitive regulation appears to be an important aspect of facilitating students' mental model transition in promoting their understanding of complex system.

Second, learning environments to facilitate complex learning should involve authentic and meaningful whole complex tasks presented in learning trajectories—not just the part tasks or subskills that make up the whole task. Given the high cognitive load imposed by whole complex tasks, they should be offered in such a way that learners are not cognitively overloaded by their complexity. That is, learners should be given the opportunity to practice simplified but increasingly complex versions of authentic whole tasks that will eventually place them on a trajectory for adaptive expertise. An appropriate model to support this type of instructional design is the 4C/ID Model (van Merriënboer 1997), which details the task analysis, sequencing, and scaffolding methods to assist with the design of holistic learning environments to support complex learning. The model is based on the idea that placing learners on a trajectory to adaptive expertise is accomplished when they are presented with multiple whole tasks that are of the same level of complexity but differ in amount of instructional support offered (from high to low support as the expertise of the learners increase); once the learners can successfully complete the first set of whole tasks without any external support providing them with the next set of whole tasks a higher level complexity, and so on until the desired level of learning and expertise is achieved.

While the 4C/ID model provides effective guidelines to design the learning activities, it mainly focuses on developing individual expertise and pays little attention to collaborative aspect of real life professional work in complex knowledge domains. Hence, as the third requirement, learning environments to facilitate complex learning should include authentic, whole task performances that require collaboration among learners replicating real life professional work. Depending on the nature of the targeted complex learning domain, learners could either assume different professional roles to solve complex problems together as a team; or they could all assume the same professional role to collaborate together to solve complex problems with guidance from expert modeling, mentoring, and legitimate peripheral participation (cf. Lave and Wenger 1991). Such an environment promotes the advancement of collective learning and support the growth of individual learning, in addition to addressing collaboration, communication, and task coordination skills (cf. Scardamalia and Bereiter 1994; Vygotsky 1978). This is in accordance with learning through participation in communities of practice perspective (cf. Lave and Wenger 1991), which emphasizes building learning communities to support shared repertoire of knowledge to be continuously developed and refined through the engagement of multiple community members in a joint enterprise, such as working together to solve complex professional problems. Shaffer (2006) further argues that through their involvement in communities of practice novices learn the structure, grammar, and ways of working of any particular profession, which he calls *epistemic frames* and include (Shaffer 2006):

- Skills: the abilities and competencies that community members are able to perform and demonstrate.
- Knowledge: the facts and information shared by community members.
- Identity: the social and cultural roles assumed by community members.
- Values: the opinions and beliefs held by community members that define what is important (and conversely, not important).
- Epistemology: the justifications and methods of proof that legitimize actions and claims within the community.

To connect this to Lave and Wenger's work (1991), new members who are at the periphery of a community of practice would have underdeveloped and loosely-linked frame elements in their epistemic frame, while expert members of the community in full participation would have well-defined epistemic frames with dense connections between and among the different frame elements. However, as the new members grow and learn in the ways of the profession, their understanding of the individual frame elements—and the relationships among them—will increase, resulting in an increasingly more sophisticated epistemic frame. In a study on instructional design expertise, Law et al. (2011) documents how building learning communities that simulate professional community of practice of instructional designers support novice designers to develop epistemic frames of the instructional design profession while collaboratively solving authentic instructional design problems.

In this section, we discussed the characteristics of situated learning environments to support desired complex learning outcomes that are representative of real-life task performance. Unfortunately, classroom-based learning environments are seldom appropriate to fulfill the required characteristics of situated learning environments discussed in this section because arranging complementary, tacit, relatively unstructured learning in complex real-world settings is difficult within the boundaries of classroom. For example, several investigators (Griffin 1995; Hendricks 2001) developed curricular activities in an attempt to validate situated learning theory but were forced to modify their research designs due to the difficulty of implementing situated learning within the constraints of a K-12 classroom. As an alternative to practices located within a school, taking students to actual professional contexts might provide an authentic, meaningful, and motivating context for students to master complex learning. For instance, Clarke and Dede (2007) attempted to bring students to a local hospital to work with epidemiologists and doctors to study an outbreak of whooping cough; yet, they found that this is not feasible for a myriad of reasons including prohibitive cost and managerial challenges.

With the advancements of computer-based technologies, the characteristics of virtual learning environments provide affordances for supporting the kinds of situated learning environments intended to facilitate complex learning. For instance, digital-game based environments such as educational massively multi-player online games (MMOG) or virtual worlds like Second Life have the potential to serve as a situated learning environment that can provide a completely immersive experience by enabling digital simulation of authentic problem-solving communities, in which learners interact with other virtual entities (both participants and computer-based agents) who have varied levels of skills. Hence, virtual worlds has the potential to provide the learners the subjective impression that one is participating in a comprehensive, realistic experience if they are willing to suspend their disbelief (Dede 2009). However, designing such realistic virtual learning environments that can provide actional, symbolic, and sensory immersion require extensive resources. In addition, students' initially high-level motivation tend to subside quickly while they are challenged with complex problem solving tasks (i.e., the novelty effect wears out quickly) in totally-immersive educational environments like massively multiplayer online games (Eseryel et al. 2011). On the other hand, augmented reality, which bridges virtual and real world environments, has the potential to open up new opportunities for supporting complex learning.

18.4 Mobile Augmented Reality and Complex Learning

The beginning of the twenty-first century sees a technological shift and a continuous progress towards powerful mobile and handheld computer devices as well as intelligent software applications. Most of these systems are GPS-enabled, location-aware, and provide wireless access to the Internet. High quality video cameras and audio functions provide the basis for future learning and instruction. Additionally, intelligent software applications can semantically interpret the learners' interactions and combine virtual objects with the real world. These new technologies are and will be shaping how people learn in the beginning of the twenty-first century in formal and informal settings (Ifenthaler 2010).

One of the most powerful technological developments within the last decade is augmented reality learning environments, which enable learners to use virtual objects in the real world. However, a consistent definition of augmented reality does not exist (Mehler-Bicher et al. 2011). In order to define augmented reality, the reality-virtuality continuum is used for clarification, which postulates a steady transition between real and virtual environments (Milgram et al. 1994). The left side of the continuum defines the real environment that contains solely real objects. The right side defines the virtual environment that contains exclusively virtual objects. Within the continuum, *mixed reality* is defined where real and

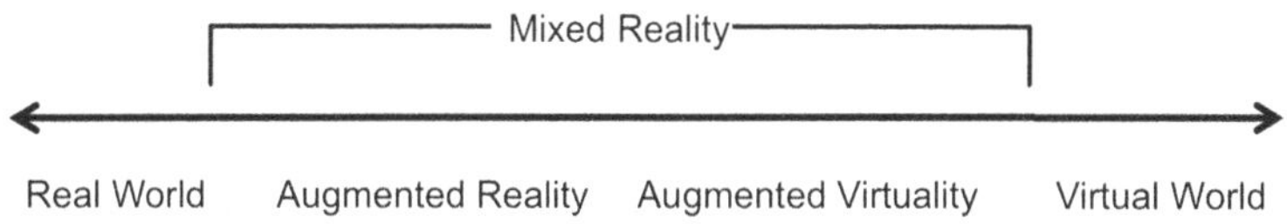

Fig. 5 Reality-virtuality continuum (Milgram et al. 1994)

virtual objects are combined arbitrary (see Fig. 18.5). For augmented reality, the real objects are predominating. Virtual objects are dominating the augmented virtuality.

Accordingly, an augmented reality learning environment features the following characteristics (Azuma 1997):

- Combines real objects and virtual objects
- Real objects are predominating
- Uses sensory input such as sound, video, graphics, or GPS-data
- Includes high interactivity
- Runs in real time
- Enables spatial registration (in any sensory dimension)

Key technologies of augmented reality (AR) include: (1) spatial augmented reality, (2) visual overlay augmented reality, and (3) self-locating augmented reality. *Spatial AR* uses digital projectors to display virtual objects and information on real objects. The key benefit is that the learner does not need to wear a head-mounted display in order to see the virtual object in the real world. This enables for a collaborative environment for multiple learners and an expanded display area (Bimber and Raskar 2005).

Visual overlay AR uses visual markers to generate visual overlays on real objects (see Fig. 18.6). A visual marker (a) is registered in the applications

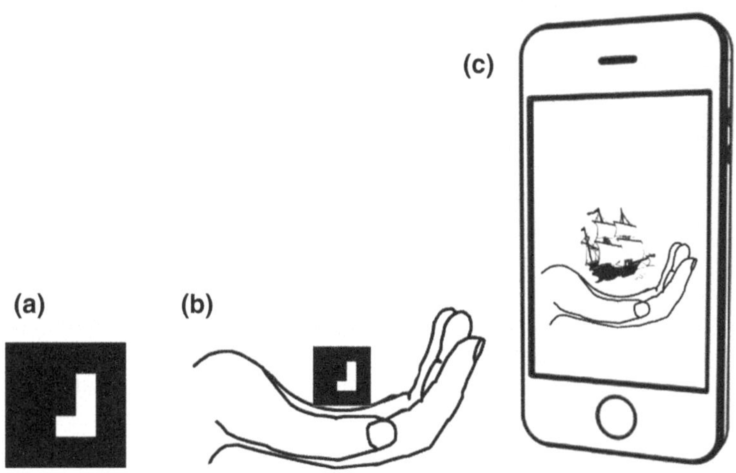

Fig. 6 Visual overlay AR process

database and connected to corresponding digital information (e.g. picture, text, etc.). The marker is placed in a real world setting (b). Through the video stream of a mobile device, the information of the registered marker is processed and transformed into a virtual object (c). Finally, the learner is able to see the ship sailing in his hand. *Self-locating AR* use the mobile devices' GPS-data and visual sensory data to calculate its spatial orientation (Ellaway 2010). This technology enables the learner to orientate within a complex environment (e.g., museum, factory) as well as locate resources and people within that environment (Ellaway 2010). Finally, mobile augmented reality learning environments (MARLE) bring virtual learning objects into the real world and allow learners to virtually interact with the combined (real and virtual) world on their mobile devises.

The potentials of AR for learning and instruction have been studied accordingly (Dunleavy et al. 2009; Haller et al. 2007; Ma and Choi 2007; Martín-Gutiérrez et al. 2010; Nischelwitzer et al. 2007). AR facilitates positive learning experiences and enhances the learner's motivation (Freitas and Campos 2008; Saforrudin et al. 2011). Other studies show potentials for formal education in biology (Gillet et al. 2004), chemistry (Fjeld and Voegtli 2002), geography (Shelton 2003), as well as informal education such as astronomy (Sin and Badioze Zaman 2009) or reading (Abas and Badioze Zaman 2011). However, the link between AR and complex learning has not been discussed in educational technology so far.

18.4.1 Facilitating Complex Learning by MARLE

Humans are good at manipulating their environments. Especially important here is the ability to manipulate the environment so that it comes to represent something by means of artifacts of technology (Seel et al. 2009). These abilities are dependent on two interacting sets of units of the cognitive system (Rumelhart et al. 1986). The *interpretation network* is concerned with the activation of schemata, and the other one is concerned with constructing a *model of the world*. It takes as input some specification of the actions we intend to carry out and produces an interpretation of what would happen if we did that. Part of this might be a specification of what the new stimulus conditions would be like. Thus, the *interpretation network* (i.e. an activated schema) takes input from the world and produces relevant cognitive (re-)actions, whereas the second module, i.e. the *model of the world*, predicts how the input would change in response to these reactions. In cognitive psychology it is common to speak of a *mental model* that would be expected to be operating in any case, insofar as it is generating expectations about the state of the world and thus *predicting* the outcomes of possible actions. However, it is not necessary for world events to have really happened. In the case that they have not, the cognitive system replaces the stimulus inputs from the world with inputs from the *mental model* of the world. This means that a *mental simulation* runs to imagine the events that would take place in the world if a particular action were to be performed. Thus, *mental models* allow one to perform entire actions internally and to judge the consequences of actions, interpret them, and draw appropriate conclusions.

In complex learning contexts, mental models have to adapt to represent each new state of the problem due to changes over time. Since mental models are ad hoc representations, they show their benefits in situations where no schema is available. Being able to monitor changes of mental models over time provides us with the necessary insight into complex problem solving—and into the representations of complex problems (Ifenthaler et al. 2011; Ifenthaler and Seel 2011). Accordingly, crucial to learning in complex domains is how learners' general and domain-specific model building skills develop and how their mental models and schemata change (Ifenthaler et al. 2007; Ifenthaler and Seel 2005). Thus, instant feedback on semantic and structural aspects of the learner's progression at all times during the learning process is a significant component for complex learning environments (Ifenthaler 2009). Such dynamic and timely feedback can promote the learner's self-regulated learning (Zimmerman and Schunk 2001). Moreover, situated learning environments require the embeddedness of learning tasks within the real world (Brown et al. 1989; Greeno 1989). Technology-mediated learning environments have the capabilities to facilitate the above-described complex processes by mediating between virtual and real world actions (Gee 2003). MARLE integrate the instructional potential of mobile learning, virtual environments and augmented reality and therefore provide a unique prerequisite for complex learning environments (Dunleavy et al. 2009).

In a resent K-12 project, iPads were handed out to over 100 students and their teachers for a daily classroom use (Ifenthaler 2011b). iPads are used in multiple ways in class:

- Digital textbooks including animations, films, and audio
- Learning management e.g., turning in homework assignments
- Corresponding with teachers and students
- Developing digital portfolios throughout a school year
- Experiments, games, and simulations
- Foreign language training (English, French)
- Instant feedback and help through teachers, peers, and technology

When using these instructional features on a daily basis, iPads are regarded as powerful and versatile tools. Moreover, this individual technology is providing multitude possibility for learning without changing the classroom setting. Yet, the project is driving the classroom beyond the four walls by integrating MARLE into teaching and learning. In a Biology class, students explore their surroundings (e.g., plants, soil) by using the camera of the iPad and visual markers (distributed all over the school campus). For example, students explore the annual rings of a tree by using visual overlays and augmenting the real tree with a simulation of the growth process. The Biology MARLE includes further instructional information about trees (e.g., habitat, plant family) and quick knowledge tests for *assessment on the fly* (Ifenthaler 2011b). In a Mathematics class, students explore practical problems of trigonometry and geodesy through topographical surveying on the school campus. Using the iPad, students can augment the school's building, the classroom, as well as the schoolyard with virtual line segments and calculate angles or solid measures. The MARLE for Mathematics includes scientific calculators, virtual surveying instruments, and quick knowledge tests for *assessment on the fly* (Ifenthaler 2011b). Within the iPad project, the acceptance of the new technology in class is currently empirically investigated Ifenthaler & Schweinbenz (in press). Further, the benefits of MARLE for complex learning will be investigated through an experience sampling technique implemented on the iPad (Ifenthaler 2011b).

18.5 Future Directions

Facilitating complex learning by mobile augmented reality learning environments (MARLE) is a challenge for researchers and practitioners in the fields of instructional design, educational technology, and computer science. This inter-disciplinary field of research is facing (1) technological, (2) theoretical, and (3) assessment challenges.

First, the rapid development of information and communication technology (ICT) has strongly influenced advances and implications for learning and instruction. Most of these systems are GPS-enabled, location-aware, and provide wireless access to the Internet. High quality video cameras and audio functions provide the basis for future learning and instruction. Additionally, intelligent software applications can semantically interpret the learners' interactions and combine virtual objects with the real world. These new technologies are and will be shaping how people learn in the beginning of the twenty-first century in formal and informal settings. The development of Web 3.0 has now been coined to describe the coming wave of innovation (Yu 2007). Accordingly, Web 3.0 will go a step further and understand or rather learn what the learner wants and suggests the information that fits to the learners' needs. This requires that all information which is available in the Internet is accessible by a certain standard and that the technology is able to *understand its meaning*. Thus, Web 3.0 is intelligent offering a data network consisting in a collection of structured data records published in the Internet in repeatedly reusable formats (e.g., XML, RDF). Besides the service-oriented architecture, Web 3.0 will be the realization and extension of the concept of the Semantic Web (Lassila and Hendler 2007; Yu 2007). Web 3.0 operations will be designed to perform logical reasoning using a multitude of rules, which express logical relationships between semantic meaning and information available in the Internet (Ifenthaler 2012).

Second, questions concerning the development of complex problem solving are still being scrutinized, even though the functions of complex problem-solving processes has attained general acceptance over the past decades (Dörner 1987, 1996; Funke 1991; Jacobson 2000; Sabelli 2006; Jonassen 2000, 2004, 2011; Spector et al. 2001). However, one of these questions has to do with Snow's (1990) verdict that theoretical constructs must be defined precisely and assessed exactly if they are to be used effectively in cognitive and instructional science. Hence, complex learning and problem solving as well as the different types of problems, interindividual and intraindividual differences among problem solvers, as well as the domain and context of problems need to be empirically investigated in laboratory and classroom settings (Ifenthaler 2011a; Ifenthaler et al. 2011; Ifenthaler and Seel 2011; Jonassen 2011).

Third, closely linked to the demand of new approaches for designing and developing up-to-date learning environments in Web 3.0 is the necessity of enhancing the design and delivery of assessment systems (Spector 2010). However, studies exploring the assessment of new technologies in the field of educational technology are rare (Dunleavy et al. 2009; Heinecke et al. 2001; Ifenthaler 2012; Ifenthaler & Schweinbenz (in press); Means and Haertel 2004). Methodologies for measuring the learning-dependent progression of mental models or inferential schemata in complex learning are still being developed and critically investigated (Seel 1999; Ifenthaler and Seel 2011). Ifenthaler and Seel (2005) also stressed the importance of measuring subjects repeatedly over extended periods of time to understand the continuous progression of learning and thinking. This suggests that measuring complex learning continuously or repeatedly during transitional stages is more effective than only measuring them before and after instruction, which is how they are typically measured in most research studies (Ifenthaler et al. 2011).

To sum up, MARLE has yet to be taken out of the laboratory and into the classroom and implemented on an everyday teaching basis. However, the potential of powerful educational interfaces will only facilitate complex learning and problem solving if the building blocks of problem solving learning-environments are understood and implemented entirely.

References

Abas H, Badioze Zaman H (2011) Visual learning through augmented reality storybook for remedial student. In: Zaman H, Robinson P, Petrou M, Olivier P, Shih T, Velastin S, Nyström I (eds) Visual informatics: sustaining research and innovations, vol 7067. Springer, Berlin, pp 157–167

Albrecht U-V, von Jan U, Krückelberg J, Behrends M, Matthies HK (2011) Medical students experience the mobile augmented reality blended learning environment (MARBLE)—an attractive concept for the net-generation? In: Sampson DG, Spector JM, Ifenthaler D, Isaias P (eds) Proceedings of the IADIS international conference on cognition and exploratory learning in the digital age. IADIS Press, Rio de Janeiro, pp 263–266

Axelrod R (ed) (1976) Structure of decision: the cognitive maps of political elites. Princeton University Press, Princeton

Azuma R (1997) A survey of augmented reality presence. Teleoperators Virtual Environ 6(4):355–385

Bechtel Power Corporation. (n.d.) (2011) Watts bar completion. Retrieved 13 Nov 2011 from http://www.bechtel.com/watts-bar-completion.html

Bimber O, Raskar R (2005) Spatial augmented reality. merging real and virtual worlds. A K Peters, Wellesley

Bransford JD, Brown AL, Cocking RR (2000) How people learn: brain, mind, experience, and school. National Academy Press, Washington
Brehmer B (1980) In one word: not from experience. Acta Psychol 45:223–241
Brown JS, Collins A, Duguid P (1989) Situated cognition and the culture of learning. Educ Res 18(1):32–42
Cavalli-Sforza V, Weiner A, Lesgold A (1994) Software support for students engaging in scientific activity and scientific controversy. Sci Educ 78:577–599
Chinn C, Malhotra B (2002) Epistemologically authentic inquiry in schools: a theoretical framework for evaluating inquiry tasks. Sci Educ 82(2):175–218
Clarke J, Dede C (2007) MUVEs as a powerful means to study situated learning. In: Chinn CA, Erkens G, Putambekar S (eds) Proceedings of the 2007 computer-supported collaborative learning (CSCL) conference, New Brunswick, pp 141–144
Dana SK, Roy PK, Kurth J (eds) (2009) Complex dynamics in physiological systems: from heart to brain. Springer, New York
de Jong T, van Joolingen WR (1998) Scientific discovery learning with computer simulations of conceptual domains. Rev Educ Res 68(2):179–202
Dede C (2009) Immersive interfaces for engagement and learning. Science 323(66):66–69
Dewey J (1938) Context and thought. In: Bernstein R (ed) On experience, nature and freedom. Library of Liberal Arts, New York, pp 88–110
Dörner D (1980) On the difficulties people have in dealing with complexity. Simul Games 11:87–106
Dörner D (1987) On the difficulties people have in dealing with complexity. In: Rasmussen J, Duncker K, Leplat J (eds) New technology and human error. Wiley, Chichester, pp 97–109
Dörner D (1996) The logic of failure: Why things go wrong and what can we do to make them right (trans: Kimber R, Kimber R). Metropolitan Books, New York
Dörner D, Wearing AJ (1995) Complex problem solving: toward a (computer-simulated) theory. In: Frensch PA, Funke J (eds) Complex problem solving: the European perspective. Lawrence Erlbaum Associates, Inc, Hillsdale, pp 65–99
Dunleavy M, Dede C, Mitchell R (2009) Affordances and limitations of immersive participatory augmented reality simulations for teaching and learning. J Sci Educ Technol 18(1):7–22
Eisenhart M, Finkel E, Marion S (1996) Creating the conditions for scientific literacy: A re-examination. Am Educ Res J 33:261–295
Ellaway R (2010) eMedical teacher. Med Teach 32:798–800
Eseryel D, Law V (2010) Promoting learning in complex systems: effect of question prompts versus system dynamics model progressions as a cognitive-regulation scaffold in a simulation-based inquiry-learning environment. In: Proceedings of the 9th international conference of the learning sciences, Chicago, IL
Eseryel D, Ge X, Ifenthaler D, Law V (2011) Dynamic modeling as a cognitive regulation scaffold for complex problem solving skill acquisition in an educational massively multiplayer online game environment. J Educ Comput Res 45(3):265–287
Fjeld M, Voegtli BM (2002) Augmented chemistry: an interactive educational workbench. In: Proceedings of international symposium on mixed and augmented reality, IEEE Computer Society
Frederiksen J, White BY (1992) Mental models and understanding: a problem for science education. In: Scanlon E, O'Shea T (eds) New directions in educational technology. Springer, New York, pp 211–226
Freitas R, Campos P (2008) SMART: a system of augmented reality for teaching 2nd grade students. In: Proceedings of the 22nd British CHI group annual conference on HCI 2008: people and computers XXII: culture, creativity, interaction. Liverpool, UK
Frensch PA, Funke J (1995) Definitions, traditions, and a general framework for understanding complex problem solving. In: Frensch PA, Funke J (eds) Complex problem solving: the European perspective. Lawrence Erlbaum Associates, Inc, Hillsdale, pp 3–26
Funke J (1991) Solving complex problems: exploration and control of complex systems. In: Sternberg RJ, Frensch PA (eds) Complex problem solving: principles and mechanisms. Lawrence Erlbaum Associates, Inc, Hillsdale, pp 185–222

Gee JP (2003) What video games have to teach us about learning and literacy. Palgrave-Macmillan, New York

Gillet A, Sanner M, Stoffler D, Goodsell D, Olson A (2004) Augmented reality with tangible auto-fabricated models for molecular biology applications. IEEE Vis 235–241

Glenberg AM (1997) What memory is for. Behav Brain Sci 20(1):1–19

Goodwin C (1994) Professional vision. Am Anthropologist 96(3):606–633

Greeno JG (1989) Situations, mental models and generative knowledge. In: Klahr D, Kotovsky K (eds) Complex information processing. Lawrence Erlbaum, Hillsdale, pp 285–318

Greeno JG (1998) The situativity of knowing, learning, and research. Am Psychol 53:5–26

Griffin MM (1995) You can't get there from here: situated learning, transfer, and map skills. Contemp Educ Psychol 20:65–87

Haller M, Billinghurst M, Thomas BH (2007) Emerging technologies of augmented reality: interfaces and design. Idea Group, Inc., Hershey

Harris M, Cullen R (2007) Learner-centered leadership: an agenda for action. Innovative High Educ 33(1):21–28

Hatano G, Inagaki K (1986) Two courses of expertise. In: Stevenson HAH, Hakuta K (eds) Child development and education in Japan. Freeman, New York, pp 262–272

Hatano G, Oura Y (2003) Commentary: reconceptualizing school learning using insights from expertise research. Educ Res 32(8):26–29

Heinecke WF, Milman NB, Washington LA, Blasi L (2001) New directions in the evaluation of the effectiveness of educational technology. Comput Schools 18(2/3):97–110

Hendricks CC (2001) Teaching causal reasoning through cognitive apprenticeship: what are results from situated learning? J Educ Res 94(5):302–311

Hogan K, Thomas D (2001) Cognitive comparisons of students systems modeling in ecology. J Sci Educ Technol 10(10):75–96

Hung W (2011) Team-based problem solving: the role of collective cognition. Paper presented at the international convention of the association for educational communications and technology (AECT), Jacksonville, FL

Ifenthaler D (2009) Bridging the gap between expert-novice differences: the model-based feedback approach. In: Kinshuk D, Sampson DG, Spector JM, Isaias P, Ifenthaler D (eds) In: Proceedings of the IADIS international conference on cognition and exploratory learning in the digital age, IADIS Press, Rome, pp 49–60

Ifenthaler D (2010) Learning and instruction in the digital age. In: Spector JM, Ifenthaler D, Isaías P, Kinshuk, Sampson DG (eds) Learning and instruction in the digital age: making a difference through cognitive approaches, technology-facilitated collaboration and assessment, and personalized communications. Springer, New York, pp 3–10

Ifenthaler D (2011a) Identifying cross-domain distinguishing features of cognitive structures. Educ Tech Res Dev 59(6):817–840. doi:10.1007/s11423-011-9207-4

Ifenthaler D (2011b) MaTS—mannheimer tablet-PC schulen. Lehrstuhl für Erziehungswissenschaft, Mannheim

Ifenthaler D (2012) Is Web 3.0 changing learning and instruction? In: Isaias P, Ifenthaler D, Kinshuk D, Sampson DG, Spector JM (eds) Towards learning and instruction in Web 3.0. advances in cognitive and educational psychology. Springer, New York, pp 11–16

Ifenthaler D, Seel NM (2005) The measurement of change: learning-dependent progression of mental models. Technol, Instr, Cogn Learn 2(4):317–336

Ifenthaler D, Seel NM (2011) A longitudinal perspective on inductive reasoning tasks. Illuminating the probability of change. Learn Instr 21(4):538–549. doi:10.1016/j.learninstruc.2010.08.004

Ifenthaler D, Pirnay-Dummer P, Seel NM (2007) The role of cognitive learning strategies and intellectual abilities in mental model building processes. Technol, Instr, Cogn Learn 5(4):353–366

Ifenthaler D, Masduki I, Seel NM (2011) The mystery of cognitive structure and how we can detect it. Tracking the development of cognitive structures over time. Instr Sci 39(1):41–61. doi:10.1007/s11251-009-9097-6

Ifenthaler D, Eseryel D, Ge X (eds) (2012) Assessment in game-based learning: foundations, innovations, and perspectives. Springer, New York
Ifenthaler D, Schweinbenz V (in press) The acceptance of tablet-PCs in classroom instruction: The teacher's perspectives. Computer in Human Behavior
Jacobson MJ (2000) Problem solving about complex systems: difference between experts and novices. In: Fishman B, O'Connor-Divelbiss S (eds) Fourth international conference of the learning sciences. Lawrence Erlbaum Associates, Inc, Mahwah, pp 14–21
Jonassen DH (1997) Instructional design models for well-structured and ill-structured problem-solving learning outcomes. Educ Tech Res Dev 45(1):65–94
Jonassen DH (2000) Toward a design theory of problem solving. Educ Tech Res Dev 48(4):63–85. doi:10.1007/BF02300500
Jonassen DH (2004) Learning to solve problems: an instructional design guide. Pfeiffer, San Francisco
Jonassen DH (2011) Learning to solve problems. A handbook for designing problem-solving learning environments. Routledge, New York
Kelso JAS (2009) Understanding complex systems. In: Dana SK, Roy PK, Kurth J (eds) Complex dynamics in physiological systems: from heart to brain. Springer, New York, pp 9–11
Kirschner PA, Sweller J, Clark RE (2006) Why minimal guidance during instruction does not work: an analysis of the failure of constructivist, discovery, problem-based, experiential, and inquiry-based teaching. Educ Psychol 41(2):75–86
Kohn LT, Corrigan JM, Donaldson MS (1999) To err is human: building a safer health system. Institute of Medicine: Committee on Quality of Health Care in America, Washington
Lassila O, Hendler J (2007) Embracing "Web 3.0". Internet Comput 11(3):90–93
Lave J, Wenger E (1991) Situated learning: legitimate periperal participation. Cambridge University Press, Cambridge
Law V, Eseryel D (2011) Cognitive regulation in a simulation-based inquiry learning environment. Paper presented at the annual convention of association for educational communications and technology (AECT), Jacksonville, FL
Law V, Ge X, Eseryel D (2011) An investigation of the development of a reflective virtual learning community in an ill-structured domain of instructional design. Knowl Manag E-Learn: An Int J 3(4):513–533
Ma JY, Choi JS (2007) The virtuality and reality of augmented reality. J Multimedia 2(1):32–37
Mackinnon AJ, Wearing AJ (1980) Complexity and decision-making. Behav Sci 25:285–296
Martín-Gutiérrez J, Contero M, Alcañiz M (2010) Evaluating the usability of an augmented reality based educational application. In: Aleven V, Kay J, Mostow J (eds) Intelligent tutoring systems, vol 6094. Springer, Berlin, pp 296–306
Mayer RE, Wittrock MC (1996) Problem-solving transfer. In: Berlinert DC, Calfee RC (eds) Handbook of educational psychology. Macmillan, New York, pp 47–62
McGinn M, Roth W (1999) Preparing students for competent scientific practice: implications of recent research in science and technology studies. Educ Res 28:14–24
Means B, Haertel GD (2004) Using technology evaluation to enhance student learning. Teachers College Press, New York
Mehler-Bicher A, Reiß M, Steiger L (2011) Augmented reality: Theorie und Praxis. Oldenbourg, München
Milgram P, Takemura H, Utsumi A, Kishino F (1994) Augmented reality: a class of displays on the reality-virtuality continuum. SPIE proceedings: telemanipulator and telepresence technologies, Boston, MA
Miller GA (1956) The magical number seven, plus or minus two: some limits on our capacity for processing information. Psychol Rev 63(2):81–97
Naylor JC, Briggs GE (1963) Effects of task complexity and task organization on the relative efficiency of part and whole training methods. J Expe Psychol 65:217–224
Nischelwitzer A, Lenz F-J, Searle G, Holzinger A (2007) Some aspects of the development of low-cost augmented reality learning environments as examples for future interfaces in

technology enhanced learning. In: Stephanidis C (ed) Universal access in human-computer interaction. Applications and services, vol 4556. Springer, Berlin, pp 728–737

Palincsar AS, Magnusson SJ (2001) The interplay of first-hand and text-based investigations to model and support the development of scientific knowledge and reasoning. In: Carver S, Klahr D (eds) Cognition and instruction: twenty five years of progress. Lawrence Erlbaum, Mahwah, pp 151–194

Peirce CS (1992) Questions concerning faculties claimed for man. In: Houser N, Kloesel C (eds) The essential peirce, vol 1. Indiana University Press, Bloomington, pp 11–27

Perkins DN, Grotzer TA (1997) Teaching intelligence. Am Psychol 52:1125–1133

Plous S (1993) The psychology of judgment and decision making. McGraw-Hill, New York

Putz-Osterloh W, Lemme M (1987) Knowledge and its intelligent application to problem solving. Ger J Psychol 11:286–303

Rumelhart DE, Smolensky P, McClelland JL, Hinton GE (1986) Schemata and sequential thought processes in PDP models. In: McClelland JL, Rumelhart DE (eds) Parallel distributed processing. Explorations in the microstructure of cognition, vol 2: psychological and biological models. MIT Press, Cambridge, pp 7–57

Sabelli NH (2006) Complexity, technology, science, and education. J Learn Sci 15:5–9

Saforrudin N, Badioze Zaman H, Ahmad A (2011) Technical skills in developing augmented reality application: teachers' readiness. In: Zaman H, Robinson P, Petrou M, Olivier P, Shih T, Velastin S, Nyström I (eds) Visual informatics: sustaining research and innovations, vol 7067. Springer, Berlin, pp 360–370

Salomon G (ed) (1993) Distributed cognitions: psychological and educational considerations. Cambridge University Press, New York

Scardamalia M, Bereiter C (1994) Computer support for knowledge-building communities. J Learn Sci 3(3):265–283

Schwartz DL, Bransford JD, Sears D (2005) Efficiency and innovation in transfer. In: Mestre J (ed) Transfer of learning from a modern multidisciplinary perspective. Information Age Publishing, Greenwich, pp 1–51

Seel NM (1999) Educational diagnosis of mental models: Assessment problems and technology-based solutions. J Struct Learning Int Sys 14(2):153–185

Seel NM (2001) Epistemology, situated cognition, and mental models: Like a bridge over troubled water. Instr Sci 29(4–5):403–427

Seel NM (2006) Mental models and complex problem solving. In: Elen J, Clark RE (eds) Handling complexity in learning environments: theory and research. Elsevier Ltd, Amsterdam, pp 43–66

Seel NM, Ifenthaler D, Pirnay-Dummer P (2009) Mental models and problem solving: technological solutions for measurement and assessment of the development of expertise. In: Blumschein P, Hung W, Jonassen DH, Strobel J (eds) Model-based approaches to learning: using systems models and simulations to improve understanding and problem solving in complex domains. Sense Publishers, Rotterdam, pp 17–40

Shaffer DW (2006) Epistemic frames for epistemic games. Comput Educ 46(13):223–234

Shelton BE (2003) How augmented reality helps students learn dynamic spatial relationships. University of Washington, Seattle

Sin A, Badioze Zaman H (2009) Tangible interaction in learning astronomy through augmented reality book-based educational tool. In: Badioze Zaman H, Robinson P, Petrou M, Olivier P, Schröder H, Shih T (eds) Visual informatics: bridging research and practice, vol 5857. Springer, Berlin, pp 302–313

Snow RE (1990) New approaches to cognitive and conative assessment in education. Int J Educ Res 14(5):455–473

Spector JM (2010) Mental representations and their analysis: an epestimological perspective. In: Ifenthaler D, Pirnay-Dummer P, Seel NM (eds) Computer-based diagnostics and systematic analysis of knowledge. Springer, New York, pp 27–40

Spector JM, Anderson TM (eds) (2000) Integrated and holistic perspectives on learning, instruction, and technology: understanding complexity. Kluwer Academic Publishers, Dordrecht

Spector JM, Christensen DL, Sioutine AV, McCormack D (2001) Models and simulations for learning in complex domains: using causal loop diagrams for assessment and evaluation. Comput Hum Behav 17(5–6):517–545

Traxler J (2009) Current state of mobile learning. In: Ally M (ed) Mobile learning: transforming the delivery of education and training. Athabasca University Press, Edmonton, pp 9–24

van Merriënboer JJG (1997) Training complex cognitive skills: a four-component instructional design model for technical training. Educational Technology Publications, Englewood Cliffs

van Merriënboer JJG, Clark RE, de Croock MBM (2002) Blueprints for complex learning: the 4C/ID-model. Educ Tech Res Dev 50(2):39–64

Vygotsky LS (1978) Mind in society: the development of higher psychological processes (trans: Cole M, John-Steiner V, Scribner S, Souberman E (eds)). Harvard University Press, Cambridge

Wenger E (1998) Communities of practice: learning, meaning, and identity. Cambridge University Press, Cambridge

Wertsch J (1998) Mind as action. Oxford University Press, New York

Wightman DC, Lintern G (1985) Part-task training for tracking and manual control. Hum Factors 27:267–284

Winn WD (2003) Learning in artificial environments: embodiment, embeddedness and dynamic adaption. Technol, Instr, Cognition Learn 1(1):87–114

Yu L (2007) Introduction to the semantic web and semantic web services. Chapman and Hall, Boca Raton

Zimmerman BJ, Schunk D (2001) Theories of self-regulated learning and academic achievement: an overview and analysis. In: Zimmerman BJ, Schunk D (eds) Self-regulated learning and academic achievement. Theoretical perspectives. Lawrence Erlbaum Associates, Mahawah, pp 1–37

Chapter 19
Mobilising Web Sites at an Open University: The Athabasca University Experience

Regina Wasti and Rory McGreal

Abstract This mobile implementation study provides a general idea of how existing Athabasca University sites work with the tested mobile devices and identifies the underlying issues as to why they work that way. Factors considered in the implementation include screen size, the use of advanced features, the display of large images, file formats and linking to embedded objects. In the effort to make the sites as mobile-friendly as possible, it is also important to consider what some possible solutions are. Redesigning all those sites carefully, with due consideration to mobile devices, is one possibility considered. This creates a huge burden of site maintenance, as we need to maintain multiple versions of the same page for different devices. Another problem with this approach is that as the capability of mobile devices changes, those sites need to be updated accordingly to reflect the device's capability. This issue is addressed to some extent by creating template-based dynamic pages, and rather than redesigning the pages whenever the device capability changes, one could change the profile of the device.

Keywords Mobile web sites · Screen size · Formatting · Style sheets · Mobile devices

---

This chapter is based on a report prepared for Athabasca University and on a paper presented at the MLearn 2012 Conference in Berlin.

R. Wasti (✉)
Athabasca, Canada
e-mail: Regina.wasti@gmail.com

R. McGreal
Athabasca University, Athabasca, Alberta, Canada
e-mail: rory@athabascau.ca

R. Huang et al. (eds.), *Reshaping Learning*, New Frontiers of Educational Research,
DOI: 10.1007/978-3-642-32301-0_19,

19.1 Introduction

Athabasca University (AU) is a leading university in Canada, providing open and distance education to more than 38,000 students per year from all over the world. Students can acquire education and degrees without ever having to be physically present at a university campus. This highlights the importance of unconventional but effective and efficient media for providing education and services to students. With the widespread availability of Internet technology, the University is now dependent on the use of the Internet to deliver course materials, to enable students to interact, to provide students with online library access, and to facilitate students in performing administrative tasks such as enrolling into or withdrawing from courses, and even writing exams, remotely.

Originally, AU websites were developed with desktop computers in mind. They have been traditionally designed with the assumption that the user accessing the website has a large, colourful screen and adequate bandwidth for downloading multimedia-rich pages. This assumption cannot be relied on anymore, given the pervasive use of small-screen, low-bandwidth mobile devices as well as the latest 3 and 4 g phones and tablets.

This study investigated the mobile-friendliness of various AU websites and some external sites that are linked from AU sites, specifically journal databases. The websites were tested for visual integrity and functionality retention using less capable mobile devices in order to ensure that students with the less capable phones could still be used if students had not upgraded. It was felt that it is not necessary to test the capacity of the different websites in supporting the more powerful 3 and 4 g phones and tablets because they can (for the most part) display the contents adequately if not better in some cases than on many larger computer screens. The less capable mobile phones have difficulty supporting more sophisticated features such as Java, JavaScript, and ActiveX. Some websites provide a fallback mechanism to accommodate these less capable mobile devices; others simply send the web page without considering what kind of device the request came from (Wasti 2006).

The objective of this study was to evaluate how well the AU websites worked with low bandwidth mobile phones with limited capabilities. The results of the study could then be used to determine how the University can make its websites useful for users with diverse choices of mobile devices. For an open university like AU, it is very important to make its online resources accessible to as wide a range of users and devices as possible.

The M-library project of the AU Library was implemented previously in an attempt to build a platform for AU to develop an effective mobile-friendly library (Cao et al. 2007). The Digital Reading Room (DRR), Digital Thesis and Project Room (DTPR), Digital Reference Centre (DRC), and AirPAC are some of the outcomes of the project (McGreal et al. 2006). These projects formed part of a research focus on mobile learning using stylesheets and proxies (Cheung et al. 2007) and building a demonstration course specifically for use on mobile phones (Ally et al. 2007).

In this investigation, a variety of low bandwidth test devices and a selection of AU websites were studied. Features at the sample websites were tested to see whether they worked as would be expected. There were two key aspects of the test: (1) visual display, and (2) functionality. Some sites rendered well, with their layout intact on small screens, but some features were "crippled" because of the limitations of the underlying device and platform. Similarly, other sites appear relatively deformed but have their features intact. The sites were evaluated for both of the above- mentioned factors.

19.2 Display Modes

Numerous types of mobile devices capable of accessing the Internet are available. Because of time and resource constraints, it was not possible to test each available device for compatibility with the websites, so for the purposes of this study, three low bandwidth smart phone devices were chosen, each with a different screen size and slightly different browsing characteristics: (1) the HP iPAQ hw6500 (iPAQ), (2) the BlackBerry 8700r (BlackBerry), and (3) the Audiovox SMT5600 (SMT). These devices were chosen specifically because they were low bandwidth older phones. Tablet computers can easily display web sites without formatting or other problems and so were not used, because the purpose of the investigation was to test the sites with the lowest common denominator types of devices.
Using these devices the following modes were generally possible

1. **Single-column mode**: In this mode, the web content was presented in a single-column format. It functioned similarly to the BlackBerry but did not use as many optimization techniques. If a table consisted of more than one column, the columns were presented vertically, one after the other. This eliminated the need for horizontal scrolling, but the original page layout was lost, sometimes resulting in pages that were more difficult to read and navigate.
2. **Desktop mode**: In desktop mode, the page was rendered as if it were being displayed on a desktop computer screen. The sizes of all page elements were kept unchanged. Viewing a page in this mode required significant horizontal and vertical scrolling to view the complete page.
3. **Default mode**: In the default viewing mode, the relative positioning of page elements was preserved, but the size of the page was proportionally reduced. The width of the resulting page can be larger than the width of the device screen, which required some horizontal scrolling. When trying to proportionally reduce the size of various elements of the page (text, tables, images), the elements sometimes overlapped.

Although some problematic web pages were viewed in different modes to find out whether the problem exists in all viewing modes, the test was primarily conducted in the default viewing mode. The default mode is the most likely choice of users and is the one that is likely to produce the best viewing experience for most websites.

There is some variation among the devices used in this study in terms of what web features and file types are supported. Some of the observations in our research represented limitations of the devices themselves and no solutions existed to remedy those limitations; other findings from our study are owing to unavailability of third-party add-on programs for that device's platform. With the exception of DocHawk Platinum and eOffice Professional for BlackBerry, no attempt was made to install third-party software that is only available by purchase. Thus, it is possible that there may be some third-party software programs available for a particular device's platform that would allow opening certain types of files or attachments from that device. Nevertheless, it should only affect the ability to open certain types of files and should have no effect on the HTML page-rendering or the look and feel of web pages when viewed on that device. It is also possible that there may be more advanced web browsers available for those devices that have better page optimization and page-rendering abilities. However, such programs are not easily available or are unavailable for free, which limits their benefit to a small number of mobile device users.

19.3 Website Testing

A varied sample of websites was tested. The sites selected were library-related sites, journal databases, hosted journal sites, and some other popular AU sites. Although these sites are mainly library- and journal-related, the results of this research are general in nature and should be applicable to most university websites.

Tests were performed on the devices by going to various AU websites and assessing them on a scale of 0–3, where 0 represents not very mobile-friendly, and 3 represents very mobile-friendly. Two factors were considered and assessed accordingly: the visual display of the website as it is rendered on the screen of the device, and the functionality of the page (links, buttons, tabs, navigation, etc.). The following scheme was used in assessing the websites:

Visual display

0 Page cannot be opened by the device at all

1 Page displays on the device with some deformation and/or requires excessive scrolling

2 Page displays reasonably well. Some scrolling may be required. Frames and fixed-size tables may cause some problems

3 The page displays perfectly and does not require horizontal scrolling.

Functionality

0 Page cannot be displayed, or none of the navigation links work

1 Only some browsing features work (e.g., many links cannot be opened, or page cannot be properly navigated)

2 Most browsing features work (e.g., most links, buttons, and navigation items work)
3 All links and all features work. Form submission and buttons, and so on, all work.

19.4 Test Results

Flash player presented a significant problem as any site using Flash would not display properly on the majority of phones. The phones also generally did not support a PDF reader, so trying to open a PDF file from any website was problematic. Such limitations are considered the limitations of the device itself and not shortcomings of the website. However, if a site primarily relied on the device being able to make use of those features, the mobile-friendliness grading of that site was reduced accordingly.

The sample pages showed the following results

Athabasca University Home Page http://www.athabascau.ca/

The BlackBerry had a default single-column view and displayed the AU home page well. The iPAQ and SMT could also display the page in single-column format that was similar to the display in the BlackBerry but looked less polished. The default mode in the iPAQ and SMT required horizontal scrolling, and the page looked slightly deformed. Regardless of the display mode, however, all navigation links worked well on all three devices.

myAU http://my.athabascau.ca

The iPAQ and SMT both display this site fairly well, and all navigation links and site logins worked as expected. On the other hand, the BlackBerry could not open this site at all. It generated a dialogue box: "HTTP error 406: Not Acceptable". This appears to be caused by a configuration problem on the server side; the server incorrectly assumed that the client device was unable to render the page and so did not send any content.

Online Registration https://tux.athabascau.ca/oros/jsp/welcome.jsp

This main registration site rendered well in all three devices. All links and form submissions worked as expected.

AU Intranet http://intra.athabascau.ca/

The BlackBerry rendered this site fairly well in its one-column layout. In the default viewing mode of the iPAQ and SMT, extensive horizontal scrolling was required and navigating was more difficult. The excessive horizontal scrolling was made necessary by the use of fixed-size tables. Setting up vacation notices and changing forwarding email addresses worked well in all three devices.

AU Webmail https://secure.athabascau.ca/webmail

Webmail worked well with the iPAQ and BlackBerry but did not open in SMT because of frames.

Research Centre http://www.athabascau.ca/research

The Research Centre site rendered well in the single-column layout of the BlackBerry and fairly well in the default layouts of the iPAQ and SMT. The site used fixed-size tables, so it requires a lot of horizontal scrolling. All links on the page worked well.

Open Journal Systems (OJS) http://www.irrodl.org/

Open Journal Systems (OJS) was tested by going to the journal site of the *International Review of Research in Open and Distance Learning* (IRRODL). This site rendered well in the BlackBerry and in the single-column format of the iPAQ and SMT. However, it rendered rather poorly in the default layout of the iPAQ and SMT: two columns of the table almost overlapped. Editing and saving submissions worked well, but files could not be uploaded through any of the tested devices.

Open Conferencing System (OCS) http://tools.elab.athabascau.ca/tools/open-conference-system

This site rendered very well on all three devices. Single-column and default views all worked well. All links on the site also opened nicely. The file-upload feature on the paper submission page was the only part of the site that did not work. Public Knowledge Project's Open Conferencing System (OCS) worked as the back end of the paper submission system; so the file-upload problem was determined to be with OCS rather than with the OCS site.

Moodle Forums http://www.athabascau.ca/moodletrain/forums.htm

The Moodle forum site displayed well on all three devices. Posting, reading, and editing messages worked well. As with other sites that required file uploads, none of the devices were able to upload files from this site.

AUSpace http://auspace.athabascau.ca/

The AUSpace site displayed well in the BlackBerry and in the single-column layout of the iPAQ and SMT. The default layout of the iPAQ and SMT required horizontal scrolling because of tables. Searching and viewing files worked well in all devices. However, when trying to submit articles to AUSpace, it was not possible to upload files because the input box for the filename and browse button were missing in all three devices. This was not a problem of the site itself but rather a limitation of the mobile devices.

AU Library Sites

Main Site—http://library.athabascau.ca/
Digital Reading Room (DRR)—http://library.athabascau.ca/drr
Digital Thesis and Project Room (DTPR)—http://library.athabascau.ca/
DTPR Digital Reference Centre (DRC)—http://library.athabascau.ca/drc

All AU Library sites tested were found to be very mobile-friendly. The DRR, DTPR, and DRC used similar layouts that are fluid, allowing a smooth flow of text. As those sites did not use fixed-size tables, the display was consistent and predictable across all the devices. AU Library sites adapted to the client device for optimal mobile-friendliness without sacrificing the richer web content. This was done by detecting what type of device was accessing the pages and then sending the appropriate version of the web page to the device.

The AU Library has integrated the mobile conversion services Google Mobile, Skweezer, and IYHY into some of the reading resources in DRRs. These third-party services work as proxy servers to provide suitable formatting of existing websites for mobile devices (Athabasca University Library 2011).

AU Library Catalogue: **AirPAC** http://aupac.lib.athabascau.ca/airpac/

This site is a mobile-optimized version of the AU Library catalogue. AirPAC formats its response for the type of device that is used to access the site. It sends a smaller version of the page to the SMT and BlackBerry to accommodate the small screen area, while it sends a larger version to the iPAQ with more screen area available. The site displayed very well in all three devices and in all view modes, and all links from this site worked flawlessly.

Journal Databases

An extensive test was performed on all journal databases linked from the AU Library website. The journal databases were assessed on a scale of 0–3, where 0 represents not very mobile-friendly, and 3 represents very mobile-friendly. The grading scheme used for assessing the journal databases was the same one used for evaluating the other AU websites. However, for the databases, the visual display and web functionally were considered together and graded accordingly. More than 120 databases were examined and their scores ranged from 0 to 3 on all devices, with varied mixes of accessibility, some being high with one device and low with another.

19.5 Discussion of Results

Based on this study's test results of the AU websites and the journal databases, the following visual display and functionality issues were identified as affecting the mobile-friendliness of the sites tested

1. Some pages were displayed with unnecessary spaces at the top of the pages and large gaps in the middle. This is normally caused by the use of complex structures in the HTML page design, such as tables, nested tables, transparent pictures used for layout, and so on. When the mobile browsers try to optimize such pages to fit a small screen, the page may be deformed in many ways, depending on the optimization method used by the browsers.
2. If a page contains fixed-width blocks, excessive scrolling is necessary when viewing through mobile devices.
3. Flash-dependent websites pose another challenge for mobile browsers. Some websites depend on Flash for navigation menus. It is impossible to successfully visit such sites through devices that do not support Flash (e.g. iPhone, iPad).
4. Because the mobile devices only partially support JavaScript, the result of visiting a JavaScript-dependent site is unpredictable. Some features may work; others may not. For example, some sites extensively use JavaScript to open new browser windows. Such links almost always fail to open in the tested mobile devices. Other sites have entirely JavaScript-dependent navigation menus. In such cases, it is not possible to visit the pages linked from the menus.
5. Extensive use of specialized file formats—such as PDF, e-book, Microsoft Word, and PowerPoint—can be problematic for some mobile devices. Some browsers do not support opening those file types, so sites making heavy use of those file formats would not be friendly to these devices.
6. The use of frames also reduces the mobile-friendliness of the site. Different mobile devices support frames to different degrees. The iPAQ does not have a problem with frames, whereas the SMT cannot open horizontal frames. The BlackBerry linearizes the frames and displays them one at a time.
7. Some web servers make assumptions about the device accessing the website. For example, in one instance, the BlackBerry could not open a site because the server refused to send content; the server assumed that the device could not render the file.
8. One major problem common to all devices is the inability to upload files. None of the tested mobile browsers allowed files to be uploaded because they could not recognize the file browsing buttons.

The following chart (Fig. 19.1) provides a mobile-friendliness score, which is the sum of the scores assigned to the different sites for individual devices. For example, adding the scores of the three devices used, the total score for the AU home page would be 14 out of the maximum 18. These scores were then normalized for each site to a maximum 100 points. Thus, the normalized score of the AU home page would be 77.77 points out of a maximum 100. The chart should be interpreted this way: "Two of the tested sites scored higher than 90, five sites scored between 80 and 90, five sites scored between 70 and 80," and so on. As we can see from the chart, in general, most AU websites are quite mobile-friendly

A similar chart (Fig. 19.2) provides a mobile-friendliness score for the more than 120 journal database sites linked to the AU Library website. The majority of websites scored 60 or higher in terms of mobile-friendliness. Some sites were

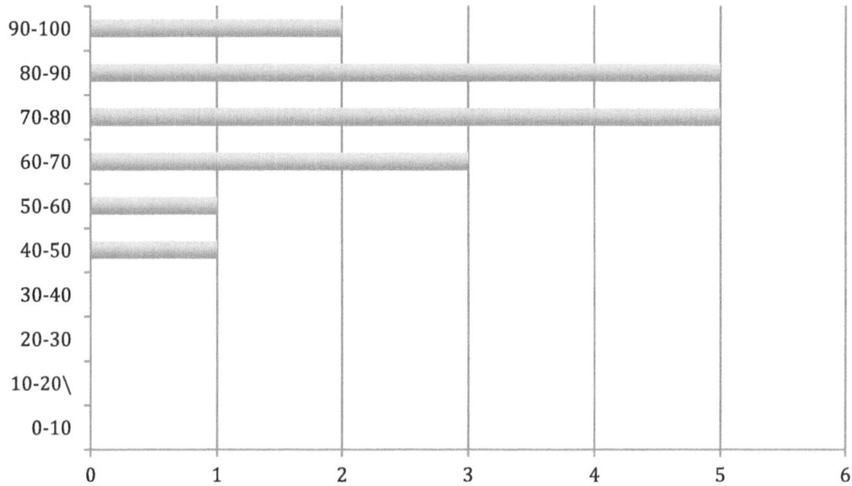

Fig. 19.1 Histogram of mobile friendliness of tested AU websites

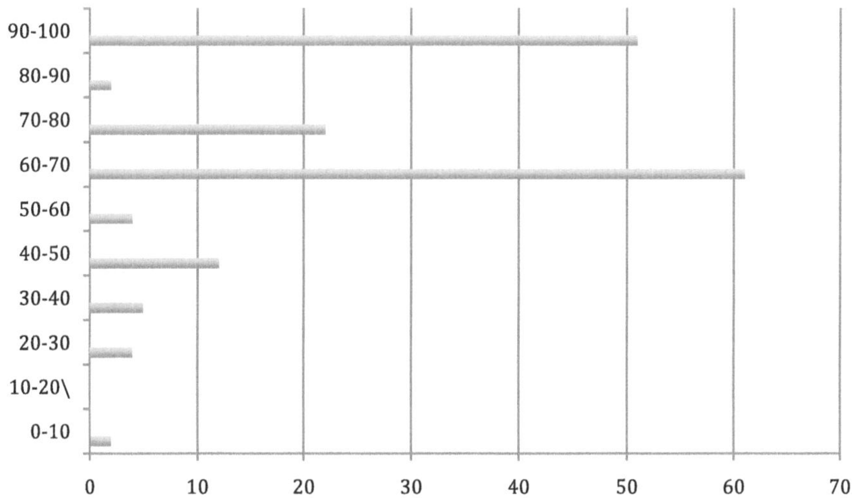

Fig. 19.2 Histogram of mobile friendliness of journal databases

problematic for the mobile devices, and scored lower than 50, so in general the external sites were not as mobile-friendly as the AU websites.

Nevertheless, overall, the websites and journal databases were found to be quite mobile-friendly. This study shows that most AU websites are viewable and operable from the tested low bandwidth mobile phones. Some sites did not retain their layout and visual design when they were viewed from the test devices but were still functional. Some sites could be rendered nicely but lost some functionality, such as their navigation links and some JavaScript-dependent features.

Some sites (especially the AU Library ones) were almost perfect visually and functionally when accessed from the smart phones.

This study determined that most of the AU Library websites (the main site, DRR, and DTPR) were designed with specific attention to the requirements of mobile devices: the server sent responses custom-tailored to the device being used to access the sites. The benefit of this approach is that mobile device users can conveniently enjoy their device's resources at the same time as desktop users can make full use of their respective capabilities, receiving multimedia-rich content and more advanced graphical display. The downside is the need to maintain different versions of the same web page for different device profiles.

19.6 Conclusion and Recommendations

Whether to characterize a website as mobile-friendly is not a simple yes or no question. There are variations in the degree to which various sites are friendly to mobile devices. Making a general statement about a website being mobile-friendly or mobile-unfriendly is not always accurate. There are so many different mobile hand-held devices with differing feature sets that it is difficult to make a generic statement about a website—while at the same time covering all possible devices and browsers that may access that site. The objective of this study was not to pronounce various sites as "mobile-friendly" or "not friendly," but to get an overall picture of how the sites are visually displayed and function when viewed through the hand-held devices that were used for testing.

The capabilities of mobile devices are also rapidly changing. Manufacturers of those devices continuously add new features, and software developers develop more capable and "smart" software solutions to overcome some of the inherent limitations of those devices. For example, even if this study found that a device currently does not support native viewing of PDF files, that capability has since been added in the more recent models, making these findings somewhat obsolete. Thus, the direct results stated in this study are time-sensitive; that is, their accuracy is valid only for the current time and only for the specific models of those devices. Even so, despite the time- and device-sensitive nature of the results, we can draw some conclusions as to what factors contribute to making a website more mobile-friendly or less mobile-friendly:

1. **Screen size considerations**: One of the main constraints of small devices such as smart phones is the screen size. So, any web page that relies on various HTML elements being displayed in a fixed size is bound to cause problems on small-screen devices. To avoid such problems, it is recommended that the use of fixed-size tables be minimized or eliminated altogether. The positioning of HTML elements should be relative as opposed to absolute, so that when the page is resized and viewed on small screens, its layout remains intact.

2. **Careful use of advanced HTML features**: Many smart phones provide only partial support for Cascading Style Sheets (CSS) and JavaScript. Thus, if a web page is intended to be viewed on both desktop computers and small-screen low bandwidth mobile devices, the page integrity can be preserved on the mobile devices by limiting the use of CSS and JavaScript features to those that are supported by both.
3. **Large images**: Avoiding the use of large images in websites helps to make the site friendlier to mobile devices. When a large image is rendered on a small screen, the device may either reduce the size of the image to fit the screen, or keep the size of the image unchanged, which then causes the need for excessive scrolling. If a large image is resized, important details of the image may be lost, defeating the purpose of the image. This is especially problematic if an image map is used for page navigation. If the image is not resized, the required excessive scrolling makes it harder to navigate the page.
4. **File format of the web content**: Excessive use of file formats that are not supported by mobile devices also makes the site less friendly to mobile devices. Most devices are capable of viewing simple HTML pages, but they may not be able to open other types of media, such as PDF files, PowerPoint files, videos, or Flash content. In such a case, even if the device is able to access some pages of that website, it cannot fully take advantage of the materials and links provided.
5. **Embedded objects**: Special care should be taken when embedding objects on websites. Embedding objects such as audios, videos, and Flash in a web page enriches the page for desktop computer users, but it assumes that all browsers accessing the site are capable of handling those embedded objects. This is a precarious assumption in terms of the access of mobile devices. Mobile browsers usually disregard embedded objects. Therefore, if the embedded object is a crucial part of the page, the rest of the page may not make sense to the mobile device user. Instead of embedding an object on the web page, it is generally better to include a link to such a file. That way, the user can download the file and open with a third- party program, if such a program exists. Even if the user chooses not to download the file, the web page integrity remains intact.

This study provides a general idea of how existing AU sites work with the tested mobile devices and identifies the underlying issues as to why they work that way. However, in the effort to make the sites as mobile-friendly as possible, it is also important to consider what some possible solutions are. Redesigning all those sites carefully, with due consideration to mobile devices, is one possibility, but it is a very impractical one. The cost of resources associated with this route can be enormous. Another possibility is creating a mobile-friendly version of each AU web page and serving those pages instead of the regular pages whenever mobile devices make page requests. This creates the huge burden of site maintenance, as we need to maintain multiple versions of the same page for different devices. Another problem with this approach is that as the capability of mobile devices changes, those sites need to be updated accordingly to reflect the device's capability. However, this issue can be addressed to some extent by creating template- based dynamic pages, and rather than redesigning the pages whenever the device capability changes, one could change the profile of the device, which in turn would be reflected in the dynamic page.

A totally different approach that is gaining some popularity is the use of an intermediary proxy- like adaptation layer for the web content. That way, there is no need to maintain multiple versions of the same website, and it also does not require redesigning existing websites. In effect, whenever a user makes requests to a web page, the request can be routed through an intermediary service that identifies the requesting device, gets the page from the web server on behalf of the device, and reformats the page—thus making it suitable for that particular device—and then passes it on to that device. The success of such an approach depends entirely on the capability of the intermediary service. One advantage of this approach is that the burden of making the web pages user-friendly now shifts to the intermediary service from the web server or the web page administrator. Another advantage is that end users do not need to make any special adjustments or install special software on their devices.

There are some websites that provide such intermediary services. Skweezer http://www.skweezer.net/, IYHY (http://www.iyhy.com/, and Google Mobile http://www.google.ca/mobile/ are examples of such services. The AU Library is experimenting with the integration of those services with some of the Digital Reading Room resources. Few AU sites employ such service at this time. In the testing, most sites that required login/authentication could not be viewed through those services. However, when those services mature and become more capable, they might make mobile web access much more comfortable.

References

Ally M, McGreal R, Schafer S, Tin T, Cheung B (2007) Use of mobile learning technology to train ESL adults, sixth international conference on mobile learning. Available from http://www.ccl-cca.ca/CCL/Research/FundedResearch/201009AllyMcGrealSchaferTinCheung.html

Athabasca University Library (2011) AU digital reading room home (integrated mobile conversion services). Retrieved from http://library.athabascau.ca/drr/mobile2.php?course=mba&id=441&sub=5

Cao Y, Tin T, McGreal R, Ally M, Schafer S (2007) Building an effective mobile-friendly digital library to support mobile learners: a case study of the Athabasca University M-library Project. Paper presented at the first international M-Libraries conference, Milton Keynes

Cheung B, McGreal R, Tin T (2007) Implementation of mobile learning using smart phones at an open university: from stylesheets to proxies. Paper presented at the IADIS Mlearn 2007 conference, Lisbon

McGreal R, Tin T, Cheung B (2006) Digital media at Athabasca University—Canada's Open University—going mobile. International Council for Distance Education (ICDE) 2006 Retrieved from http://www.icde.org/oslo/icde.nsf/CEFB5A35F7FC2EF8C1257298004C8616/$FILE/461.pdf

Wasti R (2006) A study of the mobile-friendliness of selected Athabasca University websites. Available from http://library.athabascau.ca/drr/Paper/final_web.pdf

The manufacturer's authorised representative in the EU is Springer
Nature Customer Service Centre GmbH, Europaplatz 3, 69115 Heidelberg,
Germany. If you have any concerns regarding our products, please
contact ProductSafety@springernature.com

Printed and bound by CPI Group (UK) Ltd, Croydon, CR0 4YY
01/10/2026
02225865-0016